OXFORD STUDIES ON THE ROMAN ECONOMY

General Editors

ALAN BOWMAN   ANDREW WILSON

OXFORD STUDIES ON THE ROMAN ECONOMY

This innovative monograph series reflects a vigorous revival of interest in the ancient economy, focusing on the Mediterranean world under Roman rule (c.100 BC to AD 350). Carefully quantified archaeological and documentary data will be integrated to help ancient historians, economic historians, and archaeologists think about economic behaviour collectively rather than from separate perspectives. The volumes will include a substantial comparative element and thus be of interest to historians of other periods and places.

The Economics of the Roman Stone Trade

BEN RUSSELL

OXFORD

UNIVERSITY PRESS

OXFORD
UNIVERSITY PRESS

Great Clarendon Street, Oxford, OX2 6DP,
United Kingdom

Oxford University Press is a department of the University of Oxford.
It furthers the University's objective of excellence in research, scholarship,
and education by publishing worldwide. Oxford is a registered trade mark of
Oxford University Press in the UK and in certain other countries

First Edition published in 2013
Impression: 1

Published in the United States of America by Oxford University Press
198 Madison Avenue, New York, NY 10016, United States of America

British Library Cataloguing in Publication Data
Data available

Library of Congress Control Number: 2013945561

ISBN 978–0–19–965639–4

As printed and bound by
CPI Group (UK) Ltd, CR0 4YY

For Rachel

Acknowledgements

This book began life as a doctoral thesis, submitted to the University of Oxford in 2009. I am grateful to the Oxford Roman Economy Project and the Arts and Humanities Research Council for funding it and Andrew Wilson and Bert Smith for their exemplary supervision. Rarely are students given the opportunity to be supervised by both an economic historian and an art historian, and this book has been greatly improved by their different insights. Clayton Fant and Janet DeLaine, my doctoral examiners, have also provided continual support and encouragement over the years. I have learnt an incredible amount from both of them. Simon Price first encouraged me to embark on this project and I am sorry that he could not witness its completion; he is much missed by all his colleagues, friends, and former students.

I have been working on this project for six years and in that time I have benefited enormously from the comments and advice of colleagues and friends. I am especially indebted to everyone who has read and commented on this text. Amanda Claridge has read all of it, Alan Bowman, Janet DeLaine, Clayton Fant, Bert Smith, Susan Walker, and Andrew Wilson much of it. Specific chapters were read by Anna Gutiérrez, Alfred Hirt, Lisa Fentress, Janet Huskinson, and Simon Barker. Their comments have improved this book immeasurably. For other observations, information, and suggestions I am thankful to a huge number of other individuals: at King's College London, Will Wootton; at Oxford, Allan Doig, Jaś Elsner, Jack Hanson, Kristina Glicksman, Beth Munro, Nicholas Purcell, Jo Quinn, Damian Robinson, Arietta Papaconstantinou, Peter Thonemann, Dragana Mladenović, and Christina Triantafillou; at the British School at Rome, Robert Coates-Stephens, Sophie Hay, Maria Pia Malvezzi, and Sue Russell; for discussion of stone and quarrying, Nuşin Asgari, Kıvanç Başak, Dirk Booms, Chiara Caleo, Maria Chidiroglou, Sylvian Fachard, Moshe Fischer, Lorenzo Lazzarini, Leah Long, Monica Price, Isabel Rodà, and Rolf Schneider; for sharing their work on shipwrecks, Dante Bartoli, Hélène Bernard, Igor Mihajlović, and Julia Strauss; and for answering my questions about sculptural and architectural topics, Sven Ahrens, Stine Birk, Björn Christian Ewald, Elise Friedland, Susan Kane, Michael Koortbojian, Allyson McDavid, Esen Öğüs, Jan Stubbe Østergaard, Peter Stewart, Jen Trimble, and Mark Wilson Jones. I have also worked closely with a number of practising sculptors, especially Peter Rockwell, Trevor Proudfoot, Stephen Cox, Andy Tanser, Paul Jakeman, Billy Lillywhite, Adrian Powell, and Tom Flemons. I am enormously grateful to them for the unique insight they have provided into their craft. Sections of this work were presented at conferences and workshops in Aarhus, London, Madrid, Munich, Nottingham, Paris, Philadelphia, Oxford, Rome, Tarragona, and Toulouse and I would like to thank the audiences at all of these places for their questions and observations.

Funding for travel over the years has been provided by the Arts and Humanities Research Council, the Roman Society, the Craven Committee and Meyerstein Fund of the University of Oxford, Lady Margaret Hall, and All Souls College. The Leverhulme Trust paid for me to spend a year in Rome in 2009–10, affiliated with the British School at Rome, during which most of the chapters on architectural supply and sarcophagi were completed. Without the generosity of these various bodies this project would never have got off the ground. It seems appropriate that this book should be published in the Oxford Studies on the Roman Economy series since it began its life as part of the Oxford Roman Economy Project and I would like to thank the editors of this series for accepting it. I am grateful to Taryn Das Neves and Kizzy Taylor-Richlieu at Oxford University Press for overseeing its realization and Gillian Northcott Liles for the efficient copy-editing.

Final thanks go to my parents, for whose support I will be forever grateful, and especially to my wife, who has put up with me throughout this process and without whom I could never have come even close to completing it.

Contents

List of Figures

List of Tables

List of Abbreviations

(Those used in the bibliography are taken from *L'Année Épigraphique*)

AE   *L'Année Épigraphique.* Paris (1888–).

BGU   *Berliner Griechische Urkunden (Aegyptischer Urkunden aus den Koeniglichen Museen zu Berlin).* Berlin (1895–).

CIG   *Corpus Inscriptionum Graecarum.* Berlin (1828–77).

CIL   *Corpus Inscriptionum Latinarum.* Berlin (1862–).

C.P.Herm.   *Corpus Papyrorum Hermopolitanorum.* Leipzig (1905).

Eph.Ep.   *Ephemeris Epigraphica* (Corpus Inscriptionum Latinarum Supplementum). Berlin (1872).

GIMB   *The Collection of Ancient Greek Inscriptions in the British Museum.* London (1874–1916); repr. Milan (1979).

IG   *Inscriptiones Graecae.* Berlin (1873–).

IG Bulg   *Inscriptiones Graecae in Bulgaria repertae,* 4 vols. Sofia (1956–70).

IGRR   *Inscriptiones Graecae ad res Romanas pertinentes.* Paris (1911–27).

ILAlg   *Inscriptions latines de l'Algérie.* Paris (1922–76).

ILS   *Inscriptiones Latinae Selectae.* Berlin (1892–1916).

I.Pan.   Bernand, A. (ed.) (1977). *Pan du desert.* Leiden.

IPT   *Iscrizioni puniche della Tripolitania (1927–1967).* Rome (1987).

IRC   *Inscriptions romaines de Catalogne.* Paris (1984–).

IRT   *Inscriptions of Roman Tripolitania.* London (1952).

LIMC   *Lexicon Iconographicum Mythologiae Classicae.* Zurich and Munich (1981–).

MAMA   *Monumenta Asiae Minoris Antiqua.* Manchester (1928–).

P.Amh.   *Amherst Papyri.* London (1900–1).

P.Fam.Tebt.   Von Groningen, B. A. (1950). *A Family Archive from Tebtunis.* Leiden.

P.Giss.   *Griechische Papyri im Museum des oberhessischen Geschichtsvereins zu Giessen.* Leipzig (1910–12).

P.Got.   *Papyrus grecs de la Bibliothèque Municipale de Gothembourg.* Gothenburg (1929).

P.Hib.   *The Hibeh Papyri.* London (1906–55).

P.Köln   *Kölner Papyri.* Opladen (1964–2009).

P.Lond.   *Greek Papyri in the British Museum.* London (1893–).

P.Mich   *Papyri and Ostraca from Karanis.* Ann Arbor (1931–).

P.Oxy.	*The Oxyrhynchus Papyri.* London (1898–).
RIB	*The Roman Inscriptions of Britain.* Oxford (1965–).
SB	*Sammelbuch griechischer Urkunden aus Aegypten.* Wiesbaden (1915–).
SEG	*Supplementum Epigraphicum Graecum.* Leiden (1923–).
Sel.Pap. II	Hunt, A. S. and Edgar, C. S. (eds) (1934). *Select Papyri, II: Official Documents* (Loeb Classical Library). Cambridge, Massachusetts.
TAM	*Tituli Asiae Minoris.* Vienna (1901–).

Note to the Reader

A note on nomenclature is necessary. For places mentioned in the text the best-known name is used, whether modern or ancient; hence, Lyon is used instead of Lugdunum but Assos instead of Behramkale. In terms of the spelling of ancient place names I have used the Latin conventions in the West and the Greek ones in the East, so that I use Prokonnesos instead of Proconnesus and Dokimeion rather than Docimium. In the case of materials again the most common names are used. White marbles and most granites are distinguished with reference to their origin—Prokonnesian marble or Troad granite. In the case of polychrome stones this is less easily done and so the later names created by the Italian *scalpellini* are employed. In order to avoid any confusion a short glossary is provided here of the most common stone varieties. More information about the geological classification of these materials can now be found online on the website of the Corsi Collection of Decorative Stones of the Oxford University Museum of Natural History (http://www.oum.ox.ac.uk/corsi).

Italian name	Latin name	Main source	Colour
Africano	Marmor luculleum	Teos, Turkey	Breccia with black or green matrix containing pink, white, red, and green clasts
Breccia Corallina	–	Verzirhan, Turkey	Breccia with coral red ground and cream–white clasts
Breccia di Settebasi	Marmor scyrium	Skyros, Greece	Breccia with purple ground and white, sometimes pink or orange, clasts
Cipollino	Marmor carystium	South-eastern Euboea, Greece	Streaked green and white marble
Fior di Pesco	–	Eretria, Greece	Pink–purple to brown marble streaked with white
Giallo antico	Marmor numidicum	Chemtou (ancient Simitthus), Tunisia	Breccia with a ground of purple, orange, or yellow and yellow clasts
Granito del Foro	Marmor claudianum	Mons Claudianus, Egypt	Speckled black-and-white granodiorite
Greco scritto	–	Near Ephesos, Turkey	White marble with meandering lines of black markings
Pavonazzetto	Marmor phrygium	Iscehisar (ancient Dokimeion), Turkey	Breccia of white clasts in a purple matrix

Portasanta	Marmor chium	Chios, Greece	Breccia of pink or grey clasts in a red–pink matrix
Rosso antico	Marmor taenarium	Cape Matapan, Greece	Uniformly red–brown marble
Serpentino verde	Marmor lacadaemonium	Krokeai, near Sparta, Greece	Dark green porphyritic andesite with a lighter green speckled pattern
Verde antico	Marmor thessalicum	Kassamboli, near Larisa, Greece	Breccia with light green ground and green, black, or grey clasts

1

Introduction

It would appear to be pretty generally assumed that the study of marbles
is a more or less childish diversion, which may be harmlessly taken up by
young persons in search of something pretty and attractive, but which lies
absolutely outside the limits of the legitimate antiquities of Rome.

Pullen 1894: 2

Approaches to the study of ancient stone use have changed somewhat over the
last century and a quarter. Stone objects are among the most permanent
material vestiges of Roman antiquity; like ceramics they survive well in the
archaeological record. From this durability spring practical benefits for the
historian of antiquity. Working traces on them and the geological properties of
the stone from which they were carved also reveal something of both their
manufacture and their origin. As traceable indicators of the distribution
systems through which they were moved, traded, and redistributed as commodities, therefore, stone objects can offer an insight into the mechanisms of
the wider economy. This study is concerned primarily with what a detailed
analysis of the production and distribution of these artefacts can reveal about
the Roman economy when set against the broader background of quarrying
and the demand for stone. 'The stone trade' is used here in its broadest sense to
refer to the wide range of activities underpinning ancient stone use, from the
extraction and supply of raw material to the carving of individual objects. To
this end, the first two chapters of this volume examine the context for Roman
stone use, demand first and quarrying second; the next two turn to the
transport of stone and its distribution; while the final three examine in turn
the production of architectural elements, sarcophagi, and statues.

MARBLE STUDIES

In 1951, in his defining article on the marble trade in Roman North Africa,
Ward-Perkins lamented that 'a detailed survey of the evidence for the marble

trade in other provinces during the first and second centuries AD has never been attempted'.[1] Now the picture is different and, as Fischer has recently observed, such studies are 'currently fashionable'.[2] Much of this can be credited to Ward-Perkins, whose detailed studies of individual sites and objects took place alongside, and in combination with, broader discussions of the entire trade in decorative stone, its structure and organization, as well as its historical context. The editors of his collected papers rightly credit Ward-Perkins 'as the main founder of what is now a large field of research', and his work remains the established point of reference for any discussion of Roman stone use.[3]

The editors of Ward-Perkins' collected papers, though, were equally correct to assert in 1992 that 'despite the great intrinsic interest of the subject for archaeologists, art historians and historians alike, there is so far no general and fully accessible book on the ancients' use of marble'.[4] This remains true today. Since Ward-Perkins was writing, the available datasets have increased markedly on almost all fronts. Considerable numbers of new quarrying sites have been discovered and significant progress has been made in the field of archaeometry, especially with the application of isotopic and EPR (electron paramagnetic resonance) analysis.[5] Many of the recent advances in this field have been fostered by the Association for the Study of Marble and Other Stones used in Antiquity (ASMOSIA), a consciously interdisciplinary body, the effective successor of the Marble Committee of which Ward-Perkins was a founding member.[6] A wider interest in where materials came from and how they were carved—what has been called 'the logistics behind ancient art'—can also be seen in more specifically art historical or architectural studies.[7] This is especially clear in sarcophagus studies but recent examinations of statuary have tended to follow suit.[8] Discussions of quarrying, carving, and the labour involved, are now thoroughly integrated into most work on Roman architecture.[9] Rockwell's discussions of the practicalities of stone carving have also

---

[1] Ward-Perkins 1951: 90.   [2] M. L. Fischer 1998: 7.

[3] Dodge and Ward-Perkins 1992: 1; see also Ward-Perkins 1951; 1963; 1969; 1971; 1975; 1975–6; 1980*a*; 1980*b*.

[4] Dodge and Ward-Perkins 1992: 1.

[5] On the evolution of archaeometric studies of stone, Craig and Craig 1972; Coleman and Walker 1979; Herz and Wenner 1981; Walker 1984; Herz 1990; Lapuente, Turi, and Blanc 2000; Lazzarini 2002*c*; Antonelli and Lazzarini 2004; Attanasio 2003; Attanasio, Brilli, and Ogle 2006.

[6] The published ASMOSIA volumes to date are Herz and Waelkens 1988; Waelkens, Herz, and Moens 1992; Maniatis, Herz, and Basiakos 1995; Schvoerer 1999; Herrmann, Herz, and Newman 2002; Lazzarini 2002*a*; Maniatis 2009; Jockey 2009; Gutiérrez, Lapuente, and Rodà 2012. On the Marble Committee, Monna 1988.

[7] Waelkens, De Paepe, and Moens 1988: 21.

[8] For instance: Koch 1993: 32–42; Waelkens 1982*a*: 124–7; and on statuary, Trimble 2011: 64–103.

[9] Prominent examples include: DeLaine 1997; 2001; 2006; Lancaster 1998; 2000; 2005; Barresi 2002; 2003; Wilson Jones 2000; Mar and Pensabene 2010; Pensabene, Mar, and Cebrián 2012.

helped to reinvigorate the study of artistic production and foreground it in even the most mainstream studies of Roman and Greek art.[10]

The study of Roman stone use, in sum, is booming. Despite this, research in this field remains irregularly spread and often highly targeted. There is a lot of material that needs to be drawn together. While archaeometric studies are increasingly revealing where materials came from and how and when they were used, much less work has been done on interpreting what this tells us about how the wider stone trade was organized and what it reveals about the economy more generally. This is not to say that important syntheses tackling these issues do not exist. Fant has worked extensively on the evidence for imperial stone use, while Braemer has brought together a lot of data for the more localized patterns of stone use that have tended to be ignored.[11] Pensabene, most notably of all, has produced a huge number of detailed examinations of the production and supply of stone, primarily for architectural projects.[12]

There remain, though, questions to be asked, in particular the kinds of questions routinely asked in wider economic studies. How did imperial and non-imperial stone use compare, for instance, with regard to its procurement, distribution, and scale? Did the imperial stone trade really lie 'outside of the normal orbit of trade in marbles and decorative stones', as has been proposed?[13] What can the distribution of stone reveal about wider connectivity, transport logistics, and demand for specific materials? What do stone objects, on which traces of working processes are so often preserved, add to our understanding of Roman manufacturing? Fundamentally, the basic interpretative framework originally laid out by Ward-Perkins, his influential model of the Roman 'marble trade', has rarely been challenged systematically.[14] At the heart of this model is the proposal that as demand for decorative stone swelled, notably in the first and second centuries AD, stone production was reorganized along quasi-industrial lines: production became centred on the quarries, with objects being carved in standardized forms and dimensions to stock.[15] This was a less responsive but more efficient system that can in turn be used to explain the apparently repetitive aspect of so much Roman art and architecture. New data, and the re-examination of existing material, cast serious doubt on this reconstruction.

---

[10] The key text is Rockwell 1993. Earlier works include Blümner 1912; Blümel 1927; Casson 1933; while Bessac 1986 is the best discussion of ancient tools. On these studies, see Jockey 2001: 347–58; and for a recent re-examination of carving techniques in Greek sculpture, Nolte 2006.

[11] Fant 1988; 1989a; 1989b; 1990; 1992; 1993a; 1993b; 1999; 2001; 2008a; Braemer 1971; 1982; 1984; 1986a; 1986b; 1992.

[12] Pensabene 1972; 1978; 1994; 1998a; 2001a; 2002b; 2003.

[13] Peacock 1993: 65.

[14] Ward-Perkins 1980b; 1992a; 1992b; 1992c; 1992d.

[15] See esp. Ward-Perkins 1980a: 327; 1980b: 25.

STONE IN ECONOMIC STUDIES

The impact of Ward-Perkins' model can be seen beyond the specific field of 'marble studies'. Few major studies of the Roman imperial economy now fail to include at least a brief nod in the direction of stone. About time, one might say. After all, as Jongman has noted, in most pre-industrial societies, building is the single most important non-agrarian economic activity, and in the Roman world a considerable amount of building was in stone.[16] But considering this, quarrying and the stone trade still tend to receive only cursory attention in general economic studies. In a recent volume of papers on the economy of Roman Asia Minor, of all places, 'marble' is mentioned only five times, never in detail, and quarrying only once.[17] A quick trawl through the index of the *The Cambridge Economic History of the Greco-Roman World*, arguably the most up-to-date survey of the ancient economy, is revealing.[18] Quarrying and marble and stone use are referred to on only six occasions, five of these in relation to state-organized activity: transport to and from, and investment in, the quarries of the Eastern Desert; the administration of imperially owned quarries; the exploitation of imperial property in the provinces.[19] A comparable range of focus can be identified elsewhere.[20] The testimony of the Eastern Desert quarries, of course, is particularly emotive and it is no surprise to find references to these remote enterprises liberally scattered through commentaries on the economic role of the state. This kind of activity has become as much a leitmotif for imperial excess in modern scholarship as it is in the works of ancient writers.[21]

It is crucial, however, that these choice examples are not treated as representative of the stone trade more generally; we need to be careful not to narrow our focus too greatly. Stone has the potential to illustrate a range of other aspects of the economy, as Leveau shows in his contribution to the above-mentioned volume. His words are worth quoting in full since they highlight some of the themes that will be pursued further in this volume:

> Urban and rural building work, road construction, and hydraulic works necessitated the opening of quarries and the construction of ovens to burn bricks and lime. The market was local or at most regional. Where the environment lent itself to it, quarries were opened near the building site and maintained for as long as building went on: the quarry of L'Estel near the Pont du Gard provides an example of this practice. In other cases, building programs generated local supply: the lime ovens of Iversheim sur L'Erft supplied the sites along the Rhine; the stone

---

[16] Jongman 2007: 609.   [17] Mitchell and Katsari 2005.
[18] Scheidel, Morris, and Saller 2007.
[19] Morley 2007: 585; Jongman 2007: 592; Lo Cascio 2007: 642, 644–5; Alcock 2007: 685.
[20] For example, Mattingly 2007: 224.
[21] In particular, Strabo, *Geography* XII.8.14; Pliny the Elder XXXVI.1.

from the Midi moved up the Rhône towards Lyon; brick cargoes circulated on the Guadalquivir. The precious marbles from Africa, Italy, and the east are found on sites along the Rhine.[22]

Away from the major quarries that attracted imperial attention, in other words, the stone trade was firmly rooted in the local and regional economies of the Roman world. It responded to specific demand, mainly from the construction sector, and it was shaped by the local environment and the extent of transport networks; stone was a commodity like any other. This is neither a radical re-interpretation of the Roman imperial stone trade, nor is it in conflict with the view of state-level activity most frequently remarked upon by economic historians. Rather, these two perspectives on the stone trade concern themselves with different levels of activity, different points in the same continuum. So it is vital that we do not allow our interest in one level of activity to obscure all of the other things taking place simultaneously.

This is a theme that can be recognized in much recent work on the Roman economy. In the past ten years, in particular, there has been a notable move away from the 'primitivist–modernist debate' that so characterized most twentieth-century work in this field. There is growing acceptance that to classify the Roman economy as either 'developed' or 'underdeveloped', in comparison with other historical economies, is unhelpful; as Jongman has argued, the frame of debate has been misleading.[23] The Roman economy was atypical in comparison with other pre-industrial economies precisely because the Roman Empire was atypical. Very different conclusions about its development or otherwise can be drawn depending on where we choose to look. On the one hand, the Roman economy was firmly based on agriculture, but, on the other, the Roman Empire was arguably the most urbanized of all pre-industrial societies; manufactured goods abounded, most being distributed only short distances, but staples as well as luxuries were also regularly transported long distances to feed the major centres of population and the army. The state played a central role in maintaining and organizing these long-distance redistributive supply routes, but in other areas of the economy acted only sporadically; identifying consistent economic policy is almost impossible.[24] Considering the geographical spread of the Roman Empire it is not surprising to find regional variation. Neighbouring regions had very different trajectories of development. At the same time, all of this variety needs to mapped across the more than three or four hundred years in question during which time rulers and provinces came and went, and the socio-cultural, as well as economic priorities of all levels of society, evolved in a range of

---

[22] Leveau 2007: 659–60.
[23] Jongman 2002: 32; also De Blois et al. 2002; Mattingly 2006.
[24] Bowman and Wilson 2009: 3–84.

directions. Focus has shifted, therefore, away from modelling homogeneity towards interpreting heterogeneity.[25]

Stone objects have much to contribute to this debate. Their durability means that, unlike most other commodities usually discussed in economic studies (ceramics, metals, bricks), we can see *how* they were used and often *how* they were produced. We can identify different stages of production in a way impossible for other object types. Analysis of where and how different stone types were used also offers an insight into the extent of connectivity in our period; studies of distribution and transport reveal the limits of this interconnectedness and the attempts made to overcome the natural obstacles laid down by the fragmented topography of the area. Against this background, imperial activity is especially striking. It was always consciously anomalous, standing proud from the norm, and for studies of the Roman economy, which often struggle to distinguish between state-sponsored redistribution and private commerce, this is an important point.

AIMS AND OBJECTIVES

Despite the rigid formulation of his model, Ward-Perkins was well aware that it did not explain everything. As he himself put it,

> a great deal of misunderstanding would be avoided if scholars would cease trying to squeeze into a single mould what must often have been a very wide diversity of individual practices.[26]

This study aims to follow this advice, adopting a more nuanced approach, one orientated from a similarly economic perspective but focused on highlighting and interpreting the observable variety. It takes Ward-Perkins' words, as expressed above, as its influence. Stone objects were produced and distributed as commodities but no single system determined the development of this trade. Quarrying and the production of stone objects responded to demand, which itself varied enormously both geographically and chronologically, as well as according to object type. Particular circumstances—the location of a quarry, its accessibility, material, ownership, transport links and infrastructure, the demands of the client, and the type of object required—dictated the mode of production. Although the bulk of the evidence discussed below, especially for production, comes from the largest marble quarries, such activity should be understood in a broader context. Likewise, imperial activity needs to be examined against a background of more normal, localized patterns of stone use.

---

[25] Mattingly 2007: 221–2.   [26] Ward-Perkins 1980*b*: 61.

The focus of this study, therefore, is on interpreting the observable hetero-geneity. This does not mean that any 'underlying similarity of process', to use Shaw's words, cannot be identified.[27] Stone, as a medium, limits experimen-tation and the methods adopted by different individuals at different sites, as approaches to common problems, do show similarities across the artificial boundaries that modern scholarship has imposed on the material evidence. Broader chronological changes in both the supply of, and demand for, stone are, furthermore, traceable. The rough timescale of this study, focused on the first three centuries AD, was chosen for precisely this reason, in order to encompass periods of both boom and bust. These chronological limits, though, should not be considered fixed. The fashion for imported stones had earlier origins, while many of the developments apparent in the first, second, and third centuries AD are still obvious in the fourth and even fifth centuries AD. Extensive use will be made of evidence from both earlier and later periods when relevant.

As manufactured items, stone objects were affected by the same kind of shifts in market demand and problems of supply that shaped the use of other commodities in the Roman world. However, it is also important to be aware of some of the features that distinguish many sculpted stone objects from other types of artefact. In comparison with other objects, consumer demand played a much greater role in determining the form and quality of individual stone objects. Though general demand for olive oil, therefore, might affect the mode and scale of production at a particular oilery, every batch of oil produced would be essentially identical. Certain stone objects could have been produced in this way, in response to general demand. However, stone objects with some form of sculpting, shaping, elaboration, or decoration were more likely pro-duced in response to specific demand; they were not neutral commodities. This does not mean that economic factors did not determine their mode of production, merely that we need to be able to incorporate consumer choice into any analysis of the production of sculpted stone objects; the final form of most of our evidence resulted from this choice.

---

[27] B. D. Shaw 2001: 426.

2

The Market for Stone

A stoneworker's view of his material is also concerned with its *use*.
Durability, colour and structural strength are considered in judging the
stone's suitability. No stone is rejected as such, but only in relation to a
specific purpose.

Rockwell 1993: 17

If you ask what I have to show in the way of marble, it is true that Paros,
Karystos and Prokonnesos, Phrygians, Numidians and Spartans have not
deposited here slabs from hill-faces in many colours, nor do any stone
surfaces, stained with a natural tinge among the Ethiopian crags with
their purple precipices, furnish a counterfeit imitation of sprinkled bran.
But although I am not enriched by the chill starkness of foreign rocks,
still my buildings, call them cottages or huts if you please, have their native
coolness.

Sidonius Apollinaris, Letters II.2.7[1]

Stone was put to all manner of uses in the Roman period. Roughly shaped
stone was used in rubble construction, as aggregate in concrete, for foundations, and for wall facings. Cut stone was used for ashlar construction, for
vaulting and arches, for a range of architectural elements (columns, capitals,
bases, entablature blocks), for wall veneer and floor tiles. Those stones that
could be carved to hold fine (and often not so fine) detail were employed for
free-standing statues, reliefs, urns and sarcophagi, furniture, basins and bath-
tubs, and inscriptions. Almost every variety of stone occurring naturally
within the area encompassed by Roman rule was employed, from soft sandstone to the finest grade marbles to the hardest volcanic stones, like basalt and
porphyry.

  Before turning to the evidence for the extraction and working of these
materials it is worth first considering why stone was used so widely and
extensively and how this fashion developed. To this end, this chapter examines

---

[1] As translated by W. B. Anderson.

the character of this demand for stone in the Roman world, its chronological and regional development, who was investing in this material, and how much they were spending.

DEMAND FOR STONE

In assessing whether a stone is suitable for a given project stone-workers, ancient and modern, are concerned only indirectly with its geological classification. In practice, they are more interested in stone than rock. They are concerned with the workability of particular stones, their condition, hardness, receptivity to being carved, their ability to take a polish, as well as their colour—whether they are fit for purpose or not.[2] Different types of stone require different handling, sometimes different tools. The harder the stone the harder the material used for the tools needs to be. Equally, when working hard stones, especially granites, tools tend to be held closer to perpendicular to the surface so that the stone is almost battered rather than cut as with softer stones.[3] Hardness does not necessarily relate to geological composition: there are plenty of limestones that are harder than certain marbles, and some marbles have to be worked a little like granites.[4] Rockwell, quoted above, summarizes in some detail the differences between the major stone types in terms of their reactions to tools, and his handbook should be the first port of call for anyone interested in investigating this further. For our purposes it is important to note just the essential points. Soft stones—that is soft limestones, sandstones, certain alabasters—are easy to work and tend to have few flaws running through them; they can be sawn, even without abrasive, and smoothed but not polished; they can hold certain fine detail, but not to the same extent as harder limestones or marbles. These harder limestones and marbles are obviously more difficult to carve, but they allow a far wider range of finishes, can hold a greater level of detail and can be polished, often to a high lustre. In marble, in particular, faults running through the stone can present substantial challenges. Material will often split along these lines—a fact exploited by quarrymen—and faults can be concealed within a block only to make themselves known at the final moment. Harder stones, especially igneous materials, are the hardest to carve but also the most durable and consistent, in both composition and often in colour too; they can hold detail but fine working is much harder to achieve than in marble.

Stone-workers, therefore, assess materials according to the use to which they can be put. Simply put, geologists and stone-workers classify materials

---

[2] Vitruvius II.7.1–5; Rockwell 1993: 15.   [3] Rockwell 1993: 18–19.
[4] On the hard white marble from Thasos, Rockwell 1993: 19.

according to different sets of criteria.[5] Consequently, the Greek word μάρμαρον and the Latin *marmor* referred simply to all stones capable of taking a polish, irrespective of their geological classification.[6] In terms of their petrology, therefore, many materials traditionally described as 'marbles' are in fact 'limestones'; Purbeck Marble, as it is known in Britain, is the obvious example. Indeed, the common names of many stones, both those employed nowadays and those used in the past, reveal the characteristics in which the users of these materials were interested.[7] Most of the ancient names for the best-known coloured marbles described the origin of the material, either broadly or highly specifically: so we have, for instance, *marmor numidicum* (Numidian), *phrygium* (Phrygian), *scyrium* (from Skyros) but also *marmor claudianum* (from Mons Claudianus) and *carystium* (from Karystos). In at least one instance, the famous *marmor luculleum* or *lucullum*, the name derives from Lucius Licinius Lucullus who is credited with having first brought it to Rome.[8] Only occasionally did the ancient names for these marbles include any description of the colour or composition. Exceptions include *lapis porphyrites* ('purple'), the metaconglomerate known as *lapis hecatontalithos* ('one hundred stones'), the Greek name for Aswan granite, *lithos pyrrhopoecilos* ('red-spotted'), as well as the unusual *lapis sarcophagus* ('corpse-eater').[9] In contrast, the names which are now most commonly used for these materials, those invented by the *scalpellini* of Renaissance Rome, tend to be much more descriptive, with regard to both colour (*giallo, rosso, verde antico*) and composition, with frequently poetic results (*cipollino, pavonazzetto, fior di pesco*). But the *scalpellini* also went in for geographic labels, albeit generally ones referring to sites in Rome where the materials were found, rather than distant cities or provinces: *settebasi* (after the villa on the via Tuscolana), *granito del foro* (probably the Forum of Trajan), *portasanta* (after the Porta Santa of St Peter's Basilica which was carved from this stone).

The character of demand

Some stones are naturally better suited to certain projects than others and since stone was used for all manner of work in the Roman world it is to be expected that demand for stone was also varied. While most studies of the Roman stone trade have focused on decorative stones, especially the best-known white and polychrome marbles and granites, other stones were quarried and transported

[5] Rockwell 1993: 16.
[6] Giardini and Colasante 1986: 12–13; on the range of stones quarried in the Roman period, Borghini 2001; Price 2007.
[7] For a glossary of these names, Bugini, Folli, and Ferrario 2002.
[8] Pliny the Elder XXXVI.49; see Fant 1999: 279.
[9] Pliny the Elder XXXVI.56–7, 63, 131.

in substantial quantities. Indeed one of the aims of this study is to examine the long-distance movement of decorative stones against this background of more ordinary, everyday stone use. In practice, two related trends underpin the fashion for stone use that is so characteristic of the Roman period: first, a widespread growth in aggregate demand for stone of all types, especially during the first three centuries AD; and second, a targeted and disproportionately high demand for decorative stones. Demand for stone in our period, therefore, was at once both general and specific. This distinction between ordinary stone, primarily used for building, and decorative stone has been widely noted but understanding these different levels of demand is crucial to interpreting the patterns of stone use which will be examined in the following chapters.[10]

General demand for stone naturally evolved differently across the area encompassed by Roman rule, dependent on local geology and traditions of stone-working. In areas of Greek and Punic heritage, on the one hand, urban culture and stone use had a long and close relationship. In the northern and western provinces, and in the Balkans, on the other hand, the pattern of stone use experienced a much more sudden intensification, linked to the advent of Roman rule and Roman-style urbanization. However, it would be wrong to suggest that in these areas cities and stone-use appeared simultaneously; cities did not need stone. In their earliest phases, many of the cities of Roman Gaul and Germany, for example, made use of wood and wattle and daub, local vernacular building techniques.[11] At Lugdunum Convenarum in the Pyrenees, founded by Pompey in the 70s BC, nothing is preserved prior to the Augustan period when stone buildings appear.[12] The first phases of most of the major settlements on the Rhine, all originally legionary bases, were constructed in wood. At Strasbourg the wooden ramparts were replaced with stone ones topped with a wooden superstructure after the revolt of AD 68–70; this wooden element was only finally replaced with limestone following a fire in AD 97.[13] This pattern is repeated elsewhere: away from the areas of Greek influence in the hinterland of Marseille the early years of Roman rule transformed the settled landscape of Gaul, but only by the Augustan period did this new urban character begin to be widely set in stone.[14]

Colonial foundations certainly helped to promulgate the ideology of stone use. The earliest stone-built, Mediterranean-type houses appear during the late first century BC at colonies, notably at Lyon.[15] The emergence of stone

---

[10] See Lorenz 1995: 88–9 on the distinction between 'les pierres de construction' and 'les pierres décoratives', though of course one material could fall into both categories (Aphrodisian marble, for instance); also Greene 1986: 149–50.

[11] Drinkwater 1985; Bedon, Chevallier, and Pinon 1988.

[12] Woolf 1998: 120–1.   [13] Bedon 1984: 43–4.

[14] Woolf 1998: 111 on pre-Roman Gaul as a 'world of villages'.

[15] Pelletier 1996: 172–3.

architecture in Gaul, Spain, Britain, and elsewhere, however, was first and foremost connected to public building, itself tied to patterns of elite self-display, a central feature of the way in which the local aristocracy was integrated into wider Roman society.[16] In this context, stone equalled permanence: its durability made it the perfect medium in which the socio-cultural priorities of the status quo were monumentalized; it was an expression of political allegiance, at the same time demonstrating an abnormal control of wealth, resources, and labour.[17] The use of stone for domestic building and decoration, sculpture, and funerary monuments was connected to this idea of permanence, and typically follows investment in public building. None of this was alien to any of the areas brought into the Roman Empire in our period, after all stone-built roundhouses and standing stones are a defining feature of the pre-Roman landscape of western Europe. What Roman rule stimulated was investment in stone on an unprecedented level, introducing a language of images and a framework for display and worship in which the ideology of stone was paramount.

'Foreign rocks'

Most of the stone quarried to meet general demand for ordinary architectural and sculptural projects came from the closest possible sources, as we will see further in Chapter 3. However, as stone became more valued, more fashionable, so the demand for high-quality decorative stones grew, and these often had to be brought from further afield. Where these stones came from really mattered and ideological distinctions between imported and local materials are apparent in the literary sources well into Late Antiquity. Pliny the Elder and Seneca both play on this theme, and even as late as the fifth century AD Sidonius Apollinaris draws on this idea in the passage quoted above, describing his house to a friend, celebrating its absence of 'foreign rocks'.

In fact, the Romans came to the decorative stone trade relatively late. As early as the Bronze Age, polychrome stones from the Peloponnese were put to use at Knossos.[18] The various marbles of the Cycladic islands and Prokonnesos were moved long distances to satisfy demand from the Archaic and Classical centres of the Aegean, and even beyond.[19] Naxian and Parian marble was certainly imported into Delphi in the Archaic period—for the Siphnian Treasury, for instance—while Pentelic marble was used increasingly from the

---

[16] Greene 2008: 70.

[17] For comparisons, Trigger 1990; Schoep 2004; Mackie 1990: 190: 'people inscribed things on stone to be noticed, and to be remembered.'

[18] Waterhouse and Simpson 1961: 119–21.

[19] On the Mausoleum of Halikarnassos, Walker and Matthews 1997: 53–6.

fifth century BC onwards.[20] In western Asia Minor, Vitruvius tells us that during the construction of the Artemision at Ephesos, the local council was undecided about whether to import marble from Paros, Prokonnesos, Herakleia-on-Latmos, or Thasos, before Pixodaros' discovery of local marble sources removed the need for imports.[21] There was even demand for Aegean marbles much further afield: recent analysis of the marble used for the roof of fifth-century BC Temple C (possibly the Temple of Athena) at Metapontum has shown that it was brought from Paros.[22] Although the stone trade in the Hellenistic period remains under-studied, the limited evidence available suggests that earlier processes intensified as the various rival dynasties competed to outshine each other in their varied architectural creations.[23]

In the Greek world, as Snodgrass has observed, stone was moved long distances only occasionally, and only then to offset local deficiencies.[24] This itself, however, is significant. Even where suitable stone was not available, individual communities felt it necessary to build in stone—stone buildings were proper and Greek. Stone use, therefore, whether for architecture or sculpture, is indicative of a level of cultural and economic connectedness, a sharing of common expectations and perceptions. Roman demand took this activity to an entirely new level. The metropolitan market was huge and Roman elite tastes led to the exploitation of previously untapped resources, of coloured marbles most notably. This phenomenon has its origins in the second century BC when members of the Roman elite became increasingly proactive in the use of imported marble. Alongside the continuing influx of finished objects, often booty carried in triumph, marble came to be appreciated as a raw material. The temple of Jupiter Stator, the first building in the capital to be built of imported marble, was commissioned in 146 BC by Q. Caecilius Metellus, victor in Macedonia.[25] Greek (Pentelic) marble was used, as was a Greek architect, Hermodoros of Salamis. Pentelic, in fact, was the marble of choice in this period in Rome, reflecting Athens' position as the great cultural hotspot of the Late Republic.[26] For all this Greek influence, it was Roman tradition that shaped marble use in this period. The prestige value of this material evolved in the context of elite competition. It was right, as Plutarch saw it, 'that the conquered should give place to the conquerors', and for the individual conquerors, the various *triumphatores* of this period, keen to assert their supremacy over their political rivals, eastern marbles became potent tokens of victory.[27]

---

[20] Palagia and Herz 2002: 240–1, table 1.   [21] Vitruvius X.2.15.

[22] De Siena, Cancelliere, and Lazzarini 2002.

[23] On stone-use in Attalid Pergamon, Cramer, Germann, and Heilmeyer 2002; on the Hellenistic shipwreck at Kızılburun, Carlson 2009.

[24] Snodgrass 1983: 19.

[25] Pensabene 2002*b*: 3–4.

[26] Wallace-Hadrill 2008: 390–1; S. Bernard 2010: 40–6.

[27] Plutarch, *Life of Aemilius Paullus* 28.

Elite display and public munificence were always intimately linked. In the second and first centuries BC, the newly acquired wealth of the eastern kingdoms was channelled into the urban fabric of Rome and, increasingly, into private buildings: Lucius Crassus (consul in 95 BC) erected columns of Hymettian marble in his house; Marcus Lepidus introduced *giallo antico* (in 78 BC) and Lucius Lucullus *africano* (in 74 BC); Mamurra, was the first man 'to cover with marble veneer whole walls' and 'have only marble columns' in his house.[28] In the aedileship of Marcus Scaurus (58 BC), at least 120 columns were incorporated into a temporary theatre in the city (the remaining 140 being materials other than stone). The largest, in *africano* and 38 Roman feet long (12.8 m), were then hauled to the Palatine to be built into Scaurus' own atrium; 'dragged to a private house past the earthenware pediments of temples', as Pliny puts it, a contrast between the old and the new later echoed by Suetonius' Augustus, who found a city of brick and left it one of marble.[29]

The metropolitan elites of this period were following in a well-established eastern tradition, consciously modelling their residences on the royal palaces of Hellenistic kings and notables.[30] Coloured marbles were especially sought after because they were easily identified; they spoke to the public, as much as to these elites' peers, of foreign lands and distant conquests. And for succeeding generations these materials were imbued not just with a sense of exoticism but one of class and privilege; 'our favourite marbles' Pliny calls them, the names of which even reflected their aristocratic associations—*marmor luculleum* being the best example.[31] In the Imperial period these coloured stones provided a 'material map' of the empire.[32] But in the areas where most of these materials originated, of course, these various levels of symbolism were meaningless. Such a nuisance is it to move that stone gains prestige the further away from its source it is used. One is reminded of Cicero's famous dismissal of the multicoloured marble walls of Chios—'I should be much more amazed if you had made them of stone from Tibur.'[33] In Greece and Asia Minor, where the majority of these materials originated, the fashion for coloured marbles in decorative contexts caught on only during the first and second centuries AD, influenced in part by imperial building projects in Rome and the provinces.

In Italy, the fashion for coloured marbles took hold rapidly. In first-century BC Pompeii, where supply struggled to meet demand, wall-paintings imitated coloured stones. In the latest Pompeian contexts, even the Egyptian porphyries and granites that had only appeared in the capital under Nero and the Flavian emperors are imitated. As Fant has remarked: 'the important thing to

[28] Pliny the Elder XXXVI.7, 48–50 (trans. D. E. Eichholz).
[29] Pliny the Elder XXXVI.6; Suetonius, *Augustus* 28.3.
[30] Wallace-Hadrill 2008: 144–210, esp. 190–6.
[31] Pliny the Elder XXXVI.46 (trans. D. E. Eichholz).
[32] Story et al. 2005: 163.
[33] Pliny the Elder XXXVI.46 (trans. D. E. Eichholz).

display was not necessarily the physical object, but taste itself'.[34] Fragments of various stones from the Eastern Desert do appear at both Pompeii and Herculaneum, in fact, but only in very small quantities. Slithers of porphyry are incorporated into the *cocciopesto* floor of the atrium of the Casa dell'Atrio Corinzio at Herculaneum, for example, while irregular plaques of black-and-white granite were built into the counter of the *thermopolium* at V, 9–10; green granite fragments (perhaps *Granito della sedia di San Lorenzo*) are also found on the counters of the *thermopolia* at I, 9, 4 and VI, 10, 1 at Pompeii.[35] The speed with which even the most exotic of decorative stones were adopted in Italy especially struck a particular chord with Seneca who contrasts the elegant simplicity of Scipio Africanus' villa with the more sumptuous residences of his own day, ornamented with 'marbles from Alexandria', 'mosaics of Numidian stone', and 'swimming pools lined with Thasian marble': 'we have become so luxurious that we will have nothing but precious stones to walk upon'.[36] Sidonius Apollinaris might well have been drawing directly on this passage in his much later text, quoted above.

Ancient consumers were certainly well aware of the different varieties of decorative stones. The literary sources are highly specific in their discussion of stone types, especially the poets, often remarking on their particular qualities and origins.[37] Writers were clearly able to recognize specific materials or find someone who could. Pausanias, for instance, in his description of the Temple of Olympian Zeus in Athens notes that in front of the entrance there stood two statues of Hadrian in Thasian stone and two in Egyptian stone, perhaps porphyry or granite.[38] These were important facts to be noted and epigraphic evidence shows that at least some ordinary customers had a similar knowledge: the inscription on a sarcophagus from Perge records that it was made of Prokonnesian marble; another from Konya stresses that it is carved from Dokimeian marble; and on an inscribed third-century grave plaque, presumably from the exterior of a tomb and now in the British Museum, a certain Aurelia Felicissima (spelt *Filikistima* in the Greek) records that she commissioned a sculpted sarcophagus in Prokonnesian marble and another in basalt.[39] This knowledge also extended to local materials, which were often

---

[34] Fant 2007: 343. On imitation marble in paint at Brescia, Bugini and Folli 2005: 165–7; and on the use of mosaics to recreate patterns found in marble, Michaelides 1985. Stucco, of course, is often used in place of white marble: for its use at Colchester, Blagg 1990: 34.

[35] Fant 2009*a*.

[36] Seneca, *Epistles* LXXXVI.6 (trans. R. M. Gummere).

[37] For example: Tibullus, *Elegies* III.3.13; Martial, *Epigrams* I.88; Juvenal, *Satires* XIV.307; Statius, *Silvae* I.2.148–9; Lucian, *Hippias or the Bath* 5–6.

[38] Pausanias I.18.6.

[39] On the sarcophagi, Asgari 1977: 333; McLean 2002: no. 182. For mentions of Prokonnesian, *GIMB* 1026; *CIG* 3268, 3282, 3386; Kubińska 1968: 59; Buckler 1917: 113 (from Izmir); *CIG* 4340e (Lanckoroński 1890: 162, no. 20, from Attaleia). On the British Museum plaque, *GIMB* 1026; Walker 1985*a*: 18.

highly valued. An inscription from Sagalassos, for example, notes that the monument it adorns is made in 'native stone', local limestone, and specifically not the more famous Phrygian marble.[40] At Hierapolis, where Dokimeian marble is again mentioned in several inscriptions, sarcophagi carved in the local Thiounta marble are also recorded on four funerary inscriptions.[41] The importance attached to specific materials, but also an awareness of the efforts that went into acquiring them is most clearly demonstrated in the well-known testament of Sestus Iulius Aquila from the territory of Langres in central Germania Superior.[42] Among the detailed requests that he leaves for the construction of his tomb, Aquila insists that the carved elements should be completed in the finest *lapis transmarinus*, that is stone brought from overseas, and specifically Luna marble.[43] This despite the fact that Aquila's tomb was to be built about as far from the sea as one could have got while staying within the Roman Empire.

Fine white and coloured marbles, therefore, were appreciated for their decorative qualities. The bulk of stone extracted in this period, however, was not coloured. Most of it was not even marble. Nevertheless, the fashion for coloured marble is indicative of a more widespread and deep-rooted interest in stone use that took hold in almost every region under Roman rule. By concentrating on the high-quality white and coloured marbles, the pinnacle of the stone trade, most scholars have focused on the exceptional to the detriment of the general.

Focus of demand

A growth in demand for stone generally, which went hand in hand with demand for specific decorative materials, can be noted across the Roman world in the last century BC and the first three centuries AD, then. While this fashion has its roots in Rome in the last two centuries BC its spread across the Roman world was far from even. There were important regional differences in demand but variant patterns can also be noted in what stone was used for in this period.

Most quarried stone was used for building and the increase in urbanization under the Roman empire consequently had important implications for stone consumption.[44] The foundation of new cities and the expansion of old ones necessitated extensive quarrying. The evidence provided by building dedications,

---

[40] *IGRR* III.362; Waelkens 1997: 241.
[41] For inscriptions from Hierapolis mentioning Dokimeian marble, Judeich 1898: no. 56, 158, 209, 213, 323, 335, while no. 113, 178, 312, 339b mention stone from Thiounta; also Kubińska 1968: 59.
[42] *CIL* XIII.5708; see also Le Bohec 1991.
[43] Russell 2011a: 139.
[44] Scheidel 2007: 75–80; Morley 2007: 578; for a different perspective, Hanson forthcoming.

however, shows that the chronology of construction activity varied consider-ably across the Roman world. As Jouffroy has shown, the dedication of public buildings in Italy, outside Rome, peaked in the first century AD.[45] Rome distorts this picture slightly, since construction here boomed in the first and second centuries AD but here too it slowed down almost entirely in the middle of the third century AD and never really picked up after this.[46] In contrast, in North Africa, the dedication of public buildings peaks later, in the second century AD, and in fact remains relatively stable even into the fourth and fifth centuries AD.[47] In Asia Minor, on the other hand, building activity appears to reach its zenith in the mid second century AD, then drops markedly after the Severan period, with only fortifications being added to most cities in the third century AD.[48] In Britain, as far as we can tell, investment in urban construction reached a peak in the early second century AD for civic and administrative buildings, the early to mid second century for commercial structures, the late second century for domestic buildings, and the third century for fortifications.[49]

The chronology of certain other object types follows closely that of building. French's work on the inscriptions at Amasia in northern Asia Minor, to give one example, has shown that the dated gravestones peak in the mid to late second century AD before declining after the Severan period, much like building elsewhere in the region.[50] However, this is not the pattern for all objects. Wilson has argued that honorific inscriptions, which were often erected to accompany statues, continued to be set up in large numbers across the Roman world even after public building declined. Comparing building and honorific inscriptions, primarily Latin but also some Greek ones, he shows that while building generally peaks in the mid to late second century AD, honorific inscriptions peak in the Severan period and drop away only in the early to mid third century AD.[51] MacMullen has highlighted a comparable pattern in Lydia, where again inscriptions continued to be set up in large numbers until the mid third century AD, though he makes no distinction between types of inscriptions.[52] Inscriptions were still being commissioned, then, and benefactors still being honoured, even if they were no longer paying for building projects.[53] Sarcophagus production presents a more strikingly different pattern, though again one marked by strong regional variation.

[45] Jouffroy 1977: 336–7; 1986: 459.   [46] Daguet-Gagey 1997: table 1.
[47] Jouffroy 1986: 233–7.
[48] Barresi 2003: 131–4; Mitchell 1993: 213–14; on building in the third century AD, Rambaldi 2009: esp. 111–37.
[49] Faulkner 2000: 30–1, fig. 11.   [50] French 1991: 66–8, fig. 2a.
[51] A. I. Wilson 2009: fig. 1–2; and for benefactions in Asia Minor, Zuiderhoek 2009: 17–22, esp. fig. 1.2–3.
[52] MacMullen 1986: 237, fig. 1.   [53] Mitchell 1990: 189.

Sarcophagi actually continued to be produced in large numbers well into the third century AD across much of the Roman world, even after public building trailed off. The major western centres of sarcophagus carving, like Rome and Ravenna, continued to produce for a willing market right through the third century AD, perhaps even reaching a peak of production in this period.[54] The same is true at certain eastern centres, like Tyre, where sarcophagus production remains consistent right through the third century AD and indeed into the fourth and fifth centuries AD.[55] In contrast, at Aphrodisias, where the sarcophagus corpus can be closely dated, there is an explosion in the number of locally produced sarcophagi in the early third century AD, coinciding with Caracalla's citizenship reforms of AD 212, which is then followed by a decline into the fourth century AD.[56] In this period there was more demand for stone for this kind of private commemoration than for public building and the reciprocal erection of statues. While a general boom in the numbers of all objects or monuments requiring stone can be noted across the Roman world between the late first and late second century AD, then, different chronologies can be noted according both to region and object type.

SOURCES OF DEMAND

What of the sources of demand? Who invested in stone? Was serious investment limited to the emperors or the elite, or was it more widely spread through society?

Imperial investment

The highest densities of high-quality stones are associated with imperial building projects, which have in turn attracted the bulk of scholarly attention. Fine public buildings required the best materials and imperial building projects set the tone.[57] According to Pausanias, the library that Hadrian gave to Athens had 100 columns of Phrygian marble, walls of the same material, and rooms with gilded roofs and alabaster floors.[58] When Hadrian rebuilt the

---

[54] On Ravenna, Gabelmann 1973: 91–178; Kollwitz and Herdejürgen 1979; on third- and fourth-century AD production at Rome, Eichner 1981; Koch 2000.

[55] Chéhab 1968; Koch 1989.

[56] On the connection between these reforms and sarcophagus-use, Smith 2006: 347. On the dating of these sarcophagi, Işik 2007; Reynolds and Rouché 2007.

[57] Gros 1985: 70; in emulation of imperial construction, Herod made extensive use of the highest-quality materials in his building projects (Josephus, *Jewish Wars* 404–8, 413–14, 419–25).

[58] Pausanias I.18.9.

temple of Apollo at Megara he found a brick structure and, with suitable Augustan echoes, left it marble.[59] Money for this work came directly from the emperor, or from state funds at any rate.[60] However, since structures were often dedicated in the name of the emperor, with his permission or at his request, without being paid for out of these funds, the number of imperially funded projects is easily overestimated.[61] Outside Rome, in fact, they constitute only a small minority of the total number of epigraphically attested building projects.

Imperial building was extremely targeted and by no means every city benefited from new structures put up at the emperor's expense. The evidence provided by building inscriptions, in fact, shows that most imperial building projects were concerned with improving infrastructure or providing fortifications.[62] Restoration activity also features heavily, even at Rome itself, where 54 per cent of the dedicatory inscriptions datable to between AD 180 and 305 refer to such work.[63] Building inscriptions do not provide the whole picture, of course, since imperial funds were sometimes channelled through cities. Philostratos, for instance, states that Hadrian gave 10,000,000 drachmas to Smyrna in one day, which the city then used for a range of civic buildings, while Nero gave 4,000,000 sesterces to Lugdunum after a fire.[64] Equally, the emperor could lean on members of the local elite, encouraging them to build. The portico that Dio built at Prusa, for example, was in response to Trajan's request to 'put the city into better shape and make it more impressive as a whole'.[65] As Walker has put it, with regard to the Severan period: 'it was not enough for wealthy citizens to keep their heads down and hope to avoid attention . . . the regime and its agents demanded and policed response'.[66] Imperial funds for building could also be directed through provincial officials. In Egypt, especially, the prefect was highly active: in AD 107, Vibius Maximus paid for the restoration of a bath-house and a road at Hermopolis, and in AD 128, Flavius Titianus paid for the construction or restoration of baths at Oxyrhynchus.[67] These officials could, like the emperor, also intervene to

[59] Pausanias I.42.5.
[60] For examples of each, *Historia Augusta: Life of Tacitus* 10.4–5; *Historia Augusta: Life of Pertinax* 9.1–2; see Daguet-Gagey 1997: 195–206.
[61] Mitchell 1987: 343–4; Millar 1992: 421–2.
[62] In the West, Horster 2001: 58–63 (table IIa); in the East, Millar 1992: 421. On aqueducts in Asia Minor, Naour 1978: 166–70; Malinowski and Fahlbusch 1981: 208; in North Africa, A. I. Wilson 1997: 146 (table 7); in Spain, Melchor Gil 1994: 97.
[63] See Horster 2001: 58–63 (table IIa); Barresi 2003: 133–4 (table IVc); and on the evidence from Rome, Daguet-Gagey 1997: 86–92 (table 1).
[64] Philostratos, *Lives of the Sophists* 531; Tacitus, *Annals* 16.13.
[65] Dio Chrysostom XL.5; also Jones 1978: 111–12.
[66] Walker 1990*b*: 139; also A. I. Wilson 2007: 307–13.
[67] *P.Amh.* II.64.2–3; *P.Oxy.* XLIII.3088; also Łukaszewicz 1986, 91–2.

encourage cities to build structures without actually paying for them, especially when they were deemed necessary for the functioning of civic life.[68]

Non-imperial investment in building

Despite these examples, it is clear that the bulk of ordinary civic building projects were funded by members of the local elite. Work by Frézouls and Blagg in the north-western provinces has shown that between 72 per cent (Belgica) and 97 per cent (Aquitania) of building projects attested in dedicatory inscriptions were funded by private benefactors; these were mostly holders of local magistracies or priesthoods, but also high-status freedmen and military officials, especially in frontier areas.[69] The available data from elsewhere largely follow this pattern. Even in Dalmatia, where the provincial governor and the *procurator argentariarum* were particularly active, projects funded by the administration account for no more than 15 per cent of the recorded total.[70] In Hispania Baetica, where Melchor Gil has taken this analysis further, the dominance of the *ordo decurionum* in building activity is especially striking: thirty-six members of this class are attested (59.7 per cent of the total), compared to just three of equestrian (4.8 per cent) and two of senatorial (3.2 per cent) status.[71] In North Africa too most benefactors were local office-holders; only one senatorial benefaction is recorded, for the building of a library at Thamugadi, probably in the third century AD.[72] The same is true in Italy, even if members of the senatorial elite are slightly more numerous in the epigraphic record. Pliny the Younger, of course, was especially active at Comum, building a library and adding to the baths.[73] Other senators were active at Tarquinia and Sinuessa.[74]

The view from the eastern provinces differs only in detail. In the province of Asia between the Flavians and the Severans, Barresi has shown that imperial building projects account for only 10 per cent of the total epigraphically attested constructions.[75] Overall, 59 per cent of these were paid for by private individuals, a lower proportion than in the western provinces, but this figure is distorted by the fact that private funds in the East were often channelled

---

[68] Pliny the Younger, *Letters* X.22, 90–1 (Sinope); *P.Fam.Tebt.* 15, ll. 110–29 (Arsinoe); also Van Minnen 2002: 286–7.

[69] Frézouls 1984; Blagg 1980.

[70] Glicksman 2009.

[71] Melchor Gil 1994: 169–70.

[72] *ILS* 9362; also Duncan-Jones 1982: 62–78, 125–6.

[73] Pliny the Younger, *Letters* 5.7, 7.18; *CIL* V.5262.

[74] *CIL* XI.3366; *AE* 1926, 143.

[75] These are collected by Barresi 2003: 133 (table II).

through public bodies.[76] Cities received income from rents on municipal land or property, from fees on the exploitation of monopolized resources, and from custom dues and a range of other indirect taxes which varied between communities.[77] Nevertheless, contributions from individual citizens, especially obligatory fees for office or *summae honorariae*, probably still accounted for the bulk of public funds; holders of prominent priesthoods, especially those connected to the imperial cult, were especially active benefactors.[78]

The *quid pro quo* of this kind of benefaction, of course, meant that benefactors could expect to be honoured: as Dio put it, 'they require crowns, images, the right of precedence, and being kept in remembrance'.[79] When the emperor acted as benefactor he was rewarded correspondingly; cities even vied with each other in this regard. In the precinct of the temple of Olympian Zeus at Athens, for example, where Hadrian had dedicated the temple and statue of the god, Pausanias tells us 'every city had dedicated a likeness of the emperor, and the Athenians had surpassed them in dedicating, behind the temple, the remarkable colossus'.[80] The dominance of members of the local elite in municipal benefaction, however, is reflected in the number of honorific statues. At Aphrodisias, emperors are represented fifteen times and are mentioned in thirty-four statue inscriptions; for locals these numbers rise to ninety-five and 225, giving imperial to local ratios of 1:6.5 and 1:6.3 respectively.[81] These figures are close to the ratio of imperial to private building in the province of Asia reached by Barresi, of 1:5.6, showing the very real connection between munificence and commemoration in the eastern provinces.[82] These objects, part of the urban landscape, were also repaired and restored in the same way as public buildings: numerous examples are known from Aphrodisias.[83]

The sarcophagus evidence

The evidence provided by dedicatory building inscriptions shows that in aggregate terms far more was spent on building by members of the local elite than the emperors. These data, however, tell us little about sub-elite

---

[76] Barresi 2003: 133 (table II): 22 per cent of projects in Asia were funded by public bodies; in the West, only in Gallia Belgica, where 25 per cent (only nine examples) of all projects were funded by collective bodies is such a high total attested (see Frézouls 1984: 33).

[77] Duncan-Jones 1982: 28–9; Sartre 1991: 134–5; Galsterer 2000: 353.

[78] Quaß 1993: 212–20; Smith 2006: 41.

[79] Dio Chrysostom, *Orations* XXXI.16 (trans. J. W. Cohoon and H. Lamar); also Mackie 1990: 186–7; Lendon 1997.

[80] Pausanias I.18.6 (trans. W. H. S. Jones).

[81] Smith 2006: 13.   [82] Barresi 2003: 133 (table II).

[83] Reynolds 1982: no. 29, 32; Smith 2006: no. 30–1, 39–40, 44, 46–7, 51–2, 57, 58, 94.

engagement with the stone trade. For this we need to turn to other material, in particular sarcophagi.

At the upper end of the sarcophagus market were Attic and the elaborate columnar Asiatic sarcophagi and where the purchasers of these are identified they tend to be high-ranking officials and their families.[84] Claudia Antonia Sabina, buried in an Asiatic sarcophagus at Sardis, was apparently the wife of an ex-consul.[85] A fragmentary Asiatic sarcophagus and two Attic sarcophagi (Ephesos B and C) were used in the tomb of Claudia Antonia Tatiana at Ephesos, a famous benefactor across the province of Asia but especially at Aphrodisias; one of these belonged to Quintus Aemilius Aristeides, procurator under the Severans.[86] At Rome the evidence is thinner on the ground but there are finds to show that members of the senatorial elite used the best marble sarcophagi in the second century AD in place of the more ostentatious tombs favoured in the Late Republic: the sarcophagi from the so-called 'Tomb of the Pancratii' and 'Tomb of the Valerii' on the Via Latina are cases in point, as probably also are those from the elaborate 'Licinian Tomb' near the Porta Salaria.[87]

Beyond the wealthy elite, sarcophagi were widely used by affluent tradesmen and lower-level officials. At Aphrodisias, municipal officials and their relatives are found alongside professionals: a sculptor, a painter, someone connected to the building industry, an agent of a councillor.[88] New citizens with the *nomina* Aurelius and Aurelia are especially common on sarcophagi following Caracalla's reforms of AD 212, , leading Smith to identify a 'middle-class appropriation of elite statue costumes and postures by the many new citizens'.[89] In late first- and early second-century AD Ephesos, Thomas and İçten have shown that Roman citizens, especially freedmen, played a key role in popularizing sarcophagus use alongside members of the local elite, like Tiberius Julius Celsus Polemaeanus, who was buried in one in his mausoleum.[90] Meanwhile even more modest occupants can be identified elsewhere. At Tyre, where the sarcophagi date from the second century AD until well into the fifth century AD, various tradesmen are commemorated: a wheat measurer, a baker, a banker, a carpenter, an incense merchant, a silk trader, two church officials, two overseers of the corn supply, eight murex fishermen, and a

---

[84] Ewald 2004: 236.   [85] Morey 1924: 5, 14–16.

[86] Eichler 1944–5: 128; Wiegartz 1965: 154; Rudolf 1989: 44–6, fig. 28–35; Rudolf 1992: fig. 1. On the Aphrodisias link, Smith 1998: 68.

[87] Wrede 2001: 13–21. On the Via Latina sarcophagi, Herdejürgen 2000: 213–14. On the 'Licinian Tomb' and the questions associated with it, Kragelund, Moltesen, and Østergaard 2003: 55–65, 102–4; Van Keuren et al. 2003.

[88] Reynolds and Roueché 2007: 150, no. 6, 84, 110, 137, 173, 176.

[89] Smith 2006: 73; 2008: 347–8.

[90] Thomas and İçten 2007; on the sarcophagus used by Celsus Polemaeanus, Asgari 1977: 340–1 (fig. 22), 366 (Ephesos B); Zimmermann and Landstätter 2011: 39, fig. 45.

marmorarius; two other individuals give multiple professions—a purple-dyer and banker, and a wheat measurer and murex fisherman.[91] To judge from their names and professions these were not the elite but were still wealthy members of the local community; half were wealthy enough to import the material for their sarcophagi from Prokonnesos. An undecorated chest in this same marble from Bărboşi, in Moesia Inferior (modern Romania), records that it had been purchased and dispatched by a certain Alfenus Modestus, identified by Robert as *strategos* at Kyzikos under Septimius Severus, showing that while simple chests in Prokonnesian marble appealed to middle-level buyers they also found an elite market.[92] In this case, the unknown recipient of this chest was possibly Modestus' son, Antonius Alfenus Arignotus, a senior military commander in Moesia Inferior and Dacia at that time.

At Arles, similarly, where the status of those commemorated is recorded on their sarcophagi, members of the traditional local elite are rare but moderately high-standing freedmen are relatively common.[93] One, S. Alfius Vitalis, was either a lawyer or forum official as well as a member of the corporation of *seviri Augustales*; another, M. Iunius Messianus, boasts that he was president of the corporation of the city four times, even though he died aged 28.[94] Both of these pieces are dated to the late second or early third century AD and carved in local limestone. On another sarcophagus of the same type, datable to the late second century AD and dedicated to Licinia Magna, the commissioner is recorded as T. Licinius Rusticus, a centurion in the *legio III Augusta*.[95] The sarcophagus trade operated, as far as we can tell, entirely outside of the imperial sphere but still these objects were produced and used in huge quantities.

SPENDING ON STONE

This brings us naturally to the question of cost: how much did these various individuals actually spend on stone? When considering stone use in its wider economic context some precise examples of costs would be very useful but predictably few such data are preserved. Building inscriptions, sometimes statue dedications, occasionally record costs, but what services these include and the extent to which these were symbolic sums is unclear; most of this evidence is what Duncan-Jones has described as 'the by-product of

---

[91] Chéhab 1984: no. 717, 839–40, 1208–9, 2772–3; 1985: no. 39–40, 45–6, 213–14, 217–18, 248–9, 418–19, 659–60, 668–9, 682–3, 921–2, 931–2, 935–6, 1341–2, 4020–1, 4062–3, 4950, 4078–9.

[92] L. Robert 1937: 124–7; 1960: 26, n. 5; Alexandrescu-Vianu 1970: 273, 296–7, no. 29.

[93] Gaggadis-Robin 2005: 263–4.

[94] Gaggadis-Robin 2005: 209–11 (no. 68), 221–2 (no. 73).

[95] Gaggadis-Robin 2005: 197–201 (no. 65).

munificence' and the sums recorded tend to be in whole thousands.[96] At the same time, we need to remember that a significant proportion of the materials we are discussing were probably never bought and sold like other commodities: stone is a resource which is free to those who have access to it; it was labour, to remove it from the ground and shape it, and transport costs above all that determined the final expense of a stone object. Despite all these caveats some costs are available, and in order to appreciate these it is instructive to remember that in the late first to early second centuries AD a rough minimum annual subsistence requirement can be estimated at 115–200 sesterces, while a legionary was paid a salary of 1,200 sesterces.[97] Compared to these relatively modest totals the scale of spending on stone was colossal.

Costs of architectural elements

Several sums relating to the purchase of specific architectural elements are known, though all are grounded in quite different contexts. In his attack in 70 BC on Verres' fraudulent restoration of the portico of the Temple of Castor, Cicero mentions that columns of the same size (12.5 m) for a private house, even though they had been brought a long way over bad roads, cost 40,000 sesterces each to be bought and installed.[98] The scale of this investment becomes clear when one remembers that Varro, only slightly later, tells us that three profitable estates near Rome produced annual revenues of 20,000–60,000 sesterces.[99] In our period, several documents from Egypt record contracts relating to the supply of architectural elements. In AD 117, Aquilius Polion, strategos of the Heracleopolite nome, arranged payment for 100 capitals from a nearby quarry for the reconstruction of a temple of Artemis in an undisclosed location.[100] Each capital measured roughly 0.79 × 0.97 × 0.67 m and the whole lot cost 223 drachmas, to which 168 drachmas for transport were added. This total seems very low indeed: taking the accepted rate of Egyptian drachmas to sesterces of one-to-one, this would mean each capital cost about the same as a *modius* (6.55–6.75 kg) of grain in the same period and all 100 only a little over a total typically regarded as a minimum annual subsistence level (115–200 sesterces).[101] This might be because these capitals were only roughed out or perhaps never intended to

---

[96] Duncan-Jones 1982: 64.

[97] On subsistence requirements, Hopkins 1978: 66–7; Goldsmith 1984: 268; 1987: 46; Jongman 2007: 599–600.

[98] Cicero, *Against Verres* 1.147.

[99] Varro, *Res Rusticae* III.2.7, 14–17.

[100] *P.Hib.* II 217; also Świderek 1957–8.

[101] On this conversion rate, Harl 1996: 98; Temin 2006: 44; on the price of grain, Duncan-Jones 1982: 365.

be elaborately carved. This total seems especially low in comparison with the 264 drachmas paid for each of the nine columns, with moulded bases and uncarved capitals, from the same quarry for the palaestra at Heracleopolis in AD 176–80, though this figure includes transport.[102] Unfortunately we have no idea how far these columns were transported or of their size and there is no real indication in either document whether the sums being paid are for the whole job or simply an instalment. This evidence is further complicated by a third-century AD text which seems to suggest that the buyers themselves had no real idea how much things would cost before they contacted their suppliers. During the mid third-century restoration work at Hermopolis, a certain Aurelius Hermaios was assigned the task of purchasing plaques, apparently in porphyry ($\pi\lambda\alpha\kappa[\hat{\omega}]\nu$ [$\pi o\rho\phi\nu$]$\rho\iota\tau\iota\kappa\hat{\omega}\nu$), for the gymnasium and in one document he is found requesting 5 talents to add to the 10 talents he has already been given for this project.[103] These sums are presumably inflated both by the monetary situation in this period and the high value of any porphyry that entered the open market, but they show just how unpredictable the cost of these materials might have been.

One way of dealing with the high costs of architectural elements in stone was to spread them between multiple individuals. Robert gives an example of a father and son paying for one column and the section of architrave that it supported in the theatre at Stratonikea and other examples of this practice can be pointed to elsewhere in Asia Minor, notably in the Temple of Aphrodite at Aphrodisias (Fig. 2.1).[104] A number of columns from Lepcis Magna also carry individual dedicatory inscriptions, this time in Punic.[105] There is limited evidence of this practice in the West too: a small altar from Italica, now in Seville, for example, records the gift of two columns of Karystian marble or *cipollino* for the decoration of the theatre in the early third century AD.[106] Occasionally these joint contributions give details of actual costs. At Smyrna, a Claudia Aurelia gave fifty-two columns of *cymbellita* marble for an unknown structure, apparently in place of the 10,000 denarii that the other subscribers contributed, suggesting at least a minimum value for each column equivalent to 192 denarii.[107] The mid first-century AD list of contributions made by members of the corporation of fisherman and fishmongers at Ephesos towards a new customs-house also helps to assign some relative value to different materials.[108] Those donating single columns are listed higher than those donating 50 denarii, perhaps suggesting a column cost more than this. Meanwhile the top three individuals gave four columns, 100 cubits of 'Phocaean

[102] *P.Hib.* II 217.   [103] *C.P.Herm.* 86, 94; see Łukaszewicz 1986: 106–7.
[104] L. Robert 1937: 525–7.   [105] *IPT* 68, 73, 74.
[106] González 1991: 62–5, no. 392; Rodà 1997: 156–8, fig. 1.
[107] *IGRR* IV.1431; *I.Smyrna* 697. *Cymbellita* marble is usually identified as coming from Mount Kybelon in Phrygia (Petzl 1987: 195; Chaniotis 2008: 74).
[108] *IvEphesos* 20.

Fig. 2.1. Dedicatory inscriptions on the columns of the Temple of Aphrodite at Aphrodisias (photo: author).

stone' for paving the courtyard, and three columns and paving for a tetrastyle court respectively.[109] Two individuals even clubbed together to pay for a column in coloured marble (κείονα ποίκιλον).

Since only the Egyptian documents ever tend to give dimensions for the objects concerned these prices are of little use for reconstructing costs. Even if they were all contemporary it is inconceivable that a column at Heracleopolis would cost the same as one at Ephesos; local producers had to deal with such variant circumstances (geology, logistics, local expertise, etc.) that this kind of uniformity was never a reality. Contextual details are also concealed by such documents. Claudia Aurelia, for example, might have preferred to give

---

[109] L. Robert 1937: 527; Barresi 2003: 162–3.

fifty-two columns instead of 10,000 denarii because she had privileged access to these materials—on the open-market they could have cost a lot more than this—or she intended all along to give a larger donation than the other individuals listed.

Costs of building projects

Most of the sums preserved in the epigraphic record concern whole buildings, of which only a part relates to stone. This part varied massively between projects. In the case of the Baths of Caracalla, for example, predominantly a brick and concrete building, DeLaine has argued that the cost of stone and its working accounted for no more than 15 per cent of the total cost and 80 per cent of the cost of decoration.[110] On the other hand, certain structures— especially in the eastern provinces—were built almost entirely from stone. This was often rubble or roughly squared blocks which required much less labour to produce than ashlar or sculpted objects.

What is clear, above all else, is that stone elements, particularly decorative marbles, added enormously to the cost of building. Structures that made extensive use of stone are among the most expensive recorded epigraphically. Brick was always a cheaper option, apparently even in Asia Minor: Pliny the Younger insisted that the stone-built, unfinished aqueduct at Nicomedia, which had already cost 3,329,000 sesterces, be rebuilt in either brick or reused stone to reduce its cost.[111] Indeed, stone-built aqueducts are among the most expensive of all structures.[112] The cost of bath-houses was also inflated by the expense of equipping them with suitably decorative stones: at Mandeure, in Germania Superior, a Flavius Catullus left 75,000 denarii for marble revetment for the baths, while at Vaison-la-Romaine, 50,000 sesterces were spent on ornamenting the portico in front of the baths with marble in the late first century AD.[113] These are huge sums: at Rome, 75,000 denarii could have bought enough grain to feed over 3,000 people for a year, and grain costs were probably cheaper in this region.[114] And this total is especially striking when one remembers that Flavius Catullus was paying just for revetment. Likewise, theatres, especially ones with elaborately decorated *scaenae frontes*,

---

[110] DeLaine 1997: 218–19.   [111] *Letters* X.37.

[112] On the aqueduct at Aspendos, the most expensive anywhere, *IGRR* III.804; Broughton 1939: 785, 901; on that at Bordeaux, the most expensive structure in Gaul, *CIL* XIII.596–600; Frézouls 1984: 50.

[113] *CIL* XIII.5416; *CIL* XII.1357: *ad porticum ante thermas marmoribus ornandam*. De Kisch 1979: 272 argues that this *marmoribus* refers to revetment, while Pflaum 1978: 253 thought this referred to statues.

[114] This assumes an average price per *modius* of grain at Rome of 3 sesterces and a minimum annual requirement of 37.5 *modii* per person, after Goldsmith 1984; Temin 2006.

cost incredible sums. The single largest cost recorded for part of a building in North Africa—500,000 sesterces—relates to the Antonine remodelling of the *scaenae frons* in the theatre at Lepcis Magna during which the existing limestone columns were replaced with *pavonazzetto* and *fior di pesco* shafts among others.[115]

The recording of costs, however, depended very much on local customs. The rigidity of the institution of *summae honorariae* in North Africa, in particular, meant that the recording of specific costs acquired particular prominence: of the twenty-four inscriptions recording costs on imperial statue bases, for example, all but one come from second-century North Africa.[116] Far fewer inscriptions detailing payments are available from the north-western provinces where local customs differed. De Kisch identifies only fifty from the Gallic and German provinces.[117]

Costs outside the construction industry

Costs are also common on statue bases, though again the evidence is beset with problems. In most cases, the statue referred to is now lost and only by analysing the bases themselves can the material used be ascertained. Where this has been done, especially in North Africa and Asia Minor, it is clear that many of these costs refer to bronze statues.[118] Despite this, certain patterns can be identified in the data that suggest rough orders of magnitude for statue costs, though again we should be aware that many of the sums recorded relate to acts of beneficence and are largely symbolic.

Among the 147 statue costs from Italy and North Africa catalogued by Duncan-Jones certain sums stand out: 4,000 and 5,000 sesterces are recorded nineteen and seventeen times respectively, 6,000 eleven times, 8,000 nine times, and 3,000 eight times.[119] Almost all of these costs date from the Hadrianic to Severan periods. In Spain, a similar concentration around the 4,000–6,000 sesterces mark has been noted.[120] The lower of these is again prominent in statue costs from Asia Minor. At Philadelphia, 7,000 denarii were left by a private individual to cover the costs of a statue for each of the city's seven tribes, which breaks down as roughly 1,000 denarii or 4,000

---

[115] *IRT* 534; see Duncan-Jones 1982: 68.   [116] Højte 2005: 53.

[117] De Kisch 1979: 259.

[118] On Cuicul and Timgad, Zimmer and Wesh-Klein 1989; this contradicts the assumption made in Duncan-Jones 1982: 94 that marble was used more often in North Africa. On the evidence from Kos, Höghammer 1993: 68. On the use of bronze for honorific statues in the East, Dio Chrysostom, *Orations* XXXI.9–10, 20. For more general discussion of this point, Højte 2005: 47–52; Fejfer 2008: 158.

[119] Duncan-Jones 1982: 93–9, 162–3.

[120] Melchor Gil 1994: 172; Curchin 1983: 231.

sesterces per statue.[121] These common values are suggestive but there were certainly also cheaper options. A portrait of a benefactor at Thyatira, for instance, cost 1,000 drachmas, which would translate as either 1,000 or 750 denarii depending on the type of drachma.[122] In his lambasting of the Rhodians, Dio mentions the 'mere matter of a thousand or five hundred drachmas, sums for which it is possible to erect statues'; assuming these are cistophoric drachmas this would be equivalent to roughly 750 and 375 denarii.[123]

Honorific statues, whatever their material, represented a significant investment. Applying these figures to Smith's estimates for rates of statue erection at Aphrodisias shows the expense of this activity over time.[124] If between four and ten honorific statues were erected at Aphrodisias per year over a 250 year period then one might reasonably conjecture, on the basis of the above discussion, that the city was capable of spending perhaps as much as 40,000 sesterces annually on this mode of public commemoration; this for a city with an estimated population living within the fourth-century circuit wall of around 15,000 inhabitants. This is more than was spent on a bath-house in mid second-century AD Tlos in Lykia and the same as was spent on a market in Cuicul in the same period.[125] However, as large as this sum appears, it should have been covered comfortably by payments received from office-holders annually. According to Pliny the Younger, councillors in Bithynia and Pontus often paid 1,000–2,000 denarii each. At Prusa, therefore, Dio's success in gaining 100 more members for the council might have added as much as 400,000–800,000 sesterces to the public revenues annually.[126]

We know far less about the cost of other stone objects. The price of only one sarcophagus is known—an undecorated, limestone piece from Salona. It seems to date to the late third century or later and cost 15 solidi. Based on the price of gold in the Price Edict (72 solidi = 1 pound of gold = 72,000 denarii), this sum is equivalent to a massive 15,000 Diocletianic denarii, or approximately 150 late first-century AD denarii.[127] A third-century AD limestone funerary monument of similar dimensions, discovered in 1982 near Sant'Agata in Puglia, also cost 150 denarii but again the date of this piece makes drawing comparisons difficult.[128] This monument is shaped like a lid or cover in the local style with a projecting aedicule on its front side containing

---

[121] *IGRR* IV.1632; see Barresi 2003: 161.

[122] *TAM* V.2 926; on the different drachmas, Harl 1996: 98.

[123] Dio Chrysostom, *Orations* XXXI.59 (trans. J. W. Cohoon and H. Lamar).

[124] Smith 2006: 13.

[125] On Tlos (30,000 sesterces), Balland 1981: 173–85, no. 66. On Cuicul (30,000 sesterces), *AE* 1916, 36; Duncan-Jones 1982: no. 14.

[126] Pliny the Younger, *Letters* X.112; Dio Chrysostom, *Orations* XLV.1–9.

[127] *Eph.Ep.* IV.653, where the measurements are given as 2.12 × 0.85 × 0.80 m; on the value of a *solidus*, Corcoran 2000: 226.

[128] *AE* 1994, 524; see Silvestrini 1994: 152, no. 210.

the inscription. Its cost is intriguingly close to that of two contemporary inscribed statue bases from Sigus and Tiddis, in Numidia, at 400 and 500 sesterces respectively; both were carved from local limestone and their production probably involved a similar amount of carving.[129]

Labour estimates

Another approach to calculating the cost of stone objects has been pioneered by DeLaine and, more recently, Barresi.[130] Both use the nineteenth-century building manual by Pegoretti to calculate labour requirements for a variety of construction tasks which can then be translated into costs using figures provided in Diocletian's Price Edict.[131] The general accuracy of these manuals is revealed by the similarity of the totals they record and the fact that they compare well with data derived from modern restoration projects.[132]

What later building manuals are especially useful for is highlighting how relatively time-consuming or labour intensive it was to do different types of working in different materials. This can be illustrated with the example of a monolithic column shaft, 20 Roman feet (RF) in length using the figures listed in Table 2.1. According to these totals, to quarry, rough out, dress, then flute a shaft of this size (5.90 m with a lower diameter of 0.74 m) in a hard white marble would have taken one carver at least 1,229 hours, or roughly

Table 2.1. Labour estimates for carving work relevant to the production of a column shaft in man-hours (source: Pegoretti 1844–5).

Task	Granodiorite	Cipollino	White marble	Limestone
Quarrying—by one quarryman and two assistants (hours/m³)	140–50	–	40	17.5–33.3
Roughing out (hours/m³ of material to be removed)	2,600	687.5	248.7–350	56.9–224
Rough dressing (hours/m²)	93.5	24.5	9–12.5	2.4–8
either fine dressing (hours/m²)	203.6	53.6	19.4–27.4	7.7–17.5
or fluting (hours/m²)	–	–	28.8–40.7	7–26

[129] Duncan-Jones 1982: no. 392–3.

[130] DeLaine 1997; 2001; Barresi 2002; 2003: 163–88; also Mar and Pensabene 2010.

[131] Pegoretti 1843–4; 1863–4. Other similar manuals include Morisot 1820–4; Ponza di San Martino 1841; Claudel and Laroque 1863; Fletcher 1877; Salmojraghi 1892; Ricci 1895; Rea 1902; Hurst 1903.

[132] Barker and Russell 2012; despite this, it should be acknowledged that 'there is perhaps a greater diversity of opinion as to the proper system to be adopted in estimating for stonework than is to be found in any other branch of the building trade' (Purchase 1903: 134).

Table 2.2. Labour estimates for the sawing of 1 m² panel of stone in man-hours.

Source	Porphyry	Granite	White marble	Limestone
Pegoretti 1844–5	461.4	184.4–218.4	21.3–30	8–17
Ponza di San Martino 1841	–	–	19–33	7–29
Salmojraghi 1892	400–50	175–300	20–40	7–16
Morisot 1820–4	–	–	16.7–38.2	4–21.4
Claudel and Laroque 1863	–	–	30.1	9–19

123 days.[133] Four individuals working together could perhaps have finished it in a month. In contrast, a similarly-sized shaft in granodiorite, smoothed rather than fluted, would have taken at least 6,839 hours or 684 days. What these figures show is that the most laborious stages are the finest stages of smoothing and fluting while the different labour requirements between materials are significant. Further examples of how these figures can be applied will be tested in Chapter 6.

As well as detailing labour figures for specific stages of the carving process in different materials, Pegoretti also gives several totals which are more easily applied to ancient carving projects; first, for sawing panels from a block, and second, for the carving of capitals. The labour estimates provided by Pegoretti for the sawing of 1 m² of stone are listed in Table 2.2 and match closely those given by other contemporary manuals.[134] These figures are in man-hours and since it required two sawyers to carry out this work the actual time required would have been half these totals. For the carving of capitals Pegoretti gives a series of figures listed according to the height of the capital to which totals for the quarrying and roughing out of a square block of suitable dimensions need to be added (Table 2.3 and 2.4).[135] These totals, though generalized estimates, clearly reveal the scale of labour involved in the intricate carving of the largest Corinthian capitals.

Pegoretti, and almost all of the above manuals, provide labour requirements, measured in man-hours, not costs.[136] In order to make any meaningful use of these figures, therefore, we need to translate them into ancient costs, for which we need to turn to the Diocletian's Price Edict of AD 301. This provides daily wage figures of 0.5 *MK* (*modius kastensis*) of grain or 50 Diocletianic

---

[133] Pegoretti 1843–4: 240–336. The calculations can be summarized as follows: quarrying = 40 × 3.23 m³, roughing out = 350 × 0.69 m³, dressing = 12.5 × 13.72 m², fluting = 40.7 × 13.72 m², with the quarrying figure doubled to account for the fact that the labour estimate is for one quarryman and two assistants, or one skilled and two unskilled workers. Ten-hour working days are assumed throughout, following the nineteenth-century manuals: see Barker and Russell 2012: 85.

[134] Discussions with modern stone sawyers who are used to working with traditional tools suggest that these totals are broadly accurate: I am grateful to G. De Tommasi for discussing these figures.

[135] Pegoretti 1843–4: 269–70 (= 1863–4: 397–8).

[136] Although on contemporary daily wages, Pegoretti 1863–4: 386; Skyring 1831: 84; Elsam 1826: 136.

Table 2.3. Labour estimates for the finishing of Ionic capitals in man-hours (source: Pegoretti 1844–5).

Height (m)	White marble			Limestone
	Hard	Medium	Soft	Hard
0.20	360	307.2	258.7	230.4
0.30	540	460.8	388	345.6
0.40	720	614.6	521	460.8
0.50	900	768	654.7	576
0.60	1080	921.6	784	691.2
0.70	1260	1075.2	913.3	806.4
0.80	1440	1228.8	1042.7	921.6

Table 2.4. Labour estimates for the finishing of Corinthian capitals in man-hours (source: Pegoretti 1844–5).

Height (m)	White marble			Limestone
	Hard	Medium	Soft	Hard
0.50	900	768	639.3	576
0.75	1350	1152	959	864
1.00	1800	1536	1278.8	1152
1.25	2250	1920	1598.3	1440
1.50	2700	2304	1918	1728
1.75	3150	2688	2237.8	2016
2.00	3600	3072	2557.5	2304

denarii for a skilled labourer, and half this for an unskilled labourer.[137] In order to get from Diocletianic denarii to late first-century denarii, Barresi divides the former by 100 to get totals of 0.5 and 0.25 denarii or 2 and 1 sesterces, but other evidence suggests that daily wages of 3 sesterces were common for workers in Rome and should perhaps be used instead.[138] This would mean that for labour alone the carver responsible for our 20 RF column would have to have been paid 280–420 sesterces. Using Pegoretti's figures we can also re-examine the only known sarcophagus price from a similar perspective. To quarry, hollow out, and shape the chest and lid for the sarcophagus from Salona discussed above would probably have taken no more than 50–55 days (20 for quarrying, 25 for hollowing out, 5–10 for shaping), which would imply a labour cost of 100–165 sesterces, not dissimilar

---

[137] Crawford and Reynolds 1979.
[138] Crawford and Reynolds 1979; Barresi 2003: 168.

to the sum actually paid.[139] For the more ornate varieties of sarcophagi in harder marbles, of course, the labour involved was substantially more. Wiegartz proposed that an Attic sarcophagus with *klinē* lid would take perhaps 1,000–1,200 man-days to produce or twenty times longer than our Salonitan example.[140] This is equivalent to the decoration of 5–6 Corinthian capitals 1 m in height in Pegoretti's handbook, which is not unreasonable considering the level of carving involved.[141] What this might mean is that just to cover the cost of carving an average *klinē*-lidded Attic sarcophagus the customer would have to set aside at least 2,000–3,600 sesterces, that is double to three times the annual salary of a legionary after Domitian.[142]

These totals reveal the very real cost of stone-working but we also need to remember that the carvers responsible had to make a profit from their work, which would have necessitated additional charges.[143] Equally, none of these figures give the cost of the raw material itself. In the case of the local limestone for the Salonitan sarcophagus this cost was probably quite low but for an Attic sarcophagus, carved in high-grade Pentelic, the material would have added significantly to the overall total.

The Price Edict

The only ancient source which deals in detail with the cost of decorative stones, or indeed stone of any sort, is Diocletian's Price Edict, itself a far from straightforward document. The section of the Edict dealing with marbles measures them per foot (*pedem*), but it is not clear whether this is a cubic or square foot (Table 2.5). Traditionally the cubic foot has been assumed but Corcoran and DeLaine have convincingly argued, using Pegoretti's figures for quarrying and squaring blocks, that these maximum prices are too low for this to be the case.[144] As they point out, the cubic foot measurement makes these luxury materials appear very cheap: a 40 RF column shaft in Aswan granite, for instance, would cost almost half the listed price for a first-class lion or a pound of purple silk.[145]

---

[139] Using a figure of 33.3 hours/m³ for one skilled and two unskilled workers to quarry the block, 176 man-hours/m³ to hollow it out, and 10.5 man-hours/m² to flatten the sides; see Pegoretti 1843–4: 97, 297. For more on this object, see Chapter 2: Costs outside the construction industry (pp. 28–30).

[140] Wiegartz 1974: 364–6; also Koch 1993: 110.

[141] Pegoretti 1843–4: 397–9.

[142] Lo Cascio 2007: 620.

[143] On profit and extra expenses, which can often add up to an additional 20–40 per cent, see Morisot 1820–4: 26–34; Rondelet 1867: 78; Ricci 1895: 132.

[144] Corcoran and DeLaine 1994: 270–1. For the cubic foot, Barresi 2003; Lazzarini 2010.

[145] Corcoran and DeLaine 1994: 269–70.

Table 2.5. Prices in denarii for decorative stones as listed in the Price Edict, per RF² or RF³.

Listed name	Identification	Price
Πορφυρίτης	*Porfido rosso*/Porphyry	250
Λακεδαιμόνιον	*Serpentino*	250
Νουμηδικόν	*Giallo antico*	200
Λουκούλλιον	Africano	150
Πυρροποικίλον	Aswan granite	100
Κλαυδιανόν	*Granito del Foro*	100
Ἀλαβαστρήσιον	Egyptian alabaster	75
Δοκιμηνόν	*Pavonazzetto*	200
Εὐθυδημιανόν	?	60
Ἀνακαστηνόν	?	40
Τριποντικόν	?	75
Θεσσαλόν	*Verde antico*	150
Καρύστιον	*Cipollino*	100
Σκυριανόν	*Breccia di Settebassi*	40
Ἡρακλειωτικόν	Herakleian marble	75
Λέσβιον	Lesbian marble	50
Θάσιον	Thasian marble	50
Προκοννήσιον	Prokonnesian marble	40
Ποταμογαλληνόν	?	40

In order to take this question any further we need to consider the rationale underlying this section of the Price Edict. The materials listed on the Edict are not valued according to the remoteness of their sources: *serpentino* is the same price as porphyry (250 denarii), for instance, *giallo antico* the same as *pavonazzetto* (200 denarii), and *africano* (150 denarii) more than either Mons Claudianus or Aswan granite (100 denarii).[146] They are also not valued according to their hardness, as Barresi has proposed, since the various granites listed and porphyry would be far more expensive if this was the case, as would Thasian marble (50 denarii) which is actually much harder than most other marbles.[147] However, it does makes sense that the materials listed are valued with regard to the particular use to which they are to be put; as Rockwell puts it, 'a stoneworker's view of his material is concerned with its *use*'.[148] This is partially supported by the fact that the unit of measurement is not specified. All of the various building manuals listed above make it very clear that a foot can be either a linear, squared, or cubic measurement depending on what is being described—i.e. whether a line of moulding, a section of paving, or a column shaft.[149] In the Edict the various marbles listed must have been being

---

[146] Erim and Reynolds 1970: 136.
[147] Barresi 2003: 173–4; on the hardness of Thasian marble, Herrmann and Newman 1995: 75.
[148] Rockwell 1993: 17.
[149] Langley 1735: 93: 'Masons work, which is measured by foot-measure, *viz.* either lineal, as the coping of walls (which is sometimes measured by the square foot also) or superficial, as in

valued in a particular format, rather than generically as raw materials. The apparent inflation of the prices of the most highly coloured materials, furthermore, suggests that the emphasis is on the decorative potential of these materials, not where they came from or particularly their hardness; the most expensive marbles are also the most colourful, and this is where the granites of Mons Claudianus and Aswan lose out.

In this sense, this section of the Edict is best thought of as an index of early fourth-century AD decorative tastes. If these same marbles were valued according to their suitability for monolithic column shafts the granites would surely have been priced much higher. By the early fourth century AD, and indeed even much earlier, most decorative marble was consumed as veneer and it seems reasonable to assume that the Edict was valuing these materials according to their desirability as decorative paving, and so in square feet, not cubic feet. Much of the material on the market at this date was probably also second-hand and so already cut.[150] In this sense, therefore, the Edict is a misleading source from which to generate marble costs for large volumes, indeed for anything other than veneer.

What, then, are we left with? At sixteenth-century Carrara the cost of the raw material worked out as roughly half the cost of quarrying and squaring it and these can be used in combination with Pegoretti's totals to provide rough estimates which vary according to workability.[151] If 1 m³ of medium-grained white marble cost the equivalent of 7.72 man-days, 1 m³ of granodiorite might cost 42 man-days, and 1 m³ of porphyry 55 man-days; adding quarrying and squaring one is left with absolute minimum totals of 30, 163, and 214 Diocletianic denarii/ft³. These figures are not dissimilar to those listed in the Edict and could be used to support the cubic foot proposal but they neither allow for any profit on the part of the producer nor do they make sense if the prices listed in the Edict are maxima, intended to curb rampant inflation.

Of course, all of this somewhat begs the question: was there ever a standard cost for stone that we might be able to reconstruct? In all likelihood, the cost of raw materials on the open market probably hinged on the specifics of where they were being brought from, their availability, and wider patterns of demand for them. There is abundant evidence in the ancient sources for variations in prices between cities and regions for all kinds of commodities: cities were always more expensive than the countryside and Rome always more expensive than elsewhere.[152] It seems likely, furthermore, that costs of material changed

pavements; or solid, as blocks of marble, columns, etc.' See also Peacock and Maxfield 1997: 224 on the evidence from Mons Claudianus: 'it seems probable that a foot would have the same meaning as it does among modern quarrymen: i.e. it could indicate linear, a real or cubic measure and the context would indicate what was intended.'

[150] For more on this, Barker 2011.
[151] Klapisch-Zuber 1969: 147.
[152] Martial, *Epigrams* 12.31; Apuleius, *Metamorphoses* 11.28; see Duncan-Jones 1982: 345–7.

markedly over time. Marble prices from early nineteenth-century Rome show that not only did the cost of identical materials vary year by year, but different versions of the same stone cost very different sums, depending on grain size and particular colouring.[153] The form the stone was in would also affect its price. It is significantly harder to quarry a long thin block suitable for a column, for example, than a square block of the same volume. Pricing, in short, was probably always highly unpredictable, as Aurelius Hermaios from Hermopolis, as we saw above, found out to his, and his city's, cost.[154] On the open market, stone cost what people would pay for it. By reconstructing individual costs from an artificially standardized source, therefore, we risk providing misleadingly satisfactory solutions to unsolvable problems.

CONCLUSIONS

Occasional sums for particular stone objects can be extracted from the literary and epigraphic sources, but they are too few to provide a reliable basis for reconstructing costs. It seems likely, in any case, that costs varied considerably by both region and period and depended substantially on the connections enjoyed by whoever was buying the stone. Even so, the kinds of relative costs outlined above, and the evidence for enormous sums being spent on building projects, shows that considerable capital was invested in securing stone supplies in the Roman world. Demand for stone on an unprecedented level characterizes the Roman period, the first two centuries AD in particular. Much of this demand came from the emperors directly. Imperial building projects consumed large quantities of both decorative and more ordinary stones and set the tone for much non-imperial activity. However, in aggregate terms, more stone was consumed by the non-imperial market. Local elites spent heavily, but so did individuals lower down the social spectrum, as the evidence provided by sarcophagi demonstrates. It is crucial, too, that the range of materials sought after is acknowledged: the Roman fashion for stone use was far from limited to the high-quality decorative stones that have achieved such renown. Finished structures and carving show that a huge range of stones were employed for these projects all across the Roman world but it is in the scale of quarrying activity that the impact of this broad demand is most clearly revealed, and it is to quarries that we must now turn.

[153] Pettinau 1983.   [154] See Chapter 2: Cost of architectural elements (pp. 24–7).

3

Quarrying

Mountains were made by Nature for herself to serve as a kind of framework for holding firmly together the inner parts of the earth, and at the
same time to enable her to subdue the violence of rivers, to break the force
of heavy seas and so to curb her most restless elements with the hardest
material of which she is made. We quarry these mountains and haul them
away for a mere whim; and yet there was a time when it seemed remarkable even to have succeeded in crossing them.

Pliny the Elder XXXVI.1[1]

The first step in any carving project, be it architectural or sculptural, is the
procurement of a useable block of stone and, with the exception of stones
collected from the surface or reused from earlier projects, stone must be
quarried. Stone extraction leaves behind reasonably clear traces in the archaeological record—scars and pits on the landscape that even several millennia
of abandonment often fail to conceal. The remains of many ancient quarries,
especially the larger marble quarries, have been destroyed by later, more
explosive, work; a fact that makes estimating the scale of Roman quarrying
with any precision difficult. Even so, there are a staggering number of sites at
which Roman extraction can be identified, and more turn up every year,
reflective of the massive aggregate demand for stone in this period. The
unparalleled scale of this activity was not lost on ancient commentators, as
Pliny the Elder, quoted above, remarks in one of his more rhetorical moments.

Quarrying on the scale envisaged by Pliny, of course, was never ubiquitous.
The underlying geology of the Mediterranean and its surrounding regions
determined what materials were available to the stone-workers of the Roman
world, their quantities and characteristics. Their actual extraction and use
depended on other factors. Which materials were quarried was closely related,
of course, to broader patterns of demand for stone of the kind outlined in
the previous chapter. Where quarries were opened, though, was determined
primarily by human parameters, in particular the issue of access.[2] There was

---

[1] Translated by D. E. Eichholz.   [2] Braemer 1986*b*: 287–9.

no point opening a quarry where nobody could reach it or where it was impossible to remove material from it. As we will see, most quarries were accordingly located as close as possible to where their stone was needed and/or within easy reach of established transport routes. In a sense, of course, demand played a role here too, since the more valuable a material, and the more potentially profitable its extraction, the more inaccessible a quarry could afford to be. Extra transport or infrastructure costs mattered less when there was a sizeable profit to be made. The distribution of quarries and this issue of physical accessibility will be examined in more detail in the next section. First, though, we need to consider the question of ownership.

IMPERIAL QUARRY OWNERSHIP AND ADMINISTRATION

Who owned quarries and how they controlled the material that they extracted are issues that have dominated discussion of the Roman stone trade. Especially prominent has been the question of state involvement. Most of our evidence for the organization of quarrying in the Roman period comes from those sites at which the involvement of imperial officials, mainly imperial freedmen and procurators, is epigraphically attested. Consequently, most attempts to model the stone trade in the imperial period have focused on these sites, at the risk of overshadowing all other quarrying activity.[3] Picking up on this skewed focus, there is a related tendency in the non-specialist literature to assume that these quarries are the norm or are somehow representative of quarrying activity more generally.[4] In reality, those handful of quarries at which imperial intervention is known were highly anomalous.[5] Very few sites warranted the attention of the emperor. Most quarries were probably owned by private individuals or were located on land owned by cities. In either case different levels of access are imaginable: the right to work might have been limited to members of a particular family or other group, leased out in return for a fee or a share of the output, or perhaps even open to anyone. In practice, a similar range of access levels is conceivable even at those sites seemingly under imperial control; as will be shown, the end goal of imperial

---

[3] Ward-Perkins 1980*a*; Fant 1988; 1989*a*; 1990; Pensabene 2002*b*.

[4] For example: Alcock 2007: 685: 'as with mines, most (if not definitively all) stone quarries were the property of the imperial fisc.'

[5] Ward-Perkins 1992*b*: 24; Hirt 2010: 89.

intervention at these quarries was rarely monopolization. At the same time, we should expect that arrangements changed over time, with certain quarries changing hands, perhaps even drifting from state to private ownership and vice versa.

Imperial quarrying in the Eastern Desert

The vast bulk of our evidence for the organization and administration of quarrying activities come from quarries at which imperial involvement is attested, even if these constitute only a tiny minority of the known stone quarries of the Roman world. The often highly abbreviated quarry inscriptions on quarried objects (or *notae lapicidinarum*), which attest to complex accounting systems coordinated by imperial officials, have only been found on material from the various quarries of the Eastern Desert, Chemtou, Dokimeion, and the other *pavonazzetto* quarries of the upper Tembris Valley, the *cipollino* quarries on Euboea, those at Teos, Chios, Paros, Luna, and possibly a few more (Figs. 3.1 and 3.2); though inscriptions have been found on Prokonnesian marble blocks these do not suggest imperial involvement prior to Late Antiquity.[6] Several of these sites are among the very largest quarries known from antiquity and imperial demand for decorative stones has to occupy a central part of any discussion of the scale and development of the stone trade in our period. However, in the almost every way, imperial involvement in the stone quarrying was thoroughly out of the ordinary; most quarries were run very differently and on a smaller scale.

The most detailed evidence for imperially coordinated quarrying activity comes from the remote quarries of the Egyptian Eastern Desert. The painstaking study and publication of the *ostraka* from Mons Claudianus, in the particular, has revolutionized our understanding of the operation of these sites.[7] By the second century AD the major quarries of the Eastern Desert constituted an extensive administrative unit, a *territorium metallorum* or quarrying/mining district, under the supervision of a *procurator metallorum/ἐπίτροπος τῶν μετάλλων* who could on occasion be directly involved in the procurement of blocks.[8] Within this system individual sites had their own supervisors, locked into a hierarchy which had the *praefectus Berenicidis*, possibly even the *praefectus Aegypti*, at its summit; Sulpicius Similis, prefect of

---

[6] For a list, Hirt 2010: 370–445.
[7] On these ostraka, Bingen et al. 1992; 1997; Cuvigny 2000; Bülow-Jacobsen 2009.
[8] Cuvigny 2000: 37; 2002: 242–8; Cockle 1996: 23–8; Hirt 2010: 52, 107–9.

Fig. 3.1. Inscribed block of Parian marble (inv. no. 39910) from Portus, now at Ostia (photo: author).

Fig. 3.2. Inscribed blocks of *pavonazzetto* from the quarries at Dokimeion, now in Iscehisar (photo: author).

Egypt in AD 107–12, was even personally occupied with operations at Mons Claudianus on occasion.[9] Attached to these local managers was an extensive staff in charge of ordering supplies and provisions, arranging for the employment of stone-masons and other skilled workers, and guarding the quarries and their associated settlements.[10]

Soldiers were also present. At Mons Claudianus at least twenty soldiers, most of them centurions, crop up in letters, passes or receipts, the majority dating to the second century AD.[11] These were mainly detachments seconded to the quarries from units based elsewhere in Egypt, including the fleet on the Nile. Sometimes they were brought from further afield: under Trajan, a centurion of the *legio XV Apollinaris*, Annius Rufus, is attested at the site, even though his legion was serving in Parthia then Cappadocia.[12] At Mons Porphyrites, where the epigraphic evidence is thinner on the ground, a *centurio frumentario* is mentioned in the third century AD.[13] This individual's role shows that these troops performed logistical as well as purely military tasks.[14] A number of the officers named at Mons Claudianus were responsible for granting passes for the roads in and out of the quarries and for communicating with the various *curatores* in charge of the way-stations along these routes.[15] These units probably also escorted material and supplies across the desert, while the appearance of members of the fleet might imply that the military was involved in stone transport on the Nile. These soldiers could have been guards: there are a number of references in the *ostraka* to troublesome 'infidels' (ἀνόσιοι), presumably local tribesmen.[16] The traditional view that these soldiers were there to control convicts condemned to hard labour (*damnati ad metalla*), which has persisted since antiquity, finds little support in the archaeological record.[17] It is tempting to see the *familia* mentioned on the *ostraka* from Mons Claudianus as slaves, since they are mostly unskilled labourers, but their names and the fact that they are paid for their work would suggest otherwise.[18] If convicts were used, then they worked alongside freeborn skilled workers (*pagani*): the *ostraka* from Mons Claudianus show that quarrymen were employed from as far away as Alexandria,

---

[9] *I.Pan.* 37; on this issue, Bülow-Jacobsen 2009: 178–9.

[10] Cuvigny 2000: 59–62.

[11] For Mons Claudianus, *O.Claud.* 48–71, 76–81, 148–9, 177, 286, 357–65, 368–70, 377, 383–6, 438, 540–6; *I.Pan.* 38–9, 41–2, 47.

[12] *I.Pan.* 39; see Strobel 1991: 27.

[13] *I.Pan.* 21–2, 24; see Lesquier 1918: no. 16.

[14] On the logistical tasks assigned to soldiers on public works, Mitchell 1987: 338.

[15] On this point, Strobel 1991: 26–7.

[16] Bülow-Jacobsen 2009: 180–1 (no. 850), 182 (no. 851), where they are called βαρβάροι.

[17] *Damnati* in Egypt are mentioned by Aelius Aristides (*Orations* 36.67) and Josephus (*Jewish Wars* VI.418); also Millar 1984: 137–43; Fant 2008b; Bülow-Jacobsen 2009: 2.

[18] Cuvigny 2000: 14, 42.

Arsinoe, and Memphis, as well as Aswan—no doubt a sensible place to look for experienced quarrymen.[19] Soldiers again turn up alongside freeborn workers, most from Aswan, at the Wadi Hammâmât quarries.[20]

Imperial quarrying elsewhere

Outside of the Eastern Desert, with its especially rich documentary evidence and exceptional topography and climate, detailed evidence for the administrative systems at quarries is much scarcer and it would be wrong to assume that the system was the same everywhere. Whether extensive quarrying districts like those found in the Eastern Desert existed elsewhere is especially unclear.[21] A *pagus marmorarius* apparently existed at Almadén de la Plata in Spain, to judge from an inscription mentioning *conpagani marmorarienses*.[22] This inscription has often been discussed in connection with a second from Italica which mentions a *statio serrariorum augustorum* and together these documents have been used to propose that an imperial quarrying district existed in this area managed through offices in Italica.[23] The skilled workers at Mons Claudianus, of course, are described as *pagani* in the *ostraka* which could suggest common administrative structures between these areas.[24] However, a *pagus* is simply an administrative unit and there is nothing in the first inscription to prove that this area was imperially controlled; it could just have easily have belonged to a nearby city.[25] Since the various marbles quarried at Almadén de la Plata rarely seem to have left Baetica it could be questioned whether there was any need for the imperial administration to control these quarries.[26] Whether the *serrarii* (sawyers) were working permanently for the imperial administration or temporarily, on some large building projects, and whether they were cutting up material from imperial or non-imperial quarries is altogether unclear.

---

[19] Cuvigny 2000: 11–14; 2005: 309–53; Bülow-Jacobsen 2009: 263–6.

[20] Kayser 1993: esp. 124–5.

[21] For the dubious suggestion that the central Pyrenean quarries were part of the *saltus pyrenaeus* mentioned in Pliny the Elder IV.108, see Dubois 1908: xi, 25; Lizop 1931: 247; Fabre and Sablayrolles 1995: 138–9.

[22] *CIL* II.1043.

[23] *CIL* II.1131; *serrarii* are also mentioned in *CIL* II.1132; see Dubois 1908: 26; Canto 1977–8: 175–7, 184–6.

[24] On this point, Pensabene 2002*b*: 49.

[25] Canto 1977–8: 175–6; Keay 1988: 112; Mayer and Rodà 1998: 218, 232.

[26] Almadén de la Plata marble has been found only occasionally in Tarraconensis, at Segobriga and Carranque for example (Àlvarez, Cebrián, and Rodà 2008; García-Entero and Vidal 2007), though small quantities have recently been identified at Thamusida in Mauretania Tingitana (Beltrán et al. 2011).

More secure evidence for imperial involvement is provided by the various procurators mentioned on quarry inscriptions on *pavonazzetto*. An Irenaeus, an imperial freedman and procurator, appears on two inscriptions dated to AD 137 on *pavonazzetto* blocks from the Emporium district in Rome, while a Maro—similarly titled—crops up on a further two from the quarries at Dokimeion dated to AD 194.[27] The abbreviated titles used by these officials give little away about their role. Another procurator, though, by the name of Hesperus, who is named on two inscriptions on *pavonazzetto* from Lepcis Magna, also seems to appear in a more typical procuratorial role at Aizanoi; here he is tasked with arranging a land survey by T. Avidius Quietus, proconsul in Ephesos in AD 125–6.[28] Christol and Drew-Bear argue plausibly that Hesperus and his colleagues were *procuratores Phrygiae*, in charge of all imperial property, including the quarries, in Phrygia. A certain M. Aurelius Marcio, whose career is documented on an inscription from Kaimaz in Phrygia, lists his final position as *procurator provinciae Phrygiae*, and interestingly notes that he used to be a *procurator marmorum*.[29] It would be tempting to see the two roles as connected, and indeed he might have been given this later role because of his experience in this field, but the inscription does not tell us where he was *procurator marmorum*; this could well have been a position held in Rome and between these two relevant postings he was also *procurator provinciae Britanniae* and *procurator summi choragi*. This being said, a *procurator a marmoribus*, a certain Chresimus, is attested in Asia Minor, at Tralles, Mylasa, Ephesos, and Miletos. None of these sites are particularly close to the imperial quarries in Phrygia, but it is possible that this official was tasked with overseeing transport rather than quarrying.[30] Responsibility for overseeing work at Dokimeion, then, seems to have come under the responsibility of a Phrygian procurator but other officials, like this Chresimus, might have been involved at later stages of the distribution process.

Elsewhere a similar system appears to have been in place. Several procurators are mentioned on blocks of *cipollino*—a Minic(i)us Sanctus (in AD 132) and a C. Caerialis (in the late Hadrianic period)—but again it is uncertain whether these characters were *procuratores marmorum* or *procuratores provinciae Achaiae*, a post the latter certainly held at some point; were they specifically in charge of quarrying or was this simply one of many duties

---

[27] Bruzza 1870: 190–1, no. 258–9 (= Dubois 1908: 90, no. 199–200); Christol and Drew-Bear 1991: 120–1, no. 1–2; Christol and Drew-Bear 2005: 191, 196–7.

[28] Christol and Drew-Bear 2005: 196–200; see *IRT* 794d (Lepcis Magna); *CIL* III.356 = 14191 (*IGRR* IV.571) (Aizanoi).

[29] *CIL* III.348 = *ILS* 1477; see Christol and Drew-Bear 2005: 204–5; Hirt 2010: 113–14.

[30] Hirt 2010: 115–17; the relevant inscriptions are *CIL* III.7146; *AE* 1988, 1028 = *SEG* XXXVIII.1073; *IK* 13, 856; Milet, inv. no. 288.

they attended to?[31] Only at Chemtou (ancient Simitthus) do we have more detailed evidence for the operation of individual *procuratores Augusti*; these appear on inscribed blocks of *giallo antico* and on votive inscriptions from the town in some number, their full title possibly *procurator m(armorum) N (umidicorum)*.[32] Whether all of these sites were part of imperial estates in less clear. Strubbe has questioned whether the imperial estates of central Phrygia, principally second-century foundations, included the quarries, which were functioning from the first century AD.[33] Even at Chemtou, where Khanoussi and Millar have argued for an imperial estate, the evidence is not clear-cut.[34] Nevertheless, the presence of these procurators suggests an element of close oversight.

In addition to these procurators there are scattered references to other officials: several *vilici* are known at Luna, a *dispensator* at Chemtou, and a *dispensator Augusti* near Krokeai in the Peloponnese.[35] Two officials are mentioned on a statue base from Paleochora, near Karystos, who also appear on an inscription from Rome. These are Hymenaeus Thamyrianus, who has the title *a lapicidinis Carystiis*, and Thamyrus Alexandrinus, a *dispensator Augusti* and *nutricius*.[36] On this basis, Hirt has proposed that these individuals were initially based at Rome before being assigned to the quarries at Karystos, showing that officials at the quarries and at Rome were part of the same administrative structure.[37]

Soldiers are found at Karystos and elsewhere. Sergius Longus, recorded as a centurion of both the *legio XXII Primigenia* and the *legio XV Apollinaris* is attested at Karystos; his name is found on a *cipollino* column, a lead tag attached to another block, as well as a dedication to Hercules, suggesting he was involved directly in the supervision of quarrying.[38] Tullius Saturninus of the *legio XXII Primigenia* (in AD 136/137) and Aelius Antoninus, of an unknown legion, appear at Doki-meion.[39] It is important to distinguish between these centurions—apparent specialists, operating separately from their units—and the units of troops that turn up in quarries elsewhere. On a permanent or semi-permanent frontier the procurement of building stone, suitable for defensive construction, was a pressing concern of the Roman army and detachments of soliders (*vexillarii*) are attested in

[31] Bruzza 1870: no. 1, 4; on the role held by these individuals, Hirt 2010: 114–15.
[32] Hirt 2010: 117–19; for these individuals' full titles, see Khanoussi 1996: 1011 (no. 32) = *AE* 1998, 1573.
[33] Strubbe 1975: 230; for evidence of an imperial estate near Chemtou, Khanoussi 1997: 375–7.
[34] Khanoussi 1996: 1006; Millar 1992: 420.
[35] *AE* 1980, 476; *AE* 1991, 1681 (Carrara); *AE* 1986, 674 (Chemtou); *CIL* III.493 (Krokeai).
[36] *CIL* VI.8486 (Rome); *CIL* III.563, 12289 (Palaeochora).
[37] Hirt 2010: 157–9.
[38] *ILS* 8717 (Bruzza 1870: no. 1 = Dubois 1908: no. 278); *CIL* III.12286 (Dubois 1908: no. 279); see Franke 2000.
[39] Bruzza 1870: no. 258–9 (= Dubois 1908: no. 199–200); Drew-Bear 1994: no. 15–17; Christol and Drew-Bear 1987: no. 28.

quarries throughout the Rhineland, in northern Britain, and at Enesh on the Euphrates.[40] To this material we can add papyrological evidence from Egypt showing that vexillations of the *legio III Cyrenaica* complained in their letters home at having to work at 'stone-cutting' when stationed at Petra and Bosra.[41] Stone quarrying was part of the day-to-day drudgery of military service for a good number of soldiers but these military-operated quarries are quite distinct from the major imperially owned quarries. In the Brohl Valley, in fact, quarries initially opened and worked by the military continued under private control after the Hadrianic period when the legions no longer needed them.[42]

Contractors and imperial quarrying

Ultimately, what this discussion shows is that while we have some data relating to officials at other imperially operated quarries, extrapolating evidence from the Eastern Desert for a reconstruction of practices elsewhere is potentially misleading. And this is further demonstrated by the inscriptions on quarried blocks, the primary source of evidence for the character of imperial involvement in quarrying. The inscriptions mentioning members of the *familia Caesaris* or imperial officials, and their implications, have been discussed elsewhere and it is not necessary to cover them in detail here.[43] What is important for our purposes, though, is the *raison d'être* of these inscriptions. They were clearly used to identify imperial-owned materials. Sometimes lead seals with images of the emperors on seem to have been used to perform a similar function, occasionally in combination with inscriptions. The recesses for these seals can be found on many of the blocks from Portus.[44] However, while it has become customary to use these inscriptions and seals to assert close imperial control over quarrying and the resultant material, they can in fact be used to argue for a quite different picture.[45]

Domergue's analysis of the administration of contemporary Spanish mining districts suggests that imperial involvement could be both direct and indirect, depending on whether state employees (soldiers, slaves, or salaried

---

[40] On the Rhineland: J. Röder 1957: 217; Saxer 1967: 74–9; Pétry 1978: 370–1; Bauchhenss 1986: 90; Hirt 2010: 168–85. On Britain: *RIB I*, 998–1016, 1946–52; Pearson 2006: 46–7. On Enesh: Cumont 1917: 145–59; Stoll 1998: 99–120. Military *officinae* are mentioned in *CIL* XIII.5989; *RIB I*, 1008–10.

[41] *P.Mich.* VIII.465, 466.

[42] J. Röder 1957: 228.

[43] Bruzza 1870; Dubois 1908; Baccini Leotardi 1979; 1989; Christol and Drew-Bear 1986; 1987; 2005; Fant 1986; 1989a; Drew-Bear 1994; Pensabene 1994; Hirt 2010.

[44] Pensabene 1994: 321–2, 428–9, figs. 412–13.

[45] On this point with regard to the Luna quarries, Pensabene 2012.

freeborn individuals) or private contractors were used.[46] The employment of private contractors in mineral extraction was a typical practice of the Roman imperial administration and could work in several ways. The administration could lease out the right to mine or quarry a given resource to private contractors, under a *locatio conductio rei* contract, in return for a fee or a share of the output.[47] Alternatively, the administration could hire private contractors to undertake specific work, under a *locatio conductio operis* contract.

Were private contractors present at imperial quarries? One set of possible candidates are the *rationarii* (account-holders) mentioned on inscribed blocks from Dokimeion, Chemtou, Teos, Chios, Paros, and various Euboean quarries.[48] The inscribed blocks, in such a reconstruction, would represent the material that they were contractually obliged to produce, under a *locatio conductio operis* contract, which would then have been credited to their account (*ratio*). These individuals do appear to have been contractors of some sort: on an inscription on a block of *africano* from Rome the name of one of these individuals has been erased and replaced simply with *redemptoris*.[49] Three factors, however, seem to rule out these individuals being involved in quarrying directly. First, the same individual is often mentioned in conjunction with more than one material: the name Her(-), for instance, is inscribed on two blocks of Parian at Portus (datable to AD 163 and 164) as well as on the rock-face in the quarry shaft at Marathi on Paros, but also turns up on three blocks of *africano* datable to 162 along with a certain Sext(-).[50] Second, these *rationarii* are not attested at the quarries. As Hirt has pointed out in the case of Chemtou, none of the names of the *rationarii* mentioned on blocks from this site is epigraphically attested elsewhere on the site or indeed anywhere in Africa Proconsularis (with the exception of the common name Felix).[51] In fact, even the inscriptions mentioning them are rare at the quarries: 70 per cent of the inscriptions mentioning *rationarii* come from Portus and Rome.[52] Finally, most of these *rationarii* were probably members of the *familia Caesaris*—their names being typically followed by either *Caes(aris)*, *ser(vi)*, or *lib*

---

[46] Domergue 1990: 302–5. Peter Brunt made a similar point with regard to quarrying in a letter (dated 21 June 1976) to John Ward-Perkins, stating: 'state *control* does not necessarily imply state *management*' (BSR Archive, WP.2: Box XXXV). For more on contractors in mining, Hirt 2010: 261–90.

[47] On these contracts, G. Long 1875: 710; Cuvigny 2000: 14–21; on leasing systems in agriculture, Ørsted 1994.

[48] Hirschfeld 1905: 166.

[49] Fant 1989a: 29–30.

[50] Bruno et al. 2002d: 349. On individuals associated with more than one material: a Cl(-) Zel(-) appears on a block of *africano* in 150 and three blocks of *pavonazzetto* between 146 and 150, a certain Hya(cinthi) appears on blocks of *pavonazzetto* and *portasanta*, and a Laet(-)/Lae(-) on blocks of *giallo antico* and *africano*: see Bruzza 1870: no. 140, 147, 151, 159–64, 166, 205–7, 209, 220; Baccini Leotardi 1979: no. 8, 12–13, 40; 1989: no. 10, 44, 102–3; Fant 1989a: no. 91, 91b.

[51] Hirt 2010: 305.   [52] Hirt 2010: 301–2.

(ertus) Aug(usti).[53] These individuals look like they were the contractors tasked with acquiring particular quantities of stone, often from a range of quarries, rather than the quarrymen themselves. They were probably based in Rome and were closely connected to the administration.

Better evidence for private contractors at the quarries themselves comes from those inscriptions which appear at Dokimeion between AD 136 and 236 and which provide the following information: a consular date, topographical indicators (*locus* and usually *b(racchium)* numbers), and either one or both of two names in the genitive, one preceded by *off(icina)*, the other preceded by *caes(ura).*[54] The term *officina* is conventionally translated as 'workshop/ studio' and this appears to have been the unit responsible for handling the material once it had been quarried; at Chemtou, the term *lapicaedina* is used instead of *officina* in one instance, which makes this interpretation fairly certain.[55] Interestingly, one of the *officinae* mentioned at Dokimeion is called the *officina smyrnaiorum*, which Christol and Drew-Bear have argued shows it was supervising material destined for a project at Smyrna.[56] Other *officinae* at Dokimeion seem to have connections with Ephesos and Nikaea, while most are named after individuals (Papia(-), Crescent(-), Andaev(-)), imperial figures (Commodiana, Antoni(ni)ana, Sever(-)), or other characters (Herculi, Alex(-)).[57] These *officinae* are associated with multiple *bracchia* suggesting they could draw on material from various areas of the quarries. Apparently supplying these *officinae* with the material that they needed were the *caesurae* which appear alongside them on the inscriptions at Dokimeion from AD 147 onwards.[58] A *caesura* is a place of cutting, presumably a quarry. This division of labour between one group in charge of the actual quarrying and another responsible for working the raw material (also called *officinae*), each with their own specifically defined task, is also apparent in the case of mining.[59] Though the two centurions—Tullius Saturninus and Aelius Antoninus—are attested in this period, at least early on, most of the individuals mentioned in connection with *caesurae* from Dokimeion are not members of the *familia Caesaris* and none indicate their status with the label *aug(usti)* or *Caes(aris).*[60] Though some are freedmen, the dates of the blocks suggest that most were sons of freedmen, while at least one—with the *cognomen* Maryllinus, mentioned on a

[53] Christol and Drew-Bear 2005: 196, n. 23.
[54] Fant 1989a: 17–48; Kraus 1993: 56–64; Dubois 1908: 39–45; Bruzza 1870: no. 220–35; Hirt 2010: 293–301; also Pensabene 2010: 95–104.
[55] Dubois 1908: no. 110, 112.
[56] Christol and Drew-Bear 2005: 191, n. 4.
[57] Christol and Drew-Bear 1987: 109.
[58] Hirt 2010: 293.
[59] Ørsted 2000: 73–6.
[60] Hirt 2010: 293–7, *contra* Drew-Bear 1994: 806. On the status indicators of imperial freedmen, Weaver 1972: 2.

block dated to AD 229—is linked by Fant to the *gens* Dottia of Pisidian Antioch.[61]

How were these private individuals contracted? One especially useful quarry inscription from Dokimeion shows that these individuals had to produce a certain number of blocks each year and were keen to keep up with their obligations. This inscription states that the inscribed material was being supplied by a particular *officina* in place of some stones which had previously been handed in. These other stones had been received by an individual named Titus as a temporary loan from another *caesura*.[62] These various groups were evidently eager to record exactly who had produced each block; their leases clearly depended on it. This seems to suggest that these quarrymen were contracted under a *locatio conductio operis* arrangement—in other words, that they were contracted to produce a specific amount of blocks. However, these blocks might also represent the fee paid by these contractors under a *locatio conductio rei* arrangement. Perhaps these quarrymen paid for the right to extract material in the quarries by producing a certain amount of material for the administration annually.

In his original study of the epigraphic material from Dokimeion, Fant doubted whether these contractors 'stood to realize a pure profit once they had met the cost of the lease'.[63] The fact that not every *pavonazzetto* block at Dokimeion is inscribed, however, might suggest that some of the quarried produce entered the market through what Ward-Perkins called 'regular channels of supply', outside the control of the imperial administration.[64] Uninscribed blocks were certainly traded: the cargo of the ship wrecked off Punta Scifo, in Calabria, contains blocks of *pavonazzetto* (as well as Prokonnesian), some inscribed, but others not; the wreck from Dramont, off southern France, contained small blocks of uninscribed *africano*.[65] Only a small fraction of all quarried material at Dokimeion is actually inscribed and all of this comes from the large Bacakale quarry.[66] We should not rule out the possibility, then, that these private contractors could profit from quarrying and selling *pavonazzetto* once they had met the obligations of their lease, even if only to a limited extent. The fact that almost all of the inscriptions on material from Dokimeion are found on *pavonazzetto* blocks and not white marble ones also suggests that imperial control over the quarries was never intended to be total. Since the local white marble was of little interest to the imperial administration it would have been profitable for them to lease out its extraction via a *locatio conductio rei* agreement with the cost of the lease met by a fee. It should be noted that the seventh chapter of the famous Vipasca tablets, from Portugal, refers to the extraction of schist, within the imperially controlled mining area around

---

[61] Fant 1989*a*: 34–5.   [62] Fant 1989*a*: no. 177.   [63] Fant 1989*a*: 3, 31.
[64] Ward-Perkins 1980*b*: 39.   [65] Pensabene 1978: 105–12; 2002*b*: 20.
[66] Fant 1989*a*: 3–4; Pensabene 2007*a*: 298–9

Aljustrel, by private contractors who, in this case, paid for the privilege.[67] However, we might also imagine a scenario at Dokimeion in which the cost of this lease was met by the extraction of a stated quantity of *pavonazzetto* blocks. This would have necessitated a certain amount of moving around by the quarrymen but then we know from the quarry inscriptions that *caesura*-holders were present in a range of *bracchia*, that is areas of the quarry.[68]

Elsewhere private contractors are harder to identify. At most of the other quarries from which inscribed material comes it was never felt necessary to record the names of *caesura*-holders or *officinae*; instead we continue to find *rationarii* right through the second-century AD.[69] At Chemtou a shift in notation system similar to that found at Dokimeion from AD 136 is identifiable but here it takes a slightly different form. In place of *rationarii* we find procurators, their names preceded by *sub cura*, while the name of the emperor is listed in the genitive.[70] *Caesura*-holders are not recorded until later and then they are again procurators. Does this mean that private contractors were never employed at Chemtou? It could do but we also need to question why it was felt necessary to specifically designate material as belonging to the emperor if everything from the site did. If contractors were allowed to quarry under a *locatio conductio rei* arrangement, meeting the cost of their lease with a fee rather than a set amount of quarried material, then there would be no need for the blocks produced to be inscribed. Such a set-up would leave no paper trail. Indeed at Chemtou, as at Dokimeion, not all of the blocks at the quarries are inscribed as property of the emperor and those that are have been retrieved only from the quarries operating within the boundary wall which separated them from the town, and not from those beyond this wall.[71]

Changes in the system?

In sum, the way in which the administration chose to employ these contract-ors depended very much on what they needed. If a regular supply of material was required and there were sufficient resources to allow these contractors to quarry for profit then a *locatio conductio rei* agreement with the cost met by a specific quantity of material would have made a lot of sense. It might have made even more sense if, as at Dokimeion, a distinction could be drawn between what material had to be supplied in payment (for example, the coloured *pavonazzetto*) and what could be quarried for profit (the white marble), though such a system remains hypothetical. On the other hand, at remote and awkward sites, where no private contractor could profit from selling material, the administration found it easier to simply employ workers

---

[67] Domergue 1983: 95–8.   [68] Hirt 2010: 295–6.   [69] Hirt 2010: 309–13.
[70] Hirt 2010: 305.   [71] G. Röder 1993: 20; Kraus 1993; Hirt 2010: 27.

and pay them directly. At Mons Claudianus, for instance, large numbers of freeborn Egyptians (*pagani*) were employed for quarrying and other tasks, moving between jobs as they came up.[72]

One final question needs to be asked of these quarry inscriptions: do the different epigraphic formulas found on blocks from these quarries reflect different modes of production? The inscriptions mentioning *rationarii* mentioned above do seem to place the stimulus for production with these individuals, probably based at Rome, who required specific lots of materials. Does the alternative formula, on which the individual *caesura*-holders are named, therefore reveal a production-to-stock system? Possibly. It seems clear that these individuals had to produce a set number of blocks, or quantity of material, to meet the stipulations of their lease. But this does not mean that they could not have been given particular orders to complete, and presumably even if no orders had been placed they would still have been given some guidance about what to produce. Peacock has proposed, with regard to the Mons Claudianus quarries, that 'special orders would be catered for and in the intervening periods the work-force would be employed to produce a stockpile of the commonly required dimensions'.[73] Here he is talking about columns, but most of the quarry inscriptions known from the quarries, from Portus and Rome, are on stepped blocks, suitable for cutting into veneer panels; it made much more sense to produce blocks in this form if nothing specific was required than column shafts or other objects that were distinctly less versatile. The practicalities of production-to-stock will be discussed further in Chapter 6 but suffice it to say for now that private contractors are just as likely to have been involved in production-to-order as production-to-stock; the inscriptions mentioning *caesura*-holders unfortunately tell us little about where the stimulus for production came from. It should also be noted that though *caesura*-holders appear at Dokimeion in the 130s, *rationarii* continue to be mentioned on blocks of *pavonazzetto* into the 170s; there was obviously a certain amount of overlap between accounting systems here. Elsewhere, such as in the *africano* quarries at Teos, the accounting system never changed. To argue, on the basis of the quarrying inscriptions, that there was a wholesale reorganization of imperial quarries in the second-century AD which marked a shift from production-to-order to production-to-stock, therefore, is probably to stretch the evidence too far.[74] Reliance on contractors becomes more noticeable but that is about it.

The question of imperial monopolization will be discussed further in Chapter 5. What is clear, though, is that the quarry inscriptions alone nowhere indicate imperial monopolization of a given resource. What they reveal are the complex leasing systems instigated by the imperial administration at a handful

---

[72] Cuvigny 2000: 14–52.   [73] Peacock and Maxfield 1997: 214.
[74] *Contra* Hirt 2010: 326–8.

of exceptionally valued quarrying sites across the empire; they show the mechanism which furnished imperial building projects with sufficient supplies of prestige marbles through the first to third centuries AD. The state relied on private contractors, but there is also suggestive evidence that imperial and private extraction could, and probably did, co-exist within the same quarry, as we will see.[75]

Coordinating supply

A range of imperial officials oversaw the extraction and processing of material at those quarries run by the imperial administration and specific regional oversight seems to have been coordinated through procurators who also managed staff at the quarries, including large numbers of private contractors. These officials, then, were responsible for the initial stages of the process: for securing the necessary materials, of the requisite quality and quantity. At the end of the process, meanwhile, we have scattered references to another series of officials, based at Rome, apparently charged with handling the delivery of this material. These two teams of administrators were presumably part of the same continuum of officialdom: one responsible for ensuring the safe dispatch of material, the other its receipt.

Among the officials documented at Rome are a series of *tabularii*, that is accountants or book-keepers. Two of these, a Titus Flavius Celadus and a Titus Flavius Successus, describe themselves as *tabularii marmorum Lunensium*; the latter also uses the title *tabularius rationis marmorum Lunensium* elsewhere, a variant which clarifies that this was a treasury role.[76] A Celadus, probably this same Titus Flavius Celadus, also appears as the dedicant on a funerary altar where he is described as an *actor a marmorib(us)*, probably a junior treasury official, indicating that he worked his way through the ranks before becoming a *tabularius*.[77] Two other freedmen, a Primigenius Iuvencianus and a Marcus Ulpius Martialis, describe themselves as *tabularii a marmoribus* (the second simply as *a marmoribus*), suggesting that clerical units existed for the administration of other marbles in addition to, or perhaps inclusive of, the one dealing specifically with Luna marble.[78] At least two other inscriptions also refer to a *statio marmorum* but whether this was a specific building or area, as Bruzza and Lanciani believed, or simply a clerical office is unclear.[79] The relevant inscriptions, however, record a Semnus and a Marcus Ulpius Restitutus, who describe themselves as an *optio tabellariorum stationis*

---

[75] Lambraki 1978: 32–6.   [76] *CIL* VI.8484–5; *AE* 1974, 153.
[77] Granino Cecere and Morizio 2007: 135–6.   [78] *CIL* VI.301, 8483.
[79] Bruzza 1870: 138; Lanciani 1891: 34–6; 1897: 529. On the word *statio* as referring to an abstract office, Coarelli 2002: 223–30; Maischberger 1997: 139–42.

marmorum and a *praepositus ex station(e) marmorum* respectively.[80] The latter is probably best interpreted as a supervisor, a *capo della struttura* as Granino Cecere and Morizio put it.[81]

What was the role of these officials? To judge from their titles they oversaw the delivery of quarried stone at the capital and so probably performed a similar role to the various other clerical staff attested at Rome who dealt with the influx of fiscal products of other types.[82] To judge from their names, Celadus and Successus were granted their freedom under the Flavians, Martialis and Restitutus under Trajan; Iuvencianus was a freedman of Vespasian as his dedication makes clear. Only Semnus, a Severan freedman, is later. The late first and early second centuries AD was a period of massive demand for decorative stones at Rome and indeed these officials materialize just after the first quarry inscriptions appear in the Emporium district, under Nero and the Flavians.[83] Aside from simply counting blocks, however, it is also possible that these individuals were responsible for ordering in the material being delivered. In fact, the Successus who is recorded as a *rationarius* on two blocks of *portasanta*, both dated to AD 96, could well be the *tabularius rationis marmorum Lunensium* mentioned above.[84] These *tabularii* and the *rationarii* recorded in the quarry inscriptions could be the same people, then, or at least part of the same administrative system.

Whether the various officials attested at Rome and in the quarries were part of a single centralized marble bureau, a *ratio marmorum*, as Ward-Perkins and later Fant have suggested, has been questioned.[85] Christol and Drew-Bear have suggested that it was local procurators on the ground who made the key decisions about how quarrying was organized; likewise Hirt has pointed out how varied administration systems at different quarries were.[86] However, while it is true that day-to-day decisions about how best to manage their resources and extract sufficient material must have been made by officials at the quarries, it was demand from Rome that determined the quantity and quality of material needed and the forms in which it was to be produced. These different branches of the administration must have been in constant contact.

---

[80] *CIL* VI.410; Maischberger 1997: 141; Granino Cecere and Morizio 2007: 130–3.

[81] Granino Cecere and Morizio 2007: 130–3.

[82] For other *tabularii*, *CIL* VI.8473, 8476, 8476a, 8477.

[83] Two blocks of *africano* are datable to the reign of Nero (AD 64 and 76, Bruzza 1870: no. 138–40), nine to the reign of Vespasian (AD 75–7, Bruzza 1870: no. 147–51, 153–6); a single block of *giallo antico* dates to the reign of Nero (AD 64, Bruzza 1870: no. 220), as does one block of *portasanta* (AD 67, Bruzza 1870: no. 191); one block of *cipollino* dates to the reign of Vespasian (AD 73, Bruzza 1870: no. 3); finally one block of *pavonazzetto* also dates to this period, but it was found at Dokimeion and not Rome (AD 72, Fant 1989a: no. 11).

[84] Bruzza 1870: 198–9.

[85] Ward-Perkins 1992b: 23–6; Fant 1992.

[86] Christol and Drew-Bear 2005; Hirt 2010: 351–6.

PRIVATE AND MUNICIPAL QUARRIES

Prior to the imperial period, all quarries appear to have been owned by private individuals or cities, and there is no reason to assume that this changed drastically.[87] In the past, Suetonius' much-quoted description of Tiberius' repossession of mineral extraction and tax collection rights has been used to argue for a process of 'nationalization' of extractive sites. Several factors, however, rule out an *a priori* assumption that this ever happened. For a start, Suetonius nowhere describes a universal policy; he remarks simply that 'many states and individuals were deprived of immunities of long standing, and of the right of working *metalla* [mines and/or quarries] and collecting revenues...'[88] This comment comes in the middle of a long list of examples of thefts and confiscations perpetrated by Tiberius. These were isolated attacks, often on specific 'leading men' and not part of a general process of nationalization. Later legal texts, of the first to third centuries AD, show that both private quarrying and the extraction of *vectigalia* persisted in many areas of the Roman Empire.[89] In fact, Ulpian makes the point quite clearly in his discussion of the laws relating to quarrying rights that stone resources belonged to the owner of whatever land they were found on.[90] Considering all of the above, it seems safe to say that the overwhelming majority of quarries in the Roman world operated beyond state control, as they had in earlier periods.[91]

Ownership arrangements

How quarry-owners chose to exploit the resources at their disposal is less clear. In the case of privately owned quarries the options available to the owner are fairly clear: they could work the quarry themselves, they could hire others to do it for them (*locatio operis*), or they could lease the right to work them to someone else (*locatio rei*). It is possible that the M. Ulpius Carminius Claudianus, who made many gifts to the city of Aphrodisias during the second century AD, largely of buildings and statues, was himself a quarry-owner. His various good deeds are recorded in an inscription on a statue base found in the city on which the donated statues are noted as having come from 'his

---

[87] Lambraki 1978: 33–4; Marc 1995: 33; Dworakowska 1983: 26–31; on the profitability of quarries, see Varro, *On Agriculture* 1.2.22–3.

[88] Suetonius, *Tiberius* 49 (trans. J. C. Rolfe); see Ward-Perkins 1992*b*: 24–6; Monna, Pensabene, and Sodini 1985: 16.

[89] On private quarries: Javolenus, *Digest* XXIII.5.18; Pomponius, *Digest* XXIII.3.32; Paul, *Digest* XXIV.3.8; Ulpian, *Digest* VII.1.13.5, XXIV.3.7.13, XXVII.9.3.6. On *vectigalia*, Lintott 1993: 84; Galsterer 1988: 86; Gonzalez 1986: 167; Hirt 2010: 85.

[90] *Digest* VIII.4.13.1; on this point with regard to the Thasian quarries, Marc 1995.

[91] Dworakowska 1983: 29–31; and more recently Gutiérrez 2009: 283.

Fig. 3.3. Aerial photograph of the so-called City Quarries at Aphrodisias (photo: Courtesy New York University excavations at Aphrodisias).

house'—οἴκοθεν κατεσκευακότα.[92] This might indicate a workshop or perhaps simply his estate, a hypothesis supported by the fact that the Carminii were from the village of Attouda, located north of the city on the other side of the large so-called City Quarries.[93] In fact, Reynolds has hypothesized that many other benefactors at Aphrodisias were also quarry-owners.[94] The archaeological evidence certainly does not contradict this proposal: the number of extraction sites constituting the City Quarries, their varying scale and layout, indicates a strongly decentralized process; as Rockwell puts it, private capital was probably crucial 'in industrializing the quarry process' at Aphrodisias (Fig. 3.3).[95] If the owner of a quarry did not want to extract stone themselves then they could resort to leasing out the right to work it, as a concession, to another individual, a contractor (*conductor*). The cost of this lease could be met by a fee, a share of the output, or a set amount of extracted produce. It

[92] *CIG* 2782.
[93] On the Carminii of Attouda, Macro 1979; Thonemann 2011: 227–35.
[94] Reynolds 1996: 122.   [95] Ponti 1996; Rockwell 1996: 103.

could be short-term, for the completion of a specific job, or much longer-term depending on the needs or ambitions of the concessioner.

It is also possible that some of these Aphrodisian quarries were owned by the city and access to them controlled. Securing steady income was a constant difficulty for individual municipalities; they relied principally on contributions from wealthy citizens and office-holders, indirect taxes, such as custom duties, and rents and fees from municipal monopolies.[96] The duties of the *duumviri*, as outlined in the Flavian *lex Irnitana*, from Spain, included leasing out rights to exploit certain resources on municipal land.[97] Long has even proposed that major sanctuaries could have owned quarries.[98] Provided sufficient resources were reserved for their own projects (one of the main duties of the *duumviri* in the *lex*), it made sound economic sense for the local administration, of a city or sanctuary, to lease out quarrying rights to private individuals.[99] Again these could by met by the cost of a fee or a set amount of stone. Such resources could well have been an important source of income and it is difficult to envisage a situation in which quarries were confiscated from cities by the imperial administration. In the Greek East, especially, with its long history of quarrying, stone-supply was closely linked to the autarkic ideal of the *polis*. The folklore surrounding Pixodaros, the supposed discoverer of the Ephesian marble quarries, illustrates their economic importance to the city: Vitruvius tells us that he was awarded divine honours for his find and had annual sacrifices made in his honour.[100] The Prokonnesian quarries, which had belonged to the city of Kyzikos since at least the fourth century BC, seem to have remained largely under local control as well.[101] Roman funerary inscriptions from the island show that it was under the jurisdiction of Kyzikos, and Aelius Aristides sees the citizens of this city as controlling exports from the quarries.[102] Considering all of this it is interesting to note that a block recently discovered at Lyon had a lead seal attached on which *Lugdun(um)* was inscribed, which might indicate that this was material either from a municipal quarry or for a municipal project; either way, this is a rare example of the use of a lead seal in a non-imperial context.[103]

---

[96] Galsterer 2000: 353; Sartre 1991: 134–5.   [97] Gonzàlez 1986: 212, 218–19.
[98] L. E. Long 2012*a*: 30–1.   [99] Bang 2006: 76–7.
[100] Vitruvius X.2.15.
[101] On the forceful absorption of Prokonnesos by Kyzikos in the fourth century BC, Pausanius, *Guide to Greece* VIII.46.4.
[102] Asgari 1979: 470; Walker 1985*a*: 29. For some of the inscriptions from the island mentioning the *polis* of Kyzikos, *IMT Kyz PropInseln* 1319, 1335–6, possibly also 1337–9, 1344, all of which can be viewed at http://epigraphy.packhum.org/inscriptions/ (last checked 25/11/2012). The relevant passage of Aelius Aristides is *Orations* 27.15–17; on this point, Petsalis-Diomidis 2008: 133–4.
[103] This seal was mentioned in the paper presented by D. Fellague, F. Masino, H. Savay-Guerraz, and G. Sobrà at ASMOSIA X in Rome in June 2012.

Organization of work

The inscriptions on quarried material that are so common at imperial quarries are rare at non-imperial sites. Since they were only required when one material needed distinguishing from another, when accounts needed crediting or the obligations of contractors recording.[104] In the main, then, inscriptions on quarry faces or quarried material at non-imperial sites consist of little more than numbers or ligatured initials, which seem to be control marks or simple records of orders; these were probably for the benefit of whoever was undertaking the work and never intended to be read by anyone else.[105] Sometimes clear names can be identified: in the Cape Phanari quarries on Thasos, *ΠΥΡΡΟΥ* is inscribed on the south quarry face, possibly a Greek name in the genitive, while three inscriptions found nearby, which read *OP*, have been interpreted as boundary markers perhaps marking out a specific owner's or concessioner's territory.[106]

More detailed than these abbreviated marks but less easily understood are the inscriptions and *dipinti* on the quarry faces at Saint-Boil (Saône-et-Loire). A series of painted or drawn accounts have been identified in these quarries, most largely unreadable.[107] One long inscription can be read, though. It consists of a series of apparent inventories and names with the title *ratio anglares cablonnaci*, translated by Lambert as an account (*ratio*) of either 'the stone blocks of' or even the 'stone-cutters of' *Cabillo* or *Cabillonnum*, modern Chalon-sur-Saône, the closest town to the quarries.[108] The names, it is assumed, are either those of the individuals assigned with producing stone for the city or the members of a corporation called 'The Stone-Cutters of Cabillonnum'. Another inscription from the site provides a list of apparent measurements—numbers preceded by a *P*, presumably for *pedem* (feet)—written next to the initials *CA*, possibly the *cablonnaci* again.[109] These documents seem to be rare examples of non-imperial accounting systems, presumably marked out to allow the quarrymen involved to keep track of what they were meant to be producing.

Our only other documentary evidence comes from Egypt, where a handful of papyri record contracts between individuals and quarries, which seem to be privately run. A papyrus from second-century Oxyrhynchus, records a

---

[104] Fant 1989a: 17–48.
[105] On examples from Ras et Tarf in Tunisa, Slim et al. 2004: 196–7; at Montjuïc near Barcelona, *IRC* IV.304; Gutiérrez 2009: 275; at Bois des Lens, Barutel, and Glanum, where Greek letters are also found, Bessac 1996: 293–6; at Iasos, Bruno 2012: 710.
[106] Koželj and Wurch-Koželj 2009: 59–61. Another quarry at the site contains a *dipinto* which reads *ΠΑΡ Σ-O*, which might be another ownership mark.
[107] Monthel and Lambert 2002: 106–13.
[108] Monthel and Pinette 1977: 37–61; Monthel and Lambert 2002: 118–20.
[109] Monthel and Lambert 2002: 112 (fig. 87).

contract between a certain Antonia Asclepias and a group of stone-cutters who
agree to supply cut blocks from the 'northern quarry', while another mentions
the transportation of 100 columns from the 'Ankyronon quarries' to the port
of 'Artemis' for the construction of a temple.[110] Whether these are quarry-
owners or concessioners undertaking these commissions is impossible to tell.
The same is true of the pair of workers—Quintus Iulius Iulianus and Publicius
Crescentinus—who give thanks on an altar from Marignac (near the Saint-
Béat quarries in the Pyrenees) for having safely produced and transported a
pair of 20 RF columns.[111] These men were not imperial freedmen or officials
and it seems reasonable to identify them as private quarry-owners or contractors hired for a specific job.

Mixed ownership

The presence of private contractors and other workers in imperial quarries,
some of whom might well have been producing material for their own profit,
shows that drawing a clear line between imperial and non-imperial activity is
often difficult.[112] In fact, at certain quarries there is evidence to suggest that
imperial and private quarrying took place side by side; as Ward-Perkins noted,
'there is no reason why both systems should not have operated simultaneously'.[113] The large quarrying district at Luna is one place where such a
scenario can be reconstructed.

The Luna quarries (or at least some of them) were initially controlled by the
nearby colony, to judge from the so-called *lapis Salvioni*.[114] Found inside the
quarrying district, and dated to AD 22, this stele records a list of *decuriones*
ordered by year, compiled by a certain Hilario, a *vilicus* (manager, often of a
group of slaves) and *magister* (in this context probably the head of a *collegium*).[115] Dubois showed that the names of several of these *decuriones* also
appeared in abbreviated form on inscribed blocks in the quarries, suggesting

---

[110] *P.Oxy.* III.498; *SB* XIV.11958.
[111] *CIL* XIII.38 = *ILS* 3579 = *AE* 2000, 923: *Silvano deo et/Montibus Nimidis/Q. Iul. Iulianus et
Publi/cius Crescentinus qui pri/mi hinc columnas vice/narias celaverunt/et exportaverunt/v(ota) s
(olverunt) l(ibentes) m(erito)*; though Fabre and Sablayrolles (1995: 145–8) read the inscription
as saying *claverunt* rather than *celaverunt*, which they translate as referring to a quarrying
technique. This altar is now in the Musée Saint-Raymond in Toulouse (inv. no. 31085). For a
full discussion of this text, Fabre and Sablayrolles 1995: 145–50; Hirschfeld 1905: 147, n. 5;
Pensabene 2002b: 49; Marco Simón 2003: 126.
[112] Fant 2008b: 580.
[113] Ward-Perkins 1980b: 37.
[114] *CIL* XI.1356 = *ILS* 7228.
[115] Dolci 2006: 67–9; Hirt 2010: 314–7; further *vilici* from the quarrying district are mentioned in *CIL* XI.1319–20, 1327, 6947.

that this *collegium* might well have been involved in quarrying.[116] The fact that the names of many of these individuals, including Hilario, are followed on the quarry inscriptions with the letters *COL*, has been plausibly interpreted as indicating either that the slaves for which they were responsible were *servi publici* of the *colonia Lunensis* or that they themselves were.[117] Either way, this suggests that municipal workers were engaged in quarrying at Luna. At the same time, we also know that imperial agents were present at Luna since they are named on blocks of Luna marble from Rome apparently as early as the 20s BC, and this continues through to probably the third century AD.[118]

This suggests that there was an overlap of municipal and imperial workers at Luna in the late first century BC and early first century AD. Either the two supply systems could operate side by side or the municipal workers were supplying the imperial administration, perhaps under a *locatio conductio operis* arrangement. Whichever was the case, it is entirely feasible in such a large quarrying district that different quarries were owned by different parties, be they private, municipal, or the state. Indeed Menella has argued that private quarry-workers, some ex-slaves, can be identified elsewhere in the epigraphic record from Luna, notably on altars: the example of Baebius Nymphodotus, whose slave Hermes is a *vilicus*, is a case in point.[119] The abbreviation BAE turns up on blocks in the quarries but also at Rome and Cherchel and Pensabene has pointed out that the gens Baebia were an important family at Luna.[120] Menella has also suggested that these teams of private workers were probably organized like similar teams of imperial workers, keeping detailed account of their output. This might be supported by four inscribed blocks of Luna marble from a shipwreck at Marseillan Beauséjour off southern France which seem to refer to specific individuals though give none of the information normally found on quarry inscriptions elsewhere.[121] The initials NAE which are found on Block 2 have also been found on blocks in the Olmo quarry, in the Colonnata district at Carrara; the initials RF on Block 3, perhaps R(u)F(us), have been found on blocks at Rome and again in the Olmo quarry.[122] No imperial officials are mentioned and these blocks are not given consular dates so were probably never part of the imperial distribution system. The fact that some of these blocks, inscribed with both BAE and RF, are found at Rome could further indicate that private quarrymen at Luna were supplying imperial projects. Highlighting an honorific inscription from Luna, Speidel has argued that not only was this the case but that this was a lucrative business. This inscription seems to honour P. Sulpicius Scribonius Proculus, a senior senator under

[116] Dubois 1908: 6–8.   [117] Dubois 1908: 6–8, no. 1–5, 13.
[118] Pensabene 1998*a*: 342; 2002*b*: 15.
[119] Menella 1990.
[120] Dolci 1995: 131; 1997: 41–4; 2003: 74; Pensabene 2004: 423–4.
[121] H. Bernard 2009: 514–19, figs. 5–6.
[122] Bartelletti and Criscuolo 2004: 5–12, fig. 8; Dolci 2003: 137.

Nero, in his capacity as a *curator operum publicorum* at Rome.[123] It is strange
to see a *curator operum publicorum* being honoured in this way but, as Speidel
points out, it makes complete sense if he was responsible for contracting out
work to the quarrymen of Luna; and the fact the locals honoured him so
publicly shows just how important this link to the capital was to them.

This multiple ownership system can also be proposed for Prokonnesos,
even if the quarries were under the general control of Kyzikos. Asgari and
Drew-Bear have documented forty-five inscriptions in the quarries, incised
and painted, on quarry faces and quarried material, thirty-four datable to the
Roman Imperial period, mostly the second and third centuries AD.[124] Two of
these, both on quarry faces, seem to record either an owner or worker: these
read *ΑΥΦ*, presumably *Αὐφ(ίδιος)*, and *Ἀπολλοδώρου* in the genitive.[125]
Another abbreviated name, *ΑΝΤωΝ*, presumably Antonius or Antoninus, is
also found on a series of roughed-out Corinthian capitals and one base from
the valley between Köyüstü and Yalancı Palatya on Prokonnesos; in all but two
cases this Greek name is accompanied by the abbreviation *IMR*, in Latin.[126]
The same name is found painted on three capitals and a base from in the
Silinte area of the quarries, in two cases with the same abbreviation.[127] Since
only around 10 per cent of the roughed-out objects from the Prokonnesian
quarries are inscribed this was clearly a system for recording ownership or
keeping track of orders that was only employed by a minority of workers at the
quarries. The presence of Latin inscriptions on Prokonnesos might indicate
that some of this material was being produced under imperial supervision but
it could just as easily demonstrate that Latin-speaking workers were present on
the island; none of these inscriptions, after all, mention either the emperor or
an imperial official. To judge from the large quantities of Prokonnesian marble
used in imperially funded building, the administration had direct access to
material from these quarries, but based on the above inscriptions we might
propose that this access was never exclusive.

A similar situation perhaps existed in the El Mèdol quarries near Tarragona,
if only temporarily (Fig. 3.4). The limestone from this site was used extensively
in the Provincial Forum and other major publicly funded buildings at Tarragona. At least a portion of these quarries were apparently owned or operated
by the colony: an inscription found on a quarried block reading BVCOLI likely
signifies *b(racchium) V col(onia) I(ulia)*.[128] In this case it seems reasonable to
conclude that the quarries were part of the city's *ager publicus*. Another
inscription from the quarries, however, which was found during road-works,

123 *CIL* XI.1340; Speidel 1994.
124 Asgari and Drew-Bear 2002.
125 Asgari and Drew-Bear 2002: nos. 8, 10.
126 Asgari and Drew-Bear 2002: nos. 11–15, 19, 27.
127 Asgari and Drew-Bear 2002: nos. 23–6.
128 Mar and Pensabene 2010: 513–15, fig. 6.

Fig. 3.4. The El Mèdol limestone quarries near Tarragona (photo: A. Gutiérrez).

reads simply CAES.[129] This could be short for *caesura* but it has also been
suggested that it refers to either an imperial project or one in some way
connected to the imperial administration—perhaps the Provincial Forum at
Tarragona. The quarrymen at El Mèdol could have inscribed this material to
distinguish it from blocks for ordinary projects but it is also possible that part
of the quarries were taken over for this work. Imperial building projects
needed more than just decorative stones and when built in the provinces
would have relied on local quarries to supply much of their requirements. The
administration could have taken over these sites on a temporary basis or even
confiscated them altogether but it probably would have been easier to contract
out work to them.

---

[129] Mar and Pensabene 2010: 512–13.

Exactly how work at the Göktepe quarries near Aphrodisias functioned is unclear but might present a further example of mixed ownership. The recent discovery of an inscribed block at the quarries mentioning a *rationarius* called Olympus indicates either that some material from this site was directed to imperial projects, probably at Rome, or that part or all of the quarries were under imperial supervision.[130] This same *rationarius* is attested on a series of five inscribed blocks of *pavonazzetto* found at Portus, datable to AD 96–100, and he was evidently an imperial freedman charged with securing decorative stones from Asia Minor in this period.[131] However, the high-quality white and black marbles from Göktepe were extensively used for statuary at nearby Aphrodisias, even though they lay beyond the city's territory, and Aphrodisian sculptors carved statues in this material for export.[132] It is possible then that the Göktepe quarries were exploited by both local consumers and imperial officials and that Aphrodisian carvers had a particular interest in them.

To summarize, though we have little hard data relating to how most quarries were run, it is clear that the vast majority remained in private or municipal hands throughout the imperial period. For many cities these quarries were integral elements of their urban economy and there is no reason to assume that their ownership was anything other than local. Only a minority of sites were important enough to attract imperial attention, typically those at which uniquely coloured material were extracted or those too remote to be worked by anyone else. At certain sites, however, imperial and non-imperial quarrying probably co-existed, especially at those white marble quarries where there was enough material and space for different groups of workers to be accommodated. Occasionally, as the example of El Mèdol shows, the imperial administration might even have used locally owned quarries.

QUARRY DISTRIBUTION

In order to understand how these various sites, run in very different ways, fitted into the wider landscape of quarrying it is helpful to turn to the overall distribution of quarrying sites. This is the background against which further discussions of the production and trade in stone objects have to take place. A number of detailed studies of quarrying in specific areas of the Roman world already exist and the aim here is to stitch some of these together to try and

---

[130] This inscription was presented by M. Bruno, D. Attanasio, W. Prochaska, and B. Yavuz at ASMOSIA X in Rome in June 2012; see also L. E. Long 2012*a*: 90.
[131] Fant 1989*a*: no. 83–5, 88, 92b; Baccini Leotardi 1989: no. 40.
[132] Attanasio, Bruno, and Yavuz 2009.

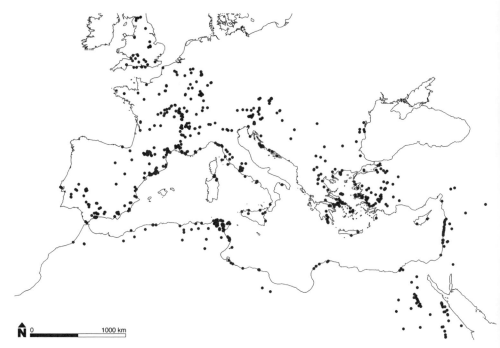

Fig. 3.5. Map of sites at which quarrying is attested in the Roman period.

understand the distribution of quarrying activity more broadly.[133] The following discussion is based on a survey of existing publications, primarily studies of Roman quarrying, art, and architecture, as well as excavation and survey reports. A total of nearly 800 sites at which Roman quarrying activity has been documented were identified in this way (Fig. 3.5), the details of which are stored in an online database on the Oxford Roman Economy Project website.[134] Such a survey can never be exhaustive but this remains a useful dataset to work with and is far more complete than any other deployed to date in this context. Several further caveats are needed. First, for a lot of these sites there is insufficient information to answer all of the questions we might want to ask; many have never been mapped, dated, or their material studied closely. Second, there are instances when we can pinpoint the origin of certain materials but any signs of Roman quarrying have been eradicated by later work; when this is the case this fact is noted in the gazetteer.

[133] Studies with a regional focus: Bedon 1984; Pearson 2006; Gutiérrez 2009. Previous overviews: Dworakowska 1983; Braemer 1986*b*; 1992.

[134] This database can be accessed at http://oxrep.classics.ox.ac.uk/databases/stone_quarries_database/.

Obviously not all quarries are alike. The sites as they are listed in the gazetteer are not individual extraction points but sites at which a particular concentration of quarrying activity is attested. Most of the larger sites included actually contain numerous individual quarry faces: the so-called City Quarries at Aphrodisias, for instance, which comprise over seventy.[135] Equally, these sites vary enormously in scale. Although the data do not exist to rank them all by surface area or the volume of material extracted we can broadly distinguish between three basic sizes of quarry. At the upper end of the scale are the very largest quarries, those covering over 5 km^2 or at which more than 120,000 m^3 of stone was quarried: Prokonnesos (at least 30 km^2 and probably well over 1,000,000 m^3), Aswan (c.20 km^2 and 220,000 m^3), Luna (probably as much as 10 km^2 and again over 1,000,000 m^3), Dokimeion (c.8 km^2 and estimated at 500,000 m^3, Fig. 3.6), Mons Claudianus (c.9 km^2), Mons Porphyrites (c.6 km^2), Penteli (at least 200,000 m^3), Chemtou (c.250,000 m^3, Fig. 3.7), and Hasançavuslar near Ephesos (c.500,000 m^3).[136] These volumes are not reliable indicators of how much usable stone was extracted at these sites since well over 70 per cent of the total quarried material would have been wasted during this process.[137] Nevertheless, these figures are useful when it comes to comparing activity at different quarries.

Smaller in scale but still significant, covering areas of 2–5 km^2 or at which between 40,000–120,000 m^3 was extracted, are many of the larger urban quarries, such as those Aphrodisias, Sardis, Belevi and Kentli Çiftliği near Ephesos, El Mex and Abu Ras near Alexandria, El Haouaria near Carthage, and probably also El Mèdol and Almadén de la Plata in Spain. At least 100 of the quarries included in the gazetteer can probably be included in this category. Even so, this means that approximately 75 per cent of the known quarrying sites were relatively small, and of course the majority of these were far smaller than the 2 km^2 or 40,000 m^3 mark. This general spread of quarry sizes seems to be representative. In her discussion of quarrying in Catalonia, Gutiérrez catalogues twenty-three Roman quarries (and eleven which might also be Roman), out of which only those at El Mèdol and Clots de Sant Julià had more than 20,000 m^3 of material extracted from them: 300–12,000 m^3 is more typical for the Catalan quarries and probably also for many of the

---

[135] Ponti 1996; Rockwell 1996.

[136] On Prokonnesos, Attanasio, Brilli, and Bruno 2008; on Luna, Dolci 1980; Attanasio 2003: 165–8; on Dokimeion, Waelkens 1990: 63; on the Egyptian quarries, Peacock and Maxfield 1997; Maxfield and Peacock 2001a; 2001b; on Penteli, Lepsius 1890: 13–14; on Chemtou, G. Röder 1988: 91–4; and on Hasançavuslar, Yavuz, Bruno, and Attanasio 2011: 223.

[137] Estimates of how much of the total stone extracted during marble quarrying was usable vary from 20 per cent (J. Röder 1971: 269), to 25 per cent (Lambertie 1962: 58), to as much as 30 per cent (Attanasio, Bruno, and Yavuz 2009: 326).

Fig. 3.6. The main Bacakale quarry at Dokimeion (photo: P. Rockwell).

Fig. 3.7. The main area of quarrying between the 'Stadtberg' and 'Gelber Berg' at Chemtou (photo: author).

quarries in North Africa, France, Britain, and the Balkans listed in the gazetteer.[138]

Moving from size to distribution, the map of the quarrying sites listed in the attached gazetteer reveals a number of interesting trends. First, there is a close correspondence between the distribution of quarries and the distribution of cities; most quarries were located in the immediate vicinity of the urban centre that was the primary market for the material extracted at them.[139] Second, the majority of those quarries not found in close proximity to an urban centre were targeting high-quality or uniquely valuable materials. Third, a considerable proportion of the quarries in this sample—both those tied into the pattern of urbanization and those not—were located on the coast or on a navigable river, while others seem to have been opened specifically to take advantage of road connections.

Quarries and urbanization

Considering what has already been said about the predominately private or municipal ownership of quarries this relationship between the distribution of quarries and cities is unsurprising (Fig. 3.8). What it shows, though, is that most quarries are best thought of as accessories to the local urban economies of the Roman world; in the case of Gaul, Goodman goes as far as to describe them as 'periurban industries'.[140] Quarrying even took place within cities: limestone was extracted at Vienne in France, for instance, while most of the early building at Sabratha was undertaken in the sandstone on which the city stood.[141] At Rome, of course, tuff was quarried in enormous quantities within the city, on its periphery, as well as throughout its immediate territory.[142]

To judge from those areas that have been closely surveyed—mainly France, Spain, Austria, Tunisia, western Turkey, and Egypt—the inhabitants of most cities relied most of the time on stone quarried no more than 20–30 km away, or a day's walk. In all of these areas customers were reliant on local resources and quarries were tied into local settlement patterns. The highest concentrations of quarries are found in the most urbanized zones. In Spain, particular clusters of quarries have been identified in the hinterlands of the cities of the southern and eastern coasts, as well as inland in the Guadalquivir valley and around Merida (Fig. 3.9).[143] As Gutiérrez has shown, in her masterful survey

---

[138] Gutíerrez 2009: 279–80.

[139] For distribution maps of cities, Scheidel 2007: 76–7 (maps 3.2–3), based on Pounds 1969: 155 (fig. 10); Jones 1937: maps II–IV; for the most up-to-date work, Hanson 2011; forthcoming.

[140] Goodman 2007: 111–12; also Leveau 2007: 659–60.

[141] Bedon 1984: 32–3; Ward 1970: 57; Chiesa 1949: 25–6; Di Vita 1999: 146–59.

[142] Ventriglia 1971; Lancaster 2005: 12–18; Jackson and Marra 2006, esp. figs. 2–3; Heiken, Funiciello, and De Rita 2005.

[143] Mayer 1992: 18–20, 99–100; Lapuente et al. 2002; Pizzo 2010.

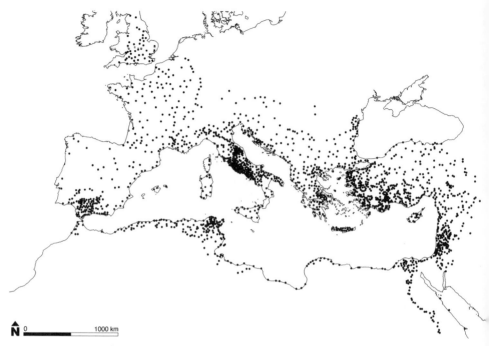

Fig. 3.8. Distribution of urban centres in the Roman Empire (source: Pounds 1969: fig. 10; Jones 1937: maps II–IV; with North African and Egyptian sites from Talbert 2000).

of quarries in Catalonia, stone in this region was rarely distributed far and quarries were opened as close as possible to where their materials were needed; such was the demand that work was sometimes undertaken on an enormous scale—as at El Mèdol.[144] In southern France, the large concentration of quarries along or close to the Mediterranean coast can actually be broken down into distinct clusters, centred on the territories of the major urban centres (Fig. 3.10): Fréjus, Marseille, Arles, Nîmes, Narbonne, and Béziers.[145] Further inland, comparable groupings of quarries can be identified in the hinterlands of Lyon, Autun, Bourges, and Paris. In the Rhineland, as the garrison towns of the *limes* grew into urban centres proper, especially after AD 70, they continued to use materials drawn from their immediate hinterlands—often the same sites previously used exclusively by the military.[146] In Tunisia, where survey has been undertaken similarly dense quarrying landscapes have been observed: Peyras' survey of the north-eastern Tunisian Tell located nineteen small limestone and marble quarries, supplying

---

[144] Gutiérrez 2009; Àlvarez et al. 2009a: 38–43, 100–5; 2009b; 2009c.
[145] Bedon 1984: 27–34.   [146] Bedon 1984: 38–49.

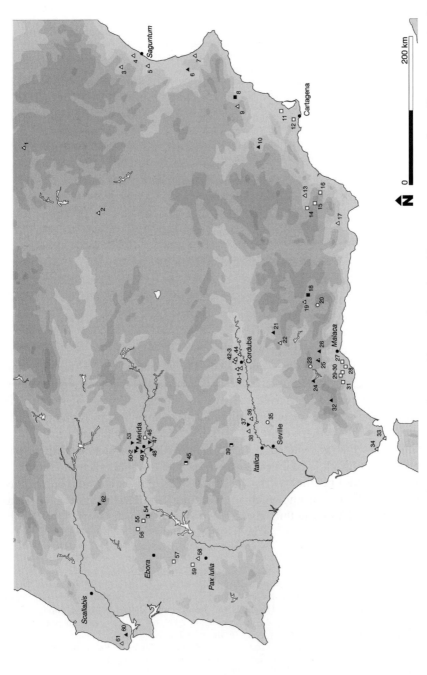

Fig. 3.9. Map of quarrying sites in southern Spain. (□ White marble; ■ Coloured marble; △ Limestone; ▲ Coloured limestone; ○ Sandstone; ▼ Igneous rocks)

Southern Spain:

1. Cerro Redondo	22. Cabra	43. Carrera del Caballo
2. *Saolicoc*	23. Cortijo de Pinedilla	44. Arroyo de Pedroches
3. Segorbe	24. Los Castillejos	45. Alconera
4. *Saguntum*	25. El Torcal (Antequera)	46. San Pedro
5. Godella	26. Sierra de las Cabras	47. Casa Blanca
6. Barxeta	27. Alhaurín de la Torre	48. El Berrocal
7. Sierra de Mondúber	28. Mijas	49. Carija
8. Novelda	29. Alhaurín el Grande	50. Proserpina
9. La Romana	30. Coín	51. Royanejos
10. Mula	31. Monda	52. Cuarto de la Jara
11. Cabezo Gordo	32. Sierra de Ronda	53. La Raposera
12. Trujilo	33. Tarfia	54. Vila Viçosa
13. Albox	34. Bolonia	55. Borba
14. Macael	35. Carmona	56. Estremoz
15. Chercos	36. Arroyo del Puerco	57. Viana
16. Lubrín	37. La Palmira	58. Trigaches
17. Gádor	38. Sierra Traviesa	59. São Brissos
18. Sierra Elvira	39. Almadén de la Plata	60. Colaride
19. Atarfe	40. Santa Maria de la Albaida	61. Sintra
20. Escúzar	41. Rodadero de los Lobos	62. Pitaranda
21. Luque	42. Puente de Hierro	

Fig. 3.9. Continued.

at least thirteen local urban centres, all relatively small but in an area of no more than 2,500 km² (Fig. 3.11).[147]

This close connection between cities and quarries can be seen in the East too, especially in Greece, western Asia Minor, and Egypt. In northern and central Greece, numerous small-scale quarries supplying local urban centres can be pointed to.[148] Across the Aegean, similar densities of sites can be identified along the western coastline of Asia Minor and in Bithynia. Inland and along the southern coast less work has been done to identify quarries but those sites that are known are again closely tied into local settlement patterns.[149] In Egypt, large limestone quarries litter the Nile valley and the 10–20 km either side of it, the area in which most of the population was concentrated (Fig. 3.12).[150] Less is known about quarrying in the Delta, but the limestone quarries at El Mex and Burg el-Arab, as well as the smaller workings along the shores of Lake Mareotis, all in the hinterland of Alexandria have received

[147] Peyras 1991: 403–4, fig. 23; on a density of quarries around Carthage, Bullard 1978a.
[148] On the north, Braemer 1986b; Vakoulis et al. 2002; on central Greece and Attica, Bommelaer 1991; Higgins and Higgins 1996; Kouzeli and Dimou 2009; on Euboea, Keller 1985: 85–6; Wallace et al. 2006: 41–3; Chiridoglou 2009; on the few Peloponnesian quarries that have been examined, Broneer 1932: 16; Braemer 1986b.
[149] On quarries in Galatia, Waelkens 1982b: 39–40; Waelkens, de Paepe, and Moens 1986; around Uşak and in the Tembris Valley, Pralong 1980: 251–62; Asgari 1981; Waelkens 1982b: 38–9; in Pisidia, Degryse et al. 2009a; 2009b.
[150] Klemm and Klemm 2008.

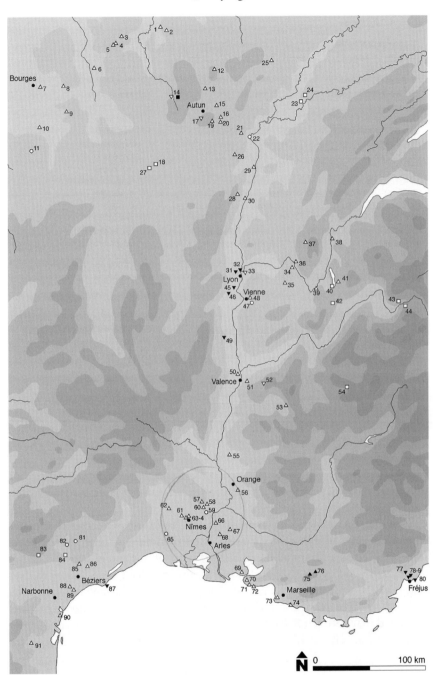

Fig. 3.10. Map of quarrying sites in southern France (key as for Fig. 3.9).

Southern France:

1. La Roche Taille	31. La Croix-Rouse	61. Barutel
2. Bois Dufour	32. Fourvières	62. Bois des Lens
3. Chevigny	33. Lyon/Yzeron	63. Canteduc
4. Bois de Minier	34. Montalieu-Vercieu	64. Roquemaillères
5. Les Fouilletières	35. Trept	65. Mus
6. Bulcy	36. Villebois	66. Beaucaire
7. Bourges	37. Hauteville	67. *Glanum*
8. Les Averdines	38. Franclens	68. Fontvieille
9. Charly	39. Fay	69. Saint-Blaise
10. La Celle	40. Bourdeau	70. Lavéra
11. Saint-Christophe-le -Chaudry	41. Antoger	71. Ponteau
12. Mont-Saint-Jean	42. Vimines	72. Cap Couronne
13. Bard-Le-Régulier	43. Villette	73. Marseille
14. Château-Chinon	44. Aime	74. Cassis
15. Saint-Léger-du-Bois	45. Montagny	75. Trets
16. Tintry	46. Saint-Andéol-le-Château	76. Pourcieux
17. Autun	47. Pont-Evêque	77. La Bouteillère
18. Gilly-sur-Loire	48. Vienne	78. Boulouris
19. Antully	49. Annonay	79. Les Petits Caous
20. Saint-Emilion	50. Crussol	80. Dramont
21. Germolles	51. Valence	81. Bédarieux
22. Chalon-sur-Saône	52. Peyrus	82. Le Poujol-sur-Orb
23. Damparis	53. La Queyrie	83. Saint-Pons-de-Thombières
24. Sampans	54. Valsenestre	84. Saint-Hilaire-de-Laderez
25. Asnières-lès-Dijon	55. Chamaray	85. Les Brégines
26. Saint-Boil	56. Courthézon	86. Servian
27. Diou	57. Bracoule	87. Emboune
28. La Lie	58. L'Estel	88. Nissan-lez-Ensérune
29. Tournus	59. La Crouzade	89. Lespignan
30. Flac	60. Les Escaunes	90. Sainte-Lucie
		91. Tautavel

Fig. 3.10. Continued.

more attention.[151] These constituted one of the densest concentrations of quarries in the eastern Mediterranean, which is unsurprising considered the size of Alexandria.

Such was the demand for stone from the larger urban centres that many supported large numbers of quarries, often of different materials, on their territories. In Asia Minor alone we have Ephesos at one end of the scale, in the territory of which more than forty separate quarries have been located to date (Fig. 3.13).[152] Cumulatively, these quarries must have furnished the Ephesians with almost all of the white and grey marble that they needed; indeed Long has estimated that between 550,000 and 660,000 m³ of marble was quarried in the territory of the city in antiquity.[153] Individually, several of these quarries were

[151] J. Röder 1967; Dworakowska 1983: 10.
[152] Monna and Pensabene 1977: 127–31; Vetters 1990: 2067–72; Attanasio 2003: 173–6; Yavuz, Bruno, and Attanasio 2011; Prochaska and Grillo 2012.
[153] L. E. Long 2012a: 183.

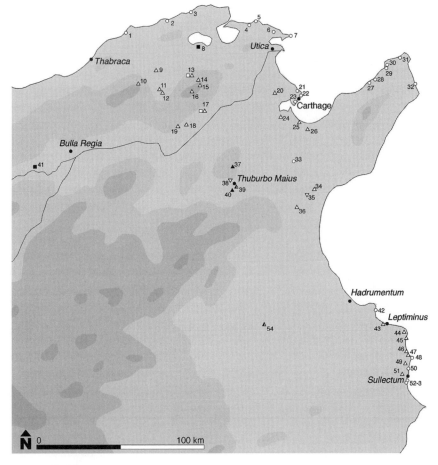

Tunisia:

1. Sidi Mechrig
2. Marsa Douiba
3. R'mel
4. Ain Demna
5. Ain el Merja
6. Sounine
7. Ras et Tarf
8. Gebel Ichkeul
9. Hara
10. *Thunigaba*
11. Henichir-Chelga
12. Smadah
13. Biha Assid
14. Toubia
15. Sidi-Abd-el-Basset
16. Vazari
17. *Uzali Sar*
18. Suas
19. Tuccabor
20. Gebel Ayari

21. Raouad
22. Carthage
23. Gammarth
24. Gebel Djelloud
25. Gebel er Rorouf
26. Gebel Keddel
27. Mraissa
28. Degla
29. Djilia
30. Sidi Daoud
31. El Haouaria
32. El Hannaker
33. Gebel Zit
34. Gebel el Hamra
35. Gebel Oust
36. Djeradou
37. Gebel Aziz
38. Gebel Raouass
39. Henchir el Kasbat
40. Gebel Kleb

41. Chemtou (*Simitthus*)
42. El Ghedamsi
43. Ghar Sebâa Sbaya
44. Zbidi
45. Cheraf
46. Ghar Tbiba
47. Ghar Sidi Messaoud
48. Mahdia
49. Ghar El Oug
50. Sidi ben Ghayada
51. Ksour Essaf
52. Borj el Mzouak
53. Henchir el Mzouak
54. Kairouan

Fig. 3.11. Map of quarrying sites in northern Tunisia (key as for Fig. 3.9).

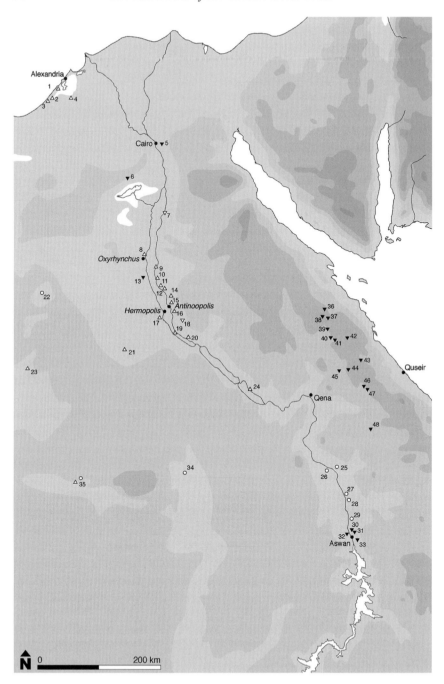

Fig. 3.12. Map of quarrying sites in Egypt (key as for Fig. 3.9).

Egypt:

1. El Mex	26. *Hierakonpolis*
2. Abu Ras	27. El Hôsh
3. Bahig	28. Gebel el-Silsila
4. Burg el-Arab	29. El Gaaphra
5. Gebel el-Ahmar	30. Gebel Gulab
6. Widan el-Faras	31. Aswan
7. Beni Suef	32. Gebel Tingar
8. Oxyrhynchus	33. Gebel Nagug
9. El Saweita	34. Kharga Oasis
10. Tehna	35. Dakhla Oasis
11. Zawiet Sultan	36. *Mons Porphyrites*
12. Wadi Sheikh Yasin	37. Wadi Umm Balad
13. Tilal-Sawda	38. Wadi Umm Towat
14. Beni Hassan	39. Wadi Umm Shegilat
15. Sheikh Ibada	40. *Mons Claudianus*
16. Deir Aba Hennis	41. Wadi Umm Huyut
17. Tuna el-Gebel	42. Wadi Bârud
18. Hatnub	43. Wadi Semna/Wadi Wikala
19. Quseir el-Amarna	44. Wadi Maghrabiya
20. Arab el-Atiat	45. Wadi Abu Gerida
21. El Maabda	46. Wadi Atalla/Wadi Um Esh
22. Bahariya Oasis	47. Bir Um el-Fawarkhir/Wadi el-Sid`
23. Farafra Oasis	48. Wadi Hammâmât (*Mons Basanites*)
24. Sidi Moussa/Gebel Tuch	
25. El Kilh	

Fig. 3.12. Continued.

sizeable: those at Hasançavuslar, most notably, but also those Belevi and Kuş-ini Tepe.[154] Further down the scale, even a relatively small city like Aphrodisias provided a market sufficient enough to support the opening of a range of quarries. The closest, the so-called City Quarries, were no more than 2 km from the city centre and probably supplied most of the stone used there (see Fig. 3.3).[155] Demand for more, though, led to the opening of a series of other quarries in the wider territory of the city, which have only recently been surveyed by Long.[156] The only material from this region, in this case outside Aphrodisian territory, which seems to have been exported is the fine-grained white and black marble from the quarries at Göktepe, 40 km to the south of Aphrodisias.[157]

Even though research on this front in other areas lags behind, the patchy data available from the Levant, Italy, and Britain indicate that this pattern of highly localized but intensive quarrying was ubiquitous.[158] Where work has

[154] Yavuz, Bruno, and Attanasio 2011: 223; Attanasio et al. 2012; Alzinger 1966–7: 61–3; Atalay 1976; 1976–7: 59–60.

[155] Ponti 1996; Rockwell 1996; Lazzarini et al. 2002.

[156] L. E. Long 2012*b*: 169–76.

[157] Yavuz et al. 2009; Attanasio, Bruno, and Yavuz 2009.

[158] On Israel, Sumaka'I Fink 2000; on Pompeii, Adam 1983; 2001: 21; Kastenmeier et al. 2010; on Puglia, Calia et al. 2002; Barbieri, Masi, and Tucci 1999; and on Britain, Blagg 1990: 33–40; J. H. Williams 1971*a*; 1971*b*; Pearson 2006; Hayward 2009.

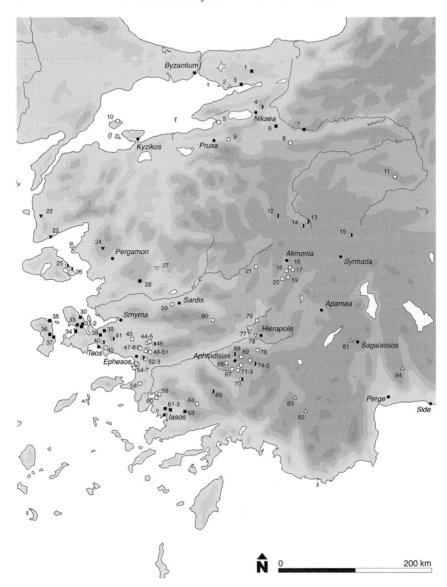

Fig. 3.13. Map of quarrying sites in Asia Minor (key as for Fig. 3.9).

Asia Minor:

1. Kutluca	43. Torbali
2. Gebze	44. Göllüce
3. Hereke	45. Aya Klıkiri
4. Iznik (*Nikaea*)	46. Hasançavuslar
5. Gemlik	47. Ahmetli Köyu
6. Verzirhen	48. Urfalidaği Tepesi
7. Harmanköy	49. Kentli Çiftliği
8. Söğüt	50. Belevi
9. Gülümbe	51. Kuş-ini Tepe
10. Marmara Adası (*Prokonnesos*)	52. Panayirdağ
11. Istiklalbaği	53. 'Farm Quarry'
12. Göynükören	54. Bülbüldağ
13. Çakırsaz	55. Ideli Tepe
14. Altıntaş	56. Pamucak
15. Iscehisar (*Dokimeion*)	57. Otusbir
16. Ulupınar	58. Priene
17. Kavacık	59. Bafa Gölü
18. Hanoğlu	60. Pinarcik
19. Eldeniz	61. Abkuk
20. Sıvaslı	62. Asin
21. Kirtaş/Selvioğlu	63. Kalınağıl
22. Çiğri Dağ	64. Stratonikeia
23. *Assos*	65. Kestanecik
24. Asagi Cuma	66. Hançam
25. Moria	67. Nargedik
26. Kourtzi	68. Yazır
27. Akhisar	69. City Quarries (*Aphrodisias*)
28. Çakmakli	70. Göktepe
29. *Sardis*	71. Çamarası
30. Azmak Tepe	72. Ören
31. Toprak Alinmis	73. Kızıl Cağıl
32. Balıklıova	74. Baba Dağ
33. Karga Tepe	75. Çamova Tepe
34. Gerence	76. Denizli
35. Margaritis	77. Gölemezli
36. Latomi	78. Hierapolis
37. Karies	79. Gözler
38. Turgut	80. Gökcealan
39. Küçükkaya	81. *Sagalassos*
40. Kara Göl	82. *Balboura*
41. Beyler	83. *Cibyra*
42. Sığacik	84. *Selge*

Fig. 3.13. Continued.

been done in central and eastern Europe the same is true: in the eastern Alps, in particular, Djurić and his team have pinpointed numerous quarries centred along the Drau/Drava valley, of which the quarries at Gummern were probably the most important (Fig. 3.14).[159] Several types of marble were also quarried in the Pohorje Mountains which were used in the cities of Celeia

[159] Djurić 1997; Djurić and Müller 2009; on quarries in Dalmatia, Škegro 2006.

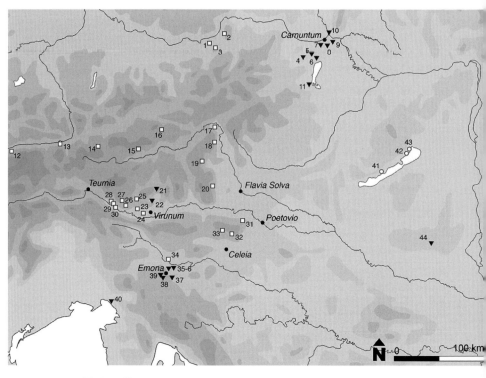

Eastern Alps:

1. Luzen	17. Galgenberg	34. Šmartno
2. Häusling	18. Kainach	35. Skopačnik
3. Hiesberg	19. Salla	36. Glince
4. Mannersdorf	20. Spitzelofen	37. Staje
5. Kaisersteinbruch	21. Kraig	38. Sv. Ana
6. Winden	22. Tentschach	39. Podpeč
7. Hainburg	23. Töschling	40. Aurisina
8. Bad Deutsch	24. Sekull	41. Balatonrendes
Altenburg	25. Tiffen	42. Alsóörs
9. Wolfsthal	26. Sattendorf	43. Balatonmaldi
10. Devín	27. Treffen	44. Gerasd
11. Fertörákos	28. Puch	
12. Rettenstein	29. Gummern	
13. Angertal	30. Wollanigberg	
14. Schaidberg	31. Planica	
15. Sölk	32. Zreče	
16. Öblarn	33. Hudinja	

Fig. 3.14. Map of quarrying sites in the eastern Alps (key as for Fig. 3.9).

and Flavia Solva, as well as at Poetovio, Emona, and even Sirmium; a series of smaller quarries opened to supply a closer market have also been identified around Emona itself.[160]

Outlying quarries

While a general correlation between the distribution of quarries and cities can be noted, this is not the whole picture. Several distinct clusters of quarrying sites in sparsely populated areas stand out. Some of these anomalous sites are extremely large. In the East, the principal cases are the *pavonazzetto* quarries around Dokimeion, the *cipollino* quarries in south-eastern Euboea, and, most noticeably of all, the quarries of the Egyptian Eastern Desert. In the West, the various marble quarries around Estremoz in Portugal, in the Sierra de los Filabres in Spain, and in the central French Pyrenees, as well as the granite quarries around the Bocche di Bonifacio and along the Tyrrhenian coast of Italy also buck the overall trend. They were all quarries targeting either especially high-quality or distinctively coloured materials.[161]

Such materials were highly valued but sources of them relatively limited. Some cities were fortunate enough to have sources of prestigious stones within their territories but most were not. Many of the cities of western Asia Minor, for instance, were blessed with high-quality white or grey marbles which they used for every project from the most mundane to the most prestigious; Ephesos and Aphrodisias are prime examples. In the West, the case of Fréjus is illuminating. Limestone, the standard building material elsewhere in France, is rare in this region and so at Fréjus a blue–grey porphyry (*granito a morviglione*) was used for construction, notably of the aqueduct. This material was later prized at Rome as an exotic import but for the builders at Fréjus it was simply the most easily sourced stone.[162] Even when cities did have access to prestigious stone within their territories, however, such was the demand for white and coloured marble and other stones that extra efforts were regularly made to bring in material from further afield; for those cities without their own resources this was the only option. Sources of prestigious stones, especially coloured ones, were deliberately sought out. This helps to explain the isolated quarrying sites listed above: the quality of materials made the remoteness of their exploitation worthwhile, since customers were more than prepared to pay extra to transport them to where they were needed. In the western

---

[160] Djurić 1997.

[161] On the Portuguese quarries, Àlvarez et al. 2009*a*: 60–7; Lamberto and Sá Caetano 2008; and on Macael, Àlvarez et al. 2009*a*: 80–5; on the Pyrenean quarries, Bedon 1984: 63–7, pl. 10; Costedoat 1995*a*: 95–9; 1995*b*.

[162] Bedon 1984: 34; Mazeran 2004: 97–103. On the aqueduct from Mons to Fréjus, Gébara and Michel 2002.

provinces there was particular demand for stones that looked superficially similar to the famous eastern stones so valued in Rome. Many of these so-called 'substitution' marbles—pink like the *portasanta* of Chios, yellow like the *giallo antico* of Chemtou, and green like *cipollino*—were quarried in the Pyrenees and across southern Spain.[163] Small quarries of coloured marbles have also been identified across northern Italy.[164]

It is no accident, of course, that included in this list of anomalous sites, isolated from obvious primary markets, are quarries at which imperial involvement is epigraphically attested. On the back of demand from ordinary customers work could be sustained at relatively (but not prohibitively) remote sites, like the quarries in the Pyrenees or the Portuguese sites discussed above. However, to sustain quarrying on any scale in inland Phrygia or Euboea, two relatively sparsely populated areas, and particularly in the Eastern Desert required investment on a wholly different scale.

Accessibility

The third conclusion that can be drawn from this distribution of quarrying sites relates to their geographical location. At least 40 per cent of the nearly 800 quarrying sites included in the gazetteer are located within 25 km of the coast, and a similar total within 25 km of a river seemingly substantial enough to have been usable for stone transport in antiquity.[165] Since the distribution of quarries largely follows that of cities, as already noted, the fact that the highest concentrations of quarries are found on coastal plains and river valleys should come as no surprise—these were the most urbanized areas of the Roman Empire. Within these concentrations, however, a more immediate connection between quarries and the coast and/or rivers can also be noted. In fact, one third of the quarrying sites in our sample are within 10 km of the coast, another third within 10 km of a sizeable river; more strikingly, half of all of these sites are within 5 km of the coast or a navigable river.

---

[163] On the Pyrenean marbles, Braemer 1971: 170; 1984; 1986b: 318; Antonelli 2002: 269–70; Antonelli and Lazzarini 2000: 111–28. For Spanish stones, Àlvarez et al. 2009a: 18–25, 114–19; Mayer and Rodà 1998: 229.

[164] Bruno and Lazzarini 1999; Bruno 2002c: 277–82; Lazzarini and Sangati 2004: 76–7.

[165] Determining which rivers were navigable is far from an exact science but in this case those included are the Struma/Strymónas in Bulgaria and Greece; the Çürüksu, Gediz, Menderes, and Sakarya in Turkey; the Orontes, Jordan, and Nile in the Levant and Egypt; the Medjerda in Tunisia; the Ebro, Guadalquivir, and the Viar in Spain; the lower stretches of the Guadiana in Portugal; the Garonne, Meuse, Moselle, Orb, Rhine, Rhône, Saône, Scheldt, and Seine in France, Belgium, and Germany; the Dee, Eden, Irthing, Medway, Nene, Severn, and Thames in Britain; the Adda, Adige, Aniene, Arno, Tiber, and Ticino in Italy; the Danube, Drau/Drava, Enns, Mur, and Sava in Austria, Slovenia, Serbia, Bulgaria, and Romania. Also included are several major lakes: Lake Balaton in Hungary and Lake Neuchâtel in Switzerland.

Fig. 3.15. The white marble quarries at Aliki on Thasos (photo: P. Storemyr).

In some cases, this focus on coasts and rivers can be explained by natural factors. Erosion can help to expose underlying rock formations, sometimes creating cliffs that can be easily targeted by quarrying. However, the prime reason for this distribution pattern must be accessibility. When the rock being extracted outcropped over a large area it was simply common sense to concentrate attention in those areas from which quarried material could be transported as easily as possible. As will be seen in the next chapter, wherever possible sea or river transport was preferred to overland alternatives. Prime examples of large coastal quarries include those at Saliara, Cape Vathy, Cape Phanari, and Aliki on Thasos, all conveniently located for the loading of stone directly onto ships (Fig. 3.15).[166] The Prokonnesian quarries, too, are centred on the natural harbour at Saraylar, ancient Palatia, which is still used for marble exports from the island today.[167] It made sense even for much smaller quarries to be located on the coast as well. The recently completed

---

[166] Brunet 1992: 40; Bruno et al. 2002*b*: 158–9; Herz 1988; Koželj and Wurch-Koželj 2009.
[167] Asgari 1979.

Tunisian–French survey of the highly urbanized coastal zone of Africa Proconsularis identified twenty-five quarries, most directly accessible from the
coast while the largest concentrations were located in the immediate hinterlands of the most important coastal centres.[168] All along the French, Italian,
and Croatian coastlines further small quarries from which material could be
loaded directly onto waiting ships can be pointed to.[169] Quarrying sites
immediately accessible by river include the majority of those concentrated in
the Nile valley—at the colossal quarries of the Gebel el-Silsila an extensive
series of loading quays and jetties have been documented, some Ptolemaic,
others dated to the Roman period—as well as across the Rhineland, in the
valleys of the Rhône, the Drava, the Sava, and the Tiber.[170]

Most of those quarrying sites not located within 25 km of the coast or a
navigable river were positioned in the immediate vicinity of cities that were
also their primary markets; they were already accessible to those that used
them. Examples include the quarries in western Phrygia (around modern
Uşak), in Lykia and Pisidia, around Palmyra, in the oases of the Egyptian
Western Desert, and in inland Tunisia and Algeria. Other sites seem to have
taken advantage of the road system. The extensive quarrying district at
Almadén de la Plata, from which material could be exported via the river
Var to the Gaudalquivir, was also close to the major road between Merida and
Seville.[171] This route also passed near the Alconera quarries. The quarries
around Estremoz were not far from the road running west from Merida to
Scallabis and were probably even closer to the smaller road which connected
Merida and Évora. In Britain, the limestone quarries at Barnack and Weldon
in Cambridgeshire and Lincolnshire, the stone from which was used as far
away as London, lay just off Ermine Street, the old Roman road between
London and York; Ancaster actually lay on this road.[172]

In practice, the only quarrying sites which are neither in the immediate
territory of an urban centre nor easily accessible from the sea, a river or major
road, are the quarries of the Eastern Desert (see Fig. 3.12). The quarries
centred on the Wadi Hammâmât lay close to the road from Coptos on the
Nile to the coast and the port at modern Quseir al-Qadim (ancient Myos
Hormos), and other roads did cross the Eastern Desert.[173] However, even
using these roads, the distances involved were enormous: the quarries at Mons
Porphyrites are 130 km from the Nile, 50 km from the Red Sea, those in the
Wadi Hammâmât over 80 km from the former and 100 km from the latter.

---

[168] Paskoff and Trousset 2004: 255–63. For more recent work, Younès and Ouaja 2009; Gaied,
Younès, and Gallala 2010; Younès, Gaied, and Gallala 2012.

[169] On French coastal quarries, Tréziny 2009; on Italian ones, R. J. A. Wilson 1988; Poggi and
Lazzarini 2005: 51–9; Williams-Thorpe and Rigby 2006: 87; Solano 1985; and on the Croatian
ones, Bulić 1900: 18–23; Fisković 1971; Škegro 2006: 161–2; Maršić 2007: 111–28.

[170] On Gebel el-Silsila, Klemm and Klemm 2008: 180–201.

[171] O. Rodríguez et al. 2012: 649.   [172] Blagg 1990: 40.   [173] Young 2001: 41–5.

Fig. 3.16. A relief showing a quarryman wielding a pick, in the Archaeological Museum of Istria, Pula (after Starac 2007: 136, reproduced with permission of A. Starac).

Due to their rich documentary record, we know more about the quarries of the Eastern Desert, and especially those at Mons Porphyrites and Mons Claudianus, than any other Roman quarries, but as this analysis shows these sites are anomalies in almost every way.

CHRONOLOGY OF QUARRYING

So far this discussion has focused on the distribution of the quarrying sites and not their chronology. Dating quarrying is often complicated by the fact that certain techniques for stone extraction changed very little between the Archaic period and the modern era, prior that is to the introduction of explosives.[174] One tool that can be tied down to the Roman period is the heavy quarry pick, which leaves characteristic festoon-shaped marks on the rock-face and, according to Waelkens, was only introduced in the late first or early second century AD.[175] A representation of a quarryman using a pick of this sort has recently been discovered at Pula in Croatia (Fig. 3.16).[176] This pick, though, is

[174] Koželj 1987; Waelkens 1990.   [175] Waelkens, de Paepe, and Moens 1988: 16.
[176] Starac 2007: 135–6.

special Karnak
Pick

not used at all Roman sites—indeed Waelkens links it to imperially stimulated work—so its absence at a particular quarry does not rule out a Roman date. Sometimes the remains left by extracted materials or abandoned objects found in quarries can be used to broadly date them. Monolithic column shafts, for instance, are rarely found in earlier or later periods; stepped blocks for cutting into veneer panels are also characteristically Roman products. Occasionally inscriptions, even more rarely *dipinti*, provide firmer dates. Our best evidence for dating the quarrying of specific stones, however, comes not from the quarries but the sites at which their materials were used; the discovery of a particular stone in primary use in a datable context allows us to state that its source was worked in that period, even if not exclusively. Combining these various dating indicators enables us to build up a good general picture of when the quarrying of certain materials begins but it is much less easy to date when it ends. What they reveal is a clear difference between the development of quarrying in the eastern and western halves of the Roman Empire, one which mirrors what has already been said about the scale of quarrying sites. In particular, against a general background of continuity with earlier periods, especially in the East, three phenomena directly related to changing patterns of demand for stone in the Roman period can be identified: first, the intensification of activity at many of these pre-existing quarries; second, the opening of quarries in the territories of new foundations; third, the massive increase in the quarrying of coloured materials.

Continuity and intensification

Most of the regions which constituted the East of the Roman Empire already had a lengthy history of stone-working by the Roman imperial period, and across this area the pattern of local quarrying probably changed little. Quarries for ordinary building stones in the Greek world had always been opened as close as possible to where their materials were needed and these continued to be of use into the Roman period; for basic building materials few builders would have to have looked more than a stone's throw away.[177] In Greece, most small local quarries continued through the Classical, Hellenistic, and Roman periods, and sometimes into Late Antiquity. Attica, in particular, had always been known for its geological resources; in the words of Xenophon: 'Nature has put in her [Attica] abundance of stone, from which are fashioned lovely temples and lovely altars, and goodly statues from the gods.'[178] These sites represent an important aspect of continuity in the Greek economic landscape and a similar picture can be noted across the Aegean, on the islands and along

---

[177] Braemer 1986*a*: 276; Cooper 1981; 2009.
[178] Xenophon, *Ways and Means* 1.4 (trans. E. C. Marchant).

the western coast of Asia Minor. Here again a certain level of continuity of quarrying activity can be noted around Ephesos, Miletos, Herakleia-on-Latmos, Priene, Sardis, Laodikea-on-the-Lykos, and Hierapolis.[179] Though the evidence is thinner on the ground on Cyprus, Classical and Hellenistic quarries were associated with the major urban centres of the island and must have continued to produce stone for them into the Roman period, even if for fine marble they were reliant on imports.[180] On the mainland Levant, to judge from a mixture of isolated survey data and literary mentions, most of the major Hellenistic foundations were supplied with local stones, which continued to be employed into the Roman period.[181] This continuity is most marked in Egypt, where almost all of the quarries in the Nile valley used in the Roman period were Pharaonic in origin; others, like those around Alexandria, were opened in the Ptolemaic period.[182] On the walls of the underground quarry galleries at Sidi Moussa *dipinti* have been found in both demotic and Latin, apparently measuring out block sizes, and at ancient Ptolemais, Latin inscriptions show that the quarries continued to be worked well after the foundation of the city.[183] The sandstone quarries at El-Hôsh were certainly worked at least until the Antonine period.[184] Equally, the alabaster quarries at Hatnub appear to have still been exploited in the Roman period; Egyptian alabaster was famous and highly valued, as Pliny the Elder notes.[185]

At those eastern quarries which were already established as good sources of white marble a striking intensification of activity can be seen in the Roman era, especially from the Augustan period onwards. A step change in the scale of quarrying activity is especially clear in the Pentelic, Parian, Prokonnesian, and Thasian quarries even though these were all sites which had previously been extensively exploited. Pentelic marble only began to be widely exported outside of Attica from the late second century BC and most of the material quarried here probably dates from after this date.[186] On Paros, work continued in the Stefani valley, where the pure white *lychnites* marble (Paros-1) was targeted, at Agios Minas and in the Choridaki valley, where coarser white marbles (Paros-2 and Paros-3) were extracted.[187] As demand increased,

---

[179] Monna and Pensabene 1977: 80–5, 104–6, 123–4, 176–82; On the Ephesian quarries, Alzinger 1966–7: 61–3; Attanasio 2003: 174; on those around Bafa Gölü, Peschlow-Bindoket 1981; on the qualities of the materials quarried around Laodikea-on-the-Lykos, Attanasio 2003: 171–3; Şimşek 2011: 337; and on Hierapolis, Scardozzi 2010; 2012.

[180] Michaelides, Herz, and Foster 1988: 159; Michaelides 1996: 139.

[181] Müller Celka and Dalongeville 2009.

[182] Fitzler 1910: 101–10; J. Röder 1967; Klemm and Klemm 2008.

[183] Klemm and Klemm 1993: 178–9; Sayce 1888: 311–17.

[184] Fitzler 1910: 103; Dworakowska 1983, 10; Klemm and Klemm 2008: 176–7.

[185] Hester and Heizer 1981; Klemm and Klemm 2008: 161–3; see also Pliny the Elder XXXVI.60.

[186] Lepsius 1890: 13–14; Pike 1999: 165–6; Attanasio 2003: 190–2.

[187] Herz 2000: 29; Schilardi 2000: 46–50.

though, further sites were opened elsewhere, suggesting that deliberate pro-spection was undertaken.[188] On Thasos and on Prokonnesos, quarrying seems to have reached a peak in the Roman period to judge from the use of the marble from these sites.[189] This phenomenon was not limited to white marble: the grey-streaked marble of Mount Hymettos was probably quarried more intensely in the Roman period than earlier—as Attanasio has shown, it is sometimes misidentified as Prokonnesian; at Ntikali, near Gortyna on Crete, the extraction of grey marble also seems to have escalated in this period.[190] The evidence from Pompeii and elsewhere shows that there was real demand for grey marble.[191]

In marked contrast with the East, there are relatively few examples of large-scale quarrying in the West prior to the Roman period. The major Punic foundations of North Africa had a long history of quarrying. Sabratha and Lepcis Magna relied on sandstone from their immediate territories in their pre-Roman phases and simply added material from new quarries—at Ra's el Mergheb and Ra's el Hammam—as the desire for better stone took hold during the course of the Roman period.[192] Carthage had its famous quarries on Cap Bon, at El Haouaria.[193] In southern Gaul, a long history of quarrying is testified to in the territory of Marseille which can be traced back to the sixth century BC.[194] Glanum also made use of fine local limestone quarries from at least the second century BC which continued to be exploited through the Roman period.[195] Further to the west, in Languedoc, Béziers did have pre-Roman quarries in its immediate vicinity, but activity at these still had to be intensified and supplies bolstered in the Roman period with material from the white marble and sand-stone quarries at St-Pons-de-Tombières, Le Pujol-sur-Orb, and Bédarieux, fur-ther afield but still accessible.[196] Outside of these areas stone quarrying certainly went on in the pre-Roman period but it was neither systematic nor widespread.

The opening of new quarries

In general quarrying in the West had a quite sudden beginning and is closely connected to the pattern of urbanization, a fact that supports what has already

---

[188] Bruno et al. 2000: 96–8.
[189] Bruno et al. 2002*b*; Attanasio, Brilli, and Bruno 2008.
[190] On Hymettian marble, Attanasio 2003: 177–8. On Ntikali, Lazzarini 2002*b*.
[191] Fant 2009*a*: 5. The distinctive grey and white striped ('zebra style') wall-painting in the service peristyle of the villa at Oplontis probably imitates panels of streaked grey marble; similar decoration can be seen on the walls of the portico to the right of the Porta Marina at Pompeii.
[192] On Sabratha, Di Vita 1999: 146–59. On Lepcis Magna, Bakir 1968: 24; Bianchi 2005.
[193] Harrazi 1995; Rakob 1984: 15–22; 1995*a*: 62–4.
[194] Tréziny 2009.
[195] Gazenbeek 1998: 97–103; Agusta-Boularot et al. 1998: 23–5.
[196] Clavel 1970: 338–40; Bedon 1984: 33–4, 61, 134.

been noted based on the spatial distribution of quarries. This is especially clear in southern Gaul where early quarries are associated principally with the foundation of colonies and are densely concentrated in Provence and along the length of the Rhône and the Saône.[197] New foundations needed considerable quantities of stone quickly and the easiest way to achieve this was to open a series of quarries that could be exploited simultaneously. As a result, whereas in the East we often find cities using the same source repeatedly throughout their history, in the West we find scatters of smaller quarries skirting urban centres. Nîmes is a good illustration of the standard situation in Gaul: built up in the Augustan period, it was supplied principally from three quarries opened at Canteduc, Roquemaillères, and Barutel, all just beyond the city walls.[198] Identical clusters of quarries have been observed in the territories of Autun, Lyon, and Paris.

This does not mean that these cities relied on the same quarries for stone throughout their histories. As in the East, as demand for stone became more nuanced and intense, so different sources were sought out. At Lyon, granite and schist quarries were opened to supply the flurry of building activity in the early years of the first century AD, but as time progressed and demand for materials more suited to carving developed, so limestone began to be imported from further up the Rhône, notably from the quarries at Franclens.[199] The city's stone-workers added other stones to their repertoires throughout the first and second centuries AD: finer limestone from Fay and Villebois on the Rhône, and Tournus on the Saône. At Volubilis, in Morocco, the pattern of stone use was probably typical of many African municipalities in this period, both in scope and chronology.[200] In the first century AD most construction at Volubilis was completed in the conveniently located sandstone from Aïn Schkor and Fertassa, just to the north of the city. However, in the boom years of the second and even third centuries AD, when the city prospered and there was demand for a better-quality stone, a hard limestone was brought in from the more distant Moulay Idriss. This trend was then reversed during the economic decline in the late third century AD and later which brought with it a gradual return to more modest sandstone construction. This is just one case in which local stone use reflected wider economic shifts from boom to bust.

In the East, evidence for the opening of new quarries targeting ordinary building stones is more limited than in the West. Most existing cities already had local stone sources. In Egypt, though, despite the large number of existing quarries in the Nile valley, new sites were certainly opened up in the Roman period. Good limestone was ubiquitous, so it made sense to quarry it as close as possible to where it was needed. As a result, following the foundation of

---

[197] Grenier 1934: 947–61.   [198] Bessac 1981; Bedon 1984: 31–2.
[199] Audin 1965: 223; Audin and Burnand 1975: 171; Bedon 1984: 27–30.
[200] Étienne 1950: 23–32; Féray and Paskoff 1966: 284–93.

Antinoopolis under Hadrian, quarries were opened at nearby Sheikh Ibada.[201] An important inscription from Philae shows that new quarries were still being opened in this region in the Severan period.[202]

Decorative stone quarrying: the East

The most striking of these three developments, however, is the surge in the number of quarries targeting coloured or other decorative materials. These stones had always been used for basic construction but only after the second century BC did they become truly sought after for their decorative effect. The effect of this shift in demand on quarrying is clearest on the island Euboea (Fig. 3.17). Demand for green veined *cipollino* (*marmor carystium*), never greatly valued prior to the Roman period, led to the eventual opening of at least 140 separate quarrying sites scattered over a 60 km arc across the south-east of the island.[203] Though often individually small, with an average size of 1,500 m³, cumulatively well over 200,000 m³ was probably extracted from these quarries (Fig. 3.18). Comparisons for a similarly sharp escalation in work at even relatively limited sources of coloured stones can be highlighted elsewhere in Greece: at the quarries of *verde antico* (*marmor thessalicum*) at Kassamboli, Thessaly; at the various quarries of *breccia di settebasi* (*marmor scyrium*) on Skyros; and famously on the Mani peninsula, where a type of *cipollino*, a dark-grey marble (*bigio antico*), several dark-grey limestones, and the red *rosso antico* (*marmor taenarium*) were quarried.[204] The popularity of coloured stones was equally seized upon in Asia Minor. Large quarries, to judge from the quantities of the mottled pink *portasanta* (*marmor chium*) found around the Mediterranean, must have been opened on Chios; so-called *breccia di Aleppo* was also quarried on the island.[205] Red *cipollino rosso* (*marmor iassense* or *carium*) was extracted on the slopes of the Cirkinçe Tepe, above Iasos.[206] The associated fashion for monolithic column shafts also had an effect on quarrying in this region. Two major sources of grey granites, which had never been especially highly prized prior to this period, were targeted in north-west Asia Minor: the first, similar to the granite

---

[201] Klemm and Klemm 2008: 83–5.   [202] *CIL* III.75; De Martino 1979: 319.

[203] Papageorgakis 1964; for more recently discovered sites, Hankey 1965: 53–4; Lambraki 1980: 31–41; Tsoflias 1982: 71–9; Vanhove 1989: 226–7; Pensabene 1998b: 311; Russell and Fachard 2012.

[204] On Kassamboli, Lambraki 1978; Jung 1961; on Skyros, Gnoli 1988: 232–5; Mielsch 1985: 47; Dworakowska 1975; Bruno 2002d; and on the Mani quarries, Bruno and Pallante 2002: 163–7; Gorgoni et al. 1992; Gorgoni, Lazzarini, and Pallante 2002: 199–200; Lazzarini 2004: 587–90.

[205] On Chios, Hunt 1940–5; Lazzarini 2007: 119–49.

[206] On Iasos, Monna and Pensabene 1977: 109–13; Andreoli et al. 2002.

Fig. 3.17. Map of quarrying sites in central and southern Greece (key as for Fig. 3.9).

Southern Greece:

1. Kassamboli	23. Myloi	45. Platsa
2. Volos	24. Kylindroi	46. Profitis Elias
3. Cape Oros	25. Aetos	47. Laghia-Dimaristika
4. Koulouri	26. Mandilou	48. Alika
5. Cape Kolona	27. Penteli (Pentelikon)	49. Kyparissos
6. Haghios Panteleimonas	28. Mount Hymettos	50. Mountanistika
7. Cape Latomio	29. Helioupolis	51. Vathia
8. Cape Marmaro	30. Akte	52. Marmaro
9. Tres Boukes	31. Brauron	53. Cape Tainaro
10. Renes	32. Agrileza	54. Mianes
11. Koprisses	33. Thorikos	55. Ntikali
12. Profitis Elias	34. Gaurion	56. Kionia
13. Eretria	35. Megara	57. Agios Nikolaos
14. Lepoura	34. Kechries	58. Apiranthos
15. Myrtia	36. Examilia	59. Kinidaros
16. Styra	37. Mauvro Spilies	60. Melanes
17. Mount Pyrgari	39. Aegina	61. Apollonas
18. Mount Vrethela	40. Doliana	62. Agios Minas
19. Mount Kionia	41. Sparta	63. Marathi
20. Mount Oberes	42. Kalyvia Sochas	64. Choridaki Valley
21. Paximadhi	43. Krokeai	65. Ghlastropi
22. Bouros	44. Kourelos	66. Mount Kynthos

Fig. 3.17. Continued.

quarried on Elba, was extracted at Asagi Cuma, near Kozak, north-east of Pergamon (modern Bergama); while the second, further north, was quarried at several sites on Çiğri Dağ (close to ancient Neandria) in the Troad.[207] The latter seems to have been used almost exclusively for monolithic column shafts from the second century AD. The literary sources, presumably reflecting wider opinion, latched onto these distinctive materials: Strabo, for instance, associates the city of Hierapolis with the popular alabaster quarried in its territory but has nothing to say about the stones used to build the city; Pausanias describes extraction of *serpentino verde* (*marmor* or *lapis lacedaemonius*) at Krokeai, south of Sparta, as a curiosity of the local area but later this material is listed as its only notable product in the *Expositio Totius Mundi et Gentium*.[208]

The contrast between the pattern of quarrying of ordinary stones for predominately local use and the quarrying of these coloured materials is especially marked in Asia Minor where they are often directly juxtaposed. At Teos, for instance, the intensive extraction and exclusive export of *africano*

[207] On *granito misio* from Kozak, Lazzarini, and Sangati 2004: 76; Lazzarini 1992; Williams-Thorpe 2008; and on the quarries in the Troad, Ponti 1995; 2002.

[208] Strabo, *Geography* XIII.4.14; Pausanias III.21.4; *Expositio Totius Mundi et Gentium* 52.16–17. On the Hierapolis quarries, Bruno 2002*a*; Scardozzi 2010; 2012; and on Krokeai, Zezza and Lazzarini 2002: 259–62.

Fig. 3.18. *Cipollino* quarries and associated debris at Styra, Euboea (photo: author).

at the Kara Gölu quarry—a pit 150 m in diameter, now filled with water and of unknown depth—progressed alongside the small-scale exploitation of the grey marble deposits to the south-west, which continued to supply the local region as they had earlier.[209] In Phrygia, this contrast is even more striking. While the numerous white marble quarries in this region supplied local urban centres, the *pavonazzetto* quarried at Dokimeion, but also Altıntaş and Çakırsaz, was extracted in wholly different quantities for a distant market.[210] Production at these quarries reached an early to mid second-century AD peak. In fact, the quarries at Altıntaş and Çakırsaz appear to have been opened in precisely this period, possibly to ease pressure on Dokimeion.[211] In Bacakale, the largest quarry at the site, *pavonazzetto* was extracted in vast quantities, including via tunnels.[212] Smaller adjacent quarries exploited the less highly valued white

[209] Ballance 1966; Fant 1989*b*; Pensabene and Lazzarini 1998. On the grey marbles also quarried around Teos, Baran and Petzl 1977–8; Türk et al. 1988.
[210] Lazzarini et al. 1985: 47–51; Waelkens 1982*b*: 38–9.
[211] J. Röder 1971: 254–5.
[212] Waelkens, de Paepe, and Moens 1986: 114.

marble, which was available in large blocks and was used to produce grave-stones, statues, and sarcophagi.[213]

Nowhere is the juxtaposition of new and old quarrying habits as obvious as in Egypt. While most of the sandstone and limestone quarries of the Nile Valley and Delta region were Pharaonic or Ptolemaic in origin, more dramatic changes can be identified in the quarrying of igneous rocks, especially the variously coloured granites and porphyries for which Egypt would become known. At existing sources of these materials, such as Aswan, work intensified, while across the Eastern Desert new sources were sought out.[214] Various materials had been extracted here under the Pharaohs and Ptolemies but in nothing like the quantities quarried in the Roman period. Repeated campaigns of prospection are the only way to explain the number and range of quarries opened in this period. One such prospector, a certain Gaius Cominius Leugas, is named on an inscribed stele from Mons Porphyrites, datable to 23 July AD 18, which records the discovery of the site.[215] Despite an initially lukewarm reception in Rome—attested to by Pliny the Elder—the quarrying of porphyry here would carry on for a further four centuries.[216] At nearby Mons Claudianus, centred on the Wadi Umm Hussein, work began at roughly the same time.[217] Skirting these core establishments, on the roads out of them, were a series of smaller quarries and to the south, and again no doubt the product of further concerted campaigns of prospection, were quarries in the Wadi Maghrabiya and the Wadi Hammâmât.[218]

Decorative stone quarrying: the West

Although most of the major sources of white and coloured stones which attracted the attention of a pan-Mediterranean market were located in the East, the impact of the demand for these materials can still be seen in the West. Demand for white marble meant that certain quarries became known for the quality of their materials in a relatively in short timeframe. A case in point is the white marble from Saint-Béat in the Pyrenees which was certainly used locally from the late first century BC but already by the early Julio-Claudian period was appreciated further afield, both across much of western and central

---

[213] Fant 1985: 656–8 (his Quarry VI is one such example); Rockwell 1993: 28.

[214] J. Röder 1965; Pensabene 1993: 182–3.

[215] Maxfield and Peacock 2001*b*: 60–2.

[216] Pliny the Elder XXXVI.57; also Maxfield and Peacock 2001*b*.

[217] Peacock 1992; 1993: 53–5; Hirt 2010: 12–24.

[218] Brown and Harrell 1995; Harrell, Brown, and Lazzarini 1999; 2002; Harrell 2005; Klemm and Klemm 2008, 290–1. On the quarries in the Wadi Semna, Sidebotham et al. 2001.

Gaul and into northern Spain.[219] An analogous situation can be posited for the various Spanish white marbles, from Mijas, from Almadén de la Plata, and from Macael.[220] High-quality white marble, as well as grey marble, was also quarried in the Gebel Filfila in Algeria and used regionally, though how widely it was exported is not clear.[221] The most intensively exploited source of white marble in the western Mediterranean, of course, were the Luna quarries.[222] Work on any significant scale did not begin here until the mid to late first century BC but already by the Augustan period Luna marble had displaced Pentelic as the material of choice at Rome and was being imported into southern Gaul and eastern Spain.[223] White marble quarrying in the western half of the Roman Empire, therefore, seems to really take off in the late first century BC and early first century AD.

Dating the quarrying of coloured stones in this same region with any precision is less easy. In the Pyrenees, the quarrying of coloured stones seems to have lagged slightly in comparison to that of white marbles. *Brèche des Romains*, extracted on the right bank of the Garonne at the La Pène-Saint-Martin quarry, only appears to have been used in any significant quantities from the Trajanic period (Fig. 3.19).[224] In roughly the same period, we begin to find *cipollino mandolato*, quarried near Campan, in contexts beyond the Pyrenees: in southern Britain in the late first century AD and Rome by the early second century AD. The *bianco e nero antico* or *Grand antique* (*marmor celticum*) of Aubert, in contrast, is only really attested in the third century AD and later.[225] In Spain, various coloured stones were certainly being quarried in the first century AD, to judge from the range of stones attested in the theatre at Italica and the Flavian sanctuary at Munigua.[226] Again, though, there is limited evidence for the export of these materials beyond the Iberian peninsula until the third century AD, when the *broccatello* of Tortosa begins to be found overseas, primarily in Italy and North Africa.[227]

The only major quarries of coloured marble in the West were those at Chemtou in Tunisia, where *giallo antico* (*marmor numidicum*) was extracted. Interestingly, these were established and worked in the pre-Roman period, under the Numidian kings, but quickly achieved wider

[219] Lizop 1931: 243–4; Bedon 1984: 36, 86; on its use in Spain, Lapuente, Turi, and Blanc 2009: 512–16.
[220] On Mijas, Beltrán and O. Rodríguez 2010: 558–61; on Almadén de la Plata, Beltrán and O. Rodríguez 2010: 561–3; O. Rodríguez et al. 2012; Àlvarez et al. 2009a: 24; on Macael, Cisneros 1988; Mayer and Rodà 1998.
[221] Toubal 1995: 57–61; Herrmann et al. 2012: 302.
[222] Dolci 1980: 31–2; Bradley 1997; Attanasio 2003: 165–8.
[223] Pensabene 1995.   [224] Bedon 1984: 64; Blanc and Blanc 2012.
[225] Braemer 1971: 170; 1984: 254; 1986b: 318; Antonelli 2002: 269–70; Antonelli and Lazzarini 2000: 111–28.
[226] Rodà 1997; Grünhagen 1978.
[227] Mayer and Rodà 1999: 49; Gutiérrez 2011: 323–7.

Fig. 3.19. The *brêche des Romains* quarry at La Pène-Saint-Martin (photo: author).

renown after the mid first century BC, reaching their peak production in the second century AD (see Fig. 3.7).[228] Stone from here was exported to many of the cities of the region (including Bulla Regia, Hippo Regius, Utica, and Carthage) and, principally, to Rome.[229] In the pre-Roman period these quarries were anomalies in a region where most quarrying was concerned with supplying basic building materials, but in the Roman period new sources of coloured stones began to be opened up. Various black limestones (*neri antichi*) were extracted across northern Tunisia, mainly in the second century AD and later: at Ain el-Ksir, close to Chemtou, and in the Gebel Aziz, further to the east.[230] The produce of most of these quarries and others in this region supplied a local luxury market, notably in *opera sectilia*, but some materials did make it to Rome in the later second

---

[228] Rakob 1993; 1994*a*; Hirt 2010: 25–7.
[229] G. Röder 1988: 91–4; 1993: 17–42; Gnoli 1988: 168. On the use of *giallo antico* at Bulla Regia, Beschaouch, Hanoune, and Thébert 1977: 18–22, 108.
[230] Lazzarini and Sangati 2004: 76–7; Lazzarini, Agus, and Cara 2006; Agus et al. 2006.

century AD; the *alabastro a pecorella* from Aīn-Tekbalet in Algeria, for instance, is found in Rome in the Severan period.[231]

Though it is difficult to date quarrying work precisely there is an important sub-category of quarries in this sample which probably had only limited lifespans, opened to supply single projects and then abandoned. In the medieval period this was standard practice.[232] The various quarries along the length of Hadrian's Wall in Britain and those at L'Estel, La Crouzade, and Bracoule, opened for the construction of the Pont du Gard in Narbonensis, are notable examples.[233] At Brean Down in Somerset the fourth-century temple was built in limestone quarried directly on site.[234] In her discussion of quarries in Catalonia, Gutiérrez notes that a reasonable proportion of the sites in her sample were probably only 'short-lived quarries, probably opened for a very specific purpose'.[235] Further east, the series of quarries at Deleni in Romania appear to have been opened to furnish the construction of the Tropaeum Traini at Adamklissi.[236]

CONCLUSIONS

What an overarching survey of this kind reveals is the heterogeneity of quarrying in the Roman imperial period. As we saw in the previous chapter, there was enormous demand for stone of all varieties for ordinary building and carving projects but also particular demand for high-quality marbles and other stones valued for their decorative effect or the fineness with which they could be carved. Quarrying reflects this. Most quarries were opened as close as possible to where their stone was needed and were owned by private individuals or municipalities.[237] Since cities were the prime consumers of stone the distribution of these quarrying sites mirrors the pattern of urbanization. In those areas with long-established histories of stone-working, quarries used in the pre-Roman period continued to be exploited and relied upon throughout the Roman period. In other areas, like the north-western provinces, quarrying on any scale intensified much more suddenly at the beginning of the Roman period and these differences are evident in the distribution and scale of quarrying in these contrasting regions. In all regions, massive demand from the emperors but also other members of the Roman elite for prestigious stones distorts the picture of small-scale localized quarrying that is ubiquitous. The

[231] Pensabene and Bruno 1998: 14.
[232] Knoop and Jones 1967: 41–3.
[233] Pearson 2006: 48–51; Bessac and Vacca-Goutoulli 2002; Bedon 1984: 32.
[234] Blagg 1990: 41.   [235] Gutiérrez 2009: 273–4.   [236] Rădulescu 1972.
[237] Braemer 1986*b*: 306–16; Dworakowska 1983: 10; Moltesen 1994: 304.

properties of different stones were understood and appreciated: deliberate prospecting was repeatedly undertaken, hard limestones and marbles favoured above all for their hardness, high tensile strength, ability to take a polish and to hold detail.[238] Sources of white marbles well connected for onward transport, such as the quarries on Prokonnesos, Thasos, or at Luna, experienced enormous demand.

A lot has been made in scholarship of imperial involvement at these sites and especially at those quarries of coloured stones where there is epigraphic evidence for the presence of imperial officials. Although the evidence is nowhere clear, at a number of these quarries imperial activity appears to have taken place alongside private quarrying—most notably at Luna—while private contractors were depended upon even at some of the most remote inland sites, such as Dokimeion. The aim of imperial involvement at these sites was to secure sufficient supplies of high-quality materials for imperial building projects; whether the aim was also to monopolize these materials will be discussed further in Chapter 5. Finally, the importance of transportation networks in determining the location of quarries should not be underestimated. Only a limited proportion of quarries in our sample could afford to be located any significant distance from either a primary market or a major transport route; most quarries clustered close to the coast or to navigable rivers. Only the imperial quarries of the Eastern Desert significantly distort this picture; the demand for these unique materials evidently merited extra efforts, financial and logistical, that only the imperial administration could sustain.[239]

[238] Bedon 1984: 28–9; see Vitruvius II.7.1–5 on the 'unequal and unlike virtues' of different stone types.
[239] Pensabene 1998a: 348.

4

Stone Transport

> Apart from the selection of suitable stone, probably the most important problem in connection with the supply of building materials was that of carriage.
>
> Knoop and Jones 1967: 45

The availability and particularly the cost of transport have always played a role in shaping the pattern of stone use, the importance of which is difficult to overstate. Stone is heavy; most of the stones moved long distances in the Roman period weighed between 2,500 and 2,700 kg/m³. On individual building projects transport could end up accounting for a massive proportion of total expenditure. In the case of the Baths of Caracalla, DeLaine has estimated that over 50 per cent of the total construction costs were eaten up by shipping and haulage.[1] Even when the source of raw materials was relatively close, transport figures would often have been the dominant expense: figures for the building of an ashlar wall in early nineteenth-century Bath, for example, give a ratio of the costs of material to transport to labour of 1:3.75:1.8.[2] The cost of transport, of course, depended on a number of variables: the distance that the cargo needed to be brought from; the intervening geography; the available means of transport; the weight and volume of the cargo.

Most discussions of transport costs in the ancient world have tended to concentrate on the freight costs detailed in Diocletian's Price Edict.[3] Using the Aphrodisian fragment of the Edict, a ratio of sea to river (downstream) to river (upstream) to overland (ox-cart) freight costs of 1:3.9:7.7:42 can be extrapolated. These rates, of course, are reflective of an economic situation peculiar to both the chronological period and geographical region in which the Price Edict was promulgated, and so need to be treated with caution. Nevertheless, these figures are not dissimilar to totals drawn from other historical periods (Table 4.1). Changes in transport technologies over time have done little to

---

[1] DeLaine 1997: 216–17.   [2] Wood 1806: 9–10.
[3] Duncan-Jones 1982: 366–8 (appendix 17); Morley 1996: 63–8.

Table 4.1. Ratios of transport costs from different historical periods.

Source	Sea:Land	Sea:River	River:Land
Price Edict, AD 301 (Erim and Reynolds 1970)	1:42	1:3.9 (downstream) 1:7.7 (upstream)	1:10.8 (downstream) 1:5.5 (upstream)
Eighteenth-century England (Duncan-Jones 1982: 368)	1:22.6	1:4.7	1:4.8
Thirteenth-century Norwich (Salzman 1967: 119)	1:34	1:2	1:16.8
Sixteenth-century Cambridge (Alexander 1995: 127)	–	–	1:8
Sixteenth-century Sens (Cailleaux 1997: 195)	–	–	1:12.5

affect the basic divergence in cost between maritime, river and overland stone transport. As recently as 1962, limestone from Portland in Dorset was cheaper to purchase at Dublin (*c.*625 km distant), to where it could be transported by sea, than at inland Birmingham (*c.*210 km distant).[4] Nevertheless, what the totals listed above clearly show is that the relative cost of different modes of transport could vary considerably, presumably depending on local topography and infrastructure, not to mention expertise. Overland transport in eighteenth-century England, therefore, appears to have been quite cheap in comparison with other periods—the consequence no doubt of the development of the turnpike road; river transport on the river Yare near Norwich in the thirteenth century also seems to have been relatively cost-effective. Localized conditions affected these costs and we should expect similar variation for the Roman period.

There are further issues with ratios of this kind. As Arnaud has noted, 'the prices of transport used to be ruled by their own logic, different from one another'; the cost of land transport depended on the weight of the cargo and the distance that it had to be carried, while the cost of sea transport depended more on cargo volumes.[5] In order to examine the peculiarities of each mode of transport, and the particular idiosyncrasies of moving stone, it is useful then to treat each in turn.

OVERLAND TRANSPORT

The efficiency of transportation is determined by two main factors: time and capacity, 'the essential elements in the problem of successful transportation,'

---

[4] Clifton-Taylor 1962: 22; Pearson 2006: 91–102.   [5] Arnaud 2007: 325.

as Westermann puts it.[6] On both counts overland transport scores poorly in comparison with maritime and fluvial transport, but this would have been of little interest to customers and producers who had no option other than to move material by land. We also have to remember that stone as a medium was favoured for so many carving and building projects because it was a heavy and durable material which was difficult to move, so transport would have been expected to take time and to have cost. How much it would cost and how long it would take depended on the size and weight of the load, the available means of transport, the topography over which it needed to be moved, and the infrastructure in place.

Capacity

Over short distances, especially within quarries and on building sites, small objects could have been carried by human porters. Loads of 50–70 kg would have been bearable over distances of no more than a kilometre, and ethnographic evidence from early twentieth-century Palestine and contemporary Syria suggests that experienced stone porters can carry two or three times this over very short distances, of 20 m or so.[7] Later building manuals, in fact, recommend the use of vehicles only for distances of over 90 m, since they tend to clog up space on site.[8] Pack animals were another option, and were well suited to rough terrain. Donkeys, mules, and horses, could carry up to 180 kg depending on the size and health of the animal.[9] Camels could probably carry up to 450 kg over short distances.[10] Pack animals, of course, could only have dealt with small loads, and the use of panniers would have limited what type of objects could be carried. For this reason, the dimensions of stone objects had to be tailored to the available means of transport. This much is clear from two fragmentary contracts preserved among the papyri from Oxyrhynchus. The first, a second century AD contract between a certain Antonia Asclepias and a group of stone-cutters specifies the supply of a series of 'squared building-stones transportable by camel.'[11] The second, a similar contract datable to the third century AD, distinguishes between four sizes of stone blocks, including two sizes of 'portable stones', perhaps one for humans, one for animals, and two sizes of 'wagon stones'.[12]

---

[6] Westermann 1928: 385–6.

[7] DeLaine 1997: 107; Raepsaet 2005: 200–2; for the higher total, see Wright 2005a: 40–1; 2005b: fig. 79; Bessac, Abdul Massih, and Valat 1997: 178–9, fig. 26.

[8] Rea 1902: 34.

[9] Raepsaet 2008: 588–9 (table 23.4); Hill 2004: 88–9; K. D. White 1984: 127–40.

[10] Orlandos 1968: 25–6; Adams 2007: 80; Raepsaet 2008: 589.

[11] *P.Oxy.* III.498, the adjective used is καμηλικός.

[12] *P.Oxy.* XXXI.2581; see Adams 2007: 67.

Over long distances, donkeys and oxen were more effective as draught than pack animals, and it seems probable that most stone moved overland around the Roman Empire was transported in vehicles. Small, two-wheeled carts could have been used for ferrying relatively small objects around building sites; a little column is depicted on a cart on the late antique mosaic from Oued R'mel, now in the Bardo Museum in Tunis (Fig. 4.1).[13] For large objects more heavy-duty vehicles would have been needed. A wagon carrying two blocks of marble drawn by a pair of oxen is depicted on the tombstone, probably datable to the late third century AD, from near Dokimeion.[14] Mitchell identifies this vehicle with the *protela*, or heavy wagons, referred to in an inscription from nearby Sülmenli.[15] The capacity of these vehicles is unknown but in fifteenth- to eighteenth-century Italy wagon-loads of up to 18 tonnes are recorded, drawn by twelve to eighteen pairs of oxen. In early twentieth-century Carrara, four-wheeled carts drawn by twelve oxen were capable of carrying 9 tonnes.[16] Since the objections raised by Lefebvre des Noëttes as to the efficiency of ancient harnessing devices have been widely dismissed, there is no reason not to assume that a single ox, or a pair of horses, could pull a load weighing as much as 800 kg; cart-loads of over a tonne seem to have been common at fourth-century BC Epidauros.[17] Harnessing oxen in pairs, one behind another or in a fan-formation could increase their traction capacity hugely.

What the maximum load capacity of an ancient wagon was, therefore, was probably determined more by the strength of the vehicle than the draught animals. Regular wagons could have coped with no more than 1–2 tonnes.[18] Specially designed, heavy-duty machines were devised for one-off projects, as Vitruvius tells us, but reinforced wagons probably also existed in regular service: Tibullus and Juvenal both complain about the disruption caused by stone-carrying wagons in the streets of Rome.[19] Much larger blocks, too big for wagons, would have to have been moved on sledges over rollers. Mussolini's Foro Italico monolith, weighing over 560 tonnes, was dragged downhill from Carrara to Marina di Carrara on a sledge by 60 oxen.[20] Large numbers of animals were needed for this kind of haulage. Even on the relatively flat

---

[13] Yacoub 1970: 20, 144, fig. 20.

[14] *MAMA* IV, no. 32; also Waelkens 1986: no. 486; Mitchell 1993: 170–1 (fig. 30).

[15] Frend 1956: 48–56.

[16] Bedon 1984: 138; Klapisch-Zuber 1969: 70. Bullocks were also used (Lee 1888: 10).

[17] Lefebvre des Noëttes 1931: 3–20, 83–8; and for dismissal of this theory, Vigneron 1968: 108–38; Spruytte 1983; Raepsaet 2008. On the Epidaurian material, Burford 1969: 187–8.

[18] The wagon capacities (330–492 kg) detailed in the Theodosian Code are likely to be underestimates, intended to prevent overloading of post-wagons of the *cursus publicus* (*Codex Theodosianus*, VIII.5.8).

[19] Vitruvius X.2.11–12 (for reconstructions, Wright 2005b: figs. 75–6), Tibullus II.3.43–4, and Juvenal, *Satires* III.257–61.

[20] Adam 1977: 49–50; for a pre-Roman parallel, Wright 2005b: fig. 74, on the sledge depicted on the Assyrian reliefs from Khorsabad.

Fig. 4.1. Detail of a Late Antique mosaic from Oued R'mel, Tunisia, now in the Bardo Museum, Tunis (photo: author, reproduced with permission of the Musée National du Bardo).

ground at Baalbek, Adam estimates that 800–825 oxen were needed to move each 800-tonne block of the trilithon of the Temple of Jupiter.[21] A set-up using pulleys and capstans would have reduced labour requirements: the 1,250 tonne base of the statue of Peter the Great at St Petersburg was transported 6 km by just sixty-four men using such a system.[22]

Timings

How long would transport using these various solutions have taken? The haulage of large blocks like those described above would have been cripplingly slow. A recent experiment on Easter Island to test how the famous *moai* statues were moved and erected found that forty people working together were able to drag a 14-tonne replica *moai* on average one mile (1.6 km) a day, using a sledge and fixed rollers.[23] Draught animals could have sped this process up but nineteenth-century records of granite quarrying in Virginia note that it could still take up to five days to haul a 50 tonne block, a considerable weight, a single kilometre using horses and oxen.[24] Adding more draught animals, as in the case of the Foro Italico monolith, would have cut this time but added to the cost and put considerable pressure on space. Wagons carrying average loads, of 1–2 tonnes, could have progressed much more rapidly, especially over level terrain. In the fourteenth century, for example, it took seventeen days to bring loads of stone by cart from Nottingham to Windsor, a distance of approximately 200 km.[25] This is a rate of about 11 km per day which is a little under that extracted by Yeo from Cato's famous description of the transporting of an olive mill.[26] The exact weight of these loads is not specified but this is probably because they were unremarkable. Over rough terrain time could vary drastically, however: in the nineteenth century it took a whole day for a team of bullocks to bring a single load of marble from the quarries at Carrara to the coast.[27]

Logistics

Roads must have helped cut transport times but controlling gradients on these roads would have been crucial if they were to be of any use for the transport of heavy loads.[28] A slope of over even 5 per cent would have made transporting

---

[21] Adam 1977: 55–6.
[22] Adam 1977: 42–5; on compound pulleys and capstans, Dibner 1970.
[23] Van Tilburg and Ralston 1999: 43–5.   [24] Russell 2008: 113.
[25] Salzman 1967: 349.   [26] Yeo 1946; also Laurence 1999: 97.
[27] Lee 1888: 10.   [28] Laurence 1999: 78–82.

heavy loads, either uphill or downhill, extremely labour-intensive and danger-ous; early railways, to give some comparison, typically had only slight gradi-ents of 0.05 per cent. To move a load in a wagon up a slope of just 1 per cent at the same speed as on level ground would have necessitated doubling the number of haulage animals. This was clearly understood. The road leading north from the quarries at Chemtou, for example, seems to have a carefully controlled slope, no more than 2–4 per cent in the places where it survives, even though it crosses mountainous terrain.[29] The switchback road between Magnesia and Ephesos, over Mount Thorax, which was built under Trajan was cut into the hillside so that its slope remained similarly gentle.[30] Both of these roads were probably used for the transport of stone but even for heavy loads of agricultural produce these attempts to limit their slopes would have been worth the effort in the long run.

Some idea of the effort that went into moving heavy blocks of stone out of the quarries is provided by the *ostraka* of Mons Claudianus. Moving quarried material around and out of the quarry was much more logistically challenging a task than extracting it in the first place. The first challenge was to get material away from the quarry face to a location where it could be sorted and loaded for onward transport. At Mons Claudianus this meant delivering stone down the hillside to the loading ramps in the wadi floor. Purpose-built slipways along which blocks were moved on rollers are mentioned in the *ostraka* and still visible on the ground.[31] The system used to winch these loads down the hillside was probably comparable to the *lizza* employed at early modern Cararra and similar slipways along which material must have been pulled have been identified in the *cipollino* quarries on Euboea (Fig. 4.2).[32] This initial stage of transport seems to have been the responsibility of the quarrymen but at the loading ramp specialist handlers (λιθοφόγοι) took over.[33] Only four of these characters are mentioned in the Hadrianic roster from the site, with ten assistants, but additional personnel involved in some way with wagons per-haps hint at a further division of labour.[34] At Mons Claudianus, with its exceptional infrastructure, an established framework existed for managing these supplies. At smaller quarries the situation can have been no different, even if operated at a smaller scale.

---

[29] Winckler 1895: 42, 44.   [30] Keil 1908: 166–7; Thonemann 2011: 103, n. 11.

[31] Bülow-Jacobsen 2009: no. 888.7, 889.5; on the remains of these slipways, Peacock and Maxfield 1997: 260–1, 267 (fig. 7.2).

[32] On Carrara, Walser 1956: 69; Adam 1989: 30 (fig. 31). In his later discussion of stone extraction in Italy, Salmojraghi 1892: 278, notes that the *lizza* is used for slopes with gradients of 6–50°, but is especially useful for slopes of 10–20°. On the slipways on Euboea, Vanhove 1996.

[33] Bülow-Jacobsen 2009, nos. 880, 888.

[34] Bülow-Jacobsen 2009: nos. 722.14, 722.21, 698.12, 699.11.

Fig. 4.2. Slipway in the Styra quarries, Euboea (photo: author).

Once the material was delivered to the loading ramp a range of vehicles enter the picture. We hear in the Antonine period alone of two- and four-wheeled carts at Mons Clanianus, and even a twelve-wheeled vehicle.[35] This machine arrives at the site with thirty-nine men, who are to be given supplies to ensure that 'they can help with the wagon'; presumably they had to pull or push it alongside animals. In fact, another *ostrakon* records an order for four 'highly necessary yoke straps' for attaching animals to wagons.[36] Adams estimates that such a wagon was probably 18 m long with an axle width of at least 2.8 m, close to the dimensions of wagon tracks known in the Eastern Desert, at Bir Salah most notably.[37] What kind of weight could such a vehicle carry? Bülow-Jacobsen, using the totals from Carrara noted above, has reasonably suggested around 30

---

[35] Bülow-Jacobsen 2009: nos. 874, 871.   [36] Bingen et al. 1992: no. 131.
[37] Adams 2001: 176; 2007: 199; Sidebotham 1996: 183.

tonnes.[38] Columns measuring less than about 30 RF could have been moved in wagons of this kind then, but for anything larger sledges and rollers would have been the only option. Large numbers of animals would have been needed to move these weights. Pharaonic texts refer to huge numbers of donkeys being sent to quarries, presumably for the movement of stone on sledges, but in the Eastern Desert in the Roman period a combination of donkeys and camels would probably have been used.[39] Various estimates, ranging from 100 to 400 animals for the movement of the largest blocks, have been proposed, and it seems to be accepted now that such numbers were not sustainable in such an arid climate; animals were certainly employed temporarily, but they were probably also used alongside men, as the above *ostrakon* indicates.[40] Whether on wagon or sledge, columns would have been especially susceptible to damage during overland transport operations, and wastage rates could well have been high. Indeed it is striking that one of the Epidaurian contracts states specifically that the stone is to be delivered 'without blemish and undamaged'.[41] In 1815, when thirty of the thirty-eight columns (reused Roman pieces) that Napoleon had taken to Paris from Aachen were returned to their original location, six were damaged during transit—in other words, 20 per cent of the load.[42]

Costs

The occasional shreds of information provided by *ostraka* and papyri, combined with comparative data from later periods, reveal the amount of effort put into stone transport. It would be useful, though, to be able to put some costs on this effort. Obviously it would be foolish to expect lists of transport costs; Roman writers, predictably, are unspecific and generally uninterested in such data. We are forced to rely again, then, on non-Roman sources and what these reveal is the impact of topography.

First, a fourth-century BC source. Sums from the accounts of the rebuilding of the Temple of Apollo from Delphi give costs for transport from the port of Kirrha to the site of 410 drachmas per block.[43] These blocks were for carving the guttering of the temple and were probably not large, weighing at a guess no more than a couple of tonnes each. Delphi is no more than 16 km by road from Kirrha, resulting in a rate of 25 drachmas/km, but it lies at over 600 m above sea level. The accounts also reveal that each of these blocks cost 61 drachmas at the quarry, over near Corinth. In other words, to move each of

---

[38] Bülow-Jacobsen 2009: 206.
[39] Saleh and Sourouzian 1987: no. 119; on textual references to donkeys, I. Shaw 2010: 123.
[40] Peacock and Maxfield 1997: 263–4.   [41] *IG* II² 1666; see Burford 1969: 188.
[42] Peacock 1997: 710.   [43] Roux 1966: 289–90.

these blocks 2–3 km overland and uphill costs the same as to purchase them in the first place.

Similar transport costs expressed in relation to the cost of the stone itself can be recovered from later Carrara. Here, between about 1475 and 1600, the cost of moving a load of marble (a *carrata*, roughly 850 kg) from the quarries to the harbour at Marina di Carrara, only 10 km distant, was fractionally more than the cost of the original block at the quarries.[44] This was a downhill trip, easier to negotiate than the Kirrha to Delphi route, but the sharpness of the descent in places still made it logistically challenging.

Over flatter terrain transport was easier and cheaper. Salzman, for example, highlights figures for medieval England which suggest that it cost the same to buy a load of stone in the quarries as it did to transport it roughly 19 km; the sixteenth-century accounts from Corpus Christi College, Cambridge, give a distance of 21 km.[45] Using evidence from early modern France, Gimpel has proposed a similar equation, this time for a distance of 18 km.[46] So many variables underlie these costs that this apparent uniformity is surprising, and probably misleading. Indeed a series of building accounts from fourteenth- and fifteenth-century northern France and Belgium give a greater variety of figures, ranging from 8 km to 30 km.[47]

Terrain played a key role in determining these costs but so to must have the relationship between the buyer and the transporter, not to mention the awkwardness of the load. The Epidaurian accounts also show marked variance, however, in transport costs for material coming from the same source: Corinthian stone for use in the *peristasis* cost on average just over 11 drachmas to transport, that for the cella just over 15 drachmas; perhaps the latter was shipped out of season, during the wetter months as Burford proposed, or perhaps it was more awkward to handle.[48] The character of the route also played a part: in his nineteenth-century manual, Morisot distinguishes between transport costs on good roads, bad roads, and lanes, the first being 14 per cent cheaper than the last.[49] As an average then, the 20 km figure seems reasonable over level ground for a regular load but the examples from Delphi and Carrara show what an impact terrain could make, and the Epidaurian material should put us off looking for uniformity.

However apparently slow and expensive, overland transport of stone must have been common. Few quarries were so fortuitously sited to allow material from them to be loaded directly onto ships, without any overland transport at all. Swapping between different means of transport, over short distances at least, was probably more trouble than it was worth. Despite all its downsides,

[44] Klapisch-Zuber 1969: 209.
[45] Salzman 1967: 119; for the Corpus Christi data, Alexander 1995: 127.
[46] Gimpel 1975: 35.   [47] Salamagne 1991.
[48] Burford 1969: 190.   [49] Morisot 1820–4: 13.

in terms of capacity and time, overland transport was still in many ways more reliable than river or sea transport. It was less affected by weather, for one thing. It was also less risky; it was easier to recover a spilled cargo from the side of a road, than from the bottom of a river or the seabed.

RIVER TRANSPORT

Estimating costs for river transport is even harder than for overland transport. The documentary sources are scarcer and provide even less usable information. The early second-century AD papyrus accounts of the rebuilding of the Temple of Artemis in the Heracleopolite nome are a case in point.[50] These record that the 100 capitals ordered from the quarries cost 223 drachmas and a further 150 to transport by river, but the distances involved are not given. Again, then, we are reliant on later sources. The sixteenth-century accounts for Corpus Christi College, Cambridge, mentioned above, suggest that to move the load of stone needed 130 km by water cost the same as to move it 16 km overland, equivalent to 75 per cent of its purchase price at the quarry.[51] On this basis one might propose that the capitals in Egypt were coming from a similar sort of distance, well over 100 km away. In reality, of course, we know nothing about the location of the quarry relative to the Nile, the availability of the boats, the conditions on the river, or the relationship between the buyers and the shippers, all factors that could add substantially to the cost of this material; in fact, we do not even know if this was a single shipment or several.

One feature of river transport that we need to be aware of when considering both costs and timings is its dependency on natural variables. Each river is best thought of, following Rieth's scheme, as a series of overlapping 'milieux navigables'.[52] Such a distinction is implicitly drawn by Pliny the Elder in his description of the Tiber: its upper reaches 'not navigable for long distance, except by rafts, or rather logs of wood'; its lower reaches 'navigable for vessels of whatever size from the Mediterranean'.[53] Weather conditions, tides, and silting also need to be considered: both high and low water-levels restrict shipping.[54] Unfortunately, the extent to which deforestation in the post-Roman period has affected the flow of rivers hampers our ability to assess the navigability of waterways in antiquity. In Gaul, numerous rivers that had their own corporations of *nautae* in the Roman period—the Ardèche, Ouvèze,

---

[50] *P.Hib.* II 217; also Świderek 1957–8.   [51] Alexander 1995: 127.
[52] Rieth 1998: 32–7.   [53] Pliny the Elder III.53–4 (trans. H Rackham).
[54] Ptolemaic granary accounts show that shipping on the Nile slowed during the annual inundation (Thompson 1983: 73). On combatting siltation, Greene 1986: 98–9; Anderson 1992: 7.

Durance—are now impassable.[55] Occasionally historical sources from the post-Roman period offer clues as to navigability of rivers which might offer insights into the situation in antiquity. The fourteenth-century accounts of Orvieto cathedral, for instance, show that loads of marble from Rome (loaded onto the Tiber at the Milvian Bridge) were transported by river as far as the harbours at Orte, Attigliano, and even Baschi.[56] It seems reasonable to expect that heavy loads could have reached this far upstream when the water level was high enough in the Roman period too. In the nineteenth century the lower reaches of the Maeander were also used for shipping marble from the sites of Miletos and Herakleia-on-Latmos, a length of river that is no longer navigable.[57]

Although the Price Edict does distinguish between upstream and down-stream travel, adverse currents could massively reduce the efficiency of fluvial travel. This much is clear from Strabo's description of the Rhône. For al-though, as he notes 'the voyage which the Rhodanus affords inland is a considerable one, even for vessels of great burden, and reaches numerous parts of the country', upstream from Lyon in particular, the river 'is swift and difficult to sail up [and] some of the traffic from here preferably goes by land on wagons'.[58]

Timings

In his discussion of the journey of Augustine of Canterbury (who died in AD 604) from Rome to Richborough, Cook estimates that a craft that could make the trip downstream from Lyon to Avignon (*c*.200 km) in two to five days might take a month to complete the return journey.[59] These figures compare well with the twenty-eight to thirty days in summer and up to two months in winter recorded by nineteenth-century authors for up-river travel from Arles to Lyon.[60] On the Nile in summer, when the winds from the north were strongest, Pliny the Elder notes that a fully laden boat could make 40 km in a day sailing against the current.[61] Without this northerly wind travel would have been significantly slower and upstream haulage required.[62] In a letter, datable to AD 300, Aurelius Isidorus, procurator of the Lower Thebaid, directs the *strategoi* of a procuratorial district further down the Nile to tend to a convoy of ships setting sail from Alexandria for the collection of a shipment of columns:

---

[55] *CIL* XII.721, 731, 3316; also Lenthéric 1892: 70–5.   [56] Riccetti 1988: 156.
[57] Rayet 1888: 140–1.   [58] Strabo *Geography* IV.1.14 (trans. H. L. Jones).
[59] Cook 1926: 386.
[60] Delacroix 1835; Lenthéric 1892: 512–13; for similar totals on the upper Rhône, see Dufournet 1976: 254.
[61] Pliny the Elder VI.102.   [62] Casson 1994: 131.

If these ships do not receive sufficient assistance from the winds ... they will exceed the time limit by which the columns must be brought to Alexandria, especially as the fall in the level of the water is increasing daily. Let every one of you, therefore, considering the absolute necessity of this task, display his own zeal, and while the ships are going up river, whenever they are not propelled by the winds, give his personal attention to seeing that they are towed by their crews and the inhabitants of the villages of the river ports, and hand them over to the next *strategos*.[63]

The logistical requirements of this kind of haulage were massive. Nineteenth-century figures for transport on the Rhône suggest that six boats with a combined cargo of 300–400 tonnes being towed together upstream required a haulage team of 30–40 horses. These figures, roughly 10 tonnes per animal, are in the same order of magnitude as those given by Pensuti for haulage by water buffalo on the Tiber (an average of 20 tonnes per pair), when one considers differences in current on each river.[64] On waterways with weaker currents, of course, the haulage capacity of animals was increased. Porteous's figures for transport in eighteenth-century England, for example, show that while a pack-horse could carry a maximum load of 127 kg of coal, the same horse could pull up to 250 times this along a canal or gentle river.[65] Even so, shippers moving upstream often had to lighten their cargoes. The sixteenth-century accounts of Sens cathedral mentioned above show that one shipper had to leave a third of his cargo of stones at the next town downriver (Montereau) in order to progress against the current; these 91 tonnes ended up being delivered a month late.[66]

Overall, these figures show that, though upstream transport was vastly more difficult than downstream travel, only in the direst of circumstances was it rendered less economical than overland transport along the same route. In fact, the purpose of the canals described by both Tacitus (between the Saône and the Moselle) and Pliny the Younger (between the Sapanca Göl and the Propontis) was to eliminate arduous overland travel.[67] The extent to which artificial waterways like these were used for commercial traffic in the Roman period remains hotly debated.[68] Overcoming elevation is likely to have been an issue. According to Parsons, 'the first device intended primarily and solely to

---

[63] Skeat 1964: Papyrus 2, lines 43–50. On the Tiber there is mention of a specialized *corpus traiec[t]us marmorariorum* but this was for the movement of personnel (*marmorarii*) and not for the haulage marble (*CIL* X.542; *ILS* 6170); see Meiggs 1973: 297.

[64] Pensuti 1925: 140: 8 *bufali* for vessels of 38 tonnes, 10 for 95 tonnes, and 12 for 140. On the *naves codicariae* used, Becatti 1961: no. 106 (complete with capstan); Casson 1965: 31–9. One of the vessels depicted on the base of the statue of the personification of the Tiber from Rome now in the Louvre (Tchernia 1997: 130–1) appears to be carrying a block of stone.

[65] Porteous 1977: 9.

[66] Cailleaux 1997: 193.

[67] Tacitus, *Annals* XIII.53; Pliny the Younger, *Letters* X.41; also Moraux 1961.

[68] Grenier 1934: 578–84; Grewe 2008: 334–6.

permit boats to overcome, on their own bottoms, a difference in elevation'—
that is, a hydraulic lock—was constructed on the Naviglio Grande (a canal
linking Milan to the Ticino river) in 1395. Interestingly it was designed to
facilitate the shipping of marble and granite from Lago Maggiore to Milan
cathedral.[69] Despite this, artificial waterways crossing reasonably level ground
were put to effective use in antiquity. Smaller waterways, intended for more
localized transport, were probably common in the northern provinces where
water-levels were more reliable. A pertinent example is the narrow channel
discovered during rescue excavations between 1994 and 1995 at the quarries at
Tendu, 6 km from the ancient town of Argentomagus.[70] This canal, 100 m
long, 2 m wide and 1 m deep, with a 1.5 m wide towpath its entire length,
connects the quarry face with the river Bouzanne where a small quay was also
excavated.

Vessels

The clear advantage that river transport had over overland transport was that
river-going vessels were certainly capable of carrying heavier loads than pack
animals or vehicles. We are lucky to have one well-preserved river vessel from
Arles which shows just how large these boats could be. The Arles–Rhône 3
boat was a flat-bottomed barge, 31 m long with a beam of 3 m, which sank with
a cargo of roughly shaped limestone blocks, probably some time in the mid to
late first century AD, perhaps even the early second century AD.[71] The stone, of
which it could have carried approximately 27 tonnes, was from the nearby
Saint-Gabriel quarries and had probably been transported down the Rhône
from Tarascon to the north.[72] Similar vessels have been excavated elsewhere
and even though none of these others contained stone cargoes they could
certainly have been put to this purpose; near-identical flat-bottomed wooden
barges were used to transport stone on Lake Geneva until relatively recently.[73]
Interestingly, just downriver from the site of the Arles–Rhône 3 wreck a
second submerged cargo was discovered in 2004, though without any remains
of the vessel carrying it.[74] This cargo (Arles–Rhône 4) consisted of two
sarcophagus chests and a lid, all datable to the fourth century AD and carved
in limestone from Beaucaire, only a short trip upriver. This is good evidence,

[69] Parsons 1939: 367; Anderson 1992: appendix E.

[70] Coulon and Tardy 1997: 200; Pichon 2002.

[71] Djaoui, Greck, and Marlier 2011: 77, 119–23, 138 (dating), 184 (dimensions); also L. Long 2008: 120.

[72] Djaoui, Greck, and Marlier 2011: 142–6 (stone type), 187 (tonnage).

[73] On the Mainz 6 and Lipe vessels, Mees and Pferdehirt 2002: 100–3, 168–72; for other examples, Bockius 2000: 110–32, esp. fig. 13; on the Lake Geneva barges, Rieth 1997: 93–5.

[74] L. Long 2008: 125–30.

Fig. 4.3. Reconstruction drawing of the Blackfriars 1 vessel (after Marsden 1994: fig. 66, reproduced with permission of the Museum of London).

as Long has put it, for micro-regional commerce along this busy stretch of river even in this later period.[75]

Alongside these finds from Arles we also have the Blackfriars 1 ship, excavated in the Thames in London, which was carrying a cargo of Kentish Ragstone and is datable to the mid second century AD (Fig. 4.3).[76] This was a quite different type of vessel, the well-preserved hull of which reveals that it was 18.6 m long, with a beam of 6.12 m, and its shape shows that it was designed for coastal as well as river transport.[77] The stone on board consisted

---

[75] L. Long 2004: 55–6.   [76] Marsden 1994: 33–96.
[77] Marsden 1967: 27–8; the route between London and the Ragstone quarries, on the Medway close to Maidstone, would have necessitated both river and coastal travel.

of irregular blocks ranging in weight between 2.7 and 31 kg and the total cargo probably amounted to around 26 tonnes.[78]

The Arles–Rhône 3 and Blackfriars 1 vessels were constructed to function in quite different environments but could probably have carried a similar quantity of stone and in both cases were used for the movement of building stone. There is suggestive evidence from elsewhere—not least the Arles–Rhône 4 site—that smaller boats also engaged in this traffic. A pair of boats have been excavated in the harbour at Toulon, for example.[79] These were both flat-bottomed, suitable for shallow water, and each contained a large block of stone; they were found in a first-century AD context and seem to have been being used as lighters for the unloading of a large vessel. Elsewhere, assemblages probably belonging to sunken vessels can be pointed to. A small cargo comprising two stelae and two sarcophagi in Ambrault limestone was recovered from the bottom of the Théols at Bommiers, not far from the quarries.[80] Though few in number, these finds are suggestive of wider practices; especially in the north-western provinces, the movement of stone by river must have been common.

OVERSEAS TRANSPORT AND THE SHIPWRECK EVIDENCE

Overseas transport, like river transport, was vulnerable to shifts in weather patterns. It was probably also seasonal. Sailing did take place throughout the winter season, the *mare clausum* was never total, but it was often avoided if the risk was considered too high; Beresford notes, in particular, that vessels with heavy cargoes were more vulnerable to the effects of bad weather.[81] Fifteenth-, sixteenth-, and seventeenth-century records from Carrara, Genoa, and Livorno show that, though marble-carrying ships continued to sail throughout the year, this traffic peaked in the spring and summer months.[82] Different routes were also favoured at different times of year. Departures of vessels from Carrara bound for southern Italy, for example, peak in April, May, and June, while arrivals of vessels from Carrara at Genoa peak in March and April and again in July, August, and September.

Estimating transport times also necessitates a consideration of weather conditions. How fast a sailing ship can travel is determined by the direction and force of the wind, as well as simply the type of vessel and what it is carrying.[83] Fast, neatly trimmed ships could probably achieve an average

---

[78] Marsden 1994: 81.   [79] Dutrait 1987.   [80] Coulon and Tardy 1997.
[81] Beresford 2005: 152–3; also Rougé 1952.
[82] Klapisch-Zuber 1969: 213–14, fig. 6.   [83] Casson 1971: 281.

speed of 4–6 knots with favourable winds.[84] We need to remember, though, that most of the ships that we are interested in were weighed down with heavy cargoes. Ships carrying stone from Alexandria to Rome probably took at least as long as the grain ships of the *annona*, which often laboured for over a month or two to make this trip, even though the return leg could be done in two to three weeks.[85] The trip from the Propontis or the northern Aegean, from the quarries on Thasos or Prokonnesos, is unlikely to have been any shorter: in the Price Edict, the freight charge for the trip between Byzantium or Thessaloniki and Rome is set at 18 denarii per *modius kastrensis*, fractionally higher than the 16 denarii for Alexandria to Rome or Asia to Rome.[86] Luna to Rome, by comparison, could probably have been managed in less than two days. One can now play with these transport figures further using the Orbis website.[87]

Costs

Again, identifying actual costs for overseas stone transport is complicated. The later data from Carrara provide some totals. Between 1475 and 1530 it cost between 1 and 1½ ducats to ship a *carrata* of marble from Marina di Carrara to Naples; this was only slightly more than the average price of the same load at the quarry and about the same as the overland transport from the quarries to the port. Between 1530 and 1580 the cost of the raw materials at the quarry stayed the same but both overseas and overland transport costs rose, to as much as 5 ducats and 3 ducats respectively.[88] Costs fluctuated therefore, but it still cost roughly the same to transport these loads 400–500 km by sea as 10 km overland, albeit over treacherous terrain. Where they are recorded, mainly in the sixteenth century, freight charges between Carrara and Rome are higher than those to Naples by half a ducat on average; this was a shorter trip but included a tiresome final upriver stretch. By way of comparison, freight charges from Carrara to Venice, a trip of about 2,000 km, varied from 3½ to 4½ ducats between 1490 and 1540. Though four times the distance, these prices are less than four times those for the Carrara–Naples route, supporting the idea that a sizable portion of all these costs covered loading and unloading and not distance travelled.

What implications do these costs have for our understanding of ancient distribution patterns? For a start, on the basis of these totals, we might

---

[84] Casson 1951: 136–48; 1971: 282–8; Arnaud 2005: 126–38.
[85] Casson 1971: 297–9; Meijer 1986: 227–8.
[86] Arnaud 2005: 139–45; 2007.
[87] This is a Stanford-based project accessible at http://orbis.stanford.edu.
[88] Klapisch-Zuber 1969: 209.

reasonably assume that a load of Luna marble roughly 1 tonne in weight would cost about three times at Rome what it did in the quarries; and it probably would have fetched a similar price in most of the ports of southern France. Had the quarries at Luna been more conveniently located, on the coast like those on Prokonnesos and Thasos, these costs could have been reduced by a third. How might the freight costs of Luna marble have compared to those of Prokonnesian and Thasian? These latter sites are roughly 2,000 km from Rome, conveniently the same distance Venice is from Carrara, so we can posit freight rates along this route of approximately three times those between Carrara and Rome. No significant overland charges need adding to this rate, meaning that a load of Prokonnesian and Thasian marble could conceivably have been only 25 per cent more expensive at Rome than an identical load of Luna marble. This differential could have been reduced further, of course, if material was cheaper on Thasos and Prokonnesos; certainly quarrying in these locations must have been easier, less logistically challenging, than at Carrara. It seems unlikely that these eastern white marbles were ever cheaper to import than Luna marble then, but if there was real demand for these distinctively foreign materials then the minimal differences in freight charges are unlikely to have put anyone off.

Shipwrecks

A certain amount of information about the probable capabilities of overland and river transport can be gleaned from the limited ancient sources, both textual and visual, from post-Roman sources, and ethno-archaeological studies. Direct archaeological evidence is thinner on the ground: a handful of stone cargoes are known from fluvial contexts but not enough to draw any great conclusions about the organization or scale of this traffic; in the case of overland transport we can only draw hypothetical conclusions. For overseas transport, in contrast, the archaeological evidence, in the form of shipwrecks, is plentiful. In fact, shipwrecks are the only real body of evidence that provides any insight into the character of stone transport between origin and destination.

Shipwrecks, however, are a complicated dataset to deal with. Site recovery rates, to begin with, vary considerably across the Mediterranean: 34 per cent (428) of the shipwrecks catalogued by Parker come from Italian waters, for example, and only 2 per cent (25) from North Africa.[89] At the same time, shipwrecks are usually only discovered in comparatively shallow waters, where

---

[89] Parker 1992a: 7 (table 2); it is also noticeable how much lower the number of shipwrecks found in Spain (10.6 per cent), Croatia (7.3 per cent), Greece (6.7 per cent), Turkey (5 per cent), and Israel (2.5 per cent) is.

diving is popular: 66 per cent (550) of the shipwrecks catalogued by Parker which have a recorded depth were found in less than 30 m of water.[90] Since 56 per cent of the Mediterranean is over 900 m deep, it is clear that our sample is extremely skewed.[91] Just because a shipwreck is known about, of course, does not mean that it is published. Many more shipwrecks are known than those published.[92] A shipwreck with a stone cargo which remains 'ancora sostanzialmente inedita' is noted by Arata off Punta Licosa, south of Salerno, for example.[93] Throckmorton described a similarly unexplored stone wreck close to Prokonnesos in a letter to Ward-Perkins in January 1964.[94] Even when publications do exist they are often rather cursory: underwater archaeology is an expensive and time-consuming business; few wrecks are systematically excavated.[95] No catalogue of ancient shipwrecks, therefore, is ever going to be definitive. The available datasets are growing at an incredible rate: Julia Strauss, in collaboration with the Oxford Roman Economy Project, has listed 273 shipwrecks identified and/or published since Parker's original catalogue, which itself contained 1,189 entries.[96] Amphorae cargoes still dominate the shipwreck record, but our knowledge about stone transport has also benefited considerably from this surge in discoveries and these new data need to be highlighted.

Existing discussions of the overseas transport of stone in the Roman period have tended to concentrate on a relatively limited number of wrecks, typically between twenty and twenty-eight.[97] For good reason, the remarkable series of large marble wrecks from southern Italy, especially Sicily, most discovered between the 1960s and 1980s, have attracted the bulk of commentary. Rougé was the first to describe these vessels as *naves lapidariae*, or specialized stone-carriers.[98] The term has since stuck, as has the assumption that these were specially constructed vessels designed to carry heavy cargoes.[99] In fact, in their publication of the Skerki F wreck, the excavators conclude that this was not 'a typical *navis lapidaria*, since such ships usually carried cargoes of building stone weighing 100–300 tonnes'.[100] If we limit our sample to the twenty-five or

---

[90] Parker 1992a: 5 (table 1). [91] Houston 1964: 37–8, 43–7.

[92] Parker 1992a: 6–7. [93] Arata 2005: 82.

[94] Archive of the British School at Rome WP-1, Box VIII; this might be the late shipwreck at Ekinlik Adası, on which, Günsenin 1997.

[95] On these issues and others relating to site recovery rates, Russell 2011a.

[96] A. I. Wilson 2011. For the online database of shipwrecks compiled by Strauss: http://oxrep.classics.ox.ac.uk; also Strauss 2007.

[97] Pensabene 2002b: 34–42; H. Bernard et al. 1998: 55–8; Maischberger 1997: 27, fig. 2.

[98] Rougé 1966: 76.

[99] References to *naves lapidariae*: Klapisch-Zuber 1969: 195; Pensabene 1972: 319; Pensabene 2002b: 34; Bedon 1984: 319; Marc 1995: 35; Gabellone, Giannotta, and Alessio 2009: 319; Petriaggi and Davidde 2010: 131. On the probable form of these vessels, Casson 1971: 173; Rougé 1981: 179–80: 'these ships were probably distinctive because they were both sturdy and slow.'

[100] McCann and Oleson 2004: 99.

so wrecks around which most discussion has centred such conclusions are not unreasonable, but this is not the whole picture. We need to widen our sample to include both newly discovered sites and sites that have been previously neglected. In practice, eighty-two shipwrecks broadly datable to between the second and fourth centuries AD can be brought into this discussion, the full details of which can be found elsewhere.[101] What these show is that the shipwreck evidence reveals activity at every level (Fig. 4.4).

Chronology

Before examining these different levels of activity a word on the chronology of these shipwrecks is necessary. Dating these sites is often problematic but of the eighty-two mapped below forty-two can be placed within a specific hundred-year period using associated ceramics, coins, or evidence provided by objects in their cargo.[102] A further eight can be dated to within two centuries.[103] Of the remainder, seventeen can be dated generally to the Roman imperial period and a further fifteen to the Roman period.[104] To graph these shipwrecks as accurately as possible we can use the probability-based system developed by Wilson, which assumes that ships had an equal chance of having been wrecked in any of the years in their date range rather than in their midpoint (Fig. 4.5).[105] What this shows is a clear peak in the third century AD. The validity of this approach can be confirmed by graphing just those forty-two shipwrecks datable to a specific hundred-year period, which shows a broadly similar pattern (Fig. 4.6).

This third-century peak is later than the overall peak in shipwrecks of all ancient periods placed by Parker in the first century BC and by Wilson in the first century AD.[106] It is also later than one might expect considering the large volumes of imported decorative stones used at Rome in the first century AD and especially the second century AD. How do we explain it? The first point to make is that demand for imported stone did peak later than demand for goods

---

[101] For a full list of shipwrecks with stone cargoes, which includes all sites datable to between the second century BC and the seventh century AD, see Russell 2013.

[102] Antikythera A, Caesarea Maritima, Camarina A, Capo Boeo, Capo Granitola A and D, Capo Rizzuto, Carry-le-Rouet, Chrétienne M(3), Dramont I, Giardini Naxos, Isola delle Correnti, Izmetište, La Maddalena, La Mirande, Ladispoli B, Lerici, Les Riches Dunes 5, Mahdia, Marseillan Beauséjour, Marzamemi A, Methone C and D, Nicotera, Paros, Porticcio A, Porto Nuovo, Punta del Francese, Punta de la Mora, Punta Scifo A and B, Rhône Delta, Salakta, San Pietro, Santa Maria, Sant Tropez A, Şile, Skerki Bank F, Sutivan, Torre Chianca, Torre Sgarrata, and Veliki Školj.

[103] Ascalon B, Ayaş, Meloria C, Jakljan, Kızılburun, Saintes-Maries 22, Tremiti Islands, and Golfo di Baratti B.

[104] These time brackets are adopted from Parker 1992a.

[105] A. I. Wilson 2011.   [106] Parker 1992a, 8–9; A. I. Wilson 2009.

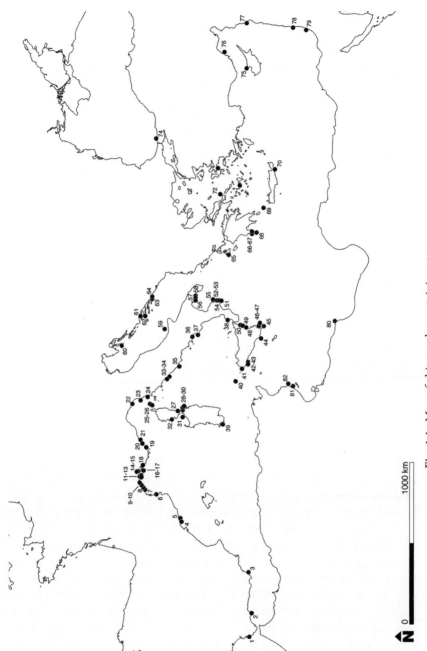

Fig. 4.4. Map of shipwrecks containing stone cargoes.

Shipwrecks key:

1. Cádiz E	31. Punta del Francese	61. Sutivan
2. Benalmadena	32. Portícolo A	62. Izmetiöto
3. Playazo de Rodalquir	33. Torre Flavia A	63. Veliki Školj
4. Punta del Milagro	34. Ladispoli B	64. Jakljan
5. Punta de la Mora	35. Anzio	65. Lixouri
6. La Mirande (Port-Vendres 5)	36. Salerno	66. Methone C
7. Les Riches Dunes 5	37. Agropoli	67. Methone D
8. Marseillan Beauséjour	38. Nicotera	68. Sapientza
9. Sète	39. Sant'Antioco B	69. Antikythera A
10. 'Les Pierres'	40. Skerki Bank F	70. Hierapetra
11. Saintes-Maries 18	41. Capo Boeo	71. Paros
12. Saintes-Maries 21	42. Capo Granitola A	72. Cavo Doro
13. Saintes-Maries 22	43. Capo Granitola D	73. Kızılburun
14. Rhône Delta	44. Camarina A	74. Şile
15. Port-de-Bouc	45. Isola delle Correnti	75. Cape Crommyon
16. Les Laurons IX	46. Marzamemi A	76. Ayaş
17. Les Laurons X	47. Marzamemi C	77. Arwad C
18. Carry-le-Rouet	48. Catania	78. Caesarea Maritima
19. Saint Tropez A	49. Giardini Naxos	79. Ascalon
20. Dramont 1	50. Capo Taormina	80. Sidi Admad
21. Chrétienne M(3)	51. Capo Rizzuto	81. Salakta
22. Lerici	52. Punta Scifo A	82. Mahdia
23. Meloria C	53. Punta Scifo B (=2)	
24. Golfo di Baratti B	54. Capo Cimiti	
25. Capraia C	55. Punta Cicala	
26. Capraia D	56. Torre Sgarrata	
27. Porto Nuovo	57. San Pietro in Bevagna	
28. Punta Sardegna	58. Torre Chianca	
29. La Maddalena	59. Tremiti Islands	
30. Santa Maria	60. Margarina	

Fig. 4.4. Continued.

transported in amphorae which are the most common object type found at shipwreck sites. The large-scale movement of decorative stone was rare prior to the Augustan period and, as we have seen, only reached its peak between the Trajanic and Severan periods. Large-scale sarcophagus production, in particular, only began in the early second century AD, reaching its zenith in the early third century AD. If we break down the graph of well-dated shipwrecks according to the type of cargo the influence of sarcophagi on this overall chronology is clear (Fig. 4.7). Although many of these third-century AD shipwrecks lack detailed dating evidence it should also be noted that most probably date to the first half of the third century AD and the Severan period in particular. However, there are also reasons to suspect that this later traffic is overemphasized in our dataset. The distribution and chronology of shipwrecks in part reflects the level of risk to shipping rather than necessarily the scale of traffic in a particular area. The further a ship sailed the more likely it was to sink and so shipments of stone from more distant origins are

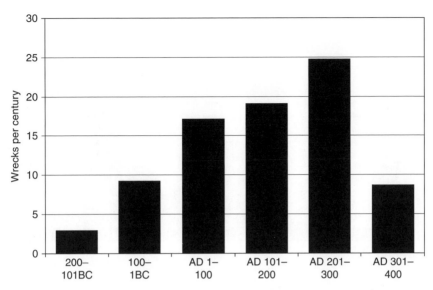

Fig. 4.5. Graph of the eighty-two shipwrecks containing stone cargoes by century, using probability per annum.

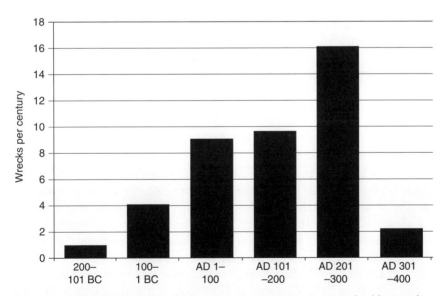

Fig. 4.6. Graph of the forty-two shipwrecks containing stone cargoes datable to within a 100-year period by century.

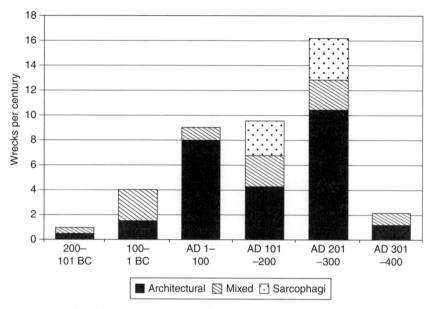

Fig. 4.7. Graph of the forty-two shipwrecks containing stone cargoes datable to within a 100-year period by century, with cargo type shown.

overrepresented in the shipwreck evidence. Consequently, evidence for medium-distance traffic, such as from Luna to Rome, is underrepresented in our sample, while long-distance activity, from the East for example, is well represented. This is especially evident when we examine the evidence from around Italy.

Supplying Rome by sea

The pull of Rome, as the largest market for imported stone in the Mediterranean, is clearly seen in the distribution of stone wrecks, the largest concentration of which is located off southern Italy, especially southern Puglia, Calabria, and eastern and southern Sicily. Most of the known wrecks in this area contain cargoes of squared blocks or roughed-out architectural elements. The largest of these are the cargoes of Prokonnesian blocks from Capo Granitola A and Isola delle Correnti, and of marble of unknown origin from Punta Scifo B (or 2), all estimated at 350 tonnes, but white marble blocks and roughed-out elements have also been found at the Marzamemi A wreck.[107] Large quantities of white marble blocks at Giardini Naxos and Capo Taormina

---

[107] Purpura 1977; Kapitän 1961; Bartoli 2008: 58–65.

were found alongside column shafts, *cipollino* ones at the former, and white marble ones at the latter.[108] Elsewhere column shafts are found by themselves, or with only a handful of other objects. A pair of *giallo antico* column shafts were found at the Camarina A wreck, while an unspecified number of granite columns were identified at the site of the Marzamemi C wreck.[109] Five and seven *cipollino* columns were found at Capo Cimiti, off Calabria, and Torre Chianca, off Puglia, respectively.[110] Finds from shipwrecks in this area, though, are not limited to roughed-out blocks and column shafts. The cargo of the Punta Scifo A wreck is a case in point. The heaviest objects in this cargo were a series of at least eight *pavonazzetto* columns of two sizes, 12 and 20 RF, as well as a group of large squared blocks, six in *pavonazzetto*, two in Prokonnesian.[111] A number of items in more finished formats were also found, including *pavonazzetto* basins and their supports, a marble table, and five altars or plinths. Three Ionic capitals and three Attic bases in white marble, all near-finished and now in the museum at Crotone, have also been linked by Pensabene to this wreck.[112] A series of roughed-out or near-finished white marble capitals, three Corinthian and two Ionic, as well as three bases, were certainly found at the site of the Capo Granitola D wreck.[113]

With the exception of the ship wrecked off Camarina, all of these vessels appear to have been carrying decorative marbles quarried in the eastern Mediterranean. Most of these cargoes also weighed over 100 tonnes (Fig. 4.8). In terms of date, for which we are largely reliant on associated ceramic finds, an equally uniform picture is apparent: Camarina A is datable to the late second century AD; Capo Granitola A and D, Giardini Naxos, Marzamemi A, and Torre Chianca to the third century AD; the Isola delle Correnti wreck to the third or fourth century AD. The only objects on any of these wrecks which are known to be inscribed, the *pavonazzetto* columns from the Punta Scifo A wreck, support this generally late timeframe; these inscriptions show that they were quarried between AD 197 and 200.[114]

Most of these ships seem to have been bound for Rome. Only the two cargoes found off Capo Granitola were conceivably destined for a different market, perhaps in North Africa. Ships travelling from the eastern Mediterranean to the capital would have skirted southern Greece as far as the Ionian Islands or Corfu, crossed to Italy and traversed the Gulf of Taranto towards the Straits of Messina. The Sapientza and Methone C ships, wrecked off the south-western corner of the Peloponnese, were probably also following this

---

[108] Basile 1988; Kapitän 1961: 304–9.
[109] Di Stefano 1991: 116–17; Kapitän 1961: 312.
[110] De Franciscis and Roghi 1961; Borricelli and Zaccaria 1995.
[111] Orsi 1921; Pensabene 1978.   [112] Pensabene 1978: 108.
[113] Pensabene 2003: 534–5.   [114] Pensabene 1978: 111.

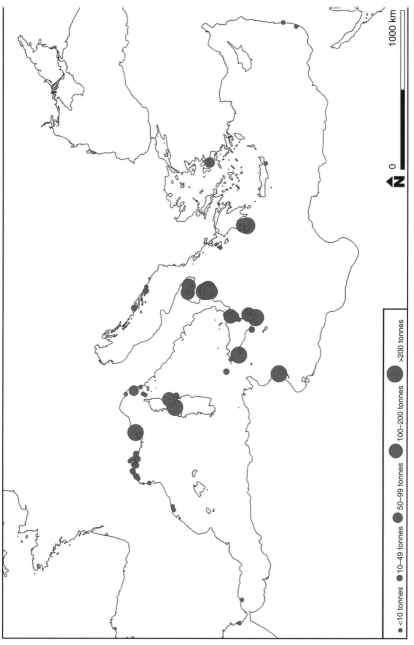

Fig. 4.8. Map of the fifty-eight shipwrecks containing stone cargoes with reconstructable weights.

route; the first was carrying a cargo of at least 300 tonnes of white marble blocks, the second at least 130 tonnes of granite columns.[115]

In addition to building supplies, considerable quantities of roughed-out sarcophagi must have passed along this route. Two shipwrecks testifying to this traffic have been identified to date, and their cargoes are discussed in more detail in Chapter 7. The largest of these was the Torre Sgarrata wreck in Puglia, datable to the very end of the second century AD. In this case, the cargo comprised eighteen roughed-out sarcophagus chests, carved in two types of Thasian marble, and twenty-three squared blocks, a total of roughly 160 tonnes (Fig. 4.9).[116] These blocks are a mixture of Thasian marble and alabaster, and were probably intended to be carved into lids for the sarcophagi or sawn into veneer. In his publication of this site, Throckmorton noted 'thousands of fragments of half-inch-thick marble sheeting' on the seabed, representing ready-cut veneer panels which had originally been stacked inside the sarcophagus chests.[117] The cargo of the nearby San Pietro in Bevagna wreck, which is slightly later in date, contains just sarcophagi, twenty-three in total; again the material used is Thasian marble (see Fig. 7.10).[118] The weight of the preserved cargo is approximately 150 tonnes. The preservation of the cargo in this case shows that clear attempts were made to economize on space. In the same way that veneer panels were stacked inside the chests on the Torre Sgarrata ship, smaller sarcophagi were placed within larger ones on the San Pietro in Bevagna ship.

All of the shipwrecks discussed so far are reasonably securely datable to the Roman imperial period. Even though, as we have seen, demand for imported material at Rome had earlier origins, few shipwrecks reflect this. In fact, the Mahdia wreck is the only real representative of the Late Republican period; despite its final resting place off eastern Tunisia, this ship was almost certainly headed for a port somewhere in central Italy before being catastrophically blown off course.[119] The cargo, composed mainly of material from Athens, and its implications for the art market in the early first century BC have been examined in detail elsewhere.[120] The finds tie in very nicely with what we know about contemporary elite Roman tastes based on archaeological finds from central Italy—notably the sculpture collection of the Villa of the Papyri

---

[115] Parker 1992*a*: 386; Throckmorton and Bullitt 1963.

[116] Throckmorton 1969; Alessio 1995; Gabellone, Giannotta, and Alessio 2009; Calia et al. 2009.

[117] Throckmorton 1969: 297: 'one sarcophagus, fortunately, stored intact seven of these fragile marble plaques.'

[118] Ward-Perkins and Throckmorton 1965; Alessio and Zaccaria 1997; Petriaggi and Davidde 2010.

[119] On a possible Numidian destination, see Ferchiou 1994.

[120] Coarelli 1983; Wallace-Hadrill 2008: 362–3; Galsterer 1994; Geominy 1994.

Fig. 4.9. Plan of the cargo of the Torre Sgarrata shipwreck off Puglia (based on Throckmorton 1972: 13, reproduced with permission of Thames and Hudson).

at Herculaneum—and the testimony of Cicero's correspondence with Atticus and ordering of statues from Greece.[121]

These shipwrecks, including Mahdia, document neatly the continued demand at Rome for prestige materials from the eastern Mediterranean. Considering, however, that most of the white marble used in Rome up until

[121] On the sculpture from the Villa of the Papyri, Warden and Romano 1994. On Cicero's collecting, see Cicero, *Letters to Atticus* 1.8.2, 1.9.2, 1.10.3.

the middle of the second century AD came not from the eastern Mediterranean but from Luna, one might expect a similar density of wrecks with stone cargoes along the northern Tyrrhenian coast of Italy. This is not the case. In fact, only five wrecks in this area can be even vaguely connected to this activity. Certainly carved in Luna marble are the blocks and one column, a total of 50 tonnes, from the first- or second-century AD Meloria C wreck.[122] The massive column drum found off Lerici, near La Sapezia, is also in Luna marble, but its date is uncertain.[123] To these we can probably add the Ladispoli B and Torre Flavia A wrecks, both containing columns, and the Capraia D wreck, with a cargo of blocks, though the white marble at these sites has not been securely identified.[124] The scarcity of shipwrecks containing Luna marble in this area must reflect the relative calmness of these waters, and the short distances involved, rather than the original volume of traffic in this area. It might even result from the size of the loads which were being ferried along the coast. Smaller cargoes are less likely to be noticed on the seabed and, though limited in number, the four cargoes that have been identified all seem to weigh less than 100 tonnes. Whatever the reasons behind them, the comparative densities of shipwrecks off the southern and north-western coasts of Italy suggest that demand for eastern marbles came at a price. The ships carrying marble from the eastern Mediterranean were forced to travel further, through significantly more dangerous waters, than those that had been working the route from Luna to Rome.

Regional patterns

Demand for high-quality white and coloured marbles was not limited to the capital. There were plenty of other customers all around the Mediterranean who actively bought into the fashion for decorative stone-use and several important concentrations of shipwrecks are revealing of this demand. Two will be highlighted here, the first off the Bocche di Bonifacio and southern France, the second in the Adriatic.

In French waters, two main concentrations of shipwrecks containing stone cargoes have been explored in recent years. First, around the Bocche di Bonifacio, on the most direct shipping route between Italy to Spain, five sites have been discovered. The best-known of these is the first-century AD shipwreck off Porto Nuovo, which contained nine squared blocks of Luna marble, approximately 138 tonnes; the largest single block in this cargo weighed 23.3 tonnes, one of the largest attested in any shipwreck.[125] Also at

---

[122] Bargagliotti, Cibecchini, and Gambogi 1997.   [123] Dolci 2006: 221–2.
[124] Gianfrotta 1981: 71–2; Parker 1992a: 127; on other finds off Capraia, see Arata 2005: 156.
[125] H. Bernard et al. 1998: 53–7.

the eastern end of the straits, two probable stone cargoes have been reported at Punta Sardegna and Santa Maria. The first of these consists of an assemblage of columns, probably in granite from the nearby Capo Testa quarries, the second of a group of white marble blocks.[126] Just to the west of the straits, at Punta del Francese, a large cargo of white marble blocks has been summarily reported, estimated at 270 tonnes; this would make it the largest cargo found to date in the western Mediterranean.[127] The Porto Nuovo and Punta del Francese wrecks testify to the long-distance movement of Luna marble in bulk; in size and composition, their cargoes bear comparison with those found off southern Italy. As well as these cargoes of building materials, the site of the Porticcio A wreck has recently produced a series of carved sculptures of members of the imperial family and other subjects, alongside a cargo of amphorae and window glass, showing that more unusual cargoes were also transported along this route.[128]

The only other cargo of Luna marble anywhere near the size of the Punta del Francese one is that of the Saint-Tropez A wreck, off the southern French coast. This contained six massive column drums, weighing at least 230 tonnes.[129] The dimensions of these drums are consistent with those used in the large temple on the hill of Les Moulinassès at Narbonne, a structure probably of Augustan date which was rebuilt in the mid second century AD.[130]

Systematic underwater survey by the Département des Recherches Archéologiques Sous-marines (DRASSM) off southern France has shown that this large vessel was not alone. Five much smaller cargoes have been recovered in recent years providing an insight into lower-level stone distribution in this region. One of these, at Marseillan Beauséjour (dépt. Hérault), was carrying a cargo of five rectangular blocks of Luna marble, with a total weight of no more than 24 tonnes, and can be dated to the later first century AD.[131] In comparison with the large wrecks elsewhere in French and Italian waters this cargo is tiny, but it was not abnormal. In 1998, three shipwrecks, each containing six or seven blocks of Luna marble (roughly 30–40 tonnes), were excavated at Saintes Maries (dépt. Bouches du Rhône); all are dated to the first or second centuries AD.[132] Finally, a cargo of one column drum and several other blocks of Luna marble, weighing less than 10 tonnes, has been identified at Sète (dépt. Hérault).[133] To judge from these finds, vessels shuttling small loads of marble along the coasts of Liguria, Provence, and Languedoc were probably relatively

---

[126] Boninu 1987.   [127] Galasso 1997.   [128] Massy 2013: 110–14.
[129] Benoit 1952; Diolé 1954.
[130] This is the so-called Capitolium; for more on the debate surrounding this structure, cf. Janon 1986: 41–6; Gros 1987: 86. On the connection between the Saint-Tropez A wreck and this building, cf. Perret 1956.
[131] H. Bernard 2001; 2009.
[132] L. Long 1999; these are Saintes Maries 18, 21, and 22.
[133] H. Bernard 2009: 510.

common. These smaller ships no doubt operated alongside larger vessels, like those wrecked at Saint-Tropez or around the Bocche di Bonifacio; booming demand for Luna marble in southern France, therefore, was probably fed by a variety of different supply routes, depending on the customers involved and the quantities of marble required.

Luna marble is not the only decorative marble found at these French wrecks. The first-century AD Dramont I wreck (dépt. Var), was carrying a cargo of three blocks of *africano*, weighing no more than 23 tonnes, as well as assorted other objects.[134] A range of white marbles, several probably of eastern origin, were also found at the Les Riches Dunes 5 wreck (dépt. Hérault).[135] This cargo comprised one large block, twenty-one panels, a small colonnette, a base, and various supports. Precut panels, in an unidentified white marble, were also found at the site of the La Mirande (Port-Vendres 5) wreck (dépt. Pyrénées Orientales).[136]

Work by the DRASSM team has also successfully highlighted the ubiquity of short- and medium-distance traffic along the French coast, precisely the kind of activity that has tended to be overlooked. One site of particular importance from this perspective is 'Les Pierres', located between the ports of Carnon and Palavas-les-Flots (dépt. Hérault).[137] This site consists of an assemblage of seventy-five blocks, including three capitals, two column drums, five columns, and five pilasters, all simply roughed out. Two stones are represented: the fine white limestone from Bois-des-Lens, near Nîmes, and a grey limestone, probably from the same area. The particular formation of this assemblage, however, remains unclear. On the one hand, it was discovered one kilometre off shore at a depth of 10 m, too deep to belong to a submerged structure. On the other hand, the assemblage is spread out in such a long line that it seems unlikely to have come from a single ship. What we might be dealing with, therefore, are a series of wrecks, perhaps even of a single convoy of small ships, all carrying the same cargo. Ordinary building stone had long been moved by sea along the southern French coast as the late second- or early first-century BC Carry-le-Rouet shipwreck shows and recently two wrecks have been found near this site, in the Roman harbour at Anse des Laurons.[138] These contained cargoes of squared blocks of Ponteau limestone, weighing 33 and 13 tonnes respectively, which had probably only just been loaded when they sank.

---

[134] Joncheray and Joncheray 1997; Joncheray 1998.

[135] H. Bernard and Jézégou 2003; initial analysis has identified the block as Dokimeian white marble, the panels as Prokonnesian, the colonnette as Luna, the base as Pentelic, and the series of supports as Thasian and Luna marble (pers. comm. Hélène Bernard).

[136] Descamps 1992.

[137] Rauzier 2001.

[138] On Carry-le-Rouet, L. Long 1985; Kainic 1986; and on Laurons IX and X, Ximénès and Moerman 1993.

Similar shipwrecks containing relatively small cargoes of stone have also been found elsewhere in the western Mediterranean. These include cargoes of tuff blocks off Anzio and Salerno, a load of granite blocks off Nicotera, and the two small columns and several large blocks, weighing no more than 9 tonnes, from the Skerki F ship.[139] An assemblage of local white marble architectural elements was found off Playazo de Rodalquir that seems to have come from a shipwreck.[140] A single Attic sarcophagus was also recovered off Punta de la Mora, near Tarragona, though whether it came from an ancient or more recent shipwreck is unclear.[141] The same is true of a fully finished Asiatic sarcophagus of the ornate columnar type, which was found off Capo Rizzuto in Calabria in 2000.[142] In general, though, underwater surveys, of the kind that might identify such shipwrecks, have been less intensively undertaken elsewhere in the western Mediterranean.

The same is true further east, though the Adriatic is one area in which this is beginning to change. Three stone wrecks, at Čavlena, Izmetište, and Margarina, have been talked about in this area for some time, though they have only recently been evaluated properly by Jurišić.[143] No traces of the purported Čavlena wreck remain, but there is better news at Margarina, where a cargo of at least twenty small white marble columns and several roughly shaped blocks is still preserved. At Izmetište, the cargo consists of ten stone blocks, nine in limestone and one in a greenish granite, alongside a large number of ceramics.[144] These blocks were probably quarried somewhere along the Dalmatian coast, but it is possible that the marble found at Margarina was imported from outside of the Adriatic. Either way, we are probably looking here at short- or medium-distance transport. Three possible sarcophagus cargoes are also known in this area. These include a series of five chests off Veliki Školj, near Mljet Island, which recent analysis has shown are carved in Prokonnesian marble; they were probably destined for Salona, Aquileia, or Ravenna (Fig. 4.10).[145] This cargo should, therefore, be counted alongside that of the Methone D ship, wrecked off the south-western Peloponnese, which was probably also supplying the Adriatic sarcophagus market: its cargo comprised six roughed-out garland sarcophagi in the distinctive andesite of Assos, the *lapis sarcophagus*, which are quite common at Ravenna.[146] The second Adriatic sarcophagus cargo catalogued by Jurišić lies off the island of Jakljan

---

[139] Parker 1992*a*: 56, 378, 289; on Skerki F, McCann and Oleson 2004.
[140] Cisneros 1988: 123.
[141] Arata 2005: 197.
[142] Arata 2005: 155–6.
[143] Vrsalović 1974: 25, 53, 240; Jurišić 2000.
[144] Jurišić 2000: 39–41, 65, 69.
[145] Jurišić 2000: 76; Miholjek and Mihajlović 2011: 217–18; the results of this analysis were presented by I. Mihajlović and I. Miholjek at ASMOSIA X in Rome in June 2012.
[146] Papathanasopoulos 1963; Throckmorton and Bullitt 1963.

Fig. 4.10. Three sarcophagi from the Veliki Školj shipwreck (photo: I. Miholjek, Croatian Conservation Institute).

and consists of three blank chests with lids, all apparently limestone.[147] A third shipwreck, dated to the early third century AD, has recently been reported off Sutivan on the island of Brač which contains at least two limestone sarcophagi chests and lids as well as fifteen stone blocks and a small column shaft.[148] As off southern France, a range of sizes and compositions of stone cargoes have been identified in the Adriatic, hinting at a combination of medium- and long-distance traffic.

It would be useful if we could test the evidence from these areas against the picture elsewhere, especially in the East, but unfortunately the available data are far too patchy to allow significant conclusions to be drawn. Isolated finds can be pointed to: two Ionic capitals, four bases, and six marble statues from off Cephalonia; a series of objects from Paroikia Bay on Paros, which might belong to one or perhaps several shipwrecks; a porphyry statue of an enthroned emperor from off Ascalon; and a single Attic sarcophagus from off Hierapetra in eastern Crete.[149] Cargoes of building stone, meanwhile, are

---

[147] Jurišić 2000: 65; Miholjek and Mihajlović 2011: 218.
[148] Mihajlović 2011; Miholjek and Mihajlović 2011: 218–19, fig. 8.
[149] On Cephalonia; Touchais 1981: 805; on Paros, Papathanasopoulos and Schilardi 1981; on Ascalon and Hierapetra, Arata 2005: 147, 166.

known from Cape Crommyon on Cyprus, Caesarea Maritima, and Dor, while a cargo of small basalt columns was found off Arwad, in Syria.[150] There remain many gaps in our knowledge that need to be filled before the exact place of these vessels in the wider pattern of stone transport in this area can be reconstructed.

One of the few shipwrecks in the East that is both datable to our period and has been closely studied is the Şile shipwreck, at the Black Sea end of the Bosphorus.[151] What is known of the cargo from this site consisted of a colossal roughed-out statue, a roughed-out bust of a woman, a sarcophagus chest and lid, a stele and two bowls, a single column base, five Ionic capitals, two large stepped blocks, and a plaque, all in Prokonnesian marble, as well as an additional stepped block and two columns in a green breccia, probably *verde antico*. Some of this material is datable to the late second century AD, but the colossal statue finds its closest parallels in the fourth century AD.[152] If this later date is correct then this looks like a cargo of odds and ends being transported alongside a single main commission.

Far better documentation exists for stone wrecks which are outside of our period but which still deserve to be mentioned. Earlier are the early first-century BC Antikythera A wreck and the second- or first-century BC Kızıl-burun wreck. The former almost certainly represents a shipment of old and new works of art; it contained thirty-six statues, as well as amphorae, a range of fine and coarse pottery, bronze, and glass vessels, as well as large numbers of Pergamene coins.[153] The ship wrecked off Kızılburun, on the other hand, was carrying a cargo of monumental column drums, as well as other assorted objects, which Carlson has plausibly connected to the construction of the Temple of Apollo at Klaros.[154]

Most of the shipwrecks discussed in this section contained cargoes of material that was being moved short- to medium-distances to satisfy demand from regional centres rather than the capital. What recent work off southern France and in the Adriatic has shown are the various levels on which the stone trade operated, from the massive vessels plying the routes to Rome, to smaller vessels shuttling both decorative and more ordinary stones relatively limited distances. What this evidence also reveals, though, is something of the organization of this activity and the ships involved.

---

[150] On Cape Crommyon, Megaw 1959: 29; on Caesarea Maritima, Raban 1992: 30; on the Dor 2001/1 wreck, datable to the fifth or sixth century AD, Kahanov and Mor 2006; and on the Arwad C wreck, Frost 1964: 72; Parker 1992a: 60–1.

[151] Beykan 1988.

[152] Parker 1992a: 404, no. 1088; pers. comm. Amanda Claridge.

[153] On the statues from this wreck, Bol 1972.

[154] Carlson 2007; 2009; Carlson and Atkins 2007.

The question of specialization

Stone objects certainly had the potential to be an awkward cargo. Their weight would have had to have been carefully distributed during stowage so as not to unbalance the ship; for large objects, which could not be split up, this had to be carefully planned. Heavier cargoes would always have been stowed towards the bottom of the hull, with lighter cargoes packed in around them, fore and aft and on top of them.[155] To stop stone shifting packing material or dunnage would have been used. A saleable product would have been preferable; indeed Lee notes that, in nineteenth-century Livorno, cargoes of stone were 'usually made up with light goods, of which pumicestone, hemp, oil, and sumac form the principal part'.[156] For extra security, blocks and columns were probably also lashed into place with ropes to stop them sliding or rolling. At those shipwrecks where the original layout of the cargo can still be seen, it is clear that columns and other long blocks were aligned lengthways, parallel to the keel.[157] On the ship wrecked off Giardini Naxos the cargo was essentially divided in two with a lighter set of columns inserted into the front of the hold and the heavier remaining blocks or columns split between its middle and rear. On top of this first layer, and on either side of it nestling against the side of the hold, were added the columns of smaller diameters and the smaller blocks.[158]

The question is, were these specially constructed vessels—the *naves lapidariae* so often mentioned in the modern literature? Were the ships responsible for carrying stone cargoes structurally different from other Roman merchant ships? In reality, though the term is widely used, there is no support in the literary record for the idea that *naves lapidariae* were a distinct category of merchant ship. The legal sources never mention *naves lapidariae*, and neither Pliny the Elder nor Ammianus Marcellinus, both of whom are usually quoted in this context, use this term.[159] Only Petronius refers specifically to a *navis lapidaria* and then only in a highly satirical passage in which a fraught character compares himself to 'a beast of burden, or a ship carrying stone'; as Fant has argued, this is a dubious passage on which reconstruct a definite category of ship.[160] In the Greek world at least ships were often identified simply by the cargo they were carrying at that specific moment; we hear, hence, of grain-carriers (ὁλκάδες σιταγωγοί), wine-carriers (ὁλκάδας οἰναγωγούς),

---

[155] Parker 1992*b*: 89–90.   [156] Lee 1888: 18.

[157] As at Capo Taormina (Kapitän 1961: 304–9), Capo Cimiti (De Franciscis and Roghi 1961), Isola delle Correnti (Kapitän 1961: 282–8), Mahdia (see the plan in Throckmorton 1972: 76, fig. 14), and Porto Nuovo (H. Bernard et al. 1998: 56, fig. 3).

[158] Basile 1988: 134–9, esp. fig. 7.

[159] Pliny the Elder XXXVI.1; Ammianus Marcellinus XVII.14.

[160] Petronius, *Satyricon* 117.12; pers. comm. Clayton Fant.

and even a stone-carrier (λιθηγὸς [ναῦς]).[161] This practice might have continued into the Roman period, but most of the references to merchant vessels
in the legal and literary sources describe them simply as *naves onerariae, or*
ships of burden.[162]

There is little in the literary sources, then, to indicate that *naves lapidariae*
were a distinct form of ship and this is supported by the archaeological
evidence. It has been proposed that ships that carried stone regularly would
have been specially reinforced or perhaps, in Casson's words, 'shorter and
sturdier' than ordinary merchant vessels.[163] Sadly, very few of the known
shipwrecks with stone cargoes have preserved hulls that might allow this
proposition to be thoroughly tested. These were certainly solid vessels and
the Torre Sgarrata ship was venerable too, but the current evidence is insufficient to prove that they were specially reinforced.[164] In this regard it is worth
noting that in most cases reinforcement would not have been essential. Most
of the known stone cargoes weigh less than 100 tonnes and could have been
carried by ordinary merchant vessels. Equally, there is some evidence to
suggest that the largest stone cargoes were being carried by vessels with
significantly larger tonnages—that these ships were travelling under-capacity,
in other words. Throckmorton's observation that 'modern practice is never to
load a ship with stone beyond about two-thirds of its gross tonnage' is
pertinent here.[165] Where hull remains do survive it is striking that actually
the cargo of stone takes up relatively little space.[166] Based on the surviving
portions of the hull of the Isola delle Correnti ship, Kapitän calculated its
length as 40–8 m, its beam at 10–12 m (quarter its length), and its height from
keel to deck at 5–6 m (half its beam).[167] In comparison, the Late Republican
ship wrecked at Madrague de Giens, had a beam of 9 m, a length of 36 m, and a
height of 4.5 m.[168] This ship, therefore, was about two-thirds the size of the
Isola delle Correnti ship. Despite this, it was carrying a heavier cargo, of
6,000–7,800 wine amphorae, equivalent to 365–475 tonnes.[169] Amphorae
could be evenly distributed through the hold, stacked to prevent shifting,
meaning that ships with them on board could travel safely much closer to
their capacity. Based on its size, and comparison with the Madrague de Giens
wreck, the Isola delle Correnti ship probably could have carried as much as

---

[161] Casson 1971: 169; the λιθηγὸς [ναῦς] is mentioned in the third-century BC *P. Cairo Zen.*
59172.6.
[162] Casson 1971: 169.
[163] Casson 1971: 173; also Meijer 2002: 152: 'the high specific gravity of marble demanded
purpose-built or at least specifically reinforced ships.'
[164] Throckmorton 1969: 300; 1989. Simone Parizzi's work on the technical aspects of ship
construction may change this picture in the near future, however.
[165] Throckmorton 1972: 76.
[166] On this point, Royal 2008: 61–2.   [167] Kapitän 1961: 286–8.
[168] Pomey and Tchernia 1978: 233–4.   [169] Pomey and Tchernia 1978: 234.

600–700 tonnes of amphorae.[170] Even if we add 50 to 100 tonnes to the weight of the stone on board to account for any perishable cargo elements, the Isola delle Correnti ship was probably travelling well under capacity. At other sites too, we can identify adroitly loaded cargoes on which the stone elements accounted for no more than a half to two-thirds of the probable gross tonnages of the vessels.[171]

Externally, then, many of the ships responsible for carrying stone probably looked no different from any other merchant ship. Perhaps this is why these vessels never earned themselves a specific name. This being said, we should not reject the idea of specialism altogether. Temporary reinforcement could certainly have taken place, even if it has yet to be identified archaeologically. More importantly, though, stone cargoes required special treatment. The loading and unloading of stone was a particular skill and shippers were clearly wary of overburdening their vessels. Certain shippers may well have specialized in the transport of stone, even if their vessels were not themselves out of the ordinary. At several of the shipwrecks in our sample, in fact, there is evidence to suggest that these vessels had been used more than once for the transport of stone. At Punta del Francese small chips of various types of marble were found alongside, and especially underneath, the main cargoes of large blocks; at Capo Granitola A similar small fragments, of at least three other stone types were found, though whether they belong to this wreck is unclear.[172] In both cases these finds have been interpreted as the remnants of previous cargoes. The same argument has been put forward for the fragments of revetment panels in various stones found on the Porto Nuovo wreck.[173] It is tempting to see the owners and operators of these vessels as experienced stone handlers, well acquainted with suppliers at the quarries, contractors or *marmorarii*, and perhaps also imperial officials responsible for overseeing the marble supply.

CONNECTIVITY

The shipwreck evidence provides a remarkably fine-grained picture of stone in transit. Nowhere else are we able to assess the quantities and conditions in which this material was routinely transported. In order to understand what these sites reveal about the organization of the shipping of stone, and what it

[170] This is the size of the Albenga ship: Pomey and Tchernia 1978: 234–5.
[171] On the Marzamemi A, Methone C, and Torre Sgarrata ships, all about 30 m in length, see Kapitän 1961: 290–300; Throckmorton and Bullitt 1963; Throckmorton 1969: 300; also Royal 2008: 60–1.
[172] Galasso 1997: 130; Pensabene 2003: 533.   [173] Mazeran 1998: 135–8.

tells us about wider Roman maritime commerce, we need to turn to the cargoes themselves.

Direct and indirect commerce

A first point to be noted is the striking dominance of stone in all these cargoes; few of these vessels were carrying anything other than stone at the moment that they sank. Of course, we have to account for perishable goods which are now invisible to us, but even so the absence of large numbers of other non-perishables at most of these sites is significant. At only seven of these shipwrecks do other non-perishable goods, or goods contained in non-perishable containers, appear to have formed an important component of the original cargo. The two most notable of these are both located in the Adriatic. At Izmetište, more than 2,500 ceramic vessels were extracted during excavation, consisting mainly of Eastern Sigillata A and Eastern coarsewares, as well as some Koan (Dressel 2–4) amphorae.[174] At Margarina, meanwhile, alongside the load of small columns and blocks, were found a large number of roof tiles, both *tegulae* and *imbrices*.[175] The statues on the Porticcio A ship were also part of a mixed cargo of amphorae and window glass.[176] To this list, though earlier than our period, we can add the Antikythera A wreck, at which over seventy Rhodian, Coan, and Lamboglia 2 amphorae were found, as well as a range of fine and coarse pottery.[177] Finally, at only two shipwrecks do the known stone objects seem to have constituted a minority of the cargo. On the La Mirande (Port-Vendres 5) wreck, the five panels of Luna veneer on board, all probably sawn from the same block, were being transport alongside a main cargo of Pascual I amphorae.[178] And at the Chrétienne M(3), the fragments of *africano* panels found at the site were accompanying a main cargo of Richborough 527 amphorae and Pompeian red-slip plates.[179] At other sites, moderate numbers of non-stone objects have been found, but only in quantities to suggest that they were shipboard items; supplies belonging to the crew.[180]

What this shows is that stone constituted the main component of the cargo of the majority of the ships in our sample, in terms of weight, volume, and probably also value. In this sense at least, stone cargoes were relatively homogeneous and this observation can be extended to the type of objects on board. Numerous cargoes included both blocks and roughed-out architectural elements; the sarcophagus chests on the Torre Sgarrata wreck were shipped

---

[174] Jurišić 2000: 65.   [175] Jurišić 2000: 69.   [176] Massy 2013: 110–14.
[177] Weinberg, Grace, and Edwards 1965.   [178] Descamps 1992.
[179] Joncheray and Joncheray 2002.
[180] For this interpretation at Torre Sgarrata, Parker 1992*a*: 429; and at Skerki F, McCann and Oleson 2004: 99–117.

alongside both blocks and ready-cut veneer panels. Rarely, though, do any of the known cargoes comprise a vast array of different types of objects. The exceptions very much stand out: the Mahdia, Şile, Sutivan, and Punta Scifo A wrecks. Even when multiple types of stone object are found within a single cargo, reasonable uniformity can be noted within each class of object, especially in terms of their finish. Objects at every stage of working are found in shipwrecks and sometimes within the same cargo; roughed-out columns are found alongside near-finished basins, and possibly capitals on the Punta Scifo A wreck, for example; finished columns were apparently shipped with roughed-out statues and blocks on the Şile ship too.[181] Very rarely, however, are objects of the same type found finished to different degrees within the same cargo. The same applies to material. We do not have cargoes of *cipollino* and *giallo antico* columns together, for example, or sarcophagi in both Thasian and Prokonnesian marble. In fact, it is noticeable that only a handful of our wrecks were carrying material from more than one source: *verde antico* and Prokonnesian at Şile; *pavonazzetto* and Prokonnesian at Punta Scifo A; *cipollino* and Prokonnesian at Giardini Naxos; Thasian and alabaster at Torre Sgarrata.[182] Two types of stone are also noted at Izmetište and at the mysterious 'Les Pierres' site, but in the latter case they seem to be from approximately the same source; likewise the Torre Sgarrata ship was carrying sarcophagi in two types of Thasian marble.[183] Overall, these sites are a small minority of the total. The Torre Sgarrata and Porto Nuovo ships, of course, were carrying bundles of veneer panels in stone from numerous sources, but these were probably all picked up together at a single location; the same applies to the assorted cargo of the Les Riches Dunes 5 ship.

Most of the ships in our sample, then, were carrying just stone, and just stone from a single source. This is supported by the composition of these cargoes, the materials on board, and even the finish of the individual object types. Even when multiple stone types are found it would appear that they were loaded together at a single location; this, in any case, is the argument made for the Punta Scifo A and Giardini Naxos wrecks.[184] This is an important observation when it comes to interpreting how this traffic was organized. It suggests that the bulk of these ships were involved in what might has been called 'direct' or 'commissioned' trade. That is, the various elements of most of these cargoes seem to have been loaded at one port for transport straight to

---

[181] Pensabene 1978: 108–10; Beykan 1988.

[182] Beykan 1988: 127; Pensabene 1978: 108; Basile 1988: 138; Gabellone, Giannotta, and Alessio 2009; Calia et al. 2009.

[183] On Izmetište, Jurišić 2000: 65; on 'Les Pierres', Rauzier 2001: 47; and on Torre Sgarrata, Gabellone, Giannotta, and Alessio 2009: 327.

[184] Pensabene 1978: 112–14, proposes either Nicomedia or an Ionian port, either Miletos or Ephesos, for the port of origin of the Punta Scifo A wreck; on the Giardini Naxos wreck, Basile 1988: 138–9.

another port; the route was predetermined, settled upon before loading began and the ship left port. Most of the cargoes in our sample had probably already been purchased, or at least ordered specifically, and were now simply being delivered. When Cicero purchased statues through agents in Greece he arranged shipping separately himself. Writing to Atticus, Cicero recommends that 'if a ship of Lentulus' is not available, put them aboard any you think fit'.[185]

The activity revealed by the known stone wrecks, therefore, was not tramping (or *cabotage* in French), whereby goods were bought and sold at various points along the route, and the market was undefined. Stone is a heavy cargo, and a high-value commodity, which is generally unsuitable for opportunistic selling. While there is little doubt that small-scale coastal tramping was ubiquitous in antiquity, it is unlikely to have played much of a role in the movement of stone.[186] Most of the stone cargoes in our sample comprise large objects, like architectural elements or sarcophagi, which were only roughed out and required significant extra work before they could be used; these are not the kind of products that people would buy on a whim off the deck of a ship. But this does not mean that there were no products suitable for such a market. The ready-cut veneer panels in the La Mirande (Port-Vendres 5) and Chrétienne M(3) wrecks, for example, were obviously not the main cargo on these ships; perhaps they had been bought by the captain for his own use or at the request of someone else, but perhaps also they were bought to be sold at the next port.[187] The similar panels on the Torre Sgarrata and Porto Nuovo wrecks could likewise have been destined for an undefined market. Most stone intended for veneer was delivered in block form and required substantial sawing and polishing. These ready-cut panels perhaps represented a more saleable version, the relative lightness of which made it a suitable complementary cargo.[188] In addition to delivering their consignments of blocks and sarcophagi, therefore, those responsible for these ships were perhaps dabbling in the sale of veneer on the side. Under life-size statues, finished rather than roughed out, are another product that one can imagine being sold in this kind of way. Only several examples have been found on shipwrecks, but there is some support in the literary sources for a trade in finished statues.[189]

Of course, not all the objects being moved around were new. Certain objects on the Mahdia and Antikythera A wrecks were old at the time of shipment;

---

[185] Cicero, *Letters to Atticus* I.8–9 (trans. D. R. Shackleton Bailey).
[186] On the normality of tramping, Horden and Purcell 2000: 365–77.
[187] Descamps 1992; Joncheray and Joncheray 2002.
[188] Russell 2008: 116–19.
[189] Examples from shipwrecks, include the statue of Diana from Benalmadena, and the female statue from the Golfo di Baratti B wreck; see Arata 2005: 148–9. Full-size and smaller statues were found in the Porticcio A wreck; see Massy 2013: 110–14. See also Chapter 8: The movement of finished statues (pp. 336–9).

both contained large number of precious works of art, many apparently antiques. At least some of the objects on the Les Riches Dunes 5 wreck were also second-hand; the column and base at least are both entirely finished and the former had been repaired at some point.[190] More interesting from this perspective is the Methone C wreck, datable to the early third century AD. In this case the cargo consisted of at least thirty-six fragmentary granite columns, apparently already broken at the time of loading since none of these pieces appear to fit together. Since the ends of these columns are finished, not left with the usual protective collars, they probably come from a ruined building, perhaps testifying to the existence of a long-distance trade in architectural scrap in this period.[191]

Origins and destinations

A considerable proportion of the traffic revealed by the shipwreck evidence seems to have originated at harbours at, or closely associated with, the quarries. Most of the objects identified in stone wrecks are roughed out or finished only to the stage at which they normally left the quarry. The remains of the loading facilities at the Aliki quarries on Thasos a well-known and studied, but it seems probable that other sites were similarly equipped.[192] During his survey of the Capo Testa quarries, on Sardinia, Wilson identified several loading stations and a quay associated with the large Capicciolu quarry; deep water channels adjacent to two of the other quarries would have allowed ships to moor alongside, and cuttings for bollards or cranes are still visible.[193] Similar cuttings for cranes have been noted on the coast close to the *breccia di settebasi* quarries at Cape Latomio on Valaxa islet, just off Skyros.[194] The Southern Euboea Exploration Project noted that several of the small *cipollino* quarries that they surveyed along the coast east of Karystos were connected by roads and slipways to loading platforms on the shore.[195] Another survey in this area identified two *cipollino* columns on the beach at Nimborio, close to the quarries, which seem to have been abandoned during loading.[196] In Euboea, however, the local urban ports were also linked into the network of quarries and their associated supply routes. Roads linked the various *cipollino* quarries with the harbours at Karystos, Marmari, and Styra, and ancient port facilities have recently also been identified at Geraistos.[197]

[190] H. Bernard and Jézégou 2003.   [191] Throckmorton and Bullitt 1963: 19.
[192] Sodini, Lambraki, and Koželj 1980.   [193] R. J. A. Wilson 1988: 104–8.
[194] Bruno 2002*d*: 31–2, fig. 19.   [195] Pers. comm. Jere Wickens.
[196] Chidiroglou 2009: 76; see also Bruno and Vitti 2012 on the quarries at Aghii.
[197] Chidiroglou 2009: 73–91.

In addition to these quarry harbours there is good reason to think that some of the cargoes in our sample originated at intermediary entrepôts. For the Egyptian stones, Alexandria would have been the only real option; the letter from the procurator Aurelius Isidorus concerning the shipping of columns on Nile, specifically mentions that their destination is Alexandria.[198] Marble was certainly shipped from Ephesos: the edict of the provincial governor Lucius Antonius Albus, dated to AD 147, explicitly bans marble-cutters from cluttering up the harbour area.[199] Ostia and Portus, though primarily points of entry for high-quality marbles destined for the capital, probably also acted as entrepôts. A likely candidate for a cargo of stone loaded at one of these sites is that of the Dramont I wreck. In addition to the three blocks of *africano* that constituted the bulk of this cargo, emery from Naxos was also found, as well as pumice from southern Italy, limited quantities of Italian (Dressel 2/4) and Spanish (Dressel 7/11 and 20) amphorae, Italian oil lamps and various copper objects associated with the cult of Isis, all of which seem to have come from Rome.[200] This spread of goods led the excavators to hypothesise a route for this ship beginning at Teos, passing Naxos, a possible Campanian port and Ostia, on its way to southern France. This was a long voyage for a ship carrying a relatively small cargo, though, and it seems much more likely that everything on board was simply loaded at Ostia or Portus in one go. Recent work on other shipwrecks sites, notably by Nieto, has shown convincingly that this kind of redistributive shipping via intermediary ports was extremely common in the Roman period.[201] If customers in the western Mediterranean wanted to get their hands on eastern marbles, and were not in direct contact with agents at the quarries, then the ports of Rome were probably the best places to look.

Transshipment

Although it is certainly true that it must have been cheaper to transport stone by sea rather than by land over a set distance, in practice most medium- to long-distance trips must have employed a combination of transportation means. This is where it is important to consider the efforts and costs involved in loading and unloading stone, something that the figures in the Price Edict ignore. Stone obviously had to be loaded once and unloaded once over any trip but transshipment, or the movement of material between one means of transport and another, added considerably to the costs involved. The Sens cathedral accounts, one of the rare cases where transshipment costs are identifiable, show that these accounted for around 30 per cent of the total

---

[198] Skeat 1964: Papyrus 2, lines 43–50.   [199] *SEG* XIX.684, XXVII.742, XXXI.1311.
[200] Joncheray 1998: 140–50.   [201] Nieto 1997.

cost of transport.[202] The thirteenth-century Norwich accounts give costs for the transshipping of stone between ships and barges at Great Yarmouth equivalent to 20 per cent of the cost of carriage between there and the building site.[203] Though he provides no figures, in his description of nineteenth-century Carrara, Lee notes that, since large ships could only dock at nearby Livorno, material from the quarries had to be loaded onto small ships (*navicelli*) at Avenza for transport along the coast: 'a considerable saving would be effected if seagoing ships could load at Avenza itself,' he states.[204]

Loading and unloading stone was expensive but also difficult. Cranes were necessary for anything over about 50–70 kg. A crane-constructor (κασιότις), in fact, is attested at Mons Claudianus.[205] Loading ramps are attested in some quarries, and are referred to as κρηπίς in the *ostraka* from Mons Claudianus.[206] In his admiring description of the stowage of marble at Livorno, Lee notes that this was a skill passed down through generations of stevedores, 'raised to the dignity of a fine art'.[207] Without the correct equipment and experience the results could be fatal, as the mildly amateurish attempts to remove material from Didyma in the late nineteenth century show.[208] Particular difficulties were caused by a large capital, weighing roughly 4 tonnes, which is now in the Louvre: twice the cranes being used to load this object onto a waiting boat broke, dumping it into the sea, and resulting in the death of one workman. Specialist workers, considerably more competent at dealing with stone objects larger than this, must have been permanently based at quarries with on-site port infrastructure. At Aliki, on Thasos, placements for cranes have been identified, cut into the bedrock along the seaward side of the quarries.[209] It has been proposed that these cranes were built on turnstiles or perhaps even on moveable tracks to allow them to reach the vessels moored

[202] Cailleaux 1997: 195; specifically, the cost of loading and unloading was 160 out of a total of 560 *s.t.* for this section of overland transport.

[203] Salzman 1967: 119.

[204] Lee 1888: 9–10.

[205] Bülow-Jacobsen 1996: 46.

[206] Peacock and Maxfield 1997: 259–61 (figs. 7.2–7.9); Maxfield and Peacock 2001*b*: 104–7, 209–14; for similar ramps at the earlier gneiss quarries in the Gebel el-Asr, I. Shaw 2010: 119–20. On the evidence from the *ostraka*, Fant 2010: 775.

[207] Lee 1888: 18; he goes on to described how 'the loading of the large ocean-going vessels from the small *navicelli* is very smartly done. A floating pontoon crane is brought into play, in which the required power is grained by means of a huge wheel. In this manner the heaviest blocks are lifted from the small vessels, and are delivered into the holds of the large craft without difficulty.'

[208] Rayet 1888: 140–1. For a similar account, though less dramatic, of the removal of the reliefs from the Great Altar at Pergamon, Humann 1959: 212–15.

[209] Sodini, Lambraki, and Koželj 1980: 111–22 (figs. 68, 76). Similar sockets for cranes have been found in many quarries; for the examples from Mons Claudianus, Peacock and Maxfield 1997: 259, fig. 7.1.

alongside the quarries.[210] No obvious quayside has been found at Aliki but the rock-face must have been padded or built out in some way to prevent these ships being smashed against it in the swell. Cranes with attached treadmills have also been hypothesized at the Cape Phanari quarries on Thasos on the basis of cuttings in the rock.[211] The major ports of the Roman world all would have been equipped with cranes of sufficient strength to handle large blocks of stone, but this would not have been true of smaller sites further down the port hierarchy. In fact, there was probably an inverse equation between the size of a stone object and the number of ports at which it could be loaded or unloaded. At a well-equipped port or loading-station transshipment would have been expensive, at a poorly equipped one near impossible.[212]

The transport of material from inland quarries would have been especially affected by these concerns. The quarries at Chemtou are a case in point. All being equal the simplest route from these quarries to the coast would seem to have been along the Medjerda river (the ancient Bagradas) to the port of Utica at its mouth. The installation of a watermill on the Trajanic bridge shows that the flow of this river could be relied upon, at least some of the year, but the riverbed here is shallow and rocky.[213] Even if the river could have been used, material still had to be moved from quarry face to river by wagon, loaded onto a suitable boat and taken downstream, then loaded straight onto a ship or, more likely, the quayside. The alternative route to the coast was via the road north to Tabarka, a distance of 60 km over mountainous terrain. On paper much more difficult, this route had the advantage that once material was loaded at Chemtou it could stay where it was until it reached the quayside. And this route was clearly used, perhaps even preferred: abandoned *giallo antico* columns found along it show that it was certainly used for the transport of stone from Chemtou; it was even either rebuilt or partially altered under Hadrian.[214]

Transport of stone from Dokimeion, though even more onerous, was affected by similar concerns. Material from these quarries could have been moved northwards, 90 km, to the Sakarya river (the ancient Sangarios), then shipped downriver, before being unloaded and transported to Nicomedia.[215]

[210] A fantastic reconstruction of this process is shown in Sodini, Lambraki, and Koželj 1980: 121 (fig. 86).
[211] Koželj and Wurch-Koželj 2009: 57.
[212] The fourth-century bc accounts of the rebuilding of the Temple of Apollo at Delphi show that large sums were spent on machines (μαχανώματα) for unloading stone for the project from ships at the port of Kirrha (Bourguet 1932: no. 19.12); clearly this investment was justified by the expense of this process. Gervase of Canterbury discusses the 'ingenious machines for loading and unloading ships' integral to the reconstruction of Canterbury cathedral in the twelfth century (Holt 1957: 56). For more on this point, Russell 2008.
[213] J. Röder and G. Röder 1993.
[214] Winckler 1895: 38; G. Röder 1993: 51; Rakob 1995b: 66; Hirt 2010: 27.
[215] For this suggestion, Ward-Perkins 1980b: 65–7; also Monna and Pensabene 1977: 71–7.

The Sakarya, however, is rapid and shallow for most of its course, and in its lower reaches funnelled through a series of narrow ravines. It is totally unsuited to the transport of stone. This proposed route would also have involved multiple transshipments, making it extremely expensive. Considering this, it seems more likely that stone from Dokimeion was channelled westwards, either down the Hermos valley to Smyrna, or via Synnada and Apamea to the Maeander valley. From Apamea, there was the option of moving material south along the via Sebaste into Pisidia and Pamphylia.[216] It could have been shipped down either the Hermos or the Maeander but it might have been preferred to keep it on land and avoid transshipment costs.[217] Silting at the mouth of the Maeander would have made it preferable to leave the river valley at Magnesia and cross over to Ephesos instead. As noted, the road between Magnesia and Ephesos, with its controlled gradient, was built under Trajan.[218] Though the distances were enormous, these various western routes, even if they did include a downriver segment, would have utilized no more than three means of transport, and potentially even just one.

CONCLUSIONS

Comparative evidence from other historical periods suggests that the transport of stone has always been an expensive business and there is no reason to assume that this way any different in Roman period. It is probably no exaggeration to state that, on average at least, to move a block of stone around 20 km overland is likely to have doubled its cost. River and sea transport were demonstrably cheaper, but the difficulty of loading and unloading awkward cargoes might have made them less cost-effective than land transport over short distances. How much it cost to bring material from them played a key role in determining the viability of quarries.[219] It is no great revelation to note that the majority of quarries opened in the Roman imperial period were located on, or close to, either the coast or a river.

Much of the above discussion has concentrated on the shipwreck evidence for obvious reasons. Our understanding of the logistics of the overland and

---

[216] On Dokimeian marble in this region, see Chapter 5: Case study 1: Asia Minor (pp. 149–50).

[217] For the argument in favour of an entirely overland route, Waelkens, De Paepe, and Moens 1988: 90.

[218] Keil 1908: 166–7.

[219] Salmojraghi 1892: 277, stresses the importance of factoring in transport when budgeting for quarrying costs: 'Il trasporto delle pietre fuor delle cave influisce grandemente sulle condizioni economiche dell'estrazione. I metodi relativi dipendono dalla posizione della cave rispetto alle vie di comunicazione e dal volume dei pezzi; sono in generale indipendenti dalla natura della roccia.'

fluvial transportation of stone is extremely limited; the archaeological evidence tells us almost nothing about how this was organized, the size of cargoes, the vehicles and vessels involved, or even the individuals responsible. Sporadic references in the papyrological corpus and occasional fortuitous finds are all that we have to work with; the comparative evidence goes some way to filling the gaps, but only some way. The shipwreck evidence reveals a striking picture. On the one hand, the draw of Rome clearly stands out. The considerable number of big ships carrying eastern marbles wrecked off southern Italy must represent a vastly larger total that made it to their destination; millions of tonnes of eastern marbles successfully entered the imperial and non-imperial market at the capital. Though there is insufficient evidence from the sites themselves to state anything definitively, most of these larger ships were probably carrying imperially owned produce. This is only part of the picture, however. What the shipwreck evidence usefully illustrates are the parallel, but sometimes interrelated, smaller-scale supply networks operating alongside the major imperially stimulated ones.[220] At one end of the scale are the short-distance coastal trips of ships like those wrecked at Carry-le-Rouet and in the harbour at Anse des Laurons, or that sunk in the Thames at Blackfriars Bridge, vessels shuttling everyday materials from quarry to city. At the other end of the scale are the considerably larger ships represented by the cargoes like that at Saint-Tropez, in the West, or Şile, in the East. Somewhere in between are the numerous ships carrying small to middling cargoes of white marble, occasion-ally high-quality limestone, along the southern French coast. A substantial proportion of the total stone moved overseas was destined for Rome, and was probably also imperially owned, but most of the ships that set sail with stone cargoes in this period were probably involved in smaller-scale, shorter-dis-tance activity.

---

[220] On this point, Russell 2012.

5

Distribution Patterns

Distributio ... is the suitable disposal of supplies and the site, and the thrifty and wise control of expense in the works. This will be guarded if, in the first place, the architect does not require what can only be supplied and prepared at great cost. For it is not everywhere that there is a supply of quarry sand or hewn stone, or fir or deal or marble. Different things are found in different places; the transport of them may be difficult and costly.

Vitruvius, *On Architecture* I.2.8[1]

On account of the present extravagance of the Romans, great monolithic pillars are taken from [the quarries] ... so that, although the transportation of such heavy burdens to the sea is difficult, still, both pillars and slabs, remarkable for their size and beauty, are conveyed to Rome.

Strabo, *Geography* XII.8.14[2]

Numerous studies over the past forty years have examined stone use at specific sites or in particular provinces or regions and with the increasing refinement of provenance studies, in the past ten to fifteen years most notably, such studies have become both more frequent and reliable. There remain large gaps in our knowledge which inhibit any overall commentary on stone use everywhere in the Roman world, but there are sufficient data from enough of a range of diverse areas to highlight certain key patterns which reveal the choices made by different groups of consumers with respect to their particular situations. While the previous chapter examined the evidence for the transportation of stone and its cost, this chapter focuses on which stones were used where, and why.

---

[1] Translated by F. Granger.
[2] Translated by H. L. Jones.

MODELLING DISTRIBUTION

For obvious reasons most studies of the distribution of stone in the Roman world have focused on the observable patterns of inter-regional traffic. This is true of both general economic studies, in which the distribution of stone is often used as an illustration of the logistical capabilities of the state, and more specialist discussions.[3] As Fant has noted, however, the 'long distance trade in stone is an improbable phenomenon.'[4] This was certainly understood in the Roman period; Pliny, of course, rails against this activity and a similar sense of excess penetrates Strabo's description of quarrying at remote Dokimeion, quoted above.[5] Even later, when the long-distance stone trade was old news, Sidonius draws a direct contrast between imported materials—'the chill starkness of foreign rocks'—and more modest, vernacular alternatives.[6] This opposition between local and imported materials is again apparent in much twentieth-century theoretical work, on architecture most notably. As Adrian Stokes, the British art historian, put it:

> [A] building, if constructed of local materials, is an expression of its neighbourhood ... The stone may have come twenty, thirty miles; no matter, it is better than three hundred miles.[7]

The long-distance movement of stone has always been both improbable and abnormal. As we saw in Chapter 3, the majority of identifiable quarries in the Roman Empire were small-scale, local suppliers, intimately linked to the pattern of urbanization; few major urban centres were located more than a long day's walk from a source of adequate building stone. In aggregate terms, then, an enormous amount of stone was moved relatively short distances in the Roman world. Between this highly localized, low-level activity and the remarkable long-distance movement of decorative stone, though, other levels of distribution can be noted which are partly revealed by the shipwreck evidence.

Layers of economic activity

This is an important point when it comes to setting the stone trade into a wider economic context and comparing the distribution of stone to that of other commodities. Several recent discussions of the Roman economy have

---

[3] See Jongman 2007: 592; Mattingly 2007: 224; and the distribution maps in Lazzarini 2004.
[4] Fant 1988: 147.
[5] Pliny the Elder XXXVI.1; Strabo, *Geography* XII.8.14 (trans. H. L. Jones).
[6] Sidonius, *Letters* II.2.7 (trans. W. B. Anderson).
[7] Stokes 1934: 44–5.

stressed the utility of distinguishing between different layers of economic activity. Most recently, Mattingly has stressed the value of considering the Roman 'economy' of the first three centuries AD as an interconnected set of three 'economies': a 'provincial economy', with a local focus within provincial or regional boundaries, operating on a free-market basis but shaped by socially embedded economic behaviour; an 'extra-provincial economy', operating on an empire-wide basis and largely free-market but including gift exchange between members of the elite; and an 'imperial economy' based around supplying the capital, the imperial household, and the army via taxation, exploitation of imperial resources, and organized redistribution.[8] As a heuristic device this division functions well, allowing the amorphous mass of what we call the Roman economy to be broken down into its key components on both a geographical and a conceptual basis. The extent to which administrative boundaries made any difference to the movement of stone, however, is questionable and it is perhaps more useful to consider these different levels of activity as shaped by geographical factors. In this sense, Mattingly's model is usefully considered alongside the observations of Bresson, who suggests that connectivity within the Mediterranean should be thought of on four geographically differentiated levels: first, local and micro-regional; second, regional or within a particular sub-zone (such as the Aegean or Adriatic); third, inter-regional but limited to the eastern or western basins of the Mediterranean; and fourth, pan-Mediterranean.[9] Bresson proposes that regional and inter-regional connectivity were the norm in our period.

The consumer and the selection of stone

In a series of influential articles in the 1980s and 1990s Braemer attempted to examine the distribution of stone in the Roman world from just such a perspective, distinguishing between five categories of stone types on the basis of their distribution.[10] First, and most numerous of these, were materials distributed in a limited area, usually within a single province; second, those distributed across a whole province or geographic zone; third, those used across several provinces or geographic zones; fourth, those used in either the eastern or western half of the Mediterranean; and finally, materials which were distributed across the whole empire. Braemer notes a number of interesting trends which are supported by various strands of evidence but other aspects of his model need to be reconsidered. Like many others, Braemer focuses on where materials from specific quarries are found: his approach is essentially quarry-centric and he argues that the distribution of these materials depended

---

[8] Mattingly 2007: 221–2.   [9] Bresson 2005: 95–100.
[10] Braemer 1986*a*; 1986*b*; 1992.

on their 'commercialization', a term which implies an active process, controlled by the quarries. Whether quarries actively commercialized their output
or not is open to debate. There is no convincing evidence that they did.
However, the key point that needs to be made here is the lack of attention
paid in this model to how the materials under investigation are used at those
sites where they are found.[11]

This, in fact, is a feature of other distribution studies, including the distribution maps of specific materials which are routinely used to document the
inter-regional distribution of the most prominent decorative stones.[12] While
such maps effectively illustrate general distribution patterns and are useful for
highlighting where certain materials are not found, they also need treating
with caution.[13] By not documenting the way in which these materials are used
at those sites where they are found important nuances in their distribution
patterns are missed. To pick just one example, column shafts were much more
logistically challenging and expensive to acquire than material for revetment
or paving and their distribution reflects this: most decorative stones were more
widely distributed for use as veneer than column shafts.[14] Several studies have
shown the benefit of integrating some of this data into traditional material-
specific distribution maps: Cisneros' distribution maps of various Spanish
stones distinguish broadly between materials employed for architecture, statuary, and inscriptions; Fischer has done something similar for Palestine.[15]
However, it is difficult to provide this kind of fine-grained detail for empire-
wide distribution maps.

Any general discussion of the distribution of stone, then, needs to be
centred around the way in which different stones were used at those sites
where they are found. This tells us much more about the processes of selection
and display, the way in which different materials were employed alongside
each other, which in turns reveals the choices made by individual consumers.
Instead of thinking of quarry-based producers targeting particular markets it
is perhaps more helpful to think of individual consumers and the stone-
workers employed by them picking from the options available.

When it comes to the selection of raw materials for a particular project,
whether a building or a carving, this process could take a number of forms,
depending on the intentions and demands of the consumer. Individual consumers might, for instance, select the materials themselves and then find
workers to carve them or pick specific workers because they were known for
working, and could supply, certain stones. Alternatively, the customer might

---

[11] Pensabene 1972; 2002*b*: 60–4.
[12] For example: Dodge 1988*a*; Lazzarini 2004.
[13] Dodge 1988*a*: 73.
[14] On this point with regard to *serpentino*, Zezza and Lazzarini 2002: 260.
[15] Cisneros 1988: 88–114; M. L. Fischer 1998: 30.

chose the stone-workers that they wanted and then request that they use particular materials: S. Iulius Aquila, mentioned in Chapter 2, who requested Luna marble for his tomb, is a prime example of one such demanding customer.[16] Even if the choice of materials was left up to the stone-worker it would still have been influenced by the demands of their customers. Stone-workers typically judge materials according to three main criteria, all of which depend on the use to which they are to be put:

1. Suitability: what kind of materials—based on an assessment of their workability, durability, ability to hold fine detail, etc.—would be suitable for the project in question?[17]
2. Aesthetics: out of the suitable materials which are the right colour or texture; which could take a polish if required; which fitted the needs of the customer?
3. Availability: which of those materials that met the above criteria could be acquired within budget?[18]

While the range of materials that could be acquired within budget clearly varied by project, depending on the types of stones needed, the location of the quarries respective to the site, and transport logistics, the experience and training of the stone-worker and their personal contacts with certain quarries probably also impacted the decision-making process. We also need to remember that certain stone objects were traded as near- or fully finished products rather than raw materials. These objects were valued differently but could also be purchased differently, as single items rather than material for a larger project. In other words, in structuring our analysis of the distribution of stone around the use to which materials are put we need to distinguish not only between sarcophagi, statuary, and stone used in building but also between different architectural elements. In this way we can also build up a picture of which materials were considered suitable for basic construction projects and which for more decorative or prestigious projects; this allows a further assessment of the level of effort that was perceived to be normal or routine and what was considered exceptional against which imperial projects can be judged.[19]

To this end, this chapter is divided into three further sections which are intended to draw out some of the patterns of stone distribution in the Roman world and are divided according both to the customer involved—whether imperial or non-imperial—and the use to which the material was put. The first of these examines stone use in primarily non-imperial architectural

---

[16] *CIL* XIII.5708; see Chapter 2: 'Foreign rocks' (p. 16).
[17] Rockwell 1993: 17; Lee 1888: 130–43 gives a long excursus on the process of selecting the right stone for a range of jobs.
[18] Pearson 2006: 70–1.   [19] Russell 2008: 119–21; Fulford 2009: 251–2.

contexts, concentrating on the impact of geography and transport logistics, and the role played by building contractors in the distribution of stone; the second, concentrates on the varying distribution patterns of other object types, notably sarcophagi and statuary, again in predominately non-imperial contexts; while the third section looks at imperial activity, at the exceptional redistribution of decorative stone for imperially funded building projects and the infrastructure employed to secure these supplies. Like Braemer—but also Bresson and Mattingly—the emphasis is placed on the layers of observable distribution patterns and the factors shaping them.

DISTRIBUTION OF STONE IN ARCHITECTURAL CONTEXTS

In his advice to prospective builders, quoted at the beginning of this chapter, Vitruvius is careful to stress the importance of selecting the right materials for the job. Particular emphasis is placed on transport costs: 'different things are found in different places; the transport of them may be difficult and costly'.[20] As we saw in the previous chapter, transport costs depended directly on the available modes of transport, the size and weight of the cargo, and the topography over which it needed to be moved. How these factors affected the distribution of stone are best examined through a series of case studies focusing on choices made by different consumers in different regions. The five case studies selected all concentrate on regions where some comparison can be drawn between stone use in coastal areas and inland areas: Asia Minor, the Levant, Spain, Gaul, the Rhineland, and Britain.

Case study 1: Asia Minor

Asia Minor provides perhaps the best evidence for contrasting patterns of stone use in coastal and inland areas, and the effect of extreme topography on the medium- and long-distance movement of stone for building. Many of the cities of central western and north-western Asia Minor, as we saw in Chapter 3, had good local stones resources and were reliant on them for building projects especially. Kyzikos had access to the Prokonnesian quarries; Miletos and Herakleia-on-Latmos had extensive local marble quarries; Ephesos probably had the largest white marble resources in its territory of any city

---

[20] Vitruvius I.2.8 (trans. F. Granger).

in Asia Minor, if not the whole Roman world.[21] While these local materials, often very high-quality, sufficed for most building and carving projects these cities were also well placed to import substantial quantities of coloured material to complement their local supplies. As Lazzarini's distribution maps of the best-known decorative marbles show, these materials were concentrated in the coastal zones of Asia Minor and were rarely moved far inland.[22]

Outside of Rome, Ephesos is perhaps richer in imported stones than any other city in the Mediterranean.[23] Almost all of the decorative stones quarried in the eastern Mediterranean are represented here in some form but *pavonazzetto* from Dokimeion is found in especially large quantities.[24] Another popular material for column shafts was Troad granite: over 200 columns of this material were used in the Tetragonos Agora, a Julio-Claudian complex (Fig. 5.1), while several others are now visible on the Marble Street.[25] A similar scheme was adopted in the agora at Smyrna and, as will see, elsewhere around Asia Minor and in the Levant.[26] The excavation of the Hanghäuser has demonstrated that this wealth of imports extended to certain private contexts: the array of decorative stones employed for the revetment and paving of the so-called Marmorsaal (Room 31) of the sixth residential unit in Hanghaus 2 is perhaps the most extraordinary display of its kind known anywhere; over 120,000 pieces of marble, of 30 different varieties, have been recovered, adding up to 350 m².[27] This room was probably first commissioned in the Hadrianic period by Gaius Flavius Furius Aptus, an important priest in the city, whose name is found on an inscription in the peristyle court of this house.[28]

Little white marble, for obvious reasons, was imported into Ephesos, but not every city in this region could call on similar resources within their own territory. In these areas, especially from the early second century AD, Prokonnesian marble was the import of choice. This is seen most notably at Pergamon, where Prokonnesian has been identified in the Trajaneum, the Temple of Asklepios, and the theatre and propylon in the Asklepieion, in the last alongside local Kozak Dağ granite.[29] Like Pergamon, the cities of coastal

[21] On Kyzikos, Barresi 2003: 105–6, 195; on the quarries around Bafa Gölü, Peschlow-Bindoket 1981: 200–11; Monna and Pensabene 1977: 123–4; on Ephesos, Yavuz, Bruno, and Attanasio 2011.

[22] Lazzarini 2004.

[23] Yavuz, Bruno, and Attanasio 2011.

[24] Lazzarini 2004: 103–18; Barresi 2003: 203; Koller 2005: 141–5; Fant 1993*a*: 154; and for statuary, see Schneider 2002: 99.

[25] Lazzarini 1987: 162; L. E. Long 2012*a*: 193.

[26] Lazzarini 1987: 162.

[27] Koller 2003; Kleber et al. 2010.

[28] Zimmermann and Landstätter 2011: 54, fig. 70.

[29] Barresi 2003: 196–9; Rohmann 1998: 8–38; on Prokonnesian marble at nearby Assos, Van der Merwe et al. 1995: 191–4, table 1.

Fig. 5.1. Troad granite columns in the Tetragonos Agroa, Ephesos (photo: author).

Pamphylia, also imported sizeable quantities of Prokonnesian marble from the early second century AD.[30] At Perge, Prokonnesian marble capitals and bases were used in combination with Troad granite column shafts in the agora, and this is a pairing replicated at nearby Side, as well as in the colonnaded street at Antioch-on-Kragos in Kilikia to the east.[31] Considering the popularity of Prokonnesian marble, and the city's coastal location, it is surprising to note that builders at Perge also looked overland to the north for high-quality stone. A Corinthian capital from near the South Baths and a Corinthianizing example from the Severan southern nymphaeum have recently been shown to be Dokimeian marble.[32] Prokonnesian marble was probably cheaper to import but Dokimeian white is a superb quality stone which was also valued for other objects.

The inland cities of Asia Minor were obviously more reliant on their local resources than coastal sites which had access to a far wider pool of material.[33] Nevertheless these cities were very differently positioned and consequently engaged with the wider stone trade in a variety of ways. A site like Aphrodisias,

[30] Waelkens et al. 2002: 375; on Prokonnesian at Side and Aspendos, Barresi 2003: 196, 201.
[31] Dodge 1990: 108; Lazzarini 1987: 162; on Antioch-on-Kragos, Borgia 2010: 294–8.
[32] Herrmann and Tykot 2009: 64–5.
[33] On local material used in prestige structures at Blaundos, Euromos, and Aizanoi see Barresi 2003: 191, 193, 309–10.

for instance, had excellent local resources. It could rely almost entirely on the white and grey marbles of its territory, as well as a range of coloured materials that have only recently been identified, including a variety of *pavonazzetto* quarried at Çamova Tepe, a mottled blue from Yazır, as well as the black and white from nearby Göktepe.[34] Materials were imported from beyond the city's territory but in relatively small quantities and were only used for revetment or paving.[35] Importing large blocks of decorative stones from the coast would have been cripplingly expensive but it was also largely unnecessary. In fact, even among those materials used for revetment and paving a preference for regional materials can be noted: *alabastro fiorito* was used extensively in the Theatre Baths and elsewhere but actually came from just over the hills near Hierapolis.[36]

At Sagalassos in Pisidia, in contrast, the local stones were much less prestigious, though they were used for architectural carving and for the numerous sarcophagi at the site.[37] They were clearly prized as local resources as the inscription celebrating this 'native stone' mentioned in Chapter 2 demonstrates.[38] In practice, though, when it came to decorative stones Sagalassos was reliant on imports, and unsurprisingly considering the location of the city few of these of any size came from the coast. Only Troad granite and *verde antico* seem to have been imported from the coast for columns and in what quantity is not clear.[39] Instead, Dokimeion was the main source of imported marble, most of which was employed for revetment, though several small columns (no more than 3.5 m tall) are known from the Antonine nymphaeum in the Upper Agora.[40] The Antonine baths in the city also made extensive use of marble revetment of various colours, including *greco scritto* and *cipollino*, but again most of it comes from Dokimeion.[41] *Pavonazzetto*, in fact, is found across central western Asia Minor, presumably because it was easier to bring it down from the Phrygian plateau than it was to import material from the coast. Hence, it is found at Aizanoi, at Hierapolis, and at Laodikeia-on-the-Lykos, in all cases as the principal non-local material.[42]

Sagalassos usefully illustrates the impact of topography on the long-distance movement of stone. Sagalassos is roughly 90 km from the coast. By comparison Sardis, though the same distance from the coast, was considerably more

---

[34] L. E. Long 2012*a*: 50–69; 2012*b*: 171–6, cat. 1, 8; also Bruno et al. 2012: 564.

[35] L. E. Long 2012*a*: 50–69; 2012*b*: 189–90.

[36] Bruno 2002*a*.

[37] Viaene et al. 1993: 85–7; Waelkens et al. 1997: 46; Köse 2005: 25–6; Degryse, Muchez, and Waelkens 2006: 11–17; Degryse et al. 2003; 2009*a*; 2009*b*.

[38] *IGRR* III.362; Waelkens 1997: 241; see Chapter 2: 'Foreign rocks' (p. 16).

[39] Corremans et al. 2012: 38–9, 43.

[40] Waelkens et al. 2002: 375.

[41] Corremans et al. 2012: 40–5.

[42] At Aizanoi, Barresi 2003: 192; at Hierapolis, Pensabene 2007*a*: 294; Barresi 2003: 200; and at Laodikeia-on-the-Lykos, Şimşek 2011.

Fig. 5.2. The so-called marble court of the Bath–Gymnasium complex, Sardis (photo: author).

open to imports: one only need point to the numerous *giallo antico*, *cipollino*, *breccia corallina*, and *pavonazzetto* columns incorporated into the palaestra and so-called marble court of the Bath–Gymnasium complex and the extensive marble revetment in the adjacent synagogue (Fig. 5.2); elsewhere *giallo antico* columns are found in the agora at Smyrna, and it is attested at Ephesos and Pergamon, but in no serious quantities anywhere further inland.[43] What made the difference for Sardis was the ease of access, via the Hermos Valley, that it enjoyed to the coast. Sardis lies at just over 100 m above sea level, while Sagalassos is at 1,490–1,600 m. While the quarries at Dokimeion (roughly 140 km distant) were further away than the Pamphylian coast they lie at 1,060 m above sea level.[44] Considering this difference in elevation, transport from Dokimeion and from the coast probably cost a similar amount but then we also need to factor in the costs of getting material to Pamphylia in the first place. Whichever way one looks at it, the white marble and *pavonazzetto* from Dokimeion would have been a more viable option for many inland cities in western Asia Minor than material from overseas, even if substantial overland transport was required.

---

[43] Barresi 2003: 202; Lazzarini 2004: 107, fig. 7; L. E. Long 2012*a*: 224–6.
[44] Corremans et al. 2012: 46.

From this very brief overview of the some of the evidence from Asia Minor a number of trends can be identified, which are replicated elsewhere: first, the dominance of local, sometimes regional, distribution patterns; second, the coastal emphasis of the observable inter-regional patterns; third, the way in which stone use at a particular site strongly depended on its location.

Case study 2: the Levant

The Levant, like Pamphylia, is not a marble-producing region and very few of the locally quarried stones were of sufficient quality to merit being moved around even regionally.[45] Nevertheless, all of the coastal cities of this region made intensive use of their local resources, even for prestigious structures like the monumental arches at Laodikeia-by-the-sea and Tyre, both late second century AD in date.[46] At the same time, the major benefactors in these cities engaged with the wider stone trade with relish, especially from the late second century AD. Coloured marbles, especially *cipollino*, are found at most major sites, usually for revetment but also columns: *cipollino* columns were used in the colonnaded streets at Tyre and Byblos and have also been found at Sidon; *pavonazzetto* and *breccia di settebasi* columns were used in the Basilica at Ascalon as part of the Severan decorative scheme.[47] The most common coloured decorative stones in the region, though, are not marbles but granites, specifically column shafts of Troad and Aswan granite, imported principally in the second century AD. The largest concentrations have been identified at Ascalon and Caesarea Maritima, where Kozak Dağ granite was also used.[48] Moving north, Troad granite columns were employed with Prokonnesian capitals and bases in the hippodrome at Tyre and the colonnaded street; in the colonnaded street and nymphaeum at Byblos; in various structures at Beirut; in the theatre at Gabala, again in combination with Aswan granite columns; and in the colonnaded street at Laodikeia-by-the-sea.[49] All of these uses can be dated to between the mid second and early third century AD, with most falling in the Severan period. These granite column shafts were usually combined with Prokonnesian marble capitals and bases, as in western and southern Asia Minor; around 80 per cent of all the imported white marble in

[45] Shadmon 1972; M. L. Fischer 1998: 29–43.

[46] On the coastal quarries, Badawi 2002; Sumaka'I Fink 2000; on the monumental arches, Pensabene 1997: 284, 385.

[47] Pensabene 1997: esp. 414–15; also 2002d: 29, fig. 2. On the basilica at Ascalon, M. L. Fischer 1995; 2002: 321.

[48] Williams-Thorpe and Henty 2000: 166, table 3; also M. L. Fischer 1996: 253–5; 1998: 52–61.

[49] Pensabene 1997: esp. 413–14.

Roman Palestine is Prokonnesian.[50] This material was also employed for entablature blocks, as in the theatre at Caesarea Maritima or the basilica at Beirut, but frequently these were carved in local limestone: the colonnaded streets at both Tyre and Byblos, and the nymphaeum at the latter, combine Prokonnesian bases and capitals, granite shafts, and limestone entablatures; the same is true of the colonnaded street at Antioch-on-Kragos in Kilikia.[51]

In comparison to Asia Minor, far greater quantities of architectural elements in imported materials have been recovered from the inland Levant. This no doubt reflects the more forgiving topography of the region, at least for the first 100 km or so from the coast, but it also probably results from the lack of high-quality local alternatives. As on the coast, granite columns are found at a considerable number of sites in Palestine, though there is certainly a drop off in their numbers as one moves inland: twelve (two Aswan, ten Troad) are known at Jerusalem; four at Tiberias and seventeen at Nazareth (all Troad); and eighteen at Hippos (five Aswan, thirteen Troad).[52] The largest concentration of imported materials in this region comes from Beth Shean in the Jordan Valley. A member of the Decapolis, this city was reshaped under the Antonine emperors and provided with a new monumental centre.[53] In this period, the local basalt was gradually replaced with the hard limestone from nearby Mount Gilboa while significant quantities of Prokonnesian marble were imported to supplement local supplies.[54] Prokonnesian was used extensively in the theatre and Williams-Thorpe and Henty also counted large numbers of granite columns: thirty-three Troad, sixteen Aswan, and three Kozak Dağ examples.[55] The range and quantity of imports compares well with those at Caesarea Maritima, and indeed most of these materials must have arrived here via this port, 70 km to the west along the road past Legio.[56]

While several of the major structures at Beth Shean were lavishly decked out in imported stones we should not overestimate the quantities of imports in inland Palestine: imported stones were still heavily concentrated in the port cities of Caesarea Maritima and Ascalon. Of the 174 white marble Corinthian capitals with a known provenance listed by Fischer, in fact, 145 (83 per cent) come from these two cities, 119 from Caesarea Maritima alone.[57] Furthermore,

[50] Pensabene 1997; M. L. Fischer 1990; 1995: 148–9; 1998: 254–5, 258; Pearl and Magaritz 1991; M. L. Fischer, Magaritz, and Pearl 1992: 214–16.
[51] On Tyre, Pensabene 1997: 286–93, figs. 6–13; on Byblos, 304–22; on Antioch-on-Kragos, Borgia 2010: 294–8.
[52] Williams-Thorpe and Henty 2000.
[53] Avi-Yonah 1962; Tsafrir and Foerster 1997: 86–99.
[54] For the 9 m columns of the pronaos of the temple, for example: Tsafrir and Foerster 1997: 89.
[55] Ovadiah and Turnheim 1994: 105, 122; Tsafrir and Foerster 1997: 89; M. L. Fischer 1998: 260–1; on the granites, Williams-Thorpe and Henty 2000: 166, table 3.
[56] Isaac and Roll 1982; Turnheim and Ovadiah 1996: 301–4.
[57] M. L. Fischer 1990: 83–97; M. L. Fischer and Grossmark 1996: 325–31.

Fig. 5.3. The Tetrapylon and its sixteen Aswan granite columns, Palmyra (photo: R. Raja).

only occasionally were large architectural elements in imported stone transported beyond the Jordan Valley. Troad granite shafts are found at Gadara in combination with Prokonnesian capitals and bases while Aswan granite was used at Jerash.[58] Here, though, they are used strategically, in the most prominent positions in the city, and in limited numbers; this far inland most coloured marbles were used for flooring and revetment only.[59] At Bosra, local limestone was used for the construction of the theatre, built or refurbished in the Severan period again, with white marble (probably Prokonnesian) used just for the capitals and bases in the *scaenae frons*.[60]

Palmyra bucks this trend. In addition to isolated Prokonnesian capitals, in the Sanctuary of Bel and along the colonnaded street, a series of monolithic columns, and fragments thereof, have been identified at Palmyra; these are in a variety of coloured stones, including *cipollino*, *pavonazzetto*, Aswan, and Troad granite.[61] As far as we can tell this material comes from two main structures—the Tetrapylon (Fig. 5.3) and the portico of the Baths of Diocletian, both major civic projects instigated by Sosianus Hierocles, the provincial governor.[62] Once again these imports were intended to contrast with the local

[58] Dodge 1990: 108–9; Pensabene 1997: 413–14.   [59] Pensabene 1997: 275.
[60] Pensabene 1997: 373–8.
[61] Dodge 1988*b*: 229.   [62] Browning 1979: 139, 184.

stones that formed the primary urban building materials in the city but the size of the monolithic columns in these complexes also set them above most other imports, which usually arrived in panel form suitable for wall revetment or paving.[63] The local granite and limestone quarries, 5 km and 10 km from Palmyra respectively, supplied the majority of the city's monumental architectural elements, as abandoned columns at them show.[64]

Numerous parallels can be drawn between urban development in Asia Minor and the Levant in the second and third centuries AD and these resulted in largely similar patterns of stone use, even if slight variations in emphasis can be noted. The main differences relate to the lack of local decorative stone sources in the Levant which reduced the range of options available to consumers, at inland sites most notably.

Case study 3: Spain

The available evidence from Spain, where contrasts can again be drawn between coastal and inland sites, largely confirms the picture in Asia Minor and the Levant. Local materials were used for most projects and imports from overseas are concentrated in the coastal zones. Differences, however, are also noticeable: first, the large-scale importation of stone in Spain begins as early as the Augustan period, earlier than in the Levant; second, Spain, like Asia Minor but unlike the Levant, has its own sources of decorative stones and these were widely quarried and moved around regionally in the Roman period.

The major cities of Spain, as elsewhere, made extensive use of their local stone resources in building and other carving projects and the clusters of quarries in the most urbanized areas of north-eastern Tarraconensis and Baetica are testament to the scale of demand from these centres. In these regions, even the most prestigious monumental projects were built primarily in local stone; at Tarragona, the Provincial Forum, the theatre, amphitheatre, and circus, for instance, were built in El Mèdol limestone.[65] Many of these structures were then faced in imported marble, though, primarily from Luna. Over 4,000 m^3 according to one estimate were used in the building of the Temple of Augustus and its surrounding complex at Tarragona in the Julio-Claudian and Flavian periods.[66] In the second century AD increasing quantities of coloured stones were also imported, alongside white marble from other sources: most notable are forty-five complete and fragmentary columns of

---

[63] Browning 1979: 139; Dodge 1988*b*: 218–23.

[64] Bounni and Al-As'ad 1987: 124–5; Bounni 1989: 258; Wielgosz et al. 2002: 389; Schmidt-Colinet 1990.

[65] Prada 1995; Mar and Pensabene 2010: 511.

[66] Mar and Pensabene 2010: 528–31; also Àlvarez et al. 2012.

Troad granite which were probably used in a Hadrianic restoration of the Provincial Forum, and seem to have been used with Prokonnesian capitals.[67] At Cartagena, meanwhile, imports of Luna marble begin in the Augustan period and the usual range of coloured stones of pan-Mediterranean origin were available here from the mid first century AD.[68]

Although large quantities of Luna marble and occasionally eastern materials were imported into eastern Spain for building from the Augustan period onwards, these imports were usually used in combination with decorative stones from closer sources. At Tarragona, for instance, the local Santa Tecla limestone was used for a range of projects, including revetment, small architectural elements, inscriptions, even sarcophagi; it was used in *opus sectile* floors in place of the similarly coloured *giallo antico*.[69] The decorative qualities of this material also led to it being used in Barcelona and throughout its territory, as well as up the Ebro to Zaragoza and south along the coast as far as Cartagena.[70] At the latter, imported Luna marble was used in conjunction with a whole series of Spanish stones, including the red travertine from Mula, used for columns in the theatre, as well as material from nearby Cabezo Gordo and Barxeta, but also from Espejón and Tortosa.[71] *Broccatello* from Tortosa was used all across north-eastern Spain, moved inland along the Ebro, as well as around the coast to sites like Italica, Corduba, and Munigua in the Guadalquivir Valley; it was used primarily for revetment, paving, and inscriptions.[72] Even though these materials were highly sought after, few of them made it as far as Rome. Only *broccatello* has been found for certain in the capital, and only then in the late third century AD, though fragments of the pinkish-yellow Buixcarró, quarried at Barxeta near Valencia, have been tentatively identified at the Villa of the Quintilii nearby.[73] Even in the nineteenth century, Lee notes that owing to 'difficulties in the matter of land carriage', Spanish and Portuguese stones, with the exception of *broccatello*, were rarely exported far.[74]

Further south the white marble quarried at Macael was used widely in Baetica, though perhaps not as much as the dolomitic marble from Mijas.[75] From the Julio-Claudian period Mijas marble began to be transported along the coast to the west and up the Guadalquivir to be used for architectural elements, statues, inscriptions, and revetment.[76] Recently these white marbles have even been identified at Thamusida in Morocco, showing the close ties

[67] Rodà, Pensabene, and Domingo 2012.   [68] Soler 2008: 136–7, fig. 4.
[69] Àlvarez et al. 2009b: 33–5; 2009c; Àlvarez, Gutiérrez, and Rodà 2010: 547–50.
[70] Lapuente, Turi, and Blanc 2009; Soler 2005.
[71] Soler 2008.
[72] Àlvarez, Gutiérrez, and Rodà 2010: 551–3.
[73] On the distribution of *broccatello*, Lazzarini 2004: 118, fig. 28; Gutiérrez 2011: 323–7; on Buixcarró, Àlvarez et al. 2009a: 26–31.
[74] Lee 1888: 71.
[75] Àlvarez et al. 2009a: 80–5.   [76] Beltrán and O. Rodríguez 2010: 558–61.

across the Straits of Gibraltar.[77] The major cities of the Guadalquivir Valley all enjoyed good access to the coast and the Mediterranean, and imported stones in some quantity, but they also relied heavily on regional quarries. Recent excavations at Seville have uncovered the typical range of pan-Mediterranean coloured stones, most used for revetment, but also significant additional quantities of material from Almadén de la Plata, Mijas, and the Portuguese quarries.[78] At Italica, the theatre uses white marble from both Almadén de la Plata and Mijas alongside a range of overseas imports, mainly used for paving and revetment but also some columns and large elements (like the perimeter wall at the front of the orchestra which is in *africano*).[79] However, it is possible that some of these apparent imports were actually brought from Almadén de la Plata and the Portuguese quarries, and even elsewhere in the Guadalquivir Valley where a variety of coloured stones were quarried: Rodríguez suggests that most of the columns were probably from these closer quarries but that two seem to be genuine *cipollino*, which would fit nicely with the altar from the site mentioning a gift of two *cipollino* columns for the theatre.[80] Among the architectural elements from Italica now in the archaeological museum in Seville, a series of Corinthian capitals in Almadén de la Plata and Estremoz marble have been identified, as well as a smaller number in Luna marble.[81] The fact that marble from Almadén de la Plata is also found at Corduba, Astigi, Munigua, and Baelo Claudia on the coast shows that this was a popular and probably relatively economical choice for cities in this region.[82]

Recent analysis of the granites employed in Baetica confirms the picture provided by these white marbles. Again imports from overseas are attested: three Troad granite shafts were used in the Casa de los Parajos at Italica, and at both Seville and Astigi columns in Troad, Kozak Dağ, Tyrrhenian, and Sardinian granites are visible in later structures and probably come from local Roman buildings.[83] At Seville, Astigi, and Munigua, however, Williams-Thorpe and Potts have identified column shafts in two sorts of Spanish granites, both possibly from the Guadalquivir Valley.[84]

Moving further inland access to overseas imports was more limited while transporting material even from regional quarries often required considerable outlay. This affected which stones were used for particular projects but it did not

---

[77] Akerraz et al. 2009.

[78] Amores, Beltrán, and González 2008; Beltrán and O. Rodríguez 2010: 569–70.

[79] Mayer and Rodà 1998: 231–4; and on other structures, León 1988: 64–79.

[80] O. Rodríguez 2008; on the coloured limestones quarried at Cabra and in the Sierra Elvira, see Cisneros 1989–90; on the altar from Italica, González 1991: 62–5, no. 392; Rodà 1997: 156–8, fig. 1.

[81] Rodà 1997: 177–9.

[82] Beltrán and O. Rodríguez 2010: 561–3; Àlvarez et al. 2009a: 24; on Munigua, Schattner and Ovejero 2008.

[83] Williams-Thorpe and Potts 2002: 183, table 3.

[84] Williams-Thorpe and Potts 2002: 183, table 3.

put customers off securing high-quality stones. The example of Merida is a case in point. Most building in this city, even monumental construction, was completed in the local granite.[85] This same material was also used for at least two columns in the Roman baths at nearby Alanje as well as one at Italica, confirming what has already been said about regional distribution patterns in Spain.[86] For finer carving projects and decorative elements at Merida white marble was brought in, from at least the middle of the first century AD, from the quarries around Estremoz to the west, with only occasional imports from further afield such as Luna.[87] Other imports were largely restricted to coloured marbles for revetment; *giallo antico*, *cipollino*, and *africano* are recorded. Elsewhere in Lusitania such overseas imports are scarce, in part because demand was met by high-quality white marble from Estremoz, violet and pink marble from Alconera, as well as several other materials.[88] Material from the former was used at Évora most notably, but also Conimbriga, Scallabis, and Pax Iulia.[89] Alconera marble is used at Badajoz (for column shafts) and Merida, and even as far away as Italica and Seville.[90]

This general picture of substantial local and regional movement of stone complemented with occasional imports is supported finally by the evidence from Segobriga, a site well over 200 km from the coast. The recent excavations of the forum have discovered large quantities of imported materials used for revetment and paving. Of these, however, only 27 per cent were imported from outside of Spain, with much of these coming from Luna (*bardiglio* was popular) and Saint-Béat.[91] The bulk of imports came instead from within Spain, especially from the coloured limestone quarries at Espejón, Tortosa (*broccatello*), and Barxeta, to the north and east, and the white marble quarries at Almadén de la Plata, to the south.[92] Almadén de la Plata marble was the only import used for anything larger than revetment or flooring panels. Initial results from Carranque, 36 km north of Toledo, indicate that this site, which seems to have been an important administrative centre in Late Antiquity, was richer in imports.[93] A range of Egyptian stones have been identified as well as substantial quantities of *giallo antico* and the most popular coloured stones. Most of this material was again used for revetment and paving though some columns have been found and this shows just how difficult it is to draw any

---

[85] Nogales, Lapuente, and De La Barrera 1999: 339; Pizzo 2010.

[86] Williams-Thorpe and Potts 2002: 183, table 3.

[87] Nogales, Lapuente, and De La Barrera 1999: 339–44; Àlvarez et al. 2009a: 66; Nogales, Rodrigues, and Lapuente 2008: 425–7.

[88] On marble from Trigaches and Viana, Mañas and Fusco 2008: 510–13.

[89] Àlvarez et al. 2009a: 60–7.

[90] Mañas and Fusco 2008: 506–10, fig. 2.

[91] Àlvarez, Cebrián, and Rodà 2008.

[92] Àlvarez, Cebrián, and Rodà 2008; also Àlvarez et al. 2009a: 26–31, 54–9.

[93] García-Entero and Vidal 2007.

strict dichotomy between inland and coastal sites; a lot of effort was taken to ornament the known structures at this site.

Case study 4: Gaul

Numerous parallels can be drawn between the picture observable in Spain and that in Gaul: there is again a reliance on local materials supplemented occasionally with high-quality stones of regional importance; the general chronology of imports is similar, as is the range of materials, and the extent to which they are moved far inland. Along the coast of southern Gaul, as in eastern Spain, the importation of white Luna marble is well attested from the Augustan period.[94] The majority of the shipwrecks from southern French waters were carrying cargoes of Luna marble, small and large, as we saw in Chapter 4. The patchy evidence from Narbonne shows that the typical coloured marbles were also used for revetment and paving, as one might expect.[95]

Despite navigational difficulties around the mouth of the Rhône many of the major cities of inland Narbonensis also contain large quantities of imports. Navigation in this area might have been eased by the major canal at the mouth of the river, the Fossa Mariana, though its trajectory is not certain. The port at its Mediterranean end, however, which is depicted on the Peutinger Table and described in the Antonine Itinerary, is possibly to be connected with the partially submerged ruins in the Golfe de Fos identified in the nineteenth century; blocks of marble, granite, and porphyry have been found at this site.[96] Some of these materials have been identified at Arles, such as the two Troad granite columns in the theatre, but larger quantities are known from Orange.[97] Most of these come from the Augustan theatre complex, where a range of columns in coloured stones are still visible.[98] Pentelic and Thasian were used alongside these columns suggesting that in the Augustan period Greece was the preferred source of white marble.[99] Although it employed vast quantities of imported materials this structure also usefully illustrates the dependence of local builders on nearby sources of stone: the core of this structure was built of locally quarried limestone which was then encased in marble. The famous Augustan triumphal arch is built from the same limestone, and the majority of the sculptural work at Orange is carved from it.[100]

---

[94] Braemer 1982: 84–5. On imports at Narbonne, Janon 1986: 41–6; Braemer 1984: 59.
[95] Braemer 1982: 84–5; 1984: 59; Janon 1986: 41–6.
[96] Lenthéric 1892: 476–9.
[97] Lazzarini 1987: 162.
[98] Antonelli and Lazzarini 2004: 12–15 identify *africano, pavonazzetto, settebasi, portasanta, cipollino, fior di pesco, giallo antico, greco scritto,* and granite from the Troad and Elba.
[99] Antonelli, Lazzarini, and Turi 2002.   [100] Bellet 1991: 11.

In southern Gaul, as in Spain, there are signs of a sizeable local traffic in ordinary building materials as well as high-quality decorative stones, especially from the Pyrenees.[101] Some of these local materials were moved by sea. Marseille drew on a number of coastal quarries (at La Couronne, Ponteau, and Lavéra) for building materials, even for massive projects like the Hellenistic city walls, as the Carry-le-Rouet shipwreck attests.[102] At Narbonne, local builders and carvers relied primarily on quarries accessible overland and by river in the direction of Béziers, notably at Nissan-lez-Ensérune, Lespignan, and Brégines.[103] However, various materials were imported from the central Pyrenees, presumably down through the Carcasonne Gap. In most cases these were used for veneer but, according to Thiers, the portico in front of the so-called 'Capitolium', the large temple on the hill of Les Moulinassès, is apparently built of columns of Pyrenean grey granite.[104] The fine limestone from the quarries at Bois des Lens, roughly 20 km north-west of Nîmes, is also found at Narbonne as well as at a range of other sites across Narbonensis. At Nîmes, a city which also had access to closer quarries, Bois des Lens limestone was the material of choice for all manner of sculptural and architectural projects as well as for minor domestic objects.[105] Slightly further afield, at Beaucaire on the Rhône, it is also used for a range of projects from high-end public to small-scale domestic. Beyond these locations, though, this limestone tends to be reserved for those projects at the higher end of the spectrum only: at Arles, Murviel-les-Montpellier to the south, and the villa at Gaujac to the north it is used for statuary and architectural carving, while at Narbonne, Fréjus, and Nice it is used only for architectural elements on the most prestigious projects.[106] Some of this limestone probably travelled south overland, presumably along the Via Domitia, but most of it to judge from its distribution was moved first to Beaucaire, and from there down the Rhône and then along the coast. The shipwreck, or series of shipwrecks, at 'Les Pierres', examined above, contains Bois des Lens limestone, in all probability on its way to Narbonne; this is the first time that this material has been identified at a shipwreck site (albeit one which is awkward to interpret).[107]

In central Gaul, though the Rhône allowed certain access with the Mediterranean, few large objects were moved up it. Consequently, at Lyon most projects were completed in locally quarried stones.[108] For fine carving projects, however, high-quality limestone was imported. It used to be thought that this was transported up the Rhône at great cost from the quarries at Glanum or

---

[101] Antonelli 2002: 267–9; Bedon 1984: 36.
[102] Tréziny 2009; on the Carry-le-Rouet shipwreck, Kainic 1986.
[103] Bedon 1984: 33; Gayraud 1981: 263.
[104] Braemer 1982: 84–5; Gayraud 1981: 263–4.
[105] Bessac 1996; Bedon 1984: 30–1.   [106] Bessac 1996: 62–3.
[107] Rauzier 2001: 47.   [108] Audin and Burnand 1975; Bedon 1984: 27–30.

Bois des Lens, but if this ever happened it only lasted a short while.[109] As Savay-Guerraz has shown, in the Julio-Claudian period high-quality limestone was brought down the Rhône from Franclens, near Seyssel, 152 km away.[110] Even when Franclens limestone was deemed unsuitable, the local carvers still looked upstream for alternatives, notably to the quarries at Fay and Villebois on the Rhône, and at Tournus on the Saône.[111] This is not to say that stone was never imported up the Rhône; Lyon was a provincial capital and its population was keen to engage with wider metropolitan fashions. Mediterranean marbles were imported from the Augustan period and are found in most of the structures that have been excavated in the city. These include column shafts in a range of coloured materials, which seem to increase in number from the Flavian period onwards, as well as entablature blocks, capitals, and pilasters in white marble. This limited picture should be fleshed out when the results of an on-going campaign of material analysis are known.[112] As the evidence stands, though, it would seem that the quantity of imports, and the number of columns especially, appear to be lower than on the coast, even if a wide range of materials are attested; most imported marble was used for revetment.[113] Perhaps the largest imported elements are the columns of Aswan granite now to be found in the church of St Martin at Ainay, which according to Fishwick might have come from the Hadrianic rebuilding of the so-called Altar of the Three Gauls.[114]

Although Lyon, as the capital of the three Gallic provinces and a colony, is likely to have been exceptional for socio-political reasons, the presence of imported marble at nearby Autun shows that the local population of this region was prepared to bear the exceptional costs of importing this material from the Mediterranean. Luna marble was used for various architectural elements at this site, including small columns, capitals, and bases from at least the Augustan period; a series of small Troad granite shafts have also been identified, though most of the remaining imports were used for revetment.[115] The largest of these imports is a column drum in Luna marble which is 1.11 m in diameter.[116] This is a large piece of stone and the column shaft for which it was intended would have been at least 10 m in height, but it is surely significant that this shaft was made up of drums rather than being monolithic;

---

[109] Bedon 1984: 28; Goodman 2007: 185.   [110] Savay-Guerraz 1997.

[111] Bedon 1984: 27–30.

[112] See Fellague 2009: 535–8; a preliminary report on this new work was presented by D. Fellague, F. Masino, H. Savay-Guerraz, and G. Sobrà at ASMOSIA X in Rome in June 2012.

[113] Braemer 1982: 87.

[114] Fishwick 1987: 105.

[115] Brunet-Gaston 2010; Brunet-Gaston et al. 2009: 413–14. Demand for Luna marble in this region is also revealed by the testament of S. Iulius Aquila from nearby Langres; see *CIL* XIII.5708.

[116] Brunet-Gaston et al. 2009: 412–13.

moving a monolithic shaft of such dimensions from Luna and then this far inland would have been enormously laborious and expensive.

Stone suppliers at Autun were clearly able to get their hands on Mediterranean stones, white and coloured, but they also drew on an extensive range of high-quality stones from the city's immediate territory. White limestone which could take a polish was brought from Gilly and Diou, 60 km away, and a pink variety from Pouillenay, 70 km away; the former was used for column drums in the city, the largest 1.10 m in diameter.[117] These materials were occasionally supplemented by coloured materials from Campan in the Pyrenees and Bourdeau in the Alps, which were used for small columns.[118] Other Pyrenean decorative stones which were imported into northern Gaul include the yellow breccia from the La Pène Saint-Martin quarry near Saint-Béat which has been identified at Paris, Meaux, and Autun.[119] Such was the local and regional demand for these materials that they rarely made it out of Gaul. In this sense the situation in antiquity probably reflects that nowadays: as Rich notes, more varieties of marble are quarried today in France than in any other country but 'much of the production has been absorbed and used within France and her exports have been less extensive than Italy's'.[120]

Case study 5: the Rhineland and Britain

Considering the likely costs involved in the transshipment of stone, it seems probable that the watershed between the rivers in Gaul which flowed into the Mediterranean and those which flowed into the Atlantic or English Channel represented a very real obstacle to the movement of stone. Either side of this dividing line, as elsewhere, local stones dominate architectural and sculptural projects.[121] However, moving north, away from the Mediterranean, it is clear that architectural imports become increasingly scarcer.[122] At both Metz and Trier a range of imported stone types are attested, but the majority used only as cut veneer.[123] For larger architectural elements at Trier basalt was imported from the Hohen Buche quarries and granite from Felsberg across the Rhine in the Odenwald.[124] Also imported across the Rhine was marble from Auerbach, used for the small columns found during excavations beneath the cathedral in Trier.[125] The sources of these stones were a long way from Trier, over 140 km overland or 280 km by river (and then 15 km overland), and after the mid third century AD were located outside of Roman territory. Despite this,

---

[117] Bouthier 2004; Brunet-Gaston et al. 2009: 410–12.
[118] Brunet-Gaston et al. 2009: 411.
[119] Blanc 1999: 250–1; Blanc and Blanc 2012: 488.
[120] Rich 1974: 227–8.   [121] J. Röder 1957; 1959; Mangartz 2000; Schaaff 2000.
[122] J. Röder 1970.   [123] Braemer 1982: 87–8; G. Röder 1992: 131.
[124] Mangartz 1998; 2000.   [125] G. Röder 1992: 132.

Felsberg granite was clearly deemed an important resource, perhaps because of its strikingly similarity to the famous granodiorite of Mons Claudianus.[126] Shipping it to Trier from across the Rhine might have been difficult but it was considerably easier than shipping it from Egypt or even the Mediterranean coast.

In the Rhineland, the imported stones that have been found are generally used for revetment, paving, or small architectural elements, like pilasters and pilaster capitals.[127] The desired decorative effect at these sites was instead usually completed in locally available coloured stones, especially the various polychrome stones of Belgium.[128] Imports were often used in conjunction with these local materials in *opera sectilia*, at the rural villas at Worringen, Froitzheim, and Jüchen, for example.[129] The primary materials used at all of the major urban centres in this region were quarried either locally or regionally and there was particular reliance on river transport to move these stones around.[130] The high-quality limestone of Norroy was imported to Bonn (250 km by river), Mainz (300 km away), Nijmegen (400 km away), and Strasbourg (450 km by river or 120 km by road).[131] In most cases the limestones that were imported from furthest away served only to supplement temporary local shortages: at Strasbourg, Trier, and Nijmegen the import of stone from far away stopped after the discovery of closer sources, even when these were of inferior materials.

In Britain, a similar picture is apparent: imports are again rare; local materials were always favoured; within the province, though, stone did move around in significant quantities.[132] In the south-east and London, in particular, where stones suitable for carving and construction were scarcer, material was brought in from elsewhere. The import of greensand (especially Kentish Rag) along the Medway and Thames is demonstrated by the Blackfriars 1 shipwreck in central London, but this material was also used around the coast of Kent.[133] Various limestones were also imported from the southern Cotswolds, and Barnack and Weldon in Lincolnshire, for prestigious projects which required high-quality material.[134] The monumental arch in London seems to have been built in Lincolnshire limestone, brought from 145 km distant, further than the materials used in any other comparable monuments

---

[126] G. Röder 1992: 131–2.

[127] On the Praetorium at Cologne, Kapitolstempel and Hafentempel at Xanten, see G. Fischer 1999: 677–9, 683.

[128] Groessens 1991: 67.   [129] G. Fischer 1999: 685.

[130] Bedon 1984: 38–52.   [131] Bedon 1984: 86.

[132] Blagg 1990: 47–8; Isserlin 1998: 125–55; Peacock and Williams 1999.

[133] J. H. Williams 1971a: 172; Marsden 1967: 36; 1994: 80–4, fig. 73–4; Stanier 2000: 13; Pearson 2006: 23–4.

[134] Hayward 2009: 86.

in the north-western provinces.[135] For decorative stones, suppliers to the London market turned to Purbeck in Dorset, where a brown–black limestone was quarried; so-called Purbeck Marble accounts for 58 per cent of the total decorative stones recovered from London from all contexts.[136] Stone was also imported from outside of the province, though generally its use was limited to revetment and paving. At least 71 per cent of these are of Mediterranean origin, the remainder coming from the Pyrenees.[137] Kentish Rag was fine for ordinary construction and various other materials could be imported for their decorative effect but the stoneworkers of London also required good stone for carving projects.

Parallels for the situation at London can be found elsewhere in the south of Britain. At Colchester, for instance, Painswick stone, from central Gloucestershire, was used, as was limestone from Lincoln.[138] A more striking series of regional imports is identifiable at the palatial villa at Fishbourne in West Sussex. Here, various local sandstones and limestones, all from easily accessible coastal quarries, were used for basic construction and supplemented with continental limestone for fine work. Calcaire Grossier, quarried in the Oise Valley, is used for column bases and capitals in the Neronian phase of the palace and alongside column drums of Caen limestone in the Flavian phase.[139] For much of south-east England quarries on the northern French coast were an easily accessible source of material; administrative boundaries were irrelevant in such matters. At Canterbury, for example, limestone from Marquise was used in the possible second-century AD temple, and the same stone is found at Richborough and Lympne, also in Kent.[140] In addition to these French stones imported decorative stones from further afield are found at Fishbourne in first-century contexts. As at London, these are limited to panel form, but unlike the situation in the capital, 97 per cent of the imported decorative stones at Fishbourne are of Pyrenean origin (*campan vert, campan rose*, and *pouillency rose*). Indeed the distribution of Pyrenean marbles within Britain suggests, as Pritchard notes, a point of entry somewhere along the southern coast and the date of these finds (first and early second century AD), therefore, might indicate the continued importance of Atlantic trading routes between southern Gaul and Britain in this period.[141] Despite this, at Fishbourne as at London, 82 per cent of the decorative stone used is Purbeck, often alongside burnt Kimmeridge shale, also quarried on the Isle of Purbeck.[142]

---

[135] Pearson 2006: 98; pers. comm. Stacey McGowen.
[136] Pritchard 1986: 185–6; Isserlin 1998: 143–4.
[137] Pritchard 1986; Williams and Peacock 2002: 136, table 1.
[138] Hayward 2009: 84–5.
[139] Hayward 2009: 87; also Cunliffe 1971: 1–4; Blagg 1990: 35.
[140] Blagg 1990: 38; Worssam and Tatton-Brown 1990; Hayward 2009: 87.
[141] Pritchard 1986: 187–8. On the question of Atlantic commerce, Cunliffe 1984: 4–5.
[142] Peacock and Williams 1999: 354, figs. 2–3.

So great was the demand for decorative stone in Britain that the coloured limestone of Purbeck appears to have been being quarried as early as the mid first century AD, very soon after the Claudian conquest.[143]

The impact of geography

A number of observations emerge from these studies. First, in all of the areas examined local materials, from no further than 20 km or so, are used for the bulk of building and carving projects. This, in practice, is true everywhere and considering the costs of transporting stone is unsurprising. However, the relative ease of importing material overseas meant that coastal cities well connected to their maritime hinterland did draw on quarries beyond their immediate vicinity, even for basic building materials. The examples of Tarragona, Marseille, and London have been mentioned but similarly located cities elsewhere did the same: the cities of eastern Africa Proconsularis, for instance, made use of the small sandstone and limestone quarries along the coast; consumers at Salona, in Dalmatia, imported substantial quantities of stone from the quarries on the nearby island of Brač.[144] Inland sites, by comparison, rarely looked more than 10 km away for sources of ordinary building stone.

A second point to note is the overwhelmingly coastal focus of the inter-regional distribution of stone. In every region examined the vast majority of imported materials are found in the major coastal cities, with few exceptions. The same pattern can be identified elsewhere. In North Africa, for example, the highest densities of imported materials are found in the coastal cities: Cyrene, Lepcis Magna, Sabratha, Carthage, Cherchel.[145] Although data from inland areas are more limited the example of Cuicul shows that, as elsewhere, there was probably more reliance on local and regional materials in these areas. The bulk of the decorative stones used here came from North African quarries: these include *giallo antico* which was used for some sculptural work and floor paving, *nero antico*, and *alabastro a pecorella* in which a series of small columns were carved.[146] The striped grey-and-white marble from the Cap de Garde and the white marble from Filfila were also used in some quantity at the site. Very little material was imported from overseas and

---

[143] Beavis 1970; Dunning 1968: 111.

[144] On the Tunisian quarries, Paskoff and Trousset 2004: 255–63; Younès and Ouaja 2009; Gaied, Younès, and Gallala 2010; Younès, Gaied, and Gallala 2012; on Brač, Bulić 1908: 86; Dworakowska 1983: 21–2.

[145] On Cyrenaica, Pensabene 2006; 2007*b*; on Tripolitania, Ward-Perkins 1993: 89; Pensabene 2001*a*; 2008: 49; on Carthage, Hurst and Roskams 1984: 218; Bullard 1978*b*; and on Cherchel, Pensabene 1982; 1986.

[146] Antonelli, Lazzarini, and Cancelliere 2010: 577–81.

what was mostly ended up as revetment: the only sizeable imports were the six columns in Kozak Dağ granite used for the so-called Temple of Venus.[147]

When it comes to the inland distribution of stone one of the major points that can be drawn from the above discussion is the importance of river networks. The significance of the Guadalquivir, the Rhône, Saône, Moselle, and Rhine for the movement of both ordinary building stone and decorative stones is clear. The Nile obviously performed an essential role in Egypt.[148] The Danube appears to have been less important for the movement of stone; very few of the imported materials found in abundance in the cities of the Black Sea coast moved upriver.[149] This might in part be explained by the difficulties associated with navigating the river, especially through the so-called Iron Gates, which would have curtailed the import of Mediterranean stones into Moesia Superior or Pannonia.[150] However, tributaries of the Danube, notably the Drava and the Sava, were certainly used for the transport of white marble from the Gummern and Pohorje quarries, from at least the first century AD.[151] Gummern marble is found at Flavia Solva, in the western Pannonian cities of Poetovio, Savaria, and Scarbantia, as well as the Danubian cities of Cetium, Lauriacum, and nearby Ovilavis.[152] At Virunum, Teurnia, and Aguntum, close to the quarries, it was used in conjunction with marble from the quarries at Tentschach, Spitzeloften, and Kraig for architectural and sculptural projects. In western Pannonia, Gummern marble was often used alongside Pohorje marble, though this never seems to have reached the Danube in the same quantities.[153]

Finally, though topography obviously played a key role in determining the cost of transporting materials, which directly affected where they were used for what, this does not mean that consumers at inland sites without river access simply absented themselves from the stone trade. Rather they engaged with wider fashions in a different way from their coastal contemporaries. Three different practices can be noted by way of demonstration. For a start, proportionally more imported stone was used for revetment or flooring as opposed to large architectural elements at inland sites than coastal ones. Even if the material for these panels was imported in block form, cutting it up into thin panels was an effective way of maximizing its surface area: as Pliny the Elder remarks, 'whoever first discovered how to cut marble and carve up luxury into many portions was a man of misplaced ingenuity'.[154] As we saw in Chapter 4,

---

[147] Antonelli, Lazzarini, and Cancelliere 2010: 577; also Dessandier et al. 2012.
[148] On the loading quays at the Aswan quarries, J. Röder 1965.
[149] Bordenache 1960; 1969a; 1969b; Ward-Perkins 1981: 249–51.
[150] Pers. comm. Dragana Mladenović.
[151] Djurić 1997; 2005; Djurić and Müller 2009; Djurić et al. 2006.
[152] Djurić and Müller 2009: 122, figs. 10–11; Gabler 1996: fig. 1.
[153] Djurić and Müller 2009: 121, fig. 9.
[154] Pliny the Elder XXXVI.51 (trans. D. E. Eichholz).

however, panels for revetment and flooring were also transported precut, light and easy to move.[155] Alongside this practice, one finds that large architectural elements, when they are used at sites inland, tend to be more restricted to the most prestigious public buildings than at comparable coastal sites: the theatres at Beth Shean, Bosra, and Orange, and the baths at Sardis and Palmyra are all examples of prominent structures which use imported stone in cities where they are otherwise scarce. The aim was to display what had been imported as prominently as possible. However, the most effective way that inland sites, but also coastal sites far from the best-known sources of decorative stones, could engage with wider fashions for stone use was simply to find alternative materials. As we have seen, a wide range of decorative stones were quarried across southern Spain, in the Pyrenees, in Belgium, and even in Britain which were rarely used beyond the region in which they were quarried. These materials are referred to in the modern literature as 'substitution marbles' because they were often coloured like the more famous eastern stones, but really they were just high-quality local equivalents and their exploitation is an important result of western customers' engagement with the wider stone trade.[156]

Building contractors and the selection of stone

Many of these observable distribution patterns can be explained on economic grounds, particularly in relation to transport logistics. Others, however, cannot be so easily explained: why was Luna marble, for example, so popular even in areas where there were local alternatives, such as the marbles quarried at Saint-Béat, Mijas, Macael, or Filfila in Algeria—a material described by Ward-Perkins in his private notes as 'the Luna marble of North Africa'?[157] Why did consumers in southern Asia Minor favour Prokonnesian marble over other alternatives, such as Thasian, Ephesian, even Pentelic? Why were the grey granites of Sardinia, Corsica, Elba, Giglio, and Nicotera not used more intensely and even overlooked in favour of eastern granites at various sites in Spain, Gaul, and North Africa?[158] Why do we find Pentelic marble used alongside Prokonnesian in the major architectural projects of the Antonine and Severan periods at Carthage, Sabratha, and Lepcis Magna?[159]

---

[155] For examples from the Torre Sgarrata and Porto Nuovo shipwrecks, see Chapter 4: Direct and indirect commerce (p. 134).

[156] Mar 2008: 181; Cisneros 2010; also Pensabene 2001*b*: 48–51.

[157] BSR Ward-Perkins Archive, WP-1, Box XXXVIII.

[158] On the distribution of the granites from Sardinia, see Williams-Thorpe and Rigby 2006; and on other granites, Williams-Thorpe 2008; on Nicotera granite, Antonelli, Lazzarini, and Cancelliere 2010.

[159] Ward-Perkins 1993; Pensabene 2001*a*; Bianchi 2009.

We can only speculate on the reasons for this, but three factors deserve consideration. First, in some of these cases the preference for one material over another can be explained in terms of the size of the outcrop and the infrastructure in place. Not every quarry had the personnel or facilities to deal with a large order of material and it took time to set these up; geological factors sometimes also restricted the sizes of blocks available at certain quarries. In addition to these practical issues, however, the symbolic value of different materials needs to be appreciated. Luna and Prokonnesian marble, as well as other high-quality marbles, are specifically mentioned by name in the epigraphic record and contemporary poetry while those from Saint-Béat, Mijas, Macael, and Filfila are not.[160] Luna, Prokonnesian, Pentelic, Parian, and Dokimeian marble were the best-known decorative stones, famed for their quality, the status of which derived in part from their widespread use in imperial projects. Finally, alongside questions of practicality and taste, we also need to consider the way in which these materials were supplied and the personnel involved, as Pensabene has stressed repeatedly.[161]

Ward-Perkins argued on several occasions that it is possible to identify 'some commercial mechanism linking the import of fine materials with that of the craftsmen needed to work them'.[162] Not every city had access to high-quality architects and building contractors (*redemptores*) who could oversee major building projects. Personnel as well as materials had to be moved around. On a detailed fourth-century AD inscription from Madaurus in Numidia a *curator* records his refurbishment of the local baths for which he imported both a range of marbles and foreign workers: *exquisitis diversorum co[lorum marmoribus], artificibus quoque peregrinis adductis*.[163] There is good evidence to indicate that overseas materials and workers often came as a package. In the fourth- and third-century BC building accounts of the Sanctuary of Asklepios at Epidauros, teams of Athenian carvers were employed to both supply and work the Pentelic marble needed, while Argive masons were hired when their local stone was used.[164] In the second century AD, teams of high-quality workers with good access to the Prokonnesian quarries can be identified on stylistic grounds: in the eastern Mediterranean, most notably, strong stylistic similarities in architectural decoration can be noted across projects at Pergamon, in Pamphylia, and all along the coast of the Levant, where Prokonnesian was the dominant import.[165]

In the western Mediterranean, by comparison, it was probably to Rome that wealthy commissioners looked for skilled workers who could also supply the necessary materials, especially in the first century AD. At Cherchel, where the monumentalization of the city under Juba II was achieved almost entirely in

---

[160] See Chapter 2: 'Foreign rocks' (pp. 15–16).
[161] For a summary, Pensabene 2002*b*: 60–7.
[162] Ward-Perkins 1980*b*: 60.   [163] *ILAlg* 1.2102; also Fagan 1999: 278, no. 131.
[164] Burford 1969: 155–6.   [165] Ward-Perkins 1980*b*: 63; Pensabene 1997; 2006: 237.

Luna marble, Pensabene has demonstrated that carvers from Italy were involved.[166] While it is possible that the material was picked first and then these workers employed to carve it, it seems more likely that the whole project was turned over to contractors from Italy who then used the material most familiar to them and most easily accessed. Cherchel was not a one-off: strong stylistic similarities can be noted between architectural elements carved in Luna marble across a range of sites in southern Gaul, eastern Spain, and elsewhere in western North Africa in the late first century BC and first century AD which seem to indicate the presence of contractors from Italy—either from Rome or perhaps Luna itself.[167]

In all of these areas these contractors could have drawn on local or regional white marble sources but they preferred to use material that they were experienced in handling from quarries where they had established contacts; they had to be confident that the material that they got hold of was of the right quality and could be supplied in the necessary quantities. This might also explain the widespread distribution of Troad granite in the second century AD, even in the western Mediterranean where there were local alternatives. The fact that Troad granite columns are usually used alongside Prokonnesian bases and capitals has been remarked upon by Dodge and may well result from the fact that the contractors responsible enjoyed similar access to the Troad quarries as they did the Prokonnesian ones; they had to effectively sail past the former, and the nearby harbour at Alexandria Troas, on their way south from the latter.[168]

Over time expertise could have been transferred, and it might have been possible for several specialists to be brought in to train local workers, but at least initially expertise in areas lacking local marble sources had to have been imported.[169] On the largest projects different groups of craftsmen probably worked alongside each other. For the construction of the colonnaded street at Perge, Heinzelmann has suggested that various teams were used, some local and some from further afield who had direct access to the required marble and granite sources.[170] A lot has been written about the fact that the major Severan projects at Lepcis Magna use both Prokonnesian and Pentelic marble and apparently also workers from both Athens and Asia Minor.[171] These were not specialist teams of imperial workers as far as we can tell but simply the best available: in fact, this combination of Prokonnesian and Pentelic is also found in the Hadrianic Baths at Lepcis Magna and in major buildings at Sabratha and Carthage from the Antonine period.[172]

---

[166] Pensabene 1982; 2004.   [167] Pensabene 1986: 297, 299; 1995; 2004.

[168] Dodge 1988*a*: 75; 1990: 108; also Pensabene 1994: 306, 311.

[169] Barresi 2003: 89–91.

[170] Heinzelmann 2003: 216.

[171] Ward-Perkins 1951: 93–4; 1980*b*: 33; 1993: 98–9; Pensabene 2001*a*; Bianchi 2009.

[172] Bianchi 2009: 46–55; Pensabene 1994: 284; 2002*b*: 45, 50, 62.

While we can often draw connections between the employment of certain teams of workers and the use of specific materials it needs to be noted that this was not a rule. Where suitable local workers existed who could handle imported materials they were used. A good example of this is the Severan theatre at Beth Shean. This complex employed substantial quantities of Prokonnesian marble for its architectural elements and both Troad and Aswan granite columns. Unlike so many other projects of this period in the Levant, however, Ovadiah and Turnheim have demonstrated convincingly that the architectural decoration was carved by local workers, not the teams from Asia Minor who seem to have handled so many of the coastal projects.[173] We should not assume, then, that Prokonnesian marble was always carved by workers brought from Asia Minor. At the same time, as Pensabene has shown, carvers from Asia Minor working overseas sometimes employed Pentelic rather than the usual Prokonnesian.[174] There was a certain flexibility to which materials were deemed right, and most easily acquired, for particular projects.

SARCOPHAGUS DISTRIBUTION AND MATERIALS FOR STATUARY

The case studies discussed above concentrated on stone use in architectural contexts only. The evidence provided by sarcophagi and statuary is deliberately treated separately. While the distribution of these objects was similarly affected by the practicalities of transportation, shaped by geography, both sarcophagi and statues were bought, used, and supplied quite differently from the raw materials for building.

Certain areas of overlap between the distribution of sarcophagi, statues, and architectural elements can be noted: since sarcophagi were big, heavy objects it makes sense that their distribution largely follows the pattern visible for similarly sized architectural elements, for instance. However, sarcophagi and statues were also produced and used in different ways from architectural elements and this affected their distribution. Most sarcophagus and statue producers, as will be discussed in Chapters 7 and 8, used their local quarries for the raw materials they needed, and in some cases these were of a high quality: as a result, the Attic sarcophagus workshops used Pentelic, the Asiatic ones Dokimeian, and the Aphrodisian workshops their local marble for both sarcophagi and statuary. Workshops which needed to import stone from further afield tended to look to the same quarries as their colleagues in the

[173] Ovadiah and Turnheim 1994: 108–11, 121–2.   [174] Pensabene 2002*b*: 65.

building industry: Prokonnesos in the East, Luna in the West. However, both sarcophagi and statues were often moved long distances part- or fully finished. These were products, not raw materials and were valued by the customers who bought them according to their form and decoration rather than just the quality of their materials. This explains why Attic sarcophagi, exported as near-finished products, were imported from Athens by customers all around the Mediterranean who would never have considered using Pentelic marble for building, and why Asiatic sarcophagi reached a wide market when Dokimeian white marble is used only sparingly for construction outside Phrygia.

One other important difference to note between these other objects and architectural elements is that while the latter had to be bought in some quantity to be useable, and required craftsmen who could handle and erect them, sarcophagi and statues could be bought singly, perhaps even finished, as one-off investments. Though expensive, sarcophagi were much less substantial investments than buildings adorned with imported materials. This helps to explain why customers at inland sites in the Levant and the north-western provinces, even as far from the Mediterranean as Britain, were prepared to import sarcophagi even when they could not (or would not) spend the sums required to import material for building. This was even more true, of course, for statues, which could be imported in a much wider range of sizes and forms.

Sarcophagus distribution in the East

To what extent do the patterns of stone use observed in architectural contexts in the eastern provinces, with their distinct focus on coastal areas, match those observable for sarcophagi? The short answer is that there are significant areas of overlap but also several noticeable divergences. One of the main differences between the inter-regional distribution of sarcophagi and material for architectural projects is their date: the sarcophagus trade reaches its peak in the late second and early third centuries AD, later than the trade in architectural materials.[175] Nevertheless, comparisons can be made.

First, in those coastal areas where a good local white marble source existed, as at Ephesos, this was used for sarcophagi.[176] In coastal areas where local white marble sources did not exist, Prokonnesian was the favoured import (Fig. 5.4): concentrations of sarcophagi in Prokonnesian marble can be highlighted around the Propontis, along the western Black Sea coast, in Pamphylia, all along the coast of the Levant, and at Alexandria.[177] At Tyre, 50–75 per cent

[175] M. L. Fischer 1998: 212.   [176] Asgari 1977: 343–5.

[177] Ward-Perkins 1992e: 82, fig. 58; on Prokonnesian garland sarcophagi, Asgari 1977: 355, fig. 53; on their distribution in the Black Sea, Conrad 2007; in the Levant, Ward-Perkins 1969; Koch 1989; Gersht and Pearl 1992; and at Alexandria, Adriani 1961: 19–31, figs. 12–82.

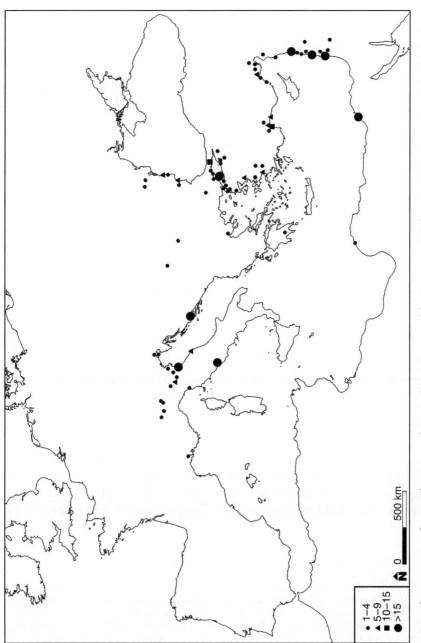

Fig. 5.4. Distribution map of sarcophagi carved in Prokonnesian marble (sources: Gabelmann 1973; Asgari 1977; Ward-Perkins 1992*e*: fig. 58).

of the imported sarcophagi, between fifty-four and eighty-one, are in Prokon-nesian marble.[178] Only in the northern Aegean, at somewhere like Thessaloniki, do we find Thasian marble being used as an imported raw material for sarcophagus production in the same way.[179] In practice, the same consider-ations that made Prokonnesian, and also Thasian, popular for building—that is, the accessibility and size of the quarries—also attracted sarcophagus producers.

In none of these regions, however, were these local products in Prokon-nesian marble the only option. In Pamphylia, Asiatic sarcophagi in Doki-meian were popular; this region contains the highest density of these sarcophagi outside of Phrygia (Fig. 5.5).[180] Since Dokimeian marble is found in architectural contexts in this region one might be tempted to assume that these materials were supplied through similar channels, but these sarcophagi are also found at sites were Dokimeian marble is absent from buildings: two examples are known from Tyre and Caesarea Maritima respectively, a third from inland Beth Shearim in the Levant.[181] The most widely distributed sarcophagi in these coastal areas, however, are Attic, carved in Pentelic marble (Fig. 5.6). These are found all around the coasts of southern Greece, southern Asia Minor, and the Levant, as well as in particular concentrations elsewhere, such as Ephesos, Thessaloniki, and Cyrene.[182] Again, these are areas where Pentelic marble is rare in architec-tural contexts.[183]

Like large architectural elements, few sarcophagi were moved far inland in Asia Minor. Attic sarcophagi are known from Pergamon, Bursa, and Termes-sos but that is it; indeed Waelkens notes that the example from Termessos, a fragment, is the only sarcophagus in Pisidia certainly imported from over-seas.[184] This gap at the upper end of the sarcophagus market was filled instead by Asiatic sarcophagi from Dokimeion. A *klinē* lid and the fragment of a chest have been found at Sagalassos, perhaps the largest imported objects at the site, and other fragments are known from Termessos and Antioch-in-Pisidia.[185] Only the very wealthiest could afford these objects, however, and most of the residents of inland Asia Minor who could afford sarcophagi at all bought locally. Huge numbers of sarcophagi were produced to meet demand from

---

[178] Chéhab 1984; 1985.   [179] Stefanidou-Tiveriou 2009.

[180] Waelkens 1982a: 9, pl. 31.

[181] Ward-Perkins 1969; Gersht and Pearl 1992: 225, 232, fig. 20; Avigad 1976: 167.

[182] On the distribution of Attic sarcophagi, Giuliano 1962; Ward-Perkins 1992e: 83, fig. 59.

[183] Though on the early use of Pentelic at Cyrene, Attanasio et al. 2006.

[184] Dodge and Ward-Perkins 1992: 83, fig. 59; Waelkens et al. 2002: 374. The fragment in question is now in Vienna; Giuliano 1962: no. 270; Koch and Sichtermann 1982: 544.

[185] Sagalassos: Waelkens 1982a: 94 (no. 163), 100 (no. 219); Termessos: Waelkens 1982a: 70 (no. 56), 87 (no. 115), 101 (no. 223); Antioch-in-Pisidia: Waelkens 1982a: 44–6 (no. 4, 7, 12, 15), 30 (no. 38, 42), 92 (no. 148), 101 (no. 226).

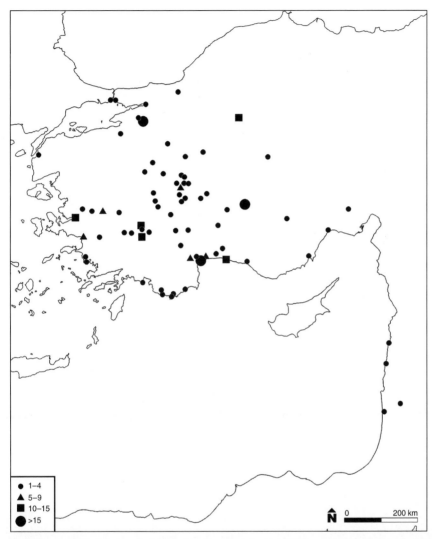

Fig. 5.5. Distribution map of Asiatic sarcophagi (sources: Ward-Perkins 1969; Avigad 1976; Waelkens 1982*a*; Gersht and Pearl 1992; Özgan 2003).

this sector at Hierapolis and Aphrodisias but a particular form of garland sarcophagus has also been documented in the Hermos Valley.[186] These sarcophagi supplied those customers who in coastal cities were increasingly

---

[186] Vanhaverbeke and Waelkens 2002 (Hierapolis); Işik 2007; Öğüş 2010 (Aphrodisias); Asgari 1979 (Hermos Valley).

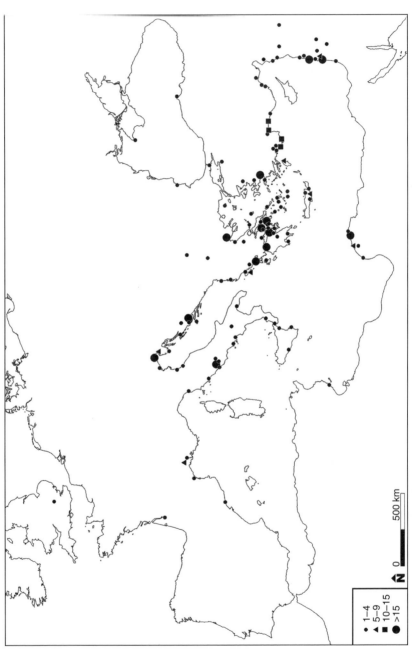

Fig. 5.6. Distribution map of Attic sarcophagi (sources: Giuliano 1962; Ward-Perkins 1992e: fig. 59).

turning to Prokonnesos if their local workshops could not satisfy them. It is very striking that when the distribution maps of different sarcophagus types are combined Attic sarcophagi and those carved in Prokonnesian marble dominate the coastal zones of Asia Minor while inland local varieties and Dokimeian sarcophagi predominate.

Several sarcophagi carved in Prokonnesian marble have also been found in Moesia Superior, showing that they were transported even to areas where imports in architectural contexts are scarce. Two fully carved garland sarcophagi in Prokonnesian marble datable to the late second century AD, as well as a third plain-sided piece, also probably Prokonnesian, have been found at Ratiaria, alongside a number of local limestone examples.[187] The well-known garland sarcophagus from Viminacium, which has an unusual *klinē* lid, is also carved in Prokonnesian marble.[188] The only other imported sarcophagi in Moesia Superior come from the south of the province, where at least three small fragments of Attic sarcophagi are known from Naissus.[189] This city was well connected by road to Ratiaria, less than 100 km distant, but the fact that another fragment of an Attic sarcophagus comes from Skopje, might indicate that these pieces were transported overland from the south rather than along the Danube.[190]

Interestingly, sarcophagi were also imported inland in the Levant, in a way which they were not in Asia Minor. Single sarcophagi in Prokonnesian marble are known from Beth Shearim and Damascus, and a Metropolitan sarcophagus which might also be carved in Prokonnesian marble has been found at Turmus Aya, 37 km north of Jerusalem.[191] Otherwise most of the sarcophagi from inland sites are Attic: these include examples from Beth Shean, Arethusa, Bosra, and Amman, seven fragmentary pieces from Beth Shearim, and four from Palmyra.[192] This relatively large number of imported Attic sarcophagi from inland sites must again be explained by the fact that there were no local high-quality alternatives. There were lower quality alternatives, in limestone, which probably explains why Prokonnesian sarcophagi were rarely imported inland, but there were no local equivalents to the Dokimeian sarcophagi which took over from Attic sarcophagi in inland Asia Minor.

---

[187] Filow 1910: 8–16, figs. 3–4; Atanasova 1972: 141–52, figs. 7–11; Mócsy 1970: 104; 1974, 237–8; also Velkov 1966.

[188] Vulić 1905: 10–12 (no. 37); Tomović 1991.

[189] Kanitz 1892: 76, fig. 52; Vulić 1941–8: 109 (no. 238), 117 (no. 259).

[190] Vulić 1931: 33–4 (no. 67).

[191] Avigad 1976: 167; Koch 1989.

[192] Avigad 1976: 167; Koch 1989: 173–5; Ward-Perkins 1992e: 83, fig. 59; Wielgosz et al. 2002: no. 12, 14, 17, 22. On locally produced sarcophagi at Palmyra, Schmidt-Colinet and al-Asʿad 2007.

Sarcophagus distribution in the West

Although the large-scale trade in sarcophagi begins in the West in the early second century AD, reaching its zenith in the early to mid third century AD, the numbers of imported sarcophagi are far fewer than they are in the East. The only exception to this rule is in the Adriatic, where large numbers have been recovered from Salona, Aquileia, and Ravenna. At Salona the majority were carved in limestone, from Brač and several of the mainland quarries nearby, but the local producers also used Prokonnesian marble for at least fifty sarcophagi.[193] Producers at Aquileia followed suit, using local Aurisina limestone with Prokonnesian marble for their high-end pieces.[194] At both sites, however, large numbers of Attic sarcophagi (most fragmentary) have been found and the discovery of others at nearby Zadar, Pula, Trieste, Torcello, Ravenna, and Rimini shows that this was the most popular import in the region.[195] However, consumers in this region were apparently well aware of all of the available options: three or four fragments of Asiatic sarcophagi have been recovered from Salona and its surroundings, while a pair of Ephesian-style garland sarcophagi are known from Aquileia.[196] To the east, at Ravenna, Prokonnesian sarcophagi are more numerous but mostly date from a period following the decline of the Attic workshops.[197] Sarcophagi were certainly being carved in this region in Prokonnesian marble in the second and third centuries AD, however, as shown by the numerous examples now in Modena, Ferrara, Bologna, and Milan, most of which Gabelmann attributes to a hypothetical Ravenna workshop.[198] In comparison, sarcophagi in Prokonnesian marble are scarcer in southern and western Italy, except at Rome, where substantial quantities of Prokonnesian, Luna, Thasian, and even Pentelic marble were imported for sarcophagus production; and though few sarcophagi from Campania and Ostia have been analysed many of these are also probably Prokonnesian marble.[199] Attic sarcophagi were also popular in this region, though again they are found in more limited numbers than further east.

Most sarcophagi found to date in both Spain and Gaul were carved in local materials but when imports are found they are concentrated in the major cities on or close to the coast. In Spain, the most common imports are Metropolitan sarcophagi, though overall imported sarcophagi are much scarcer than in

---

[193] Cambi 1998: 169.   [194] Gabelmann 1973: 79–83.

[195] Ward-Perkins 1992e: 83, fig. 59; on Salona, Cambi 1988; 1998: 169; Ciliberto 1996; 1998; 2007; also Ward-Perkins 1963.

[196] Cambi 1998: 169; Brusin 1941: 51–6, fig. 22.

[197] Gabelmann 1973: 91–191; Kollwitz and Herdejürgen 1979.

[198] For example, Gabelmann 1973: no. 57, 59–62, 65, 68–72, 74–8, 80–2, 86–90, 93, 95, 98, 99.

[199] On the Campanian producers, Valbruzzi 1998; on Ostia, Bonanno Aravantinos 2008; for more on the materials used for sarcophagus production at Rome, Chapter 7: Sourcing raw materials: the evidence from the quarries (p. 260).

the East.[200] The highest concentration of finds comes from Tarragona and its territory, the nearby cities of Barcelona and Girona; most of these date between the Hadrianic period and the late third century AD.[201] Two Attic sarcophagi, including the one from the Punta del Mora shipwreck, are also known from Tarragona, both datable to the early to mid third century AD.[202] Later, in the fourth or fifth centuries AD, Rodà has shown that a limited number of limestone sarcophagi were imported from Carthage.[203] Although most of these imports, of all periods, are concentrated in the north-eastern coastal region, isolated Metropolitan sarcophagi are also known from far inland: from Husillos and Covarrubias.[204] All three could have been brought up the Ebro from the east, or even the Duero from the west. Fragments of a marble sarcophagus, apparently carved in Parian marble and probably a Metropolitan product, have also been found at Carranque, a site which, as we have seen, was remarkably rich in imported decorative stones considering its location.[205] The picture is largely the same in Baetica, where Metropolitan sarcophagi are again the most common imports. Here, though, the largest concentration of them—albeit just twenty fragments—is found at Corduba (and nearby Madinat Al-Zahra, where a lot of material from Corduba was reused), the provincial capital which was accessible from the coast via the Guadalquivir.[206] Interestingly, sarcophagi are much scarcer at the large cities of Seville and Italica until the fourth or fifth centuries AD.[207] To the west, in Lusitania, two whole Metropolitan sarcophagi, a lid, and several other fragments have been found at coastal sites around Lisbon.[208] One complete Metropolitan sarcophagus and two fragments have been recovered from near Évora, showing that these objects were imported inland, but only a handful of fragments are known from Merida.[209]

In southern Gaul, most sarcophagi were again carved in local limestone, though there is some evidence that Pyrenean marble was used occasionally; Pyrenean white marble was certainly used across this region for sarcophagus production in Late Antiquity.[210] Only at a handful of sites have a sizeable

---

[200] On the distribution of Metropolitan sarcophagi in the West, see Koch 1977: 255–69.

[201] Claveria 1998: 139–43; 2001: 3–39; 2007: 198–200.

[202] Claveria 1998: 140–1, pl. 72.6–7.

[203] Rodà 1998: 158–61.

[204] García y Bellido 1949: nos. 249, 276; Claveria 2007: 199, fig. 1.

[205] García-Entero and Vidal 2007: fig. 5.

[206] Beltrán 2001: 94–100; 2007: 234–40; and on the examples from Corduba specifically, Beltrán, García, and P. Rodríguez 2006: 164–74. On sarcophagi in local stones in Baetica, see P. Rodríguez 2001.

[207] Beltrán, García, and P. Rodríguez 2006: 72–92.

[208] García y Bellido 1949: nos. 256, 260, 269–70; De Souza 1990: nos. 136, 139–40, 158.

[209] On the finds from near Évora, De Souza 1990: no. 69–71; on Merida, García y Bellido 1949: nos. 266, 425; Claveria 2007: 201.

[210] Immerzeel 1995; Mérel-Brandenburg, Blanc, and Blanc 2009: 423–5; Antonelli 2002: 267; Rodà 2001: 63–5.

number of imports been found. These include Arles, where Gaggadis-Robin has identified two whole and six fragmentary sarcophagi in Prokonnesian marble, two whole and fourteen fragmentary Attic sarcophagi, and five whole and twenty-three fragmentary Metropolitan examples; recent archaeometric analysis even suggests that at least one sarcophagus at Arles is carved in Pyrenean marble.[211] Two Metropolitan sarcophagi are known from Narbonne and the same number from Marseille, while Attic sarcophagi have been identified at Narbonne and Nîmes.[212] To the north, an even smaller number of imported sarcophagi are known, though as in the Levant it is again clear that they were brought further inland than large architectural elements. At least five imported sarcophagi have been found at Lyon, all Metropolitan products, while further examples have been recorded at Autun, Paris, and several sites in the valley of the Seine.[213] These objects were certainly also transported over the watershed to the north: a complete Metropolitan sarcophagus, and several unassociated fragments, have been found at Cologne, and further fragments have been catalogued at Trier and Mannheim.[214] Several sarcophagi in imported materials have been found in Britain on the other hand: two strigillated Metropolitan sarcophagi, from Englefield Green (Surrey) and Clapton (London), and a possible Attic sarcophagus from a mausoleum in Welwyn (Hertfordshire).[215] To stress how exceptional these finds are: these three sarcophagi are probably the largest single pieces of stone imported into Britain in the Roman period. Most sarcophagi were carved in local limestone, albeit stone that was sometimes moved long distances: sarcophagi have been found in London carved in limestone from Lincolnshire and examples in Essex seem to have been carved in material from Oxfordshire.[216]

Materials for statuary

The final category of material to bring into this discussion are other carving projects, and in particular free-standing statuary. Three key points can be made about the distribution of statues in imported materials: first, they are found at a wider range of sites than architectural elements or sarcophagi in similar materials; second, where these materials have been tested it is clear that specific materials were often used for statuary that were not used for other

---

[211] Gaggadis-Robin 2005: nos. 1–53, 67, 69, 71, 83–4, 92; Gaggadis-Robin et al. 2009.

[212] Koch 1977: 258–61; Koch and Sichtermann 1982: 268, fig. 4; Ward-Perkins 1992e: 83, fig. 59.

[213] On Lyon, Espérandieu 1910: no. 1770–5; on the finds from other sites, Koch 1977: 258–61.

[214] Deckers and Noelke 1980: 163–5, fig. 8; Koch 1977: 257–8; Koch and Sichtermann 1982: 300–1. On the locally produced sarcophagi of the Rhineland, Rodenwaldt 1942.

[215] Toynbee 1964: 210–11; Rook, Walker, and Denston 1984: 149–60; also Russell 2010: 3.

[216] Russell 2010: 4–6; also Dimes 1980: 198–200; Toynbee 1964: 211.

objects; and thirdly, raw materials were drawn from a huge variety of sources for statue production.

In the East, the major coastal and inland centres containing large quantities of decorative stones in other contexts all also contain statues, but so too do other centres, such as Samaria-Sebaste, Beth Shearim, Jerash, Bosra, and Amman.[217] At the Sanctuary of Pan at Caesarea Philippi in the Golan Heights at least twenty-eight marble statues have been found.[218] The majority of these statues depicted deities or members of the imperial household and were clearly intended to contrast with the locally produced alternatives that were the normal medium of display. This is especially clear at Palmyra, where the thirty or so statues in imported materials contrasted sharply in subject and style with the locally produced carvings.[219] In the West, too, statues in imported materials have been recovered from certain sites where marble architectural elements are rare, such as Trier, Metz, Cologne, and various sites in Britain.[220]

More striking differences emerge if we turn to the specific materials used for these statues. For a start, many stones which were used for neither architectural elements nor sarcophagi turn up being employed for statuary. Thasian marble, for instance, was a popular material for statuary: examples carved in white dolomitic marble from Cape Vathy have been identified from Ephesos, Pergamon, and Nicomedia.[221] Large sculptures in the same stone are also known from Gaza (a colossal Zeus) and Byblos (an over-lifesize Poseidon), both dated to the second century AD.[222] The popularity of Thasian marble for high-quality commissions, and especially colossal statues, can also be seen in the West. At Vienne, a number of statues in dolomitic Thasian marble are known, including a colossal Juno, a torso of Venus, a head of Eros, and another of Apollo or Bacchus, all late first or second century AD in date.[223] A toe of a colossal statue in this material has also been recovered from the Provincial Forum complex at Tarragona which might belong to a large imperial statue.[224] Three second-century AD statues from Utica—a cuirassed Trajan, Hercules, and an unidentified deity—were also carved in the same

[217] M. L. Fischer 1998: 134–63; Wielgosz 2008; Friedland 2003: 415–17; 2012.

[218] Friedland 1999; 2012; M. L. Fischer 2002: 321–2.

[219] On the imports, Wielgosz et al. 2002; on Palmyrene art generally, Colledge 1976.

[220] On Trier and Metz, Espérandieu 1913; 1915; on Cologne, Noelke 1980: 144–7; G. Fischer 1999: 681; on the examples from Britain, Cunliffe and Fulford 1982: no. 2, 89–90, 92, 98, 113, 152; Tufi 1983: no. 13, 15, 132; Keppie and Arnold 1984: no. 57; Brewer 1986: no. 31, 115: Henig 1993: no. 1–16; Huskinson 1994: no. 26, 96; Toynbee 1962: 128–43, 153 (on the Walbrook mithraem), 149; Toynbee 1964: 46, 50, 59–62; Crummy 1997: 95.

[221] Herrmann and Newman 1999: 294–6; 2002: 219–21.

[222] Herrmann and Newman 2002: 219.

[223] Herrmann and Newman 1999: 298–302.

[224] Àlvarez et al. 2012: 202 (Sample 7).

stone.[225] Further fragments of statuary in Thasian marble have been identified in the Carthage, Mactar, and Sousse museums, all datable to the second century AD.[226] Even at Athens, where one might expect Pentelic to dominate, statues carved in Thasian marble have been identified; indeed Pausanias mentions that two portraits of Hadrian erected in the temenos of the temple of Olympian Zeus were carved in Thasian marble.[227]

This is not a phenomenon unique to this one material. It is striking that at Thessaloniki, in fact, where one might expect just Thasian marble to be used for statuary as it usually is for architectural elements and sarcophagi, we find Pentelic and Parian being used as well.[228] In Spain and Gaul, furthermore, where local white marbles are used for architectural elements, a lot of effort was put into acquiring the highest-quality eastern white marbles for statuary. At Cartagena, as early as the Augustan period, Luna, Pentelic, and Parian are used for statuary; a *peplophora* in *giallo antico* has even been identified.[229] At Italica, Parian was the most popular choice for high-quality carving projects, followed by Luna and Pentelic, with Almadén de la Plata used only occasionally.[230]

Only really in southern Asia Minor can we draw any direct link between the materials used for architectural elements, sarcophagi, and statuary. In Pamphylia, Dokimeian marble was used for at least some statues, to judge from limited analysis of material in Antalya Museum.[231] At Sagalassos, one statue in Dokimeian marble is known from the north-west Heroon and two from the Antonine nymphaeum, both of the latter signed by a Dokimeian sculptor, Glykon son of Alkimos.[232] However, Aphrodisian marble also turns up at Sagalassos: two statues of Dionysos, from the nymphaeum were carved in this material, possibly by Aphrodisian sculptors.[233] At Aphrodisias itself all of the statuary was carved in local marble, though the fine-grained white marble from Göktepe became increasingly favoured during the course of the second century AD.[234]

---

[225] Two are in the Rijksmuseum van Oudheden in Leiden (Herrmann 1992: 96), while the third is at the site museum (Herrmann, Van Den Hoek, and Nerman 2002: 359–61).

[226] Herrmann, Van Den Hoek, and Nerman 2002: 361.

[227] Pausanias I.18.6–7; on Thasian marble statues in Athens, as well as at Patras and on Crete, see Herrmann and Newman 1995: 82, table 3; 2002: 219–20.

[228] Tykot et al. 2002; Pike, Herrmann, and Newman 2002.

[229] Noguera and Antolinos 2002: 126–49; Soler 2008: 139–43, fig. 9; Noguera and Ruiz 2006: 214–16.

[230] Rodà 1997: 177–9.

[231] Herrmann and Tykot 2009: 66

[232] Waelkens et al. 2002: 371; Moens, De Paepe, and Waelkens 1997: 373; Horsley 2007: no. 22, 201.

[233] Moens, De Paepe, and Waelkens 1997: 373; Waelkens et al. 2002: 373–4.

[234] On Göktepe, see Attanasio, Bruno, and Yavuz 2009.

Finally, at single sites, it is common to find materials being used for statuary from a wide range of quarries. This is true at both coastal and inland sites. In the East, Prokonnesian and Pentelic have been identified at Ascalon, and perhaps also Dokimeian marble, while at Caesarea Maritima, where 40 per cent of the marble statuary in Roman Palestine has been found, Prokonnesian, Pentelic, Dokimeian or Aphrodisian, and Thasian marble are known.[235] At Bosra, where imports date from the Hadrianic period, Dokimeian, Parian, and Pentelic marble have been identified; at Shahba, Dokimeian and Pentelic; at Amman, Pentelic, Prokonnesian, and other materials from Asia Minor; at Beth Shean, Dokimeian or Aphrodisian; and at Palmyra, Thasian, Prokonnesian, Dokimeian, Pentelic, and Parian.[236] An even wider range of sources have been proposed for the material from Caesarea Philippi, though in this case the preference was for material from Asia Minor: from Prokonnesos, Dokimeion, Ephesos, Uşak, Aphrodisias, and perhaps even smaller quarries like those at Mylasa, Herakleia-on-Latmos, and Denizli.[237]

Where sufficient material has been tested it would appear, perhaps unsurprisingly, that customers in central Italy were also able to get hold of a wider range of materials. At Cosa analysis has identified statues in Pentelic, Parian, and Thasian marble alongside local Luna marble.[238] Two recent programmes of analysis of the statuary from Hadrian's Villa have identified material from Paros, Thasos, Prokonnesos, Dokimeion, Penteli, Luna, and potentially also Göktepe.[239] At Ostia, meanwhile, statuary in Parian, Pentelic, Thasian, Aphrodisian, and Dokimeian marble, in addition to Luna and Prokonnesian have been identified, with Luna and Parian, especially in the first and second centuries AD, the most popular.[240] At Nemi, Parian and perhaps Dokimeian marble are used for statues between the second century BC and the first century AD, with Luna marble appearing during the first century AD.[241] Although fewer statues have been found at Pompeii a similar range of stones have been identified in other contexts. Sampling at the Casa dei Vettii, for example, has demonstrated that most of the garden ornaments were carved in Parian (Paros-2) and Pentelic marble but that Luna, Thasian, Prokonnesian, and grey Lesbian marble were also present.[242] Similar work in the Casa del Bracciale d'Oro and the Casa di Polibio has identified Parian (Paros-2), Luna,

[235] Pearl and Magaritz 1991; M. L. Fischer 1998; 2002; and especially Friedland 2012.
[236] Wielgosz 2008; Wielgosz and Degryse 2008: 69–73; Friedland and Tykot 2012; M. L. Fischer 2002: 320–2; Wielgosz et al. 2002.
[237] Friedland 2012.
[238] Collins-Clinton, Attanasio, and Platania 2008.
[239] Pensabene et al. 2012; Lapuente et al. 2012.
[240] Lazzarini et al. 2007; also Pensabene 2007c.
[241] Moltesen, Bald Romano, and Herz 2002.   [242] Fant et al. 2002.

dolomitic Thasian, and Pentelic marble being used for revetment, small architectural elements, and a small herm.[243]

Less work to date has been done on analysing statuary in other materials to see whether they were also moved around. Exceptions to this rule are the various campaigns of analysis undertaken by Hayward on Romano-British sculpture.[244] An important result of this work is the confirmation that the funerary monument of M. Favonius Facilis, datable to the Neronian period, was carved in limestone from Norroy in north-eastern Gaul.[245] Facilis was a centurion of the *legio XX Valeria Victrix* and it is possible that at this early date in Britain he was forced to look to established workshops in the Rhineland for precisely the monument that he wanted. Even so, this material, perhaps even the monument itself, travelled a long way. More recently a newly discovered relief in the form of a cylinder from Fittleworth in West Sussex, not far from Bignor Villa, has been shown to have been made in imported limestone.[246] This relief depicts the story of Iphigenia in Tauris and is carved in Middle Eocene limestone from the Paris Basin. More analysis of limestone carvings in this area might reveal similar examples elsewhere.

The range of materials used for statuary across all of these regions should alert us to the fact that stone for statuary and stone for architecture were supplied, in most cases, in quite different ways. This divergence might also result, as has been proposed for sarcophagi, from the fact that some of these statues could well have been imported as part-finished or finished works rather than raw materials, a hypothesis that will be examined further in Chapter 8.

'Overseas agencies' and customer choice

Breaking down our analysis of distribution into three categories (architecture, sarcophagi, statuary) based on the use to which material was put reveals some important patterns which have wider implications for understanding the mechanisms of this activity. In Ward-Perkins' model of the marble trade, structured as it is around the quarries and their role in the process of distribution, a lot of emphasis is placed on what he labelled 'overseas agencies' or 'branch workshops'. These were offices established by individual quarries which Ward-Perkins saw as coming into existence 'in the first instance to facilitate the processes of ordering and of distribution, but which, once established, inevitably tended in their turn to shape the patterns of that distribution'.[247] Sarcophagus evidence featured heavily in this model. In particular, the fact that certain sarcophagus types are vastly preferred over

[243] Fant 2009*b*; Cancelliere, Lazzarini, and Turi 2002: 304.   [244] Hayward 2006; 2009.
[245] Hayward 2006.   [246] Black et al. 2012.   [247] Ward-Perkins 1980*b*: 25.

others at certain sites was explained by Ward-Perkins as evidence for 'systematic commercial activity', which he credited to these overseas agencies. To illustrate this point Ward-Perkins drew on the examples of Cyrene and Alexandria and their contrasting patterns of sarcophagus use. The dominance of Attic sarcophagi at Cyrene, Prokonnesian at Alexandria, he argued resulted from the fact that these two producers deliberately targeted different markets through their overseas representatives.[248] There is room for customer choice in this model but not much of it: 'an individual who wished to shop outside the framework of these monopolies was at perfect liberty to do so—if he could establish contact with other sources and could pay the price. But in the event the ordinary client accepted the market situation.'[249]

The distribution patterns examined above cast serious doubt on this reconstruction. In fact, there is very little evidence for single materials dominating particular markets across all object categories. In architectural contexts consumers often employed a range of stones of similar type: the combination of Prokonnesian and Pentelic in many North African cities is a case in point but we might also consider the use of Dokimeian marble alongside Prokonnesian at Perge or the range of white marbles found at Italica. Even when only single materials are found their use is usually easily explained on either geographic grounds or because they were the favoured materials of a particular team of contractors. When it comes to sarcophagi and statuary even greater diversity can be observed. At most major Mediterranean centres, especially in the East, a wide range of imported and local sarcophagus types are attested—a point Ward-Perkins himself acknowledged.[250] The distribution patterns of different sarcophagus types overlap considerably and when they do not this is easily explained in economic terms, as resulting from transport costs most obviously. The range of materials employed for statuary shows that consumers clearly exercised considerable choice when it came to buying these objects or commissioning sculptors. All of this shows that 'the ordinary client', as Ward-Perkins labelled them, did not simply *accept* the market situation, they *shaped* it.

A simpler solution for the contrasting patterns of sarcophagus use at Cyrene and Alexandria presents itself if we simply turn the problem around and focus not on the quarry or quarry-based workshop but on the customer and the choices made by them. Cyrenaican buyers clearly favoured the more elaborate Attic sarcophagi, with their full blown Classical-style decoration; perhaps this reflects the continued connections (real or perceived) between the local elite and mainland Greece, or perhaps it results from the close relationship between

---

[248] Ward-Perkins 1980*a*: 80–1; 1992*d*: 39.
[249] Ward-Perkins 1980*b*: 45–8; for a recent study of statue distribution which places similar emphasis on the decisions of quarry-based producers, Trimble 2011: 108–16.
[250] Ward-Perkins 1980*b*: 44.

local stone-workers and the Pentelic quarries, revealed by statuary from the city.[251] Whatever the case, Prokonnesian marble was certainly used at Cyrene in prestigious buildings in the second century AD: this was clearly not a material off limits to Cyrenaicans and contacts between the city and the quarries must have existed.[252] At Alexandria, meanwhile, there seems to have been more demand for the plainer chests that could be acquired from the Prokonnesian quarries; these were more flexible forms that could be altered and elaborated according to local tastes.[253] We should probably not be surprised that the imports at two neighbouring cities could vary so considerably: Cyrene and Alexandria were quite different cities, with distinct histories, as well as socio-cultural and ethnic compositions.

How individual consumers went about securing the materials or objects that they required will be discussed in the next three chapters with regard to different object types. Suffice it to say for now, the lack of evidence for 'overseas agencies' is more than made up for by attestations of private stone suppliers and craftsmen who specialized in the carving and probably also transporting of stone: *marmorarii, redemptores marmorarii*, in one case a *negotiator marmorarius*; these were the individuals to whom ordinary consumers turned and who maintained the link between consumer and producer.

IMPERIAL REDISTRIBUTION

What the series of case studies examined above show quite clearly is the normality of the local and regional distribution of stone in the Roman imperial period. Privately funded building projects rarely made use of non-local stone for the bulk of their construction need; in this sense they followed the advice of Vitruvius, spelled out in the passage quoted at the beginning of this chapter. Ordinary distribution was shaped by geographic and topographic parameters, the limitations of transportation and infrastructure, the availability of particular workers, all of which moderated the cost and practicality of picking a particular stone for a given project.

Against this background imperial activity was self-consciously atypical. With the enormous resources available to it, the Roman state was capable of both maintaining and supplying quarrying districts in remote locations and coordinating the movement of vast quantities of quarried material towards

---

[251] On the import of Pentelic marble for statue production at Cyrene, see Kane 2000; on the influence of Attic styles at Ptolemais, Fabbricotti 1985.

[252] On Prokonnesian marble at Cyrene, see Ward-Perkins 1992*d*: 39, n. 3; Pensabene 2006; 2007*b*.

[253] Adriani 1961: 19–31.

Rome on a scale that, as Weigall put it, was well beyond the reach 'of all save the rulers of the earth'.[254] This, of course, was precisely the point: it was important not only that the state overcome those obstacles that otherwise limited ordinary trade, but that they be seen to do so.

Imperial projects at Rome

Rome, of course, was the locus of imperial display *par excellence*. The capital contained the largest concentration of decorative stones anywhere and the fashions established here, notably in imperial building projects, influenced stone use everywhere else. Quantifying the amount of stone used in building projects at Rome is impossible, though the fact that Corsi was able to catalogue around 7,000 columns in the city in 1833 gives some impression of the scale of imports.[255] Corsi identified seventy-two different stone types in his list, revealing the sheer breadth of materials on display. The most common materials he identified were *granito bigio* (1,546; 25.5 per cent) and *bigio antico* (742; 12 per cent), grey granites and grey marbles; these granites were probably mainly from Kozak Dağ, Elba, and Giglio, possibly also the Troad, while the main sources of *bigio antico* are Lesbos and perhaps also Iznik.[256] After these come a number of easily distinguished coloured stones: *granito rosso* from Aswan (602; 10 per cent), *cipollino* (446; 7 per cent), *pavonazzetto* (232; 3.8 per cent), *verde antico* (218; 3.6 per cent), *granito del Foro* (182; 3 per cent), *portasanta* (181; 2.9 per cent), *giallo antico* (159; 2.6 per cent), and *porfido rosso* (158; 2.6 per cent). The popular combination of grey and pink granite and the widespread use of *cipollino* that we have seen in the Levant and elsewhere, then, is echoed at Rome. Corsi also counted at least 705 white marble columns, though the quarries he connects them with are questionable.[257] A far higher number of columns must originally have existed in Rome—we know that many were shipped out in the Medieval period—and equally considerable quantities of imports were used for other architectural elements, revetment, and flooring.[258]

Many of these stones were first introduced to the capital during the Late Republican period, mainly in the first century BC: *giallo antico*, *pavonazzetto*, *portasanta*, *cipollino*, and *africano*, which is represented by 107 columns in

[254] Weigall 1909: 90; also Mattingly 2007: 224.
[255] Corsi lists 6,067 in the second edition of his work (1833: 293–386) and 7,012 in the third (1845: 293–393).
[256] Williams-Thorpe 2008: 80; on the sources of *bigio antico*, Gnoli, Marchei, and Sironi 2001: 158–9; Pensabene 1998*b*: 175; Yavuz, Bruno, and Attanasio 2012.
[257] Corsi 1833: 82–4.
[258] Greenhalgh 2006: 80; Russell 2008: 115.

Corsi's catalogue.[259] However this list continued to be added to; indeed many of the most numerous materials in Corsi's catalogue are either rare or absent prior to the Flavian period. Aswan granite, for example, though used in Pharaonic and Ptolemaic Egypt is not used significantly at Rome before the late first century AD. Serious interest in the various *bigi antichi*, the *granito del Foro* from Mons Claudianus, even porphyry is also hard to identify prior to the Flavian or Trajanic periods, while during the course of the second century AD we see the introduction of grey granites from the Troad, Kozak Dağ, and the Tyrrhenian islands, as well as coloured stones like *verde antico*. Suppliers in the capital, no doubt bolstered by imperial demand, were continually updating and expanding their repertoires.

Changes in the supply of white marbles can also be noted through systematic analysis of the major imperial monuments in Rome, as several key archaeometric studies have shown. A general development can be noted in which the primary white marble used shifts from Pentelic in the Late Republican period to Luna in the Augustan through to Flavian periods, with only small quantities of other stones having been identified.[260] Pentelic re-emerges in the arches of Titus and Domitian, as well as the Domitianic phase of the Porticus of Octavia, but Luna remains dominant, being used in the Colosseum, Temple of Vespasian, the Forum Transitorium, and the Forum and Column of Trajan.[261] Although first attested in the Flavian period, the use of Prokonnesian really takes off from the mid Hadrianic period onwards: it is used in significant quantities in the Temple of Venus and Roma, the Hadrianeum, the Temple of Antoninus and Faustina, and the Arch of Septimius Severus; most Severan restorations of earlier structures use Prokonnesian too.[262] This shift towards Prokonnesian was far from total—Luna was still used throughout the Antonine period—but the awkwardness of acquiring material in quantity from the Luna quarries probably counted against them as alternatives from the East became more intensively exploited.[263]

This being said, it should be noted that many of the major building projects in Rome used multiple white marbles, especially in the second century AD. Pentelic and Luna are found in the Pantheon and Prokonnesian and Luna on

[259] On these dates, Gnoli, Marchei, and Sironi 2001.
[260] On the Late Republic, S. Bernard 2010; on the introduction of Luna marble, Fant 1999; Pensabene 2008: 28–31; and on its use, Bruno et al. 2002*a*; De Nuccio et al. 2002; Amadori et al. 1998; Lazzarini et al. 1997; Gorgoni et al. 2002.
[261] On Pentelic in this period, Bruno, Gorgoni, and Pallante 1999: 165–7; Bruno et al. 2002*a*: 291; Lazzarini et al. 1997; and on the continued use of Luna, Lazzarini et al. 1988; Amadori et al. 1998; Bruno et al. 2002*a*; Bianchi and Bruno 2009: 105.
[262] Bruno et al. 2002*a*: 293–7; Claridge 1982; Bruno, Gorgoni, and Pallante 1999.
[263] On Luna in Antonine monuments, Bruno et al. 2002*a*: 295; 1999 (on the reliefs now on the Arch of Constantine); on the benefits of Prokonnesian over Luna, see Walker 1988; Attanasio, Brilli, and Bruno 2008: 748–54.

the Temple of Antoninus and Faustina and the Arch of Septimius Severus.[264] Even the Severan restoration of the Temple of Bellona appears to have been carried out with low quality Luna marble as well as Prokonnesian.[265] A recent study of the Baths of Caracalla demonstrated that most of the white marble was Prokonnesian and Pentelic but a few blocks of Luna and Dokimeian marble, perhaps leftovers from earlier projects, were also identified.[266] Luna and Pentelic seem to have still been valued for their beauty. On the Arch of Septimius Severus, Luna marble is employed for the primary relief panels and at Lepcis Magna many of the most prominent architectural details are finished in Pentelic.[267] It is possible that this mixing of materials also reveals an attempt to spread the burden of demand across multiple suppliers.

Imperial projects outside of Rome

Outside of Rome, as we saw in Chapter 2, most building projects were paid for by members of the local elites and by public funds controlled by cities themselves; only around 10 per cent of building projects probably received assistance from the state. Where imperially funded projects can be identified, though, they typically employ a wealth of imported materials. The Severan building projects at Lepcis Magna are almost certainly imperially funded, even if we have no direct epigraphic evidence to prove this, and epitomize the potential scale of investment: enormous quantities of Prokonnesian and Pentelic marble were employed for these structures, alongside a range of coloured materials.[268] Ward-Perkins counted nearly 450 column shafts of *cipollino* in the Severan Forum, Basilica, and Colonnaded Street, as well as at least seventy-eight columns of Aswan granite in the Severan Temple, Basilica (Fig. 5.7), and Nymphaeum.[269] Imported materials had been introduced to the city earlier in the second century AD, most notably in the Hadrianic Baths, and continued in popularity through the Antonine period, but the scale of decorative stone use in the Severan projects overshadowed everything that had come before.[270] Severan munificence was not limited to Lepcis Magna and Rome. Several prominent cities of the Levant, as we have seen, were thoroughly rejuvenated in this period, importing large quantities of Prokonnesian marble as well as *cipollino* and various granites, the same range of materials in other

---

[264] Bruno et al. 2002*a*: 293–4; Bruno et al. 1999.   [265] De Nuccio et al. 2002.
[266] Bruno, Gorgoni, and Pallante 2009: 390.
[267] Bruno et al. 1999; Attanasio, Brilli, and Bruno 2008: 753.
[268] On the white marbles, Pensabene 2001*a*; Attanasio, Brilli, and Bruno 2008: 753; Bianchi et al. 2009; on the granites, see Williams-Thorpe, Webb, and Thorpe 2000.
[269] Ward-Perkins 1993: 89; Pensabene 2008: 49; on granite use in the city, Lazzarini 1987: 162; Williams-Thorpe, Webb, and Thorpe 2000.
[270] Bianchi 2009: 46–55; Pensabene 2002*b*: 65.

Fig. 5.7. Aswan granite columns in the Severan Basilica at Lepcis Magna (photo: W. Wootton).

words as we find at Lepcis Magna. Several of these cities, notably Tyre, had backed Septimius Severus in his civil wars against Pescennius Niger in AD 193–4 and it is tempting to connect this building boom to imperial acknowledgement of their loyalty.[271]

While Lepcis Magna stands out as the exemplar of imperial beneficence beyond the capital, imperial projects elsewhere are similarly anomalous. The use of monolithic columns in the Tetrapylon and the portico of the Baths of Diocletian at Palmyra are cases in point. Both projects were instigated by Sosianus Hierocles, the provincial governor, and it seems reasonable to assume were at least part-funded by the state.[272] At the other end of the empire, in Britain, the monumental arch at Richborough in Kent is equally jarring in its local context. Apparently dedicated in AD 90 to celebrate Domitian's final pacification of the province, and paid for either by the state or by someone closely associated with the emperor, it was built of local materials (flint, tuff, and sandstone) and some imported limestone from Marquise, and then apparently faced with Luna marble, which is found in some quantity at the site and in the surrounding area.[273] If this material does come from the

---

[271] Pensabene 1997: 283–4.   [272] Dodge 1988b: 229; Browning 1979: 139, 184.
[273] Blagg 1984: 73; Pearson 2006: 23–4.

arch and was used as a facing all over it then approximately 400 tonnes would have been required. Nowhere else in Britain do we find imported stones in anything approaching these quantities.

Similarly, the only three sites in the inland Danubian provinces to have produced noticeable quantities of Mediterranean imports are all are connected in some way with the imperial administration. At Romuliana, the fortified palace of the emperor Galerius, imported granite and coloured marbles, possibly also Prokonnesian marble, have been identified in late third- and fourth-century contexts.[274] Another site to have received special attention in this period was Naissus, the supposed birthplace of the emperor Constantine.[275] Several small marble architectural elements and a large number of marble statues have been discovered at the nearby villa at Mediana, which possibly belonged to a high-ranking imperial official, if not the imperial family itself.[276] Two of these statues, depicting Asklepios and Hygieia, are in porphyry.[277] All of the other porphyry statues to have come to light in Moesia Superior are connected to the imperial administration, either by find location or theme: these include fragments of a seated male statue from the large fortified site at Vrelo and two portrait heads, one from Romuliana, the other from Naissus.[278] Finally, the only site in Pannonia to have produced architectural elements in imported Mediterranean materials in any quantity is the Flavian colony and third-century imperial capital of Sirmium.[279] In marked contrast to other sites in this area, column shafts in a variety of Mediterranean materials have been identified (including red and black porphyry, *cipollino*, and *pavonazzetto*) alongside substantial quantities of panels for revetment and paving; in addition to the Egyptian materials the presence of *giallo antico* revetment is striking considering the site's location.[280]

The Danubian provinces were not rich in imported decorative stones but as Pensabene has noted, even in areas were such materials abounded, such as Campania, imperial projects are still notable for their lavishness. Many privately or publicly funded buildings in Campania employed imported stones from at least the Augustan period: coloured marble revetment was used in the Augustan phases of the theatres at Pompeii and Herculaneum, *africano* columns at the latter; columns in *cipollino* and *portasanta* are found in the theatre at Cales; while the amphitheatre at Pozzuoli was adorned with at least seventy-two columns of Prokonnesian marble at some point in the second

[274] Vasić 1993: 118–47.
[275] For references to his time in the city: *Codex Theodosianus* II.15.1, II.16.1, XI.27.1.
[276] Petrović 1993: 55–81.
[277] Tomović 1993: no. 111, 112.
[278] Janković 1980; Srejović 1992–3; M. Vasić 2000; also Bergmann 1977: pl. 48.6.
[279] Popović 1993: 13–26; Mirković 2004: 151–5.   [280] Djurić et al. 2006: 104, fig. 1.

century AD.[281] Despite the relative wealth of these projects they are all over-shadowed by two structures which benefited from imperial munificence, the theatres at Sessa Aurunca and Teano.[282] The former, originally constructed under Augustus, was spectacularly rebuilt following an earthquake by Matidia Minor, a close relative of Trajan and Hadrian and great-aunt of Marcus Aurelius, in the mid second century AD, while the latter underwent a comparable transformation in the Severan period.[283] A vast array of imported materials was employed at both sites, especially in the elaborate *scaenae frontes*. Eighty-four columns, in *cipollino*, *breccia di settebasi*, *pavonazzetto*, *portasanta*, *giallo antico*, *fior di pesco*, and Troad granite were incorporated into this structure at Sessa Aurunca; at Teano, red Aswan granite and *granito del foro* columns made up the lower order and *pavonazzetto*, *africano*, *giallo antico*, and *portasanta* the upper order.[284] In each case the white marbles used seem to be a combination of Luna and primarily Prokonnesian, and both ensembles were finished off with spectacular wall revetment and *opus sectile* flooring. In the scale of imports but also their range, these complexes totally eclipsed those in neighbouring cities funded through the typical channels of non-imperial beneficence.

The imperial transport system

How did the imperial administration go about securing these enormous quantities of material and delivering them to the sites where they were needed? The scale of this activity hints at the existence of specialist supply routes. Imperial officials, as we saw in Chapter 2, can be identified at either end of the redistributive process, overseeing both quarrying and the receipt of stone at Rome, and they must have coordinated efforts to secure the necessary supplies for building projects.[285] However, we are less well informed about who took charge of physically moving this material.

No imperial officials connected to the transport of stone have been identified to date. Chresimus, the *procurator a marmoribus* discussed above is the only likely candidate, simply because he is attested at a range of sites more plausibly explained as transport hubs than quarrying sites.[286] It is noteworthy,

---

[281] On these examples, and others from Cumae, Misenum, and Herculaneum, Pensabene 2005: 80–6, 86–91, 134–5; on Pozzuoli, Demma 2004; Barresi 2004.

[282] Pensabene 2005: 136, tables 1–2; the theatres at Benevento, Capua, and perhaps Nocera might also have benefited from imperial financing.

[283] Cascella 2009: 21–3; Sirano et al. 2002; Sirano and Beste 2005.

[284] On Sessa Aurunca, Cascella 2009: 25, 27, 28–37; on Teano, Sirano et al. 2002: 328; Sirano and Beste 2005: 411, 413–17, table 4, figs. 15–16; Antonelli, Lazzarini, and Cancelliere 2010: 934.

[285] See Chapter 3: Coordinating supply (pp. 51–2).

[286] See Chapter 3: Imperial quarrying elsewhere (p. 43).

though, that we hear of no imperial shippers of stone. Did such individuals ever exist or did the state contract out this work to private shippers? In the absence of further data, useful parallels can be found in the case of other state-driven redistributive systems, most obviously that of grain. In this case, as Casson has put it, 'the state's interest in Rome's grain extended only to fulfilling the needs of the dole and of government personnel; the rest it left to private dealers'.[287] Various inducements were offered by the state—notably special privileges or the avoidance of liturgies—to make involvement in the grain supply profitable to private individuals, whatever their position.[288] Shippers involved in state redistribution were sometimes also freed from port charges on merchandise carried alongside state-owned products, at least by the late fourth century.[289] There is nothing in the legal sources, however, to indicate that what applied to shippers of imperial grain also held for shippers of decorative stones and we should be wary of pushing this comparison too far.[290] Even without inducements, though, it would still have been easy within the existing framework of maritime law for the state to hire from private shippers either space on their vessel or their whole vessel as necessary, perhaps even for multiple trips.[291]

Only in one instance is there any reference in the documentary sources to the use of imperially owned ships for the movement of stone. This is on the Nile, and then only in the letter of Aurelius Isidorus discussed in Chapter 4.[292] Here, the ships that are the subject of the letter are being sent up the Nile 'since the ten state ships sent to Syene for the transport down river of the columns are insufficient to carry all of them'. The first fleet of ships was probably state-owned, therefore, but the second group, sent to assist them, seem not to have been. The prefect in Egypt must have had the option of hiring privately owned ships to supplement the state-owned fleet, especially at harvest time. The requisitioning of boats, in fact, is alluded to in the Edict of Germanicus, issued in AD 19.[293] In the Ptolemaic period, many of the largest grain ships on the Nile were owned by wealthy Alexandrians, and this is a practice that probably continued.[294]

Shipping on the Nile, of course, was a carefully controlled affair but requisitioning means of transport was an option always open to the imperial administration; this was one way in which it could access a far larger pool of manual labour than most private individuals. Requisitioning was normally only turned to for the movement of military personnel and other officials but in Egypt requisitioned camels were frequently used for non-military ventures;

[287] Casson 1980: 29.
[288] Suetonius, *Claudius* 18; *Digest* V.3, VI.6.5–6, VI.6.8–9, L.3.9; also Garnsey 1983: 121–8.
[289] *Codex Theodosianus* XIII.5.24 (ad 395); also Jones 1964: 828.
[290] On this point, Fant 2012: 528–9.
[291] Fant 2012: 529.   [292] Skeat 1964: Papyrus 2, lines 43–50.
[293] *Sel.Pap.* II.211; also Lewis 1983: 143; Adams 2001: 186.   [294] Thompson 1983: 67.

in fact, individuals had to declare their camels annually so the administration could keep track of the number of animals at its disposal.[295] The whole process, in typical fashion, was documented by punctilious officials, and the resulting 'camel-returns' reveal both where the animal was used and to what end. Camels from the Fayum were routinely used in the Eastern Desert. According to his camel-return, datable to AD 163, an inhabitant from Soknopaiou Nesos had two of his camels requisitioned in a single year, one for use on the caravan between Berenike and the Nile, another for the movement of a porphyry column; in both cases the requisition was authorized by the prefect.[296] An individual from the same town also provided one of his four camels for work transporting material from Mons Porphyrites.[297] In both of these cases the animals were hired, that is paid for, for the specific task listed and used for no longer than a year.

Another document illustrates the food requirements of this requisitioning. This letter is addressed to the *strategos* of the Heptakomia Apollonipolites nome (Upper Egypt) who was probably stationed at Qena. It requests that 'all the barley currently in the nome' be dispatched immediately in order to supply the 'great number of animals for the purpose of bringing down a fifty-foot column' (probably from Mons Claudianus).[298] Alongside the animals, quarrymen also needed supplies and two further documents refer to the supply of grain from cities in the Fayum to soldiers in the Thebaid and workers at the quarries of the Eastern Desert.[299] Soldiers and quarrymen, in this case at least, were supplied through the same system.

Records from Asia Minor highlight another aspect of requisitioning: the obligations of local communities. The Sülmenli inscription, from near Dokimeion, records a third-century dispute between two villages regarding the allocation of *angareia*, that is, the supply of animals and manpower for the *cursus publicus* or public transport service.[300] Each village was tasked with responsibility for transportation along defined stretches of road, calculated in proportion to the amount of *apophora* or ground tax they paid; both were required to supply fodder for the animals.[301] The mention of heavy wagons, or *protela*, on this route might indicate that these local villages were also partially responsible for supplying the *cursus clavularis* or transport system responsible for heavy items. Considering the location of these communities, it is possible

[295] *P.Lond.* II.304, 309, 327–8, 368, 376, 443; also Lesquier 1918: 369–75; Mitchell 1976: 125; Leone 1988: 127–38; Adams 2007: 120–30.

[296] *P.Lond.* II.328; also Lesquier 1918: 372–3. Even the roads along which this activity took place, and associated wells, fortlets and staging posts, were maintained by imperial mandate— *ILS* 2453 (Augustan) and *IGRR* 2.1142 (Hadrianic); on this point, Mitchell 1987: 337.

[297] *BGU* III.762.

[298] *P.Giss.* 69; see Peña 1989.

[299] Youtie 1978: 251–4 (= *P.Mich.* inv. 6767); *P.Oxy.* XLV.3243; also Adams 2001: 177–9.

[300] Frend 1956.   [301] Pekáry 1968: 135–55.

that the heavy loads in question comprise stone from the imperially controlled areas of the quarries at Dokimeion.[302] Synnada is mentioned in the inscription, as too is Dokimeion, apparently as the place to which the villagers could appeal against this burden, though the context is unclear. In general these obligations mirror those imposed on the citizens of Sagalassos who were required, according to a first-century AD bilingual edict, to 'provide a service of ten wagons and as many mules for the necessary use of people passing through . . . as far as Cormasa and Conana', that is, across the whole territory of the city.[303] This edict was intended to curb abuses of the system and re-emphasizes the fact that, in this period at least, requisitioned transport, unlike accommodation, had to be paid for.

Even considering the necessary payments involved in the requisitioning of animals, the cost of the medium- to long-distance movement of stone in these areas must have been comparatively low for the imperial administration.[304] As Adams observes, 'the transport of stone was not so much a financial achievement as a technological and logistical one'.[305] What these documents make very clear is that there was an established infrastructure for the movement of imperially owned goods and imperial officials that could be used for stone transport as and when required. It is noticeable, for example, that the official sent to collect feed for the animals moving the fifty-foot column in the Eastern Desert, described above, had been sent to the same town the preceding year for the collection of a consignment of cloaks. It was this ability to draw at will on the immense combined resources of each and every city, town, and village in this way that allowed for the efficient functioning of the imperially orchestrated redistributive system, be it of grain or stone.

The nature of imperial intervention

Most of the materials used in imperially funded building projects came from quarries at which imperial involvement is epigraphically attested. However, these materials were also used elsewhere and not just in the hinterland of the capital or in projects demonstrably financed by imperial officials. It was clearly possible for private customers, provided they had the wherewithal to do so, to purchase most, perhaps even all, of the best-known decorative stones, even those from imperial quarries. This begs the question, why did the imperial

---

[302] Pekáry 1968: 136; Kolb 2000: 96–7.

[303] *SEG* XXVI.1392; see Mitchell 1976: 117–23; Horsley 2007: no. 335; the term used for a wagon in this case is *carrum*.

[304] Mitteis and Wilcken 1912: 374 even argue that no payment was made for requisitioned animals.

[305] Adams 2001: 188.

administration intervene in the quarrying and movement of stone at all? Why did the state not simply buy the stone that it needed on the open market?

The answer, presumably, is that the more symbolic marble and other coloured stones became, the more necessary it was for the emperors to ensure that they had sufficient supplies of them. Imperial building projects consumed these materials in such quantities that defined sources had to be secured to prevent their exhaustion by the non-imperial market as well as to avoid potential inflation of prices by suppliers. Equally, many of the most exotic, visibly distinctive materials favoured by the emperors came from quarries simply too remote to have been operated by anyone other than the administration; Mons Claudianus and Mons Porphyrites are the prominent examples but it is doubtful that quarrying at Dokimeion, even Chemtou, could have been maintained on any significant scale with private financing alone. It was simply expedient, therefore, for the state to maintain a hand in this process.

Whether imperial involvement also aimed at preventing these materials from entering the non-imperial market, at monopolization, is much less certain, though it has been suggested. Fant has pointed to Dio Chrysostom's comment that Teos, Karystos, and 'certain Egyptian and Phrygian cities' are 'no better or more fortunate than any of the very lowly and pitiful cities' despite their wealth in coloured stones and used it to argue that imperial control of these quarries deprived these cities of their own resources.[306] Using this evidence, combined with the data for decorative stone usage at Rome, Fant argued that the polychrome stones from imperially owned quarries were the monopoly of the emperor, that they were sent exclusively to Rome, from where they were only redistributed secondarily to Italy and the provinces.[307] The surge of studies of provincial stone use in recent years casts serious doubt on this model, however; it is now clear that considerable quantities of decorative stones from imperial quarries were used in non-imperial projects across the Roman world and not shipped via Rome.[308]

This being the case, what then was Dio Chrysostom talking about? An alternative reading of this text, which perhaps fits better in the context of Dio's rhetoric more generally, is that these luxury polychrome stones, in contrast to good government, contributed nothing to the true 'wealth' of a city; it is not that these cities are prevented from accessing these resources but that they are no better off for having them. Karystos is a significant example to draw on. A small, largely inconsequential urban centre, Karystos was only famous for the distinctive *marmor carystium* or *cipollino* quarried in its hinterland; however luxurious this material, then, nobody in Dio's audience would have

---

[306] Dio Chrysostom, *Orations* LXXIX.2–3 (trans. J. W. Cohoon and H. Lamar); also Fant 1989*b*: 211–13.
[307] Fant 1988; 1989*a*; 1989*b*; 1990; 1993*a*; 1993*b*.
[308] Paton and Schneider 1999: 293–4.

considered Karystos a tempting holiday destination. No comment is being made about the distribution of this material. *Cipollino* is actually the most widely distributed of all coloured stones, and was used extensively on Euboea for everyday construction.[309] *Pavonazzetto*, likewise, which Dio is presumably referring to in regard to his 'Phrygian cities', is found at sites across western Asia Minor and all around the Mediterranean. Even *africano*, from Teos, though scarce in the immediate vicinity of the quarries, is found nearby at Ephesos, Iasos, Patmos, Pergamon, Aphrodisias, and across Italy.[310] Equally, we know that there was particular demand for *africano* from the imperial administration—the quarries at Teos seem to have been exhausted during the second century AD and an alternative source, probably on Chios or elsewhere in the territory of Teos, sought out; it might simply have been the case that any of this material that became available was quickly consumed by the imperial market.[311]

All this being said, it is important that the qualitative and quantitative difference between imperial and non-imperial consumption of these materials is noted, as already discussed. Demand first from Rome, secondly from imperial projects in the provinces, and only thirdly from the private market, shaped the pattern of extraction and distribution of these prominent decorative stones. For this reason certain materials were extremely scarce on the non-imperial market, especially the various Eastern Desert stones. These are rare outside Rome, unlike the granites from the Troad, Kozak Dağ, and even Aswan.[312] Such was the demand for porphyry that it was probably particularly hard to acquire. Even so, small pieces of porphyry are found in floors at Pompeii and Herculaneum, and vessels carved in porphyry turn up in various non-imperial contexts; a striking porphyry bowl and vase, dated by the excavators to the first century AD, have been found as far away as Begram in Afghanistan.[313] The evidence of Aurelius Hermaios at Hermopolis, discussed in Chapter 2, seems to show (depending on how the text is interpreted) that porphyry could be bought on the open market, at least in the mid third century AD, though at an extortionately high price.[314] The *Historia Augusta* even contains a passage describing Antoninus Pius' admiration for a set of porphyry columns belonging to M. Valerius Homullus, consul in AD 152, who had set them up in his house.[315] What this suggests is that imperial involvement in quarrying did not necessarily lead to the situation, envisaged by Peacock,

---

[309] Lazzarini 2007: 283–8; and on its use on Euboea, Chiridoglou 2009; Russell and Fachard 2012.

[310] Lazzarini 2004: 109.

[311] Fant 1989*b*; and on the quarries around Teos, Türk et al. 1988; Bruno et al. 2012: 567–8.

[312] Williams-Thorpe 2008: esp. 80, fig. 3; Williams-Thorpe and Henty 2000.

[313] Hiebert and Cambon 2011: 201 (no. 103–4).

[314] *C.P.Herm.* 86, 94; see Chapter 2: Cost of architectural elements (p. 25).

[315] *Historia Augusta: Life of Antoninus Pius* 11.7.

whereby materials from imperial quarries 'lay outside of the normal orbit of trade in marbles and decorative stones', but imperial demand may well have substantially skewed the market.[316]

Imperial stones on the non-imperial market

The papyrus from Hermopolis reveals little about where Hermaios went looking for his desired porphyry panels, but we might imagine several situations in which this material, and others from imperial quarries, entered the non-imperial market.[317] As noted in Chapter 3, at those sites where private quarrying contractors were employed there was scope for them to sell material once they had met the cost of their lease. We might expect, though, that only what was not needed by the administration would have been let go.[318] At the same time, it was probably always the case that a certain amount of private quarrying took place alongside or around the edge of imperially directed work, especially at large sites like Dokimeion and Chemtou. Private contractors and such unregulated quarrying were not present in the Eastern Desert, however. The whole infrastructure in this region was maintained to support the redistribution of state-owned produce from both mines and quarries, as well as to sustain the caravans running between the Nile and Red Sea.[319] There was little room in this set-up for an entrepreneurial quarryman selling the odd bit of porphyry here and there. The direct sale of this stone, therefore, of the kind Hermaios engaged in had to have been above board. It seems probable that, as Ward-Perkins suggested, limited amounts of quarried stone could have been sold by imperial officials, as well as their subordinates, either at the quarries, at ports before they were shipped, or at their final destination; he never regarded this as a watertight system.[320] A Hadrianic quarry inscription has been found on the rear side of one *pavonazzetto* revetment panel in residential unit 6 of Hanghaus 2 at Ephesos, suggesting that the owner had bought in, or perhaps been given, this material.[321] A similar inscription on a *pavonazzetto* panel from the Bath-Gymnasium at Sardis has also been identified.[322] Private individuals certainly paid for *pavonazzetto* architectural elements as part of public building programmes at Ephesos: donations of both revetment panels and columns are recorded.[323]

A recent re-examination of the ornamental stone collected by the South Etruria Survey has also suggested that certain quantities of material from imperial quarries were secondarily redistributed from Rome; there was

[316] Peacock 1993: 65.   [317] Barresi 2003: 97–9.   [318] Pensabene 2003: 535–6.
[319] Kayser 1993: 111.   [320] Ward-Perkins 1980a: 74–5; Lazzarini 2010: 488–9.
[321] Zimmermann and Landstätter 2011: 48, fig. 57.
[322] L. E. Long 2012a: 226.   [323] *IvEphesos* 430, 661.

enormous demand from villa-owners around the capital for this material.[324] This seems entirely reasonable, but it is questionable whether this was ever an institutionalized trade. Officials could turn a quick profit this way, and excess or off-cuts could probably have been bought, but there was little incentive for the imperial administration to engage actively in this kind of commerce. The fifteen talents that Aurelius Hermaios needed for his porphyry plaques might have seemed a lot to him, and to his disgruntled council who were actually paying, but this was small change to the emperor, even in the third century AD. Perhaps these plaques were simply off-cuts—waste material not needed by Rome that could be sold off for a quick profit by enterprising officials. There is always, of course, the possibility that the plaques Hermaios was buying were second-hand.

Imperial gifts

Overall, this suggests that the rationale behind imperial involvement in quarrying was not to deprive the non-imperial market but to guarantee imperial projects sufficient supplies of prestigious building material.[325] It is in this light that the famous gifts of columns given by Hadrian to Athens and Smyrna need to be considered. In the case of Smyrna, this gift is recorded at the end of a long list of contributions from local bigwigs to the city and is the result of the agency of one Antonius Polemo.[326] The columns were given along with numerous other privileges: a second title of Neokoros (temple guardian of the imperial cult), Sacred Games, immunity from taxation, panegyrists of the gods, singers of hymns, 1.5 million drachmas, and seventy-two columns of *pavonazzetto*, twenty of *giallo antico*, and six of porphyry for the anointing room.[327] Fant has argued that 'neither the request for columns nor the gift make sense unless the crucial issue was not cost but access to these prestigious building materials'.[328] Hadrian's gifts to Athens—100 columns of Numidian marble for the library and 100 columns of Phrygian marble for another colonnade—might support this view; at a later date, the emperor Tacitus is also supposed to have given 100 columns of Numidian marble to Ostia.[329] However, the later description, in the sixth-century chronicle of John Malalas, of Antoninus Pius' gift of stone to Antioch suggests rather that the prohibitive cost of materials might have been behind this activity. For the paving of the street of the great colonnades, so we are told, 'he used basalt, generously contributing stone from the Thebaid out of his own resources, and the remaining expenses too from his own pocket.'[330]

---

[324] Clarke 2008: 696–7. [325] Carrié 1994: 178–9; Harris 1993a: 17; 2003: 295.
[326] *IGRR* IV.1431. [327] Fant 1993a: 155–6. [328] Fant 1993a: 156.
[329] Pausanias I.18.8–9; *Historia Augusta: Life of Tacitus* 10.5.
[330] John Malalas, *Chronicle* 11.24.

Other imperial gifts of stone also suggest that this activity needs to be seen in the broader context of typical imperial beneficence. Marble and granite were given for the restoration of the portico above the *summa cavea* of the amphitheatre at Capua in the Hadrianic period, for example.[331] An unnamed emperor also gave paving stone to Kourion, probably in the late first century AD.[332] In none of these cases is the exact material specified but it seems likely that this was not stone from the large, imperially owned quarries discussed above. Gifts from officials and private individuals to cities were common and do not always indicate monopolistic ownership of the sources of the donated materials. There is nothing to indicate, for example, that the two black marble blocks given to Lepcis Magna by Fulvius Plautianus were from a monopolized source; these were fancy stones that this official was simply well placed to be able to get hold of.[333] The same was probably true of the marble that Chresimus, the procurator mentioned in Chapter 2 and above, donated for the construction of a gymnasium at Tralles.[334] Paying for stone, as opposed to whole buildings, was not a common act of euergetism, but there are certainly attestations of it: gifts of marble for civic building projects by private individuals are documented at Lepcis Magna and at Ephesos, for example.[335] The case of M. Ulpius Carminius Claudianus, who made many gifts to the city of Aphrodisias during the second century AD, largely of buildings and statues, has already been noted.[336] These gifts were generous not because nobody else had access to identical or similar sources of marble, or because this material was not for sale, but because Carminius was supplying it free of charge.

Gifts of marble, therefore, were probably intended to reflect the generosity of the emperor, his access to exotic materials, and his unbounded wealth. In the case of Athens such gifts also reflect this particular emperor's desire to furnish the capital (newly rejuvenated) of the Greek world appropriately.[337] These donations relieved the cities concerned of the exorbitant costs of transporting columns in such numbers from these distant quarries. They also provided these cities with material that was in such demand from imperial building projects that there would have been very little chance of them securing what they needed otherwise.

CONCLUSIONS

The imperially coordinated movement of stone, especially the fanciest coloured marbles and granites, was never entirely divorced from the ordinary,

---

[331] *CIL* X.3832 (Capua).   [332] *IvKourion* 106.
[333] *IRT* 530a–b.   [334] *CIL* III.7146; also Hirt 2010: 115–16.
[335] *IRT* 601; *IvEphesos* 430, 661.   [336] *CIG* 2782.
[337] Spawforth and Walker 1985; Mitchell 1987: 357–60.

non-imperial stone trade. This is true even at the quarries: as we have already seen, private contractors, themselves probably quarrying material for their own profit, played a key role in the imperial quarry system.[338] The quarrying of *pavonazzetto* under the guidance of imperial officials at Dokimeion and the production of sarcophagi at or close to the quarries, probably by private artisans, were intimately related activities even if there is no convincing evidence for imperial control of these sarcophagus workshops. Equally the close relationship between the imperial and non-imperial spheres is apparent in terms of demand: imperial tastes, on show for all to see in the form of elaborate public building projects, established wider fashions, creating precisely the kind of intense demand that the non-imperial stone trade fed. Despite this, imperial engagement with the stone trade operated on a different scale from most non-imperial activity. The emperors, or rather the officials working for them, could draw on enormous reserves of manpower, requisitioning animals and vehicles where needed. They simply had far more resources to expend on the transport of stone than ordinary customers. This explains why imperially funded building projects so often stand out against the normal pattern of stone use that is revealed by the kind of case studies detailed above.

Outside of the imperial sphere, local materials were preferred for most projects, architectural or sculptural, so long as suitable stones and the craftsmen to work them were available. This is in no way an attempt to belittle the regional and long-distance trade, apparent in all of the regions examined, in decorative stones, both in the form of raw materials and carved products. Customers all across the Roman world often went to extraordinary lengths, and expense, to engage in the wider fashions of stone use. Demand for these prestigious materials was enormous, but the cost of actually importing them varied considerably according to geography, localized topography, access to transport, and also object type. It is especially striking that outside imperial contexts, statues and sarcophagi tend to move the greatest distances. The reasons for this are primarily economic, determined above all by decisions made by the customer. Unlike architectural elements, statues and sarcophagi were objects that could be purchased singly and which functioned without need for other imported materials. The same is not true of columns, capitals or bases, which had to be imported in large numbers. It is striking that those marble statues and sarcophagi that did penetrate far inland tend to be of the highest quality—consumers were willing to spend far more to import an Attic sarcophagus, for instance, than any cheaper alternative. What this clearly

---

[338] See Chapter 3: Contractors and imperial quarrying (pp. 45–9).

shows is the importance of distinguishing between object types, even those carved in the same stone. Different types of object were valued, used, and consequently purchased quite differently. For this reason, the next three chapters, which concentrate on production, are divided according to object type, focusing in turn on architectural elements, sarcophagi, and statues.

6

Building and Stone Supply

Considerable quantities of the stone quarried in the Roman world were used as rubble, aggregate, or basic ashlar, but a substantial proportion of it also ended up being carved into more complex forms. The production of these objects is rarely discussed in wider economic studies of Roman manufacturing which tend to limit themselves to other categories of non-perishable artefacts which are considered more everyday, in particular ceramics. Stone objects, though, deserve more attention in this regard. Not only do traces of working on these items often reveal how they were made, but finds at quarries, in shipwrecks, and at sites all around the Roman world allow a detailed reconstruction of their production to be formulated. As Rockwell has stated: 'any object worked in stone is a document that, correctly understood, describes its own manufacture'.[1] This basic assumption underlies much of what follows in the next three chapters, each of which deals with a different category of evidence: architectural elements, sarcophagi, and statues. These categories are treated separately because the way in which these objects were commissioned, made, and used often varied significantly even if certain similarities of approach can be noted in their production.

Most of the stone quarried in the Roman world ended up in buildings and it is the production of those architectural forms central to the Roman builder's repertoire that are the focus of this chapter: columns, capitals, and bases. Architectural elements have received considerable attention before from this perspective. Indeed, what he regarded as the serial production of column shafts formed a central plank in Ward-Perkins' model of the Roman stone trade.[2] This is the light in which the primary data have tended to be viewed. Conclusions derived from finds of architectural elements at the quarries in particular have been used to back up this notion of a closely controlled system orientated around the production-to-stock of standardized objects. This viewpoint has even entered wider scholarship on Roman architecture.[3]

---

[1] Rockwell 1993: 5. [2] Ward-Perkins 1980*b*; 1992*b*. [3] Wilson Jones 2000: 155.

The purpose of this chapter is to re-examine the evidence on which these conclusions have been drawn and reconsider how the process of supplying architectural elements might have functioned, from the initial decisions made by the customer to the final finishes applied on the building site. The emphasis placed on quarry-based production-to-stock, it will be argued, is misplaced. Although this is a common practice in many mechanized modern quarries it is rarer at more traditionally operated sites.[4] While blocks for sawing into panels and perhaps certain other objects of non-specific form were probably produced in the Roman period without specific buyers in mind this is unlikely to have been the case with more complex architectural elements. Rather we should imagine a more responsive system in which the majority of architectural elements were produced from scratch in reaction to specific demand from suppliers working for architects and their customers or from these individuals directly.

THE ARCHITECTURAL PROJECT

The series of processes that lead to a finished building began first and foremost with decisions made by the commissioner, whether they were an individual, group of individuals, or a collective body, such as a city council.[5] During this first phase of planning the type of building, its location, and the available budget were decided and an architect selected. This could have been done by either approaching someone specific or opening the contract up to competitive tender.[6] It was up to the architect to realize the demands of their client and one gets a good sense of how they might respond and adapt to these requests in Vitruvius' description of the basilica which he designed at Fano—a structure which was forced to be innovative so as to avoid obstructing existing buildings while remaining sufficiently light and airy to be usable.[7]

Managing building projects

While architects might have brought teams of workers with them, the usual practice appears to have been for them to contract out responsibility for the actual construction work to dedicated building contractors or *redemptores*,

---

[4] On this point, Bessac, Abdul Massih, and Valat 1997: 164.

[5] For a detailed discussion of the individuals involved in commissioning a public building, Mar 2008.

[6] On this process, Duncan-Jones 1982: 75–6; Taylor 2003: 16–17.

[7] Vitruvius V.1.6.

who would take over the hiring and organization of the workforce and the supply of materials, subcontracting out parts of the job to other specialists as necessary.[8] These contractors provided the link between, on the one hand, the workforce and the on-site foremen in charge on a day-to-day basis and, on the other hand, the architect, who could involve themselves in the actual building process as much or as little as they liked. At Fano, Vitruvius tells us that he 'superintended the building', and it is likely that other architects oversaw the entire construction process, from initial design through to final finish. Several legal documents suggest that the commissioner themselves might sometimes take responsibility for overseeing building work, contracting workmen and suppliers directly.[9] Dio Chrysostom took it upon himself, when building his contentious stoa at Prusa, to supervise the supply of materials, for example; he moans, in particular, about having to visit the 'mountains', perhaps to oversee quarrying.[10] On publicly funded projects, meanwhile, on which every decision would have gone through the local council, this oversight was provided by an official.[11] These curators of public building (*curatores operum publicorum* or ἐπιμελέται) were responsible for chasing up promises of materials or funds from different donors, managing the *redemptores* involved, and liaising with the architect. Plutarch describes how he performed this role, 'standing and watching tiles being measured or mortar or stones being delivered'.[12] This was evidently a supervisory position but we also hear of public officials taking a more active role. A priest, who was also a municipal official, is attested ordering columns, capitals, and bases for a palaestra at Heracleopolis in the Antonine period; the same individual also takes responsibility for arranging their transport.[13] The Aurelius Hermaios, mentioned in Chapter 2, who over-spent so alarmingly on porphyry slabs, was a public official tasked specifically with securing materials for several third-century building projects at Hermo-polis.[14] Several contracts between suppliers of building materials and repre-sentatives of city councils also survive from elsewhere in Egypt.[15]

Picking the right *redemptores* for the job would have been a critical decision and would presumably have been shaped by the type of project, the desired finish, and the materials required, as well as the available budget. Employing local contractors when the work was to be completed in local materials would

---

[8] For a full discussion of the relationship between architect and contractors on site, see Barresi 2003: 51–81; for an example of a contract, for the building of a wall in second-century BC Puteoli, see *ILS* 5317; also Taylor 2003: 16.

[9] *Digest* 19.2.22 (Paul), 19.2.59 (Javolenus), 19.2.60 (Labeo).

[10] Dio Chrysostom, *Orations* XL, 7.

[11] For more detail, see Barresi 2003: 68–77; Mar 2008: 180–1; Lazzarini 2010: 490.

[12] Plutarch, *Praecepta gerendae reipublicae* 15; also Jones 1940: 237–8; Łukaszewicz 1986: 104.

[13] *P.Hib.* II.217.

[14] *C.P.Herm.* 86, 94; also Łukaszewicz 1986: 106–7.

[15] *P.Got.* 7; *P.Köln* 52; *P.Oxy.* I.55, XII.1450; on orders placed by *curatores operum pub-licorum*, see Kolb 1993: 114–21.

obviously have been the most cost-effective option—and one Vitruvius would certainly have approved of.[16] However, as we saw in Chapter 5, commissioners of large projects often turned to skilled contractors from elsewhere who could supply both high-quality materials and the workers needed to carve them. Teams of carvers from Greece, carving in Pentelic marble, can be identified in Rome and North Africa, while others from Asia Minor, working primarily but not exclusively in Prokonnesian, were present in the Levant, North Africa, and Italy.[17] Carvers from Italy on the other hand apparently worked all across the western Mediterranean in the first century AD.[18] Prominent architects probably had trusted *redemptores* to whom they returned again and again and who they knew had the right network of associates to acquire both sound materials and reliable workmen. Eastern architects, who are likely to have had close contacts with carvers and suppliers connected to the eastern quarries, were certainly sought after in the second century AD; as Trajan informs Pliny the Younger in one of his more terse letters, 'you cannot lack architects: every province has skilled men trained for this work. It is a mistake to think that they can be sent out more quickly from Rome when they usually come to us from Greece'.[19] An architect honoured at Olbia, in Ukraine, was a citizen of both Tomis (Costanţa) and Nicomedia. Considering that most of the imported white marble in this area came from Prokonnesos, close to Nicomedia, it is tempting to draw some connection here between the choice of architect and material.[20]

Specialist contractors

Redemptores and the subcontractors working for them could be employed in a number of ways, to oversee the completion of either part of a project or the whole thing, to supply materials, to work them, or to do both. Regrettably, about the status or identities of these individuals who played such a key role in the process of architectural production, providing the link between quarry and customer, we know relatively little. Several *redemptores marmorarii*, presumably contractors specializing in supplying and working marble, however, are attested in inscriptions: C. Avillius December at Puteoli, M. Vipsanius

---

[16] Vitruvius I.2.8 on 'the thrifty and wise control of expense in the works' (trans. F. Granger).

[17] On Athenian architectural carvers, Walker 1979. On architectural carvers from Asia Minor, Ward-Perkins 1980*b*: 63; in the Levant, Pensabene 1997; and at Cyrene, Pensabene 2006: 237. On the mix of workers at Lepcis Magna, Ward-Perkins 1993; Pensabene 2001*a*; Bianchi 2009.

[18] Pensabene 1986: 297, 299; 1995; 2004.

[19] Pliny the Younger, *Letters* X.40 (trans. B. Radice); for more on the origins of architects, Toynbee 1951: 9–15.

[20] *IGRR* I.854; Ward-Perkins 1980*b*: 34, no. 7.

Clemens at Lepcis Magna, and another individual at Rome.[21] Rawson high-lighted the example of one family, the Cossutii, that appears to have been involved in building, stone supply, and carving over an extended period of time.[22] The first prominent member of this family known to us was Decimus Cossutius, the architect employed by Antiochus IV Epiphanes to complete the construction of the Olympieion at Athens in the second century BC.[23] Over the following two centuries, members of this family are attested at Erythrae and Eretria, on Delos, Ios, Paros, and Kos, most apparently engaged in building and stone supply.[24] Later members of the family branched out into other areas of stone-working: in the first century BC, freedmen of the Cossutii are known from signatures on three statues from Italy; an M. Cossutius is recorded as *marmorarius* on a first-century AD inscription from Pisa; stone-carvers' tools are depicted on a funerary inscription from Rome set up by Cn. Cossutius Agathangelus for his wife Cossutia Arescusa and his brother Cn. Cossutius Cladus in the late first or second century AD; and two Cossutii even appear at Chemtou in the second century AD.[25] This one family's involvement in stone supply lasted well over 400 years and comparisons can be drawn with the later Frugone family in Italy. Two members of this family (Stefano and Jacopo) are listed as specialist marble transporters in sixteenth-century documents from Carrara; in the middle of the next century another two (Filippo and Giovanni Battista) supplied marble to Bernini, Algardi, and others in Rome; and at the end of the seventeenth century we hear of a certain Giovanni Martino Frugone supplying marble for the French Academy in Rome and the Lateran, among other projects.[26]

Even if the contractors employed did not have direct access to sources of the required materials specialist suppliers also existed and probably performed a similar role to many of the later Cossutii. One the most famous such suppliers is Marcus Aurelius Xenonianus Aquila, a Bithynian based at the Horrea Petroniana in Rome, in the third century AD, who describes himself as a seller of stone ($\lambda\iota\theta\acute{\epsilon}\mu\pi o\rho os$), on an inscription in Prokonnesian marble.[27] A second Bithynian, this time from Nicomedia, who describes himself as a $\lambda\iota\theta\acute{\epsilon}\nu\pi o\rho os$, is

---

[21] *CIL* X.1549 (Puteoli), VI.33873 (Rome); *IRT* 275 (Lepcis Magna).

[22] On the Cossutii, Rawson 1975: 36–9; Torelli 1980: 313–17; Hatzfeld 1919: 107; Coarelli 1983: 46.

[23] Decimus Cossutius is mentioned by Vitruvius (VII.Pref.) and on a statue base from the site of the Olympieion (*IG* III.1.561).

[24] Keil 1910: no. 25 (Erythrae); *IG* XII Suppl. 557 (Eretria); Roussel and Launey 1937; no. 1738–9, 1767 (Delos); *IG* XII.5.11 (Ios); *IG* XII.5.1049 (Paros); *IGRR* IV.1092 (Cos).

[25] On the signatures: British Museum cat. no. 1666, 1667; *IG* XIV.1250; Pisa, *CIL* XI.1415; Rome, *CIL* VI.16534a–b; on Chemtou, *CIL* VIII.14628–9.

[26] On the Frugone family, Klapisch-Zuber 1969: 190, 203; Weil 1974: 136–8, no. 5; Olszewski 1986: 660–2.

[27] *SEG* IV.106; also Ward-Perkins 1980*b*: 33.

attested at Terni in the same period.[28] Nicomedians involved in the stone trade are relatively well represented in the epigraphic record. A Nicomedian *marmorarius* is attested at Lepcis Magna and an association (*synodos*) of Nicomedian sculptors existed at Nicopolis-ad-Istrum.[29] This led Ward-Perkins to propose that these Nicomedians controlled output from the Prokonnesian and possibly other quarries and were perhaps centrally organized.[30] While there is no evidence for the latter, Nicomedian stone-workers were well placed to access both the Prokonnesian quarries and the granite quarries in the Troad and like their colleagues from Athens, Dokimeion, and Aphrodisias were clearly sought after for their services overseas.

Whether the Nicomedian *marmorarius* at Lepcis Magna, Asclepiades son of Asclepiades, was involved simply in the carving of stone or its supply as well is unclear. On one level *marmorarius* clearly meant just 'marble-worker'.[31] In the well-known Constantinian edict (*De Excusationibus Artificum*) releasing artists from compulsory public services, *marmorarii* and *lapidarii* are listed alongside *quadratarii* (stone-squarers) and *sculptores* (sculptors), as craftsmen.[32] However, some *marmorarii*, as we have seen, also describe themselves as *redemptores*, and a tantalizing inscription from Rome mentions a *negotiator marmorarius*.[33] This suggests that *marmorarius* was an overarching title which covered numerous specialisms. Asclepiades was at Lepcis Magna under either the Antonines or Severans, depending on how one reads the inscription, but in both periods Prokonnesian marble (alongside Pentelic) was used in vast quantities and it seems likely that Nicomedians like him were present because of their ties to the quarries.[34] *Marmorarii* elsewhere must also have been able to secure the materials that they needed in order to do their work. The same might have been true of *lapidarii*. This term again, however, covered a range of proficiencies: a *lapidarius quadratarius* is attested at Rome, *fabri lapidarii* at Bologna and Narbonne, a *lapidarius subaedianus* at a site in Bosnia Herzegovina, an *opifex lapidarius* at Vaison-la-Romaine, and a *lapidarius structor* at Saintes.[35] Even if *lapidarii*, probably more often than *marmorarii*, worked in whatever materials were available locally, they would still have to have been able to supply materials as well as their expertise. In sum, it seems reasonable to assume that both *marmorarii* and *lapidarii* could

---

[28] *IG* XIV.2247; this individual, Aurelius Andronikos, is recorded on an epitaph, now lost.

[29] *IRT* 807, 275; *IGBulg* II.674.

[30] For the full elaboration of this argument, see Ward-Perkins 1980*b*.

[31] For attestations of *marmorarii*, see Calabi Limentani 1961*b*.

[32] *Codex Theodosianus* XIII.4.2.

[33] *CIL* VI.33886.

[34] Ward-Perkins 1951: 93–4; 1980*b*: 33; 1993: 98–9; on the use of imported marble in the Hadrianic and Antonine periods, see Pensabene 2001*a*; Bianchi 2009.

[35] *CIL* VI.9502; *CIL* XI.6838; Espérandieu 1929: no. 580; *AE* 1913, 137; *CIL* XII.1384; *CIL* XIII.1034; see Calabi Limentani 1961*a*.

be more than simply carvers and probably oversaw the supply of material as well.

Some of these specialist contractors are likely to have had connections at the quarries to which they returned again and again. Certainly the major teams of workers attested throughout the eastern Mediterranean in the second century AD enjoyed access to the Prokonnesian quarries, perhaps also the Troad granite quarries. Some of these contractors might even have owned quarries, while others were probably able to acquire material from a range of sources, including ones further afield. Either way, in dealing with the demands of their clients, these contractors had three main options available to them for securing the required stone: they could order the material that was needed to be produced from scratch at the quarries; they could supply it from their own stock, if they had anything suitable; or they could acquire it from some other stockpile, at a quarry, at a building yard perhaps, or from another specialist supplier. The same range of options was available to commissioners or officials who were keen to oversee this process themselves, except of course that they are unlikely to have had any stock of their own (though in the case of public officials we should not rule this out).

ORDERING FROM THE QUARRIES

The assumption that a considerable quantity of the materials used in any structure—and especially the largest imperial complexes—was supplied from stock has become something of a commonplace in discussions of Roman building.[36] The conventional argument is that it would have been more expensive and time-consuming to order the materials needed to be produced from scratch, particularly when they often came from distant quarries. Indeed Ward-Perkins regarded the widespread production-to-stock of building materials as one of the key characteristics of the Roman stone trade that distinguished it from earlier Greek practices whereby most stone came from local quarries and was ordered 'quite literally block by block'.[37] This contrast between Roman and earlier practices, however, should not be overstated. As noted throughout the preceding chapters, most building projects continued to be supplied from local quarries even in the Roman period. Furthermore, a responsive production-to-order system, not dissimilar to that identified by Ward-Perkins in the Greek world, should not be so quickly dismissed for the

---

[36] For examples, Dodge 1988*b*: 215–17; Barresi 2002: 71–2; 2003: 64; Wright 2005*a*: 39. On the impact of Ward-Perkins' model of production-to-stock, Dodge 1991: 36–7. For scepticism about this issue, Fant 2008*a*: 131.

[37] Ward-Perkins 1980*b*: 24.

later Roman period, even when quarry and customer were located at some distance from each other. The quarry data, so often used to argue in favour of production-to-stock, can be interpreted quite differently and to this we can add new documentary material from Mons Claudianus to suggest that production-to-order in fact remained common. Before examining these data-sets, though, it is first worth considering how ordering material from the quarries might have functioned in practice.

The logistics of commissioning

How did those contracted to supply building projects communicate with quarries that were often (and increasingly in our period) far away? Occasionally, of course, the contractor might themselves have had direct access to a quarry in which case the solution was simple. This must have been quite common when the quarry was local, but we should not rule out the possibility that more long-distance links were established over time as the example of the Cossutii mentioned above shows. If the contractors involved did not have these kind of long-standing connections with the quarries then they could either subcontract the job to others who did or contact the necessary quarry-men themselves. This last option, of course, would have been difficult when there were significant distances involved; the order would have to have been sent either in written form via a third party or with a worker who could then have stayed to oversee its completion and delivery. The first of these options required less effort on the part of the contractor but for this system to function effectively the request would have to have been relatively standard or explained via some form of drawing. A certain amount of trust would have to have existed between these parties too: it would be difficult to describe a complex three-dimensional form remotely in this way and impossible for the contractor to ensure that suitable-quality material was used for the project. The responsibility for any substandard material would fall ultimately on the shoulders of the contractor, as would the potential cost of replacing it.

Sending a skilled worker with the order who could then stay and supervise work would eliminate most of these issues. This individual could explain what was needed, select materials, and check on progress but also negotiate and arrange payment in a way that a third party could not. A contractor of any standing would certainly have been able to afford dispatching one worker to the quarry for several months even if they could not do without a larger team. It is tempting to see the very precisely shaped objects recovered from a range of quarry sites, as will be demonstrated below, as having been worked on by carvers under the oversight of such an individual. An intriguing find from the Prokonnesian quarries suggests that sometimes at least these visiting workers brought with them models from which to work. This is the single Corinthian

Fig. 6.1. Corinthian capital in Aurisina limestone from Prokonnesos, now in the open-air museum at Saraylar (photo: author).

capital, itself already used, in a style common only at the northern Italian city of Aquileia, which is carved not in Prokonnesian marble but in the limestone quarried at Aurisina to the east of Aquileia (Fig. 6.1).[38] In this case the order was presumably for a set of capitals like this but in the more prestigious Prokonnesian marble. When the commission was completed there must have seemed little point paying for this model to be returned too; alternatively, perhaps the commission was cancelled and this model abandoned.

A system of specialized, quarry-based workers completing orders under the supervision of visiting contractors or their agents would have functioned well for most kinds of commissions. The larger the project or the more awkward the request, though, the more strain this system would have been put under. In these cases, it might have been ultimately more cost-effective for a contractor to dispatch an entire team of workers to the quarry, so ensuring that exact requirements were met and material supplied promptly. Fifteenth-century

[38] Pensabene 2002*b*: 50; for the argument in favour of such models at Pergamon, Rohmann 1998: 28.

records from Venice show that stonemasons were sent to the quarries in Istria to oversee quarrying of the material they needed; the convent of San Zaccaria even hired accommodation close to the quarries for the masons in its employ.[39] In the Roman period, such teams could have purchased or leased a concession from the quarry-owners or even arranged some other deal with local subcontractors to work their quarry faces. For really large building projects, like the various imperial ones, extra workers must have been sent to the quarries to supplement the existing workforce. It is notable in this regard that recent analysis of the marble used in the Baths of Caracalla suggests that all of the Prokonnesian and all of the Pentelic objects originated from the same extraction points within these respective quarrying zones, regardless of their final use.[40] All of the Luna marble used in the Building with Three Exedras at Hadrian's Villa also came from the same district of those quarries, again indicating a single campaign of extraction for this project.[41] These particular quarry faces were either new ones opened specific-ally to supply this project or existing ones turned over to the task. This opening up of new quarry faces would almost certainly have been accompan-ied by an influx of workers.

Which of these options was preferred would have depended very much on the type of commission, its timescale, and the relationship between the contractor outside the quarry and the subcontractors within it. The prime concern for the contractor, and especially the architect and customer above them, was that the material acquired was of suitable quality—that is was up to the job. This has an impact on the way we understand quarries operating. Rather than closed sites run by single enterprises these were varied locations at which different groups of personnel would have interacted. The inscriptions from Prokonnesos discussed in Chapter 3 seem to support this. Different quarry faces here appear to have been owned by different individuals or groups: we know that one quarry in the Mandıra district was owned at some point by an Apollodoros, another perhaps by a certain Aufidius, who had a Latin name but abbreviated it in Greek.[42] We can also hypothesize different working systems operating at the same time. While 90 per cent of the roughed-out material on Prokonnesos was left uninscribed, one producer or set of producers was clearly more fastidious. The series of inscriptions, mainly on roughed-out Corinthian capitals mentioning an Antonius or Antoninus (in Greek), often along with the initials IMR (in Latin), come from two distinct areas of the quarries: the valley between the Köyüstü and Yalancı Palatya hills (where they are inscribed) and the Silinte district (where they are painted). As Asgari and Drew-Bear put it, 'this inscription had a function not in the general production of Corinthian capitals [on Prokonnesos], but in the particular

---

[39] Connell 1988: 99–100.   [40] Attanasio, Brilli, and Bruno 2008: 753.
[41] Attanasio et al. 2009: 363.   [42] Asgari and Drew-Bear 2002: nos. 8, 10.

circumstances of a single workshop or artisan in a single area of the quarries'.[43] Different conventions for keeping track of output seem to have been used by other individuals: two column shafts, for instance, from the Silinte district have a sort of hourglass symbol, comprising a pair of triangles, incised on their ends, and seem to have been part of the same project.[44]

In addition to the Aufidius mentioned above there were other individuals on Prokonnesos, revealed by their funerary epitaphs, whose names betray their distant origin: Gaius Culcius Rufus, Laevius Soterius, and Aurelius Octacilius Crispus and his wife who had their sarcophagus inscribed in both Greek and Latin; an individual named Chrestos even states that he is a Nicomedian.[45] We should probably imagine that at any one moment in time most large quarries contained workers based there permanently, responding to orders placed with them by contractors elsewhere (sometimes with and sometimes without supervisors sent by them), as well as teams working there on a short-term basis for the completion of a specific project. In his analysis of the limestone quarries at Bois des Lens near Nîmes, Bessac argued for a similar scenario, with small teams of workers being sent to the quarries from the building site, often for limited periods of time, for the extraction of specific quantities of material.[46] It is just possible that this is less of an exceptional arrangement than Bessac originally thought and that the distinction between working practices at these relatively small limestone quarries and those at the major white marble quarries of the Roman world has been drawn too sharply.

Documentary evidence

Remarkable testimony to the process of ordering architectural elements directly from the quarries is provided by a series of newly published *ostraka* from Mons Claudianus. Although this site was quite exceptional and this activity was clearly not undertaken during its peak period of operation, there is enough comparable data from elsewhere to indicate that this evidence is representative of broader trends. Two separate sets of correspondence relate to the ordering of columns by imperial officials. The first of these is a draft letter addressed to Antonius Flavianus, a prefect, probably the *praefectus Berenicidis*; the document is dated roughly to the late second century and reports on progress fulfilling an order:

---

[43] Asgari and Drew-Bear 2002: 8.   [44] Asgari and Drew-Bear 2002: nos. 20–1.
[45] *IvKyzikos* I.270, 273, 380, 487; see Hasluch 1910: cat. nos. 5.76, 89, 255, 270.
[46] Bessac 2002: 51.

To Antonius Flavianus, prefect, from the foremen and the stonemasons, Sir, greetings. With the help of our lord Sarapis and the Tyche of Claudianus and your Tyche we announce that we have finished one of the two 25 foot columns on the 26th day of Hathyr. If you please, Sir, and with the accord of our master the procurator, if steel and charcoal be sent to us, we shall finish the other one faster, if we can work without hindrance. From the moment you send us (it, and if) all the infidels (will leave us in peace) ... (we shall we able to finish it).'[47]

We can date this letter because these same columns seem to be mentioned again in a set of letters addressed to an imperial procurator named Probus, who was certainly operating in Egypt during the reign of Commodus.[48] The first of these, a fairly fragmentary text, seems to record the placing of an order for at least one 26 RF column, though the precise details are unclear.[49] This is followed up later by a progress report, which responds directly to a request from the procurator for more information about proceedings:

To Probus, procurator of the Lord Caesar, from the stonemasons, foremen, and smiths working in the quarry of Claudianus, Sir, greetings. We announce to you, Sir, the good tidings that Sarapis willing and with the help of the Tyche of Claudianus and your Tyche, we have accomplished the first column by the 26th of the current month Hathyr, ... Egyptian cubits. You write, Sir, to tell you from which quarry. We do not know the name of the quarry, but it is the quarry far from the *praesidium*, lying towards Porphyrites, which we have given the name 'Philoserapis'. When we were well arrived at the quarry ... [50]

The fact that the column mentioned is completed on the same date as the one described in the above text seems to suggest that these are the same object, even if there is a little confusion about whether it is 25 or 26 RF long. A third draft letter is filed nineteen days later stating that a second column, part of the same order, has also been completed.[51] Probus, though, was not satisfied and in a fourth letter the stonemasons are forced to respond to his complaints:

We have received your letter, Sir, in which you reproach us about the *caurasia* [broken stone?] because we have made them conterminous [fitted them together?]. However, as we (had learnt) from your letter that there was iron in the store, we used all the colour-mixing, like the people of old (taught us).[52]

---

[47] Bülow-Jacobsen 2009: no. 850; on the identification of Antonius Flavianus as *praefectus Berenicidis*, as opposed to *praefectus Aegypti*, cf. Bülow-Jacobsen 2009: 178–9.

[48] Bülow-Jacobsen 2009: 183.

[49] Bülow-Jacobsen 2009: no. 855.

[50] Bülow-Jacobsen 2009: no. 853; in this case the site named Porphyrites is probably not Mons Pophyrites but a single extraction site at Mons Claudianus, which crops up again in several *ostraka* relating to the distribution of personnel at the site (no. 704–6).

[51] Bülow-Jacobsen 2009: no. 856: 'To Probus, the procurator of Caesar. Tithoes and the foremen, Sir, greetings. We announce to you the good tidings that on the 14th of the current month Choiak we have finished the second of the [two 26-foot columns] ...'.

[52] Bülow-Jacobsen 2009: no. 854.

The obscure terminology employed here seems to describe the piecing together of two parts of this column using iron clamps, a not unusual solution; the 'colour-mixing' might refer to a technique for concealing the join. Probus was irked by the end result, but starting from scratch was apparently not an option. In fact, the not insignificant number of columns repaired in this way that actually entered the supply stream adds further support to the idea that these objects were not simply selected from stock—a lot of work had gone into their manufacture and accidental damage could not be allowed to hold up proceedings.

Interestingly, the workers that we encounter in the second of these *ostraka* appear to have been sent to the quarries for the completion of a single commission. Their ignorance when it comes to the names of the quarries shows an unfamiliarity with this region, while their complaints about hostile locals indicate that the quarries did not have a permanent population at this date.[53] Earlier *ostraka* show that the quarries had a much larger workforce in the Trajanic period at least and one that could probably have dealt with quite significant orders coming in, but by the later second century this appears to have changed.[54]

To this list of fairly complete texts we might add a more fragmentary subset of *ostraka* which apparently also relate to the ordering of material from the quarries. A register of stone plaques (πλάκες) from the 'Dionysos' quarry, confusingly accompanied by a set of incomprehensible numbers or dimensions, makes sense as an order and is dated to the Antonine period.[55] Likewise, an abbreviated Latin text, dated to the Trajanic period, mentioning a 33 RF column from the 'Sozusa' quarry might be the receipt of an order, part of a progress report like those discussed above, or a note of the completion of a project.[56]

Though the correspondence between the workers at Mons Claudianus and their overseers evidently took place over some distance (Antonius Flavianus was probably based at Berenice), the detail and frequency of the letters shows that close ties were maintained. There was an established infrastructure in the Eastern Desert, coordinated by the imperial officials on hand, which must have made this kind of long-distance coordination fairly unproblematic. To judge from other *ostraka* at other Eastern Desert quarries there was regular traffic along the roads between the Red Sea and the Nile.[57] Personnel at other

[53] Fant 2010: 777.
[54] Cuvigny 2005; for more on this, see below: Chapter 6: Timescales and manpower (pp. 230–2).
[55] Bülow-Jacobsen 2009: no. 844.
[56] Bülow-Jacobsen 2009: no. 846; no. 848, another Trajanic text, seem to refer to the supply of a number of other objects of unspecified type, though columns seem a reasonable bet since only two dimensions are listed.
[57] On gifts sent along these roads by quarrymen and soldiers at Wadi Hammâmât and elsewhere, including food and wine, Kayser 1993: nos. 22, 28–9.

imperially controlled quarries could presumably also have taken advantage of similarly well-established communication channels.

From non-imperial quarries documentary evidence is understandably more limited but the inscriptions from Marignac and Saint-Boil, both discussed in Chapter 3, could be interpreted as recording the completion of specific commissions.[58] The workers responsible from the Marignac inscription appear to have been at the quarries for the completion of a single job—the carving and transport of a pair of 20 RF columns—and give thanks to Silvanus and the spirits of the mountains for its safe completion. The Saint-Boil inscription meanwhile appears to assign certain amounts of material to specific workers, probably for a particular project; although the interpretation of this text is far from certain these individuals seem not to have been simply producing material on a continual basis.

Finds from the quarries

Support for the notion that work at quarries was undertaken in close correspondence with a range of individual contractors and sometimes even under their direct supervision can be found at the quarries themselves. Considerable quantities of partially worked architectural elements are known from Roman quarrying sites, including blocks, column shafts, capitals, bases, and sometimes more complicated objects. In some cases finishing even took place within the quarries: completed capitals and bases are known from both the Prokonnesian and Pentelic quarries.[59] As will be demonstrated, in the precision of the carving undertaken on these objects, the range of their sizes and levels of finish, this material reveals just how varied and responsive to different requests this initial stage of working was.

These data, though, are not usually discussed in this light. Finds from the quarries have traditionally been interpreted as the vestiges of carefully managed stockpiles resulting from the serial production of standardized products to stock for contractors and architects elsewhere to select from. Ward-Perkins was the first to speculate on such a system, arguing that this should be understood as a vital step—'the fundamental innovation'—taken to ensure demand was met and major building projects were supplied on time.[60] The evidence from the quarries, though, can be read differently. Indeed, several important studies since Ward-Perkins was writing have cast serious

---

[58] See Chapter 3: Organization of work (p. 57).
[59] Asgari 1988: 118; Pensabene 2001a: 79–83, 87–9; a finished base from the Pentelic quarries was mentioned by F. Bianchi and M. Bruno at ASMOSIA X in Rome in June 2012.
[60] Ward-Perkins 1980a: 327; 1980b: 25.

doubt on the idea of quarry-based serial production.[61] The main argument against this model is the demonstrable absence of almost any identifiable set of standard sizes of architectural elements, without which an effective production-to-stock orientated system could not have functioned. Before examining this issue in detail, though, it is useful to re-examine the material recovered from the quarries.

The reasons for roughing out quarried material within the quarries, prior to transport, are generally agreed upon. One benefit was that this preliminary working helped identify any flaws in the stone as early as possible. Michelangelo describes the discovery of one such flaw in a section of rock from which a nearly completely rounded column shaft was being extracted; this forced him, as he put it, 'to work back into the hill the whole thickness of the column' in order to avoid it.[62] The prime motivation for roughing out major architectural elements at the quarry, though, was weight reduction. It is especially easy to explain in the case of column shafts: a shaped column shaft weighs over 20 per cent less than a roughly rectangular block of the same height and width; for a shaft measuring 8 × 1 m, this represents a weight reduction of roughly 4,500 kg. Even prior to the Roman fascination with monolithic column shafts, column drums were regularly roughed out in the quarries for precisely this reason; the best-preserved examples, dating to the fifth century BC, come from the Cave di Cusa near Selinunte on Sicily (Fig. 6.2).[63] At this site, as at later Roman quarries, drums and shafts were usually cut straight from the rock-face in a roughly rounded form. Three sides of the shaft could be shaped before separation leaving only the fourth side to be smoothed off, an activity which leaves behind characteristic curved recesses.

Identifying any faults within the rock as early as possible in this process was an absolute priority in the case of monolithic shafts. These turn up surprisingly often at larger quarries. Most can be dated only broadly, to the Roman period, and then only because monolithic column shafts were rare prior to the first century BC, while newly quarried ones are scarce after the third century AD. For more specific dates we are reliant on inscriptions, themselves quite limited in number and restricted generally to the late first and second centuries AD. Despite this patchy data, it would seem that it was normal to rough out column shafts throughout the Roman period. The nine columns at the Kylindroi quarry near Karystos are the most spectacular examples, but other shafts can be seen in the granite quarries at Yedi Taşlar in the Troad, at Mons Claudianus, at Chemtou, at Luna, at Capo Testa,

---

[61] See esp. Asgari 1990: 117.   [62] Stone and Stone 1962: 96.
[63] Peschlow-Bindoket 1990. For column drums from Carrara, Dolci 1980: 200–1; 2006: no. 175, 212.

Fig. 6.2. Roughed-out column drums still attached to the bedrock in the Cave di Cusa quarries near Selinunte, Sicily (photo: author).

at Göktepe, at Felsberg in Germany, and on Thasos, to name but a few (Figs. 6.3, 6.4, and 6.5).[64] These were typically worked with the point chisel all over; the surfaces of their shafts carefully curved. To guard against bangs and knocks during onward transit, these shafts were usually produced with wide collars at either end, out of which the final moulded projections (the astragal and flare) could be carved at their destination.[65] The entasis of each shaft had to be defined at this early stage in the process to ensure that they were produced to precisely the right dimensions, albeit with an extra layer of stone left to allow for further carving and polishing (a *gras de taille* in the

---

[64] On the Troad, Ponti 2002: 293; on Mons Claudianus, Peacock and Maxfield 1997: 201–14; on Chemtou, G. Röder 1993: 46–7 (fig. 20, pl. 47c–d); on Luna, Dolci 1980: 200–1; on Capo Testa, Poggi and Lazzarini 2005: on Göktepe, Attanasio, Bruno, and Yavuz 2009: 315–18; on Felsberg, G. Röder 1992: 135, fig. 1; on Thasos, Sodini, Lambraki, and Koželj 1980: 103, 105, 109 (figs. 46–7, 57); Pensabene 1998c: 312–13. For examples from Gaul, Bedon 1984: 115.

[65] For examples at Karystos, Hankey 1965: 58; Wilson Jones 2000: 130–2. For Prokonnesos, Asgari 1992: 41. For Nicotera, Solano 1985: 87.

Fig. 6.3. Abandoned *cipollino* column shafts in the Kylindroi quarries on Mount Ochi, Euboea (photo: courtesy Hellenic Ministry of Education and Religious Affairs, Culture and Sports/Archaeological Receipts Fund/IA EPKA (from the personal archive of M. Chidiroglou)).

Fig. 6.4. Abandoned *cipollino* column shaft in the Kylindroi quarries on Mount Ochi, Euboea (photo: courtesy Hellenic Ministry of Education and Religious Affairs, Culture and Sports/Archaeological Receipts Fund/IA EPKA (from the personal archive of M. Chidiroglou)).

Fig. 6.5. Abandoned *giallo antico* column shaft still attached to the bedrock in a quarry on the 'Gelber Berg' at Chemtou (photo: author).

Fig. 6.6. Bundle of four *pavonazzetto* column shafts from Portus, now at Ostia (photo: author).

French quarrying terminology).[66] Column shafts were occasionally also produced in bundles, like the examples of four and two columns of *pavonazzetto* from Portus (Fig. 6.6).[67] Presumably this was done to protect them during transport but it was only really practical for relatively small shafts; the longest of the examples from Portus are 3.38 m in length, and similar sets from the quarries at Dokimeion and Mons Claudianus are shorter than this.[68]

Ensuring that this initial stage of shaping was done accurately was absolutely vital if these objects were to be of any use in a final structure. The carvers responsible for this roughing out had to have the exact final measurements to hand and these had to be applied equally to all the column shafts intended for a single project. As Wilson Jones has shown, even in the relatively rigid Corinthian order, where the ratio between shaft height and diameter is usually around 1:8, values of 1:7 and even 1:9 are attested.[69] All of the shafts employed for a single project needed to have near-identical proportions to avoid disharmony and individual architects might have had particular preferred proportional arrangements. On a purely practical note, all of this would have made producing column shafts to stock difficult, unless a standard set of proportions were employed, and as Wilson Jones's data show, this appears not to have been the case.

This was also true for the capitals and bases which had to be combined with these column shafts in any final construction. Roughed-out Corinthian (or Composite) capitals are one of the most common architectural elements found in the quarries in this period, reflecting what has already been said about the popularity of the Corinthian order: seventeen are known from the Luna quarries, datable broadly to between the first and third centuries AD, and forty-three from Prokonnesos, most probably from the second century AD, though others could be later.[70] At Dokimeion, three roughed-out Corinthian capitals have been identified.[71] The various forms of these capitals and the working carried out on them will be examined in more detail below. Elsewhere, three roughed-out Corinthian capitals are known from the limestone quarry near Xylophagou on Cyprus.[72] Ionic capitals are scarcer but

---

[66] On guidelines of the carving on entasis found on columns in the quarries, Pensabene 1998c: 313; Wilson Jones 2000: 130–2, with reference to the columns from Kylindroi. On examples from the Tiber and the Colosseum, Pensabene 1992. On the *gras de taille*, Noël 1965: 192.

[67] Pensabene 1994: 73 (no. 18–19).

[68] A set of three white marble columns from Dokimeion is now held in the Afyon Archaeological Museum; for the set from Mons Claudianus, Peacock and Maxfield 1997: 201 (fig. 6.26).

[69] Wilson Jones 2000: 224–5, table 2.

[70] Dolci 2006: 220–1; Asgari 1988: 115.

[71] Waelkens, de Paepe, and Moens 1986: 114, fig. 5; the latter two were seen by Amanda Claridge in 1989 and 1998 and I am grateful to her for sharing her photographs of them with me.

[72] Karageorghis 1969: 498–9 (fig. 135–6); now in the museum at Larnaca (inv. no. 1–3).

have been found on Prokonnesos.[73] There is no question that almost identical Ionic capitals were produced at the Thasian quarries, in the fourth century AD in particular.[74] Roughed-out capitals of various types were also produced alongside roughed-out column shafts in certain limestone quarries in Gaul.[75]

Alongside capitals, bases have been found on Prokonnesos and at Luna, and also in the *bigio* quarries on Lesbos.[76] A variation on the standard column base, the pedestal, is also represented in several roughed-out forms on Prokonessos, and at Dokimeion; rectangular types, a variation found at both quarries, were used at Lepcis Magna, in the interior of the portico of the Severan Forum.[77] To this list of column shafts, capitals and bases we can add a limited corpus of more idiosyncratic objects which received some roughing out in the quarries. This includes the remarkable theatre or stadium seat from Prokonnesos as well as the roughly delineated entablature blocks from the same site which Asgari compares to those employed in the theatre at Perge.[78]

As with column shafts, the carvers responsible for roughing out these objects had to have detailed measurements to hand. The theatre seat and entablature blocks were clearly produced in response to a specific order, and were probably even worked on by carvers familiar with their final destination and what was required. The forms and sizes of capitals and bases too could only be planned out with any accuracy if the exact dimensions of the column shafts that they were to be combined with were known. The canonical form of the Corinthian capital was established by a relatively consistent vertical relationship between: the lower diameter of the column shaft and the diameter of the astragal; the diameter of the apophyge of the shaft, the axial width of the abacus, and the diameter of the kalathos; and the diagonal width of the plinth and the diagonal width of the abacus.[79] The design of a typical Corinthian column was organized around a limited set of proportions common to capital, shaft, and base, and so the production of any one of these items had to take account of, and had to be able to be accommodated with, any of the other of these pieces. This had important consequences when shaft and base and capital were carved, as was often the case, from different materials.[80]

---

[73] Asgari 1990: 120–2.   [74] Hermann and Sodini 1977: 471–511.
[75] Duval 1953: 188–9.
[76] Asgari 1990: 117–18; Dolci 2006: 221, 236–7; Pensabene 1998a: no. 27 (pl. 9.1–2). For Thasian examples from Ostia, Baccini Leotardi 1989: no. 116–17; Pensabene 1994: no. 66 (fig. 13–17).
[77] Ward-Perkins 1993: 7–22 (esp. fig. 11).
[78] Asgari 1990: 124.
[79] Wilson Jones 1989; 1991. These relationships differ slightly from those detailed by Vitruvius (IV.1.1–12). For more on the proportions of the Corinthian capital, Gros 2001: 471; Heilmeyer 1970: 13.
[80] Coloured marble shafts (red Aswan granite, *cipollino* or *pavonazzetto*) were normally combined with white marble bases and capitals, which explains the high number of capitals and bases relative to column shafts recovered from Prokonessos (Asgari 1992: 74).

Reassessing the quarry evidence

All of these roughed-out objects were produced with a clearly defined set of final dimensions in mind; they were bespoke materials which were intended to be used in combination with other equally carefully carved objects. Some alteration could have been carried out to cut them down into smaller objects but the main dimensions of column shafts especially were fixed early on and recutting was laborious and often resulted in a loss of proportion. Plutarch makes this point with regard to the columns from Athens reused in the Flavian reconstruction of the Temple of Jupiter Capitolinus: 'when re-cut and shaped at Rome, [these columns] did not gain as much in polish as they lost in symmetry and beauty, and now look too slender and thin'.[81] This general observation has important implications for the production-to-stock model. A streamlined system, orientated around production-to-stock, could only have functioned if the objects being produced were of both standardized dimensions and forms; architects and the contractors working for them had to know exactly what was available in stock and if they needed material from more than one quarry then they had to know that the same sizes would be available everywhere. Certain sizes would also have to have been prioritized since too great a range of standard sizes would have spread supplies too thinly, so undermining the whole system. If such standardized sizes were a reality then they should show up in our dataset.

Drawing together the data relating to 117 columns shafts from eleven different quarrying sites where such information has been collected reveals an interesting picture (Fig. 6.7).[82] Shafts of almost every size up to around the 30 RF mark are attested, which in itself casts serious doubt on the standardization model. However, at the upper end of the size spectrum certain groupings of sizes can be noted. A distinct cluster just above 20 RF is noticeable, as are others around the 30 RF, 38 RF, 40 RF, and 45 RF marks. Some of these represent groupings at specific quarries: there are three roughly 20 RF shafts at Chemtou, seven roughly 40 RF shafts at the Kylindroi quarries, as well as the pair of 45 RF ones at the nearby Aetos quarries, the three roughly 30 RF and three 20 RF ones at Mons Claudianus, and fifteen 37–9 RF ones at the Yedi Taşlar quarries in the Troad. These are roughed-out pieces of course, so their intended final dimensions would have been slightly smaller, and approximately half of these lengths are reconstructed from the diameter of fragmentary shafts. Even so, the data from the quarries largely reflects those collected by Wilson Jones from finished structures, primarily in Rome (Fig. 6.8), and by

---

[81] Plutarch, *Life of Publicola* XV.4 (trans. B. Perrin): these columns were probably from the Temple of Olympian Zeus.

[82] The quarries in question are Aliki on Thasos, Capo Testa, Chemtou, Aetos and Kylindroi near Karystos, Mons Claudianus, Mons Porphyrites, Moria, Nicotera, Prokonnesos, and Yedi Taşlar.

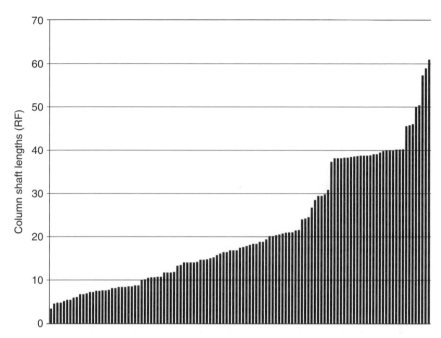

Fig. 6.7. Lengths of 117 column shafts, complete and reconstructed, from eleven quarrying sites (sources: Sodini, Lambraki, and Koželj 1980; Solano 1985; R. J. A. Wilson 1988; Asgari 1992; Kraus 1993; G. Röder 1993; Peacock and Maxfield 1997; Bruno 1998; Pensabene 1998*b*; 1998*c*; Maxfield and Peacock 2001*a*; Ponti 2002).

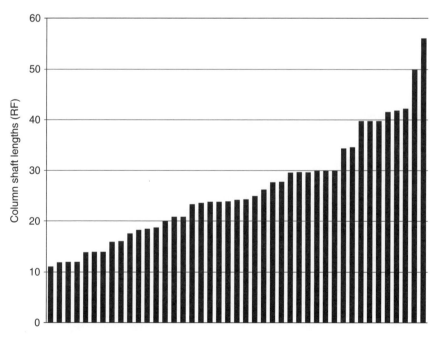

Fig. 6.8. Lengths of forty-four column shafts in finished structures in Rome (source: Wilson Jones 2000: 224–5, table 2).

Barresi.[83] Again, the largest column shafts, over about 30 RF, appear to have been routinely designed to be multiples of 5 or 10 RF, while 24 RF was also popular.

This popularity of column shafts in multiples of 4, 5, or 10 RF was remarked upon by Ward-Perkins and used to support his standardization and stock model.[84] The range of sizes of smaller column shafts seems to counter this, though. Perhaps only larger column shafts were produced to stock while smaller ones were not, but this would be odd since relatively few structures ever used column shafts over 30 RF; if this was a step taken in response to enormous demand then one might expect more standardization lower down the size spectrum. In practice, a much more simple explanation for this phenomenon emerges from Wilson Jones's work on the Roman Corinthian order.[85] As he has shown, the internal proportions of the Corinthian order became increasingly standardized during the course of the Roman period, with the principal ratio of the total height of the column (i.e. base, shaft, and capital) to that of the shaft, in particular, becoming fixed at around 6:5.[86] Beginning with a shaft that was produced in a multiple of 5 or 10 RF straight away made a considerable amount of the remaining calculations much easier, something that would have been particularly valuable on the largest projects. It meant that for a 30 RF shaft, the capital and base had to equal 6 RF in height, for a 40 RF shaft 8 RF. The popularity of sizes in multiples of 4 RF can be explained similarly, since, as Wilson Jones notes, the favoured slenderness ratio for Corinthian columns was 1:8; this meant that an 8 RF shaft usually had a lower diameter of 1 RF, a 12 RF shaft of 1.5 RF, and a 24 RF shaft of 3 RF. The internal dimensions of the shaft, in other words, were much more easily worked out for these lengths.[87]

Even if not all of the roughed-out column shafts from the quarries were destined for use as part of a Corinthian order, the vast majority probably were; 'Corinthian is the Roman order', as Wilson Jones puts it.[88] This popularity of larger column shafts in multiples of 5 or 10 RF in other words perfectly reflects contemporary architectural practice. We might even speculate on an ideological aspect to this practice, reflecting the repeated use of whole dimensions in the planning of buildings.[89] There is no need to stretch the evidence to make it fit a more complicated model of standardization and stock. Though many have shown unease with this model, few have rejected it altogether. Wilson

[83] Wilson Jones 2000: 222–5 (table 1–2); Barresi 2002: 70–2.
[84] Ward-Perkins 1980a: 327–8; 1981: 117–88; 1992b: 25–6.
[85] Fant 2008a: 131.
[86] Wilson Jones 2000: 147–8.
[87] Wilson Jones 2000: 155.
[88] Wilson Jones 2000: 135.
[89] Packer 1997: 260–3; Wilson Jones 2000: 163, fig. 8.4; DeLaine 1997: 47–56.

Jones, for instance, rules out the idea that major projects were supplied in this way and shows that column shafts were produced in all sorts of sizes, but still allows that standardization and production-to-stock might have taken place occasionally.[90] Dodge, too, expresses reservations with this model and attempts to turn it around, noting, albeit in parentheses, that it is 'likely that standardized designs by architects produced more standardized production in quarries'.[91] This could be put much more forcefully: it was precisely the decisions made by architects that determined what was produced because it was being produced in response to specific demand from them and according to their requirements.

Further support for this assertion comes from the dimensions of the known capitals which, where they have been recorded, show no convincing evidence for standardization. The thirty-six roughed-out Corinthian capitals from Prokonnesos for which at least these dimensions have been recorded vary in height between 0.47 and 1.06 m, and in lower diameter between 0.41 and 0.95 m.[92] These observations have led Nuşin Asgari, one of the key experts in this area, to conclude that there is no evidence for a system of standard sizes on Prokonnesos and the dimensions of these objects resulted from choices made by individual commissioners.[93]

Rejects and wastage

If we accept that commissioning material from scratch was the norm then we also need to explain why so much of this material, represented by the roughed-out objects examined above, was apparently abandoned in the quarries. If these are not the vestiges of stockpiles then what are they? In practice, most of these objects are rejects, damaged or flawed in some way, cast aside during carving. Quarrying and roughing out objects that had to be a specific size was a wasteful process. Over-cutting was a constant risk and would have made an object useless. Column shafts were especially vulnerable to both flaws and damage, and this perhaps explains why so many examples are known from the quarries. There are numerous examples of column shafts abandoned even before they had been completely extracted from the rock-face. An interesting anecdote in the tenth-century compendium of the Arab writer Mas'ūdī, describes just one such shaft on the quarries at Aswan:

---

[90] Wilson Jones 2000: 155.   [91] Dodge 1991: 36.

[92] Asgari 1988: 118, table 1; Wilson Jones 1991: 150, appendix 7.

[93] Asgari 1990: 117: 'toutes les observations démontrent que les mesures devaient être spécifiées par le client.'

I have seen . . . one in the mountains of Aswan, marked out and worked on: it has not been detached from the mountain, and the visible part has certainly not been polished. Indeed, before they polished a column, they detached it from the mountain, and then transported it to its destination.[94]

The series of 40 RF shafts lying in the Kylindroi and Aetos quarries on Euboea are probably examples of such rejects, abandoned due to flaws. Shafts of this size do have parallels in Rome: the *cipollino* shafts used for the Temple of Antoninus and Faustina measured just under 40 RF, and the recent excavations in the Forum of Trajan have shown that at least four 40 RF *cipollino* column shafts were also employed in the monumental wall flanking the southern side of the piazza, in combination with another four *pavonazzetto* and eight *giallo antico* shafts of the same size.[95] Despite these examples, columns of this size, in *cipollino* or any stone, were never common and it would have been pointless producing such items to stock. Rather most of these shafts appear to have been flawed in some way and it seems much more likely that they are leftovers from a major commission, perhaps of the scale of the Forum of Trajan. Repairs were attempted, stitching iron clamps, shaped like enormous staples, across their faults.[96] Industrious officials at these quarries were presumably under great pressure to salvage any materials they could lay their hands on. Similar repair projects or attempts to recycle column shafts by cutting them up can be found elsewhere.[97] Interestingly, salvage efforts can be identified on a number of the shafts recovered from Portus, suggesting that some faults only became apparent after shipping.[98]

It would be wrong, though, to suggest that all of the material still visible at the quarries can be explained in this way. Others must be the result of customers defaulting on their commissions or of building projects being cancelled. The series of monolithic column shafts from the granite quarries at Yedi Taşlar in the Troad are a case in point (Fig. 6.9). Fifteen of these column shafts appear to have been designed to be between 37 and 39 RF in length, while another fifteen columns range between 11 and 18 RF in length. Only a few show signs of damage, so these were not rejects. Clearly they were abandoned for other reasons. Ponti, falling back on the traditional standardization and stock model, argues that we are looking here at the effect of a drop in market demand for monolithic column shafts that these quarries had become accustomed to producing to stock; 'faced with an excess of twenty

---

[94] Mas'ūdī 794 (trans. Greenhalgh 2006: 84).
[95] Meneghini and Santangeli Valenzani 2007: 93–5.   [96] Monthel 2009.
[97] Fant 1989a: no. 10, 50a–b, 58; Dolci 2006: no. 182. On an attempt to cut one of the smaller Kylindroi columns down into veneer, Pensabene 1998c: 314–15.
[98] For examples from Portus, Fant 1992: 116; Pensabene 1994: 54 (no. 4–5, figs. 66–9), 73 (no. 17, fig. 86), 85 (no. 28, figs. 107–9).

Fig. 6.9. Abandoned granite column shafts in the Yedi Taşlar quarries in the Troad (photo: author).

items, it is difficult to presume that the columns were part of an order on commission', he reasons.[99]

On top of what has already been said about the unconvincing evidence for standardization and stock production at the quarries generally, there are several further reasons for doubting this reconstruction for the Yedi Taşlar material. First, there is nothing about the sizes of the shafts found at these quarries to indicate that they were part of some broader system of standard sizes: there are none around the popular 20, 30, or 40 RF marks; the shafts between 37 and 39 RF are, in fact, a slightly awkward size, perhaps intended for full Corinthian columns (i.e. including capital and base) of 45 RF. Secondly, most of these shafts are finished to the same degree and lined up in the quarries, where they clearly obstruct further work. If a shift in demand led to their abandonment then this must have occurred just at the point when work on all of these had been finished but no others of the same

[99] Ponti 1995: 315.

size yet begun; all of the evidence for interrupted quarrying activity comes from quarries at which the main groups of columns are not found.[100] Thirdly, column shafts in Troad granite of the largest size found at the quarries, 37–9 RF, are extremely rare. The enormous database of 1,176 granite columns compiled by Williams-Thorpe shows this quite clearly.[101] This contains 324 shafts of Troad granite, 202 of which have recorded diameters, taken at the mid-point of their shaft. The base diameters of the 37–9 RF shafts at the quarries range between 1.48 and 1.66 m, equivalent to on average about 1/7 or 1/8 their length, while their mid-point diameters range between roughly 1.40 and 1.55 m. In comparison, none of the shafts in Williams-Thorpe's dataset have diameters over 0.94 m. This is largely confirmed by the recent work by Rodà, Pensabene, and Domingo who have studied Troad granite column shafts in Spain, North Africa, and Egypt.[102] The only examples that they have identified over 30 RF in length are the eight from the frigidarium of the Antonine Baths at Carthage, which are 40 RF. These data show that, though there were probably larger column shafts in Troad granite in existence, on the current evidence there are more shafts of the 30–40 RF size in the quarries than outside of them.[103]

If these quarries were simply churning out column shafts around the 38 RF mark then either they have all disappeared or whoever was responsible for this decision badly misjudged their market. This seems unlikely and, in practice, these column shafts look much more like several batches of commissioned material awaiting transport than they do material that had been produced to stock until work was suddenly halted. We can only speculate, of course, as to the reasons for their abandonment but the calling off of the building project for which they were intended, presumably quite late in the day, might fit the bill; perhaps the commissioner had a change of heart and opted for a more prestigious material. At what date this happened is impossible to say for sure but Troad granite continued to be used well into the fourth century AD; since little activity seems to have taken place at the largest quarries in the area after the extraction of these columns it seems reasonable to at least suggest that we should be thinking about a fourth-century date.[104] It is entirely possible that more of these column shafts were originally produced as part of this commission and transported off later for reuse elsewhere; as Ponti notes at least one 38

---

[100] For example, in Ponti's Quarry A1/6, Yarık Taş, where a series of four or five blocks were marked out and partially shaped but not separated from the bedrock (Ponti 1995: 303).

[101] Williams-Thorpe 2008.

[102] Rodà, Pensabene, and Domingo 2012; additional material from North Africa and Egypt was presented at ASMOSIA X in Rome in June 2012.

[103] The 'large' column is no. SPET6, while those with diameter of 0.93–4 m are no. CHR1–4, all from Paphos.

[104] On the use of Troad granite, Lazzarini 2002c: 246.

RF column was found near Alexandria Troas harbour, where it was awaiting shipment, though to date no columns in this material have been found in shipwrecks.[105]

Timescales and manpower

One of the main criticisms levelled at this kind of reconstruction, which sees commissioning and production from scratch as the norm for complex architectural elements, is that it would have been simply too slow. We know that imperial building projects, in particular, were completed rapidly, especially in the capital. The Temple of Peace, for instance, was built in roughly five years (AD 70–5), the Baths of Trajan in five years (AD 104–9), the Forum of Trajan in around six (AD 106–12), the Hadrianeum in no more than seven (AD 138–45), the Baths of Caracalla in five to six (AD 211–17). Some projects dragged on a little longer—the Temple of Venus and Roma, begun in AD 121, was inaugurated by Hadrian in AD 135 but not actually finished until AD 141—but most were finished with startling speed. The question, then, is whether these incredible building schedules are incompatible with a system that supplied material primarily from scratch rather than stock.

In responding to this, the first thing to note is that supplying large quantities of material can never have been easy and we should not expect it to have been. Both contractors and quarry-based workers would have been put under enormous strain; huge amounts of time and labour went into these building projects. This is why suppliers would probably have been forced to send additional workers to the quarries to help speed up production at times of peak demand. A second point is that, though the times in which these major imperial projects were built are impressive, they are also exceptional. Most ordinary, non-imperial projects took a lot longer to complete. Duncan-Jones refers to several projects paid for by benefactors in North Africa which were finished decades later, and in one case by the original commissioner's grandchildren.[106] Pliny the Younger famously despairs of the time taken over building projects in Bithynia.[107] Finally, and most importantly for the current discussion, it is worth noting that columns and other marble elements, primarily wall and floor veneer, were always among the first features to be planned at the design stage of a building project and among the last to be

---

[105] This column measures 11.44 m or 38.64 RF (Ponti 1995: 312) and was not the only one apparently moved out of the quarries: Schliemann 1880: 57, describes three columns among the dunes near to Alexandria Troas which he says are the same as those at Yedi Taşlar.

[106] Duncan-Jones 1982: 87–8; and on the slow construction of temples at Mustis and Muzuc, see *CIL* VIII.15576, 12058. On attempts to speed up this process, see *Digest* 50.10.5.

[107] Pliny the Younger, *Letters* X.37, 39.

incorporated into the final structure, maximizing the time available for their manufacture.[108]

The only way to really answer this question, of course, is to attempt some calculations. In this respect, the Forum of Trajan is a useful case study. Construction on this site began in AD 106–7 and it was dedicated in AD 112. The principal imported stones used on this project were *pavonazzetto* from Dokimeion, *granito del Foro* from Mons Claudianus, *giallo antico* from Chemtou, and white marble from Luna. Interestingly, this range of materials helped to spread the burden, ensuring that no single quarry was overwhelmed—an accidental by-product of the fashion for polychrome finishes. In terms of volume, most of these imports were used in the form of column shafts, supplied principally from Dokimeion and Mons Claudianus. Using the labour figures given by Pegoretti in his nineteenth-century building manual we can begin to estimate manpower requirements for the quarrying and roughing out of these shafts in the quarries. A maximum total of 184 column shafts in *pavonazzetto* were deployed in the Forum of Trajan, in five different sizes (following the reconstruction of the Basilica Ulpia by Packer).[109] Using Pegoretti's figures for the quarrying, roughing out and rough dressing of hard marble one arrives at totals of 3,285 days for quarrying (one quarryman and two assistants) and 9,200 man-days for carving. This suggests that working ten-hour days a team of thirty at the quarry face (quarrymen and assistants) and thirty carvers would be able to carry out all of this work in a year, assuming at least 320 days of work. In addition to these column shafts at least forty pilaster shafts and 70 m³ of material for veneer also had to be supplied from the quarries at Dokimeion for the Forum of Trajan, which might account for the labour of a further twenty quarrymen and twenty carvers.[110] Extra workers would be required for moving these shafts, sharpening tools, and clearing spoil but still a workforce of 150 would probably have been sufficient. In reality this was a six-year project, and if we assign a year at the beginning to planning and mobilization of the workforce, a year to transport, and two years at the end to the finishing of all this material on site, then two years could probably

---

[108] I owe this observation to Janet DeLaine. For more of the dynamics of site management and the supply of materials, DeLaine 1997; Triantafillou forthcoming.

[109] Packer 1997: appendices 4–6, 8: the columns included are the forty of the lower and forty of the upper interior orders of the Libraries (4.78 m and 3.53 m respectively), the four of the columnar screens of these structures (5.17 m), the sixteen of the peristyle surrounding the Column (*c.* 7.05 m), the fifty-eight of the East and West Colonnades (7.05 m), as well as sixteen others along the southern façade of the Basilica Ulpia (8.83 m).

[110] These pilasters are 7.05 m; the figure for veneer is calculated as enough to cover 2,788 m² (Packer 1997: 264; Vitti 2002: fig. 1), assuming that from a 1 m³ block of marble one could get 40 m² of veneer (DeLaine 1997: 180).

have been dedicated to quarrying work. Our total workforce could be reduced, therefore, by as much as half.

What this exercise reveals is the very real effect that increasing the workforce has on production times. There is no need to imagine vast battalions of workers being sent off to the quarries but the number of specialist quarrymen and carvers must have been stepped up in these periods. The available space would naturally have limited the extent to which the workforce could be continually augmented so it also would have been necessary to find somewhere to put these new arrivals to work. Perhaps this is why we begin to find so much activity at the other quarries around Dokimeion in the Trajanic period: this influx of workers had to be put to use somewhere to be in any way effective and so a temporary expansion of the actual area being quarried was needed.

Judging the accuracy of these workforce totals for Dokimeion, of course, is impossible; we have no idea how many personnel were working in these quarries at any one point. However, we do have figures for Mons Claudianus and again the evidence provided by the *ostraka* is crucial. One document in particular, a list specifying all those who required water rations, gives us a fantastic picture of the make up of the quarry population at a single point in time—in this case one day in the middle Trajanic period, probably in AD 110, though it might be earlier (Fig. 6.10).[111] Out of a (quite staggering) total population of 917 individuals, 349 stone-masons are listed. The distinction here between quarrymen and carvers is blurred but it is the total that matters. If we attempt the same exercise carried out above for *pavonazzetto* we can see how this real total compares with our theoretical workforce. A total of 108 *granito del Foro* column shafts were employed in the lower order of the Basilica Ulpia, each measuring 8.84 m in height (*c.*30 RF) with a lower diameter of 1.10 m.[112] Applying Pegoretti's figures for granodiorite, we end up with totals of 160 days for quarrying (one quarryman and two assistants) and 633 days for roughing out per shaft.[113] Assuming that all of the individuals involved were of the same status (i.e. that quarrymen and assistants are equal), we can estimate that to produce one roughed-out shaft would have taken 1,115 man-days, and to produce all 108 a total of 120,420 man-days. This means that our workforce of 349 workers could have handled all of these shafts in 345 days, or roughly a year and a quarter, assuming that they had some days off. Extra work, of course, needs adding to this since material for veneer also had to be supplied, but this would probably have accounted for no more than two to three months extra. What this means is that, even if quarrying did not start till mid AD 107 these shafts could have been

---

[111] *O. Claud. Inv.* 1538, 2921; see Cuvigny 2005; Bülow-Jacobsen 2009: 263–6.
[112] Packer 1997; Claridge 2007: 74.   [113] Pegoretti 1843–4: 78, 240–5.

Fig. 6.10. Water distribution list (*O. Claud. Inv.* 1538 and 2921) from Mons Claudianus (photo: A. Bülow-Jacobsen, courtesy of H. Cuvigny and A. Bülow-Jacobsen).

ready by early AD 109 and potentially in Rome for early AD 110. This would have left nearly two years for finishing work on site.[114]

Even though this *ostrakon* is tentatively dated to AD 110, when most of the supply work for the Forum of Trajan would have been finished, it seems reasonable to assume that the number of workers stayed this high through Trajan's reign. The use of *granito del Foro* in the Forum of Trajan was unparalleled until work began on the Temple of Venus and Roma in AD 121 and it would have made no sense to increase the workforce between these projects. In later periods, in fact, when there was less demand for this material, Bülow-Jacobsen has suggested that the numbers of personnel employed dropped away sharply; certainly the letter quoted above, datable to the reign of Commodus, indicates a vastly curtailed workforce.[115] These are not intended to be definitive totals but what they show is that it would have

---

[114] On the organization of work on the Forum of Trajan, Triantafillou forthcoming; and for more on these totals, Russell forthcoming.
[115] Bülow-Jacobsen 2009: 263.

been possible to supply major building projects with material from scratch even in the short times available simply by increasing the numbers of workers involved. What the Mons Claudianus *ostraka* show is that the quarry population varied considerably year on year and in periods of peak demand was more than large enough to supply major building projects on a lavish scale.

STOCK

The discussion so far has focused on the evidence for the ordering of building materials in tailored forms and sizes and their production from scratch at the quarries in response to this demand. Simply because production-to-order seems to have been more common than has been previously assumed and the evidence for widespread production-to-stock less than convincing should we dismiss the idea of stock altogether? Did stocks of building material exist, either at the quarries or elsewhere, that contractors could make use of if required?

Unintentional and intentional stock at the quarries

First, we need to distinguish between intentional and unintentional stock, that is between material produced deliberately for stockpiling—usually in standardized forms—and material produced to order which then simply found its way into stock. Unintentional stockpiles must have built up over time at quarries. Wastage during quarrying is unavoidable.[116] Indeed, as already noted, often faults which rendered whatever was being worked on unusable only revealed themselves during roughing out, perhaps even during loading for onward transport. Alongside these out and out rejects would have been leftovers from earlier projects or material on which purchasers had defaulted. Some of this material could have been pressed into service without much difficulty but other pieces would have needed reworking to make them in any way appealing.

Direct evidence for unintentional stockpiles of discarded or leftover material of this sort comes from both Dokimeion and Mons Claudianus, where the epigraphic record bears close scrutiny. At both sites, inventories of this material appear to have been carried out on a fairly regular basis, presumably to ensure that nothing that could be put to use was overlooked. At Dokimeion, Fant has identified a particular series of inscriptions which he

---

[116] Lambertie 1962: 58.

identifies as inventory marks—his Type II. They are highly abbreviated and tend to cluster, with multiple inscriptions of different dates on a single block.[117] No blocks inscribed in this way appear to have left the quarries and most are extremely weathered and often damaged. To judge from the dates on these inscriptions, in the period of intense demand for *pavonazzetto*, between the middle of Domitian's reign and the middle of Trajan's, inventories of material lying around the quarries were carried out every other year.[118]

A series of apparent stock-lists are also preserved among the *ostraka* from Mons Claudianus. The most detailed of these, Antonine in date, lists at least forty blocks, their location and dimensions, and apparently also whether they are squared or unworked; most are documented at extraction sites, more than twenty of which are inspected, but others were found discarded next to the loading ramps or by the roadside.[119] This was a running total with repeated corrections and alterations, and the documented blocks vary considerably in size, the largest measuring $16 \times 7 \frac{3}{4} \times 3 \frac{1}{2}$ RF (11.27 m³, over 28 tonnes), the smallest just $2 \frac{3}{4} \times 2 \times 1 \frac{1}{4}$ RF (0.18 m³, less than half a tonne).[120] There is nothing about the scattered location and random sizes of these blocks to support the idea of an organized stockpile of choice materials: this was a list of, as Bülow-Jacobsen has put it, 'usable stones that had been left over from the production of larger building elements'.[121] The largest block listed, in fact, is specifically designated ἀργ(ός) or unworked, probably because it was abandoned soon after extraction due to a fault; similarly 'unworked' are a series of blocks that must originally, to judge from their dimensions, have been intended for columns.[122] The two other known stock-lists from the site, one in Greek and one in Latin, both also Antonine, are much more fragmentary and add little to this picture.[123] A similar list of material, again on an *ostrakon*, has been found at the Wadi Hammâmât quarries, though whether it is a stock-list or an order is less clear.[124] Between fifteen and seventeen blocks (λίθος) are mentioned, with two sets of dimensions, apparently length and width; depth is mentioned only once, perhaps because a set thickness was specified somewhere else. Again they vary hugely in size, the largest being 6 RF long, the smallest 3 RF.

Was an intentional stock of material also accumulated at the quarries? It has already been suggested that the roughed-out architectural elements found at many Roman quarry sites are likely the remnants of orders and discards rather

---

[117] Fant 1989a: 17, 29.   [118] Fant 1989a: 29.

[119] Bülow-Jacobsen 2009: 163–72, no. 841; most of the blocks are described as ν(όμαιος), which Bülow-Jacobsen plausibly suggests means that they were of regular form, i.e. squared or roughed out, but some are labelled simply λίθος (stone) or πέτρα (boulder), while at least one ν(όμαιος) is called ἀργ(ός) (unworked) and another ἄχρηστος (useless).

[120] Bülow-Jacobsen 2009: no. 841.27–8, 58.

[121] Bülow-Jacobsen 2009: 163; also Fant 2010: 778.

[122] Bülow-Jacobsen 2009: no. 841.15, 29, 47.

[123] Bülow-Jacobsen 2009: no. 842–3.   [124] Kayser 1993: no. 20.

than the vestiges of stockpiles. The same, though, cannot be said with such certainty for the stepped blocks intended for sawing into veneer that are commonly recovered from quarrying sites. These blocks could have been put to a range of uses unlike the more defined architectural elements and so had a large undefined market. Even in a system orientated around production-to-order there would always have been occasions when production-to-stock made sense. Hunting down material suitable for large architectural elements would always have necessitated the clearance of unsuitable stone, that is material with closely spaced breaks or the wrong colouration, and this could easily have been put to one side for use as blocks rather than discarded. In the absence of specific commissions a quarry foreman might also need to keep their workers busy or a contractor might need to continue producing material to meet the cost of their lease.[125] During such lulls in specific demand it would make far more sense for these individuals to have their workers produce blocks that could be put to a range of uses rather than columns or capitals. This is backed up by the epigraphic evidence from blocks of *pavonazzetto* and white marble from Dokimeion. These inscriptions, as noted in Chapter 3, appear to indicate that contractors working for the imperial administration at Dokimeion had to produce a certain quantity of material annually. When they did not have specific commissions to produce then stepped blocks appear to have been the favoured product: of the 225 inscribed blocks catalogued by Fant in the Dokimeian quarries, 199 are parallelepipeds, or roughed-out blocks stepped on one or two sides so that as much of the roughly quarried block was useable.[126] There was, then, scope for the production-to-stock of certain elements in the quarries but this needs to be understood alongside the mass of evidence indicating that most complex forms were not produced so speculatively.

Stockpiles at Rome and elsewhere

As at the quarries, accumulations of unintentional stock must have built up elsewhere. Large quantities of material would have been available from demolished structures which could have been reused in its existing form, cut up or carved into something new. This was a practice that was probably much more often turned to in the imperial period than has been acknowledged, as Barker has demonstrated.[127] Particularly large-scale demolition projects, such as under the Flavians when many of Nero's projects were dismantled or after the purposeful clearing of structures immediately preceding the construction of the Aurelianic Walls, must have flooded the market with secondhand

---

[125] Peacock and Maxfield 1997: 213–14.
[126] Fant 1989*a*.   [127] Barker 2011; 2012.

material and these contractors would have been well placed to take advantage of this glut. In addition to material from demolished structures there must have been a lot of roughed-out blocks or architectural elements around which had been damaged during transit or discovered to contain faults and so could not be used in the project for which they were intended. There was plenty of scope for cutting up such rejects and tailoring them to new demands. Equally, the cancelling of a project part way through the construction process would have released material onto the open market. In major cities, in particular, all of these sources would have contributed to a general accumulation of stock.

These bits and pieces of leftovers and discards could have been used to satisfy limited demand quickly but it would never have been possible to supply an entire building project in this way; unless, that is, the project was designed entirely with the available supplies in mind from the beginning. Assuming that they had sufficient capital to do so, it might have made sense for contractors supplying building projects on a regular basis to build up a deliberate stock of certain materials. Blocks of stone that could be put to a variety of uses—of the kind that were probably produced to stock in major quarries when orders were not being handled—could have been bought in anticipation of demand and worked on as required: sawn into flooring or wall veneer, shaped into capitals, bases, column drums, or simply used for ashlar. The ubiquity of stone veneer and the popularity of coloured marbles in our period would have meant that any contractor could be sure of getting a good return on an investment in blocks of this material. As we have already seen, though, the same does not apply to architectural elements which were produced in fixed dimensions and were thus less adaptable. A contractor would have to have been pretty certain of being able to shift it in order to consider investing any capital upfront in stock of this sort.

In addition to this kind of small scale, flexible stock that most contractors probably built up, alongside their more unintentional accumulated materials, there is a possibility that larger stockpiles—or stone yards—existed to which contractors could turn. It is widely accepted, in fact, that there were several centralized stockpiles at Rome (and even elsewhere) that were continually replenished with blocks and architectural elements in set forms and that the imperial administration, and perhaps others, could dip into at will.[128] Usually highlighted in support of this assemblage—the *enormo accumulo*, as Fant characterizes it—are the assortments of inscribed blocks recovered from Portus and the Tiber bank of the Emporium district in Rome. From the former, at least 340 items, most inscribed, have been recovered, mainly from

---

[128] For example, Lazzarini 2010: 489 on 'grandi depositi di marmi presso i porti principali', among which he lists Alexandria, Miletos, Nicomedia, and Ostia; for further discussion and criticism, see Fant 2001: 177.

the bottom and banks of the Fossa Traiana; more remain at the site unstudied and they continue to be found.[129] At the Emporium, Bruzza includes 204 items in his catalogue of inscriptions, but well over 300 marble objects were given inventory numbers during Visconti's excavations in this area between 1868 and 1870, and the project diaries mention the discovery of thousands, perhaps even tens of thousands, of small fragments of different marbles.[130]

Though impressive in scale, these are awkward datasets to work with and it would be wrong to assume that they offer unambiguous evidence of the stockpiling of different types of objects. For a start, most of the objects found at these two sites are squared or stepped blocks and not roughed-out architectural elements. In Bruzza's catalogue only thirteen column shafts are listed, alongside five pieces of 'marmi lavorati', while most of the rest are blocks or slabs.[131] At Portus, Pensabene catalogues fourteen column shafts and thirty-four fragments compared to 155 whole and fifty-one fragmentary blocks; only three bases and two capitals were found.[132] If these were stockpiles at all, then they were primarily stockpiles of blocks for sawing into veneer panels—essentially raw materials that could have been produced to stock with little risk—and not large quantities of architectural elements in predetermined forms.

Another reason to doubt the identification of these assemblages as deliberately amassed stockpiles is the quality of the material in them. As Fant has shown, most of these objects are cracked, broken or faulty; many of the column shafts reveal the efforts made to repair them in antiquity.[133] We have no idea, of course, what proportion of the original material from these assemblages was removed in the post-Roman period.[134] The Emporium was certainly a prime source of marble in later periods; it was these supplies after which this neighbourhood, the Marmorata, was later known.[135] Even so, it seems unlikely that what is left is simply what was sifted through and rejected in these later periods. At both Portus and in the Emporium much of this material was recovered from underwater, in the Fossa Traiana and the edge of the Tiber, where it lay hidden from later prospectors. And even if this material had been visible and accessible there is no obvious reason why the Roman *scalpellini* would have rejected it since their main market was in cutting such blocks down into thin panels for floors and table tops; the kind of faults present in so many of these objects would not have hindered this work too greatly.

---

[129] Baccini Leotardi 1979; 1989; Pensabene 1994; Maischberger 1997: 39–54. Pieces are still being recovered from along the edge of the Fossa Traiana (pers. comm. Simon Keay).

[130] Bruzza 1870; 1877; Dubois 1908; Maischberger 1997: esp. 71–86.

[131] Bruzza 1870; Maischberger 1997: 74.

[132] Pensabene 1994: 422; he also lists eight whole and eight fragmentary 'fusti per altri usi'.

[133] Fant 1992; Pensabene 1994: 423.

[134] Pensabene 2001b: 47–8; Brandenburg 1996: 15; Hansen 2003: 15.

[135] Maischberger 1997: 67.

The Portus and Emporium assemblages, in sum, might more plausibly be interpreted as the remains of dumps of discards, similar in composition to the unintentional accumulations we find at the quarries, than as the remnants of carefully managed stockpiles. Presumably certain faults only revealed themselves over time and/or after shipment. Vast quantities of imports must naturally have led to a large amount of wastage. Corsi catalogued nearly 7,000 ancient columns reused in the churches of Rome, presumably only a fraction of the original total imported into the city, and if only 1 per cent of these developed faults during transport then one would be looking at a considerable amount of material that needed storing, repairing, or dumping.[136]

Most of the architectural elements from the Emporium and Portus assemblages, then, should probably be categorized as unintentional rather than intentional stock. The same might be said for other objects that have traditionally been used to argue for the existence of stockpiles but are more obviously interpreted as leftovers or excess from previous projects. The Aswan granite Column of Antoninus Pius is one example. According to the abbreviated and confusing quarry inscription on one of its ends it appears to have been quarried in AD 105–6 but we know that it was not actually erected till the middle of the second century AD.[137] One possible explanation for this time lag is that this was a column quarried and sent to a stockpile in Rome, where is then stayed for half a century. However, this was a 50 RF shaft, of which there are few in Rome, and it would be a strange object to go to the trouble of producing without a specific destination in mind. The inscription on it, too, shows that it was part of a pair, or a specific commission.[138] Perhaps this second column was damaged and the original project for which both were intended called off or perhaps this pair of shafts were destined for a larger project and then one or both not needed. It is possible that the *giallo antico* blocks found in a destruction context datable to AD 394 in the so-called Edificio fuori Porta Marina at Ostia, the inscriptions on which show that they were quarried under Domitian, should be interpreted in the same way.[139] Considering the evidence for accidental damage and the emergence of defects discussed already, it seems reasonable to suppose that a surplus of architectural elements, especially column shafts, must have been deliberately produced for every major building project in Rome. Over time these spare pieces must have built up. Precisely this point has been made in a recent analysis of the marble architectural elements in the Baths of Caracalla, a colossal project for which excess material must have been ordered in. Even so, a number of roughed-out objects were put to use in the final building that seem to have been brought in from elsewhere to replace defective pieces. One of these, a

---

[136] Corsi 1833: 293–386; 1845: 293–393; also Napoleone 2001.
[137] Ward-Perkins 1976.   [138] Ward-Perkins 1980*b*: 26.   [139] Becatti 1969: 22–5.

Fig. 6.11. Stockpile of column shafts in the Temple of the Fabri Navales, Ostia (photo: author).

block in white Dokimeian marble, has an inscription on it datable to AD 206, several years before building at the site began.[140] This block, and others like it, the investigators reason, probably came from a store of leftovers from previous projects rather than a stockpile of new blocks in set form; certainly white Dokimeian marble is otherwise rare at Rome.

In reality, the only excavated collection of material that looks anything like a stockpile of architectural elements is that from the Temple of the Fabri Navales at Ostia (Fig. 6.11). A total of forty-six column shafts, twenty-one bases, and five Ionic and four roughed-out Corinthian or Corinthianizing capitals, in a mix of Thasian and Prokonnesian marble, were found stacked at this site.[141] The collection itself, though not necessarily the material, is datable to the fourth century AD, and appears to have supplied the local building market; the name of one customer, Rufus Volusianus, is inscribed on five of

[140] Bruno, Gorgoni, and Pallente 2009: 389. This block was previously listed as Parian in both Bruzza 1870: 193, no. 279; Dubois 1908: 113, no. 270.

[141] Calza 1940: 76; Bloch 1953: 272; Becatti 1969: 160; Pensabene 1973: 545–8; Pensabene et al. 1999.

the shafts and appears again on material from the so-called Christian Basilica, while a similarly roughed-out Corinthian capital appears in the apsidal hall of the Thermae of Mithras in the city.[142] Unfortunately we know nothing about the formation of this stockpile. Does it represent a stock of material built up over time or was all this material part of a single shipment in the process of being distributed to various building projects? It is equally possible that these objects were originally ordered in for a structure that was never built and were simply being stored until some use could be found for them.

PRODUCTION METHODS: FROM QUARRY TO BUILDING SITE

The lack of any convincing evidence for the sustained production-to-stock of roughed-out architectural elements shows that securing materials quickly was less important than acquiring the right materials, in the form and especially the dimensions required by both architect and commissioner. A system orientated around production-to-stock would have to have traded in responsiveness for efficiency. This does not mean, however, that efficiency was not important. The patent pressure under which the beleaguered workers revealed in the Mons Claudianus *ostraka* were operating shows that the speed with which material was produced really did matter. As the labour exercise attempted above demonstrates, the easiest way to increase the speed of production was to increase the workforce involved. For most imperial projects this was probably the option preferred; the imperial administration, of course, had the resources to pay an enormous workforce as well as sources of further manpower, in the form of slaves, if required.

Adding to the workforce, however, while it might increase the speed with which a certain result was achieved would not increase overall productivity, that is the amount of work that each individual worker was able to complete. Several ways in which productivity could have been improved can be hypothesized. Improving the tools used would have been one way and indeed we do find harder iron tools in the Roman period and references to steel; the introduction of the heavy quarry pick has already been mentioned.[143] Experiments with new types of saw were also carried out. Water-powered stone-cutting saws have been excavated in Late Antique contexts at Ephesos and Jerash (Figs. 6.12 and 6.13); these are almost certainly machines of the kind described by Ausonius installed on the banks of the Moselle.[144] Both of the

---

[142] Pensabene et al. 1999: 147.   [143] See Chapter 3: Chronology of quarrying (pp. 81–2).
[144] On hand-operated saws, Schwander 1991; on the water-powered ones from Ephesos and Jerash, Mangartz 2006; 2010; Seigne 2002; Ausonius, *The Moselle* 363–4.

Fig. 6.12. Reconstructed water-powered stone-cutting saw at Jerash (photo: K. Glicksman).

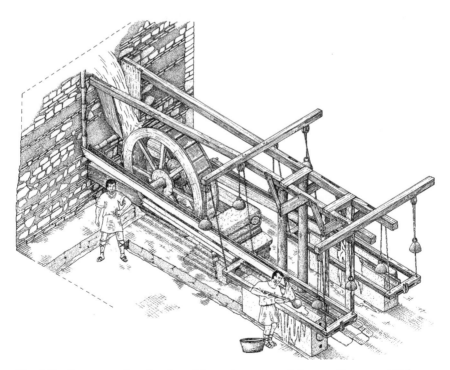

Fig. 6.13. Reconstruction drawing of the water-powered stone-cutting saw at Ephesos (Mangartz 2010: fig. 41, reproduced with permission of the Römisch-Germanisches Zentralmuseum (RGZM), Mainz).

exacavated examples have two sets of saw blades, powered by a central waterwheel. A recently published relief on one end of a sarcophagus lid from Hierapolis depicts a similar machine in meticulous detail, suggesting these devices were in use earlier, at least in the third century AD when this sarcophagus was produced.[145]

The simplest way to increase productivity, however, would have been to rationalize the production methods employed, dividing them as much as possible between different workers so as to increase their specialization.[146] This would have been most easily achieved when the form of the object being produced was relatively standard, meaning that each individual worker would have been responsible for the same task again and again. This concept of labour division, as Wilson has noted, was certainly understood in other industries in the Roman period.[147] To what extent can this kind of rationalization be identified in the case of stone objects? There is some evidence for the production in series of small statuettes and vessels in the six-aisled hall, the so-called *fabrica*, next to the quarries at Chemtou.[148] The materials handled here were small, though, and could easily have been passed between workers, unlike architectural elements or sarcophagi. While it is unlikely that these larger objects were produced in series in this way, certain features of their production can be highlighted which suggest that attempts were made to increase productivity.

Repeated designs

The first point that can be made concerns the forms of many of the architectural elements widely used in the Roman period and, in particular, the way in which they were roughed out. Finds from the quarries show that common approaches were taken to roughing out particular objects again and again, both within single sites and across multiple ones, which suggest a level of specialization.

This phenomenon has been examined in most detail in the case of the roughed-out Corinthian capitals from Prokonnesos, where Asgari has identified a series of repeated production processes.[149] Most of these capitals were roughed out to a stage which left them with defined upper and lower surfaces, a delineated abacus, two blocked-out rows of acanthus leaves as well as space for the central flower of the abacus (Figs. 6.14 and 6.15). Corinthian capitals

---

[145] Ritti, Grewe, and Kessener 2007.
[146] On this, see Adam Smith, *On the Wealth of Nations*, I.1.
[147] A. I. Wilson 2008.
[148] Rakob 1994*b*: 51–140; Rakob 1995*a*; 1997; Rüger 1997; Mackensen 2000; 2005.
[149] Asgari 1988: 118, table 1; also Wilson Jones 1991: 134–9, appendix 7.

Fig. 6.14. Roughed-out Corinthian capitals from Prokonnesian quarries, now in Saraylar (photo: author).

Fig. 6.15. Roughed-out Corinthian capital from Prokonnesian quarries, now in Saraylar (photo: author).

are intricate, complex forms, and it is not surprising that a set of guides which might limit human error in the carving process developed over time, particularly it would appear in the period of greatest demand, that is in the second century AD.[150] Based on their form, thirty-one of the Corinthian capitals on Prokonnesos can be argued to have been roughed out in the same way, repeatedly making use of these two sets of dimensions: the height of the capital and the lower diameter of the column shaft for which it was intended. Most of these capitals passed through four main phases of working, which can be further broken down into approximately nine distinct steps, before they left the quarry (Fig. 6.16).[151] It is worth stressing that not all the Corinthian capitals roughed out on Prokonnesos were produced in the same way. Asgari notes that twelve of the forty-three examples studied in detail to date were worked completely differently from the rest.[152] At least three capitals, furthermore, were carved to an almost finished condition, though these could have been models for the carvers to work from.[153] In any case, this variety lends support to the idea that the quarries on Prokonnesos were, at any one point in time, full of a mix of carvers, some permanent residents, others passing through for a specific job, who sometimes worked in different ways.

In comparison, seventeen roughed-out capitals, all designed for final carving into either Corinthian or Composite forms, are known from the Luna quarries.[154] Two distinct groups can be noted. First, a series of large capitals, all between 1.24 and 1.43 m, consisting of three defined parts: a cylindrical band on the underside corresponding to lower diameter of the capital, a slightly wider cylindrical band above this at the level of the top of the first row of acanthus leaves, and a rectangular section the lower corners of which are cut back into four oblique triangular planes (Fig. 6.17). These examples are very similar in form to the majority of the roughed-out Corinthian capitals from Prokonnesos. In comparison, those of the second type from Luna are smaller, rarely over a metre in height, and are much less defined in form (Fig. 6.18). All of the known examples of this type have a rounded base and squared top, sometimes with the depth of the abacus marked out, but their sides tend to be simply flattened surfaces. None of these capitals was found in a securely stratified context, but the first type can be dated broadly to the Roman period through comparison with an example in Rome, now in the Antiquario del Celio.[155] The second type can be dated by the inscriptions on them, four of which carry the ligatured initials BAE and another two the initials

---

[150] Wilson Jones 1991: 127: the Corinthian capital was 'the most complex and three dimensional element of the classical architect's repertoire.'

[151] Asgari 1988: 118 (table 1).

[152] Asgari 1988: 115.

[153] Asgari 1988: 118 (table 1): these three capitals are no. 41, 47, 92.

[154] On the examples in the Museo del Marmo, Carrara, Dolci 2006: 220–1.

[155] Pensabene 1994: 202 (no. 19, fig. 229).

The Economics of the Roman Stone Trade

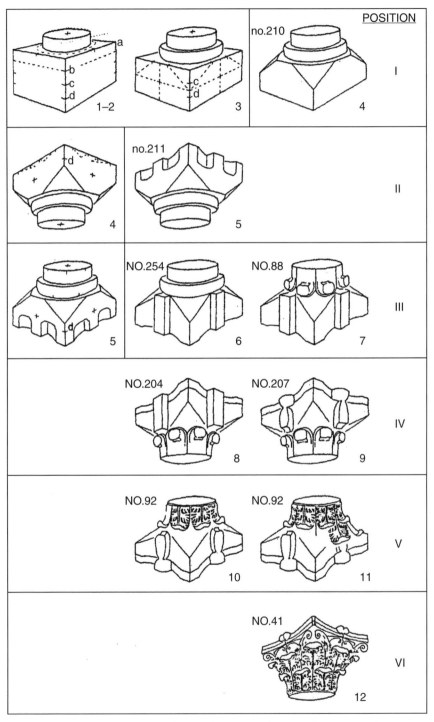

Fig. 6.16. Stages of production of Corinthian capitals on Prokonnesos (after Asgari 1988: 122, fig. 1 (drawn by M. Beykan), reproduced with permission of Springer).

Fig. 6.17. Roughed-out Corinthian capital from the Luna quarries, now in the Museo del Marmo, Carrara (photo: author, used with permission of the Museo del Marmo, Carrara).

Fig. 6.18. Roughed-out Corinthian capitals from the Luna quarries, now in the Museo del Marmo, Carrara (photo: author, used with permission of the Museo del Marmo, Carrara).

HILAR. These seem to be names, probably Bae(bius) and Hilar(ius), attested at the quarries in the first century AD, though they probably continue later.[156]

Perhaps the most striking feature of the first type of roughed-out Corinthian capitals from Luna is their similarity with the numerous examples from Prokonnesos, but also those few recovered from Dokimeion. One capital at an early stage of working and two others in style a more fully articulated roughed-out form have been recovered from these last quarries.[157] This common approach could be used to argue for centralized control of these sites but it seems more likely that this was a system honed over time at a range of sites that a carver could memorize and apply by rote, so translating the shaping of a complicated form into a handful of individually simple tasks. Perhaps unsurprisingly considering this, the basic way of completing a Corinthian capital using traditional tools seems not to have changed significantly over the past 2,000 years. Modern carvers still break down the production process of a Corinthian capital into stages almost identical to those observable on the roughed-out capitals from Luna and Prokonnesos; it is still part of the training of many stone-carvers, at least in the United Kingdom, to practise and memorize these stages.[158] There is no direct link, of course, between the way in which carvers are trained today and how they were trained in antiquity; many of these skills were lost and had to be rediscovered in the Renaissance. What this shows is that it is the form of the object that determines the mode of production and not vice versa. This common approach emerges out of the intense demand for Corinthian capitals in the Roman period which forced carvers to rationalize their working processes. It was demand that was common to all these quarries, not any form of central control. This was not the only way to rough out a Corinthian capital but it was the most popular one and it was, in essence at least, the one that later carvers would also go on to rediscover and develop in the Renaissance.

Corinthian capitals provide the clearest evidence for these repeated designs but similar approaches can be identified in the case of bases and even monolithic column shafts. On Prokonnesos, for instance, most bases seem to have passed through four distinct working phases, the first two of which simply blocked out the shape before the final two defined the exact form.[159] Features of roughed-out column shafts that are common to examples from multiple quarries are the characteristic collars of stone left at either end and the way in which concentric bands of flat chisel work was applied to the

---

[156] Dolci 1995: 131; 1997: 41–4; 2003: 188–92, no. 20–3 (first type), 216–18, no. 31–2 (second type).

[157] Waelkens, de Paepe, and Moens 1986: 114, fig. 5; pers. comm. Amanda Claridge.

[158] I am grateful to Adrian Powell and Mark Lillywhite for this information.

[159] Asgari 1990: 117–18.

surface of the shaft to assist with the laying out of the entasis.[160] The repeated production techniques apparent at these quarries must, in Wilson Jones's words, have 'oiled the process, facilitating communication and checking, and so reducing the risk of misunderstanding and error'.[161] Crucially, they limited the risk of overcutting. However, it also seems reasonable to assume that they helped to speed up the production process. A carver working on the same thing again and again is naturally bound to become quicker; it is much easier to produce a given quantity of objects of identical form than the same number of one-off pieces.[162] Whatever the dimensions required, standard proportional relationships of the kind identified on capitals on Prokonnesos must have contributed towards increased productivity.

On-site work

In his analysis of the loci of artistic and architectural production in antiquity, Heilmeyer notes that the main working places for stone carving were 'on the one hand the stone quarries, on the other the place of installation'.[163] Architectural elements were usually roughed out at the quarries to a state in which their weight was reduced as much as possible without any details being shaped that might get damaged during transport. Further detailed work would be undertaken on the building site; this included the finishing of capitals, the smoothing and/or fluting of column shafts, the sawing of blocks into panels for wall revetment and flooring. Whether the finishing of these objects on site was still the responsibility of the contractor tasked with supplying them is uncertain and probably varied between projects. Even in those cases, probably relatively few, when architectural elements were imported fully finished—as Pensabene has proposed for certain examples in the Severan complexes at Lepcis Magna—carvers would still have been needed to fix them in place and adjust them as necessary.[164]

Established and repeated production processes were just as useful during finishing work, when it was required, as during earlier stages of carving. Capitals would have gone through a similar series of steps on site to those identified in the quarries. Finds from the site of the Central Baths at Pompeii show that the finishing of the simple Tuscan capitals was split into at least three stages: an initial one devoted to modelling the rough shape of the piece onto the roughed-out import; a second one which focused on the addition of acanthus leaves to the body of the capital; and a final one which involved the laying out of the remaining details.[165] The second stage of this process, at

---

[160] Pensabene 1992.   [161] Wilson Jones 1991: 139.
[162] Pers. comm. Peter Rockwell.   [163] Heilmeyer 2004: 404.
[164] Pensabene 2001a: 79–89.   [165] Bruno et al. 2002c: 282–6.

which the design was laid out but not finished, is also visible on Corinthian capitals from a range of other locations, including Lepcis Magna and Rome, not to mention among the more finished examples from the quarries on Prokonnesos.[166] Guidelines incised on stone objects are another manifestation of this practice of repetitive production. The lines incised on the series of roughed-out Ionic capitals from the Şile shipwreck, for example, seem to have been used by the carvers responsible to define the shape and size of the volutes on these pieces.[167] Relatively standard guidelines can also be found on Corinthian and Composite capitals from a range of sites which were used for laying out their detailed decoration.[168] Guidelines for the planning of fluting can also be found on column shafts which show that the craftsmen responsible endlessly adapted accepted methods dependent on the desired end result.[169]

Even when the material being handled had been commissioned specially a certain amount of on-site alteration must always have been necessary as well. In an era prior to widespread mechanization it would be foolish to expect everything to have arrived on site in precisely the form and size that was needed. Capitals often had to be cut down to compensate for overly long column shafts. This was the case in the Severan Basilica at Lepcis Magna and the Hadrianeum in Rome.[170] During the anastylosis of both the Sebasteion and the Tetrapylon at Aphrodisias, both carved entirely in local marble, a similar variety in capital heights was noted.[171] On the Tetrapylon, however, the required shortening of the capitals in question seems to have taken place following their finishing, resulting in the removal of the lower portion of their acanthus leaves. Typically measures were less extreme. Column shafts could not be trimmed much but the square plaque on the upper surface of the abacus of most Corinthian capitals could be cut back if necessary.[172]

Where this work was done, whether in place or on the ground, would have depended on the overall organization of the building site. In order to maximize productivity it would have made sense to have as many carvers working at any one point as possible. This might have meant some working on

---

[166] Heilmeyer 1970: pl. 1.6, 51.1–6; on part-finished capitals from Lepcis Magna, Bianchi 2009: fig. 7, 11, 15–17.

[167] Beykan 1988: 129; on the laying out of volutes on Ionic capitals, Andrey and Galli 2004.

[168] Toma forthcoming; for examples at Ostia, Pensabene 1973: pl. 72–3, 89, 92, 96; at Sabratha, Tomasello 1983: 87–103; and at Lepcis Magna, Pagello 1992: 235–52.

[169] On fluting guidelines at Pompeii, De Haan and Wallat 2008: 21–2, fig. 9; on the Temple of Vespasian at Rome, Rockwell 1987–8; see also Wilson Jones 2000: 7–9.

[170] Ward-Perkins 1993: 13, 56–9, pl. 31b; Wilson Jones 1991: 136.

[171] Paul 1996: 209–10.

[172] On columns, Hankey 1965: 18; Waelkens 1990: 65; on capitals, Packer 1997: 253; Wilson Jones 2000: 151, n. 54.

material in place and others carving different elements on the ground for later insertion, but it might also have meant as much work as possible being undertaken in place.[173] A relief from the amphitheatre in Capua, for instance, shows a carver working a Corinthian capital on the ground while the column for which it is intended is lifted into place.[174] The famous wall-painting from the Villa di San Marco at Stabia, the most complete surviving depiction of a Roman construction site, shows both types of work being carried out.[175] On the right, three carvers square rough blocks, a column shaft ready for erection lying next to them, while in the centre a further three carvers work on ladders at the top of a number of standing columns, putting the finishing touches to either the shafts themselves or their capitals. Capitals and entablature blocks would have to have been put up whenever they were needed, whatever their condition, so as not to hold up work overall. They could then be finished in place, but if they looked adequate when erected then that would often have sufficed. The fluting of columns, meanwhile, is a task that could only have been completed once they were in place and has always been time-consuming (Fig. 6.19).[176]

Time and cost were clearly high priorities to the commissioners of these structures. In the wider context of civic munificence, they represented real political capital; it was not acceptable for them to drag on, like the cathedrals of medieval England, for several centuries. At Aphrodisias several signs of expediency can be noted. Despite the proximity of the quarries, it was still felt preferable to adjust the already carved capitals on the Tetrapylon rather than order new blocks, for example, while one of the spiral-fluted columns on its western side was carved back-to-front, its spiral running the wrong way (Fig. 6.20).[177] This was an error, and a relatively obvious one, but one which was overlooked in the interest of getting the job done. Even at Aphrodisias, marble, if not as expensive elsewhere, was still time-consuming and laborious to work, and it was impractical to simply start over again. This is clear on the most prestigious of all sculptural projects at the city, the Sebasteion, where what was deemed an acceptable level of finish appears to have changed during the course of the project; as Rockwell notes, speed and legibility were more important than a uniform finish.[178]

---

[173] On this point, and the related costs of ground costs, see Morisot 1820–4: 26–34; Rondelet 1867: 78; see also Taylor 2003: 114, 239–40.

[174] Adam 1989: 48 (fig. 92).

[175] Adam and Varène 1980: 216–17, fig. 2.

[176] Taylor 2003: 241; on the fluting of the column for the restored Stoa of Attalos, Mauzy 2006: 65; and on the cost of fluting provided by the Erechtheum accounts, Caskey 1927: 411–13.

[177] Paul 1996: 211–12, fig. 10.

[178] Rockwell 1990: 118.

Fig. 6.19. Fluting of the columns of the reconstructed Stoa of Attalos, Athens (photo: courtesy Agora Excavations, The American School of Classical Studies at Athens).

Division of labour

Repeated production processes can be identified in the roughing out and even finishing of a range of different architectural elements and these must have helped to make the manufacturing of these items more efficient. At the same time, it is possible to identify a clear distinction between the kind of work carried out at the quarries and that undertaken on building sites. To what extent, though, were the individual stages of production of these objects divided between different workers? Is it possible, in other words, to argue for a division of labour between specialists that might have helped to increase productivity further?

At one end of the scale a highly articulated process can be imagined: a single Corinthian capital, for instance, could have passed through the hands of a

Fig. 6.20. Tetrapylon at Aphrodisias, viewed from the south-east (photo: author).

quarryman, a series of carvers responsible for roughing it out at the quarry, several further carvers on site, a detailed foliage specialist, perhaps also a drill-worker. Asgari has proposed that the most common form of roughed-out Corinthian capital on Prokonnesos was turned five times as it was shaped and it is possible that each of these steps could have been divided between specialists.[179] Likewise Wilson Jones assumes that 'formative capitals must have passed through a number of pairs of hands as work progressed'.[180] Although feasible, we should be wary of assuming this was necessarily always the case. Breaking down production into clearly defined stages was intended to simplify the process and reduce the risk of overcutting but dividing these steps between multiple workers could simply have increased the potential for confusion and error. All of the modern carvers spoken to about this point agreed that it is easier and simpler for one carver to complete all of the work or at least all of one type of work, such as quarrying, roughing out, or finishing.[181] Particular efforts should be taken, they also stressed, to minimize the number of times that the capital should be moved or turned over, since this is a waste of time and energy. There is no need to further complicate this activity.

Most Corinthian capitals probably passed through the hands of at most three carvers and a similar number is plausible for bases. In the case of column shafts the obvious stages of work which could have been divided between different workers were again quarrying, roughing out, and finishing, though fluting might have been an additional specialism. The obvious way, then, to divide labour would have been along geographical lines, between carvers repeatedly roughing out in the quarry and others continually finished on the building site. When quarry and building site were near each other or when it was felt necessary to send workers to the quarry to assist with a major commission then it is entirely possible that the same carvers were involved right the way through the production process. Even then, though, it would still have made sense to split roughing out and finishing work between different groups of specialists: the former is best suited to workers who are quick and strong, the latter to ones who are patient and careful, with a good understanding of geometry.[182] This level of labour division would also have allowed a certain amount of work on site and in the quarries to have taken place simultaneously—with carvers on site finishing a first batch of roughed-out material while their colleagues at the quarries prepared their next batch. This kind of overlapping of labour would have been a necessity for the largest building projects.

---

[179] Asgari 1988: 115–17.   [180] Wilson Jones 1991: 136.
[181] I am grateful to Trevor Proudfoot and Adrian Powell at Cliveden Conservation, who are responsible for stone conservation work at Aphrodisias among other projects, for discussion of this point.
[182] Pers. comm. Trevor Proudfoot.

One type of on-site work that would probably have been handed over to distinct specialists is sawing. In later periods stone sawyers were marked as specialists, like quarrymen and sculptors, and often paid a different wage.[183] Sawyers required special equipment and space. As already noted, in most cases material for revetment or flooring arrived at the building site in the form of stepped blocks of the kind common at quarries and on shipwrecks, sometimes squared blocks too.[184] If specialist sawyers were not available then precut panels could be imported, or material sent elsewhere for sawing. Precut panels have been found on shipwrecks, as noted above, and during the recent excavation of the villa of the Sulpicii family at Murecine, near Pompeii, over 200 newly cut white marble panels were found stacked in the kitchen, ready for use in the unfinished bath complex.[185] Charcoal labels on the surfaces of roughly half of these panels, many including the initials SVL, presumably a reference to the Sulpicii family, might indicate that they were sawn elsewhere and then delivered to the villa.[186]

To summarize, the potential for the division of labour in architectural production should not be overemphasized. A basic division between quarrymen, carvers, sawyers, and perhaps fine-detail carvers can be imagined but it is unlikely that single elements passed through a huge number of hands. That is, unless they were large enough that multiple carvers could work on them simultaneously. Increasing the workforce in this way would have been highly effective, as the manpower estimates attempted above for the Basilica Ulpia showed.[187] There are even signs on some objects that this was done. Rohmann notes that many of the Corinthian capitals of the Trajaneum at Pergamon have slightly different finishes on their different sides, which could result from a pair of carvers working on them at the same time, and Lipps has suggested the same for the capitals of the Hadrianeum in Rome.[188] For column shafts we should expect a whole team of carvers. For the finishing of long lines of mouldings a series of carvers could work side by side as long as they had clear directions or guidelines to work from. The best example of this is the guide section carved into one end of the entablature block from the Temple of Vespasian in Rome, now built into the substructures of the Tabularium, part of the Capitoline Museums. On this example, studied in detail by Rockwell,

---

[183] Ponza di San Martino 1841: 26–52.

[184] On sawn blocks from the site of the Temple of Venus at Pompeii, Bruno et al. 2002c; Fant 2008a: 132; and on the examples from the 'Edificio fuori Porta Marina' at Ostia, Becatti 1969: 22–5.

[185] See Chapter 4: Direct and indirect commerce (p. 134); on the Murecine finds, De Simone and Ciro Nappo 2000: 49–75, 58, 190.

[186] I am grateful to Antonio De Simone for talking me through his photographs of these labels.

[187] See above: Chapter 6: Timescales and manpower (pp. 228–32).

[188] Rohmann 1998: 26–7; Lipps 2010–11: 118–21; on carvers working in pairs on capitals in the convent of San Zaccaria in fifteenth-century Venice, Connell 1988: 175–6.

the rough profile of the mouldings which had to be carved all along the block were provided by a 0.1 m wide finished section at one end.[189] This acted as a model from which the carvers could take calliper measurements but would have been hidden in the final arrangement.

Maximizing the number of workers employed on a project was the easiest way to increase the speed with which it was completed but the evidence for limited division of labour and, in particular, the use of repeated designs and methods demonstrate that attempts were made to rationalize production. These should not be exaggerated—this was not serial production in the modern industrial sense—but the workers responsible for supplying the above materials would certainly have been working under enormous pressure, whether at the quarries, on building sites, or at both. Crucially, none of these attempts to rationalize production impinged upon the character of what was being produced. What the customer or architect required was fixed, it was up to the producers to do what they could to respond as well as they could to their requests.

CONCLUSIONS

Quarries, like building sites at the other end of the process, were places where different groups of carvers, trained in different traditions, would have met, worked side by side, occasionally together. They were important nodes for the transmission of techniques and skills, focal points for craft specialization; 'nurseries for stone-workers' as Knoop and Jones put it.[190] The largest quarries, though, were to judge from their output rarely single, centrally controlled enterprises; only a handful of imperially controlled quarries, like those in the Eastern Desert, should be thought of in this way. Production at individual quarries varied according to the orders coming in and the workers carrying them out. Common approaches to completing certain objects can be noted within single quarries and between multiple ones and we should not dismiss the idea that large specialist producers dominated activity at certain sites. This does not mean, though, that we should think of Prokonnesian or Dokimeian producers as single bodies of workers.

To judge from the evidence at the quarries, in the form of roughed-out and sometimes finished objects, but also the various strands of documentary evidence, most architectural elements were produced in response to specific demand in the Roman imperial period. Production-to-stock might have had a role but probably only for blocks for cutting into veneer or other undefined

---

[189] Rockwell 1987–8; 1993: 99–100.   [190] Knoop and Jones 1967: 67.

objects that did not need to have specific dimensions. Large stocks of leftovers or rejected material were built up over time but these were not deliberate, carefully managed assemblages and can rarely have furnished enough for whole projects. There is little convincing evidence for the deliberate standardization of the sizes of architectural elements that would have been necessary for production-to-stock to be feasible. Instead, we need to accept that the production of these complex forms in expensive and durable materials, often from distant quarries, would simply have taken a long time. They would have to have been ordered at the beginning of the building process, in the very early planning stage. Even then, for ordinary building projects this would have been a long, drawn out procedure. Stone-workers themselves clearly adapted under pressure, finding ways to work which increased their efficiency, and no doubt settled into routines that enabled a certain amount of increased productivity. However, the only real way to increase output dramatically would have been to add to the workforce. As the Mons Claudianus *ostraka* show, the imperial administration had access to the labour required and was more than capable of accommodating and nourishing hundreds of workers even at the remotest quarrying sites. This is what marked out imperial building from the norm in this period but also what distinguishes it from later activity. It is striking, in fact, that only around 300 masons were employed at any one time during the building of Santa Maria del Fiore in fifteenth-century Florence, fewer than were working just at Mons Claudianus in one year under Trajan.[191] Even on a structure that was built mainly in brick, like the Baths of Caracalla, DeLaine has estimated that 500–600 specialist marble-carvers would have been employed on the building site, out of an average workforce of approximately 7,200 over the four years of construction.[192] This is a workforce which dwarfs those of most other preindustrial construction projects for which we have figures.[193]

[191] Sanpaolesi 1977: 21.   [192] DeLaine 1997: 192–4.
[193] For examples, DeLaine 1997: 193–4.

7

The Sarcophagus Trade

Nowhere is discussion of production as commonplace as in sarcophagus studies (or *Sarkophagforschung*). Sarcophagi, in form but also decoration, lend themselves to typological analyses and, since the earliest studies, much of this analysis has focused on matching the resultant types to individual production centres.[1] In most cases this match is made on the basis of stylistic details, distribution patterns, and occasionally the materials used. In order to examine how these production centres functioned and the links between them and the quarries from which they acquired their materials, this chapter traces the production of sarcophagi from quarry through to final finishing. As for architectural elements, there is now enough data from the quarries, from shipwrecks, and from sites all around the Roman world to be able to reconstruct the trajectories followed by different types of sarcophagi during their production. However, in the same way that the production of architectural elements varied according to the contractors involved, their relationship with the quarries and the customer, the location of the project, and the time in which it had to be completed, so modelling sarcophagus production is a complicated affair. Different sarcophagus types were used by very different markets, to satisfy a range of needs, and their production reflects this. At the same time, though it is often assumed that most sarcophagi were bought at the last minute, and perhaps often without much thought, the decision to purchase a sarcophagus, when to acquire one, and how to have it decorated, were very personal choices which are not easily itemized.

BUYING A SARCOPHAGUS

There were a range of choices available to the customer looking to purchase a sarcophagus. The simplest option would be to approach a local workshop. By

---

[1] On this issue of identifying 'workshops' more generally, Heilmeyer 2004; Bejor 2011.

Fig. 7.1. Sarcophagi in the North Necropolis at Hierapolis in Phrygia (photo: author).

the late second century AD there were numerous such producers located in, or close to, urban centres across the Roman world, working in whatever materials were easily available and specializing in local forms and decorative schemes. At least half of all extant sarcophagi (well over 6,000) came from workshops which fall into this category. The thousands of sarcophagi documented at Hierapolis in Phrygia are cases in point, even if their numbers are somewhat exceptional (Fig. 7.1).[2] The products of similarly local workshops have been identified across the Roman world.[3] Like so much else about stone supply in this period, the sarcophagus trade was dominated by localised activity.

A more expensive option, if the choice of materials mattered especially to the customer, was to approach a workshop which sourced superior stone from further afield. Catering to a customer base keen to engage with wider fashions

[2] Vanhaverbeke and Waelkens 2002.
[3] On regional workshops in Asia Minor, Koch 1993: 169–91; in Egypt, Ambrogi 1993: 103–9; in the Levant, Foerster 1998; Parlasca 1998; in North Africa, Fournet-Pilipenko 1961–2; in Pannonia, Pochmarski 1998; in Spain, Rodà 2001: 65–71; P. Rodríguez 2001; Claveria 1998: 143–9); in Gaul, Ward-Perkins 1960: 25–34; Gaggadis-Robin 2005: 175–251; in Britain, Russell 2010.

in relation to both the form and material of their funerary monument but reluctant to dispense with traditional, local decorative schemes and motifs, numerous producers from the mid second century AD onwards turned to the major white marble quarries for raw materials. Prokonnesian (sometimes Thasian) marble, the quarries of which were comparatively accessible by sea, was the material of choice for workshops in the northern Balkans, northern Italy, and the Levant.

The final option was to acquire a sarcophagus from a workshop elsewhere. Various sarcophagus types, famed for the quality of their carving and distinctive character, found wide appeal during the course of the second century AD. Prominent among these are Attic and Asiatic sarcophagi, carved by workshops close to the Pentelic and Dokimeian quarries. The producers of Metropolitan sarcophagi too, though primarily rooted in the Roman market, occasionally worked for customers further afield, in the western provinces most notably but sometimes also the Levant. Exactly which options were available to each customer, of course, depended on where they were based and their financial clout. Not everywhere were there local sarcophagus workshops with access to suitable materials.

Time of purchase

How the producer responded to the customer's request also probably varied according to their situation. It is often assumed that most sarcophagi were purchased fully finished 'off the shelf'—that they were usually carved to stock with only certain details (inscription and portrait) left for personalization on purchase.[4] The rationale behind this will be dealt with in detail below, but it is worth considering here the main argument usually put forward in support of this suggestion, which is that sarcophagi were often needed urgently, following a sudden death. There was rarely time to commission a sarcophagus from scratch, so this hypothesis goes.[5]

A crucial point to understand here is that sarcophagi were not simply functional containers for the corpse of the deceased. At those sites where we have extensive epigraphic records, generally in the Greek East, it is clear that most sarcophagi were purchased during the lifetime of the planned occupant, and not in a rush following their death. In Asia Minor especially, it was common to record in the inscription whether the individual was alive or dead when the sarcophagus was either set up or inscribed. Of the eight inscribed sarcophagi at Kalchedon, five were installed but not inscribed when the client was alive (ζῶν follows the name), two were installed and

---

[4] Stewart 2008: 37.   [5] Koch and Sichtermann 1982: 613–14; Stewart 2008: 37.

inscribed (ζῆ is used), while only one was installed after the individual had died (ζήσας is used).[6] In their study of the inscriptions on the garland sarcophagi at Aphrodisias, Reynolds and Roueché argue that almost all the extant examples were purchased during the lifetimes of those commemorated.[7] Epitaphs regularly use the future tense to refer to the individual or individuals who will be buried within a particular sarcophagus.[8] At Tyre it was common to write who a particular sarcophagus was 'reserved' for on it—the verb used was διαφέρω—and individuals bought multiple chests in anticipation of future need.[9]

This was not a practice limited to the East, even if the bulk of our evidence for it comes from there. At Arles, the inscription on the sarcophagus of S. Alfius Vitalis states quite clearly that this monument was erected during his lifetime for himself and his descendants.[10] On funerary reliefs from around Rome it was also common for monuments to be erected when the individual commemorated was still alive; in this case, the formula *vivus sibi fecit* or *viva sibi fecit*, or sometimes just *V*, was used.[11] No concrete rule governed when the inscription was added: it could be added when the first member of a family died, commemorating both the deceased and those still alive, or it could be added by an heir or third party when the last member of a family died.[12]

Multiple occupancy

What these examples also show is that sarcophagi, like tombs, were often intended for multiple occupants, especially in the Greek East; in fact, the Greek terms used for sarcophagi are the same as those used for tombs.[13] In Asia Minor they were sometimes produced with small projecting ledges on their insides on which a shelf could be rested to divide them into levels.[14] At Aphrodisias, the average number of individuals commemorated on the

---

[6] Asgari and Fıratlı 1978: 35–6.   [7] Reynolds and Roueché 2007: 149.

[8] Öğüş 2008: 174.

[9] For example: Chéhab 1985: 485 (no. 879–80), 492 (no. 923–4), 495 (931–2), 496 (no. 937–8), 568 (no. 4062–3), 740 (no. 31–2), 741 (no. 33–4), 757 (no. 213–14), 761 (no. 205–6).

[10] Gaggadis-Robin 2005: 209–11 (no. 68).

[11] Carroll 2006: 86–7.

[12] SR. 9 at Kalchedon records the death of a certain Flavius Eutyches who set up the sarcophagus during his own lifetime but commemorates also his son, whose full name is left uninscribed, presumably because he was still alive (Asgari and Fıratlı 1978: 33–4). Another example is a funerary relief of four family members in the cloister of S. Giovanni in Laterano, three of whom are described as still living (*CIL* VI.9411; Zanker 1975: 294–6, fig. 32; Carroll 2006: 87).

[13] Kubińska 1968: 32–57.   [14] At Aphrodisias: Öğüş 2008: 172.

inscription is four.[15] At Kalchedon between two and four individuals, usually
of the same family, is the norm, though in all but one case, more skeletons
were found inside the sarcophagus during excavation than there were individ
uals listed in the inscription.[16] This should remind us that sarcophagi often
carried on being used by other people even after the death of the purchaser. At
Tyre, one sarcophagus was found to contain at least thirty-eight skeletons with
coins dating from the reigns of Elagabalus to Arcadius, a period of at least 173
years.[17] Individuals occasionally anticipated this future need, buying multiple
sarcophagi for their whole family which could be put to use as required.
Several inscribed sarcophagi from Tyre record how local notables jostled
for space in the crowded necropolis, reserving both plots and sarcophagi for
themselves and their families: a purple fisherman named Heraclitos, for
example, installed three sarcophagi in his name.[18] The point here is that a
considerable amount of planning went into the purchase of a sarcophagus; like
buying a plot of land, building a tomb, or making a will, purchasing a
sarcophagus was part of the process of planning for death.

SOURCING RAW MATERIALS: THE EVIDENCE FROM THE QUARRIES

The distance between the individual workshops responsible for carving sarcophagi and the sources of their raw materials could vary significantly, as
could the relationship between them. The Metropolitan workshops, in particular, were reliant on imported materials brought from some distance away,
and separate campaigns of archaeometric analysis of sarcophagi in Rome
suggests that they cast their nets wide, commonly using Luna, Prokonnesian,
Pentelic, and Thasian.[19] The quarries, therefore, supplied these production
centres with raw materials; we should not rule out the possibility, even, that
representatives from these centres travelled to, or even worked in, the quarries.
Finds of roughed-out sarcophagus chests and lids at the quarries reveal the
condition in which these raw materials were supplied; what they do not
necessarily show is that the quarries themselves had any role in deciding the
form or design of the object in question.

---

[15] Smith 2008: 349–50.
[16] Asgari and Fıratlı 1978: 32–4.   [17] Chéhab 1984: 234–7 (nos. 823–4).
[18] Chéhab 1985: 666–7 (nos. 1341–2), 675–6 (nos. 4864, 4950).
[19] On examples in Rome, Van Keuren et al. 2011; Stowel Pearson and Herz 1992; on those in
the British Museum, Walker 1990a: 15–36; and on the use of Thasian dolomitic marble,
Herrmann and Newman 1995: 82–3; 1999: 300–2; Herrmann 1999: 57–69.

Quarry-based shaping

In most cases, the work undertaken on a sarcophagus at the quarry consisted of nothing more than the rough squaring and hollowing out of the chest, and sometimes the shaping of the lid. This level of working made more sense for sarcophagi than for almost any other object type; it could reduce the weight of the chest alone by almost half, or as much as 2,000 kg for an averagely sized example.[20] Work was usually carried out with the point chisel and the pick, traces of which can be found on sarcophagus interiors. As with architectural elements, roughing out occurred even when the sarcophagus did not need to be moved far. For example, even though 90 per cent of the catalogued sarcophagi at Hierapolis in Phrygia were carved from the local travertine, they were still supplied in roughed-out form from the quarries.[21]

As with architectural elements, a large portion of our data for quarry-based shaping of sarcophagi comes from Prokonnesos. At least 112 sarcophagi or sizeable fragments thereof have been identified to date at the quarries and in the small neighbouring necropolis here (Fig. 7.2).[22] The majority of these chests were simply hollowed out and roughly smoothed on their exterior sides with the pick and point chisel. The results of the archaeometric studies on Metropolitan sarcophagi already mentioned show that considerable quantities of these blank chests ended up in Rome, but this was also the imported material of choice for sarcophagi in much of coastal Asia Minor and the Levant, the Balkans, and north-eastern Italy.[23] Across almost all of these areas they were combined with gable or saddle-roof type lids with corner acroteria which are well represented in roughed-out form at the quarries.

These chests and lids were not some sort of distinctive Prokonnesian 'type'. The example of Hierapolis has already been mentioned, but similar chests have been found in quarries elsewhere.[24] This was simply the first stage in the production process, one designed to make these objects more manageable for onward transportation. Even the highly elaborate chests of Asiatic sarcophagi began life as simply hollowed-out blank chests, as an example from the Dokimeian quarries demonstrates.[25] What distinguishes the blank chests carved in Prokonnesian marble from these other examples is their distribution. Demand for high-quality white marble in regions lacking obvious local sources forced producers to look further afield, and due to their island location, the quarries on Prokonnesos were an accessible alternative. The

---

[20] Wurch-Koželj and Koželj 1995: 45.
[21] Vanhaverbeke and Waelkens 2002; Ronchetta 1987: 105.
[22] Asgari 1990: 110–15; also Ward-Perkins 1975: 42.
[23] See above: Chapter 7: Sourcing raw materials: the evidence from the quarries (pp. 260–73).
[24] At, for example, Dokimeion (Waelkens 1988), Sagalassos (Köse 2005: 25–6), and in Dalmatia (Cambi 1988).
[25] Fant 1989c: 113.

Fig. 7.2. Sarcophagi at Saraylar on Prokonnesos (photo: author).

arrangement of quarrying on the island allowed large blocks to be quarried, shaped, and loaded onto ships more quickly and efficiently than at either Penteli or Luna. The same, of course, can be said about the quarries on Thasos, and here too roughed-out sarcophagus chests are common. Rectangular chests, in particular, are found in at least seven distinct quarries on the island, including both the calcitic marble quarries at Aliki and the dolomitic ones on Cape Vathy.[26]

Further work in the quarries

Hollowed-out chests are not the only form of roughed-out sarcophagi found at the quarries. Work was often taken further, which in turn provides more of an insight into the relationship between these quarries and the sarcophagus producers using them. Sometimes this extra work was extremely simple; examples are found on Prokonnesos, and at Hierapolis, on which this extra

---

[26] Koželj et al. 1985; Wurch-Koželj and Koželj 2009.

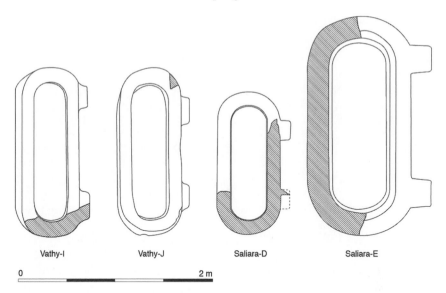

Vathy-I   Vathy-J   Saliara-D   Saliara-E

0   2 m

Fig. 7.3. Roughed-out *lēnos* sarcophagus chests I and J from the quarries at Vathy and D and E from the quarries at Saliara on Thasos (based on Wurch-Koželj and Koželj 1995: fig. 3b, 4a, 7b, 8b, with permission of the authors).

level of definition consisted of nothing more than the shaping of a lower socle, and occasionally also the addition of an upper profile.[27] The examples from Prokonnesos with a pronounced lower socle were possibly destined for northern Italy where this format was especially popular, as examples in Ivrea, Modena, and Ravenna show.[28]

In other cases, the form of the sarcophagus received far more definition at this early stage. The round-ended, so-called *lēnos* (λην́ός) or tub-shaped, chests are a case in point. There were two basic roughed-out forms of this sarcophagus type: the first with sides of an even thickness all the way around, the second incorporating projecting bosses on its front. These bosses were intended for carving into either lion-head protomes or relief lions with raised heads, two of the canonical forms of the so-called 'lion sarcophagus' or *Löwensarkophag* (for an image of which, see Fig. 7.20).[29] A reasonable number of these objects have been found in the quarries on Cape Vathy and at Saliaria on Thasos, but this was not a distinctly Thasian form (Figs. 7.3 and 7.4).[30] *Lēnos* sarcophagi are not used on Thasos, where more simple rectangular chests were preferred, nor are they found anywhere locally.[31] This was a product destined primarily for the Roman market, a creation of the Metropolitan producers,

---

[27] Asgari 1990: 110–15: Types C and D.   [28] Gabelmann 1973: no. 61, 55, 68, 71, 63.
[29] Chiarlo 1974; Stroszeck 1998.   [30] Koželj et al. 1985; Wurch-Koželj and Koželj 1995.
[31] Koželj et al. 1985: 77.

Fig. 7.4. Roughed-out *lēnos* sarcophagus chest F in the quarries at Saliara on Thasos (photo: T. Koželj).

who were using these Thasian quarries as a source of raw materials. These same producers used other quarries too. Nearly half of the *lēnos* sarcophagi in the collections of the British Museum were identified as Prokonnesian.[32] In fact, a handful of roughed-out *lēnos* sarcophagi have been found at these quarries, though they remain unpublished.[33] Recent analysis of a *lēnos* sarcophagus in the collection of the Museum of Fine Arts in Boston, furthermore, reveals that Pentelic marble was also occasionally used for this type.[34] A roughed-out *lēnos* sarcophagus, in this case presumably for local use, has even been found in the Vila Viçosa quarries near Estremoz in Portugal.[35] Again, there appears to be no defined link in this case between material and sarcophagus type.

In comparison to these *lēnos* sarcophagi the well-known roughed-out forms of Asiatic garland sarcophagi were much more precisely defined before they

[32] Walker 1985*b*: 61; 1990*a*: 15–36; for an example in the Toledo Museum of Art, Knudsen, Craine, and Tykot 2002: 237.

[33] Pers. comm. Nuşin Asgari.

[34] Comstock and Vermule 1976: 154–5 (inv. 1975.359); and on the analysis of its material, Van Keuren et al. 2011: 169.

[35] Mañas and Fusco 2008: 495; this was found alongside a rectangular chest.

Fig. 7.5. Roughed-out garland sarcophagus in andesite from Assos (photo: author).

left the quarry. The curiously geometric blocked-out form of these pieces, usually worked with the point chisel, began life as a stage in the production process; this was when the decorative format was planned and fitted to the shape of the chest, before detailed carving was begun. However, this scheme became popular in its own right; it was even imitated on rock-cut tombs, as at Anazarbos in Kilikia.[36] Interestingly, the garland sarcophagi carved in the maroon andesite of Assos were produced in a similar form and only one or two of the known examples of these were ever fully ornamented (Fig. 7.5).[37]

Typological work by Asgari and Işik has enabled the identification of five distinct varieties of Asiatic roughed-out garland sarcophagi carved in white marble.[38] Each of these types, it has been argued, is the product of a different production centre, three of which can be confidently identified as being based on Prokonnesos (Fig. 7.6), at Ephesos (Fig. 7.7), and at Aphrodisias (see Figs. 7.18 and 7.19); indeed three examples have been found at the

[36] Waelkens 1990: 68, fig. 34; Koch 2011: 15.
[37] On the examples at Assos, Serdaroğlu 1990: 3; also Clarke, Bacon, and Koldewey 1902: pl. 8; on the analysis of their material, Lazzarini and Visonà 2009.
[38] Asgari 1977; Işik 1992; 1998; 2007.

Fig. 7.6. Roughed-out garland sarcophagus at Saraylar on Prokonnesos (photo: author).

Fig. 7.7. Roughed-out garland sarcophagus at Ephesos (photo: author).

Fig. 7.8. Roughed-out Asiatic *klinē* lid from the quarries at Dokimeion (photo: P. Rockwell).

quarries on Prokonnesos.[39] The distribution patterns of the remaining two types are centred on coastal Karia and the Hermos valley respectively. The discovery of an abandoned roughed-out garland sarcophagus in the quarry at Selvioğlu, near Uşak, might indicate the origin of the latter.[40] Whether there were single workshops responsible for all the known pieces from each in these locations is impossible to say—the numbers are certainly not too great to rule this out—but it should be noted that until further archaeometric work is carried out we cannot be sure that the close connection drawn between each of these types and their respective production centres is accurate.

The level of detailed roughing out apparent on garland sarcophagi was not limited to chests. At Dokimeion, the source of the fine white marble favoured by the producers of the elaborate columnar sarcophagi, four roughed-out *klinē* lids complete with reclining figures have been found to date (Fig. 7.8).[41] To this list we can add a roughed-out gable lid with corner acroteria that has also been found at the quarries.[42] These objects, especially the *klinē* lids were produced to the absolute requirements of the sarcophagus workshops; it

[39] Asgari 1990: 115.   [40] Pralong 1980: 254–5, figs. 4a–b.
[41] Fant 1985: 659.   [42] Fant 1989c: 113.

seems probable, in fact, that the *klinē* lids on Attic sarcophagi were similarly roughed out in the Pentelic quarries, though no examples have been found to date.

These finds of carefully roughed-out chests and lids in various forms at a range of quarries, often alongside simply hollowed-out blank chests, shows that different modes of production co-existed even at the same site. In some cases even detailed finishing work took place at the quarries. Three examples of this are known from Prokonnesos. The first is a near-finished child's *lēnos* sarcophagus on which the front surface is decorated with the double strigil pattern.[43] Since this decorative format is most popular at Rome and children's sarcophagi are absent from the Greek East in general, this object was presumably either destined for a customer in the capital or for use on the island, but in either case it would seem to point to the presence of carvers from Rome at the quarries. A similar conclusion could be drawn for a pair of fragmentary lids, both of the gable type with corner acroteria, which also bear traces of detailed finishing. On the first of these, the triangular gable end of such a lid, the surface has been smoothed, the framing profiles modelled, and the head of a gorgon carved into the central boss.[44] On the second example, this time with a blank gable end, a detailed female portrait bust has been carved onto the forward-facing acroterion (Fig. 7.9).[45] The face of this bust is now damaged and it is impossible to say whether it was finished or not, but the modelling of the curved surface behind the bust finds close parallels on lids from northern Italy.[46] This latter example certainly seems to indicate the presence of north Italian carvers at the quarries. Again, it is possible that these objects were finished to this state so as to be ready for use on the island, but we should not rule out their being exported in this condition: a garland sarcophagus in Prokonnesian marble, finished on all four sides, was found at the site of the Şile shipwreck.[47] Whether the carvers responsible were based at the quarry permanently, in an established workshop, or only temporarily, perhaps even for the completion of a single job, can only be hypothesized; it is even possible that these were practice pieces or models, like the Aurisina capital mentioned in Chapter 6.

This brief survey of the evidence for the roughing out, and sometimes finishing, of sarcophagi (chests and lids) at the quarries shows that even within individual quarries a spectrum of modes of production are identifiable. It was simply not the case, as Ward-Perkins would have had it, that certain quarries produced 'certain particular shapes, and in some cases even certain particular

[43] This chest is in the open-air museum at Saraylar and is due to be published by Nuşin Asgari.
[44] This lid is also in the open-air museum at Saraylar and is currently unpublished.
[45] Asgari 1990: 113, fig. 6.
[46] For examples: Gabelmann, 1973: no. 59, 62, 65.   [47] Beykan 1988.

Fig. 7.9. Sarcophagus lid at Saraylar on Prokonnesos (photo: author).

designs'.[48] The range of finds from the quarries instead reflects the variety of demand for sarcophagi.

Orders and stock at the quarries

Who actually undertook this roughing out and at whose behest no doubt varied: these could have been specialist carvers based permanently at the quarries working either for customers directly or producers further away placing orders with them; or perhaps they were temporary visitors to the quarries, there for the completion of a single commission. Whether distant producers preferred to contract others at the quarries to complete orders for

---

[48] Ward-Perkins 1980*b*: 25.

them or travel there themselves to oversee or undertake the whole process must have depended on their relationship with the quarry-based workers in question and the character of the commission. In practice, the range of options were similar to those available to building suppliers outlined in Chapter 6. For one-off commissions of unusual scale or form it might have been necessary to send workers specifically to the quarries to secure the required materials and rough them out. While this was a possibility, it must be admitted that for the bulk of sarcophagi this kind of careful oversight of quarrying and roughing out would have been immaterial. The quarrying, squaring, and hollowing out of a chest would have presented few challenges to a skilled quarryman. Even the shaping of a *lēnos* sarcophagus would have been unproblematic. All these workers would have needed were rough dimensions and the number of objects needed which could have been sent via a middleman or a specialist supplier, perhaps a *negotiator marmorarius* or someone similar.[49]

The relatively formulaic roughed-out forms of most, if emphatically not all, sarcophagus chests and lids recovered from the quarries raise a further issue. Could certain quarry-based workers specialized in roughing out sarcophagi simply have produced these objects continually to stock? Did they have to wait for specific orders from more distant producers to filter through? On the face of it, simply squared, hollowed-out chests were relatively flexible products that could be carved with almost any design after export from the quarries. Production-to-stock in this case would have posed little risk to a quarry-based workshop, one might argue, considering the size of the market for chests adaptable to any design in the second and third centuries AD.[50] This argument can be extended to the more elaborated roughed-out types, the Asiatic garland sarcophagi and the *lēnos* varieties.

While all of this is true at least theoretically, we should be careful not to assume that production-to-stock was the norm. Squared and hollowed chests, in fact, were not simply blank canvases. They vary substantially in size: Prokonnesian chests at the quarries, at Tyre, and in northern Italy vary in length between 1.37 and 2.68 m, and in width and height between 0.62 and 2.28 m; those used by the Metropolitan producers tend to be shorter, usually less than 2.20 m, and rarely more than 0.70 m in width or height.[51] Their wall thicknesses, which in part determine the decoration that can be carved on them, as well as their proportions are also often quite different.[52] There was no standard type of Prokonnesian blank chest, in other words. Rather, production

[49] See Chapter 6: Specialist contractors (pp. 204–7).
[50] Ward-Perkins 1980a: 326–7; Asgari 1990: 115.
[51] Asgari 1990: 110–11; Chéhab 1984; 1985; Gabelmann 1973; Walker 1990a: 15–36.
[52] On the importance of wall thicknesses, Asgari 1990: 111; Vanhaverbeke and Waelkens 2002: 141.

responded to, and adapted to, the demands of individual workshops, which were presumably placing orders, either single or bulk, at the quarries.

A similar scenario has recently been proposed by Stefanidou-Tiveriou for the Thasian quarries, on the basis of the evidence from Thessaloniki.[53] The preference here, as in the Propontis, was for large inscriptions and small figured relief scenes; most of the sarcophagi have rectangular frames on three or fewer of their sides, and often a lower socle. Thasian marble, due to the proximity of the quarries, was the preferred material and the chests, as well as probably lids, were imported from the island squared and hollowed with a defined lower socle. Several factors suggest that these chests were not simply a standard type purchased from stock on Thasos. First, most of the sarcophagi found on Thasos and used on Thasos are simply squared, plain-sided pieces lacking a lower socle. Second, almost all of the sarcophagi from Thessaloniki which have been analysed were carved from the calcitic marble of Aliki, and not the dolomitic marble from which most of the sarcophagi used on Thasos itself were carved; this might have been a deliberate choice based on the ease of transportation from Aliki.[54] Stefanidou-Tiveriou has even shown that three distinct chest lengths are noticeable among the sarcophagi at Thessaloniki, clustering around 2.10, 2.36, and 2.65 m, roughly equivalent to 7, 8, and 9 RF; since the Roman foot was not used on Thasos, this might suggest that the dimensions for these objects were specified at Thessaloniki.[55] There is good reason, as a result of all these factors, to argue that the roughing out of these chests was undertaken in response to a specific order from producers based at Thessaloniki, according to their requirements, and possibly even overseen by them.

The shipwreck evidence

The roughed-out chests from the Torre Sgarrata shipwreck off Puglia, datable to the late second or early third century AD, support this suggestion.[56] A total of eighteen rectangular chests were found at this wreck of two different types, one with rectangular interior cavities, one with round-ended ones. Analysis has shown that the chests of the first type are carved in the dolomitic marble of Cape Vathy, while those of the second type are carved in the calcitic marble of Cape Phanari.[57] These chests vary in length between 1.93 and 2.45 m, with

---

[53] Stefanidou-Tiveriou 2009.   [54] Stefanidou-Tiveriou 2009: 21.
[55] Stefanidou-Tiveriou 2009: 22; for a similar argument with regard to *lēnos* sarcophagi at the Saliara quarries, Wurch-Koželj and Koželj 1995: 46.
[56] Throckmorton 1969.
[57] Gabellone, Giannotta, and Alessio 2009; Calia et al. 2009.

those of the first type being higher and wider than those of the second type. But a number of specific details also show that these were not simply stock pieces. One of the chests of the first type, for instance, has a moulded socle on one of its short sides. Another, of the same type, has a much thicker wall along one of its long sides which might well have been to allow for planned relief decoration. Two of the chests of the second type, meanwhile, are joined together, presumably intended for sawing apart on arrival.[58] This cargo also contained sixteen blocks of white Thasian marble, a mixture of calcitic and dolomitic, some of which were stepped for sawing into veneer, but the rest of which were probably intended for the production of lids. Therefore, not only were some of these chests already individualized but a considerable amount of work was still needed to make these objects usable. Again, the stimulus for the production of these chests seems to be coming for elsewhere, probably Rome.

A broadly similar case can be made for the cargo of the San Pietro in Bevagna shipwreck, from off southern Puglia (Fig. 7.10). Wrecked in the early third century AD, this ship was carrying a sizeable cargo (roughly 150 tonnes) of twenty-three sarcophagi, all carved in Thasian dolomitic marble.[59] These comprised three main types: ten *lēnos* sarcophagi, seven with projecting protomes and three without; nine rectangular chests; and four rectangular chests with round-ended interior cavities.[60] Six of these were stacked in pairs, a smaller one within a larger one to economize on space during transit; a further six were produced in joined pairs, for separation after arrival; while at least two had lids attached to one of their long sides. As Ward-Perkins and Throckmorton originally noted, the fact that one of these lids (no. 11) was not meant for the sarcophagus to which it was attached but for a smaller chest (no. 7) in the cargo showed that these two pieces at any rate were destined for the same producer, who would then have been responsible for sawing this lid free and putting it with the right chest.[61] This also proves that this one chest at least was not a stock piece. The same can be proposed for the examples joined in pairs, which would require significant additional work to separate, but were structurally stronger in this form. Overall it seems unlikely that the range of chest-types from the San Pietro in Bevagna wreck could have been supplied from stock, especially considering the different sizes represented—essentially three of each type. This cargo probably represents at least one large order of material placed by a producer, or multiple producers, with the quarries on Thasos.

---

[58] Gabellone, Giannotta, and Alessio 2009: 323–5.
[59] Herrmann 1999: 63.
[60] Alessio and Zaccaria 1997: 215, fig. 2.
[61] Ward-Perkins and Throckmorton 1965: 205–7.

Fig. 7.10. Plan of the cargo of the San Pietro in Bevagna shipwreck, Puglia (plan: author, based on Alessio and Zaccaria 1997: 215, fig. 2).

PRODUCTION CENTRES BEYOND THE QUARRIES

The work carried out on sarcophagus chests and lids in the quarries was usually only the first stage in the production process; rarely did it progress beyond roughing out. So fashionable were sarcophagi in imported materials, however, that often no further work was undertaken on these roughed-out chests; these were still usable and prestigious containers for the dead. There are plenty of such minimally decorated sarcophagi in the necropolis at Tyre.[62] Sometimes a further level of smoothing was all that was required to satisfy their buyers.[63] In most cases, though, these roughed-out chests would have passed through a series of further stages of working before being passed by the workshop on to the customer.

Local producers and imported materials

The roughed-out chests identified on Prokonnesos were destined primarily for sarcophagus producers in the northern Aegean, the Balkans, northern Italy, and the Levant. The way these chests were handled across these areas varied greatly since, though working in the same material, these producers were catering to different markets. Around the Propontis and up the western coast of the Black Sea, especially between the mid second and late third centuries AD, the preference was for inscribed *tabulae ansatae* and small indented relief panels cut into the sides of the chest.[64] A more elaborate formulation of this type is the so-called 'chest sarcophagus' (*Truhensarkophag*), found again in various areas of the northern Balkans, on which the whole field is framed on all four sides by projecting consoles with figures, usually *genii*, holding the *tabula*. These designs were carved into the sides of blank-sided chests and not roughed out before they left the quarries as is shown by a fragmentary, part-finished chest from Tomis, on which the first stage of carving is still preserved.[65] A similar working process can be seen on a sarcophagus from Alexandria on which a considerably more complicated scene, depicting Dionysos and Ariadne on Naxos, was carved into the flat surface of another simply squared and hollowed-out chest in Prokonnesian marble, as the part-finished left-hand short side reveals.[66]

A variation on the elaborate version of the *Truhensarkophag* is found in northern Italy, where a range of architectural chest types were produced in Prokonnesian marble between the second and fourth centuries AD.[67] The similarities between certain sarcophagi in this region and contemporary examples in the Balkans should not necessarily lead us to assume, as Asgari and Fıratlı have, that their designs were roughed out before they left the quarries.[68] No roughed-out *Truhensarkophage* have been found at the quarries

---

[62] Ward-Perkins 1969: no. PR1, PR3–4, PR8, PR11, PR14, PR17, PR19, PR20, PR22–6.

[63] For a tooth-chiselled example: Asgari and Fıratlı 1978: 27 (SR 9).

[64] Koch and Sichtermann 1982: 343–6, pl. 367–71; Barbu 1963: 553–9; Rădulescu, Coman, and Stavru 1973: 247–9.

[65] Alexandrescu-Vianu 1970: no. 15.

[66] Adriani 1961: 29, figs. 65–72.

[67] Gabelmann 1973: 40–1, 207–10, 221–6 (Types I–III).

[68] Asgari and Fıratlı 1978: 41.

on Prokonnesos and, in any case, there is no unifying structure to the design scheme that might suggest some level of determination prior to export.[69] This became a popular scheme, and the motif of two *genii* holding a *tabula* a favourite funerary motif all across the Roman world, but in every region it was refined and adapted in a slightly different way.[70] A nice example from Arles, the sarcophagus of Attia Esyche, again carved in Prokonnesian marble, shows this very clearly.[71] The front side of this sarcophagus depicts two winged *genii* supporting an inscribed *tabula*, but the corner consoles usually found on *Truhensarkophage* are absent; the sides, meanwhile, are decorated with eagles holding garlands below gorgon heads. Gaggadis-Robin has no hesitation in assigning this sarcophagus to a local workshop based on the carving techniques employed.

The majority of the sarcophagi carved in Prokonnesian marble in northern Italy were not of the *Truhensarkophag*-type but of a more elaborate architectural formulation.[72] This focus on architectural forms is not found to the same degree in the northern and eastern Balkans, though it is popular in Dalmatia (Fig. 7.11).[73] It might reflect the influence of the columnar schemes popular on contemporary sarcophagi in Asia Minor but it seems more likely that this style originated closer to home: identical architectural motifs are common on north Italian funerary stele of the first century AD, and were usually employed to frame portraits of the deceased.[74] Here, and indeed elsewhere, the imports consisted of simply squared, hollowed-out chests in Prokonnesian marble with no predetermined, roughed-out decorative format; the only details of the design that seem to have been shaped before they left the quarries were their lower socles and their lids.

In many of the areas where Prokonnesian marble was the imported material of choice for sarcophagus producers we also find roughed-out garland sarcophagi, usually but not always in Prokonnesian marble. These objects were roughed out on Prokonnesos, apparently by a workshop based there to judge from their standard form, but they also seem to have passed through the hands of local workshops beyond the quarries who adapted them to the particular demands of their clients. The holders of the garlands could be finished in various ways—carved into bucrania, rams' heads, putti, giants, eagles, Victories—as could the disks above them; rosettes, gorgons' heads, and dramatic masks were fashionable, as were simple paterae, but this space could also be used for portrait busts or more complicated figured scenes.[75] Occasionally specific

[69] For the contrary argument, Asgari 1990: 112, fig. 3: Types F–H.
[70] For examples, Gaggadis-Robin 2005: 219–27; Toynbee 1964: 211, pl. 50; Pochmarski 1998.
[71] Gaggadis-Robin 2005: 215–18 (no. 71); with Gaggadis-Robin et al. 2009: 138–9.
[72] Gabelmann 1973: 40–1.
[73] Cambi 1998: 171–2; Cambi 2000: 239–44.
[74] Pflug 1989: 39–46.
[75] Asgari 1977; Koch 1989; Koch and Sichtermann 1982: 484–97; Işık 1998.

Fig. 7.11. Sarcophagi in the Manastirine necropolis at Salona (photo: author).

motifs of local significance were included: two Prokonnesian garland sarcophagi from Ratiaria in Moesia Superior have depictions of so-called 'Thracian
Horseman' in their central *tabulae*.[76] Often these chests were simply left in
their roughed-out state. Occasionally the design was carefully dressed and
smoothed with the tooth chisel and flat chisel or outlined; on two examples—
this time from Ephesos—found in the necropolis at Aquileia, the design was
so flat that it never could have been intended for further work.[77]

When it comes to lids we find significantly less local variation in terms of
overall form: most customers, it would appear, were content with gabled lids
with corner acroteria, a form also used for limestone sarcophagi across the
regions under consideration.[78] These were adapted in various ways to local
tastes, with both gables and acroteria carved in a range of ways. Other lid types
were also experimented with, though. A Prokonnesian garland sarcophagus

[76] Filow 1910: 8–16, fig. 3–4; Atanasova 1972: 141–52, fig. 8–11; Koch and Sichtermann 1982:
335, pl. 357.
[77] Asgari 1977: 331–2: examples from Çanakkale and Gelibolu (A and B); on the pair of
Ephesian garland sarcophagi from Aquileia, Brusin 1941: 51–6, fig. 22.
[78] Examples: Cambi 1998; Gaggadis-Robin 2005: 176–251.

from Viminacium in Moesia Superior, for example, has a *klinē* lid in Prokonnesian marble.[79] A curious hybrid lid, combining elements of both a *klinē*- and gable-type lid with large corner acroteria, is known from several examples in Dalmatia and was also carved in Prokonnesian marble.[80] These examples show that there was not simply one 'Prokonnesian' lid type for these scattered producers to work with; it was up to them what they imported and how they worked it.[81]

The Metropolitan producers

These various producers were firmly rooted in the local markets to which they were responding. Though handling imported materials they specialized in decorative schemes which appealed to very specific markets. In many ways the various sarcophagus producers based at Rome were similarly located in close proximity to their customer base: most Metropolitan sarcophagi were used in the capital and were tailored primarily to that market.[82] These producers imported roughed-out chests in a variety of forms from a series of quarries and finished them in Rome. We cannot rule out the possibility that these producers also imported unshaped blocks from the quarries but this seems unlikely considering the implications of this extra weight; most sarcophagi probably arrived in the capital in the form of those recovered from the Torre Sgarrata and San Pietro shipwrecks.[83] A handful of rectangular chests in several sizes can be found in the collections of the Museo Nazionale Romano, all neatly squared with the point chisel but not worked further.[84] These are similar to the Torre Sgarrata examples though the origin of their marble is unknown. Another chest in the same collection is sawn on all sides, a feature that is common on Metropolitan sarcophagi, though whether this was done at the quarries or at Rome is unclear; saws were certainly used at a range of quarries.[85] In addition to simply squared and hollowed-out chests, the Metropolitan workshops also dealt with roughed-out imports in more complicated forms, of course. The most distinctive of these are the round-ended *lēnos* sarcophagi, but a roughed-out rectangular sarcophagus chest, with lid, datable to the third or early fourth century and again in the collection of the Museo Nazionale Romano, might indicate that other objects arrived in the capital

[79] Vulić 1905: 10–12, no. 37; 1941–8: 147–8, no. 317; Koch and Sichtermann 1982: pl. 355–6.
[80] Cambi 1994; for more on this lid type, see Chapter 7: Multi-purpose forms pp. (300–1).
[81] On Prokonnesian production for local workshops, Koch 2011:13.
[82] Koch and Sichtermann 1982: 267–72.
[83] On the argument in favour of importing blocks, Ward-Perkins 1975–6; 1992d: 42.
[84] Giuliano 1982: no. III.9, VI.36; 1984: no. XIII.18, XX.1, XX.3, XXI.4.
[85] Giuliano 1982: no. III.13. On saws in the quarries at Kassamboli and in Gaul, Lambraki 1982; Bedon 1984: 127–8; and on sawn objects at Dokimeion, Mellink 1977: 317.

roughed out.[86] This chest, and its accompanying lid, are coarsely worked with the point chisel all over, but their edges are defined by smooth, flat-chiselled strips, as is the outline of a central *clipeus* medallion at the centre of the chest.

Metropolitan carvers were responsible for a dizzying array of sarcophagus forms and designs but a number of features are common to their products. First, most Metropolitan sarcophagi are only decorated on their front and two short sides, with most attention being devoted to the front. Second, sarcophagi in the capital tend to be much lower to the ground, rarely more than 0.80 m high, than examples in the East. These producers also specialized in certain forms (*lēnos* sarcophagi) and decorative schemes (strigillated façades) which never really caught on elsewhere. What these factors all show is that, though these producers were importing roughed-out sarcophagi from distant quarries, the form of these objects and the way in which they were handled responded to local patterns of demand.

Asiatic sarcophagi

The various sarcophagi produced all across the Roman world in imported materials were designed for local markets. The so-called Attic and Asiatic (or Dokimeian) sarcophagi were different. These were renowned products, aimed at the very highest end of the sarcophagus market; their ornate decoration, on all four sides of their chests, and the quality of finish made them the most expensive option available to elite commissioners. Their dating also suggests that they were produced over roughly the same period: Asiatic sarcophagi appear in the mid second century AD and reach their peak numbers in the Severan period, dropping away in the early to mid third century AD; production of Attic sarcophagi begins slightly earlier, reaching an Antonine to Severan peak, but also ceases in the mid third century AD.[87] Wider awareness and appreciation of these sarcophagi is revealed by the attempts made to imitate them: locally produced versions of the columnar Dokimeian sarcophagi can be found in Bithynia, including examples now in the museum at Iznik, and at Aphrodisias; the impact of Attic forms can be seen in numerous Metropolitan sarcophagi.[88] The elaborate *klinē* lids of both types were also copied: Ward-Perkins identified a *klinē*-lidded strigillated sarcophagus at Tyre as 'copying Attic models' but carved in Prokonnesian marble.[89]

---

[86] Giuliano 1984: no. IX.4.
[87] Waelkens 1982a: 7–104; Özgan 2003: 34–44 with Schwertheim 2003: 87–92; Giuliano 1962: 15.
[88] Wiegartz 1965: 161–2, pl. 38–9; Pensabene 2007a: 299; Öğüş 2010: 167–85; Koch and Sichtermann 1982: 76–80.
[89] Ward-Perkins 1969: no. PR 18.

Fig. 7.12. Asiatic sarcophagus from Sidamara (Istanbul B) now in Istanbul Archaeological Museum (photo: author, used with permission of Istanbul Archaeological Museum).

Of the two, Attic sarcophagi were much more widely distributed than their Asiatic counterparts, as we have seen.[90] Rarely, though, were they imported far inland. In contrast, sarcophagi in Dokimeian marble, though only occasionally shipped overseas, were widely distributed throughout central and western Asia Minor; particular concentrations have been found in Phrygia, Bithynia, and Pamphylia.[91] As Waelkens has convincingly argued, in addition to referencing contemporary architectural tastes for sweeping columnar facades, the carvers responsible for these Asiatic sarcophagi also drew on motifs common to a range of other artefacts produced in and around the Dokimeian quarries (Fig. 7.12); most notably, in the early imperial period, the famous 'door-stone' stele (*Türsteine*).[92] Waelkens saw a single workshop as responsible for these sarcophagi, of which well over 300 examples survive.[93]

---

[90] Chapter 5: Sarcophagus distribution in the East, fig. 5.6; Ward-Perkins 1992*e*: 83.
[91] Waelkens 1982*a*: 9, pl. 31.
[92] Waelkens 1982*a*: 40–2; 1986; 1988; Wiegartz 1965: 13–14.
[93] Russell 2011*b*: 127–31.

Whether this was actually the case is unknown; an alternative model sees these objects as the products of a number of nucleated workshops, all still working in a similar way and for the same market but without any overriding direction. While roughing out might have taken place at the quarries, as it did for other sarcophagus types, there is less evidence to tell us where the finishing work took place. Did the carvers responsible finish them close to the quarries and ship them in this state or did they finish them elsewhere, either where they were to be used or in another intermediary place?[94]

Waelkens is keen to see the final decorative scheme conceived, laid out, and almost completely carved at the quarries, with only portraits and inscriptions left blank for later finishing.[95] This requires us to assume that these sarcophagi were transported considerable distances overland (on bumpy wagons down from the Phrygian plateau) in a near-finished form. While this would have been risky, and we should remember the steps taken to protect column shafts during transit, considerably more fragile products were also moved around in this way.[96] The only real alternative to finishing them in advance was for the producers to transport these sarcophagi from the quarries in their roughed-out form, and finish them once they had been safely delivered. Unfortunately, we have very few part-finished Asiatic sarcophagi from which a reconstruction of the production process might be attempted. Portraits, though, were occasionally left unworked: on the couple on the short side of the enormous Istanbul B sarcophagus, for example, and on several *klinē* lids.[97] These show that the carving of portraits was a separate stage of work but not necessarily that it was completed in a different location from the rest of the carving, as Waelkens (and before him Wiegartz) proposed; there were other reasons why portraits might be left blank, as will be discussed below.[98] Examples found in their original context are also too few to reveal whether or not their finish took account of their final surroundings. One was found in the tomb of Claudia Antonia Tatiana at Ephesos but is too fragmentary to be useful in this regard.[99] In his analysis of the sarcophagus from the tomb of Claudia Antonia Sabina at Sardis, however, Morey was keen to note that the right short side 'shows distinct neglect in the finish', which he argued showed it was finished in place.[100] Sadly, the exact location of the sarcophagus is not known; there was space for at least two sarcophagi in the porch of this tomb,

[94] Wiegartz 1974: 345.   [95] Waelkens 1982a: 124–7.
[96] Wiegartz 1974: 350; on the shipping of finished capitals, Pensabene 1972: 322; Heilmeyer 1970: 169; and on cargoes of window glass and glass vessels, Foy and Jézégou 2003.
[97] Wiegartz 1965: 156–7; Morey 1924: 40–2, fig. 67. Blank portraits are only found on the Afyon K, Cumae, and the two Naples lids (Waelkens 1982a: 90; Stroka 1971), while on an example from Perge the female portrait was finished but not the male one (Demirer 1999).
[98] See Chapter 7: Blank portraits (pp. 301–7).
[99] Eichler 1944–5: 128; Wiegartz 1965: 154; and for a plan of the findspot, Rudolf 1992: fig. 1.
[100] Morey 1924: 5.

either side of the door, and Morey's reconstruction of this example is itself based on the finish of its short ends. In any case, the differences between the two short sides are overstated.[101]

The evidence, then, is far from conclusive. In one sense it would appear simpler for Dokimeian carvers based at the quarries to field orders and send out near-finished sarcophagi from there. At the same time, if this were the case, one might expect to find more unworked portraits than one actually does; in fact, it is striking how few of these objects bear any traces of unfinish. Of course, if a team of carvers travelled with each commission this would have added considerably to their expense but only a small minority of the super rich could have afforded these objects anyway.[102] For these high-end products it would be wrong to rule out this possibility on the basis of cost alone. The carvers responsible, furthermore, would not have had to cover enormous distances: as noted, few of these sarcophagi actually left Asia Minor.[103] Dokimeian carvers do turn up outside of Phrygia: two (brothers, Limnaios and Diomedes) are attested at Konya, for instance.[104]

Attic sarcophagi

The carvers of Attic sarcophagi, like their counterparts in Asia Minor, were trained in a common tradition, in this case one rooted in the Neo-Attic style— what Giuliano calls 'l'atticismo ateniese'.[105] At Athens, they were close both to the source of their raw materials (the Pentelic quarries), their primary market, and the major harbour of Piraeus; they were far better positioned geographically to respond to widespread demand for their products than the carvers of Asiatic sarcophagi. In terms of the condition in which these objects were shipped, the debate is largely the same as that outlined already for Asiatic sarcophagi; were they produced near-finished at Athens and shipped in that state or transported roughed out and completed *in situ* by teams of travelling carvers?

Unlike Asiatic sarcophagi, Attic ones often exhibit a range of finishes, both on their chests and their lids. As Rodenwaldt first noted, with regard to the examples from Xanthos, a considerable number have lower and rougher relief carving on their rear and one short side (compare Figs. 7.13 and 7.14).[106] The socles, profiles, and corner consoles on these sides were typically left as rough strips or bosses, delineated for further decoration, and the main friezes

---

[101] Morey 1924: 12–13, and compare fig. 11 and 12; also Cormack 2004: 284–7.

[102] On the extra expense of travelling sculptors, in this case with regard to Attic sarcophagi, Wiegartz 1974: 366.

[103] Chapter 5: Sarcophagus distribution in the East, fig. 5.5; Ferrari 1966: 87–8; Wiegartz 1974: 379.

[104] McLean 2002: no. 45; Hall and Waelkens 1982; L. Robert 1962: 41–3; see also Chapter 8: Migrant carvers (pp. 332–4).

[105] Giuliano 1962: 14.   [106] Rodenwaldt 1933: 181–213.

Fig. 7.13. Front side of the Attic sarcophagus from Punta de la Mora now in Tarragona (photo: Neg. D-DAI-MAD-D743).

Fig. 7.14. Rear side of the Attic sarcophagus from Punta de la Mora now in Tarragona (photo: Neg. D-DAI-MAD-D718).

shallower and more schematic than on the other sides.[107] Sometimes this finish was very rough indeed, as on an example now in Split.[108] Work on these sides clearly halted at an early stage in the carving process, after the bulk of the content had been decided and the composition arranged but before any carving in depth had begun. In noting this phenomenon, Rodenwaldt suggested it resulted from specifications supplied by the commissioner, who was aware of where the sarcophagus would be displayed: according to this reconstruction Attic sarcophagi were carved in Athens but with those sides that would never be visible finished to a lower level; they were transported, then, in a near-finished state.[109] Reluctant to believe that such fragile objects might be shipped, Ward-Perkins preferred to see the low relief sides as vestiges of the overall roughed-out condition in which these sarcophagi were exported.[110] Only once the sarcophagus was delivered, he proposed, and its final position known, were the visible sides fully finished. This finish was applied either by an accompanying team of carvers, or by a local 'branch workshop', closely connected to the Athenian producers.[111]

Whether this uneven finish was a result of *in situ* finishing, as Ward-Perkins suggested, or of specific cliental demands, as Rodenwaldt would have had it, remains unclear. Few Attic sarcophagi have been found in their original context and on those that have been there is no convincing connection between the level of finish of their sides and their placement. Two sarcophagi, from Delphi and the Kerameikos in Athens, both of which were probably displayed against walls, do have lower levels of finish on their rear sides.[112] However, the four Attic sarcophagi from a tomb at Kephissia near Athens, two others from Ladochori near Igoumenitsa, as well a fifth (Ephesos F) from Ephesos are finished evenly on all four sides, even though they were placed up against walls (or other sarcophagi) where their rear sides would not have been visible.[113] The examples found *in situ* in the necropolis at Tyre, on the other hand, most of which were originally displayed outside and were visible from multiple angles, do tend to have the uneven finish remarked upon above.[114]

---

[107] For examples: Giuliano and Palma 1978: pl. 25.63 (Boston), 26.65 (Agrigento), 30.73 (Apollonia), 40.97 (Cyrene), 58.143 (Budapest); Rogge 1995: pl. 9 (Tyre), pl. 22–3 (Beirut), 80 (Istanbul).

[108] Koch 1975: pl. 139.

[109] Rodenwaldt 1933: 181–213.

[110] Ward-Perkins 1956: 10–16; also Giuliano 1962: 16; Ferrari 1966: 20; and for criticism, Wiegartz 1965: 18; 1974: 348–50.

[111] Ward-Perkins 1963: 119–20.

[112] Flämig 2007: 127–8, pl. 8.1–3 (no. 2a, Kerameikos), 140–2, pl. 27–31 (no. 17a, Delphi).

[113] Kephissia: Flämig 2007: 133–5, pl. 15–19 (no. 10); and on the sarcophagi, Tschira 1948–9: 83–97, fig. 1–3 (sarcophagus 1); Schauenburg 1967: 50–1, fig. 8–10; Toynbee 1934: pl. 51.3 (sarcophagus 2); C. Robert 1890: 9–10, pl. 3 (sarcophagus 3). Ladochori: Flämig 2007: 145–6, pl. 40–3 (no. 21a–b). Ephesos: Keil 1932: 68–71; Rudolf 1989: 33–5, fig. 22–7.

[114] Linant de Bellefonds 1985: 13, 18–20 (no. 954), 22–3 (no. 330); also Chéhab 1968: pl. 1, 4, 7 (no. 607), 8–12 (no. 954), 35c (no. 383, 330), 36–40 (no. 907).

Other finds are unfortunately too poorly documented or too fragmentary to be of assistance, but even based on this limited dataset there is little to indicate that the finish of these pieces was tailored to their surroundings; this further suggests that the form in which most Attic sarcophagi are found was probably the form in which they were exported from Athens.[115] The Attic sarcophagus recovered from the sea off Punta de la Mora, just north of Tarragona, was in exactly this condition but unfortunately it is not clear whether this comes from a Roman shipwreck or a more recent one (Figs. 7.13 and 7.14).[116] The fact that these sarcophagi were probably not finished *in situ* by teams of travelling sculptors is further indicated by the large number of Attic *klinē* lids which have unworked portraits and the fact that when these are carved they seem to have been finished by local sculptors and vary considerably in quality.[117]

If Attic sarcophagi were not completed *in situ* then how do we explain the uneven finish on their sides noted by both Rodenwaldt and Ward-Perkins? Since most of the sarcophagi on which this phenomenon can be noted have *klinē* lids, a format introduced into the Attic carvers' repertoire in the later second century AD, it seems plausible that this uneven finish relates to the function of this particular format.[118] These *klinē*-lidded sarcophagi were frontal monuments, with the reclining figures on their lids made to be seen primarily from the front or from the foot end of the *klinē*.[119] As a result far more attention was paid to finishing the prominent sides of these chests, with the remaining sides being left serviceable but not nearly as ornate.[120] There was nothing to stop the customer having these other sides carved fully but this does not seem to have been the default finish, perhaps reflecting the fact that most Attic sarcophagi ended up in tomb buildings anyway.[121] The balance of the evidence indicates, therefore, that Attic sarcophagi were shipped largely finished, often but not always with a lower level of finish on their less prominent sides, and with blank portraits on their *klinē* lids if they were of this type. There was no need for a team of sculptors to be dispatched with each and every commission.

---

[115] Examples with poorly recorded locations: those from Xanthos tomb (Rodenwaldt 1933: 181–2; Cormack 2004: 328–9); from Photike near Paramythia and Magoula near Sparta (Flämig 2007: 150–1, 172–3, pl. 53, 78 (no. 30a, 70a)). Too fragmentary: Ephesos B and C sarcophagi (Rudolf 1989: 44–6, fig. 28–35; 1992: fig. 1; Cormack 2004: 219–21); those from Agia Pelagia in Epirus and Messene (Flämig 2007: 144–5, 178–9, pl. 39.3–4, 90.1–2 (no. 20a, 78a–b)).

[116] The erosion on the breaks on this chest might indicate that it was already old when it was deposited on the seabed; see Ventura y Solsona 1949; Domenech Miró 1961.

[117] Compare Rogge 1995: pl. 46–7 (no. 24, Rome), pl. 52–3 (no. 6, Beirut); Koch and Sichtermann 1982: fig. 420 (Paris); Koch 1989: fig. 35 (Arethusa), 47 (Tyre).

[118] Wiegartz 1977: 386–7; Rogge 1993: 111.

[119] Linant de Bellefonds 1985: 10–11.

[120] Wiegartz 1974: 360–3; Linant de Bellefonds 1985: 10–13.

[121] Flämig 2007: 82–3.

This means that there would have been no need for the 'branch workshops' hypothesized by Ward-Perkins. Indeed, in their attempt to categorize Attic sarcophagi on stylistic grounds, Giuliano and Palma were able to distinguish no distinctive regional groupings that might be connected to any such 'branch workshops'.[122] The sarcophagi of northern Italy share no distinct set of characteristics that are not also common to the sarcophagi of Syria, in other words.[123] Occasionally pairs of sarcophagi with very common features can be identified at a single site but these tend to be close in date and could easily have been ordered at the same time, or by related individuals at slightly different times, from the same producer at Athens.[124] Athens, it would seem, remained the hub of this activity and the place to which prospective buyers needed to turn. Individual customers could have done this by travelling to Athens and discussing a commission in person, by sending someone to do this for them, or by hiring a middleman or specialist stone supplier who could communicate their wishes. In this respect it is worth noting that most of the purchasers of Attic sarcophagi who can be identified were high-status individuals who no doubt had a range of contacts on which they could draw.

The producers of Attic and Asiatic sarcophagi specialized in the export of highly crafted, culturally expressive sculpture; the uniformity of their respective types demonstrates that their decorative form was established by a limited core of sculptors trained in a defined artistic tradition. Purchasers of these sarcophagi were buying into this tradition and appear to have been content to select from the relatively limited range of decorative schemes that these workshops excelled at. There was room for adaptation and individualisation, as the range of motifs employed on the various sarcophagi carved in Dokimeian marble show. Originality, though, was by no means the primary requirement of most commissioners. These sarcophagi were statements of wealth and cultural belonging and arguably the more stereotypical the decoration the more forcefully these messages could be communicated.

PRODUCTION METHODS

Part-finished sarcophagus chests and lids at the quarries but also at sites around the Roman world allow us to reconstruct on a broad scale where the major stages of production were undertaken. Typically the system was fairly simple: hollowing out and basic roughing out were carried out at the quarries,

---

[122] Giuliano and Palma 1978: 13–14, 30–4.
[123] Compare the examples in Ciliberto 1996; 1998; Linant de Bellefonds 1985.
[124] For a pair from Antioch, dated to the mid 150s and mid 160s AD respectively, see Giuliano and Palma 1978: 13–14.

further finishing as close as possible to where the sarcophagus was to be put to use, though in the case of Attic sarcophagi this appears to have taken place at Athens. The traces of working and tool marks still visible on a number of sarcophagi, however, allow an even more fine-grained analysis of the stages of production. What they reveal are the approaches taken to finishing these monuments by a range of carvers which in turn provides an insight into the organization of production.

Working stages and techniques

On Attic sarcophagi, especially those which have the uneven finish described above, a number of working stages can be reconstructed: first, the chest was squared and hollowed out with the point chisel, perhaps also the pick; second, the design on all four sides was roughed out, the main figures on the frieze defined in shallow relief and the mouldings blocked out, with point and flat chisel; third, the profile and socle were decorated and the carvers worked into the frieze, carving around the front series of figures, adding in background figures and details of scenery with various grades of flat chisel, rasps, and even abrasives. More segmented production stages are visible on Metropolitan sarcophagi, which exhibit a wide range of technical approaches, presumably reflecting the variety of producers involved.[125] Rockwell has drawn attention to the early fourth-century boar-hunt sarcophagus in the Centrale Montemartini in Rome, on which the part-finished lid reveals at least three working stages (Fig. 7.15).[126] This lid (of the L-shaped type) was first sawn, as shown by traces on the frontal panel and rear slab, then the figured scene was carved into this surface.[127] Two phases of work can be seen on the frontal panel: on the left, the outlines of the figures were first sketched out and the spaces between them gently hollowed with the point chisel; on the right, where work was taken further, the figures were shaped with the flat or round-ended chisel and the details of the background defined. Carving was aborted at this stage, but to judge from the chest, the drill would then have been used to give depth to the background foliage and define details of the figures, before finishing work with rasp and abrasives.[128]

In this example, as on Attic sarcophagi, 'the carver's reference plane was always the front plane of the stone', to quote Rockwell.[129] A similar approach can be identified on several Aphrodisian examples.[130] The carver worked from front to back, freely excavating between the figures, shaping and detailing

---

[125] Ward-Perkins 1975–6.   [126] Inv. MC 837; Rockwell 1993: 109–10.
[127] On lid types: Koch and Sichtermann 1982: 68, fig. 1.
[128] On the drill: Ward-Perkins 1992d: 48, fig. 35; Rockwell 1993: 37, 44–5, 59, fig. 5 (no. 7).
[129] Rockwell 1993: 109–10.   [130] Öğüş 2010: 113–14, figs. 97–9 (nos. 44–6).

Fig. 7.15. Boar-hunt sarcophagus now in the Centrale Montemartini, Rome (photo: Neg. D-DAI-Rom 1541, digitally modified (restored)).

them, before moving on to the spaces around them and adding depth to these. This was a flexible way to work, allowing for the addition of more detail as carving progressed, but it also meant that the key features of the design were finished first so that if the sarcophagus had to be pressed into use suddenly the scene would still be legible. Other Metropolitan sarcophagi show a slightly different sequence of working stages—including the mid second-century AD Triumph of Dionysus sarcophagus in Baltimore, studied by Ward-Perkins— but still this general approach is evident.[131]

Different decorative schemes demanded other approaches. On the architectural designs so popular in northern Italy work focused initially on these structural elements, leaving till later the figured scenes framed by them. The rear of the sarcophagus of Bruttia Aureliana from Modena, on which the remains of an aborted design are still visible, shows that the planned design was first outlined using a point chisel.[132] Next the key architectural elements

---

[131] Ward-Perkins 1975–6: 220–3 (figs. 24–8); 1992*d*: 45–9 (figs. 36–8).
[132] Gabelmann 1973: no. 59 (pl. 26).

were defined, starting with the corner pilasters and progressing to the upper profile, lower socle, then the columns, all the time leaving rough bosses for later figurative details.[133] On several sarcophagi the capitals of the corner pilasters and of the smaller columns on the front were left for finishing later.[134] Only once all the structural details were completed did work start on the figured scenes: first, the rough panels were blocked out more precisely (Figs. 7.16 and 7.17); then the figures or other decoration were roughly worked with the point chisel and perhaps also the tooth chisel and flat chisel; and finally these figures were finished with a fine flat chisel.[135] These north Italian examples are mainly carved in Prokonnesian marble but these working stages can also be noted in sarcophagi carved in local limestone in this region. The short sides of the sarcophagus of Baburius Anthus in Grado show that the architectural framework was defined all over before work began on the figural scenes.[136] A similar approach was taken to lids. As the lid of the sarcophagus of Sosia Herennia from Modena reveals, when portraits were added to the acroteria these were first roughed out with the point chisel, with the clothing then being tackled with the flat chisel before the portrait was done.[137]

The final body of evidence that can be brought to bear on this question are the series of part-finished garland sarcophagi in Asia Minor. Guidelines for the laying out of this scheme are still visible on several of these distinctive sarcophagi, especially at Aphrodisias (Fig. 7.18).[138] These were based around simple proportional relationships which allowed this quite complicated design to be applied to any chest, regardless of its exact dimensions; this was a system that could be memorized and transferred, much like that described for Corinthian capitals in Chapter 6. Following this the geometric forms were blocked out using the point and further details, if required, of the principal features of the design (garland, grapes, rosettes, supports—Victories or putti) were shaped first with the point chisel, then probably the tooth chisel. An example now on the lawn outside the museum at Aphrodisias (which has a sawn short side) preserves traces of this stage of work on its short sides; carefully controlled tool marks, distinguishable from the rougher point chiselling, can be seen around the finished bunches of grapes on both sides (Fig. 7.19).[139] To judge from other examples, the drill was then often used to add definition to

---

[133] Definition of the corner consoles: Gabelmann 1973: no. 13 (pl. 9.2, Grado), 59 (pl. 26, Modena); and for those with all their architectural forms defined, see no. 22 (pl. 11.3, Poreč); no. 70 (pl. 35, Bologna).

[134] Gabelmann 1973: no. 67 (pl. 34.3, Ravenna), no. 71 (pl. 38, Modena), no. 74 (pl. 40, Milan).

[135] The first of these stages can be seen on sarcophagi in Modena and Bologna (Gabelmann 1973: pls. 35, 36.1, 36.2, 38); the second is visible on the panels depicting *genii* on the sarcophagus of T. Canius Restitutus from Grado (Gabelmann 1973: no. 13 (pl. 9.2))

[136] Gabelmann 1973: no. 11 (pl. 8).

[137] Gabelmann 1973: no. 71 (pl. 38.1), no. 74 (pl. 40.1).

[138] Işik 2007: nos. 20–1, pl. 44.1–8.

[139] Işik 2007: no. 48, pl. 29.1–4.

Fig. 7.16. Front side of the sarcophagus of Sosia Herennia in the Museo Civico, Modena (photo: Schwanke, Neg. D-DAI-Rom 83.877).

Fig. 7.17. Short side of the sarcophagus of Sosia Herennia in the Museo Civico, Modena (photo: Schwanke, Neg. D-DAI-Rom 83.878).

Fig. 7.18. Garland sarcophagus from Aphrodisias with guidelines for roughing out preserved (photo: author).

Fig. 7.19. Left short side of a garland sarcophagus from Aphrodisias (photo: author).

the foliage in the garland, the grapes and rosettes, before finishing work with the flat chisel. The background was usually left relatively rough and signs of the rasp or abrasives are rare.

Division of labour

On few other stone objects can these stages of work be broken down so accurately as on sarcophagi and this encourages speculation as to how this work was organized. Should we be thinking of these objects passing through multiple hands, moving along a sort of production line, or were these different stages of work all undertaken by the same carver?

It is theoretically possible that each of the stages of work identified above was carried out by a different craftsman and even that individual workshops contained specialists in particular subject matter: architectural-carvers, figure-carvers, portrait-carvers, etc. We might even consider the possibility of carvers specialized in the use of certain tools. The sculptor Eutropos who chose to depict himself on his grave plaque from Rome (now in Urbino) drilling the details on a lion's head protome of a strigillated *lēnos* sarcophagus might have been a specialist drill operator, but we have no way of telling this for sure (Fig. 7.20).[140] Perhaps Eutropos was just proud of his strap-drill and the fact that he had an apprentice or slave to operate it with him.

In his analysis of Constantinian sarcophagi in Rome, Eichner distinguishes nine stages in the production process, each of which could be further subdivided, and proposes that these could quite simply have been split between different workers.[141] There can little doubt that such a set-up would have been efficient. One worker performing the same task again and again would no doubt become quicker at it over time. However, this kind of highly articulated division of labour would also have required a large workforce and a market sufficient enough to sustain them. Division of labour on such a scale only makes sense if all the workers involved could be kept occupied simultaneously; if a continual supply of new commissions was passing through, in other words. Only very large workshops could ever have afforded to structure their production in such a way. The smaller the workshop the more flexible the carvers had to be. Adam Smith, of course, made precisely this point in his discussion of the relationship between the division of labour and the size of the market:

> As it is the power of exchanging that gives occasion to the division of labour, so the extent of this division must always be limited by the extent of that power, or, in other words, by the extent of the market... When the market is very small, no

---

[140] Strong and Claridge 1976: 200, fig. 327; Koch 1993: 37, figs. 26–8.
[141] Eichner 1981: 103–4.

Fig. 7.20. Detail of the grave plaque of the carver Eutropos, from Rome and now in the Palazzo Ducale, Urbino (photo: Rossa, Neg. D-DAI-Rom 75.1102).

person can have any encouragement to dedicate himself entirely to one employ-ment ... A country carpenter deals in every sort of work that is made of wood; a country smith in every sort of work that is made of iron. The former is not only a carpenter, but a joiner, a cabinet-maker, and even a carver in wood, as well as a wheelwright, a ploughwright, a cart and wagon maker.[142]

On one hand, then, the feasibility of labour division depends on the size of the market, which in turn has an effect on the size of the workforce. However, we should also consider the extent to which it would have made sense to divide certain stages of work between different carvers. The carvers of figured scenes on sarcophagi, as already noted, worked relatively fluidly from the front plane of the chest inwards, switching between tools as they went. One worker could carve the figures in the foreground and leave the background to another, but the set of skills required for each area was the same and handing over responsibility in this way might only introduce potential for confusion. In practice, all of the individual stages of work identifiable on sarcophagi can be grouped into three phases of activity: basic shaping and hollowing out, usually

---

[142] Adam Smith, *On the Wealth of Nations*, I.3.

done at the quarry; roughing out and shaping of the design; and detailed finishing, including the addition of portraits and an inscription if required. Sometimes the middle phase could have been split in two: on the north Italian architectural sarcophagi, for instance, we might imagine an architectural specialist working with a figure-carver. Certainly portraits often seem to be carved in a slightly different way than the rest of the decoration: Rockwell has noted that one sometimes finds portraits on which the drill was never used on chests on which extensive drilling is visible elsewhere.[143] Despite this, most sarcophagi probably passed through no more than three or four sets of hands, and many could conceivably have been worked on by the same carver throughout.

Even if it would not always have been easy to divide each stage of work between different carvers, it would certainly have been possible to have more than one carver working on a sarcophagus at a time. On a large Attic or Asiatic sarcophagus there is no reason why four workers could not have been employed simultaneously. The finish on several Metropolitan sarcophagi seems to indicate the presence of multiple carvers. On the so-called Childhood sarcophagus in Baltimore, Ward-Perkins noted that the two short sides were worked in different ways (one quite roughly), even though both were finished with a rasp; the lid, meanwhile, was finished on one end but only roughed out on the other.[144] The lid of the boar-hunt sarcophagi in the Centrale Montemartini discussed above might also have been being worked on by two different carvers, perhaps separately from the chest. Increasing the number of carvers working on a particular chest would certainly have been one way of speeding up its production—a point that has already been made for architectural elements.[145]

CUSTOMER DEMAND AND PRODUCTION-TO-STOCK

The ease with which sarcophagi can be catalogued (due to their seemingly predictable forms and often repetitive iconography), alongside the routinely unfinished appearance of many, has contributed to the widely held assumption that they were in general produced in standardized forms to stock.[146] Prospective purchasers simply walked into their local workshop and selected one, literally, off the shelf. Many never bothered to have any further work undertaken, such as the addition of portraits or inscriptions, content with

[143] Pers. comm. Peter Rockwell.
[144] Ward-Perkins 1975–6: 223–30, figs. 29–34; 1992d: 48–51, figs. 39–42.
[145] See Chapter 6: Division of labour (pp. 250–4).
[146] Stewart 2008: 3; for the implication of this argument, Russell 2011b: 119–21.

them as they were—to our eyes unfinished. Just because a series of sarcophagi look the same, of course, does not mean that we should think of them as 'standardized'. This term suggests a conscious process, decided by their purchasers, which is probably far from the reality. Stone objects of similar or near-identical design, and often size, are relatively common in the Roman period. The most obvious examples are architectural, but the precise replication of popular statue types was also widespread. There was, in fact, massive consumer demand for such objects in what might be regarded as 'standard' forms; this is arguably one of the most striking characteristics of Roman art and architecture.[147] Customers in this period wanted their statues or their sarcophagi to look the same, and often to be of the same (or similar) size; these objects were required to function in very specific ways in a social context which had an accepted visual language. In other words, objects produced in standard forms could just as easily be commissions as stock pieces. The fact that there was demand for objects in increasingly common form and approximate dimensions must have facilitated their manufacture, enabling a degree of specialization, but this was an accidental consequence.

While the direct connection between apparently 'standard' forms of sarcophagi and production-to-stock can be dismissed, then, this does not mean that the idea that certain sarcophagus producers did manufacture sarcophagi to stock should be rejected altogether.

Unintentional and intentional workshop stock

Like contractors supplying building materials, specialist sarcophagus carvers would over time have built up a stock of roughed-out or near-finished chests ordered for customers who had then failed to pay; they might even have had access to stock of other sorts, including leftovers from building projects, damaged blocks, or material from dismantled structures that could be cut up and reused. The famous Badminton sarcophagus was carved from an old entablature block, as the marks on its rear demonstrate, and it is tempting to see this as having come from such a stock.[148] Bartman draws attention to a Hadrianic child's sarcophagus chest carved from an entablature block and a Severan sarcophagus lid carved from a segment of coffering.[149] The back of another sarcophagus, this time a Dionysiac one in Baltimore, has a series of sketches of horses' heads carved into its rear sides, as well as incised circles and guidelines for the laying out of a design.[150] This looks very much like a chest or

[147] On this point with regard to statuary, Bieber 1962; 1977; Trimble 2000; Daehner 2007.
[148] Bartman 1993: 58–60.
[149] Herdejürgen 1988: 87–90, figs. 1, 4 (Djursholm); Bartman 1993: 58 n. 12 (San Antonio).
[150] Bartman 1993: 62–3, fig. 5.

block that had spent some time lying unused in the corner of a carving workshop. If the customer was not especially concerned about the exact form of their sarcophagus or wanted it quickly then supplying a chest out of this kind of accumulated stock could have been a mutually beneficial solution.

The key question is whether sarcophagus producers went further than this: did they build up a deliberate stock of sarcophagi to cater for this kind of demand? If so, were these simply roughed out or were they nearly finished, as is often assumed? Ordering chests one at a time from the quarry in response to specific demand from their customers would have been fine for producers in their immediate vicinity but for those located further afield it would have been time-consuming and expensive. It might have been preferable to order a number of chests at a time, roughed out according to specific requirements, in anticipation of defined demand rather than in response to it. This would have required a substantial capital outlay, which must have made it difficult for smaller producers, but for larger enterprises this kind of bulk order would have made a lot of sense. As long as the undefined market was such that they could be certain of selling these chests (as it was in the second and third centuries AD) this would have presented little risk. The sarcophagi from the San Pietro in Bevagna shipwreck could be interpreted as comprising a kind of bulk order of stock chests or, alternatively, as several orders, made by different producers, which were being shipped together.[151]

Investing in a stock of roughed-out chests, which could still be finished according to the specific demands of the client, was a quite different exercise from producing fully worked sarcophagi to stock. The more defined the product, the more reduced the potential marketplace for it. If a workshop was to invest the capital, time, and labour to carve a sarcophagus in anticipation of demand, then they had to be very certain of selling the final product. Would this risk have been worth it? It certainly would have enabled the workshop to respond more rapidly to demand, a service for which they presumably could have charged a premium. Even though, as we have seen, most customers probably bought their sarcophagus while still alive, there would always have been others who needed a sarcophagus immediately. Children's sarcophagi, Huskinson has argued, must have been acquired from stock in almost all instances.[152] Occasionally adults too must have died before they had time to fully-prepare their sarcophagi. Even in these situations, however, customers would not have been forced to buy from a stock of finished products. The inscription on a late fourth-century AD sarcophagus in the cathedral of Tolentino states that the deceased was not interred in his monument until forty days after his death.[153] Bodies could have been put in

---

[151] See Chapter 7: The shipwreck evidence (pp. 271–3), and fig. 7.11.

[152] Huskinson 1996: 79–80.

[153] Märki-Boehringer, Deichmann, and Klauser 1966: 39; Koch 2000: 79.

terracotta, lead, or most likely wooden coffins and placed in their tomb while their sarcophagus was being carved. This temporary container could then have been moved into the finished monument when it was ready or the body transferred.

Multi-purpose forms

This does not mean, though, that sarcophagus producers were not prepared to undertake any work before receiving specific commissions. Assuming that they had a stock, however limited, of roughed-out or blank chests, there was plenty of work that a workshop could carry out that did not overly limited the final choices of the client. This would have been especially true for producers specializing in the most popular sarcophagus types, such as strigillated sarcophagi in third-century Rome. Since all of their clients could be expected to request a strigillated format, workshops known for these products could conceivably have completed the strigillated panels in advance, leaving the central or side panels rough for individualization according to the wishes of the customer. A fragment of the front of a strigillated sarcophagus now attached to the interior wall of the cloister of San Paolo fuori le Mura in Rome was left in just this state (Fig. 7.21): it has neatly squared, point-chiselled bosses at its centre and left end, and presumably had another on its now lost right end, while the S-shaped stigillated panels between these are fully finished.[154] Another strigillated sarcophagus, found during excavations on the Via Trionfale in Rome, shows that one possible further stage of this process involved the complete finishing of the central figured panel before work on the side ones was even begun.[155] Another sarcophagus in Rome which is roughed out with a delineated *clipeus* medallion could also have been awaiting personalization.[156] One might even reconstruct a comparable scenario at the north Italian workshops, producing similarly formulaic schemes, this time architectural; roughed-out panels of the kind found on sarcophagi in Bologna, Modena, and Poreč in Istria, for example, set no limit on the choices available to the client, provided they were happy with the overall form of the chest.[157] Asiatic garland sarcophagi could perhaps also have been roughed out to stock, since their basic design still allowed for a range of decorative motifs to be incorporated at a later stage and at the behest of the client.

---

[154] Russell 2011*b*: 138–9, fig. 4.5; and for another example, Giuliano 1984: no. XII.16.
[155] Mineo and Santolini 1985: 188, fig. 149.
[156] Giuliano 1984: no. IX.4.
[157] Gabelmann 1973: no. 22 (pl. 11.3), 68 (pl. 36.1–2), 70 (pl. 35), 71 (pl. 38).

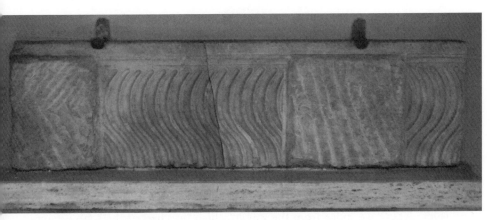

Fig. 7.21. Fragment of a strigillated sarcophagus in the cloister of San Paolo fuori le Mura, Rome (photo: author).

This does not mean, however, that sarcophagi which were never carved beyond this simple roughed-out format were necessarily purchased from stock. There might have been an intention to finish them that was never fulfilled or perhaps the roughed-out form was considered a reasonable finish, as was certainly the case with many garland sarcophagi. In fact, there is good reason to believe that many Asiatic garland sarcophagi might have been commissions and not stock purchases. These objects were not nearly as standardized as the existing typological studies of them would suggest: at sites like Ephesos and Aphrodisias a huge range of garland sizes and arrangements are found and there was no single type that buyers at these sites were forced to pick from. Outside of Asia Minor, this notion receives further support from the sixteen garland sarcophagi in Prokonnesian marble from Alexandria. Ten of these are of the typical form found elsewhere in Prokonnesian marble, with roughed-out or finished garlands on all four sides, but six have blank rear sides.[158] Most sarcophagi at Alexandria were displayed within tombs and, as at Rome, usually against a wall, so it makes some sense that these sarcophagi were not worked on their rear sides. Importantly, though, these examples show that the roughed-out garland format was not an unalterable scheme that purchasers simply had to accept. Asgari and Fıratlı were keen to see these atypical garland sarcophagi as products manufactured on Prokonnesos purposely for the Egyptian market.[159] While this must be the case, there is no reason to assume, as they did, that this shows sarcophagus producers at the quarries targeting specific markets. Again, it is simpler and more plausible to see the workshops at the quarries responding to the specific

[158] Adriani 1961: 19–31, fig. 12–82.   [159] Asgari and Fıratlı 1978: 41.

demands of customers at Alexandria, some of whom wanted garlands on four sides, others on just three.[160]

Another category of sarcophagi often identified as stock products are those on which some alteration of the design seems to have taken place. A good example is the garland sarcophagus from Parion, now in Istanbul, on the front side of which the garland design was carved away and replaced with a lengthy inscription and a depiction of a nude male with his horse, both on statue bases.[161] A second example in Istanbul, originally from Tripoli in Lebanon, was reworked on three sides to depict scenes from the myth of Phaedra and Hippolytos, inspired by Attic models, with only its rear side betraying its original format.[162] Perhaps the best-known example of such alteration is the third-century AD Endymion *lēnos* sarcophagus now in the British Museum (Fig. 7.22).[163] To judge from the way in which the chest of the central figure was carved back and a socket for the insertion of a penis added this sarcophagus must have originally depicted Ariadne. At some point, then, the sex of the figure was changed. Another sarcophagus in the same collection, datable to the late third or early fourth century AD, appears to have had its *clipeus* portrait altered at some point from that of a woman to that of a young boy.[164] Like the other examples listed above, it is usually argued that these chests were purchased from stock because nothing else was available and then altered to suit the particular client—who in these cases, presumably, were men rather than women. Whether this was actually what happened is impossible to say for certain, but other explanations can be imagined. The British Museum chests could well have been produced for female clients who then reneged on the deals and so the chests had to be sold off cheaply, or perhaps they were bought by families and ended up being used by someone other than was originally planned. In particular, there is no way of knowing whether these alterations took place immediately after purchase or considerably later, perhaps by someone who bought the chest secondhand. As noted, sarcophagi had long lives and were continually reused. There is even evidence for those that were no longer needed being sold on. A garland sarcophagus from Aphrodisias, originally produced with three garlands hanging between four roughed-out busts on its façade, shows how this process might have worked (Fig. 7.23): according to its inscription this piece was ceded by the original commissioners to the eventual owner, one Aemilius Aristeas, who then removed the central garland to make space for this inscription and completed the middle two busts

---

[160] Ward-Perkins 1969 notes that the Alexandrian craftsmen were likely responsible for deciding on this format, even if elsewhere he argues in favour of quarry-based producers targeting specific markets.

[161] Asgari 1986: 220, fig. 22; Koch 1993: 138–9, fig. 76; also Pensabene 2002*b*: 58.

[162] Mendel 1912–14: no. 26.   [163] Walker 1990*a*: 38, no. 43.

[164] Walker 1990*a*: 33–4, no. 36, pl. 13.

Fig. 7.22. Detail of the *lēnos* sarcophagus in the British Museum showing the transformed central figure (photo: © The Trustees of the British Museum).

Fig. 7.23. Sarcophagus of Aemilius Aristeas and family, Aphrodisias (photo: author).

Fig. 7.24. The Good Shepherd sarcophagus in the Archaeological Museum, Split (inv. no AMS D-13, photo: author, used with permission of the Arheološki Muzej u Splitu).

with his portrait and that of his wife, Carminia Philemation.[165] We should not simply assume, in sum, that altered sarcophagi were certainly stock pieces.

An intriguing variation on the standard production-to-stock scenario has been proposed for the roughed-out lid of the so-called Good Shepherd sar-cophagus from the Manastirine necropolis at Salona in Dalmatia (Fig. 7.24).[166] This curious object, in Prokonnesian marble, is a hybrid of two different lid types: on three sides it is of the standard gable type with corner acroteria, but along its front side it is carved as a *klinē* with roughed-out figures. A near-identical lid is known from Benkovac, inland from Zadar.[167] Cambi's suggestion is that these were a variety of editable, multi-purpose stock lid, with could be kept in this form and then finished, at short notice, as either a gable- or *klinē*-lid as the client desired.[168] This is an appealing suggestion but whatever option the

---

[165] Işik 2007: no. 6; Reynolds and Roueché 2007: 152–3. [166] Cambi 1994.
[167] Cambi 1994: 114 (fig. 7–8).   [168] Cambi 1994: 13–15.

customer plumped for would have involved considerable work for the carver and wastage of material. So it is perhaps not a surprise to see that two newer discoveries, both from the necropoleis of Salona, reveal that these lids were not stock pieces at all: on both the reclining figures, *klinē*, gables, and acroteria are fully decorated.[169] This was not a multi-purpose roughed-out form but a genuinely hybrid lid-type, drawing on Attic and Asiatic motifs alongside the more traditional gable and acroteria combination favoured at Salona.[170] This distinctive lid-type was apparently a speciality of the Salonitan workshops and we might hypothesize that they were roughed out on Prokonnesos, according to the requirements of the Salonitan producers, and shipped in this form.

None of this is intended to suggest that production of sarcophagi to stock never happened. There were occasions when it was perfectly feasible. However, production-to-stock was probably never the norm and it would certainly be wrong, in interpreting sarcophagus use and decoration, to assume that most sarcophagi were simply bought 'off the shelf'.

Blank portraits

'Unfinished' or blank portraits on sarcophagi, that is portraits that received one or more stages of roughing out but were not taken any further, are frequently brought to bear on the question of production-to-stock. Such portraits are especially common on Metropolitan sarcophagi (Fig. 7.25), though they are not exclusive to them: they are found on the chests of several high-end Asiatic sarcophagi, on north Italian sarcophagi, on Attic and Asiatic *klinē* lids (Fig. 7.26), and they are ubiquitous on Aphrodisian sarcophagi (Fig. 7.27).[171] Considering the Roman 'obsession with personal immortality', the number of such 'unfinished' portraits is striking.[172] Indeed a trawl through the *Die Antiken Sarkophagreliefs* volumes shows that, perhaps surprisingly, they are most often found on decorative schemes in which the portrait was the principal focus. For example, 22.5 per cent of the recorded *clipeus* portraits, that is portraits mounted on a shield or roundel, were left blank; this compared

---

[169] One is mentioned in Cambi 2000: 240; the second piece was found in 2008 and is unpublished but both are visible in the Manastirine necropolis at Salona.

[170] The *klinē* of the most recently discovered lid is decorated with scenes of hunting *putti* and marine creattures, copied from Attic models, while the *putti* reclining on the mattress follow Asiatic prototypes.

[171] Asiatic examples: Waelkens 1990: 70 (Istanbul B); and on *klinē* lids, Waelkens 1982a: 90; Demirer 1999 (Perge); Stroka 1971: fig. 26–9 (Naples A and B); on Attic *klinē* lids: Pietrogrande 1930 (Cyrene); Koch 1993: fig. 56 (Thessaloniki); Rogge 1995: pl. 52.1 (Tyre); on North Italian sarcophagi: Gabelmann 1973: no. 74 (pl. 40), no. 71 (pl. 38.1); and at Aphrodisias: Smith 2008: 347.

[172] Bianchi Bandinelli 1970: 105.

Fig. 7.25. Blank portrait on a Metropolitan Nereid sarcophagus in the Museo Nazionale Romano–Terme di Diocleziano, Rome (photo: Faraglia, Neg. D-DAI-Rom 29.273).

Fig. 7.26. Attic sarcophagus with lid and four unjoined fragments, unknown maker, c. AD 180–220 (used with permission of the The J. Paul Getty Museum, Villa Collection, Malibu, California).

Fig. 7.27. Sarcophagus of Aurelia Tate, Aphrodisias (photo: courtesy New York University excavations at Aphrodisias).

to 43 per cent of *parapetasma* portraits, that is portraits displayed in front of a curtain.[173] On the so-called Seasons sarcophagi, popular in the late third and early fourth centuries, and the type most frequently incorporating the *clipeus* motif, a third of all the portraits are left blank.[174] Even 'biographic' scenes of couples show a high ratio of blank to fully worked portraits: 22.5 per cent (sixteen examples) of sarcophagi with *dextrarum iunctio* scenes, for example, and four out of the twenty-one sarcophagi which contain magistracy scenes.[175] On *klinē*-lids, where the individuals depicted are again the centre of attention, blank portraits are also well-attested; examples include the lid of the Meleager sarcophagus now in the Capitoline Museum, as well as the lids of two Metropolitan sarcophagi in the Levant, one from Ascalon, one from Tyre.[176] Perhaps most importantly, this is a phenomenon largely restricted to sarcophagi—'unfinished' portraits are extremely scarce on other forms of

[173] Data from Andreae 1980; Reinsberg 2006; Amedick 1991; Kranz 1984; 1999; Wegner 1966; Stroszeck 1998; Herdejürgen 1996; where it is impossible to tell if the portrait is blank or damaged it is ignored.

[174] Huskinson 1998: 135–8; and on Seasons sarcophagi, Kranz 1984: nos. 11–12, 34, 42–4, 48, 57, 62, 64, 74, 77–9, 93, 121, 156, 159, 161, 166–8, 171, 178, 181, 185, 335, 531, 547; possibly also 36, 39, 54, 89, 157, 164, 363.

[175] Reinsberg 2006: no. 45–60; on *dextrarum iunctio* scenes, nos. 13, 41, 52 (= Kranz 1984: no. 11), 60 (= Kranz 1984: no. 12), 61, 71, 85, 87, 110, 116, 119, 128–9, 140, 150, 157; on magistracy scenes, nos. 24, 41, 62, 169 (= Sichtermann 1992: no. 168).

[176] Koch 1975: no. 67, pl. 56, 60 (Rome); 1989: fig. 6–7 (Tyre and Ascalon).

funerary monument—and one most apparent only in the late second and into the third century AD.[177]

Three main explanations for these 'unfinished' portraits have been proposed. The first links them directly to a perceived shift in sarcophagus manufacturing away from a responsive production-to-order system towards production-to-stock. These portraits were not carved with the rest of the decoration, so this explanation goes, because the customer at this point was not known. They were left for individualization, but for some reason were never finished: perhaps the customer could not afford the extra expense or had no particular desire to have them finished.[178] The implication here is that if these were commissions, carefully considered and produced to the specific requirements of the client, then surely they would have been finished; why go to all that effort only to leave your sarcophagus part-finished? In support of this argument one might note that 'unfinished' portraits are more common on the most formulaic sarcophagus types, notably third-century strigillated sarcophagi: of the thirty-eight known *Löwensarkophage* with a central *clipeus*-portrait, fourteen (37 per cent) have 'unfinished' portraits and thirteen of these are of the strigillated variety.[179] As noted above, with strigillated sarcophagi at least half of the ornamentation could quite reasonably have been completed prior to purchase, irrespective of client demands; they were well suited, in other words, to production-to-stock. All this being said, the connection between 'unfinished' portraits and production-to-stock should not be pushed too far. Plenty of sarcophagi with particularly idiosyncratic decoration or form have 'unfinished' portraits, even though they must have been commissions: the Portonnacio and the Istanbul B sarcophagi, for instance.[180] The sarcophagus of Aurelia Tate from Aphrodisias combines 'unfinished' portraits with a one-off scene of a blacksmith's workshop—presumably a reference to the profession of the deceased; this was a personalized commission even if the portraits on it were never completed (see Fig. 7.27).[181] At Aphrodisias generally, a city of no more than 15,000 inhabitants, it is doubtful that the market was large enough to sustain stock production, yet 'unfinished' portraits are very common.[182] Additionally it is worth asking why an individual who had no intention of having the portrait finished would purchase a sarcophagus from stock with space for a

---

[177] Among the examples in Frenz 1985 and Kockel 1993 only Kockel 1993: no. N8 was left unfinished.

[178] Floriani Squarciapino 1943–4: 267: the 'facile contentatura dei committenti'; also Eichner 1977: 130–1.

[179] Matz 1968: no. 196, 230, 241, 256, 296, 302, 307, 311, 318, 322, 325, 334, 352, 395, 406. For *dextrarum iunctio* scenes with 'unfinished' portraits on strigillated sarcophagi, Reinsberg 2006: no. 71, 110, 116, 119, 150, 157.

[180] Koch and Sichtermann 1982: 92, pl. 76; Wiegartz 1965: pl. 34a; also Russell 2011*b*.

[181] Smith 2008: 374–6.

[182] Smith 2008: 347; Russell 2011*b*: 139.

portrait? There were plenty of other choices available, probably cheaper ones too. In fact, sarcophagi with portraits, roughed out or finished, are in a minority; one really had to go out of one's way to buy one of these objects.

The second explanation for these 'unfinished' portraits acknowledges this point: the purchasers of these sarcophagi—whether they had commissioned them from scratch or bought them from stock—really did want to add portraits of themselves to their purchase but for whatever reason never managed to. The intent was there but events intervened; perhaps the sarcophagus was pressed into service hastily or the heir could not afford to finish it; perhaps the heir too had died or the sarcophagus could not be accessed in a crowded tomb. Numerous changes in circumstance can be imagined.[183] This explanation gains credence, of course, if these portraits were routinely not completed until after the subjects themselves had died, perhaps following their funeral or as part of it. If this was the case then many of these sarcophagi would have been sitting around waiting to be used, and it is easy to see how, when the moment finally came, the completion of these portraits might have been low on the priorities list of those left behind. The inscriptions from Kalchedon discussed above certainly show that it was common to set up sarcophagi and only inscribe or ornament them further once they were actually put to use.[184] The sarcophagus from Aphrodisias mentioned above which was ceded from one family to another is also interesting in this regard.[185] Since the inscription specifies that other individuals were to be added when they died it seems reasonable to assume that the two blank busts on the chest were left for these later occupants.

Two criticisms can be levelled at this explanation. First, if the lack of finish results from chance factors, then why do we not see 'unfinished' portraits across all periods, or indeed on other types of funerary monument? Second, the assumption that these 'unfinished' portraits were unintentional, and that their lack of completion was a sort of negligence, is quite inconsistent with what we know of Roman funerary practice, which placed enormous emphasis on preserving the memory of the deceased. Both criticisms are valid, however neither completely undermines this overall hypothesis. Even without detailed information about funerary practices it would be wrong to assume that habits never changed. It might well have been the case that the practice of finishing portraits posthumously, rather than while the individual was still alive, resulted from superstitions that only took hold in the later second century AD. If more portraits were being left to be finished later, we might expect to find more that were never finished. With regard to the second point, the obligations of the heir were certainly enshrined in law and are frequently

---

[183] Andreae 1984; Blanck 1969: 105.
[184] See Chapter 7: Multiple occupancy (pp. 259–60).
[185] Reynolds and Roueché 2007: 152–3.

recorded in epitaphs.[186] However, this does not mean that the law was always upheld. Neglect on the part of heirs must have been common. Pliny the Younger famously laments the unfinished condition of Verginius Rufus' tomb ten years after his death; and this was a man better connected than most.[187] While on paper then the requirements of heirs might well have been clear, the situation on the ground, in practice, was less certain. Crowded necropoleis, often chaotically laid out, were no doubt full of part-finished monuments, some abandoned, others to be returned to; modern cemeteries are no different.[188]

The third explanation for the phenomenon of 'unfinished' portraits, though, skirts this problem, taking a more positive view of this material. Perhaps, it is suggested, these portraits were deliberately left in this state by the individual tasked with finishing them. These are not 'unfinished' but strictly 'blank' portraits, then; their 'unfinish', in other words, was the desired finish and not an accidental result. This was neither indifference nor neglect but a positive statement, a definite choice. Perhaps they were kept in their roughed-out state so that those left behind could avoid fixing the final image of their loved ones.[189] To suggest that they were meant to appear blank, like the aniconic busts and statues from Late Classical and Hellenistic Cyrene and the later stelai from Pompeii, however, would probably be to push this suggestion too far.[190] These were not carefully smoothed, deliberately aniconic representations but rather roughed-out busts that could be finished if necessary.

Several scholars have been tempted to draw comparisons between blank portraits on sarcophagi and similar levels of unfinish on major architectural or sculptural projects. Huskinson points to the Ara Pacis and Arch of Titus at Rome.[191] A distinct lack of finish is so obvious on the major monuments of Aphrodisias as to appear deliberate.[192] Perhaps this results from superstition— a desire to avoid attracting the evil eye—or maybe it was a way for the stone-carvers involved to reveal, and so celebrate, the mechanics of their work.[193] Most likely, the level of unfinish observable on so many major architectural or sculptural projects results from time constraints and a

---

[186] The legal responsibilities of the heir are outlined in some detail in Book 35 of the Digest.

[187] Pliny the Younger, *Letters* VI.10.

[188] The recently excavated sections of necropolis discovered during the Autoparco excavations in the Vatican illustrate just how cluttered these environments could be: Liverani 2010: 161–97, esp. fig. 14–17, 23.

[189] Huskinson 1998: 152–5; also Marrou 1939: 202. On the connections between this practice and wider abstraction in third-century AD Roman art: Andreae 1980; 1984: 125.

[190] On the Cyrenean examples, Chamoux 1953: 293–300, pl. X, XIII; Cassels 1955: 4–6, pl. VIII.e, IX.a. On the problem of dating these images, Rosenbaum 1960: 14–15. On the Pompeian stelai, Kockel 1983: 16–18.

[191] Huskinson 1998: 129.

[192] On unfinished works elsewhere in the city, Rockwell 1990: 101–3.

[193] I am grateful to R. R. R. Smith for discussing these theories with me.

different attitude to what constituted 'finished'. When one considers the number of these blank portraits found on sarcophagi it is clear that they were not considered unacceptable and did not detract significantly from the overall value of the monument. Busts or full-length statues were popular motifs on sarcophagi and like garlands, columns, and *tabulae* were rooted in the very public context of elite display and civic life. While only the prominent few had honorific statues erected in their honour anyone who could afford it could have them carved on their sarcophagus. Whether finished or not, then, these motifs were symbolically potent and since many sarcophagi were intended for multiple occupants leaving them blank was by no means an act of negligence.

There is, as Huskinson has put it, 'no hard and fast explanation for these unfinished portrait heads'.[194] All of the explanations given above have their own strengths and weaknesses and, to some extent, the phenomenon of 'unfinished' portraits must result from a combination of factors.[195] What should be clear, though, is that the connection often drawn between these portraits and the purchasing of sarcophagi from stock is too simplistic. Equally, it should be acknowledged that sarcophagi often had long lives; they were not always used in the way in which they were originally intended, or even by the individuals who commissioned them. There was plenty of scope, therefore, for plans to be left unfulfilled. On this point an intriguing passage of Ulpian preserved in the *Digest* might be significant.[196] The regulation in question states that:

> If a man's remains have been buried in a monument which is said to be incomplete, nothing prevents it from being finished. But if the place has already become religious, the priests must establish how far the need to put the structure in proper shape can be met without offending against religion.

If this rule extended to sarcophagi within tombs then it might indicate that sometimes details of finish were left uncompleted for religious reasons. Whatever the precise reasons for this phenomenon it should be stressed that even with apparently 'unfinished' details these were still exceptionally prestigious and expensive monuments; it seems quite reasonable that the 'unfinish' that strikes us as so unusual would not have so bothered an ancient viewer.

CONCLUSIONS

The evidence provided by sarcophagi, especially part-finished sarcophagi from which we can reconstruct the working methods employed, reveals a

---

[194] Huskinson 1998: 154.   [195] Koch and Sichtermann 1982: 614.
[196] *Digest* 11.8.5.

remarkably varied picture. Sarcophagi for predominately local markets were produced all around the Roman world in whatever materials were to hand. At the same time, though, those with the wherewithal to do so also sought out local or regional producers working in the finest materials, often imports, as well as more distant carvers famed for the quality of their products. In this sense, the sarcophagus trade is a useful illustration of the different levels of demand for stone that so characterized the Roman market. Although certain centres of production were famed for their sarcophagi and certain major white marble quarries were respected sources of raw materials for sarcophagus carving, there is no evidence to indicate that this trade was controlled by the a small handful of mega-producers. The Attic, Asiatic, and Metropolitan producers might all have worked respectively in ways which allow them to be categorized as major producers but they are much more plausibly explained as belonging to clusters of independent workshops than large quasi-industrial enterprises.[197] The exact role of the quarries in sarcophagus production should also be reconsidered. Certain sarcophagus producers based themselves at or close to the quarries but multiple workshops could be associated with a single quarry. As argued in the previous chapter, the largest quarries were probably open to a range of workers, might perhaps have been owned by different groups, and could perform a variety of services depending on the demands of their customers. Prokonnesos is the best example of this, a site that was used both by local producers who were probably based on the island permanently as well as a range of producers working elsewhere, in the Levant, in Egypt, in Italy, and in the Balkans. Whether these overseas carvers dispatched personnel to quarry their supplies or ordered what they needed from established quarrymen it is clear that the form and size of the material they acquired were decided by them; they were not picking from a limited range of types decided by the quarry-based producers but placing specific orders with them. As part of this arrangement production was often divided between places, sometimes across enormous distances, revealing a remarkable level of connectivity. There are important overlaps here with what was observed for architectural elements in the previous chapter.

When it comes to the exact relationship between carver and customer a similar level of responsiveness can also be identified. Sarcophagi were often produced in highly repetitive forms and this has lent weight to the assumption that they were usually carved to stock, leaving little option for individualization of the part of the customer. To quote Ward-Perkins once again, 'the ordinary client accepted the market situation'.[198] What has been shown above is that this link between repetitive forms, and sometimes imagery and production methods, has been overstated. Even the most common sarcophagus types are actually far

---

[197] Russell 2011*b*: 127–31.   [198] Ward-Perkins 1980*b*: 48.

more varied it their details than is usually acknowledged even if their overall forms are not. The widespread typological approach to sarcophagus classification often plasters over these differences. Blank chests were almost certainly bought for stockpiling by producers based far from the sources of their raw materials and certain varieties were carved further than this, with their basic design sketched in before any definite buyer had been secured: the examples of Asiatic garland sarcophagi and certain formats of strigillated sarcophagi have been examined above. However, it seems to have been rare for carvers to take their products much beyond this stage without a specific customer confirmed. These were expensive objects for both parties and there was no point wasting material and energy on a sarcophagus that would then need to be adapted. Not all sarcophagi were purchased before they were needed but many, perhaps even most were, and even when a monument was needed suddenly there is no reason to assume that a stock product would have been the only option, as outlined above. The similitude of so many Roman sarcophagi, in sum, cannot be explained away as the result of production factors alone. Customer choice clearly played an important role: individual buyers wanted their monuments to look like those of their peers. In this sense they are usefully understood alongside honorific statues and other objects types which were produced in the same form again and again and carried a set of messages which were easily read and understood by a wide audience. Most sarcophagus users employed them to stand out from the crowd through their membership of a particular class of wealthy, erudite, and tasteful citizens, which included but was not limited to members of the elite; to quote Smith, 'they gain effect and power as monumental expressions of group membership'.[199]

The sarcophagus trade is one sector of wider stone production that operated entirely beyond imperial control, as far as we can tell. The imperial ownership of the Dokimeian sarcophagus workshops, proposed by both Waelkens and Fant on the basis of their distribution and evidence for imperial involvement at the Phrygian quarries, can probably now be dismissed.[200] The prime market for these sarcophagi was the local elite of Asia Minor and as we have seen there is no reason to assume that all of the output of the Dokimeian quarries was imperial property. Imperial involvement in the sarcophagus trade has also been posited for later periods and on similarly slender evidence. Eichner, for instance, has argued that the scale and organization of sarcophagus production at Rome in the fourth century AD shows that it was controlled by the state.[201] In practice, the stylistic and technical range of these sarcophagi shows that, as earlier, production was probably divided between a series of competing, private workshops.[202] Others have drawn attention to the intriguing early sixth-century AD letter preserved by

[199] Smith 2008: 349.   [200] Waelkens 1982a: 124–7; Fant 1985: 660–1.
[201] Eichner 1981: 91–2.   [202] Koch 2000: 79–80.

Cassiodorus in which Theodoric grants a certain Daniel the right to supply marble sarcophagi to the citizens of Ravenna.[203] While this text reveals a level of state interference in this trade not previously attested it is less clear whether Daniel was being granted a monopoly, as some have suggested; rather Daniel appears to have been being given the official seal of approval and is warned not to overinflate his prices.[204] The state had little to gain from the sarcophagus trade directly. Even the profits that could be made by selling the highest-quality pieces would have been insignificant when compared to imperial income from other sources. The main drivers of the sarcophagus trade, then, were the wealthy individuals who purchased these objects and the independent carvers and traders who supplied them.

---

[203] Cassiodorus, *Variae* III.19; see Dresken-Weiland 1995.
[204] For a sensible discussion of this text, see Marano forthcoming.

8

Statue Production

Like the previous two chapters this one focuses on the production of a single artefact type, in this case free-standing statues. There is, though, considerably less useable evidence for reconstructing how statue production was organized in comparison to architectural elements and sarcophagi. There are also many more signs of individuality, of carvers adopting thoroughly different approaches depending on their circumstances and the demands of their customers. This has been demonstrated already in Chapter 5 by the variant distribution patterns of the materials used for statuary when compared to other artefact types. In order to explore these issues, this chapter is divided into four main sections which deal in turn with the processes underpinning the purchase of a statue, the supply of materials for statuary, the distribution of statues and the movement of their carvers, and the evidence for the organization of production.

THE BUYING PROCESS

The relationship between the different parties involved in the production of a statue and the location of each respective to the other played a crucial role in shaping how this process was organized. The two main parties were obviously the customer and the carver and while pinpointing exactly how much of a finished work is attributable to decisions made by each of these parties is impossible it is important that we acknowledge the role played by both.[1]

Commissions

Typically the carver was working directly for a customer and it was their job to provide satisfaction as best they could. Naturally the specific demands of the

---

[1] Smith 2002: 71: a statue is best seen as 'the crystallised product of infinite and continuous oscillations between buyers, workshops and public'.

customer must always have been moderated by the abilities of the carver, the price being paid, and the time available; a reasonable amount of consultation and negotiation must have underlain any commission. In a letter to Vestricius Spurinna and his wife Cottia, in which he asks for guidance in the composition of his *laudatio* for their son, Pliny the Younger makes reference to just this kind of interaction between artist and customer:

> As you might instruct a sculptor or painter who was making an image of your son what he ought to emphasize and what he should correct, thus also please guide and correct me as I attempt to form an image not fragile and perishable but immortal.[2]

How the physical process of actually commissioning a statue worked depended ultimately on the relationship between customer and carver and especially the location of the latter. The simplest option would have been for the customer to approach a local carver, with whom they could discuss their plans, inspect the work, and negotiate a budget. A number of sculpting workshops—*officinae*—are recorded on inscriptions carved on statues (signatures or, more accurately, makers' marks), most of which have been catalogued by Calabi Limentani.[3] However, the only sculptor's workshop to have been systematically excavated is the one from Aphrodisias (Fig. 8.1).[4] This was a small, centrally located workshop datable to the 4th century AD, though it was perhaps open earlier. It operated in an open space behind the Bouleuterion, a site where new customers might pass by and existing ones come to check on progress.[5] Rockwell even suggested that some of the sculpture found in this workshop had been on display next to the doors, as if to advertise the talent and repertoire of the proprietors.[6]

Commissioners around the Roman world were under no obligation to patronize their local workshops, though. If they wanted something different they could look elsewhere, to a neighbouring city perhaps or a well-known centre for sculpture production, like Athens. Cicero, of course, ordered most of his art from Greece by mail via his close friend Atticus. Without a conveniently placed agent, however, customers were probably forced to travel to meet with sculptors themselves or go through some sort of middleman, a *marmorarius* of the kind who supplied material for building perhaps or a specialist art dealer, like the *negotiator artis lapidariae* attested at Cologne.[7]

---

[2] Pliny the Younger, *Letters* III.10 (trans. E. W Leach); see Leach 1990: 22–3.
[3] Calabi Limentani 1958: 159–66; 1961b: 873–5.
[4] Rockwell 1991; Van Voorhis 1999; on the difficulties of identifying workshops, Nolte 2006: 239–41; Heilmeyer 1986; 2004; Bejor 2011.
[5] Rockwell 2008: 93; Smith 2011: 64.
[6] Rockwell 1991: 141.
[7] AE 1904, 23; for more on *marmorarii*, see Chapter 6: Specialist contractors (pp. 204–7).

Fig. 8.1. The Sculptor's Workshop at Aphrodisias comprising the row of rooms to the north of the Bouleuterion (photo: author).

Stock

Not all statues, of course, would have been commissions. We hear of Cicero in the first century BC buying finished statues, probably all antiques, and in the second century AD Philostratos describes a merchant in the Piraeus setting sail with a cargo including votive statuettes (gold, stone, and ivory) to be sold along the Ionian coast.[8] Even carvers producing material for this kind of opportunistic selling, however, had to consider their prospective customers and focus on what would sell. They were responding, in other words, to *undefined* rather than *defined* demand.

How did carvers build up such stock? Here, again, it is useful to distinguish between the intentional and unintentional accumulation of this material, as we have done in previous chapters. The finds from the Aphrodisian Sculptor's Workshop show that the unintentional assembling of stock would have been a reality for any carver. Customers defaulting on orders must have been a fairly common occurrence, as it was later: Michelangelo complains about Piero de'

---

[8] Cicero, *Letters to Atticus* 1.8.2, 1.9.2, 1.10.3; Philostratos, *Life of Apollonios of Tyana* V.20.

Medici failing to pay for a block which he then puts to use in another project.[9] Another source of stock would have been the secondhand market. Honorific statues were occasionally removed and reused. Usually they were reworked before re-erection; indeed, a bust in the process of being recut was discovered in the Sculptor's Workshop.[10] However, Dio Chrysostom complains in the late first century AD about statues being re-inscribed without appropriate alteration and in his Rhodian Oration even suggests that honours are applied so readily by the Rhodians to their local notables precisely because they have 'an abundant supply of statues'—though in this case he is probably talking of bronzes.[11] If an honorific statue, particularly if only the body, was required quickly such stores could be dipped into. While some of the material recovered from the Sculptor's Workshop at Aphrodisias is demonstrably fourth century AD in date other pieces are more plausibly dated to the second and third centuries AD and might even predate the workshop itself.[12] Rather than being leftovers these pieces could well have been bought secondhand or removed from public sites for repair or to be sold off. There are plenty of examples of statues that have been recarved into something quite different.[13]

If carvers were regularly producing the same sort of object then they could also acquire a stock of blocks from the quarries, much as sarcophagus producers could have built up a stock of roughed-out chests. This would have required investing capital up front—something that even a sculptor of Michelangelo's status was reluctant to do—but it would have allowed them to respond quicker to their customers' demands. Such blocks could also be used for other projects—architectural elements or statue bases, for example. Crucially, the steps taken by the sculptor or workshop to rationalize their production never deprived the client of choice within limits accepted by both parties.

Production-to-stock

Considering the level of demand for statues of particular mythological subjects or standard honorific portrait types could carvers have gone one stage further and produced finished or near-finished statues to stock? The evidence provided by Cicero and Philostratos has already been mentioned and shows that there was clearly a market for finished statuary, in this case of mythological

[9] Stone and Stone 1962: 16–17.   [10] Smith 2006: no. 136.
[11] Dio Chrysostom, *Orations* XXXI, XXXVII (trans. J. W. Cohoon and H. Lamar).
[12] Van Voorhis 1999: 103–4.
[13] Barker 2011: 104; a paper on this topic was presented by S. Barker at ASMOSIA X in Rome in June 2012. On an example from Ptolemais, Fabbricotti 1985: pl. 18.III, 3–4.

and divine subjects, to be bought off the shelf.[14] Can this evidence be extended to other forms of statuary, including portraits? When the identity of the subject was already known—in the case of the emperor, for example—this kind of production-to-stock was also theoretically possible. Indeed, it has been suggested that the statues requested by Arrian in his famous *periplus* are to be supplied from stock. In the passage in question, Arrian describes to Hadrian the condition of a temple containing several statues, including one of the emperor, in Trapezus on the Black Sea:

> Though your statue has been erected in a pleasing pose—it points out to the sea—the work neither resembles you nor is beautiful in any other way. So I have sent for a statue worthy to bear your name, in the same pose; for that spot is very well suited to an everlasting monument. The temple has also been built in squared stone, not without care; but the image of Hermes is worthy neither of the temple nor of the place itself. If you approve, send me a statue of Hermes about five feet tall—for that seems to be proportionate to the temple—and another, four feet tall, of Philesios . . . [15]

Ward-Perkins went so far as to describe this as an example of 'mail-order statue shopping', though of course we have no idea what material these statues were made of.[16] One could take this argument further and suggest that even for statues of private individuals, which were also routinely carved in repetitive poses, a certain amount of production-to-stock could have gone on.[17] These objects could have been turned out with blank spaces left for the finishing of their portraits at the moment of sale, much as on sarcophagi. Perhaps this is why there is so often a clear difference in finish between the portraits on these statues and the rest of the body—not simply because they were done by different carvers but because they were done at completely different points in the production process.[18]

The obvious question here, though, is whether this practice would have brought any real benefits? Why bother producing this kind of material to stock? It is no accident that the merchant in Philostratos' tale is setting sail from Piraeus and that his cargo consists of votive statues for sale overseas.[19] Images of deities or mythological characters of canonical type were well-suited to this kind of stock production and Athens was a well-known artistic centre. To judge from the inscriptions on finished statues, on which Athenians often recorded their hometown, the tag evidently carried a certain cachet. As already

---

[14] See above: Chapter 8: Stock (pp. 313–14).
[15] Arrian, *Periplus* 1.4–2.1 (translation from Liddle 2003: 50–3); Philesios was probably a local god or hero, see Marvin 2008: 236.
[16] Ward-Perkins 1992*b*: 29.
[17] Trimble 2011: 92–9.
[18] For examples from Cyrene, Rosenbaum 1960: no. 43 (Pl. XXXI.1), 90 (Pl. LVI.3–4).
[19] Philostratos, *Life of Apollonios of Tyana* V.20.

noted in the case of sarcophagi, however, building up stock required capital outlay and involved a certain amount of risk. The carver had to be sure that they could sell what they produced. Philostratos' merchant had acquired or produced a stock of material because he planned to sell them overseas but whether it was worth sculptors like the occupants of the Aphrodisian workshop building up a similar stock is questionable.

For large projects which would have cost a lot and taken time to complete the answer is that it was probably not worth the trouble; the customers for such pieces would have been prepared to wait for them to be carved and would also have expected some say over the exact form or finish of the piece. Even in a city like Aphrodisias, a high-quality, life-size satyr and Dionysus group of the kind found in the Sculptor's Workshop could only have been afforded by a handful of discerning individuals.[20] If there was enormous demand for statues in the city then such a centrally located workshop would probably have been kept busy enough handling commissions for portraits and other projects—far too occupied, one might suspect, to be producing such pieces on the off chance that they would find a buyer. For honorific portraits too, it seems doubtful that there was ever really a need for these items to be ready immediately and despite the large number of the best-known statue types that have survived from antiquity, it is doubtful whether there was ever enough of a defined market in any one place to sustain production-to-stock. Even at Aphrodisias, probably no more than four to ten honorific statues were erected annually.[21] It would have been far too risky, expensive, and ultimately pointless, for producers to second-guess demand.

Finally, there is nothing in the much-quoted Arrian passage to indicate that stockpiles of imperial and other statues existed. Arrian asks specifically for a statue of the emperor 'in the same pose' as the one that already exists and specifies the sizes of the others based on the dimensions of the temple. Ward-Perkins claimed that this imperial statue was 'obviously one of a recognised series of standard poses' but there is no reason to assume this.[22] This is a carefully thought out order for new statues, not material from stock. What is important is simply that the statues, in poses and sizes appropriate for the context, are dispatched as soon as possible and are of suitable quality. All in all, while we should not rule out production-to-stock, this was a mode of production best-suited to small carvings of common forms, much like the statuettes and other items produced in the Chemtou *fabrica*, which could turn a quick profit but required little upfront investment of capital or time, not large commissions.[23]

---

[20] Rockwell 1991: 140; Erim 1974: 768–9.   [21] Smith 2006: 13.
[22] Ward-Perkins 1992b: 29.   [23] Rakob 1994b: 51–140, pls. 115–22.

SUPPLYING MATERIALS AND
THE QUARRY EVIDENCE

Regardless of whether they were undertaking a commission or producing an object to stock, carvers could have acquired the material needed in a number of different ways: they could have travelled to the quarries to select and perhaps rough it out themselves; they could have placed an order with specialist quarrymen to get either a block of sufficient dimensions or even have it roughed out; or they could have bypassed the quarrying process altogether and acquired a pre-quarried block from stock, either at the quarries or somewhere else. The decision made probably depended a lot on where they were based, the material that they wanted, the location of its quarries, and the contacts that they had there. It seems probable that our Aphrodisian carvers routinely walked the 2 km out of the city to the quarries to get hold of the material that they needed; they might even have owned a quarry for this purpose.[24] Over longer distances, though, this would obviously have been unfeasible. We should also note that a statue is physically quite different from an architectural element, or even a sarcophagus, and that this fact too might have affected the decisions made by these carvers. Columns, capitals, and sarcophagus chests could, and often did, have their rough form shaped at the quarry with little difficulty; a limited set of dimensions could be supplied and the results predicted—not every detail of the final design needed to be transmitted to the workers at the quarry. In contrast, the final form of a statue had to be known from the very earliest stage of the carving process. A statue could be absolutely any shape or size, and any level of roughing out had to be carefully considered since it would limit the final form of the piece.

Importing blocks

Since it would have been difficult to communicate demands for the roughing out of a statue over long distances and awkward to trust this work to someone else this is unlikely to have been an option often turned to. Instead, carvers who needed to import raw materials but could not go to the quarries themselves probably ordered in unshaped or only roughly squared blocks. In the large assemblage of quarried blocks recovered from the Fossa Traiana at Portus only thirteen unshaped blocks were found, but these are all of Parian marble and were probably destined for carving into small statues (see Fig. 3.1).[25] A series of almost identically shaped white marble blocks have

---

[24] On the Aphrodisian quarries, Ponti 1996; Rockwell 1996.
[25] Bruno et al. 2002*d*: 348–50; Pensabene 1994: 121–2, no. 54–60.

been found adandoned in the quarries at Göktepe; both the white and black marble from this site was favoured for statuary at nearby Aphrodisias, but also further afield, notably at Rome.[26]

Roughly squared blocks could also have been imported and are a common find on Roman shipwrecks. At Cyrene, Kane and Carrier have identified two phenomena relating to the size of statues which they connect to the import of blocks in a particular size: first, Cyrenaican statues in imported marble, regardless of type, tend to be extremely thin; second, the smaller statues from the city appear to have been produced from blocks calculated as integer divisions of those from which the largest statues were carved.[27] These blocks were of reasonably standard sizes, then, suitable both for the carving of full-size honorific statues and for subdividing into smaller works. Parian and Pentelic are the most common materials imported.[28] These quarries were a long way away and it was evidently felt easier to simply order in blocks rather than communicate more specific requests. At Cyrene and elsewhere, blocks could probably also have been bought from middlemen, *marmorarii*. There is little evidence for such a practice in the archaeological record but in later periods this was certainly an option, albeit one that came with risks. Occasionally Michelangelo was forced to deal with stone suppliers in Rome, but he always struggled to acquire material of suitable quality; his Bacchus was carved from an inferior block and he mentions in one letter buying another block for 5 ducats which proved to be unusable.[29] It is noticeable, in fact, that the stone from which a lot of statues at Cyrene were carved is of inferior quality, perhaps because carvers closer to the quarries took all the best material for themselves and Cyrenean carvers had to settle for whatever was left over.[30]

Carvers at the quarries

The risk of being supplied with substandard stone meant that it was probably in the interest of the carver where possible to travel to the quarries to pick out the materials themselves. For major commissions especially it would simply have been far too risky to entrust this work to anyone else. This might have been true even if all that was needed were blocks; a damaged or faulty block could jeopardize the whole project and if the commission consisted of a series of individual pieces it would have been vital to ensure that the material for all the component parts was of the same quality. Whenever possible,

---

[26] Yavuz et al. 2009: 95; Attanasio, Bruno, and Yavuz 2009: 323–4.
[27] Kane and Carrier 1988: 204.
[28] Kane 2000: 480; Attanasio, Kane, and Herz 2009: 352.
[29] Scigliano 2005: 54–6; Stone and Stone 1962: 16–17.
[30] Kane and Carrier 1992: 124.

Michelangelo preferred to select material himself at the quarries—he travelled to Carrara at least twenty times. If he could not go to the quarries himself then he was prepared to entrust the initial stages of work (quarrying and roughing out) to other carvers but these were always close associates, usually from his hometown of Settignano: Domenico di Giovanni da Settignano (known as Topolino) was one of his men at Carrara whom he worked with again and again; but he also became increasingly reliant on other specialist quarrymen/transporters at Carrara, notably Matteo Cucherello and Guido d'Antonio di Biaggio.[31] Michelangelo's trust in the skills of these men was built up over time and in person, during months of work at the quarries.

Michelangelo was not alone. The sculptor Vincenzo Danti, working under pressure at Seravezza in 1568, even wrote to his Medici patron explaining how long the process of stone selection took.[32] This kind of detailed documentary evidence is simply not available for the Roman period but we can be reasonably confident, for the reasons outlined above, that this was not a practice restricted to the Renaissance. It is striking, in fact, that analysis of all the marble used for the sculptural programmes of the Nymphaeum of Herodes Atticus at Olympia suggests that it came from a single extraction point within the quarries on Penteli. This is a very high-quality variety of Pentelic marble and it seems likely that this source was specially selected for this project.[33]

Roughed-out statues at the quarries

Our best evidence for carvers working in the quarries in the Roman period is provided by finds from these sites. Relatively few statues have been recovered from quarrying sites but most of those that have been are simply roughed out, like the architectural elements and sarcophagi so often found at these sites. These include a pair of roughed-out busts in *pavonazzetto* and porphyry from the quarries at Dokimeion and Mons Porphyrites respectively.[34] Both were shaped roughly to a state which still allowed for the inclusion of a range of hairstyles and distinctive facial features, much like the roughed-out busts on sarcophagi.[35] These objects could simply have been being worked on by carvers in the quarries who planned to finish them there but never got around to it. However, the similarity in finish between these pieces and a female bust from the Şile shipwreck, which was probably shaped to this state on Prokonnesos, indicates that they were having their first phase of carving done in the

---

[31] Scigliano 2005: 74, 77, 162.   [32] Klapisch-Zuber 1969: 62.
[33] Kane et al. 1999: 322–3.
[34] Bruno 2002*b*: 186, 189, fig. 10; Maxfield and Peacock 2001*b*: 109–10, fig. 3.73.
[35] For an example, see Fig. 7.26.

quarries ready for onward transport.[36] Unfortunately, none of these examples is easily dated, all probably falling somewhere between the second and fourth centuries AD.[37]

More definitively roughed out than these busts are four statues, datable to the second century AD (perhaps even earlier), from the limestone quarries near the village of Xylophagou on Cyprus (Figs. 8.2 and 8.3).[38] These consist of a cuirassed emperor, a draped female, and a nude male, all just over life-size, as well as a smaller female statue of the Small Herculaneum type. All were in the process of being carved out of squared blocks when they were abandoned. The carvers clearly progressed from the front of the block to the back and their rear sides are still unworked.[39] A similarly finished togate statue, just over life-size, was found recently in one of the quarries around Vila Viçosa near Estremoz in Portugal. This statue is carved with the point chisel all over, with the key details of its drapery carefully marked out, but work had also begun with the flat chisel in certain places.[40] Unlike the Xylophagou statues this piece was designed to have a separately inserted head, but just like these other examples it was carved from a roughly rectangular block. Other fragmentary roughed-out statues from quarrying sites include a nude male from the Saliara quarries on Thasos (now lost), a fragment of a female statue from the Parian quarries, and other less certain forms from the quarries at Kavacık near Akmonia and Pessinus.[41] Palagia recently published a roughed-out statue of a dog from the Pentelic quarries which may well be Roman, though this is far from certain; the statue is roughed out all over with several different sizes of point chisel while a substantial strut of raw stone has been left behind the rear legs.[42]

Not found at a quarry but in a roughed-out form similar to the examples listed above are a pair of roughly life-size statues from Mala Dubočica near Leskovac, in southern Serbia. These pieces are included in Tomović's catalogue of statuary from Moesia Superior but are otherwise unpublished.[43] The pair appear to represent a male and a female. Though only very roughly shaped with the point chisel their general form is clear. Both stand upright with clothing tightly wrapped around their bodies. The male figure's left arm is folded across his chest while his right rests by his side. The arrangement of the female figure's arms is less clear: the left one seems to cross the chest but it is possible that the right one does too; Tomović suggests that it is a version of the Herculaneum Woman type but both of the canonical forms of this type have their right arms across their chests. In scale, pose, and clothing these statues would have suited a funerary or even honorific context. Typically for this

---

[36] Asgari et al. 1983: 134–5, no. B.373.   [37] Pensabene 2002*b*: 42.
[38] Karageorghis 1969: 494–7, figs. 130–3.   [39] Hollinshead 2002: 227
[40] Mañas and Fusco 2008: 493–5, fig. 4.
[41] Koželj 1988: 10, pl. 12, ill. 18; Waelkens et al. 1988: 108, n. 137; Asgari 1981: 44, fig. 46.
[42] Palagia 2011.   [43] Tomović 1993: 21, 123 (no. 232–3), figs 48.2, 48.4.

Fig. 8.2. Roughed-out statue of a draped female from the Xylophagou quarry on Cyprus, now in Larnaca Archaeological Museum (photo: M. Hollinshead, used with permission of the Department of Antiquities Cyprus).

Fig. 8.3. Roughed-out statue of a cuirassed male from the Xylophagou quarry on Cyprus, now in Larnaca Archaeological Museum (photo: M. Hollinshead, used with permission of the Department of Antiquities Cyprus).

region they appear to have been carved in a coarse grey–white marble from a nearby quarry. Their discovery some distance from any known Roman site might indicate that they were abandoned during transport and, while we cannot be absolutely certain, it seems reasonable to assume that they were carved to this stage at or close to the quarry at which they originated.

Colossal roughed-out statues

The roughed-out statues discussed above are all around or a little over life-size but there are also a series of much larger statues that seem to have been roughed out in the quarries. These include, most notably, the colossal statue of a cuirassed emperor in Prokonnesian marble recovered from the Şile ship-wreck (Fig. 8.4).[44] This massive figure, over 4.50 m high, is roughly point chiselled all over with various details of the design schematically outlined: the folds of the paludamentum on the left shoulder and hanging over the left arm, the line of pteryges at the bottom of the cuirass. This wreck is conventionally dated to the second century AD, but the form of this figure finds its closest parallel in the cuirassed statue of Constantine II now on the south-west balustrade of the Piazza del Campidoglio in Rome, dated to the early fourth century AD.[45] Whether this figure was roughed out in the quarry or at a workshop somewhere else is impossible to say for sure. The Şile ship was also carrying a pair of *verde antico* columns and other objects that clearly did not come straight from the quarries on Prokonnesos; this was a mixed cargo of bits and pieces of stone. The level of finish on the Şile cuirassed statue is closely paralleled on a roughed-out statue of a seated figure from the Penteli quarries. This enormous piece of stone, 3.50 m long and 2.53 m at its widest point, has received little attention and appears to be lost now, but is again worked with the point chisel and was probably intended to represent a Late Roman emperor.[46]

Two similarly massive roughed-out statues of horsemen have also been found near a quarry close to Breifurt in Saarland, Germany (Figs. 8.5 and 8.6).[47] These sandstone statues, roughly 3 m high and 5 tonnes in weight, the largest Roman statues north of the Alps, are now displayed outside the front of the Historisches Museum der Pfalz in Speyer. Like the Şile statue they are roughed out with the point chisel all over, with the space between the horses' legs hollowed out but with unworked stone left around the legs. Certain details are again delineated, including the front hooves of the horses, their faces and bridles, as well as the boots and cloaks of the riders. Their scale has led to the identification of these individuals as emperors—Valentinian I and his son Gratian are a popular choice, but others have been proposed—though they could also represent local notables.[48]

Whoever they represent exactly, what the horsemen from Breitfurt show is that the practice of roughing out large statues at the quarry was neither limited to the major quarries of the Mediterranean nor restricted to works in marble. The Breifurt, Şile, and Penteli statues were roughed out to the same stage as many architectural elements and sarcophagi also found at the quarries, but they were also major commissions for which carvers must have been sent to the quarries specially. The Breifurt horsemen are particularly unusual, since it

---

[44] Asgari 1990: 125–6, fig. 28.
[45] Fittschen and Zanker 1985: 145–7, no. 121, pls. 149–50.
[46] Wiseman 1968; Carpenter 1968: pl. 98.
[47] J. Röder 1960.   [48] J. Röder 1960; Kolling 1992; Stinsky 2011.

Fig. 8.4. Roughed-out colossal statue from the Şile shipwreck, now in Istanbul Archaeological Museum (photo: author, used with permission of Istanbul Archaeological Museum).

was rare to carve rider and horse from a single block of stone. On the basis of this small sample it is impossible to draw any significance from their date but the size of these statues is relevant: the weight savings to be gained by this initial stage of roughing-out were substantial in these cases (especially in the case of the Breifurt horsemen). Earlier cases, like the famous sixth-century BC roughed-out *kouroi* abandoned in the Melanes quarries and the colossal Dionysos in the Apollonas quarry, both on Naxos, show that large statues had been handled like this from the beginning.[49] Indeed comparisons can even be drawn with practices on Easter Island in the south-eastern Pacific, where

---

[49] Nolte 2006: cat. 11–12, 18 (pls. 9–10, 78–9); Ortolani 2001: 27 (fig. 9).

Fig. 8.5. Cast of a roughed-out statue of a horseman from near Breitfurt, now in the Römermuseum Schwarzenacker (photo: C. Witschel, reproduced with permission of the Römermuseum Schwarzenacker).

Fig. 8.6. Cast of a roughed-out statue of a horseman from near Breitfurt, now in the Römermuseum Schwarzenacker (photo: C. Witschel, reproduced with permission of the Römermuseum Schwarzenacker).

the iconic *moai* were also roughed out before being fully separated from the bedrock.[50]

Near-finished statues at the quarries

Alongside this handful of finds attesting to the occasional roughing out of large and sometimes small statues at the quarries, further examples show that detailed work was occasionally also undertaken at this point. There was no single rule governing what work was and was not best carried out at the quarries. The best-known example of a near-finished statue found in a quarry is the statue of a Dacian prisoner discovered by Cox in 1926 in the *pavonazzetto* quarry at Çakırsaz in the upper Tembris valley.[51] This piece is similar to those other, originally Trajanic, *pavonazzetto* Dacians reused on the Arch of Constantine, but it is actually closest in form to the pair of Dacians from the

---

[50] Van Tilburg and Ralston 1999: 43–5.
[51] Buckler, Calder, and Cox 1928: 22–3; Waelkens 1985.

Eastern Baths at Ephesos.[52] This statue was either worked on by carvers sent out from Ephesos or by Dokimeian carvers assigned to the task. If the former then it is surprising that they decided to carve it beyond roughing out; perhaps because it was a relatively compact form it was felt that there would be little risk of damage. However, we should not rule out the possibility that carving workshops in this area were capable of handling major commissions. The Çakırsaz quarry has also produced a part-finished statue of a standing male in white marble, apparently carved out of a discarded stepped block.[53] A roughed-out statuette with a columnar support on its rear side has also been found at this quarry, similar in form to numerous statuettes from around Dokimeion.[54] It is even possible that a team of Ephesian carvers travelled to the quarries to carve a single Dacian which then acted as a model for the others which could have been carved by Dokimeians.

In terms of overall finish, the closest parallels to the Çakırsaz Dacian come from the Prokonnesian quarries. These include two partially worked herms, one of which is published; in both cases the details of the faces are carefully modelled, and almost finished, while the bodies are only roughly shaped.[55] A closer parallel, though, is provided by the pair of over life-size statues of cuirassed emperors from Prokonnesos (Fig. 8.7). Both were finished to an advanced stage with the flat chisel all over, with only the head left roughed out.[56] Their portraits were presumably intended to be finished by a specialist, though whether at the quarries or elsewhere is unclear. What is evident is that they are probably fourth century AD in date, to judge from the details of their clothing and the style of their finish, and were intended to be a pair, perhaps an Augustus and his Caesar, or a father and son. Unlike the Çakırsaz Dacian, though, these are not compact forms that were well-suited to transport; their legs, carved in the round, would have been vulnerable to damage and indeed the head on one of them has been broken off in recent years. In the same period we have the Şile and Breifurt statues showing that transporting statues roughed out was still an option. Why, then, was work on these examples taken so far at the quarries? One possibility is that they were to be shipped, perhaps as imperial gifts, to a destination where the presence of suitable carvers could not be relied on; if this were the case, though, we have to assume either that

[52] On the Rome examples, Curtius 1944: 50, pl. 103, 105; Waelkens 1985: 645–8; on the Ephesian ones, Schneider 1990: 251–3, Pl. 71.1–2; Aurenhammer 1990: 162–4, no. 144–5.

[53] Identified as Harmodios in Pensabene 2002a: 206–7, fig. 4; Bruno 2002b: 186–7, fig. 9a–b; as Herakles in Pensabene 2010: 87; but it most likely represents Marsyas—see *LIMC*, Marsyas I 11.

[54] Fant 1989c: 112.

[55] Asgari 1990: 126, fig. 27.

[56] Asgari 1990: 126, fig. 29; Attanasio 2003: pl. 28.1. One of these statues is now in the open-air museum at Saraylar; its head was stolen in 2001 but recovered in 2005 in Munich and is now in Ankara. The location of the other statue is unclear.

326 *The Economics of the Roman Stone Trade*

their heads were meant to be finished before export and were for some reason not or that a specialist portrait-carver was meant to travel with them. We know, from the famous Constantinian edict to the effect, that there was a huge shortage of skilled sculptors in the early fourth century AD.[57] It would make sense in such a scenario to concentrate workers close to the quarries. Indeed we know from the story of the four saints in the *Passio Sanctorum Quattuor Coronatorum*, which Peacock suggests refers to the Mons Porphyrites quarries, that sculptors were based more permanently at these quarries in the early fourth century AD at least.[58] Perhaps, in the case of our Prokonnesian statues, it was considered too expensive and time-consuming for those carvers that there were to accompany each and every work, particularly examples like these that were reasonably formulaic—unlike the Şile and Breifurt statues.

Prefabrication

As with other stone objects found in roughed-out forms at the quarries there has been a temptation to interpret these statues as prefabricated objects, their forms decided by quarry-based sculptors aiming their products at known markets. Several scholars have explored the idea that the repetitive forms of the best-known statue types used in the Roman imperial period resulted from contemporary modes of production, especially at the quarries.[59] Were these types used again and again, in other words, because this is what the quarries were producing in roughed-out form for sculptors elsewhere to finish? This is an intriguing suggestion which has been widely accepted for other object types, as we have seen in the previous two chapters. However, both the material from the quarries and the evidence of finished statues, even of the most common types, shows that we should not overstate the role of this quarry-based work.

Unlike the sarcophagi and architectural elements for which this argument has also been made, statues found at quarrying sites are hugely varied. To date, no two identical roughed-out or near-finished statues have been recovered from the quarries, with the exception of the pair of emperors from Prokonnesos which were probably part of the same job. All of these pieces are more easily explained as commissioned projects being worked on by carvers who were either sent there for this purpose or based there permanently. The Breifurt, Şile, Penteli, and Çakırsaz statues were thoroughly out-of-the-ordinary projects, so too the Prokonnesian emperors. Analysis of the working traces on the Xylophagou statues, furthermore, shows that these were not being

---

[57] *Codex Theodosianus* XIII.5.2

[58] *Passio Sanctorum Quattuor Coronatorum*, 1–2; see Wattenbach 1870:324–8; Peacock 1995.

[59] A. I. Wilson 2008: 402–5; Trimble 2011: 64–103.

Fig. 8.7. One of the pair of near-finished statues of emperors from Prokonnesos, now in the open-air museum at Saraylar (photo: J. C. Fant, taken before the head was stolen).

prepared to a standard roughed-out form.[60] Certain details of the design, such as the drapery on the smaller female and various details on the nude male, were carefully modelled by the carver as they moved into the block. These examples at least were simply being carved in the normal way when for some reason work on them was called off. There was no overseas market for this limestone and these statues, probably a single commission much like the family group found behind the Bouleuterion at Aphrodisias, were simply being worked on by a carver active in the quarry, perhaps one who was

[60] Hollinshead 2002: 228–9.

based there permanently; the intention was most likely to carve them to a near-finished state before finishing them *in situ*.[61] Likewise, the Vila Viçosa *togatus* was probably intended for a relatively local client, since the white marble from this area was only really used for high-end statuary in the cities of central and eastern Lusitania, notably Merida.[62] It seems unlikely that there was a large enough market for marble *togati* in this region to encourage quarry-based sculptors to prefabricate them.

When it comes to the finished works, a quick comparison between two series of statues from Olympia and Cyrene shows that similar forms were not decided in the quarries. At both sites a number of Small and Large Herculaneum Woman types have been discovered which are carved in Pentelic marble. If these had been purchased as prefabricated forms by carvers working at both sites then one might expect to see some similarities beyond simply their overall form, in terms of their dimensions or the quality of their material. Instead, those from Cyrene tend to be around a third smaller than those from Olympia and carved in markedly lower-quality marble, particularly during the Antonine period.[63]

An additional point about the connection between quarries and statue types is also worth noting. That is that while certain sarcophagus types (Attic and Asiatic) were routinely produced in the same marble there is no obvious connection between particular statue types and particular materials. As Trimble has noted, statues of the Large Herculaneum Woman type have been identified in Prokonnesian, Pentelic, Parian, Thasian dolomitic, and Aphrodisian marble, as well as limestone.[64] Only occasionally can such a connection be made, as in the case of the series of table supports (*trapezophoroi*) depicting Eros which were all carved in Thasian dolomitic marble. In addition to a fragmentary example from Thasos itself, Herrmann and Newman have identified a further three of identical form which are certainly also dolomitic marble, in collections in Rome, Thessaloniki, and Leiden, while another two which have not been tested are in the Vatican Museums.[65] Even in this case, though, there is no evidence to indicate that these pieces were prefabricated at the quarries on Thasos; rather we are probably dealing with the products of a workshop on Thasos which used its local material.

In sum, a number of statues were roughed out before they left the quarries and others worked to a more finished condition, but there is no convincing evidence to suggest that these were prefabricated by quarry-based carvers without specific customers in place. This work was done, as with other object types, to reduce the weight of the piece as much as possible for onward

[61] On the Aphrodisian group, Hallett 1998.
[62] Pensabene 2004: 425–7, figs. 11–15.
[63] Kane and Carrier 1992; Kane et al. 1999.   [64] Trimble 2011: 64–74.
[65] Herrmann 1992: 95, 100, figs. 5–6; Herrmann and Newman 1995: 78–80, figs. 13–15.

transportation and the individuals responsible were probably either the carver undertaking the whole project, present permanently or temporarily at the quarries, or someone working for them. The widely replicated forms of the most popular statue types were not decided by quarry-based workshops, in other words; indeed this is further indicated by the fact that this replication extends well beyond simply their form down to the precise details of their roughed-out finish, which would not have been carved in the quarries.[66]

THE MOVEMENT OF CARVERS AND STATUES

Some of these finds from the quarries were clearly intended for local customers. The limestone quarried at Xylophagou was certainly not widely valued and the statues from these quarries were probably for one of the nearby cities (perhaps Larnaca?). Likewise the Breifurt and Mala Dubočica statues, carved in unspectacular materials, were probably never meant to be moved far. In these cases the carvers responsible could easily have travelled with them and finished them in place. Was this also the case, however, for statues that were being moved much longer distances? Was there a team of carvers with the statues on the ship wrecked at Şile, for example, who had been tasked with finishing them wherever it was they were heading? Turning the question around, how do we know whether marble statues at somewhere like Palmyra were carved locally using imported raw materials (by a migrant or Palmyrene carver), carved by an itinerant carver who arrived with the material, or carved elsewhere altogether and imported fully finished? The short answer, of course, is that it is usually impossible to know for certain since the evidence is often far from conclusive. A case in point is the famous epitaph of the sculptor Novius Blesamus from Rome which states that he 'decorated the city and the whole world with statues' (*hic olim statuis urbem decoravit et orbem*).[67] Novius, apparently an Italian of Celtic origin, was evidently keen to celebrate his prolific career but whether he spent most of it on the road or simply exported his works widely from Rome is unclear.

In Philostratos' text mentioned above, Apollonios draws a specific distinction between carvers who travel to complete specific commissions with raw material supplied by someone else and carvers who produce finished statues for sale, like the merchant he is addressing:

... the image-makers of old behaved not in this way, nor did they go round the cities selling their gods. All they did was to export their own hands and their tools for working stone and ivory; others provided the raw materials, while they plied

---

[66] Trimble 2011: 99.　　[67] *CIL* VI.23083.

their handicraft in the temples themselves; but you are leading the gods into harbours and markets just as if they were wares of the Hyrcanians and of the Scythians—far be it from me to name these—and do you think you are doing no impiety?[68]

A chronological distinction is drawn here between these two approaches but there are bodies of evidence to indicate that a variety of practices existed in the Roman period. Apollonios might disapprove of the shipping of these votive statues, even going so far as to compare it to the slave trade apparently (the wares of Scythians and Hyrcanians?), but the dichotomy he sets up here is a false one. Migrant carvers sometimes moved to regions where there was demand for their services, carvers did travel to complete specific commissions, and also a lot of statues were shipped fully finished to their customers. The range of ways in which the supply process could function helps explain why the distribution pattern for materials used in statuary differs so markedly from those used in building or sarcophagus production.

Carvers and their materials

Before turning to the evidence for these different practices, the link between materials and carvers should be considered. Rockwell has often stated that carvers tend to work only those materials they are most familiar with.[69] While this is probably true and Thasian carvers, as a result, are likely to have worked predominately in Thasian marble, this does not mean that all statues in Thasian marble were necessarily carved by Thasian carvers. Contrasting the stylistic differences between statues in Thasian dolomitic marble from Macedonia and from Ephesos, Herrmann and Newman conclude that 'it appears that different regions tended to use Thasian dolomite in different ways in keeping with their local traditions'.[70] This material was used as a raw material by local producers in these two areas. In fact, at Ephesos, the same authors have noted that this marble was especially favoured for large-scale works: the colossal portrait of Titus and various statues from the Nymphaeum of Pollio, dated to AD 93, are in Thasian dolomitic marble, as apparently is the Great Antonine Altar.[71] It seems unlikely that a city like Ephesos, with its rich artistic tradition, would have relied on Thasian carvers for these projects which in any case differ greatly from sculpture on Thasos in their stylistic details. Interestingly, this same material was also popular for imperial portraits, especially in the mid to late first century AD. Tests performed by

---

[68] Philostratos, *Life of Apollonios of Tyana* V.20 (transl. F. C. Conybeare).
[69] Rockwell 1990: 221; 1993: 2–5.
[70] Herrmann and Newman 1995: 75–8, figs. 5–9.
[71] Herrmann and Newman 1995: 78.

Herrmann and Newman showed that three of the seven portraits of imperial women in the Ny Carlsberg Glyptotek were carved in Thasian dolomitic marble, as was the colossal Nero in the Munich Glyptothek.[72] These pieces were almost certainly carved in Rome, probably by carvers based there. On one level this choice of Thasian marble is a curious one. It is arguably the most awkward of the white marbles to carve and certainly the hardest, rated at 3.5–4 on the Mohs scale, 0.5–1 more than most other white marbles used for statuary.[73] However, it is more uniformly white than other options and has a distinctive reflective quality that is often remarked upon in the scholarship. Its hardness might also have been considered an advantage, especially in the carving of the elaborate Flavian and Trajanic female hairstyles for which it was often used.[74]

The same holds true for all marble types. While carvers were probably most comfortably working in those materials with which they were most familiar, carving similar stones would have presented no major difficulties and they could even have experimented with quite different ones. A carver used to working in Luna marble could just as easily have handled most other white marble, then, even if it took a while to adjust to the idiosyncrasies of each. When selecting which marble to use for a particular project, the carver concerned would have considered the sizes of blocks that could be quarried, the consistency of the material and its colouring, its hardness, and its reflectiveness. Since all white marbles differ slightly in these respects, a single carver might conceivably have worked in a variety of stones, importing them directly from the quarry or buying them from middlemen.

For these reasons we should also not assume that all marble carving in areas without local marble sources was done by foreign workers. At Ptolemais in Cyrenaica, for example, where an Athenian sculptor named Asklepiades is recorded on a maker's mark, the widespread use of Pentelic marble has been used to assert that he was likely one of many immigrant Athenian carvers.[75] However, marble statues were widely used in the Cyrenaican cities in the Classical and Hellenistic periods and it is inconceivable that there would not have been local carvers capable of working marble by the Roman period; indeed Kane has drawn attention to a statue base from the Sanctuary of Demeter at Cyrene signed by a certain Aristis Tabalbios who was almost certainly a local Cyrenean.[76] Equally in the Levant, another area lacking local marble reserves, there is evidence for local marble carvers. The finish

---

[72] Herrmann and Newman 1995: 75–6, fig. 4; 2002: 220.

[73] Herrmann and Newman 1995: 75; Peter Rockwell, who has carved Thasian marble, confirms this.

[74] Herrmann and Newman 2002: 220–1.

[75] Fabbricotti 1985: 221–2.

[76] D. White 1977: 185; Kane 1985: 243; 1988: 134; 2000: 479.

on the Large Herculaneum Woman from the 'Senate House' at Palmyra, which is carved in Prokonnesian marble, shares many similarities with locally produced statuary and funerary reliefs and seems to indicate Palmyrene carvers were capable of handling marble sculpture, at least by the Severan period.[77] At Beth Shean, Ovadiah and Turnheim have shown that architectural decoration of the theatre, which is also Severan in date, was almost certainly undertaken by local carvers working again in imported Prokonnesian.[78] In both the Levant and Cyrenaica marble-working skills would have been transferred from immigrant carvers to local ones over time and by the Roman period it might often have been difficult distinguishing between these groups.

Migrant carvers

While a significant amount of stone, especially white marble, did probably move around as raw materials for carving projects, there is evidence to show that carvers also travelled. We know from the literary sources that numerous Greek carvers were present in Rome in the Late Republic, among them Pasiteles and Arkesilaos, and we can reasonably assume that this practice continued.[79] It was not just the capital that attracted carvers, though. As already noted, an association of Nicomedian sculptors is attested at Nicopolis-ad-Istrum.[80] The fact that they formed themselves into an official group implies they were there for the long-term rather than for the completion of a single commission. Other candidates for permanent residents include a pair of Dokimeian sculptors named on a dedication from Konya: 'the brothers, Limnaios and Diomedes, statue carvers and carvers of Dokimeian marble, Dokimeians'.[81] In these cases, the carvers attested moved from areas with well-known carving and quarrying traditions to regions without sources of marble. There was clearly demand for their services in these areas and they appear to have based themselves there permanently or at least long-term.

The numerous makers' marks on finished statues, especially those on which the carver records their hometown (or ethnicity), provide more ambiguous evidence for the movement of carvers. This practice was generally limited to carvers from a small series of cities—Athens and Aphrodisias most notably, but also Nicomedia, Rhodes, Miletos, Dokimeion, and Alexandria. It was clearly intended as a mark of quality since these were all famous cities with

---

[77] Trimble 2011: 89, 427, no. 133.   [78] Ovadiah and Turnheim 1994: 108–11, 121–2.
[79] Toynbee 1951: 18–26.   [80] *IG Bulg* II.674; see Ward-Perkins 1980b: 34, no. 4.
[81] McLean 2002: no. 45; Hall and Waelkens 1982.

fine artistic traditions.[82] However, these inscriptions do not tell us where the inscribed statue was actually carved: there is really no way of telling for sure whether these carvers travelled with their materials and carved these pieces *in situ*, were based permanently at the sites where their works are found, or never left their hometowns, simply inscribing their works before dispatching them. While the brothers Limnaios and Diomedes, then, were possibly resident at Konya (Iconium), it is much less clear whether the Glykon who signed two statues at Sagalassos or the Menandros who signed one at Pisidian Antioch lived in these cities or were based in Dokimeion.[83] Although in most cases carvers appear not to have recorded their origin when working in their hometown, a sculptor named Polyneikes, who carved one of the two statues of third-century AD boxers now in the museum at Aphrodisias, was so proud of his Aphrodisian roots that he chose to record them even when working there.[84] Slightly more useful are several makers' marks from the western provinces on which carvers record their places of origin apparently for no reason other than to indicate where they came from and that they were working far from home. At Bath, a certain Priscus son of Toutus is attested who describes himself as a *lapidarius cives Carnutenus*, that is from northern Gaul; in artistic terms this statement of origin carried no particular weight (unlike 'Athenian' or 'Aphrodisian') and there was no reason for Priscus to celebrate this unless he was present in Bath.[85] The same might be said for a pair of Gallic sculptors, Samus and Severus, who signed the Jupiter Column at Mainz.[86]

Sometimes the materials used by these carvers also allow a more accurate reconstruction of events. The two togate statues from the forum at Merida, the makers' marks on which assign them to the *officina* of Gaius Aulus, and a third of similar form, are cases in point.[87] Two of these have recently been shown to be carved in Luna marble and all are carved in a typically Italian style, similar in finish to contemporary examples from Flavian Rome. While it would be tempting to see these as pieces carved in Italy and imported near-finished (with only their portraits left to be worked) it is now clear that the third of

---

[82] On Athenians, Palagia 2010: 435–7; Trimble 2011: 121–6; Toynbee 1951: 23–6; Fabbricotti 1985: 219; on Aphrodisians, Floriani Squarciapino 1943: 12–17; Roueché and Erim 1982; on Nicomedians, L. Robert 1960: 35–6; Traversari 1993: 22–3; on Rhodians, Nocita 2007: 1036–7; on Alexandrians, Donderer 2001: 176–9, no. 3–7; and on a Milesian and the surprising absence of Ephesians, Donderer 1996: 97–104.

[83] Waelkens et al. 2002: 371; L. Robert 1962: 41–3.

[84] Inan and Rosenbaum 1979: 217–21, no. 190–1; Roueché and Erim 1982: 102–3. For an Aphrodisian sarcophagus on which the individual describes himself as an Aphrodisian, see Reynolds and Roueché 2007: 167–8, no. 120.

[85] Toynbee 1951: 26; Pearson 2006: 67; for a local sculptor at Bath, Sulinus son of Brucetus, see *RIB* I, 151.

[86] *ILS* 9235; *CIL* XIII.11806; Toynbee 1951: 26.

[87] This signed ones are García y Bellido 1949: 184, 188, nos. 207, 215; for images of these and the third piece, and information about their materials, see Pensabene 2004: 425–7, figs. 11–15.

these statues is carved in Estremoz marble from the nearby quarries: Gaius Aulus, or a member of his team at least, was present at Merida, then. Though far from certain, it is tempting to see Gaius Aulus as an Italian-trained carver who originally arrived in Merida to carry out a specific commission along with several blocks of Luna marble but was then commissioned to undertake a third, for which he employed Estremoz marble. Whether he then returned to Italy or stayed is unclear but the fact he is attested in connection with an *officina* suggests a level of permanence. At the other end of the empire, a certain Antoninos son of Antiochos, an Alexandrian, is attested on two makers' marks from Jerash. Again the materials used for these objects, both statue bases, can be used to show that Antoninos was present in the city: the first, in imported white marble, comes from the North Hall of the East Baths, while the second, from an unknown context, is carved in the local yellow limestone.[88] Both are datable to the early second century AD. Antoninos would certainly not have been using this local limestone unless he was in the city and had little option. Alexandrian carvers are attested widely in the Hellenistic period but they are less well known in the Roman period, even though several makers' marks mentioning Alexandrians are known from Messene, datable to the early Imperial period.[89]

Itinerant carvers

The epigraphic evidence shows that carvers did move and were sometimes resident in areas far from their places of origin, presumably because there was demand for their services. As we have seen, when these carvers worked in areas distant from the sources of their raw materials they could have ordered in blocks or perhaps even dispatched requests for roughed-out material to be sent to them. It is also possible, though, that carvers travelled just to complete single or multiple commissions. Conlin points to the passages of Pliny and Plutarch mentioning Vulca, the Etruscan sculptor, who travelled from Veii to Rome to undertake several projects in terracotta for Tarquinius Priscus in the sixth century BC.[90] In the previous chapter it was proposed that the elaborate columnar sarcophagi carved in Dokimeian marble might have been accompanied by a team of sculptors who finished them in place.[91] There is also evidence for major building projects being worked on by teams of carvers brought in temporarily.[92] Sometimes itinerant workers employed on building

---

[88] Weber 1990: 352; Donderer 2001: 178–9, nos. 6–7; Friedland 2003: 413, 417, fig. 3, 439–41; 2012: 107–8, fig. 1.

[89] Donderer 2001: 176–7, nos. 3–5.

[90] Conlin 1997: 35; Pliny the Elder XXXV.157; Plutarch, *Life of Poplicola* 13.

[91] See Chapter 7: Asiatic sarcophagi (pp. 278–81).

[92] See Chapter 6: Managing building projects (pp. 202–4).

projects also carved statues. Kleiner has convincingly argued that the same team of carvers was responsible for the Augustan mausolea of the Julii at Glanum and of the Salonii at Lyon, as well as a series of reliefs elsewhere in southern Gaul which probably originally belonged to other tombs.[93] These carvers undertook both the building of these structures and the carving of the statues and reliefs that adorned them to judge from similarities of style and technique between these elements. As Kleiner notes, these 'were rare and costly memorials, and their patrons must have been few and dispersed. It was necessary for the workshop to be mobile in order to earn a livelihood'.[94]

The team of carvers identified by Kleiner concentrated themselves in southern Gaul, in a relatively restricted area, and they worked in local materials. Identifying instances in which carvers travelled longer distances with their materials for single commissions is much harder. For big projects, like the major civic structures that are such a feature of the cities of the eastern empire in the second century AD, commissioners may well have been forced to bring in craftsmen from further afield. Huge complexes like the Sebasteion at Aphrodisias, the Great Antonine Altar at Ephesos, and the Severan theatre at Hierapolis might well have been worked on by both local and foreign carvers, much like the major building projects at places like Rome and Lepcis Magna.[95] On the very largest construction sites sculptors would have been needed in large numbers, to complete both relief decoration and the necessary plethora of free-standing statuary, and we might imagine a close connection between architectural and sculptural specialists.

Good evidence for an itinerant carver is provided by a fortuitous find from the Porto Nuovo shipwreck off Corsica. A bundle of tools was recovered here, including a number of tools inscribed with initials (showing that they were possessions not new items), some suitable for carving soft stones which are most commonly attested in the Levant, as well as a series of tools clearly belonging to a sculptor.[96] In this case, the cargo consisted of blocks of Luna marble not roughed-out statues. Whether this carver or team of carvers were travelling to complete a single commission, however, or migrating with a stash of materials—perhaps like Gaius Aulus—is unclear. Equally uncertain is whether carvers were accompanying the roughed-out colossus from the Şile shipwreck. This was an exceptional project and it would have made sense for at least one carver to oversee its carving from start to finish but there are no finds from the site to demonstrate that such oversight was provided. Alternatively, it is possible that this statue was being transported to a separate group of carvers who would undertake its finishing. There is some suggestive evidence for this practice elsewhere. At Palmyra, Wielgosz has argued that two second-century

---

[93] Kleiner 1977.   [94] Kleiner 1977: 674.
[95] On 'big-project workshops', Smith 2011: 71.
[96] H. Bernard et al. 1998: 58–66.

AD statues of Apollo and Dionysos from the Baths of Diocletian and the Colonnaded Street respectively were imported part-completed.[97] The fact that they were never worked beyond this stage, she uses to propose that 'at least in the second century AD there were no workshops in Palmyra able to complete the work'.[98] It seems unlikely that, if this were the case, the buyer of these statues would not have got them fully finished first; other statues of this period at Palmyra are fully carved so it must have been possible. More likely these pieces were rushed into use or the commissioners cancelled the contract; we do not, after all, know when they were actually set up, and it could have been long after they were initially ordered.

The movement of finished statues

If there were no carvers at the destination capable of finishing the Şile colossus then the only alternative to dispatching workers with it would have been to finish it close to the quarries, like the pair of smaller emperors from Prokonnesos. While this might well have been a cheaper option for such a large project, which would in any case already have been exorbitantly expensive, it can hardly have been worth the risk of exposing it to damage during transport. In practice, when long distances were involved and the project was large, complicated or especially delicate, it would probably have been more cost effective for carvers to travel with their materials either roughed out or in block form and undertake the bulk of carving *in situ*. It would certainly have been necessary when a portrait needed to be carved at the destination. For most smaller commissions, however, particularly those of compact form which required no final adjustments, it might have been preferable to simply dispatch them fully completed—or perhaps part-finished, with only their portraits to be finished. The lower the value of the commission the more proportionately expensive it would have been to have the carver travel with it.

Finished statues would have been delicate objects to ship but Philostratos' text quoted at the beginning of this section shows that they were moved long distances; the Arrian passage discussed above also assumes that the required statues will be dispatched completed. Even if these texts are unspecific about the size or materials of the statues they discuss, isolated finds of finished or near-finished statues at remote quarries, like those at Çakırsaz and on Prokonnesos, confirm what they say. The risk of damage during transport did not always put carvers off finishing their works at the quarries. Several finished or very nearly finished statues have been recovered from shipwrecks as well. Six marble statues, all apparently made for the insertion of heads, were

<hr>

[97] Wielgosz 2000: 96–8, figs. 1a–c, 2a–c.   [98] Wielgosz et al. 2002: 398.

found off Cephalonia, and other finds of finished statuary have been made in Paroikia Bay on Paros, off Ascalon, and off Benalmadena in Spain, all apparently coming from shipwrecks.[99] The Porticcio A wreck off Corsica has marble busts of a third-century AD emperor and his wife, probably Philip the Arab and Otacilia Severa, as well as two honorific statues and numerous small statuettes of various subjects.[100] A portrait of Augustus was also found in the Étang de Berre at the mouth of the Rhône, though whether it comes from a shipwreck is uncertain.[101] Not all of these statues are demonstrably new products. Some could have been secondhand. Pliny talks at length about the quantity of old statues imported into Rome and this continued later, the Baths of Caracalla being full of such pieces.[102] Even greater numbers of ancient works were moved to Constantinople to adorn the new capital.[103] Some of these finds from shipwrecks, notably those from the Porticcio A wreck, might also have been in the process of being moved by their owners rather than on their way to new markets.

Nevertheless, it is interesting that imperial portraits figure prominently in this sample. How controlled the production of imperial portraits actually was remains highly contentious.[104] It is possible to identify a core group of high-quality portraits for most emperors which may well have been the products of workshops in Rome favoured by the administration. Models based on these prototypes, in either plaster or terracotta, or perhaps even finished marble examples could have been circulated, to act as models for carvers outside of Rome. The portraits from shipwrecks could represent lost models of this kind. However, this should not be pushed too far. The variation in imperial portraiture indicates that even if models did exist many carvers were confident to stray far from them.[105] Fronto famously remarks in a letter to Marcus Aurelius that 'everywhere there are likenesses of you, badly painted most of them to be sure, and modelled or carved in a plain, not to say sorry, style of art, yet at the same time your likeness'.[106] The imperial portraits from shipwrecks might simply represent treasured possessions being taken home or commissions from the best metropolitan workshops.

What the shipwreck evidence certainly reveals is that just because statues were fragile does not mean that they were not transported fully finished. Indeed when works by particular carvers were widely sought after it made

[99] On those off Cephalonia, Touchais 1981: 805; off Paros, Papathanasopoulos and Schilardi 1981; and off Ascalon and Benalmadena, Arata 2005: 147, 149.

[100] Parker 2008: 421; Massy 2013: 110–14.

[101] Brentchaloff and Salviat 1989.

[102] Pliny the Elder XXXVI.9–43; and on the sculpture from the Baths of Caracalla, DeLaine 1997: 78–83; Gasparri 2010.

[103] Bassett 2004: 37–49.

[104] On this question, see Fittschen 1971; Pfanner 1989; Stewart 2006.

[105] Smith 1996.   [106] Fronto, *Ad M. Caesarem* IV.12.4

sense for them to meet this demand with finished pieces rather than continually travelling to complete jobs. Carvers based on Thasos, or elsewhere in Asia
Minor but using Thasian marble, certainly seem to have adopted this approach. Dolomitic Thasian marble was a popular choice for high-quality
statuary, especially over life-size projects, and Hermann and his colleagues
have identified statues in this material all around the coasts of the Aegean, in
the Levant, in North Africa, Italy, and even southern Gaul.[107] Some of these
statues were certainly carved locally by non-Thasians, as already noted, but in
other cases a strong stylistic similarity can be identified which indicates that
they were carved in Asia Minor, perhaps at Ephesos. Herrmann and Newman
point to several statues from Vienne in southern France, notably a colossal
head of a goddess, which shares certain traits with the statues from the
Nymphaeum of Pollio at Ephesos, carved in the same stone.[108] On similar
grounds Fischer has argued that three statues in white Dokimeian marble
from Ascalon and Caesarea in Palestine were probably carved close to the
quarries and imported fully finished; Wielgosz has argued the same for the
pair of statues in Dokimeian marble from Bosra, as have Walda and Walker
for the examples from Lepcis Magna.[109] There is no way of affirming these
hypotheses but the fact that high-quality statues in Dokimeian marble are
found at a wide range of sites and that statue carving certainly took place close
to the quarries lends some support to them. Furthermore, an intriguing
inscription from near Prusa in Bithynia records the dedication of a statue to
Zeus which the dedicant's son had 'brought from Dokimeion'.[110] This was
evidently a work finished by a carver at Dokimeion and then transported fully
finished, escorted by this individual, to the site at which it was to be erected.

On occasion, then, statues were transported fully finished. This was not a
practice limited to earlier periods, as often assumed. This does not mean,
however, that these statues were necessarily stock pieces. A carver in Dokimeion would have been unlikely to produce a large-scale statue on a whim,
hoping that a buyer would turn up. The finished statues (if indeed they were
finished) in Dokimeian marble that arrived in the Levant and North Africa,
and perhaps also some of the Thasian ones found elsewhere, were probably
still commissions, ordered from known producers at great cost by well-
informed buyers. The range of materials used for statues at different sites, as
discussed in Chapter 5, shows that these commissioners often reached out to a
variety of different carving workshops. The decision to ship these statues fully
finished was based ultimately on the location of the producer and the buyer

[107] Herrmann 1992; 1999; Herrmann and Newman 1995; 1999; 2002; Herrmann, Van Den Hoek, and Nerman 2002.
[108] Herrmann and Newman 1999: 298–300.
[109] M. L. Fischer 1998: no. 103, 120, 136; Wielgosz 2008: 58; Walda and Walker 1984: 83–6.
[110] L. Robert 1962: 42.

respective to each other and the time that the former could afford to devote to the project—or the fact that they were secondhand.

Aphrodisians and their products

Aphrodisian carvers present an interesting case study in this context. Aphrodisians, as we have seen, regularly noted their place of origin when signing their works. Where they worked, however, is unclear, despite important new discoveries that have crucial bearing on this question. Aphrodisians were certainly based overseas, permanently but perhaps also temporarily too. One such migrant is recorded epigraphically at Rome, in this case on a herm of Hadrianic date now in the Vatican Museums. This carver, an Aphrodisian named Zenon, states that he has built a tomb for his family at Rome but that before this he had worked in many other cities.[111] This herm dates to precisely the same period as the famous centaurs from Hadrian's Villa, now in the Capitoline Museums, which were carved and signed by the Aphrodisians Aristeas and Papias. Interestingly the black marble used for these pieces has recently been identified as the black marble from Göktepe.[112] If Aristeas and Papias were based at Rome, like Zenon, then, they continued to use raw materials from the area of their hometown.

Demand for Aphrodisian products at Rome, from at least the Hadrianic period, was probably enough to sustain a number of carvers but whether Aphrodisians migrated elsewhere is less clear. The ongoing campaign of analysis of fine-grained white and black marble statues all around the Mediterranean prompted by the discovery of the Göktepe quarries has shown that material from this source was widely used in the second and early third centuries AD for high-quality statuary. The team responsible for this work have provisionally identified statues in Göktepe marble in Asia Minor, Greece, North Africa, Italy, Spain, and southern Gaul. There are a number of other statues in black marble in North Africa which betray strong stylistic similarities with examples from Aphrodisias, including the black child from Sousse and a dancer from El Jem.[113] Göktepe marble, furthermore, was not the only material from the region around Aphrodisias used for statuary overseas: as we saw in Chapter 5, white marble from the so-called City Quarries has been identified at several sites in the Levant, notably at Caesarea Maritima and Caesarea Philippi.[114] Not all of these works seem to have been carved by Aphrodisians: some of the statues identified as having been carved in Göktepe

---

[111] *CIG* III.6233; Toynbee 1951: 27, 31; Strong and Claridge 1976: 195.
[112] Attanasio, Bruno, and Yavuz 2009; also Floriani Squarciapino 1943: 32–3.
[113] De Chaisemartin 2007: 207–12, 216–21.
[114] See Chapter 5: Materials for statuary (p. 181); also Friedland 2012.

marble show no stylistic similarities at all with Aphrodisian work. However, the majority can be linked with some confidence to Aphrodisians, either on stylistic or epigraphic grounds. If these statues were carved in the place where they were displayed then the carvers responsible clearly brought their materials with them or ordered them in from the quarries close to their hometown. However, we should also not rule out the possibility that some were simply dispatched from Aphrodisias fully finished. Aphrodisias was a medium-sized town and it seems unlikely that it could ever have produced enough sculptors to populate all of the sites at which these materials were used. There was apparently a wide market for Aphrodisian products, a fact further attested to by inscriptions from Apateira and Hypaipa in Asia Minor referring to Aphrodisian carvings—though of what sort is not clear.[115] These inscriptions have been interpreted variously as referring either to the type of product, the marble of these objects or the carvers responsible, but considering the evidence from elsewhere both marble and carvers might have been Aphrodisian.

Perhaps the most famous Aphrodisians is this context are Flavius Zenon and Flavius Chryseros who are named on the bases of several of the statues of the famous Esquiline group, now in the Ny Carlsberg Glyptotek (Figs. 8.8, 8.9, and 8.10).[116] This group includes five statues, representing a satyr with the infant Dionysos, Hercules, Poseidon, Helios, and another god, perhaps Zeus, as well as three further plinths and several fragments of legs.[117] Zenon is named on the plinths of the satyr and the Hercules and Chryseros on those of the Poseidon and the Helios, as well as two of the additional plinths. These pieces were all found broken up and reused in a series of walls exposed during building work on the Esquiline in Rome in 1886. Other fragments were found alongside them which never made in to Copenhagen, including inscriptions mentioning these two sculptors again, as well as two other Aphrodisians, a Flavius Andronikos and a Polyneikes.[118] These walls have been dated to the fourth century AD by La Rocca, a period in which much of this area on the Esquiline was rebuilt.[119] This date is intriguing because, though these statues have been widely dated to the second century AD on stylistic grounds, their inscriptions appear to be later. Flavius Zenon, in fact, is named on one of the other inscriptions found on the Esquiline as a high priest and *perfectissimus* (διασημότατος) and is also attested at Aphrodisias as a high priest and *comes* in two further inscriptions.[120] For a provincial to use the title *perfectissimus* is unknown before the fourth century AD, while the term *comes* was only used

[115] These inscriptions come from Apateira and Hypaipa: *IvEphesos* 3214, 3803; Drew-Bear 1980: 535–6 n. 120; De Chaisemartin 1999: 264. The adjective is Ἀφροδεισιακός.

[116] Moltesen 2000; Smith 2011: 74.

[117] Moltesen 2000: 112–21.

[118] Moltesen 2000: 126–7.

[119] La Rocca 1987: 11.

[120] Roueché and Erim 1982: 103–9; Floriani Squarciapino 1983; Moltesen 2000: 123.

Fig. 8.8. Statue of a satyr and the infant Dionysos signed by Flavius Zenon from the Esquiline, now in the Ny Carlsberg Glyptotek, Copenhagen (photo: author, used with permission of the Ny Carlsberg Glyptotek).

Fig. 8.9. Detail of the inscription mentioning Flavius Zenon on statue of a satyr and infant Dionysos in the Ny Carlsberg Glyptotek, Copenhagen (photo: author, used with permission of the Ny Carlsberg Glyptotek).

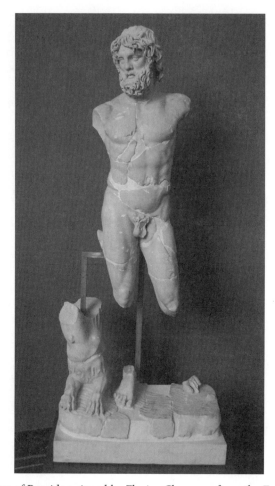

Fig. 8.10. Statue of Poseidon signed by Flavius Chryseros from the Esquiline, now in the Ny Carlsberg Glyptotek, Copenhagen (photo: author, used with permission of the Ny Carlsberg Glyptotek).

for imperial companions prior to AD 320. Interestingly, Flavius Andronikos, one of the other other Aphrodisians named in the fragments from the Esquiline, is honoured as a *perfectissimus* in his hometown.[121] We have already seen that a sculptor named Polyneikes is attested at Aphrodisias in the third century AD.[122]

These inscriptions, then, all appear to date to the fourth century AD—or, in the case of Polyneikes, perhaps the third century AD. This means that either the stylistic dating of the statues is wrong, and they are in fact later than is

[121] Roueché and Erim 1982: 104–9.   [122] Roueché and Erim 1982: 102–3.

often assumed, or these inscriptions were simply added to old statues.[123] Zenon and Andronikos were certainly not ordinary carvers, to judge from their social standing, and were at the very least workshop-owners.[124] However, we might also imagine a new role for these individuals, as neither carvers nor even workshop-owners but dealers in secondhand, or rather 'antique', statues. Works of this kind, many of them quite old, were continually moved and re-erected, sometimes adjusted, throughout Late Antiquity at Aphrodisias and it is possible that Flavius Zenon took advantage of this activity to sell certain prominent pieces on the Rome art market.[125] The statue depicting the satyr and infant Dionysos, of course, is almost identical in form to the pair in two sizes from the Sculptor's Workshop at Aphrodisias, both of which appear to have been old statues taken down, repaired, and awaiting resale.[126]

Analysis of the material that these statues were carved in adds another dimension to this debate. Initial isotopic analysis suggested they were Luna marble, a finding which was used to support the theory that they were carved by immigrant Aphrodisians in Rome.[127] However, recent reanalysis, making use of improved comparative datasets, has shown that they are actually carved in marble from Göktepe, near Aphrodisias.[128] This changes things consider-ably for while it is still possible that they were carved in Rome by Aphrodisian sculptors importing Göktepe marble, it is also possible that they were simply carved in Aphrodisias and exported fully finished. While this does not answer the question of when or where they were carved it certainly opens up a series of possibilities.

What these examples demonstrate, in sum, is that Aphrodisians were well known for their skill in carving and their products were highly sought after. Individual carvers exploited this renown in different ways, some clearly operating out of their home city, others probably travelling to complete commissions, and at least a few basing themselves permanently overseas. Their preference, in all of these cases, was for their local marble from the City Quarries or the higher-quality material from Göktepe. These sculptors were independent craftsmen and how they worked no doubt depended on their connections overseas, the demands of their clients, and the quality of their products, rather than any centrally determined policy. Such was the demand for Aphrodisian products at Rome that even as late as the fourth

---

[123] On the fourth-century AD date, see Hannestad 1990: 516–17.

[124] Roueché and Erim 1982: 113–14; Smith 2011: 65.

[125] On the redeployment of statues at Aphrodisias, Smith 2006: no. 52, 57, 58 (from the Agora Gate), 30, 31, 39, 40, 51 (from the theatre); 2007 (from the Hadrianic baths).

[126] On the Copenhagen piece, Poulsen 1951: 363–4, no. 521; Moltesen 1990: 139; and on the Aphrodisian statues, Erim 1974; Rockwell 1991: 130.

[127] Moltesen 1988: 436–9; 1990; Matthews and Walker 1990.

[128] The results of this reanalysis were presented by M. Bruno, D. Attanasio, W. Prochaska, and B. Yavuz at ASMOSIA X in Rome in June 2012.

century AD Flavius Zenon and his colleagues were potentially profiting from the trade in old masterpieces.

WORKSHOP PRACTICES AND PRODUCTION METHODS

Moving from questions of quarrying and distribution to how statue carving was actually undertaken, it is striking how little good evidence we have for this. This is partly because of the comparative scarcity of part-finished statues in comparison to the large number of sarcophagi and architectural elements preserved at all stages of working. While a part-finished sarcophagus or even column or capital was still useable, a roughed-out statue was not. They were usually discarded or carved into something else. At the same time, finds from the quarries suggest that it was comparatively rare for statues to be roughed out prior to onward transport. Despite this, certain conclusions can be drawn about the general approaches taken by carvers to transform these raw materials into statues.

Stages of production

There were a wide range of ways in which a carver could complete a statue and a range of tools at their disposal. In the Roman world most carvers used the point chisel for roughing out and then progressed to the flat or round-headed chisel for finer work, finishing the surface with rasps or abrasives.[129] A tooth chisel was often used between point and flat chisel and the drill was widely employed for achieving depth, though these tools were by no means employed by every carver. Which tools were used, and how they were used, varied by region but also between individual carvers.[130]

How carvers approached the blocks from which they were to carve their products also varied, though some general approaches can be recognized. Analysis of the series of roughed-out statues from the Xylophagou quarries shows that the carvers responsible worked with the point chisel from the front of the block to the back, defining the figure as they went; this meant that the design could be changed if a flaw was discovered in the stone but also that the mass of stone left at the back supported the object while it was being worked on.[131] There are parallels here with what has already been observed on

---

[129] On the tools employed, Rockwell 1993: 31–54.
[130] Claridge 1985: 113–16.   [131] Hollinshead 2002: 225–7.

sarcophagi. The collection of part-finished material from the Sculptor's Workshop at Aphrodisias is also illuminating from this perspective. This workshop was probably running up until the end of the fourth century AD, but when it was established is less clear; it could date from as early as the mid second century AD.[132] Most of the finds from this site consist of portraits and ideal statues, that is of mythological subjects.[133] Again work seems to have progressed from front to back, roughing out completed with the point chisel, followed by more detailed carving with the round-headed and flat chisel. The tooth chisel, interestingly, seems not to have been used much at all, but this might be a result of the relatively late date of these pieces since this tool was certainly used at Aphrodisias earlier.[134] The nature of this work means that it is often difficult to tell whether unfinished pieces carved in this way were meant to be reliefs or statues in the round when completed. The unfinished relief of an athlete of the Polykleitan Diskobolos type now in the museum at the site, found in the area of the Bouleuterion, was aborted midway through this process, with the direction of work from front to back clearly visible (Fig. 8.11). In this case the background, which is still to be cut away, bears the marks of the point chisel, while the body of the athlete has already been detailed and smoothed with flat chisel and rasp. These two stages, then, seem not to be divided between carvers but carried out in steps by the same individual. If this was to be a statue in the round then the next stage would have been to carve away the background with the point chisel before modelling and smoothing the rear side of the statue.

Our only detailed visual evidence for how these workshops might have been organized is the decorated fragment of a sarcophagus from Ephesos, now in Istanbul (Fig. 8.12).[135] Three working scenes are represented: from left to right, a seated master carver, wearing a tunic, puts the finishing touches to a statue of a man wearing a himation; next a standing assistant polishes a carved table leg on a work bench; and finally a standing master carver again finishes the detailed drapery of a bust, with an assistant behind him holding his tools. The structure of the scenes is reminiscent, albeit in miniature form, of the baking scenes on the monument of M. Virgilius Eurysaces at Rome.[136] Ancient carving workshops are usually assumed to have been small enterprises with only a handful of workers. Certainly the evidence provided by inscriptions on bronze statues from Rhodes from the fourth century BC to first century AD suggests that most workshops were essentially family units.[137] Dentzer has identified families of sculptors stretching over

---

[132] Van Voorhis 1999: 40–3.   [133] Van Voorhis 1999: 7–9, 44–67.
[134] Van Voorhis 1999: 111; also Rockwell 1991: 141–2. On the tooth chisel, Nylander 1991; and its use on the Sebasteion, Rockwell 1990.
[135] Mendel 1912–14: no. 13; also Bouras 2009: 497; Smith 2011: 67.
[136] Petersen 2003.   [137] Goodlett 1991: 676–78; also Conlin 1997: 30.

Fig. 8.11. Part-finished relief of an athlete from Aphrodisias (photo: courtesy New York University excavations at Aphrodisias).

Fig. 8.12. Fragment of a sarcophagus base depicting workshop scenes from Ephesos, now in Istanbul Archaeological Museum (photo: author, used with permission of Istanbul Archaeological Museum).

multiple generations in the epigraphic record of the town of Sī in Syria, while on a funerary altar from Kirgil in Turkey a stonemason Euprepes credits his father Trophimos and mother Asklepiodora with teaching him his trade.[138] Even though they are unreliable sources, most representations of carving workshops also tend to depict no more than a few workers.[139] Just because

---

[138] Dentzer 1986: 414; *MAMA* IX, no. 198a.
[139] Zimmer 1982: 35–7, 153–61 (nos. 75–83).

one or two workers are represented does not mean more were never employed, of course, but still the focus on small groups of carvers is suggestive.

Division of labour

What the images on the Ephesos sarcophagus fragment suggest, in particular, is at the very least a basic division of labour, in this case between sculptor, assistant, and also—assuming he is not the same assistant—polisher. Van Voorhis, in her study of the material from the Sculptor's Workshop at Aphrodisias, notes that the portraits seem to have passed through two main stages of work: they were first roughed out and carved until almost finished using the point and flat chisel but then left for separate working with the drill and polishing. The unfinished Late Antique statue of a magistrate from the workshop never received this second stage of work on its head, even though the body was finished, further indicating that these two parts of the figure were treated separately (Fig. 8.13).[140] This broad division between rough and fine work again finds parallels in later periods and notably the work of Michelangelo. In one of his letters Michelangelo mentions a contract with a group of carvers at Carrara to rough-out eight blocks of marble for eight statues of two basic sizes (for the façade of the basilica of San Lorenzo in Florence).[141] Exactly how much work they were meant to carry out is not stated but Michelangelo was evidently still responsible for the detailed finishing work.

At Aphrodisias, the initial stages of roughing out might well have been undertaken by apprentices or junior carvers. In their hypothetical reconstruction of the statue-carving process Boschung and Pfanner assume the presence of both master carvers and assistants, the latter responsible for the bulk of the carving right up until the final stages.[142] In his analysis of the Apadana reliefs at Persepolis, Roaf proposed a similar division with the master carvers working on the most important details of each scene and their assistants completing the rest.[143] At Aphrodisias, we know a little about how these apprentices or assistants were trained. Numerous roughly carved feet, either single or in pairs, and occasionally hands, have been found at Aphrodisias and appear to be training pieces used by apprentices to hone their skills.[144] Even nowadays aspiring carvers at Carrara have to carve these same complex body parts as part of their education.[145] At least one abandoned statue found in the Sculptor's Workshop also became a practice block for apprentices keen to

---

[140] Van Voorhis 1999: 116–18.   [141] Stone and Stone 1962: 104.
[142] Boschung and Pfanner 1988: 13–15, esp. fig. 7.   [143] Roaf 1983: 27.
[144] Van Voorhis 1998; on possible apprentice pieces at Laodikeia-on-the-Lykos, Şimşek 2011: 338–9; on apprentice quarrymen at Mons Claudianus, Bülow-Jacobsen 2009: no. 864.
[145] Pers. comm. Peter Rockwell.

Fig. 8.13. Part-finished statue of a Late Antique magistrate from the Sculptor's Workshop, Aphrodisias (photo: courtesy New York University excavations at Aphrodisias).

experiment with newly learnt techniques.[146] The young Lucian, of course, was very briefly apprenticed to his uncle, a famous sculptor, and describes the beating he received on his first day for breaking a marble panel with the first strike of his chisel.[147] While the character of the uncle is described specifically as a sculptor (ἑρμογλύφεύς, literally a carver of herms), the young apprentice is to be educated by him as a stone-cutter (ἑργάτης λίθου), mason (σύναρμοστής λίθου), and sculptor, suggesting a broad-based approach to training.

We might also speculate on a certain division of labour between carvers with different specialities. Portrait carvers, for instance, were perhaps distinct from carvers of decorative forms or drapery.[148] There is certainly good

---

[146] Van Voorhis 1999: 128–31; 1998; also Conlin 1997: 30–4.

[147] Lucian, *The Dream or Lucian's Career* 2.

[148] On this point with regard to the Sculptor's Workshop, Van Voorhis 1999: 135–6; see also, Boschung and Pfanner 1988: 15.

evidence on architectural reliefs elsewhere in the city to support such a division. The blocks making up the well-known mask and garland frieze from the South Agora went through a number of hands. An initial stage of roughing out with the point chisel, which could have been carried out at the quarries, was followed by the carving of the garland, with space for the mask left rough. These masks, finished in a range of styles and using various models, were then presumably carved by the most skilful carver within each workshop.[149] Again, as already discussed with sarcophagi, the ability of these carvers to divide stages in the working process between multiple specialists depended ultimately on the size of their market.

There is, though, good evidence for the cooperation, probably within a single workshop, of craftsmen of different media. In the early third century AD at Aphrodisias, a statue-maker (ἀγαλματογλύφος) named M. Aurelius Glykon was buried in the same sarcophagus as a paint-supplier (πῖμεντάριος), suggesting that they worked together, probably in the same workshop; statue production, of course, required paint in some quantity.[150] Letter-carvers could also have been separate specialists. A bilingual inscription from Palermo advertises the skills of one letter-carver: 'inscriptions laid out and cut here for religious buildings and public works'.[151] However, this is unlikely to have been any carver's sole focus, as another advertisement from Rome makes clear: 'if you need inscriptions cut for tombstones, or any sort of stonework done, this is the place'.[152] Inscriptions were this individual's speciality but he could turn his hand to anything else that the customer required.

Dividing work between carvers of different specialities would certainly have increased productivity. There were, though, few other ways in which this could be done. The carving of detailed forms in stone is laborious and time-consuming process and there were no mechanical solutions that could have made it any quicker in the Roman period. On larger projects, though, it would have been possible to employ more than one carver on the same statue. In the specialist temple carving workshops in modern India it is common to find two carvers working together on carvings no more than 2 m in height, though they tend to lie them on the ground.[153] Considering this, two or more carvers could comfortably have worked side by side on the Breifurt and Şile statues. In addition, improved tools would have helped speed up the carving process. Claridge has suggested that tools, in fact, did improve, and that probably from the first century BC harder iron chisels became more common;

---

[149] De Chaisemartin 1999: 264–7, who disagrees slightly about the order the mask and garland were carved in but, nevertheless, notes that they were probably done by different carvers.

[150] Smith 2011: 65.

[151] *CIL* X.7296 (translation after Ireland 1983: 220).

[152] *CIL* VI.9556 (translation after Carroll 2006: 105).

[153] Pers. comm. Choodie Shivaram and Peter Rockwell.

steel tools are mentioned in one of the *ostraka* from Mons Claudianus discussed in Chapter 6.[154]

Aside from adding to the number of workers involved and the quality of the tools used, the only way that Roman carvers might have substantially increased their efficiency, though not necessarily the speed of their work, would have been through the use of more sophisticated measuring tools. Raised measuring knobs have been found on lots of Roman statues, a considerable number of which have been catalogued by Pfanner.[155] It has generally been argued that these knobs were used to assist the carver during the copying process and that they corresponded to marked points on the model, usually assumed to have been in clay, plaster, or wax.[156] They are typically found in groups of three and acted as points of reference from which the carver could layout the rest of the design and ensure that it was correctly proportioned. Whether an instrument like the modern 'pointing machine', a T-shaped device to which a jointed mobile arm is attached, was used for this transferral of measurements is doubtful; there are none of the characteristic drill holes left by this instrument visible on Roman statues.[157] More likely a simple frame was employed from which a plumb line could be suspended and measurements taken with a ruler.[158] It is worth noting, though, that these knobs are found on statues which seem not to have been copies, such as private portraits or other subjects which are unparalleled: the early third-century AD male portrait in the Munich Glytothek discussed by Pfanner is a good example.[159] In this case and others, these measuring knobs seem simply to have been used by the carver to assist with laying out the features of the portrait. While established measuring systems did exist, then, there is no evidence for any specific tool to rival the modern 'pointing machine', itself probably developed in the eighteenth century.[160]

CONCLUSIONS

As Apollonios of Tyana, in Philostratos' biography of him, is said to have observed:

---

[154] Pers. Comm. Claridge; see also Chapter 6: Documentary evidence (pp. 212–13).

[155] Pfanner 1989: 236–51.

[156] Blümel 1955: 44–56; clay models by the famous sculptor Arkesilaos, which were highly sought after by other artists, are mentioned in Pliny the Elder XXXV.155; on this point, see also Hollinshead 2002: 228–9.

[157] Strong and Claridge 1976: 202–3; Rockwell 1993: 118–20.

[158] Blümel 1955: 54, fig. 42.

[159] Pfanner 1989: 244–5, fig. 45a–b (inv. 542).   [160] Rockwell 1993: 118–20.

All the arts that exist among mankind have different spheres of action, but all aim at money, whether little or much, or simply enough to subsist on. This includes not only the menial arts, but all the others too, the learned ones and the semi-learned ones alike, except for that of true wisdom . . . and by the 'semi-learned' [I mean] those of painting, sculpture, of statue makers, of pilots, of farmers as long as they follow the seasons, since these arts too are not far removed from learning.[161]

Carvers, like other craftsmen, had to live off their work. They were skilled workers who needed to make a profit from the sale of their products and as such would always have looked for ways to increase their efficiency and reduce their overheads. Improved tools and working methods were certainly explored and their can be little doubt that there was sufficient demand for statuary in the Roman world to sustain a large population of carvers. It is also clear that carvers, especially in the first two centuries AD, adapted to meet demands from their customers for the highest-quality materials. Like sarcophagus producers, statue carvers in regions without local marble sources increasingly imported materials, usually in unworked form but perhaps occasionally also roughed out according to their specific instructions. There is no convincing evidence to suggest that statues were routinely part-finished at the quarries in anticipation of demand, though. The statues that are known from quarrying sites are varied in form, scale, and level of finish. These were pieces being worked on by carvers who would then have travelled with them to where they would be finished or dispatch them to another team with whom they were in close communication. Carvers did travel. They certainly migrated to areas where there was demand for their services, sometimes permanently but perhaps also on a temporary basis for the finishing of particular commissions. Carvers apparently travelled in large numbers to work on major building projects, and the contractors responsible for supplying these projects would probably always have needed both architectural and sculptural specialists, so we might reasonably suppose that at any one point in time there would have been a significant population of stone carvers in transit in the Roman world. Even so, there would have been occasions when it was preferable to dispatch finished works, a practice attested to by both the shipwreck and literary evidence.

---

[161] Philostratos, *Life of Apollonios of Tyana* VIII.7.3 (translated by F. C. Conybeare).

9

Final Remarks

The use of stone in vast quantities is a ubiquitous and defining feature of the material culture of the Roman world. In aggregate terms, far more stone was quarried and consumed in building and sculptural projects between the beginning of the first century BC and the end of the third century AD than at any time previously and for at least 1,000 years afterwards. As Walker has put it, the fortunes of the trade in stone objects 'cannot be separated from the wider currents of the economic history of the empire'.[1] Stone was a commodity much like any other and the geographical and chronological development of the stone trade strongly reflect wider economic patterns. In particular, the regional and long distance trade in decorative stones as well as more ordinary materials reaches its zenith in the second century AD, when the trade in all commodities appears to peak, and similarly trails away after the second quarter of the third century AD. Despite this, the stone trade and its potential to further inform our understanding of the Roman economy is often neglected in wider studies of this topic. Much of this potential has been highlighted in the preceding chapters and it is the aim of this final chapter to draw some of this together, in particular as it relates to the role of the state, connectivity, and manufacturing.

THE ROLE OF THE STATE

A significant amount of the discernible distribution patterns of material goods in the Roman world are the result of imperially orchestrated redistributive mechanisms, the importance of which in the wider economy is difficult to overstate.[2] The exceptionally long-distance movement of decorative stones from imperially controlled quarries to imperially funded building projects is

---

[1] Walker 1988: 192.
[2] On this point, in the context of the ceramic evidence, Peacock and D. F. Williams 1986: 57.

one of the more spectacular illustrations of this fact and has been widely remarked upon as such, even in mainstream economic studies.[3] As we saw in Chapters 3 and 5, the imperial administration went to enormous efforts, in terms of finances and manpower, to secure access to the sources of the most prestigious decorative stones and to ensure that they could be moved in quantity all around the Mediterranean. The fruit of this labour can be seen in the impressive array of materials employed at Rome, a site entirely lacking local decorative stone quarries, and other set-piece projects across the empire, foremost among them Lepcis Magna. In supplying these structures the parameters that so clearly shaped the distribution of stone outside of the imperial orbit were routinely overcome; in practice, limits to imperial redistribution, even of that most bulky and awkward of cargoes, were few.[4]

This was the prime purpose of imperial involvement in the stone trade: to ensure that imperial building projects were supplied with the range and quantity of decorative stones that reflected their intended majesty. The deliberate monopolization of these resources was probably never the aim. Officials at imperial quarries controlled exploitation, often through the strategic use of private contractors, and once demand from imperial projects was met materials from these sites did enter the non-imperial market. As the example of the hapless Aurelius Hermaios showed, even porphyry could be bought.[5] As Lo Cascio has put it, with regard to other imperially orchestrated distributive systems, where 'there is no complete control of resources . . . there is no total redistribution'; some of this material, in other words, would always have entered the open market.[6] What this meant in practice was that the most sought after polychrome stones were also likely to have been difficult and expensive to acquire in bulk, such was the demand for them from imperial projects.

The model initially constructed by Fant, which saw material from imperial quarries redistributed first to Rome and only secondarily from there elsewhere, in many ways echoes that proposed by Hirschfeld and others concerning grain.[7] On the basis of a passage in Josephus, in which Herod is recorded paying for the right to import grain from Egypt after a bad harvest, Hirschfeld argued that this grain was strictly controlled and only exceptionally distributed elsewhere than Rome.[8] Imperially authorized grain imports, attested at

---

[3] Jongman 2007: 592; Mattingly 2007: 224.

[4] For an interesting illustration of how 'construction projects undertaken by the Roman state need not have followed the general principles of cost utilized by archaeologists and historians', in this case with regard to road building in the Tiber valley, Black, Browning, and Laurence 2008: 708–14, 722–7.

[5] See Chapter 2: Cost of architectural elements (p. 25).

[6] Lo Cascio 2006: 218; Fant 2008b: 580; on what 'state' control might mean in this period more generally, Hirschfeld 1905: 174–6; Fitzler 1910: 112–13; Millar 1963: 29–30.

[7] Casson 1980: 21–5.   [8] Hirschfeld 1905: 235.

Tralles and Ephesos, could be used to support such a reconstruction.[9] But
these texts need to be set in context. The reply of a second-century emperor in
response to complaints from the grain-traders of Ephesos makes it clear that
restrictions on access to Egyptian grain were only in place when there were
shortages resulting from inopportune flooding.[10] In fact imperial gifts of grain
were part of a broader spectrum of gifts of grain from members of the local
elite. Permission was not normally required and gifts resulted not from
monopolistic ownership of Egyptian grain but from a desire by the emperor
both to ensure the supply of grain to Rome and to engage in the normal
currency of elite beneficence.[11]

Imperial quarries, then, were often worked by private contractors, who
probably sold on at least some of the material that they produced, and it
seems likely that non-imperial personnel were also responsible for shipping
the decorative stones used at Rome in such quantities. There is no evidence at
all for imperially owned transport ships and indeed the shipwreck data
indicate that a range of sizes of vessels were used to move stone. The imperial
administration probably paid private shippers to ship small consignments of
material alongside their other cargo or hired whole ships for larger jobs.[12]
What this shows is that drawing too sharp a distinction between imperial and
non-imperial activity in the stone trade can be misleading.[13] As Paterson has
put it, with regard to other economic sectors, 'they are often part of the same
continuum, but reflect the preoccupations and perceptions of people at different points in the chain'.[14] In his discussion of the different levels of economic
activity Mattingly also stresses this point: while we can identify distinctive
patterns stimulated by imperial demand and driven by state-coordinated
efforts, these often overlap and connect with non-imperial activity.[15]
The imperial administration relied on private quarrymen, shippers, and
stone-workers to achieve their vast building projects and imperial financing
would have represented an important source of revenue for all of these parties.
It was not only those who handled prestigious materials who were set to
benefit. For all the decorative stones employed in imperial projects these
were still structures firmly rooted in their local environment and they made
substantial use of local materials. The examples of the Tetrarchic structures at
Palmyra and the various third-century complexes in Moesia Superior and
Pannonia are cases in point.[16] In addition, as seen in Chapter 3, at certain
quarries imperial and non-imperial quarrying appears to have taken place side

[9] *CIG* II.2927, 2930; Casson 1980: 31 n. 20; Strubbe 1987.   [10] *AE* 1968, 478.
[11] Strubbe 1989: 106–8.   [12] Fant 2012: 529.
[13] On this point, Fant 2008*b*: 580; Ward-Perkins 1980*b*: 37.
[14] Paterson 1998: 157.
[15] Mattingly 2007: 221–2.
[16] On the local stones used in building the palace at Sirmium, Rižnar and Jovanović 2006;
Djurić et al. 2012.

by side. While the imperial redistribution of decorative stones took place on a scale which was unprecedented and has probably never since been replicated, it would be wrong to separate it entirely from the ordinary stone trade which it influenced so greatly.

DISTRIBUTION AND CONNECTIVITY

At the same time, we should be careful not to overstate the wider impact of the imperial redistribution of decorative stone. While the highest concentrations of decorative stones are associated with imperial building projects, it is clear that in aggregate terms far more stone was moved all distances to satisfy demand from the non-imperial sector.[17] Most quarries were small-scale enterprises rooted in their local markets, often set up directly to supply specific cities or even one-off projects. They were predominately under private or perhaps municipal control. Even the most prestigious white marble quarries stayed, in part at least, under local control: those at Luna under the nearby colony, those on Prokonnesos in the hands of Kyzikos.[18] At both of these sites, a range of different users were present at any one time, among them representatives of the imperial administration.

The predominately local or regional distribution of stone is entirely in keeping with what has been observed for other commodities. As Bresson has noted, relatively few materials were moved all around the Mediterranean in the Roman period.[19] To quote Horden and Purcell, 'the movement of goods associated with connectivity across "short distances" take up a far larger portion of the overall picture than the usual narrative would suggest'.[20] In the case of the stone trade, the weight of most stone objects put significant limitations on the extent to which they were transported overland in particular. Monolithic columns made distinctly awkward cargoes. At inland sites, far from the well-known sources of decorative stones, most imports were employed for revetment and flooring, sawn up to be put to maximum effect. Commissioners at coastal sites were able to engage far more intensively with this trade, drawing on materials from a wider area, both for decorative and more functional purposes. Since stone is so difficult to move, which materials were used where and for what purposes is revealing of both the connectedness of the Roman world and the financial clout of the customers who had to pick up the bill.

---

[17] On the need to contextualize imperial activity, Harris 1993*b*.
[18] See Chapter 3: Private and municipal quarries (pp. 53–61).
[19] Bresson 2005: 95–100.   [20] Horden and Purcell 2000: 150.

All this being said, what is remarkable in the first three centuries AD, and even after, is the extent to which customers were prepared to pay these costs, to pay the vast sums necessary to move large columns far inland—to Autun, Sagalassos, and Palmyra, for instance—and transport carved marble sarcophagi enormous distances both by sea and overland. These were high-quality, symbolically charged artefacts for which the substantial costs involved were evidently considered worth paying. At Rome, but also at other large urban centres on the Mediterranean, the use of imported decorative stones became normalized in this period. This clearly astounded contemporary authors, among them Strabo, Pliny the Elder, and Seneca.[21] However, the ideology of stone use even filtered down beyond the limited sphere of the most prestigious decorative stones and an awareness of the suitability of more ordinary materials for different jobs can also be noted. Limestones which could hold fine detail, appropriate for sumptuous architectural carving and sculpture, were routinely moved long distances: stone from the Bois des Lens quarries was used all across southern Gaul, while Norroy limestone was shipped down the Moselle to the cities of the Rhineland and even as far as Britain, where again we find a range of limestones being moved around regionally, even very early on in the Roman period.[22] At Hierapolis and Sagalassos, as we have seen, the use of local stones was deemed worth celebrating in inscriptions.[23] These were high-quality stones in their local and regional contexts, even if they were fairly ordinary when compared to the finest Mediterranean marbles.

The shipwreck evidence adds crucial insight into these different levels of activity: the short-distance movement of building stone of the kind revealed by the Carry-le-Rouet and Blackfriars 1 shipwrecks; the regional shipping of higher-quality materials, as seen in the numerous relatively small shipwrecks off southern France; and the long-distance transport of decorative stones, both architectural elements and sarcophagi, much of which was centred on Rome. Shipwrecks are also revealing of the mechanisms underlying these patterns. Most stone was probably only transported long distances when it had a buyer secured and indeed the known stone cargoes are relatively homogenous, in terms of the origins of materials on board and the finish of the artefacts. This suggests that this material was predominately shipped directly from the quarries or nearby ports to as close as possible to where it was intended to be used. Stone, especially decorative stone, was an expensive and heavy cargo, awkward to load and unload, and was unsuited to indirect commerce. While this was probably the rule for large objects there are exceptions. Small blocks of decorative stone, precut veneer panels of the kind found at the Torre Sgarrata and Porto Nuovo shipwrecks, and even carved statues to judge

---

[21] Strabo, *Geography* XII.8.14; Pliny the Elder XXXVI.1; Seneca, *Epistles* LXXXVI.6.
[22] See Chapter 5: Case study 5: the Rhineland and Britain (pp. 162–3).
[23] See Chapter 2: 'Foreign rocks' (p. 16).

from Philostratos' text discussed above, could all have been produced with no specific buyers in mind and distributed via merchants engaged in coastal tramping. It would be wrong, in sum, to assume that any single mode of distribution dominated.

The physical movement of stone of all types reveals the scale of financial and logistical investment that sustained this trade. However, it also demonstrates the awareness of both stone carvers and their customers of the materials available to them and their willingness to explore their potential. While stones themselves were moved long distances, knowledge about them and their qualities travelled further. Ordinary customers were well informed and there evidently developed a class of merchants specialized in supplying them with the materials that they wanted, providing the connection between these individuals and the increasingly disparate quarries. References to these merchants, and the contractors who supplied building materials, are scant in the epigraphic record but they are presumably to be associated with the various *marmorarii*, of different specialisms, who turn up all across the Roman world.[24]

MODELLING PRODUCTION

Aggregate demand for stone increased enormously between the first century BC and second century AD, and disproportionately high demand in this period was placed on the handful of major quarries which targeted high-quality or coloured marble and/or were well suited to supply distant markets. While in most cases new quarries could be opened to supply specific demand on a local level, expansion at these major sites which supplied a much larger market was often limited by geology and logistics. The model developed by Ward-Perkins sought to explain how producers at these sites were able to meet this upsurge in demand and it remains highly influential.[25] In particular, the notion that the major quarries of the Roman world engaged in a form of serial or mass production of standardized objects to stock is widely held.

There can be little doubt that certain objects in the Roman world were produced in this way: ceramic vessels, glassware, metal objects (arms and armour, vessels, nails, and coins), and bricks.[26] These objects were indeed produced in series, the work broken into stages divided between different workers, the product highly standardized. We might even describe their production as quasi-industrial: as Harris has noted, 'any production of artefacts in large numbers can without great discomfort be called *industry*', and

---

[24] Calabi Limentani 1961*b*.   [25] See especially Ward-Perkins 1980*a*; 1980*b*.
[26] On ceramic production, Marichal 1988; on weaponry, Sim 1995; on bricks, Helen 1975; and on mass production in general, A. I. Wilson 2008.

this highly articulated division of labour is the basis of mass production, which Wilson simply defines as 'the production of very large quantities of the same artefact, or of essentially similar artefacts, by the same production means'.[27] Whether stone objects can be legitimately classed as mass produced in the Roman period, though, is far from clear. They were certainly produced in large quantities and smaller items—vessels, items of furniture, statuettes—probably did pass through the hands of multiple highly specialist workers, much like ceramics or other manufactured commodities. However, individual carving workshops probably remained relatively small and larger stone objects— architectural elements, sarcophagi, statues—were expensive, complicated projects that consumed enormous quantities of labour and material, and usually had to be tailored to the specific needs of the customer.[28] The evidence presented in Chapters 6, 7, and 8 does not need repeating here but shows that production-to-stock of these objects was probably never the norm. In the main such items were entirely ill-suited to this mode of production, with the possible exception of roughly squared blocks or perhaps simply hollowed-out sarcophagus chests. Quarrying and production was more responsive than Ward-Perkins' model allowed and heavily determined by very specific patterns of customer demand.

This does not mean, though, that the producers of stone objects did not take steps to rationalize their production in the face of massive customer demand. As Stokes has put it, 'every artist has more than a passing interest in labour'.[29] Adding to their workforce was one way of increasing output, and it is clear that vast numbers of workers must have been involved in both quarrying and building, especially at imperially controlled sites, but it was also the case that over time techniques developed which would also have contributed to increased productivity. The practice of roughing out objects at the quarries before transporting them on for finishing elsewhere could well have led to a level of specialization, especially when the distances involved were too great for the same workers to be responsible for all of this work. Likewise, demand for objects in repetitive forms, whether architectural elements or statuary, would have facilitated production, further enabling specialization. These were largely accidental consequences of the patterns of demand which underpinned the long-distance stone trade but they would still have contributed towards productivity. To describe the latter as 'standardization', though, is misleading. These repetitive forms were not a result of production methods, of attempts to simplify forms and increase efficiency, but rather part of an established visual repertoire which individual commissioners bought into. Part-finished objects show that carvers tackled these forms in the same way again and again, often laying out guidelines to assist them during this work. Workers at different sites

---

[27] Harris 1980: 127; A. I. Wilson 2008: 394; and for objections, Pucci 1973: 261–5.
[28] On the size of workshops, Russell 2011*b*: 127–31.   [29] Stokes 1934: 109.

routinely approached these objects in the same way, as in the case of Corinthian capitals on Prokonnesos and at Luna, even if they exported them at different stages.[30] This is unsurprising: stone-working is a conservative and highly specialized craft and in order to avoid over-cutting, much more of a concern to a sculptor than to a bronze-, clay-, or even wood-worker, the carving process needs to be meticulously planned; a well-planned process eliminates waste, of both time and money.[31] What the material from the quarries, as well as finished structures, reveals is just how streamlined this planning and carving process became, especially by the second century AD.

EPILOGUE

The necessarily limited chronological focus of this study has meant that changes affecting the production and trade in stone objects after the end of the third century AD have not been considered in detail. However, this later period merits further attention. By the early fourth century AD, the golden age of public munificence at the local level had passed and this had an important impact on the aggregate market for stone. After a number of high profile materials had ceased to be quarried, additional steps were taken in the fourth century AD to stimulate renewed quarrying, both imperial and private.[32] In addition, a lack of demand for their services had made architects and stone-workers scarce. On 2 August 337, in an attempt to remedy this pressing skills shortage, the following edict was issued in the name of the recently deceased emperor Constantine:

> Artisans who live in each city and who practise the skills included in the appended list shall be free from all compulsory public services, since indeed their leisure should be spent in learning these skills whereby they may desire the more to become more proficient themselves and to instruct their children.[33]

Included in the appended list were architects, stone-cutters, stone-masons, painters, sculptors, statue-makers, mosaicists, and marble-workers. Three years earlier, Constantine had issued a similar edict urging 'those youths in the African provinces who are eighteen years old and have a taste for the liberal arts' to be encouraged to train as architects: 'there is a need of architects, but they do not exist'.[34] The contrast with the early second century AD could not be greater: this was a time when Trajan could advise the younger Pliny that

---

[30] See Chapter 6: Repeated designs (pp. 241–7).
[31] Rockwell 1993: 12–13; Varène 1975: 54–8.   [32] Carrié 1994; Padilla 1999.
[33] *Codex Theodosianus* 13.5.2.   [34] *Codex Theodosianus* 13.5.1.

'you cannot lack architects, for every province has skilled men trained for this work'.[35]

This apparent slump in activity, however, needs to be understood in context. The long-distance trade in decorative stones did not cease. The Marzamemi B and Ekinlik Adası shipwrecks, and possibly also the Dor 2001/1 wreck, attest to such a traffic.[36] Indeed, the number of shipwrecks datable to between the fourth and seventh centuries AD has been underestimated to date.[37] Imperial activity, in particular, boomed once more. Coloured stones were the mark of imperial power as never before and the moving of the capital eastwards appears to have reinvigorated production at the Aegean quarries.[38] New demand for architectural elements during the fourth century AD and later is especially clear on Prokonnesos.[39] Additionally, in his analysis of the production of Ionic capitals in Late Antiquity, Herrmann stresses that workshops continued to engage in the kind of specialization identifiable earlier and, despite its political redundancy, Rome remained a key player in this trade and a highly competitive market.[40]

Importantly, the long-distance transport of stone of all varieties did not end with the fall of Rome. As Greenhalgh has stressed, there were periods between the ninth and eleventh centuries when more stone was potentially moved around the Mediterranean than in similar periods in the first to third centuries AD.[41] And though the end points of this traffic and the motivation behind it were different, Arab sources from this later period offer a literal reflection of distributive practices in antiquity. They demonstrate, in a period that is far better documented, the continued importance of maritime transport dynamics for the distribution of stone objects and the enduring ideology of stone use.[42] As Ibn Khaldun observed, urbanity, stone use, and civilization remained intimately connected:

> When a city has been founded it has few houses, few construction materials and few wall coverings... Then the city grows, its population and its civilization develops. Construction materials increase, as do projects to be undertaken and the number of craftsmen, up to the point where a ceiling is reached. And then the decline begins, prosperity diminishes and the population falls. In consequence, people lose the habit of building elegant and solid structures. Available labour diminishes at the same time as the number of inhabitants. Scarcely any stone, marble or other materials are to be found. Second-hand stones are re-used, taken from empty buildings... The same materials are perpetually re-used, from palace

---

[35] Pliny the Younger, *Letters* X.40 (trans. B. Radice).
[36] Kapitän 1969; 1971; Günsenin 1997; Kahanov and Mor 2006.
[37] Russell 2013.
[38] Downey 1959 on the tombs of the Byzantine emperors.
[39] Asgari 1979.
[40] Herrmann 1988: 165–7; Herrmann and Newman 1995: 73.
[41] Greenhalgh 2006; 2008.   [42] Russell 2008: 107–8.

to palace, from house to house, until they are completely used up ... When cities fail, civilization then recedes, and the decrease in people entails a decrease in crafts, so that solid buildings are no longer constructed and ornamented. Materials such as stone, marble, and other things are now being imported scarcely at all and become unavailable.[43]

---

[43] Ibn Khaldun, *Al-Muqaddina* II.712 (translation from Greenhalgh 2006: 78).

Bibliography

Adam, J.-P. (1977). 'À propos du trilithon de Baalbek. Le transport et la mise en oeuvre des mégalithes', *Syria* 54: 31–63.

Adam, J.-P. (1983). *Dégradation et restauration de l'architecture pompéienne*. Paris.

Adam, J.-P. (1989). *La construction romaine: matériaux et techniques*. 2nd edn. Paris.

Adam, J.-P. and Varène, P. (1980). 'Une peinture romaine représentant une scène de chantier', *RA*: 213–38.

Adams, C. E. P. (2001). 'Who bore the burden? The organization of stone transport in Roman Egypt', in D. J. Mattingly and J. Salmon (eds), *Economies Beyond Agriculture in the Classical World*. London and New York, 171–92.

Adams, C. E. P. (2007). *Land Transport in Roman Egypt. A study of Economics and Administration in a Roman Province*. Oxford.

Adriani, A. (1961). *Repertorio d'arte dell'Egitto Greco-Romano, Serie A, Volume I*. Palermo.

Agus, M., Cara, S., Lazzarini, L., and Mola, M. (2006). 'Laboratory characterisation of black limestones (*neri antichi*) from Zeugitania (Tunisia)', *Marmora* 2: 71–82.

Agusta-Boularot, S., Gazenbeek, M., Marcadal, Y., and Paillet, J.-L. (1998). '*Glanum*, l'extension de la ville et sa périphérie', *Dossiers d'Archéologie* 237: 20–5.

Akerraz, A., Papi, E., Perugini, D., Poli, G., Gliozzo, E., Turbanti Memmi, I., and Dallai, L. (2009). 'I reperti in marmo', in E. Gliozzo, I. Turbanti Memmi, A. Akerraz, and E. Papi (eds), *Sidi Ali Ben Ahmed—Thamusida: 2. L'archeometria*. Rome, 73–84.

Alcock, S. E. (2007). 'The eastern Mediterranean', in W. Scheidel, E. L. Morris, and R. P. Saller (eds), *The Cambridge Economic History of the Greco-Roman World*. Cambridge, 671–97.

Alessio, A. (1995). 'Pulsano (Taranto), Torre Sgarrata', *Taras* 15.1: 149–51.

Alessio, A. and Zaccaria, A. (1997). 'Nuove ricerche sul relitto di San Pietro in Bevagna (Manduria—Taranto)', in *Atti del Convegno Nazionale di Archeologia Subacquea*. Bari, 211–24.

Alexander, J. S. (1995). 'Building stone from the East Midlands quarries: sources, transportation and usage', *Medieval Archaeology* 39: 107–35.

Alexandrescu-Vianu, M. (1970). 'Les sarcophages romains de Dobroudja', *RESE* 8.2: 269–328.

Àlvarez, A., Cebrián, R., and Rodà, I. (2008). 'El mármol de Almadén de la Plata y los *marmara* importados del foro de *Segobriga*', in T. Nogales and J.Beltrán (eds), *Marmora Hispania: explotación y uso de los materiales pétreos en la Hispania romana* (Hispania Antigua, Serie Arqueológica 2). Rome, 101–20.

Àlvarez, A., Domènech, A., Lapuente, M. P., Pitarch, À., and Royo, H. (2009a). *Marbles and Stones of Hispania: Exhibition Catalogue*. Tarragona.

Àlvarez, A., García-Entero, V., Gutiérrez, A., and Rodà, I. (2009b). *El marmor de Tarraco: explotació, utilització i commercialització de la pedra de Santa Tecla en època romana/Tarraco Marmor: The Quarrying, Use and Trade of Santa Tecla Stone in Roman Times* (Hic et Nunc 6). Tarragona.

Àlvarez, A., Gutiérrez, A., Lapuente, M. P., Pitarch, À., and Rodà, I. (2009c). 'The *marmor* of Tarraco or Santa Tecla stone (Tarragona, Spain)', in P. Jockey (ed.), *Leukos lithos. Marbres et autres roches de la Méditerranée antique: études interdisciplinaires. ASMOSIA VIII.* (Collection l'atelier méditerranéen). Paris, 129–40.

Àlvarez, A., Gutiérrez, A., and Rodà, I. (2010). 'Las rocas ornamentales en las provincias del imperio: el caso del Broccatello y la piedra de Santa Tecla', in S. Camporeale, H. Dessales, and A. Pizzo (eds), *Arqueología de la construcción II. Los procesos constructivos en el mundo romano: Italia y provincias orientales* (Anejos de Archivo Español de Arqueología 57). Madrid, 539–54.

Àlvarez, A., Marcias, J. M., Muñoz, A., Pitarch, À, Teixell, I., and Menchon, J. J. (2012). '*Marmora* used in the imperial cult area of Tarraco (Hispania Citerior)', in Gutiérrez, A., Lapuente, P., and Rodà, I. (eds), *Interdisciplinary Studies on Ancient Stone. ASMOSIA IX* (Documenta 23). Tarragona, 196–203.

Alzinger, W. (1966–7). 'Ritzzeichnungen in den Marmorbrüchen von Ephesos', *JÖAI* 48: 61–72.

Amadori, M. L., Lazzarini, L., Mariottini, M., Pecoraro, M., and Pensabene, P. (1998). 'Determinazione della provenienza dei marmi usati per alcuni monumenti antichi di Roma', in P. Pensabene (ed.), *Marmi antichi II: cave e tecnica di lavorazione, provenienze e distribuzione* (Studi Miscellanei 31). Rome, 45–56.

Ambrogi, A. (1993). 'Sarcofagi in granito di produzione egiziana', *Xenia Antiqua* 2: 103–10.

Amedick, R. (1991). *Die Sarkophage mit Darstellungen aus dem Menschenleben: Vita Privata* (Die antiken Sarkophagreliefs 1.4). Berlin.

Amores, F., Beltrán, J., and González, D. (2008). '*Marmora de Hispalis*: studio de los materiales pétreos recuperados en las excavaciones arqueológicas de "La Encarnación" (Sevilla)', in T. Nogales and J. Beltrán (eds), *Marmora Hispania: explotación y uso de los materiales pétreos en la Hispania romana* (Hispania Antigua, Serie Arqueológica 2). Rome, 212–29.

Anderson, J. D. (1992). *Roman Military Supply in North-East England. An Analysis of and Alternative to the Piercebridge Formula* (BAR British Series 224). Oxford.

Andreae, B. (1980). *Die Sarkophage mit Darstellungen aus dem Menschenleben: die römischen Jagdsarkophage* (Die antiken Sarkophagreliefs 1.2). Berlin.

Andreae, B. (1984). 'Bossierte Porträts auf römischen Sarkophagen: ein ungelöstes Problem', in B. Andreae (ed.), *Symposium über die antiken Sarkophage* (Marburger Winckelmann-Programm 1984). Marburg, 109–28.

Andreoli, A., Berti, F., Lazzarini, L., and Pierobon Benoit, R. (2002). 'New contributions on Marmor Iassense', in L. Lazzarini (ed.), *Interdisciplinary Studies on Ancient Stone. ASMOSIA VI.* Padua, 13–18.

Andrey, D. and Galli, M. (2004). 'Geometric methods of the 1500s for laying out the Ionic volute', *Nexus Network Journal* 6.2: 31–48.

Antonelli, F. (2002). 'I marmi della Gallia e dell'Iberia importati a Roma', in M. De Nuccio and L. Ungaro (eds), *I marmi colorati della Roma imperiale*. Padua, 267–76.

Antonelli, F. and Lazzarini, L. (2000). 'Le "Marbre Campan": histoire, diffusion et archéométrie', *Revue d'Archéométrie* 24: 111–28.

Antonelli, F. and Lazzarini, L. (2004). 'La caratterizzazione minero-petrografica e geochimica delle rocce', in L. Lazzarini (ed.), *Pietre e marmi antichi. Natura, caratterizzazione, origine, storia d'uso, diffusione, collezionismo*. Padua, 33–45.

Antonelli, F. and Lazzarini, L. (2004). 'Les marbres de couleur des monuments d'*Arausio* (Orange, Provence)', in P. Chardron-Picault, J. Lorenz, P. Rat, and G. Sauron (eds), *Les roches décoratives dans l'architecture antique et du Haut Moyen Âge* (Archéologie et d'histoire de l'art 16). Paris, 9–24.

Antonelli, F., Lazzarini, L., and Cancelliere, S. (2010). '"Granito del Foro" and "Granito di Nicotera": petrographic features and archaeometric problems owing to similar appearance', *Archaeometry* 52.6: 919–36.

Antonelli, F., Lazzarini, L., and Turi, B. (2002). 'The provenance of white marble used in Roman architecture of *Arausio* (Orange, France): first results', in L. Lazzarini (ed.), *Interdisciplinary Studies on Ancient Stone. ASMOSIA VI*. Padua, 265–70.

Arata, F. P. (2005). *Opere d'arte dal mare. Testimonianze archeologiche subacquee del trasporto e del commercio marittimo di prodotti artistici*. Rome.

Arnaud, P. (2005). *Les routes de la navigation antique. Itinéraires en Méditerranée*. Paris.

Arnaud, P. (2007). 'Diocletian's Price Edict: the prices of seaborne transport and the average duration of maritime travel', *JRA* 20: 321–36.

Asgari, N. (1977). 'Die Halbfabrikate kleinasiatischer Girlandensarkophage und ihre Herkunft', *AA* 1977: 329–80.

Asgari, N. (1979). 'The Roman and early Byzantine marble quarries of Proconnesus', in E. Akurgal (ed.), *Proceedings of the 10th International Congress of Classical Archaeology, Ankara–Izmir*. Ankara, 467–80.

Asgari, N. (1981). 'Uşak selçiker ve çevresinden Roma çağı lahitleri ve mermer ocakları', *Türk Arkeoloji Dergisi* 25.2: 11–47.

Asgari, N. (1986). 'Prokonnesos-1986 Çalışmaları', *Araştırma Sonuçları Toplantısı* 5.1: 135–46.

Asgari, N. (1988). 'The stages of workmanship of the Corinthian capital in Proconnesus and its export form', in N. Herz and M. Waelkens (eds), *Classical Marble: Geochemistry, Technology and Trade* (NATO ASI series E: Applied Sciences 153). Dordrecht, 115–26.

Asgari, N. (1990). 'Objets de marbre finis, semi-finis et inachevés du Proconnèse', in M. Waelkens (ed.), *Pierre Éternelle du Nil au Rhin. Carrières et Prefabrication*. Brussels, 106–26.

Asgari, N. (1992). 'Obsevations on two types of quarry-items from Proconnesus: column-shafts and column-bases', in M. Waelkens, N. Herz, and J.-L. Moens (eds), *Ancient Stones: Quarrying, Trade and Provenance* (Acta Archaeologica Lovaniensia, Monographiae 4). Leuven, 73–80.

Asgari, N. and Drew-Bear, T. (2002). 'The quarry inscriptions of Prokonnesos', in J. J. Herrmann Jnr, N. Herz, and R. Newman (eds), *ASMOSIA 5. Interdisciplinary Studies on Ancient Stone*. London, 1–19.

Asgari, N. and Fıratlı, N. (1978). 'Die Nekropole von Kalchedon', in S. Şahin, E. Schwertheim, and J. Wagner (eds), *Studien zur Religion und Kultur Kleinasiens. Festschrift F. K. Dörner* (Études Preliminaries aux Religions Orientales dans l'Empire Romain 66), vol. 1. Leiden, 1–92.

Asgari, N., Madra, B., Soysal, M., Atasoy, S., and Parman, E. (eds) (1983). *The Anatolian Civilisations, II: Greek/Roman/Byzantine, St. Irene, Istanbul, May 22–October 30, 1983.* Istanbul.

Ashmole, B. (1970). 'Aegean marble: science and common sense', *ABSA* 65. 1–2.

Atalay, E. (1976-7). 'Antiker Marmorsteinbruch bei Ephesos', *JÖAI* 51: 59–60.

Atalay, E. (1976). 'Kuşini Mermer Ocaği hakkinda ön rapor', *Türk Arkeoloji Dergisi* 23.1: 13–15.

Atanasova, J. (1972). 'Нов паметник на надгробьната пластика от Рациария (Un nouveau monument de la plastique funéraire de Ratiaria)', *Bulletin de la Société Archéologique Bulgare* 33: 141–52.

Attanasio, D. (2003). *Ancient White Marbles. Analysis and Identification by Paramagnetic Resonance Spectroscopy* (Studia Archaeologica 122). Rome.

Attanasio, D., Brilli, M., and Bruno, M. (2008). 'The properties and identification of marble from Proconnesus (Marmara Island, Turkey): a new database including isotopic, EPR and petrographic data', *Archaeometry* 50.5: 747–74.

Attanasio, D., Brilli, M., and Ogle, N. (2006). *The Isotopic Signature of Classical Marbles* (Studia Archaeologica 145). Rome.

Attanasio, D., Bruno, M., and Yavuz, A. B. (2009). 'Quarries in the region of Aphrodisias: the black and white marbles of Göktepe (Muğla)', *JRA* 22.1: 312–48.

Attanasio, D., Kane, S., and Herz, N. (2009). 'New isotopic and EPR data for 22 sculptures from the extramural sanctuary of Demeter and Persephone at Cyrene', in Maniatis, Y. (ed.), *ASMOSIA VII* (BCH Suppl. 51). Athens, 343–56.

Attanasio, D., Kane, S., Platania, R., and Rocchi, P. (2006). 'Provenance, use, and distribution of white marbles at Cyrene', in E. Fabbricotti and O. Menozzi (eds), *Cirenaica: studi, scavi e scoperte. Parte I: nuovi dati da città e territorio. Atti del X Convegno di Archeologia Cirenaica, Chieti 24–26 Novembre 2003* (BAR International Series 1488). Oxford, 247–60.

Attanasio, D., Mesolella, G., Pensabene, P., Platania, R., and Rocchi, P. (2009). 'EPR and petrographic provenance of the architectural white marbles of three buildings at Villa Adriana', in Y. Maniatis (ed.), *ASMOSIA VII* (BCH Suppl. 51). Athens, 357–69.

Attanasio, D., Yavuz, A. B., Bruno, M., Herrmann Jnr., J. J., Tykot, R. H., and Van den Hoek, A. (2012). 'On the Ephesian origin of Greco Scritto marble', in A. Gutiérrez, P. Lapuente, and I. Rodà (eds), *Interdisciplinary Studies on Ancient Stone. ASMOSIA IX* (Documenta 23). Tarragona, 245–55.

Audin, A. (1965). *Lyon, miroir de Rome dans les Gaules.* Paris.

Audin, A., and Burnand, Y. (1975). 'Le marché lyonnais de la pierre sous le haut-empire romain', in *Archéologie Minière.* Paris, 157–80.

Aurenhammer, M. (1990). *Die Skulpturen von Ephesos. Bildwerke aus Stein. Idealplastik I.* Vienna.

Avi-Yonah, M. (1962). 'Scythopolis', *IEJ* 12: 123–34.

Avigad, N. (1976). *Beth She'arim. Volume III, Report on the Excavations during 1953–1958: Catacombs 12–13.* New Brunswick, NJ.

Baccini Leotardi, P. (1979). *Marmi di cava rinvenuti ad Ostia e considerazioni sul commercio dei marmi in età romana* (Scavi di Ostia X). Rome.

Baccini Leotardi, P. (1989). *Nuove testimonianze sul commercio dei marmi in età imperiale.* Rome.

Badawi, H. (2002). 'Les carrières littorales de la Phénicie romaine', in M. Khanoussi, P. Ruggeri, and C. Vismara (eds), *L'Africa romana XIV. Lo spazio maritimo del Mediterraneo occidentale: geografia storica ed economica*, vol. 1. Rome, 305–22.

Bakir, T. (1968). *Historical and Archaeological Guide to Leptis Magna*. Tripoli.

Ballance, M. (1966). 'The origin of *africano*', *PBSR* 24: 79–81.

Balland, A. (1981). *Inscriptions d'époque impériale du Létôon* (Fouilles de Xanthos VII). Paris.

Bang, P. F. (2006). 'Imperial bazaar: towards a comparative understanding of markets in the Roman empire', in P. F. Bang, M. Ikeguchi, and H. G. Ziche (eds), *Ancient Economies, Modern Methodologies. Archaeology, Comparative History, Models and Institutions* (Pragmateiai 12). Bari, 51–88.

Baran, M. and Petzl, G. (1977–8). 'Beobachtungen aus dem nordöstlichen Hinterland von Teos', *MDAI(I)* 27–8: 301–8.

Barbieri, M., Masi, U., and Tucci, P. (1999). 'Petrographic and geochemical character-ization of calcareous archaeological materials from the Roman town of Herdonia, Apulia (Southern Italy) and probable stone provenance', in M. Schvoerer (ed.), *Archéomatériaux: marbres et autres roches. ASMOSIA IV*. Bordeaux, 27–34.

Barbu, V. (1963). 'Monumenti funerari con inscrizioní rinvenuti a Tomis', *Dacia* 7: 553–67.

Bargagliotti, S. (2002). 'Rinvenimenti sottomarini di età imperiale sulle secche delle Meloria e alla foce del rio Ardenza (Livorno), 1993–98', in P. A. Gianfrotta and P. Pelagatti (eds), *Archeologia Subacquea III*. Rome, 227–42.

Bargagliotti, S., Cibecchini, F., and Gambogi, P. (1997). 'Prospezioni subacquee sulle Secche della Meloria (LI): alcuni risultati preliminari', in *Atti del Convegno Nazio-nale di Archeologia Subacquea*. Bari, 43–54.

Barker, S. (2011). *Demolition, Salvage and Re-Use in the City of Rome, 100 BC–AD 315*. DPhil. thesis, University of Oxford.

Barker, S. (2012). 'Roman marble salvaging', in A. Gutiérrez, P. Lapuente, and I. Rodà (eds), *Interdisciplinary Studies on Ancient Stone. ASMOSIA IX* (Documenta 23). Tarragona, 22–30.

Barker, S. and Russell, B. (2012). 'Labour figures for Roman stone-working: pitfalls and potential', in S. Camporeale, H. Dessales, and A. Pizzo (eds), *Arqueología de la Construcción III. Los procesos constructivos en el mundo romano: la economía de las obras* (Anejos de Archivo Español de Arqueologa 64). Madrid and Merida, 83–94.

Barresi, P. (2002). 'Il ruolo delle colonne nel costo degli edifici pubblici', in M. De Nuccio and L. Ungaro (eds), *I marmi colorati della Roma imperiale*. Padua, 69–81.

Barresi, P. (2003). *Province dell'Asia Minore: costo dei marmi, architettura pubblica e committenza* (Studia Archaeologica 125). Rome.

Barresi, P. (2004). 'Anfiteatro flavio di Pozzuoli, portico in summa cavea: una sima dei costi', in E. C. De Sena and H. Dessales (eds), *Metodi e approcci archeologici: l'industria e il commercio nell'Italia antica* (BAR International Series 1262). Oxford, 262–7.

Bartelletti, A. and Criscuolo, A. (2004). 'Ipotesi intorno ad iscrizioni romane recente-mente scoperte nelle cave di Carrara', *Acta Apuana* 3: 5–12.

Bartman, E. (1993). 'Carving the Badminton sarcophagus', *MMJ* 28: 57–75.

Bartoli, D. (2008). *Marble Transport in the Time of the Severans: A New Analysis of the Punta Scifo A Shipwreck at Croton, Italy*. PhD dissertation, Texas A&M University.

Basile, B. (1988). 'A Roman wreck with a cargo of marble in the bay of Giardini Naxos (Sicily)', *IJNA* 17.2: 133–42.

Bassett, S. (2004). *The Urban Image of Late Antique Constantinople*. Cambridge.

Batista-Noguera, R., Molist, N., Rovira Port, J., and Vilalta, M. (1991). 'La cantera romana de Olèrdola (Barcelona), aspectos tecnicos y funcionales', in J. Lorenz and P. Benoit (eds), *Carrières et constructions en France et dans les pays limitrophes*. Paris, 383–98.

Bauchhenss, G. (1986). 'Hercules Saxanus, ein Gott der niedergermanischen Armee', in *Studien zu den Militärgrenzen Roms, III*. (Forschungen und Berichte zur Vor- und Frühgeschichte in Baden-Württemberg 20). Stuttgart, 90–5.

Beavis, J. (1970). 'Some aspects of the use of Purbeck Marble in Roman Britain', *Proceedings of the Dorset Natural History and Archaeological Society* 92: 181–204.

Becatti, G. (1961). *I mosaici e i pavimenti marmorei* (Scavi di Ostia IV). Rome.

Becatti, G. (1969). *Edificio con opus sectile fuori Porta Marina* (Scavi di Ostia VI). Rome.

Bedon, R. (1984). *Les carrières et les carriers de la Gaule romaine*. Paris.

Bedon, R., Chevallier, R., and Pinon, P. (1988). *Architecture et urbanisme en Gaule romaine. Tome 1: L'architecture et les villes en Gaule romaine*. Paris.

Bejor, G. (2011). 'Produzioni e scuole: uno sguardo alla questione', in F. D'Andria and I. Romeo (eds), *Roman Sculpture in Asia Minor* (JRA Suppl. 80). Portsmouth, RI, 30–6.

Bellet, M. É. (1991). *Orange antique: monuments et musée* (Guide archéologique de la France). Paris.

Beltrán, J. (2001). 'El uso del sarcófago en la Bética durante los siglos II–III d.C.', in J. M. Noguera and E. Conde (eds), *El sarcófago romano. Contribuciones al estudio de su tipología, iconografía y centros de producción*. Murcia, 93–105.

Beltrán, J. (2007). 'Sarcofagi decorate con rilievi di tema pagano della *Provincia Baetica* (Secc. II–IV d.C.)', in G. Koch (ed.), *Akten des Symposiums des Sarkophag-Corpus 2001* (Sarkophag-Studien 3). Mainz, 233–40.

Beltrán, J., García, M. A., and Rodríguez, P. (2006). *Los sarcófagos romano de Andalucía* (Corpus Signorum Imperii Romani: España I.3). Murcia.

Beltrán, J. and Rodríguez, O. (2010). 'Los materiales lapídeos de la província *Baetica*: estado de la cuestíon y líneas actuales de investigación', in S. Camporeale, H. Dessales, and A. Pizzo (eds), *Arqueología de la construcción II. Los procesos constructivos en el mundo romano: Italia y provincias orientales* (Anejos de Archivo Español de Arqueología 57). Madrid, 555–70.

Beltrán, J., Rodríguez, O., López, P., Ontiveros, E., and Taylor, R. (2011). 'Las canteras romanas de Almadén de la Plata (Sevilla)', in V. García-Entero (ed.), *El marmor en Hispania: explotación, uso y difusión en época romana*. Murcia, 239–56.

Benoit, F. (1952). 'L'archéologie sousmarine en Provence', *Rivista di Studi Liguri* 18.3–4: 237–307.

Beresford, J. (2005). *A Reassessment of the Ancient Sailing Season: the Case for Wintertime Seafaring on the Graeco-Roman Mediterranean*. DPhil. thesis, University of Oxford.

Bergmann, M. (1977). *Studien zur Römischen Porträt des 3. Jahrhunderts n. Chr.* Bonn.

Bernard, H. (2000). 'Die Marmorwracks der französischen Kusten', *Skyllis* 3: 114–25.

Bernard, H. (2001). 'Hérault. Au large de Marseillan', *Bilan scientifique de département des recherches archéologiques sous-marines*: 45.

Bernard, H. (2009). 'Épaves antiques de marbre sur les côtes du Languedoc: l'épave de Marseillan Beauséjour', in P. Jockey (ed.), *Leukos lithos. Marbres et autres roches de la Méditerranée antique: études interdisciplinaries. ASMOSIA VIII.* (Collection l'atelier méditerranéen). Paris, 509–25.

Bernard, H., Bessac, J.-C., Mardikian, P., and Feugère, M. (1998). 'L'épave romaine de marbre de Porto Nuovo', *JRA* 11: 53–81.

Bernard, H. and Jézégou, M.-P. (2003). 'Hérault. Carte archéologique', *Bilan scientifique de département des recherches archéologiques sous-marines*: 52–6.

Bernard, S. G. (2010). 'Pentelic marble in architecture at Rome and the Republican marble trade', *JRA* 23: 35–54.

Beschaouch, A., Hanoune, R., and Thébert, Y. (1977). *Les ruines de Bulla Regia* (Collection de l'École française de Rome 28). Paris.

Bessac, J.-C. (1981). 'Les carrières de Nîmes. La pierre, matériau de base dans l'expression monumentale antique de Nîmes', *Histoire et Archéologie. Les Dossiers* 55: 58–67.

Bessac, J.-C. (1986). *L'outillage traditionnel du tailleur de pierre, de l'antiquité à nos jours* (RAN Suppl. 14). Paris.

Bessac, J.-C. (1996). *La pierre en Gaule Narbonnaise et les carrières du Bois des Lens (Nîmes). Histoire, ethnologie et techniques* (JRA Suppl. 16). Ann Arbor.

Bessac, J.-C. (2002). 'Les carrières romaine du Bois des Lens (Gard)', *Gallia* 59: 29–51.

Bessac, J.-C., Abdul Massih, J., and Valat, Z. (1997). 'De Doura-Europos à Aramel: étude ethno-archéologique dans des carrières de Syrie', in P. Leriche and M. Gelin (eds), *Doura-Europos. Études IV, 1991–1993* (Bibliothèque Archéologique et Historique 149). Beirut, 160–98.

Bessac, J.-C. and Vacca-Goutoulli, M. (2002). 'La carrière romaine de L'Estel près du Pont du Gard', *Gallia* 59: 11–28.

Beykan, M. (1988). 'The marble architectural elements in export-form from the Şile shipwreck', in N. Herz and M. Waelkens (eds), *Classical Marble: Geochemistry, Technology and Trade* (NATO ASI series E: Applied Sciences 153). Dordrecht, 127–38.

Bianchi, F. (2005). 'La decorazione architettonica in pietra locale a Leptis Magna tra il I e il II sec. d.C. Maestranze e modelli decorativi nell' architettura pubblica', *ArchClass* 56 (n.s. 6): 189–223.

Bianchi, F. (2009). 'Su alcuni aspetti della decorazione architettonica in marmo a Leptis Magna in età imperiale', *Marmora* 5: 45–70.

Bianchi, F. and Bruno, M. (2009). 'Flavian amphitheatre: the cavea and the portico: comments about the quality, quantity, and the working of its marbles', in Y. Maniatis (ed.), *ASMOSIA VII* (BCH Suppl. 51). Athens, 103–11.

Bianchi, F., Bruno, M., Gorgoni, C., Pallante, P., and Ponti, G. (2009). 'The pilasters of the Severan Basilica at Leptis Magna and the School of Aphrodisias: new archaeometric and archaeological data', in P. Jockey (ed.), *Leukos lithos. Marbres et autres roches de la Méditerranée antique: études interdisciplinaries. ASMOSIA VIII.* (Collection l'atelier méditerranéen). Paris, 329–49.

Bianchi Bandinelli, R. (1970). *Rome: The Centre of Power*. London.

Bieber, M. (1962). 'The copies of the Herculaneum Woman', *PAPhS* 106.2: 111–34.

Bieber, M. (1977). *Ancient Copies. Contributions to the History of Greek and Roman Art.* New York.

Bingen, J., Bülow-Jacobsen, A., Cockle, W. E. H., Cuvigny, H., Rubinstein, L., and Van Rengen, W. (1992). *Mons Claudianus: Ostraca Graeca et Latina I (O. Claud. 1 à 190)* (Documents de Fouilles de l'Institut Français d'Archéologie Orientale 29). Cairo.

Bingen, J., Bülow-Jacobsen, A., Cockle, W. E. H., Cuvigny, H., Kayser, F., and Van Regen, W. (1997). *Mons Claudianus: Ostraca Graeca et Latina II (O. Claud. 191 à 416)* (Documents de Fouilles de l'Institut Français d'Archéologie Orientale 32). Cairo.

Bishop, A. C., Woolley, A. R., and Hamilton, W. R. (2005). *Philip's Guide to Minerals, Rocks and Fossils.* London.

Black, E., Edgar, J., Hayward, K. M. J., and Henig, M. (2012). 'A new sculpture of *Iphigenia in Tauris*', *Britannia* 43: 243–9.

Black, S., Browning, J., and Laurence, R. (2008). 'From quarry to road: the supply of basalt for road paving in the Tiber Valley', in F. Coarelli and H. Patterson (eds), *Mercator Placidissimus. The Tiber Valley in Antiquity.* Rome, 705–30.

Blagg, T. F. C. (1980). 'Roman civil and military architecture in the province of Britain: aspects of patronage, influence and craft organization', *World Archaeology* 12.1: 27–42.

Blagg, T. F. C. (1984). 'Roman architectural ornament in Kent', *Archaeologia Cantiana* 100: 65–80.

Blagg, T. F. C. (1990). 'Building stone in Roman Britain', in D. Parsons (ed.), *Stone: Quarrying and Building in England, AD 43–1525.* Chichester, 33–50.

Blanc, A. (1999). 'Observations préliminaires sur les marbres et riches décoratives de quelques monument gallo-romains du nort de la France', in M. Schvoerer (ed.), *Archéomatériaux: marbres et autres roches. ASMOSIA IV.* Bordeaux, 249–54.

Blanc, A. and Blanc, P. (2012). 'Ancient uses of the Roman breccia (Brèche des Romains) in Gaul', in A. Gutiérrez, P. Lapuente, and I. Rodà (eds), *Interdisciplinary Studies on Ancient Stone. ASMOSIA IX* (Documenta 23). Tarragona, 487–92.

Blanck, H. (1969). *Wiederverwendung alter Statuen als Ehrendenkmäler bei Griechen und Römern* (Studia Archeologica 11). Rome.

Bloch, H. (1953). 'Ostia—Iscrizioni rinvenute tra il 1930 e il 1939', *NSA*: 239–306.

Blümel, C. (1927). *Griechische Bildhauerarbeit* (JDAI Erganzungseft 11). Berlin.

Blümel, C. (1955). *Greek Sculptors at Work.* Glasgow.

Blümner, H. (1912). *Technologie und Terminologie der Gewerbe und Künste bei Griechen und Römern.* 2nd edn. Leipzig.

Bockius, R. (2000). 'Antike Schwergutfrachter—Zeugnisse römischen Schiffbaus und Gütertransports', in *Steinbruch und Bergwerk: Denkmäler römischer Technikgeschichte zwischen Eifel und Rhein.* Mainz, 110–32.

Bol, P. C. (1972). *Die Skulpturen des Schiffsfundes von Antikythera* (MDAI(A) Beihefte 2). Berlin.

Bommelaer, J.-F. (1991). *Guide de Delphes. Le site* (École Française d'Athènes. Sites et Monuments 7). Paris.

Bonanno Aravantinos, M. (2008). 'Sarcofagi di Ostia', *ArchClass* 59: 147–82.

Boninu, A. (1987). 'Notizie dei rinvenimenti subacquei lungo la costa della Sardegna centro-settentrionale', in F. Sisinni (ed.), *Archeologia Subacquea 3* (Bolletino d'Arte Suppl. 37–38). Rome, 55–62.

Bordenache, G. (1960). 'Attività edilizia a Tomi nel II secolo dell'e.n.', *Dacia* 4: 255–72.

Bordenache, G. (1969a). *Sculture greche e romane del Museo Nazionale di Antichità di Bucharest. Volume I: statue e rilievi di culto, elementi architettonici e decorativi.* Bucharest.

Bordenache, G. (1969b). 'Römische Kunst und römische Kunstgewerbe auf dem Boden der Dobrudscha', in *Römer in Rumänien.* Cologne, 71–3.

Borghini, G. (ed. 2001). *Marmi antichi.* 4th edn. Rome.

Borgia, E. (2010). 'I cantieri delle vie colonnate nell'oriente romano', in S. Camporeale, H. Dessales, and A. Pizzo (eds), *Arqueología de la construcción II. Los procesos constructivos en el mundo romano: Italia y provincias orientales* (Anejos de Archivo Español de Arqueología 57). Madrid, 281–99.

Borricelli, D. and Zaccaria, A. (1995). 'Porto Cesareo (Lecce), Torre Chianca', *Taras* 15.1: 151–2.

Bortolaso, G. and Appolonia, L. (1992). 'The polychrome marble of *Augusta Praetoria*', in M. Waelkens, N. Herz, and J.-L. Moens (eds), *Ancient Stones: Quarrying, Trade and Provenance* (Acta Archaeologica Lovaniensia, Monographiae 4). Leuven, 129–30.

Boschung, D. and Pfanner, M. (1988). 'Antike Bildhauertechnik. Vier Untersuchungen an Beispielen in der Münchner Glyptothek', *Münchner Jahrbuch der bildenden Kunst* (Series 3) 39: 7–28.

Bounni, A. (1989). 'Palmyre et les Palmyréniens', in J. M. Dentzer and W. Orthmann (eds), *Archeologie et Histoire de la Syrie, II. La Syrie de l'époque achéménide à l'avènement de l'Islam* (Schriften zur Vorderasiatischen Archäologie 1). Saarbrücken, 251–66.

Bounni, A. and Al-As'ad, K. (1987). *Palmyre. Histoire, monuments et musée.* 2nd edn. Damascus.

Bouras, C. (2009). 'La circulation des pierres et le port d'Éphèse', in P. Jockey (ed.), *Leukos lithos. Marbres et autres roches de la Méditerranée antique: études interdisciplinaries. ASMOSIA VIII.* (Collection l'atelier méditerranéen). Paris, 495–508.

Bourguet, É. (1932). *Les comptes du IVe siècle* (Fouilles de Delphes 3, Epigraphie: Fascicule 5). Paris.

Bouthier, A. (2004). 'Éléments décoratifs en pierre des établissements ruraux gallo-romains du nord-est de la Nièvre', in P. Chardron-Picault, J. Lorenz, P. Rat, and G. Sauron (eds), *Les roches décoratives dans l'architecture antique et du Haut Moyen Âge* (Archéologie et d'histoire de l'art 16). Paris, 69–88.

Bowman, A. K. and Wilson, A. I. (2009). 'Quantifying the Roman economy: integration, growth, decline?', in A. K. Bowman and A. I. Wilson (eds), *Quantifying the Roman Economy: Methods and Problems* (Oxford Studies on the Roman Economy 1). Oxford, 3–84.

Bradley, F. (1997). *Guida alle cave di marmo di Carrara.* Carrara.

Braemer, F. (1971). 'Les marbres à l'époque romaine', *RA*: 167–74.

Braemer, F. (1982). 'La décoration en matériaux nobles (marbes, porphyres . . .) des édifices de la Gaule et des régions limitrophes durant le Haut-Empire et la basse Antiquité', in *Mosaïque. Recueil d'hommages à Henri Stern.* Paris, 81–92.

Braemer, F. (1984). 'Le commerce des matériaux d'architecture et de sculpture de part et d'autre de la châine des Pyrénées dans les provinces de Terraconaise, de Narbonnaise et d'Aquitaine', in *Archéologie pyrénéenne et questions diverse.* Paris, 57–72.

Braemer, F. (1986a). 'Les gisements de pierres dans l'antiquité romaine. Problémes de méthode, état de la question', in F. Braemer (ed.), *Les resources minérales et l'histoire de leur exploitation* (Colloques du Comité des Travaux Historiques et Scientifiques 2). Paris, 267–86.

Braemer, F. (1986b). 'Repertoire des gisements de pierre ayant exporté leur production à l'époque romaine', in F. Braemer (ed.), *Les resources minérales et l'histoire de leur exploitation* (Colloques du Comité des Travaux Historiques et Scientifiques 2). Paris, 287–328.

Braemer, F. (1992). 'Les principaux gisements au Haut-Empire romain', *Les Dossiers d'Archéologie* 173: 8–15.

Braemer, F. (2004). 'Le rôle des pierres précieuses et nobles dans l'ornamentation dans l'Antiquité et le Haut Moyen Âge', in P. Chardron-Picault, J. Lorenz, P. Rat, and G. Sauron (eds), *Les roches décoratives dans l'architecture antique et du Haut Moyen Âge* (Archéologie et d'histoire de l'art 16). Paris, 89–120.

Brandenburg, H. (1996). 'Die Verwendung von Spolien und originalen Werkstücken in der spätantiken Architektur', in J. Poeschke (ed.), *Antike Spolien in der Architektur des Mittelalters und der Renaissance*. Munich, 11–48.

Brentchaloff, D. and Salviat, F. (1989). 'Une tête colossale d'Auguste trouvée en mer', *Archeologia* 245: 18–22.

Bresson, A. (2005). 'Ecology and beyond: the Mediterranean paradigm', in W. V. Harris (ed.), *Rethinking the Mediterranean*. Oxford, 94–116.

Brewer, R. J. (1986). *Wales* (Corpus Signorum Imperii Romani: Great Britain I.5). Oxford.

Broneer, O. (1932). *Corinth. Volume X: The Odeum*. Cambridge, MA.

Broughton, T. R. S. (1939). 'Roman Asia Minor', in T. Frank (ed.), *An Economic Survey of Ancient Rome*, vol. 4. Baltimore, 499–918.

Brown, V. M. and Harrell, J. A. (1995). 'Topographical and petrological survey of ancient Roman quarries in the Eastern Desert of Egypt', in Y. Maniatis, N. Herz, and Y. Basiakos (eds), *The Study of Marble and Other Stones Used in Antiquity. ASMOSIA III*. London, 221–34.

Browning, I. (1979). *Palmyra*. London.

Brunet, M. (1992). 'Les carrières de marbre de Thasos', *Les Dossiers d'Archéologie* 173: 40–5.

Brunet-Gaston, V. (2010). 'Le marbre de Carrare dans les programmes architecturaux d'Augustodunum—Autun (France)', in S. Camporeale, H. Dessales, and A. Pizzo (eds), *Arqueología de la construcción II. Los procesos constructivos en el mundo romano: Italia y provincias orientales* (Anejos de Archivo Español de Arqueología 57). Madrid, 491–508.

Brunet-Gaston, V., Blanc, A., Blanc, P., Chardron-Picault, P., Gaston, C., Lamotte, D., and Lorenz, J. (2009). 'Les pierres de décoration et de construction à Augustodunum (Autun, France)', in P. Jockey (ed.), *Leukos lithos. Marbres et autres roches de la Méditerranée antique: études interdisciplinaries. ASMOSIA VIII*. (Collection l'atelier méditerranéen). Paris, 409–20.

Bruno, M. (1998). 'Su un fusto colossale di cipollino sopra le cave di Kylindroi nel distretto di Myloi', in P. Pensabene (ed.), *Marmi antichi II: cave e tecnica di lavorazione, provenienze e distribuzione* (Studi Miscellanei 31). Rome, 327–30.

Bruno, M. (2002a). 'Alabaster quarries near Hierapolis (Turkey)', in L. Lazzarini (ed.), *Interdisciplinary Studies on Ancient Stone. ASMOSIA VI.* Padua, 19–24.

Bruno, M. (2002b). 'Considerazioni sulle cave, sui metodi di estrazione, di lavorazione e sui trasporti', in M. De Nuccio and L. Ungaro (eds), *I marmi colorati della Roma imperiale.* Padua, 179–94.

Bruno, M. (2002c). 'Il mondo delle cave in Italia: considerazioni su alcuni marmi e pietre usati nell'antichità', in M. De Nuccio and L. Ungaro (eds), *I marmi colorati della Roma imperiale.* Padua, 277–90.

Bruno, M. (2002d). 'The quarries at Cape Latomio on Valaxa Island, Skyros (Greece)', in J. J. Herrmann Jnr, N. Herz, and R. Newman (eds), *ASMOSIA 5. Interdisciplinary Studies on Ancient Stone.* London, 27–35.

Bruno, M. (2012). 'Quarry blocks in *marmor iassense* from the Balık Pazarı at Iasos (Turkey)', in A. Gutiérrez, P. Lapuente, and I. Rodà (eds), *Interdisciplinary Studies on Ancient Stone. ASMOSIA IX* (Documenta 23). Tarragona, 706–14.

Bruno, M., Cancelliere, S., Gorgoni, C., Lazzarini, L., Pallante, P., and Pensabene, P. (2002a). 'Provenance and distribution of white marbles in temples and public buildings of Imperial Rome', in J. J. Herrmann Jnr, N. Herz, and R. Newman (eds), *ASMOSIA 5. Interdisciplinary Studies on Ancient Stone.* London, 289–300.

Bruno, M., Conti, L., Lazzarini, L., Pensabene, P., and Turi, B. (2002b). 'The marble quarries of Thasos: an archaeometric study', in L. Lazzarini (ed.), *Interdisciplinary Studies on Ancient Stone. ASMOSIA VI.* Padua, 157–62.

Bruno, M., Conti, L., Pensabene, P., and Turi, B. (2002c). 'Pompeii after the AD 62 earthquake: historical, isotopic, and petrographic studies of quarry blocks in the Temple of Venus', in J. J. Herrmann Jnr, N. Herz, and R. Newman (eds), *ASMOSIA 5. Interdisciplinary Studies on Ancient Stone.* London, 282–88.

Bruno, M., Elçi, H., Yavuz, A. B., and Attanasio, D. (2012). 'Unknown ancient marble quarries of western Asia Minor', in A. Gutiérrez, P. Lapuente, and I. Rodà (eds), *Interdisciplinary Studies on Ancient Stone. ASMOSIA IX* (Documenta 23). Tarragona, 562–72.

Bruno, M., Gorgoni, C., and Pallante, P. (1999). 'I marmi dell'Arco di Settimio Severo: composizione strutturale, volumetria e analisi archeometriche', in P. Pensabene and C. Panella (eds), *Arco di Costantino tra archeologia e archeometria* (Studia Archeologica 100). Rome, 157–69.

Bruno, M., Gorgoni, C., and Pallante, P. (2009). 'On the provenance of white marbles used in the Baths of Caracalla, Rome', in Y. Maniatis (ed.), *ASMOSIA VII* (BCH Suppl. 51). Athens, 385–98.

Bruno, M. and Lazzarini, L. (1999). 'Discovery of the Sienese provenance of *Breccia Dorata*, and *Breccia Gialla Fibrosa*, and the origin of *Breccia Rossa Appenninica*', in M. Schvoerer (ed.), *Archéomatériaux: marbres et autres roches. ASMOSIA IV.* Bordeaux, 77–82.

Bruno, M., Lazzarini, L., Pensabene, P., Soligo, M., and Turi, B. (2002d). 'Provenance studies of the white marble blocks and architectural elements from Porto and their contributions to the history of the marble trade', in J. J. Herrmann Jnr, N. Herz, and R. Newman (eds), *ASMOSIA 5. Interdisciplinary Studies on Ancient Stone.* London, 347–58.

Bruno, M., Lazzarini, L., Soligo, M., Turi, B., and Varti-Matarangas, M. (2000). 'The ancient quarry at Karavos (Paros) and the characterisation of its marble', in D. U. Schilardi and D. Katsonopoulou (eds), *Paria Lithos: Parian Quarries, Marble and Workshops of Sculpture*. Athens, 95–103.

Bruno, M. and Pallante, P. (2002). 'The "Lapis Taenarius" quarries of Cape Tainaron (Mani Peninsula, S. Peloponnesus, Greece)', in L. Lazzarini (ed.), *Interdisciplinary Studies on Ancient Stone. ASMOSIA VI*. Padua, 163–76.

Bruno, M., Panella, C., Pensabene, P., Preite-Martinez, M., Soligo, M., and Turi, B. (1999). 'Determinazione dei marmi dell'Arco di Costantino su base archeometrica', in P. Pensabene and C. Panella (eds), *Arco di Costantino tra archeologia e archeometria* (Studia Archeologica 100). Rome: 171–84.

Bruno, M. and Vitti, M. (2012). 'Cipollino marble quarries south of Karystos at Aghii (Euboea, Greece)', in A. Gutiérrez, P. Lapuente, and I. Rodà (eds), *Interdisciplinary Studies on Ancient Stone. ASMOSIA IX* (Documenta 23). Tarragona, 604–11.

Brusin, G. (1941). *Nuovi monumenti sepolcrali di Aquileia* (Associazione Nazionale per Aquileia, Quaderno 1). Venice.

Bruzza, L. (1870). 'Inscrizione dei marmi grezzi', *Annali dell'Instituto di Corrispondenza Archeologia* 42: 106–204.

Bruzza, L. (1877). 'Gli Scavi dell'Emporio', in *Triplice Omaggio alla Santità di Papa Pio IX nel suo Guibileo Episcopio*. Rome, 39–46.

Buckler, W. H. (1917). 'Lydian records', *JHS* 37: 88–115.

Buckler, W. H., Calder, W. M., and Cox, C. W. M. (1928). 'Asia Minor 1924. V—Monuments from the Upper Tembris Valley', *JRS* 18: 21–40.

Bugini, R. and Folli, L. (2005). 'Sull'uso di marmi colorati antichi in Lombardia (Italia settentrionale)', *Marmora* 1: 145–68.

Bugini, R., Folli, L., and Ferrario, C. (2002). 'A glossary of some coloured marbles—comparison between ancient and modern terms', in L. Lazzarini (ed.), *Interdisciplinary Studies on Ancient Stone. ASMOSIA VI*. Padua, 177–81.

Bulić, F. (1900). 'Ritrovamenti antichi sull' isola Brazza risguardanti il Palazzo di Diocleziano a Spalato', *Bullettino di Archeologia e Storia Dalmatia* 23: 18–23.

Bulić, F. (1908). 'Materiale e provenienze della pietra, delle colonne, nonchè delle sfingi del Palazzo di Diocleziano a Spalato e delle colonne ecc. delle basiliche cristiane a Salona', *Bullettino di Archeologia e Storia Dalmatia* 31: 86–127.

Bullard, R. G. (1978a). 'The environmental geology of Roman Carthage', in J. H. Humphrey (ed.), *Excavations at Carthage, 1975, conducted by the University of Michigan*, vol. 2. Ann Arbor, 3–25.

Bullard, R. G. (1978b). 'The marbles of the *opus sectile* floor', in J. H. Humphrey (ed.), *Excavations at Carthage, 1975, conducted by the University of Michigan*, vol. 2. Ann Arbor, 167–88.

Bülow-Jacobsen, A. (1996). *Mons Claudianus. Organisation, administration og teknik i et romersk stenbrud fra kejsertiden*. Copenhagen.

Bülow-Jacobsen, A. (2009). *Mons Claudianus: Ostraca Graeca et Latina IV—The Quarry Texts: O. Claud. 632–896* (Documents de Fouilles de l'Institut Français d'Archéologie Orientale 47). Cairo.

Burford, A. (1969). *The Greek Temple Builders at Epidauros. A social and economic study of building in the Asklepian sanctuary, during the fourth and early third centuries BC*. Liverpool.

Cailleaux, D. (1997). 'Un chargement de pierres de Saint-Leu pour le chantier de la cathédrale de Sens a la fin du Moyen Age', in J. Lorenz, P. Benoit, and D. Obert (eds), *Pierres & Carrières. Géologie—Archéologie—Histoire. Textes réunis en hommage à Claude Lorenz*. Paris, 191–8.

Calabi Limentani, I. (1958). *Studi sulla società romana: il lavoro artistico*. Milan and Varese.

Calabi Limentani, I. (1961a). 'Lapidarius', in R. Bianchi Bandinelli and G. Becatti (eds), *Enciclopedia dell'arte antica, classica e orientale*, vol. 4. Rome, 475.

Calabi Limentani, I. (1961b). 'Marmorarius', in R. Bianchi Bandinelli and G. Becatti (eds), *Enciclopedia dell'arte antica, classica e orientale*, vol. 4. Rome, 870–5.

Calia, A. Giannotta, M. T., Lazzarini, L., and Quarta, G. (2009). 'The Torre Sgarrata wreck: characterization and provenance of white marble artefacts in the cargo', in Y. Maniatis (ed.), *ASMOSIA VII* (BCH Suppl. 51). Athens, 333–42.

Calia, A., Giannotta, M. T., Quarta, G., and Alessio, A. (2002). 'Ancient coastal quarries south-east of Taranto: identification and preliminary characterization of the lithotypes exploited', in L. Lazzarini (ed.), *Interdisciplinary Studies on Ancient Stone. ASMOSIA VI*. Padua, 183–91.

Calza, G. (1940). 'Una basilica di età constantiniana scoperta ad Ostia', *RPAA* 16: 63–98.

Cambi, N. (1988). *Atički Sarkofazi u Dalmaciji* (Biblioteka Znanstvenih Djela 27). Split.

Cambi, N. (1994). *Sarkofag Dobroga Pastira iz Salone i njegova Grupa/The Good Shepherd Sarcophagus and its Group*. Split.

Cambi, N. (1998). 'Sarkophage aus salonitanischen Werkstätten', in G. Koch (ed.), *Akten des Symposiums '125 Jahre Sarkophag-Corpus'* (Sarkophag-Studien 1). Mainz, 169–81.

Cambi, N. (2000). 'Les sarcophages de Manastirine: sarcophages décorés et typologie/ Sarkofazi na Manastirinama: ukrašeni sarkofazi i tipologija', in M. Bonačić Man-dinić, N. Cambi, P. Chevalier, N. Duval, J. Mardešić, E. Marin, and A. Šarić-Bužančić (eds), *Salona III: Manastirine* (Collection de l'École française de Rome 194/3). Rome and Split, 227–57.

Cancelliere, S., Lazzarini, L., and Turi, B. (2002). 'White marbles and coloured stones in the House of Polibius at Pompeii', in J. J. Herrmann Jnr, N. Herz, and R. Newman (eds), *ASMOSIA 5. Interdisciplinary Studies on Ancient Stone*. London, 301–7.

Canto, A. (1977–8). 'Avances sobre la explotación del Marmol en la España romana', *Archivo Español de Arqueología* 50–1: 165–87.

Carlson, D. N. (2007). 'An uplifting summer: the 2006 excavations season at Kızılburun, Turkey', *INA Quarterly* 34.1: 3–10.

Carlson, D. N. (2009). 'A marble cargo of monumental proportions: the late Hellenistic shipwreck at Kızılburun, Turkey', in P. Jockey (ed.), *Leukos lithos. Marbres et autres roches de la Méditerranée antique: études interdisciplinaries. ASMOSIA VIII*. (Col-lection l'atelier méditerranéen). Paris, 475–93.

Carlson, D. N. and Atkins, C. E. (2007). 'Leaving no stone unturned: the 2007 excavation season at Kızılburun, Turkey', *INA Annual*: 1–7.

Carpenter, R. (1968). 'The unfinished colossus on Mt. Penteli', *AJA* 72.3: 279–80.

Carrié, J.-M. (1994). 'Les échanges commerciaux et l'État antique tardif', in *Économie Antique. Les échanges dans l'Antiquité: le rôle de l'État* (Entretiens d'Archéologie et d'Histoire, Saint-Bertrand-de-Comminges). Toulouse, 175–212.

Carroll, M. (2006). *Spirits of the Dead. Roman Funerary Commemoration in Western Europe* (Oxford Studies in Ancient Documents). Oxford.

Cascella, S. (2009). 'Uso del marmo nella decorazione architettonica del teatro romano di Sessa Aurunca (CE)', *Marmora* 5: 21–43.

Caskey, L. D. (1927). 'The inscriptions', in J. M. Paton (ed.), *The Erechtheum*. Cambridge, MA, 277–422.

Cassels, J. (1955). 'The cemeteries of Cyrene', *PBSR* 23 (New Series 10): 1–43.

Casson, L. (1951). 'Speed under sail of ancient ships', *TAPhA* 82: 136–48.

Casson, L. (1965). 'Harbour and river boats of ancient Rome', *JRS* 55: 31–9.

Casson, L. (1971). *Ships and Seamanship in the Ancient World*. Princeton.

Casson, L. (1980). 'The role of the state in Rome's grain trade', in J. D'Arms and E. C. Kopff (eds), *The Seaborne Commerce of Ancient Rome: Studies in Archaeology and History* (MAAR 36). Rome, 21–34.

Casson, L. (1994). *Ships and Seafaring in Ancient Times*. London.

Casson, S. (1933). *The Technique of Early Greek Sculpture*. Oxford.

Chamoux, F. (1953). *Cyrène sous la monarchie des Battiades*. Paris.

Chaniotis, A. (2008). 'Twelve buildings in search of locations: known and unknown buildings in the inscriptions of Aphrodisias', in C. Ratté and R. R. R. Smith (eds), *Aphrodisias Papers 4: New Research on the City and its Monuments* (JRA Suppl. 70). Portsmouth, RI, 61–78.

Chéhab, M. H. (1968). 'Sarcophages à Tyr', *BMB* 21: 7–91.

Chéhab, M. H. (1984). *Fouilles de Tyr. La nécropole II: description des fouilles* (BMB 34). Paris.

Chéhab, M. H. (1985). *Fouilles de Tyr. La nécropole III: description des fouilles* BMB 35). Paris.

Chiarlo, C. (1974). 'Sul significato dei sarcofagi a ληνος decorati con leoni', *ASNP* (3rd series) 4.4: 1307–45.

Chidiroglou, M. (2009). 'New data on the ancient quarries in southern Euboea, Greece', in P. Jockey (ed.), *Leukos lithos. Marbres et autres roches de la Méditerranée antique: études interdisciplinaries. ASMOSIA VIII.* (Collection l'atelier méditerranéen). Paris, 73–91.

Chiesa, C. (1949). 'Sui materiali da construzione di provenienza locale usati dagli antichi in Tripolitania', *Reports and Monographs of the Department of Antiquities in Tripolitania* 2: 25–8.

Christol, M. and Drew-Bear, T. (1986). 'Documents latins de Phrygie', *Tyche* 1: 39–87.

Christol, M. and Drew-Bear, T. (1987). 'Inscriptions de Dokimeion', in B. Rémy (ed.), *Anatolia Antiqua/Eski Anadolu. Recueil de travaux publiés par l'Institut Français d'Études Anatoliennes d'Istanbul* (Varia Anatolica 1). Istanbul and Paris, 83–137.

Christol, M. and Drew-Bear, T. (1991). 'Les carrières de Dokimeion à l'époque sévérienne', *Epigraphica* 53: 113–74.

Christol, M. and Drew-Bear, T. (2005). 'De Lepcis à Aizanoi: Hesperus Procurateur de Phrygie et l'administration des carrières de marbre', in J. Desmulliez and C. Hoët-Van Cauwenberghe (eds), *Le monde romain à travers l'épigraphie: méthodes et pratiques*. Villeneuve d'Ascq, 189–216.

Ciliberto, F. (1996). *I sarcofagi attici nell'Italia settentrionale* (Hefte des Archäologischen Seminars der Universität Bern 3. Beiheft). Bern.

Ciliberto, F. (1998). 'Sarkophage in Oberitalien: Importe und Nachahmungen', in G. Koch (ed.), *Akten des Symposiums '125 Jahre Sarkophag-Corpus'* (Sarkophag-Studien 1). Mainz, 240–8.

Ciliberto, F. (2007). 'Die Sarkophage der Region von Friuli-Venezia Giulia', in G. Koch (ed.), *Akten des Symposiums des Sarkophag-Corpus 2001* (Sarkophag-Studien 3). Mainz, 159–63.

Cisneros, M. (1988). *Marmoles Hispanolos: su Empleo en la España Romana* (Monografias Arqueologicas 29). Zaragoza.

Cisneros, M. (1989–90). 'Sobre la explotación de calizas en el sur de España en época romana: canteras de Gádor (Almería), Atarfe (Granada), Antequera (Málaga) y Cabra (Córduba)', *Caesaraugusta* 66–7: 123–42.

Cisneros, M. (2010). 'Reflexiones sobre los mármoles Hispanos: revisando la expresión "mármoles de sustitución"', *Marmora* 6: 135–50.

Claridge, A. (1982). 'Le scanalature delle colonne', in L. Cozze (ed.), *Tempio di Adriano: lavori e studi di archeologia 1*. Rome, 27–30.

Claridge, A. (1985). 'Sulla lavorazione dei marmi bianchi nella scultura dell'età romana', in P. Pensabene (ed.), *Marmi antichi: problemi d'impiego, di restauro e d'identificazione* (Studi Miscellanei 26). Rome, 113–26.

Claridge, A. (2007). 'Hadrian's lost temple of Trajan', *JRA* 20: 54–94.

Clarke, J. T., Bacon, F. H., and Koldewey, R. (1902). *Investigations at Assos: Drawings and Photographs of the Buildings and Objects Discovered during the Excavations of 1881–1882–1883*. London.

Clarke, W. (2008). 'Perspectives on Rome's enigmatic marble trade: restudying the South Etruria Survey data', in F. Coarelli and H. Patterson (eds), *Mercator Placidissimus. The Tiber Valley in Antiquity* (Quaderni di Eutopia 8). Rome, 687–703.

Claudel, J. and Laroque, L. (1863). *Pratique de l'art de construire*, 3rd edn. Paris.

Clavel, M. (1970). *Béziers et son territoire dans l'antiquité* (Centre de Recherches d'Histoire Ancienne 2). Paris.

Claveria, M. (1998). 'Roman sarcophagi in Tarragona', in G. Koch (ed.), *Akten des Symposiums '125 Jahre Sarkophag-Corpus'* (Sarkophag-Studien 1). Mainz, 138–49.

Claveria, M. (2001). *Los sarcófagos romano de Cataluña* (Corpus Signorum Imperii Romani: España I.1). Murcia.

Claveria, M. (2007). 'El sarcófago romano en la peninsula Ibérica', in G. Koch (ed.), *Akten des Symposiums des Sarkophag-Corpus 2001* (Sarkophag-Studien 3). Mainz, 197–204.

Clifton-Taylor, A. (1962). *The Pattern of English Building*. London.

Coarelli, F. (1983). 'Il commercio delle opera d'arte in età tardo-repubblicana', *Dialoghi di Archeologia* (3rd series) 1: 45–53.

Coarelli, F. (2002). 'Gli spazi della vita sociale', in E. Lo Cascio (ed.), *Roma imperiale. Una metropoli antica*. Rome, 221–48.

Cockle, W. E. H. (1996). 'An inscribed architectural fragment from Middle Egypt concerning the imperial quarries', in D. M. Bailey (ed.), *Archaeological Research in Roman Egypt* (JRA Suppl. 19). Ann Arbor, 23–8.

Coleman, M. and Walker, S. (1979). 'Stable isotope identification of Greek and Turkish marbles', *Archaeometry* 21: 107–12.

Colledge, M. (1976). *The Art of Palmyra*. London.

Collins-Clinton, J., Attanasio, D., and Platania, R. (2008). 'Sculptural marbles from Cosa (Tuscany, Italy) and their provenance by EPR and petrography', *Marmora* 4: 19–55.

Comstock, M. B. and Vermeule, C. C. (1976). *Sculpture in Stone. The Greek, Roman and Etruscan Collections of the Museum of Fine Arts, Boston*. Boston.

Conlin, D. A. (1997). *The Artists of the Ara Pacis. The Process of Hellenization in Roman Relief Sculpture*. Chapel Hill.

Connell, S. (1988). *The Employment of Sculptors and Stonemasons in Venice in the Fifteenth Century*. London and New York.

Conrad, S. (2007). 'Die Sarkophage aus Moesia Inferior. Der Herakles-Sarkophag aus Čavdarci (Lădžane)', in G. Koch (ed.), *Akten des Symposiums des Sarkophag-Corpus 2001* (Sarkophag-Studien 3). Mainz, 255–62.

Cook, A. S. (1926). 'Augustine's journey from Rome to Richborough', *Speculum* 1.4: 375–97.

Cooper, F. A. (1981). 'A source of ancient marble in the southern Peloponnese', *AJA* 85: 190–1.

Cooper, F. A. (1988). 'The quarries of Mt Taygetos in the Peloponnese', in N. Herz and M. Waelkens (eds), *Classical Marble: Geochemistry, Technology and Trade* (NATO ASI series E: Applied Sciences 153). Dordrecht, 65–76.

Cooper, F. A. (2009). 'Limestone quarries for Greek cities and sanctuaries', in P. Jockey (ed.), *Leukos lithos. Marbres et autres roches de la Méditerranée antique: études interdisciplinaires. ASMOSIA VIII.* (Collection l'atelier méditerranéen). Paris, 161–76.

Corcoran, S. (2000). *The Empire of the Tetrarchs: Imperial Pronouncements and Government AD 284–324*. Revised edn. Oxford.

Corcoran, S. and DeLaine, J. (1994). 'The unit measurement of marble in Diocletian's Prices Edict', *JRA* 7: 263–73.

Cormack, S. (2004). *The Space of Death in Roman Asia Minor* (Wiener Forschungen zur Archäologie 6). Vienna.

Corremans, M., Degryse, P., Wielgosz, D., and Waelkens, M. (2012). 'The import and use of white marble and coloured stone for wall and floor revetment at Sagalassos', in A. Gutiérrez, P. Lapuente, and I. Rodà (eds), *Interdisciplinary Studies on Ancient Stone. ASMOSIA IX* (Documenta 23). Tarragona, 38–51.

Corsi, F. (1833). *Delle pietre antiche*. 2nd edn. Rome.

Corsi, F. (1845). *Delle pietre antiche*. 3rd edn. Rome.

Costedoat, C. (1995a). 'Aperçu géologique des Pyrénées: quelques données sur le méta-morphisme pyrénéen', in J. Cabanot, R. Sablayrolles, and J.-L. Schenk (eds), *Les marbres blancs des Pyrénées: approches scientifiques et historiques*. Toulouse, 95–100.

Costedoat, C. (1995b). 'Recherches sur les marbres pyrénéens', in J. Cabanot, R. Sablayrolles, and J.-L. Schenk (eds), *Les marbres blancs des Pyrénées: approches scientifiques et historiques*. Toulouse, 101–18.

Coulon, G. and Tardy, D. (1997). 'Argentomagus: l'approvisionnement en pierre d'une agglomération secondaire des Biturges', in J. Lorenz, P. Benoit, and D. Obert (eds), *Pierres & Carrières. Géologie—Archéologie—Histoire. Textes réunis en hommage à Claude Lorenz*. Paris, 199–202.

Craig, H. and Craig, V. (1972). 'Greek marbles: determination of provenance by isotopic analysis', *Science* 176: 401–3.

Cramer, T., Germann, K., and Heilmeyer, W.-D. (2002). 'Petrographic and geochemical characterization of the Pergamon Altar (Telephos Frieze) marble in the Pergamon Museum, Berlin', in L. Lazzarini (ed.), *Interdisciplinary Studies on Ancient Stone. ASMOSIA VI.* Padua, 285–91.

Crawford, M. and Reynolds, J. (1979). 'The Aezani copy of the Prices Edict', *ZPE* 34: 163–210.

Crummy, P. (1997). *City of Victory—the story of Colchester: Britain's first Roman Town.* Colchester.

Cumont, F. (1917). 'Les carrières romaines d'Énesh. Arulis et Ourima', in F. Cumont (ed.), *Études syriennes.* Paris, 151–72.

Cunliffe, B. (1971). *Excavations at Fishbourne 1961–69. Volume 2: The Finds* (Reports of the Research Committee of the Society of Antiquaries of London 27). London.

Cunliffe, B. (1984). 'Relations between Britain and Gaul in the first century BC and early first century AD', in S. Macready and F. H. Thompson (eds), *Cross-Channel Trade, between Gaul and Britain in the Pre-Roman Iron Age* (The Society of Antiquaries of London, Occasional Paper (New Series) 4). London, 3–23.

Cunliffe, B. and Fulford, M. G. (1982). *Bath and the Rest of Wessex* (Corpus Signorum Imperii Romani: Great Britain I.2). Oxford.

Curchin, L. (1983). 'Personal wealth in Roman Spain', *Historia* 32: 227–44.

Curtius, L. (1944). *Das antike Rom.* Vienna.

Cuvigny, H. (2000). *Mons Claudianus: Ostraca Graeca et Latina III—Les reçus pour avances à la familia: O. Claud. 417 à 631* (Documents de Fouilles de l'Institut Français d'Archéologie Orientale 38). Cairo.

Cuvigny, H. (2002). 'Vibius Alexander, praefectus et épistratège de l'Heptanomie', *CE* 77: 238–48.

Cuvigny, H. (2005). 'L'organigramme du personnel d'une carrière impériale d'après un ostracon du Mons Claudianus', *Chiron* 35: 309–53.

Daehner, J. (2007). 'The statue types in the Roman world', in J. Daehner (ed.), *The Herculaneum Women. History, Context, Identities.* Malibu, 85–112.

Daguet-Gagey, A. (1997). *Les opera publica à Rome (180–305 ap. J.-C.). Construction et administration* (Collection des Études Augustiniennes. Série Antiquité 156). Paris.

De Blois, L., Pleket, H. W., and Rich, J. (2002). 'Introduction', in L. de Blois and J. Rich (eds), *The Transformation of Economic Life under the Roman Empire* (Impact of Empire (Roman Empire) 2). Amsterdam, ix–xx.

De Chaisemartin, N. (1999). 'Technical aspects of the sculptural decoration at Aphrodisias in Caria', in M. Schvoerer (ed.), *Archéomatériaux: marbres et autres roches. ASMOSIA IV.* Bordeaux, 261–8.

De Chaisemartin, N. (2007). 'Le commerce des sculptures dans l'empire romain: témoinages sur les échanges artistiques des ateliers d'Aphrodisias avec l'Afrique', in A. Laronde and J. Leclant (eds), *Colloque—La Méditerranée d'une rive à l'autre: culture classique et cultures périphériques: actes* (Cahiers de la Villa 'Kérylos' 18). Paris, 201–29.

De Franciscis, A. and Roghi, G. (1961). 'Esplorazione sottomarina al Capo Colonne ed al Capo Cimiti presso Crotone', *Klearchos* 3.11: 55–61.

De Haan, N. and Wallat, K. (2008). 'Le Terme Centrali a Pompei: ricerche e scavi 2003–2006', in P. G. Guzzo and M. P. Guidobaldi (eds), *Nuove ricerche archeologiche nell'area vesuviana (scavi 2003–2006)* (Studi della Soprintendenza archeologica di Pompei 25). Rome, 15–24.

De Kisch, Y. (1979). 'Tarifs de donations en Gaule romaine d'après les inscriptions', *Ktema. Civilisations de l'Orient, de la Grèce et de la Rome Antique* 4: 259–80.

De Martino, F. (1979). *Storia economica di Roma antica* (Pensiero Storico 75). Florence.

De Nuccio, M., Bruno, M., Gorgoni, C., and Pallante, P. (2002). 'The use of Proconnesian marble in the architectural decoration of the Bellona Temple in Rome', in L. Lazzarini (ed.), *Interdisciplinary Studies on Ancient Stone. ASMOSIA VI*. Padua, 293–302.

De Siena, A., Cancelliere, S., and Lazzarini, L. (2002). 'The architectural marbles of the Athenaion of Metapontum and their identification', in L. Lazzarini (ed.), *Interdisciplinary Studies on Ancient Stone. ASMOSIA VI*. Padua, 303–8.

De Simone, A. and Ciro Nappo, S. (eds 2000). . . . *Mitis Sarni Opes. Nuove indagine archeologica in località Murecine*. Naples.

De Souza, V. (1990). *Portugal* (Corpus Signorum Imperii Romani). Coimbra.

Deckers, J. G. and Noelke, P. (1980). 'Die römische Grabkammer in Weiden', in *Führer zu vor- und frühgeschichtlichen Denkmälern, 39: Köln III*. Mainz, 156–67.

Degryse, P., Bloxam, E., Heldal, T., Storemyr, P., and Waelkens, M. (2009a). 'Conservation of ancient quarry landscapes: a survey of the area of Sagalassos (SW Turkey)', in P. Jockey (ed.), *Leukos lithos. Marbres et autres roches de la Méditerranée antique: études interdisciplinaries. ASMOSIA VIII*. (Collection l'atelier méditerranéen). Paris, 189–201.

Degryse, P., Muchez, P., Loots, L., Vandeput, L., and Waelkens, M. (2003). 'The building stones of Roman Sagalassos (SW Turkey): facies analysis and provenance', *Facies* 48: 9–22.

Degryse, P., Muchez, P., Trogh, E., and Waelkens, M. (2009b). 'The natural building stones of Hellenistic to Byzantine Sagalassos: provenance determination through table isotope geochemistry', in Y. Maniatis (ed.), *ASMOSIA VII* (BCH Suppl. 51). Athens, 571–80.

Degryse, P., Muchez, P., and Waelkens, M. (2006). 'Geology and archaeology of late Hellenistic limestone quarries at Sagalassos (SW Turkey)', *Marmora* 2: 9–20.

Delacroix, M. (1835). *Statistique du département de la Drôme*. 2nd edn. Valence.

DeLaine, J. (1997). *The Baths of Caracalla: a Study in the Design, Construction, and Economics of Large-Scale Building Projects in Imperial Rome* (JRA Suppl. 25). Portsmouth, RI.

DeLaine, J. (2001). 'Bricks and mortar: exploring the economics of building techniques at Rome and Ostia', in D. J. Mattingly and J. Salmon (eds), *Economies Beyond Agriculture in the Classical World*. London and New York, 230–68.

DeLaine, J. (2006). 'The cost of creation: technology at the service of construction', in E. Lo Cascio (ed.), *Innovazione tecnica e progresso economico nel mondo romano. Atti degli incontri capresi di storia dell'economia antica* (Pragmateiai 10). Bari, 237–52.

Demma, F. (2004). 'Anfiteatro flavio di Pozzuoli, la decorazione marmoreal nella storia edilizia: tipologia e stile, restauri, officine e artigiani', in E. C. De Sena and

H. Dessales (eds), *Metodi e approcci archeologici: l'industria e il commercio nell'Italia antica* (BAR International Series 1262). Oxford, 243–61.

Demirer, Ü. (1999). 'Perge nekropolü'nde kurtarma kazısı', in *IX. Müze Kurtarma Kazıları Semineri (27–29 Nisan-Antalya)*. Ankara, 75–89.

Dentzer, J.-M. (1986). 'Conclusion: développement et culture de la Syrie du Sud dans la période préprovinciale (Ier s. avant J.-C.–Ier s après J.-C.)', in J.-M. Dentzer (ed.), *Hauran I: recherches archéologiques sur la Syrie du sud a l'époque Hellénistique et Romaine*. Vol. 2. Paris: 387–420.

Descamps, C. (1992). 'L'épave antique de La Mirande a Port-Vendres', in J. Rieucau and G. Cholvy (eds), *Le Languedoc, le Roussillon et la mer (des origines à la fin du XXe siècle)*, vol. 1. Paris, 79–97.

Dessandier, D., Antonelli, F., Lazzarini, L., Varti-Matarangas, M., Leroux, L., Hamiane, M., Riache, C., and Khalfallah, C. (2012). 'An introductory study to the ornamental and building stones of the Djemila (Algeria) archaeological site', in A. Gutiérrez, P. Lapuente, and I. Rodà (eds), *Interdisciplinary Studies on Ancient Stone. ASMOSIA IX* (Documenta 23). Tarragona, 68–74.

Di Stefano, C. A. (1991). 'La nave delle colonne', *Archeo* 73: 115–18.

Di Vita, A. (1999). 'Sabratha', in R. Polidori, A. Di Vita, G. Di Vita-Evrard, and L. Bacchielli (eds), *Libya. The Lost Cities of the Roman Empire*. Cologne, 146–82.

Dibner, B. (1970). *Moving the Obelisks*. London.

Dimes, F. G. (1980). 'Petrological Report', in C. Hill, M. Millett, and T. F. C. Blagg (eds), *The Roman Riverside Wall and Monumental Arch in London* (London and Middlesex Archaeological Society Special Paper 3). London, 198–200.

Diolé, P. (1954). *4,000 Years under the Sea: Excursions in Undersea Archaeology*. London.

Djaoui, D., Greck, S., and Marlier, S. (2011). *Arles-Rhône 3: le naufrage d'un chaland antique dans le Rhône, enquête pluridisciplinaire*. Arles.

Djurić, B. (1997). 'Eastern Alpine marble and Pannonian trade', in B. Djurić and I. Lazar (eds), *Akten des IV. internationalen Kolloquiums über Probleme des provinzialrömischen Kunstschaffens* (Situla 36). Ljubljana, 73–86.

Djurić, B. (2005). 'Poetovio and the Danube marble trade', in M. Mirković (ed.), *Römische Städte und Festungen an der Donau*. Belgrade, 75–82.

Djurić, B., Davidović, J., Maver, A., and Müller, H. W. (2006). 'Stone use in Roman towns. Resources, transport, products and clients. Case study Sirmium. First report', *Starinar* 56: 103–36.

Djurić, B., Maver, A., Rižnar, I., Jovanović, and Davidović, J. (2012). 'Sirmium's main limestone quarry at Dardagani (Bosnia and Herzegovina)', in A. Gutiérrez, P. Lapuente, and I. Rodà (eds), *Interdisciplinary Studies on Ancient Stone. ASMOSIA IX* (Documenta 23). Tarragona, 471–9.

Djurić, B. and Müller, H. W. (2009). 'White marbles in Noricum and Pannonia: an outline of the Roman quarries and their products', in P. Jockey (ed.), *Leukos lithos. Marbres et autres roches de la Méditerranée antique: études interdisciplinaries. ASMOSIA VIII.* (Collection l'atelier méditerranéen). Paris, 111–27.

Dodge, H. (1988a). 'Decorative stones for architecture in the Roman Empire', *OJA* 7.1: 65–80.

Dodge, H. (1988b). 'Palmyra and the Roman marble trade: evidence from the Baths of Diocletian', *Levant* 20: 215–30.

Dodge, H. (1990). 'The architectural impact of Rome in the East', in M. Henig (ed.), *Architecture and Architectural Sculpture in the Roman Empire* (Oxford University Committee for Archaeology, Monograph 29). Oxford, 108–20.

Dodge, H. (1991). 'Ancient marble studies: recent research', *JRA* 4: 28–50.

Dodge, H. and Ward-Perkins, B. (eds 1992). *Marble in Antiquity: Collected Papers of J. B. Ward-Perkins* (Archaeological Monographs of the British School at Rome 6). London.

Dolci, E. (1980). *Carrara. Cave Antichi: materiali archeologici. Relazione delle campagne di rilevamento dei beni culturali del territorio promosse dal Comune di Carrara, anni 1977–1978–1979.* Carrara.

Dolci, E. (1995). 'Due capitelli semilavorati da una cava lunense', *Quaderni del Centro Studi Lunensi* (New Series) 1: 127–36.

Dolci, E. (1997). 'Un' *officina* imperiale nelle cave lunensi: il sito del monte Strinato a Carrara', *Quaderni del Centro di Studi Lunensi* (New Series) 3: 27–46.

Dolci, E. (1998). 'Una cava lunense scoperta di recente a Carrara: il sito della Scalocchiella', *Quaderni del Centro di Studi Lunensi* (New Series) 4: 115–38.

Dolci, E. (2003). *Archeologia Apuana: iscrizioni—lavorazioni—cave antiche a Carrara.* Carrara.

Dolci, E. (2004). 'Sui marmi lunensi recentemente scoperti', *Quaderni del Centro di Studi Lunensi* (New Series) 8: 47–78.

Dolci, E. (2006). *Museo del Marmo, Carrara. Catalogo-guida.* Pontedera.

Domenech Miró, J. (1961). 'Arqueología submarina en la costa tarraconense', in *Atti del II Congresso Internazionale di Archeologia Sottomarina, Albenga 1958.* Bordighera, 256–61.

Domergue, C. (1983). *La mine antique d'Aljustrel (Portugal) et les tables bronzes de Vipasca* (Publication du Centre Pierre Paris (E.R.A. 522), 9/Collection de la Maison des Pays Iberiques 12). Paris.

Domergue, C. (1990). *Les mines de la péninsule Ibérique dans l'Antiquité romaine* (Collection de l'École française de Rome 127). Paris.

Donderer, M. (1996). 'Bildhauersignaturen auf griechischer Rundplastik', *JÖAI* 65: 87–104.

Donderer, M. (2001). 'Bildhauer in und aus Alexandria', in K. Geus and K. Zimmermann (eds), *Punica–Libyca–Ptolemaica: Festschrift für Werner Huß* (Orientalia Lovaniensia Analecta 104; Studia Phoenicia 16). Leuven, 167–83.

Downey, G. (1959). 'The tombs of the Byzantine emperors', *JHS* 79: 27–51.

Dresken-Weiland, J. (1995). 'Riflessioni sulla scultura tra V secolo e VI secolo in Italia', in *Atti del convegno di studi 'Storia antica in Val Bidente: l'ultima stagione.* Galeata, 20–2.

Drew-Bear, T. (1980). 'An act of foundation at Hypaipa', *Chiron* 10: 509–36.

Drew-Bear, T. (1994). 'Nouvelles inscriptions de Dokimeion', *MEFRA* 106.2: 747–844.

Drinkwater, J. F. (1985). 'Urbanization in the Three Gauls: some observations', in F. Grew and B. Hobley (eds), *Roman Urban Topography in Britain and the Western Empire* (CBA Research Report 59). London, 49–55.

Dubois, C. (1908). *Études sur l'administration et l'exploitation des carrières marbres, porphyre, granit, etc. dans le monde romain.* Paris.

Dufournet, P. (1976). 'Pierre blanche et carrières antiques de Seyssel', in *Archéologie Occitane. Préhistoire et Antiquité*. Paris, 245–72.

Duncan-Jones, R. (1982). *The Economy of the Roman Empire: Quantative Studies*. 2nd edn. Cambridge.

Dunning, G. (1968). 'The stone mortars', in B. Cunliffe (ed.), *Fifth Report on the Excavations of the Roman Fort at Richborough, Kent*. London, 110–14.

Dutrait, L. (1987). 'Toulon: deux bateaux romains dans le port antique', *Archeologia* 229: 6–7.

Duval, P.-M. (1953). *La vie quotidienne en Gaule pendant la paix romaine (Ier–IIIe siècle après J.C.)*. Paris.

Dworakowska, A. (1975). *Quarries in Ancient Greece* (Academia Scientiarum Polona, Bibliotheca Antiqua 14). Warsaw.

Dworakowska, A. (1983). *Quarries in Roman Provinces*. Warsaw.

Dyson, R. W. (ed. 1998). *Augustine: The City of God Against the Pagans*. Cambridge.

Eichler, F. (1944–5). 'Zwei kleinasiatische Säulensarkophage', *JDAI* 59–60: 125–36.

Eichner, K. (1977). *Die Werkstatt des sogen. dogmatischen Sarkophags. Untersuchungen zur Technik der konstantinischen Sarkophagplastik in Rom*. Mannheim.

Eichner, K. (1981). 'Die Produktionsmethoden der stadtrömischen Sarkophagfabrik in der Blütezeit unter Konstantin', *JbAC* 24: 85–113.

Elsam, R. (1826). *The Practical Builder's Perpetual Price-Book*. London.

Erim, K. (1974). 'The Satyr and young Dionysus group from Aphrodisias', in E. Akurgal and U. Bahadir Alkim (eds), *Mansel'e Armağan/Mélanges Mansel*, vol. 2. Ankara, 767–75.

Erim, K. and Reynolds, J. (1970). 'The copy of Diocletian's Edict on Maximum Prices from Aphrodisias in Caria', *JRS* 60: 120–41.

Espérandieu, E. (1910). *Recueil général des bas-reliefs de la Gaule romaine. Tome troisième: Lyonnaise, I.* (Collection de documents inédits sur l'histoire de la France). Paris.

Espérandieu, E. (1913). *Recueil général des bas-reliefs de la Gaule romaine. Tome sixième: Belgique, I.* (Collection de documents inédits sur l'histoire de la France). Paris.

Espérandieu, E. (1915). *Recueil général des bas-reliefs de la Gaule romaine. Tome sixième: Belgique, II.* (Collection de documents inédits sur l'histoire de la France). Paris.

Espérandieu, E. (1929). *Inscriptions latines de Gaule (Narbonnaise)*. Paris.

Étienne, R. (1950). 'Les carrieres de calcaire dans la region de Volubilis (Maroc)', *BCTH* 16: 23–32.

Ewald, B. C. (2004). 'Men, muscle, and myth. Attic sarcophagi in the cultural context of the Second Sophistic', in B. E. Borg (ed.), *Paideia: the World of the Second Sophistic*. Berlin, 229–76.

Fabbricotti, E. (1985). 'Influenza Attica a Tolemaide nel 2 sec. d.C.', in G. W. W. Barker, J. Lloyd, and J. Reynolds (eds), *Cyrenaica in Antiquity* (Society for Libyan Studies Occasional Papers 1; BAR International Series 236). Oxford, 219–29.

Fabre, J.-M. and Sablayrolles, R. (1995). 'Le dieu Erriape et les isotopes stables: les carrières antiques des Pyrénées, entre terrain et laboratoire', in J. Cabanot, R. Sablayrolles, and J.-L. Schenk (eds), *Les marbres blancs des Pyrénées: approches scientifiques et historiques*. Toulouse, 131–68.

Fagan, G. G. (1999). *Bathing in Public in the Roman World*. Ann Arbor.

Fant, J. C. (1985). 'Four unfinished sarcophagus lids at Docimium and the Roman imperial quarry system in Phrygia', *AJA* 89: 655–62.

Fant, J. C. (1986). 'Three seasons of epigraphical survey at the Roman Imperial quarries at Docimium (Iscehisar) 1983–85', *Araştırma Sonuçları Toplantısı* 4: 127–32.

Fant, J. C. (1988). 'The Roman emperors in the marble business: capitalists, middlemen or philanthropists?', in N. Herz and M. Waelkens (eds), *Classical Marble: Geochemistry, Technology and Trade* (NATO ASI series E: Applied Sciences 153). Dordrecht, 147–58.

Fant, J. C. (1989a). *Cavum Antrum Phrygiae. The Organization and Operations of the Roman Imperial Marble Quarries in Phrygia* (BAR International Series 482). Oxford.

Fant, J. C. (1989b). 'Poikiloi Lithoi: the anomalous economics of the Roman imperial marble quarry at Teos', in S. Walker and A. Cameron (eds), *The Greek Renaissance in the Roman Empire* (BICS Suppl. 55). London, 206–18.

Fant, J. C. (1989c). 'New sculptural and architectural finds at Docimium', *Araştırma Sonuçları Toplantısı* 7: 111–18.

Fant, J. C. (1990). 'Les carrières des empereurs romains', in M. Waelkens (ed.), *Pierre Éternelle du Nil au Rhin. Carrières et Préfabrication*. Brussels, 147–58.

Fant, J. C. (1992). 'The Roman imperial marble yard at Portus', in M. Waelkens, N. Herz, and J.-L. Moens (eds), *Ancient Stones: Quarrying, Trade and Provenance* (Acta Archaeologica Lovaniensia, Monographiae 4). Leuven, 115–20.

Fant, J. C. (1993a). 'Ideology, gift, and trade: a distribution model for the Roman imperial marbles', in W. V. Harris (ed.), *The Inscribed Economy: Production and Distribution in the Roman Empire in the Light of Instrumentum Domesticum* (JRA Suppl. 6). Ann Arbor, 145–70.

Fant, J. C. (1993b). 'The Roman imperial marble trade: a distribution model', in R. Francovich (ed.), *Archeologia delle attività estrattive e metallurgiche*. Florence, 71–96.

Fant, J. C. (1999). 'Augustus and the city of marble', in M. Schvoerer (ed.), *Archéomatériaux: marbres et autres roches. ASMOSIA IV*. Bordeaux, 277–80.

Fant, J. C. (2001). 'Rome's marble yards', *JRA* 14: 167–98.

Fant, J. C. (2007). 'Real and painted (imitation) marble at Pompeii', in J. J. Dobbins and P. W. Foss (eds), *The World of Pompeii*. London and New York, 336–46.

Fant, J. C. (2008a). 'Quarrying and stoneworking', in J. P. Oleson (ed.), *The Oxford Handbook of Engineering and Technology in the Classical World*. Oxford, 121–35.

Fant, J. C. (2008b). 'Marble workshops at *Simitthus*', *JRA* 21.2: 577–80 (review of Mackensen 2005).

Fant, J. C. (2009a). 'Bars with marble surfaces at Pompeii: evidence for sub-elite marble use', *Fasti Online* 159: 1–10.

Fant, J. C. (2009b). 'White marbles in the summer triclinium of the Casa del Bracciale d'Oro, Pompeii', in Y. Maniatis (ed.), *ASMOSIA VII* (BCH Suppl. 51). Athens, 53–7.

Fant, J. C. (2010). 'Quarrying granite for Rome: glimpses behind the scenes in Egypt's Eastern Desert', *JRA* 23.2: 773–9 (review of Bülow-Jacobsen 2009).

Fant, J. C. (2012). 'Contracts and costs for shipping marble in the Roman Empire', in A. Gutiérrez, P. Lapuente, and I. Rodà (eds), *Interdisciplinary Studies on Ancient Stone. ASMOSIA IX* (Documenta 23). Tarragona, 528–32.

Fant, J. C., Cancelliere, S., Lazzarini, L., Preite-Martinez, M., and Turi, B. (2002). 'White marble at Pompeii: sampling the Casa dei Vettii', in L. Lazzarini (ed.), *Interdisciplinary Studies on Ancient Stone. ASMOSIA VI.* Padua, 309–15.

Faulkner, N. (2000). *The Decline and Fall of Roman Britain.* Stroud.

Fejfer, J. (2008). *Roman Portraits in Context* (Image and Context 2). Berlin and New York.

Fellague, D. (2009). 'Les ateliers d'architecture à *Lugdunum*', in V. Gaggadis-Robin, A. Hermary, M. Reddé, and C. Sintes (eds), *Les ateliers de sculpture régionaux: techniques, styles et iconographie. Actes du Xe Colloque International sur l'Art Provincial Romain.* Arles and Aix-en-Provence, 533–40.

Féray, G. and Paskoff, R. (1966). 'Recherches sur les carrières romaines des environs de Volubilis', *BAM* 6: 279–300.

Ferchiou, N. (1994). 'Recherches sur les éléments architecturaux', in G. Hellenkemper-Salies, H. von Prittwitz und Gaffron, and G. Bauchhenβ (eds), *Das Wrack. Der antike Schiffsfund von Mahdia*, 2 vols. Cologne, 195–208.

Ferrari, G. (1966). *Il commercio dei sarcofagi asiatici.* Rome.

Filow, B. (1910). 'Избрани паметници на античното изкуство въ България (Monuments choisis de l'art antique en Bulgarie)', *Bulletin de la Société Archéologique Bulgare* 1: 1–22.

Fischer, G. (1999). 'Köln als Mittler des Marmorluxus im römischen Rheinland?' *KJ* 32: 677–87.

Fischer, M. L. (1990). *Das korinthische Kapitell im Alten Israel in der hellenistischen und römischen Periode. Studien zur Geschichte der Baudekoration im Nahen Osten.* Mainz.

Fischer, M. L. (1995). 'The Basilica of Ascalon: marble, imperial art, and architecture in Roman Palestine', in J. H. Humphrey (ed.), *The Roman and Byzantine Near East. Some Recent Archaeological Research* (JRA Suppl. 14). Ann Arbor, 121–50.

Fischer, M. L. (1996). 'Marble, urbanism, and ideology in Roman Palestine', in A. Raban and K. G. Holum (eds), *Caesarea Maritima. A Retrospective after Two Millennia.* Leiden, 251–61.

Fischer, M. L. (1998). *Marble Studies: Roman Palestine and the Marble Trade.* Konstanz.

Fischer, M. L. (2002). 'Marble studies in Israel since Lucca 1988: a balance as the millennium turns', in L. Lazzarini (ed.), *Interdisciplinary Studies on Ancient Stone. ASMOSIA VI.* Padua, 317–24.

Fischer, M. L. and Grossmark, T. (1996). 'Marble import and *marmorarii* in Eretz Israel during the Roman and Byzantine periods', in R. Katzoff (ed.), *Classical Studies in Honour of David Sohlberg.* Ramat Gan, 319–52.

Fischer, M. L., Magaritz, M., and Pearl, Z. (1992). 'Isotopic and artistic appraisal of Corinthian capitals from Caesarea Maritime: a case study', in *Caesarea Papers. Straton's Tower, Herod's Harbour, and Roman and Byzantine Caesarea* (JRA Suppl. 5). Ann Arbor, 214–21.

Fishwick, D. (1987). *The Imperial Cult in the Latin West. Studies in the Ruler Cult of the Western Provinces of the Roman Empire, I.1.* Leiden.

Fisković, I. (1971). 'Ranokršćanske crknive na Sutvari, Gubavcu i Lućnjaku kraj Majsana u Pelješkom kanalu', *Vietsnik Hrvatskoga Arheološkoga Društva* 65–7: 141–68.

Fittschen, K. (1971). 'Zum angeblichen Bildnis des Lucius Verus im Thermen-Museum', *JDAI* 86: 214–52.

Fittschen, K. and Zanker, P. (1985). *Katalog der römischen Porträts in den Capitolinischen Museen und den anderen kommunalen Sammlungen der Stadt Rom. Band I. Kaiser- und Prinzenbildnisse*. 2 vols. Mainz.

Fitzler, K. (1910). *Steinbrüche und Bergwerke im ptolemäischen und römischen Ägypten* (Leipziger historische Abhandlungen 21). Leipzig.

Flämig, C. (2007). *Grabarchitektur der römischen Kaiserzeit in Griechenland* (Internationale Archäologie 97). Rahden.

Fletcher, B. (1877). *Quantities: a Text-Book for Surveyors in Tabulated Form*. London.

Floriani Squarciapino, M. (1943). *La scuola di Afrodisia*. Rome.

Floriani Squarciapino, M. (1943–4). 'Sarcofagi romani con ritratti riadattati', *RPAA* 20: 267–86.

Floriani Squarciapino, M. (1983). 'La scuola di Aphrodisias (40 anni dopo)', *ArchClass* 35: 74–87.

Foerster, G. (1998). 'Sarcophagus production in Jerusalem from the beginning of the Common Era up to 70 CE', in G. Koch (ed.), *Akten des Symposiums '125 Jahre Sarkophag-Corpus'* (Sarkophag-Studien 1). Mainz, 295–310.

Folli, L. and Ferrario, C. (2002). 'Preliminary investigations on white marbles used in Roman architecture of Brixia (Brescia—northern Italy)', in L. Lazzarini (ed.), *Interdisciplinary Studies on Ancient Stone. ASMOSIA VI*. Padua, 325–7.

Fournet-Pilipenko, H. (1961–2). 'Sarcophagues romains de Tunisie', *Karthago* 11: 77–169.

Foy, D. and Jézégou, M. P. (2003). 'Sous les vagues, le verre: l'épace de l'île des Embiez', in D. Foy (ed.), *Coeur de verre. Production et diffusion de verre antique*. Gollion, 150–71.

Franke, T. (2000). '*Legio XXII Primigenia*', in Y. Le Bohec and C. Wolff (eds), *Les légions de Rome sous le Haut-Empire* (Collection du Centre d'Études Romaines et Gallo-Romaines. Nouvelle Série 20), vol. 1. Lyon, 95–104.

French, D. H. (1991). 'Dated inscriptions at Amasia', in H. Malay (ed.), *Erol Atalay Memorial* (Arkeoloji Dergisi 1). Izmir, 65–70.

Frend, W. H. C. (1956). 'A third-century inscription relating to *angareia* in Phrygia', *JRA* 46: 46–56.

Frenz, H. G. (1985). *Römische Grabreliefs in Mittel- und Süditalien* (Archaeologica 37). Rome.

Frézouls, E. (1984). 'Evergétisme et construction urbaine dans le Trois Gaules et les Germanies', in *Mélanges offerts à E. Will* (Revue du Nord 66). Lille, 27–54.

Frézouls, E. (1985). 'Les resources de l'evergétisme. Le cas d'Opramoas de Rhodiapolis', in P. Leveau (ed.), *L'origine des richesses dépensées dans la ville antique*. Aix-en-Provence, 249–51.

Friedland, E. A. (1999). 'Graeco-Roman sculpture in the Levant: the marbles from the Sanctuary of Pan at Caesarea Philippi (Banias)', in J. H. Humphrey (ed.), *The Roman and Byzantine Near East, Volume 2: Some Recent Archaeological Research* (JRA Suppl. 31). Portsmouth, RI, 7–22.

Friedland, E. A. (2003). 'The Roman marble sculptures from the North Hall of the East Baths at Gerasa', *AJA* 107: 413–48.

Friedland, E. A. (2012). 'The carving of classical sculpture in the Roman Near East', in T. M. Kristensen and B. Poulsen (eds), *Ateliers and Artisans in Roman Art and Archaeology* (JRA Suppl. 92). Portsmouth, RI, 101–18.

Friedland, E. A. and Tykot, R. H. (2012). 'Quarry origins, commission, and import of marble sculptures from the Roman theater in Philadelphia/Amman, Jordan', in A. Gutiérrez, P. Lapuente, and I. Rodà (eds), *Interdisciplinary Studies on Ancient Stone. ASMOSIA IX* (Documenta 23). Tarragona, 52–60.

Frost, H. (1964). 'Rouad, ses récifs et mouillages. Prospection sous-marine', *Annales Archéologiques de Syrie* 14: 67–74.

Fulford, M. (2009). 'Approaches to quantifying Roman trade: response', in A. K. Bowman and A. I. Wilson (eds), *Quantifying the Roman Economy: Methods and Problems* (Oxford Studies in the Roman Economy 1). Oxford, 250–8.

Gabellone, F., Giannotta, M. T., and Alessio, A. (2009). 'The Torre Sgarrata wreck (south Italy): marble artefacts in the cargo', in Y. Maniatis (ed.), *ASMOSIA VII* (BCH Suppl. 51). Athens, 319–31.

Gabelmann, H. (1973). *Die Werkstattgruppen der oberitalischen Sarkophage.* Bonn.

Gabler, D. (1996). 'Marmorverwendung im nördlichen Teil Oberpannoniens. Zusammenhänge zwischen Kunst und Wirtschaft', in G. Bauchhenss (ed.), *Akten des 3. internationalen Kolloquiums über Probleme des provinzialrömischen Kunstschaffens* (BJ Beihefte 51). Cologne, 39–44.

Gaggadis-Robin, V. (2005). *Les sarcophages païens du Musée de l'Arles antique.* Arles.

Gaggadis-Robin, V., Maniatis, Y., Sintès, C., Kavoussanaki, D., and Dotsika, E. (2009). 'Provenance investigation of some marble sarcophagi from Arles with stable isotope and maximum grain size analysis', in Y. Maniatis (ed.), *ASMOSIA VII* (BCH Suppl. 51). Athens, 133–46.

Gaied, M. E., Younès, A., and Gallala, W. (2010). 'A geoarchaeological study of the ancient quarries of Sidi Ghedamsy island (Monastir, Tunisia)', *Archaeometry* 52.4: 531–49.

Galasso, M. (1997). 'Rinvenimenti archeologici subacquei in Sardegna sud-occidentale e nord-occidentale', in *Atti del Convegno Nazionale di Archeologia Subacquea.* Bari, 121–34.

Galsterer, H. (1988). 'Municipium Flavium Irnitanum. A Latin town in Spain', *JRS* 78: 78–90.

Galsterer, H. (1994). 'Kunstraub and Kunsthandel im republikanischen Rom', in G. Hellenkemper-Salies, H. von Prittwitz und Gaffron, and G. Bauchhenβ (eds), *Das Wrack. Der antike Schiffsfund von Mahdia*, 2 vols. Cologne, 857–66.

Galsterer, H. (2000). 'Local and provincial institutions and government', in A. K. Bowman, P. Garnsey, and D. Rathbone (eds), *The Cambridge Ancient History, Second Edition. Volume XI: The High Empire, AD 70–192.* Cambridge, 344–60.

García-Entero, V. and Vidal, S. (2007). '*Marmora* from the Roman sie of Carranque (Toledo, Spain)', *Marmora* 3: 53–69.

García y Bellido, A. (1949). *Esculturas romanas de España y Portugal*, 2 vols. Madrid.

Garnsey, P. (1983). 'Grain for Rome', in P. Garnsey, K. Hopkins, and C. R. Whittaker (eds), *Trade in the Ancient Economy.* London, 118–30.

Gasparri, C. (ed. 2010). *Le sculture Farnese, III: Le sculture delle Terme di Caracalla, relieve e varia.* Naples.

Gayraud, M. (1981). *Narbonne antique des origines à la fin du IIIe siècle* (RAN Suppl. 8). Paris.

Gazenbeek, M. (1998). 'Prospections systématiques autour de *Glanum* (Bouches-du-Rhône): l'extension de l'agglomération', in *Suburbia. les faubourgs en Gaule romaine et dans les regions voisines* (Caesarodunum 32). Limoges, 83–103.

Gébara, C. and Michel, J.-M. (eds 2002). *L'aqueduc romain de Fréjus: sa description, son histoire et son environnement* (RAN Suppl. 33). Montpellier.

Geominy, W. (1994). 'Der Schiffsfund von Mahdia und seine Bedeutung für die antike Kunstgeschichte', in G. Hellenkemper-Salies, H. von Prittwitz und Gaffron, and G. Bauchhenβ (eds), *Das Wrack. Der antike Schiffsfund von Mahdia*, 2 vols. Cologne, 927–44.

Gersht, R. and Pearl, Z. (1992). 'Decoration and marble sources of sarcophagi from Caesarea', in *Caesarea Papers. Straton's Tower, Herod's Harbour, and Roman and Byzantine Caesarea* (JRA Suppl. 5). Ann Arbor, 222–43.

Gianfrotta, P. A. (1981). 'Il commercio del marmo', *Mondo Archeologico* 57: 27–31.

Gianfrotta, P. A. (1982). 'Archeologia sott'acqua. Rinvenimenti sottomarini in Etruria Meridionale', in G. B. Triches (ed.), *Archeologia Subacquea* (Bollettino d'Arte Suppl. 4). Rome, 68–92.

Gianfrotta, P. A. and Pomey, P. (1981). *Archeologia Subacquea. Storia, tecniche, scoperte e relitti*. Milan.

Giardini, G. and Colasante, S. (1986). *Le collezioni di pietre decorative antiche 'Federico Pescetto' e 'Pio de Santis' del Servizio Geologico d'Italia. Studio critico sistematico* (Memorie per servire alla descrizione della Carta Geologica d'Italia, Volume 15), vol. 1. Rome.

Gimpel, J. (1975). *La révolution industrielle du Moyen âge* (Collection Points, Série Histoire 19). Paris.

Giuliano, A. (1962). *Il commercio dei sarcofagi attici*. Rome.

Giuliano, A. (ed. 1982). *Museo Nazionale Romano: le sculture—I,3*. Rome.

Giuliano, A. (ed. 1984). *Museo Nazionale Romano: le sculture—I,7*. 2 vols. Rome.

Giuliano, A. and Palma, B. (1978). *La maniera ateniese di età romana. I maestri dei sarcofagi attici* (Studi Miscellanei 24). Rome.

Glicksman, K. (2009). *The Economy of Roman Dalmatia*. DPhil. thesis, University of Oxford.

Gnoli, R. (1988). *Marmora Romana*. 2nd edn. Rome.

Gnoli, R., Marchei, M. C., and Sironi, A. (2001). 'Repertorio', in G. Borghini (ed.), *Marmi antichi*. 4th edn. Rome, 131–302.

Goldsmith, R. W. (1984). 'An estimate of the size and structure of the national product of the early Roman empire', *Review of Income and Wealth* 30: 263–88.

Goldsmith, R. W. (1987). *Premodern Financial Systems. A Historical Comparative Study*. Cambridge.

González, J. (1986). 'The lex Irnitana. A new copy of the Flavian municipal law', *JRS* 76: 147–243.

González, J. (1991). *Corpus de inscripciones Latinas de Andalucía II/II. Sevilla (La Vega, Itálica)*. Seville.

Goodlett, V. C. (1991). 'Rhodian sculptural workshops', *AJA* 95: 669–81.

Goodman, P. J. (2007). *The Roman City and its Periphery. From Rome to Gaul.* London and New York.

Gorgoni, C., Filetici, M. G., Lazzarini, L., Pallante, P., and Pensabene, P. (2002). 'Archaeometry of two important marble monuments of the Republican and Early Imperial periods in Rome: the Tempio Rotondo and the Pyramid of Cestius', in J. J. Herrmann Jnr, N. Herz, and R. Newman (eds), *ASMOSIA 5. Interdisciplinary Studies on Ancient Stone.* London, 308–15.

Gorgoni, C., Kokkinakis, I., Lazzarini, L., and Mariottini, M. (1992). 'Geochemical and petrographic characterisation of "rosso antico", and other white-grey marbles of Mani (Greece)', in M. Waelkens, N. Herz, and J.-L. Moens (eds), *Ancient Stones: Quarrying, Trade and Provenance* (Acta Archaeologica Lovaniensia, Monographiae 4). Leuven, 155–66.

Gorgoni, C., Lazzarini, L., and Pallente, P. (2002). 'New archaeometric data on "Rosso Antico" and other red marbles used in Antiquity', in L. Lazzarini (ed.), *Interdisciplinary Studies on Ancient Stone. ASMOSIA VI.* Padua, 199–206.

Granino Cecere, M. G. and Morizio, V. (2007). 'Nuove testimonianze sull'amministrazione dei marmi nella Roma imperiale', in E. Papi (ed.), *Supplying Rome and the Empire* (JRA Suppl. 69). Portsmouth, RI, 127–37.

Greene, K. (1986). *The Archaeology of the Roman Economy.* Berkeley.

Greene, K. (2008). 'Learning to consume: consumption and consumerism in the Roman Empire', *JRA* 21: 64–82.

Greenhalgh, M. (2006). *Islam and Marble from the Origins to Saddam Hussein.* Canberra.

Greenhalgh, M. (2008). *Marble Past, Monumental Present: Building with Antiquities in the Mediaeval Mediterranean* (Medieval Mediterranean 80). Leiden.

Grenier, A. (1934). *Manuel d'archéologie gallo-romaine. Deuxième partie: l'archéologie du sol. Tome II: navigation—occupation du sol.* Paris.

Grewe, K. (2008). 'Tunnels and canals', in J. P. Oleson (ed.), *The Oxford Handbook of Engineering and Technology in the Classical World.* Oxford, 319–36.

Groessens, É. (1991). 'Les marbres et pierres blanches de Belgique', in J. Lorenz and P. Benoit (eds), *Carrières et constructions en France et dans les pays limitrophes.* Paris, 65–78.

Gros, P. (1985). '"Modèle urbain" et gaspillage des ressources dans les programs édilitaires des villes de Bithynie au début du IIème s. apr. J.-C.', in P. Leveau (ed.), *L'origine des richesses dépensées dans la ville antique.* Aix-en-Provence, 69–85.

Gros, P. (1987). 'Remarques sur les fondations urbaines de Narbonnaise et de Cisalpine au début de l'empire', in *Atti del Convegno 'Studi Lunensi e prospettive sull' occidente romano'* (*Quaderni del Centro di Studi Lunensi* (New Series) 10–11–12). Carrara, 73–96.

Gros, P. (2001). *L'architecture romaine du début du IIIe siècle av. J.C. à la fin du Haut-Empire* (Les manuels d'art et d'archéologie antiques), 2 vols. Paris.

Grünhagen, W. (1978). 'Farbiger Marmor aus Munigua', *Madrider Mitteilungen* 19: 290–306.

Günsenin, N. (1997). '1996 yılı Marmara Adaları yan taramalı sonar araştırması Ekinlik Adası mermer batiği', *Araştırma Sonuçları Toplantısı* 15.1: 295–306.

Gutiérrez, A. (2009). *Roman Quarries in the Northeast of Hispania (Modern Catalonia)* (Documenta 10). Tarragona.

Gutiérrez, A. (2011). 'The exploitation of local stone in Roman times: the case of north-eastern Spain', *World Archaeology* 43.2: 318–41.

Gutiérrez, A., Lapuente, P., and Rodà, I. (eds) (2012). *Interdisciplinary Studies on Ancient Stone. ASMOSIA IX* (Documenta 23). Tarragona.

Hall, A. and Waelkens, M. (1982). 'Two Dokimeian sculptors in Iconium', *Anatolian Studies* 32: 151–5.

Hallett, C. H. (1998). 'A group of portrait statues from the civic center of Aphrodisias', *AJA* 102.1: 59–89.

Hankey, V. (1965). 'A marble quarry at Karystos', *BMB* 18: 43–59.

Hannestad, N. (1990). 'The classical tradition in Late Roman sculpture', in *Akten des XIII. Internationalen Kongresses für klassische Archäologie, Berlin 1988*. Mainz, 516–17.

Hansen, M. F. (2003). *The Eloquence of Appropriation. Prolegomena to an Understanding of Spolia in Early Christian Rome* (ARID Suppl. 33). Rome.

Hanson, J. W. (2011). 'The urban system of Roman Asia Minor and wider urban connectivity', in A. Bowman and A. Wilson (eds), *Settlement, Urbanization, and Population* (Oxford Studies in the Roman Economy 2). Oxford, 229–75.

Hanson, J. W. (forthcoming). *The Urban System of the Roman Empire*. DPhil. thesis, University of Oxford.

Harl, K. W. (1996). *Coinage in the Roman Economy, 300 B.C. to A.D. 700*. Baltimore and London.

Harrazi, N. (1995). *Les carrières antiques d'El Haouaria*. Tunis.

Harrell, J. A. (2005). '*Porfido rosso laterizio* and the discovery of its source in Wadi Abu Gerida (Egypt)', *Marmora* 1: 37–48.

Harrell, J. A., Brown, V. M., and Lazzarini, L. (1999). 'Two newly discovered Roman quarries in the Eastern Desert of Egypt', in M. Schvoerer (ed.), *Archéomatériaux: marbres et autres roches. ASMOSIA IV*. Bordeaux, 285–92.

Harrell, J. A., Brown, V. M., and Lazzarini, L. (2002). '*Breccia Verde Antica*: sources, petrology and ancient uses', in L. Lazzarini (ed.), *Interdisciplinary Studies on Ancient Stone. ASMOSIA VI*. Padua, 207–18.

Harris, W. V. (1980). 'Roman terracotta lamps: the organization of an industry', *JRS* 70: 126–45.

Harris, W. V. (1993a). 'Between Archaic and Modern: problems in Roman economic history', in W. V. Harris (ed.), *The Inscribed Economy: Production and Distribution in the Roman Empire in the Light of Instrumentum Domesticum* (JRA Suppl. 6). Ann Arbor, 11–30.

Harris, W. V. (1993b). 'Production, distribution, and *instrumentum domesticum*', in W. V. Harris (ed.), *The Inscribed Economy: Production and Distribution in the Roman Empire in the Light of Instrumentum Domesticum* (JRA Suppl. 6). Ann Arbor, 186–9.

Harris, W. V. (2003). 'Roman governments and commerce, 300 BC–AD 300', in C. Zaccagnini (ed.), *Mercanti e politica nel mondo antico*. Rome, 275–306.

Hasluch, F. W. (1909). 'The Marmara island', *JHS* 29: 6–18.

Hasluch, F. W. (1910). *Cyzicus*. Cambridge.

Hatzfeld, J. (1919). *Les trafiquants Italiens dans l'Orient Hellénique*. Paris.

Hayward, K. M. J. (2006). 'A geological link between the Facilis monument at Colchester and first-century army tombstones from the Rhineland frontier', *Britannia* 37: 359–63.

Hayward, K. M. J. (2009). *Roman Quarrying and Stone Supply on the Periphery— Southern England. A Geological Study of First-Century Funerary Monuments and Monumental Architecture* (BAR British Series 500). Oxford.

Heiken, G., Funiciello, R., and De Rita, D. (2005). *The Seven Hills of Rome. A Geological Tour of the Eternal City*. Princeton and Oxford.

Heilmeyer, W.-D. (1970). *Korinthische Normalkapitelle: Studien zur Geschichte der römischen Architekturdekoration* (MDAI(R) Ergänzungsheft 16. Heidelberg.

Heilmeyer, W.-D. (1986). 'Antike Kunst und Kunstproduktion—Werkstattforschung in der klassischen Archäologie', *Jahrbuch Preußischer Kulturbesitz* 23: 95–124.

Heilmeyer, W.-D. (2004). 'Ancient workshops and ancient "art"', *OJA* 23.4: 403–15.

Heinzelmann, M. (2003). 'Städtekonkurrenz und kommunaler Bürgersinn: die Säulenstraße von Perge als Beispiel monumentaler Stadtgestaltung durch kollektiven Eurgetismus', *AA* 2003.1: 197–220.

Helen, T. (1975). *Organization of Roman Brick Production in the First and Second Centuries A.D. An Interpretation of Roman Brick Stamps* (Acta Instituti romani Finlandiae 9). Helsinki.

Henig, M. (1993). *Roman Sculpture from the Cotswold Region with Devon and Cornwall* (Corpus Signorum Imperii Romani: Great Britain I.7). Oxford.

Herdejürgen, H. (1988). 'Sarkophagrückseiten', *AA* 1988: 87–96.

Herdejürgen, H. (1996). *Stadtrömische und italische Girlandensarkophage: die Sarkophage des ersten und zweiten Jahrhunderts* (Die antiken Sarkophagreliefs 6.2.1). Berlin.

Herdejürgen, H. (2000). 'Sarkophage von der Via Latina. Folgerungen aus dem Fundkontext', *MDAI(R)* 107: 209–34.

Herrmann Jnr, J. J. (1988). *The Ionic Capital in Late Antique Rome*. Rome.

Herrmann Jnr, J. J. (1990). 'Thasos and the ancient marble trade: evidence from American museums', in M. True and J. Podany (eds), *Marble: Art Historical and Scientific Perspectives on Ancient Sculpture*. Malibu, 73–100.

Herrmann Jnr, J. J. (1992). 'Exportation of dolomitic marble from Thasos: evidence from European and North American collections', in M. Waelkens, N. Herz, and J.-L. Moens (eds), *Ancient Stones: Quarrying, Trade and Provenance* (Acta Archaeologica Lovaniensia, Monographiae 4). Leuven, 93–104.

Herrmann Jnr, J. J. (1999). 'The exportation of dolomitic marble from Thasos. A short overview', in C. Koukoule-Chrusanthake, A. Muller, and S. Papadopoulos (eds), *Thasos. Matière premières et technologie de la préhistoire à nos jours*. Paris, 57–74.

Herrmann Jnr, J. J., Attanasio, D., Tykot, R. H., and van den Hoek, A. (2012). 'Characterization and distribution of marble from Cap de Garde and Mt. Filfila, Algeria', in A. Gutiérrez, P. Lapuente, and I. Rodà (eds), *Interdisciplinary Studies on Ancient Stone. ASMOSIA IX* (Documenta 23). Tarragona, 300–9.

Herrmann Jnr, J. J., Herz, N., and Newman, R. (eds) (2002). *ASMOSIA 5. Interdisciplinary Studies on Ancient Stone*. London.

Herrmann Jnr, J. J. and Newman, R. (1995). 'The exportation of dolomitic marble from Thasos: evidence from Mediterranean and other collections', in Y. Maniatis, N. Herz, and Y. Basiakos (eds), _The Study of Marble and Other Stones Used in Antiquity. ASMOSIA III._ London, 73–86.

Herrmann Jnr, J. J. and Newman, R. (1999). 'Dolomitic marble from Thasos near and far: Macedonia, Ephesos, and the Rhône', in M. Schvoerer (ed.), _Archéomatériaux: marbres et autres roches. ASMOSIA IV._ Bordeaux, 293–303.

Herrmann Jnr, J. J. and Newman, R. (2002). 'New sculptures in Thasian dolomite: Turkey, Greece, Egypt, Italy', in J. J. Herrmann Jnr, N. Herz, and R. Newman (eds), _ASMOSIA 5. Interdisciplinary Studies on Ancient Stone._ London, 215–24.

Herrmann Jnr, J. J. and Sodini, J.-P. (1977). 'Exporations de marbre Thasien à l'époque paléochrétienne: le cas des chapiteaux ionique', _BCH_ 101: 471–511.

Herrmann Jnr, J. J. and Tykot, R. H. (2009). 'Some products from the Dokimeian quarries: craters, tables, capitals, and statues', in Y. Maniatis (ed.), _ASMOSIA VII_ (BCH Suppl. 51). Athens, 60–75.

Herrmann Jnr, J. J., Van Den Hoek, A., and Newman, R. (2002). 'New sculptures in Thasian dolomite: Ukraine, Tunisia, and questions of style', in L. Lazzarini (ed.), _Interdisciplinary Studies on Ancient Stone. ASMOSIA VI._ Padua, 357–62.

Herz, N. (1988). 'Classical marble quarries of Thasos', in G. A. Wagner and G. Weisgerber (eds), _Antike Edel- und Buntmetallgewinnung auf Thasos_ (Der Anschnitt, Zeitschrift für Kunst und Kultur im Bergbau 6). Bochum, 232–40.

Herz, N. (1990). 'Greek and Roman marble: provenance determination and artifact reconstruction', in P. G. Marinos and G. C. Koukis (eds), _The Engineering Geology of Ancient Works, Monuments and Historical Sites: Preservation and Protection._ 4 vols. Rotterdam, 1987–94.

Herz, N. (2000). 'The classical marble quarries of Paros: Paros-1, Paros-2 and Paros-3', in D. U. Schilardi and D. Katsonopoulou (eds), _Paria Lithos: Parian Quarries, Marble and Workshops of Sculpture._ Athens, 27–34.

Herz, N. and Waelkens, M. (eds 1988). _Classical Marble: Geochemistry, Technology and Trade._ NATO ASI series E: Applied Sciences 153. Dordrecht.

Herz, N. and Wenner, D. (1981). 'Tracing the origins of marble', _Archaeology_ 34: 14–21.

Hester, T. R. and Heizer, R. E. (1981). _Making Stone Vases, Ethnoarchaeological Studies at an Alabaster Workshop in Upper Egypt._ Malibu.

Hiebert, F. and Cambon, P. (2011). _Afghanistan: Crossroads of the Ancient World._ London.

Higgins, M. D. and Higgins, R. (1996). _A Geological Companion to Greece and the Aegean._ London.

Hill, P. (2004). _The Construction of Hadrian's Wall_ (BAR British Series 375). Oxford.

Hirschfeld, O. (1905). _Die kaiserlichen Verwaltungsbeamten bis auf Diokletian._ 2nd edn. Berlin.

Hirt, A. M. (2010). _Imperial Mines and Quarries in the Roman World: Organizational Aspects, 27 BC–AD 235_ (Oxford Classical Monographs). Oxford.

Höghammer, K. (1993). _Sculpture and Society: a Study of the Connection between the Free-Standing Sculpture and Society on Kos in the Hellenistic and Augustan Periods_ (Boreas 23). Uppsala.

Højte, J. M. (2005). *Roman Imperial Statue Bases: from Augustus to Constantine.* Aarhus.

Hollinshead, M. B. (2002). 'From two to three dimensions in unfinished Roman sculpture', in J. J. Herrmann Jnr, N. Herz, and R. Newman (eds), *ASMOSIA 5. Interdisciplinary Studies on Ancient Stone.* London, 225–30.

Holt, E. G. (1957). *A Documentary History of Art. Volume I: The Middle Ages and the Renaissance.* Garden City, NY.

Hopkins, K. (1978). 'Economic growth and towns in classical antiquity', in P. Abrams and E. A. Wrigley (eds), *Towns in Societies: Essays in Economic History and Historical Sociology.* Cambridge, 35–77.

Horden, P. and Purcell, N. (2000). *The Corrupting Sea: a Study of Mediterranean History.* Oxford.

Horsley, G. H. R. (2007). *The Greek and Latin Inscriptions in the Burdur Archaeological Museum* (Regional Epigraphic Catalogues of Asia Minor 5/The British Institute at Ankara, Monograph 34). London.

Horster, M. (2001). *Bauinschriften römischer Kaiser. Untersuchungen zu Inschriftenpraxis und Bautätigkeit in Städten des westlichen Imperium Romanum in der Zeit des Prinzipats* (Historia Einzelschriften 157). Stuttgart.

Houston, J. M. (1964). *The Western Mediterranean World. An Introduction to its Regional Landscapes.* London.

Humann, C. (1959). *Der Pergamon Altar endeckt, beschrieben und gezeichnet* (Schriften der Hermann-Bröckelschen-Stiftung, Carl Humann zum Gedächtnis). Dortmund.

Hunt, D. W. S. (1940–5). 'An archaeological survey of the island of Chios', *ABSA* 41: 29–47.

Hurst, H. R. and Roskams, S. P. (1984). *Excavations at Carthage: The British Museum, Volume I,1. The Avenue du President Habib Bourguiba, Salammbo: The Site and Finds other than Pottery.* Sheffield.

Hurst, J. T. (1903). *A Handbook of Formulae, Tables and Memoranda for Architectural Surveyors and Others Engaged in Building.* 15th edn. London.

Huskinson, J. (1994). *Roman Sculpture from Eastern England* (Corpus Signorum Imperii Romani: Great Britain I.8). Oxford.

Huskinson, J. (1996). *Roman Children's Sarcophagi: their Decoration and Social Significance.* Oxford.

Huskinson, J. (1998). '"Unfinished portrait heads" on later Roman sarcophagi: some new perspectives', *PBSR* 66: 129–58.

Immerzeel, M. (1995). 'L'emploi du marbre pyrénéen pour la production de sarcophages paléochrétiens en Gaule: la Provence et les Pyrénées', in J. Cabanot, R. Sablayrolles, and J.-L. Schenk (eds), *Les marbres blancs des Pyrénées: approches scientifiques et historiques.* Toulouse, 207–22.

Inan, J. and Rosenbaum, E. (1979). *Römische und Frühbyzantinische Porträtplastik aus der Türkei: neue Funde.* 2 vols. Mainz.

Ireland, R. (1983). 'Epigraphy', in M. Henig (ed.), *A Handbook of Roman Art: A Survey of the Visual Arts of the Roman World.* London, 220–33.

Isaac, B. and Roll, I. (1982). *Roman Roads in Judaea I. The Legio—Scythopolis Road* (BAR International Series 141). Oxford.

Işik, F. (1992). 'Zum Produktionsbeginn von Halbfabrikaten kleinasiatischer Girlandensarkophage', *AA* 1992: 121–45.

Işik, F. (1998). 'Zu produktionsbeginn und Ende der kleinasiatischen Girlandensarkophage der Hauptgruppe', in G. Koch (ed.), *Akten des Symposiums '125 Jahre Sarkophag-Corpus'* (Sarkophag-Studien 1). Mainz, 278–94.

Işik, F. (2007). *Girlanden-Sarkophage aus Aphrodisias* (Sarkophag-Studien 5). Mainz.

Isserlin, R. M. J. (1998). 'A spirit of improvement? Marble and the culture of Roman Britain', in R. Laurence and J. Berry (eds), *Cultural identity in the Roman Empire*. London and New York, 125–55.

Jackson, M. and Marra, F. (2006). 'Roman stone masonry: volcanic foundations of the ancient city', *AJA* 110.3: 403–36.

Janković, D. (1980). 'Etudes des monuments de Vrelo, Šarkamen', *Starinar* 31: 88–93.

Janon, M. (1986). 'L'ensemble "Capitolium-forum"', in Y. Solier (ed.), *Narbonne (Aude). Les monuments antiques et médiévaux, le Musée Archéologique et le Musée Lapidaire*. Paris, 41–5.

Jockey, P. (2001). 'L'artisanat de la sculpture antique: une conquête historiographique?', in J.-P. Brun and P. Jockey (eds), τέχναι. *Techniques et Sociétés en Méditerranée. Hommage à Marie-Claire Amouretti*. Paris, 347–66.

Jockey, P. (ed. 2009). *Leukos lithos. Marbres et autres roches de la Méditerranée antique: études interdisciplinaries. ASMOSIA VIII.* (Collection l'atelier méditerranéen). Paris.

Joncheray, A. (1998). 'Dramont I: une épave de marbres d'Asie Mineure', in É. Rieth (ed.), *Méditerranée antique: pêche, navigation, commerce*. Paris, 139–58.

Joncheray, A. and Joncheray, J.-P. (1997). 'Dramont I, description et étude de la coque d'une épave de marbres d'Asia Mineure du premier siècle après J.-C.', *Cahiers d'Archéologie Subaquatique* 13: 165–95.

Joncheray, A. and Joncheray, J.-P. (2002). Chrétienne M, trois épaves distinctes, entre le cinquième siècle avant et le premier siècle après Jésus-Christ', *Cahiers d'Archéologie Subaquatique* 14: 57–130.

Jones, A. H. M. (1937). *Cities of the Eastern Roman Provinces*. Oxford.

Jones, A. H. M. (1940). *The Greek City from Alexander to Justinian*. Oxford.

Jones, A. H. M. (1964). *The Later Roman Empire, 284–602. A Social, Economic and Administrative Survey*. Oxford.

Jones, C. P. (1978). *The Roman World of Dio Chrysostom*. Cambridge, MA, and London.

Jongman, W. (2002). 'The Roman economy: from cities to empire', in L. de Blois and J. Rich (eds), *The Transformation of Economic Life under the Roman Empire* (Impact of Empire (Roman Empire) 2). Amsterdam, 28–47.

Jongman, W. (2007). 'The early Roman Empire: consumption', in W. Scheidel, E. L. Morris, and R. P. Saller (eds), *The Cambridge Economic History of the Greco-Roman World*. Cambridge, 592–618.

Jouffroy, H. (1977). 'Le financement des constructions publiques en Italie: initiative municipale, initiative impériale, évergétisme privé', *Ktema* 2: 329–34.

Jouffroy, H. (1986). *La construction publique en Italie et dans l'Afrique romaine* (Groupe de Recherche d'Histoire Romaine de l'Université des Sciences Humaines de Strasbourg. Études et Travaux 2). Strasbourg.

Judeich, W. (1898). 'Inschriften', in C. Humann, C. Cichorius, W. Judeich, and F. Winter (eds), *Altertümer von Hierapolis* (Jahrbuch des kaiserlich deutschen archäologischen Instituts, Ergänzungsheft 4). Berlin, 67–180.

Jung, D. (1961). 'Die Geologie des Gebietes von Chasampali (Thessalien)', Πρακτικα της Ἀκαδημιας Ἀθηνων (*Praktika tes Akademias Athenon*) 36: 149–56.

Jurišić, M. (2000). *Ancient Shipwrecks of the Adriatic: Maritime Transport during the First and Second Centuries AD* (BAR International Series 828). Oxford.

Kahanov, Y. and Mor, H. (2006). 'The Dor 2001/1 wreck', in L. Blue, F. Hocker, and A. Englert (eds), *Connected by the Sea*. Oxford, 84–8.

Kainic, P. (1986). 'Deux epaves antiques livrent leur cargaison', *Archeologia* 209: 6–9.

Kane, S. (1985). 'Sculpture from the Cyrene Demeter Sanctuary in its Mediterranean context', in G. W. W. Barker, J. Lloyd, and J. M. Reynolds (eds), *Cyrenaica in Antiquity* (Society for Libyan Studies Occasional Papers 1; BAR International Series 236). Oxford, 237–48.

Kane, S. (1988). 'Sculpture from Cyrene in its Mediterranean context', in J. C. Fant (ed.), *Ancient Marble Quarrying and Trade* (BAR International Series 453). Oxford, 127–38.

Kane, S. (2000). 'Parian sculpture in the Greco-Roman city of Cyrene, Libya', in D. U. Schilardi and D. Katsonopoulou (eds), *Paria Lithos: Parian Quarries, Marble and Workshops of Sculpture*. Athens, 479–86.

Kane, S. and Carrier, S. (1988). 'Relationships between style and size of statuary and the availability of marble at Cyrene', in N. Herz and M. Waelkens (eds), *Classical Marble: Geochemistry, Technology and Trade* (NATO ASI series E: Applied Sciences 153). Dordrecht, 197–206.

Kane, S. and Carrier, S. (1992). 'Relationships between style and size or statuary and the availability of marble in the eastern Roman Empire', in M. Waelkens, N. Herz, and J.-L. Moens (eds), *Ancient Stones: Quarrying, Trade and Provenance* (Acta Archaeologica Lovaniensia, Monographiae 4). Leuven, 121–8.

Kane, S., Polikreti, K., Herz, N., Carrier, S., and Maniatis, Y. (1999). 'Investigation of the Pentelic marble sculptures of the *Nymphaeum* of Herodes Atticus in Olympia, Greece', in M. Schvoerer (ed.), *Archéomatériaux: marbres et autres roches. ASMOSIA IV*. Bordeaux, 317–24.

Kanitz, F. (1892). *Römische Studien in Serbien. Der Donau-Grenzwall, das Strassennetz, die Städte, Castelle, Denkmale, Thermen und Bergwerke zur Römerzeit im Königreiche Serbien* (Denkschriften der kaiserlichen Akademie der Wissenschaften in Wien. Philosophisch-Historische Classe 41). Vienna.

Kapitän, G. (1961). 'Schiffsfrachten antiker Baugesteine und Architekturteile vor den Küsten Ostsiziliens', *Klio* 39: 276–318.

Kapitän, G. (1969). 'The church wreck off Marzamemi', *Archaeology* 22: 122–33.

Kapitän, G. (1976). *Das Kirchenwrack von Marzamemi*. Hamburg.

Karageorghis, V. (1969). 'Chronique des fouilles à Chypre en 1968', *BCH* 93: 431–569.

Kastenmeier, P., Di Maio, G., Balassone, G., Boni, M., Joachimski, M., and Mondillo, N. (2010). 'The source of stone building materials from the Pompeii archaeological area and its surroundings', *Periodico di Mineralogia, Special Issue*: 39–58.

Kayser, F. (1993). 'Nouveaux textes grecs du Ouadi Hammamat', *ZPE* 98: 111–56.

Keay, S. (1988). *Roman Spain*. London.

Keil, J. (1908). 'Zur Topographie der ionischen Küste südlich von Ephesos', *JÖAI* 11 (Beiblatt): 135–68.

Keil, J. (1910). 'Forschungen in der Erythraia I', *JÖAI* 13 (Beiblatt): 1–80.

Keil, J. (1932). 'XVI. Vorläufiger Bericht über die Ausgrabungen in Ephesos', *JÖAI* 27 (Beiblatt): 5–71.

Keller, D. (1985). *Archaeological Survey in Southern Euboea, Greece: A Reconstruction of Human Activity from Neolithic Times through the Byzantine Period*, PhD dissertation, University of Indiana.

Keppie, L. J. F. and Arnold, B. J. (1984). *Scotland* (Corpus Signorum Imperii Romani: Great Britain I.4). Oxford.

Khanoussi, M. (1996). 'Les officiales marmorum Numidicorum', in M. Khanoussi, P. Ruggieri, and C. Vismar (eds), *L'Africa Romana. Atti de XII convegno di studio, Olbia, 12–15 dicembre 1996*, 3 vols. Sassari, 997–1016.

Khanoussi, M. (1997). 'Le saltus philomusianus et les carrières de marbre numidique', *MDAI(R)* 104: 375–7.

Klapisch-Zuber, C. (1969). *Les maîtres du marbre: Carrare, 1300–1600*. Paris.

Kleber, F., Diem, M., Sablatnig, R., and Kampel, M. (2010). 'Proposing features for the reconstruction of marble plates of Ephesos', in *VSMM 2010–16th International Conference on Virtual Systems and Multimedia, 20–23 October 2010, Seoul, South Korea*. Seoul, 328–31.

Kleiner, F. S. (1977). 'Artists in the Roman world. An itinerante workshops in Augustan Gaul', *MEFRA* 89.1: 661–96.

Klemm, R. and Klemm, D. (1993). *Steine und Steinbrüchen im Alten Ägypten*. Berlin.

Klemm, R. and Klemm, D. (2008). *Stones and Quarries in Ancient Egypt*. Revised edn. London.

Knoop, D. and Jones, G. P. (1967). *The Mediaeval Mason. An Economic History of English Stone Building in the Later Middle Ages and Early Modern Times*. 3rd edn. Manchester.

Knudsen, S. E., Craine, C., and Tykot, R. H. (2002). 'Analysis of classical marble sculptures in the Toledo Museum of Art', in J. J. Herrmann Jnr, N. Herz, and R. Newman (eds), *ASMOSIA 5. Interdisciplinary Studies on Ancient Stone*. London, 231–9.

Koch, G. (1975). *Die mythologischen Sarkophage, 6: Meleager* (Die antiken Sarkophagreliefs 12.6). Bonn.

Koch, G. (1977). 'Ein Endymionsarkophag in Arles', *BJ* 177: 245–70.

Koch, G. (1989). 'Das Import kaiserlicher Sarkophage in den römischen Provinzen Syria Palaestina und Arabia', *BJ* 189: 161–211.

Koch, G. (1993). *Sarkophage der römischen Kaiserzeit*. Darmstadt.

Koch, G. (2000). *Frühchristliche Sarkophage* (Handbuch der Archäologie). Munich.

Koch, G. (2011). 'Sarcofagi di età imperiale romana in Asia Minore: una sintesi', in F. D'Andria and I. Romeo (eds), *Roman Sculpture in Asia Minor* (JRA Suppl. 80). Portsmouth, RI, 9–29.

Koch, G. and Sichtermann, H. (1982). *Römische Sarkophage* (Handbuch der Archäologie). Munich.

Kockel, V. (1983). *Die Grabbauten vor dem Herkulaner Tor in Pompeji* (Beitrage zur Erschliessung hellenistischer und kaiserzeitlicher Skulptur und Architektur 1). Mainz.

Kockel, V. (1993). *Porträtreliefs stadtrömischer Grabbauten. Ein Beitrag zur Geschichte und zum Verständnis des spätrepublikanisch-frühkaiserzeitlichen Privatporträts*

(Beiträge zur Erschließung hellenistischer und kaiserzeitlicher Skulptur und Architektur 12). Mainz.

Kolb, A. (1993). *Die kaiserliche Bauverwaltung in der Stadt Rom. Geschichte und Aufbau der cura operum publicorum unter dem Prinzipat.* Stuttgart.

Kolb, A. (2000). *Transport und Nachrichtentransfer im Römischen Reich* (Klio, Beihefte Neue Folge 2). Berlin.

Koller, K. (2003). 'Marmorwandausstattungen—stummes Zeugnis privater Repräsentation im Hanghaus 2 in Ephesos', in B. Asamer and W. Wohlmayer (eds), *Akten des 9. Österreichischen Archäologentages am Institut für klassiche Archäologie der Paris Lodron-Universität Salzburg, 6.-8. Dezember 2001.* Vienna, 109–14.

Koller, K. (2005). 'Zur Marmorwandvertäfelung aus der Nordostecke der Temenoshallen des "Serapeions" in Ephesos', in B. Brandt, V. Gassner, and S. Ladstätter (eds), *Synergia. Festschrift für Friedrich Krinzinger*, vol. 1. Vienna, 137–45.

Kolling, A. (1992). 'Die Reiterstatuen von Breitfurt und der antike Name von Schwarzenacker', *Saarpfalz* 1992.1: 51–62.

Kollwitz, J. and Herdejürgen, H. (1979). *Die Sarkophage der westlichen Gebiete des Imperium Romanum: die ravennatischen Sarkophage* (Die antiken Sarkophagreliefs 8.2). Berlin.

Köse, V. (2005). *Nekropolen und Grabdenkmäler von Sagalassos in Pisidien in hellenistischer und römischer Zeit* (Studies in Eastern Mediterranean Archaeology 7). Turnhout.

Kouzeli, C. and Dimou, E. (2009). 'Building materials (except Pentelic marble) used in ancient Athens', in P. Jockey (ed.), *Leukos lithos. Marbres et autres roches de la Méditerranée antique: études interdisciplinaries. ASMOSIA VIII.* (Collection l'atelier méditerranéen). Paris, 291–308.

Koželj, T. (1987). 'Les carrières de marbre dans l'antiquité. Techniques et organisation', in D. Vanhove (ed.), *Marbres helléniques de la carrière au chef-d'oeuvre.* Brussels, 20–33.

Koželj, T. (1988). 'Les carrières des époques grecque, romaine et byzantine', in J. C. Fant (ed.), *Ancient Marble Quarrying and Trade* (BAR International Series 453). Oxford, 3–79.

Koželj, T., Lambraki, A., Muller, A., and Sodini, J. O. (1985). 'Sarcophages découvertes dans les carriers de Saliari (Thasos)', in P. Pensabene (ed.), *Marmi antichi: problemi d'impiego, di restauro e d'identificazione* (Studi Miscellanei 26). Rome, 75–82.

Koželj, T. and Wurch-Koželj, M. (1993). 'Les transports dans l'antiquité', in R. Francovich (ed.), *Archeologia delle attività estrattive e metallurgiche.* Florence, 97–142.

Koželj, T. and Wurch-Koželj, M. (2009). 'Les carrières du Cap Phanari à Thasos', in P. Jockey (ed.), *Leukos lithos. Marbres et autres roches de la Méditerranée antique: études interdisciplinaries. ASMOSIA VIII.* (Collection l'atelier méditerranéen). Paris, 49–71.

Kragelund, P., Moltesen, M., and Østergaard, J. S. (2003). *The Licinian Tomb: Fact or Fiction?* Copenhagen.

Kranz, P. (1984). *Jahreszeiten-Sarkophage: Entwicklung und Ikonographie des Motivs der vier Jahreszeiten auf kaiserzeitlichen Sarkophagen und Sarkophagdeckeln* (Die antiken Sarkophagreliefs 5.1). Berlin.

Kranz, P. (1999). *Die stadtrömischen Eroten-Sarkophage, 1: Dionysische Themen* (Die antiken Sarkophagreliefs 5.2.1). Berlin.

Kraus, T. (1993). 'Steinbruch- und Blockinschriften', in F. Rakob (ed.), *Simitthus I: die Steinbrüche und die antike Stadt*. Mainz, 55–64.

Kubińska, J. (1968). *Les monuments funéraires dans les inscriptions grecques de l'Asie Mineure* (Travaux du Centre d'Archéologie Méditerranéenne de l'Academie Polonaise des Sciences 5). Warsaw.

La Rocca, E. (1987). *L'auriga dell'Esquilino*. Rome.

Lambertie, R.-M. (1962). *L'industrie de la pierre et du marbre*. Paris.

Lamberto, V. and Sá Caetano, P. (2008). 'Marble stones from *Lusitania*: the quarries of the Estremoz anticline', in T. Nogales and J. Beltrán (eds), *Marmora Hispania: explotación y uso de los materiales pétreos en la Hispania romana* (Hispania Antigua, Serie Arqueológica 2). Rome, 467–81.

Lambraki, A. (1978). *Les roches vertes. Étude sur les marbres de la Grèce exploités aux époques romaine et paléochrétienne*, Thèse de troisième cycle, Université de Paris I—Pantheon-Sorbonne.

Lambraki, A. (1980). 'Le cipolin de la Karystie. Contribution à l'étude des marbres de la Grèce exploités aux époques romaine et paléochrétienne', *RA*: 31–62.

Lambraki, A. (1982). 'L'emploi de la scie lisse en tant qu'outil de carrier, en Grèce, à l'époque paléochrétienne', in *Troisièmes Journées de l'Industrie Minérale: le Marbre* (Bulletin des Musées Royaux d'Art et d'Histoire, Bruxelles 53.2). Brussels, 81–8.

Lancaster, L. (1998). 'Building Trajan's Markets', *AJA* 102: 283–308.

Lancaster, L. (2000). 'Building Trajan's Markets 2: the construction process', *AJA* 104: 755–85.

Lancaster, L. (2005). *Concrete Vaulted Construction in Imperial Rome: Innovations in Context*. Cambridge.

Lanciani, R. (1891). 'Officina marmoraria della Regione XIII', *BCAR* 4: 23–36.

Lanciani, R. (1897). *Ruins and Excavations of Ancient Rome: A Companion Book for Students and Travellers*. London.

Lanckoroński, K. (1890). *Städte Pamphyliens und Pisidiens*, 2 vols. Vienna.

Langley, B. (1735). *The Builder's Vade-Mecum: or, A Complete Key to the Five Orders of Columns in Architecture*. London.

Lapuente, P., León, P., Nogales, T., Royo, H., Preite-Martinez, M., and Blanc, P. (2012). 'White sculptural materials from Villa Adriana: study of provenance', in A. Gutiérrez, P. Lapuente, and I. Rodà (eds), *Interdisciplinary Studies on Ancient Stone. ASMOSIA IX* (Documenta 23). Tarragona, 364–75.

Lapuente, P., Preite-Martinez, M., Turi, B., and Blanc, P. (2002). 'Characterization of dolomitic marbles from the Malaga province (Spain)', in J. J. Herrmann Jnr, N. Herz, and R. Newman (eds), *ASMOSIA 5. Interdisciplinary Studies on Ancient Stone*. London, 152–62.

Lapuente, P., Turi, B., and Blanc, P. (2000). 'Marbles from Roman Hispania: stable isotope and cathodoluminescence characterization', *Applied Geochemistry* 15.10: 1469–93.

Lapuente, P., Turi, B., and Blanc, P. (2009). 'Marbles and coloured stones from the theatre of *Caesaraugusta* (*Hispania*): preliminary study', in Y. Maniatis (ed.), *ASMOSIA VII* (BCH Supplement 51). Athens, 509–22.

Laurence, R. (1999). *The Roads of Roman Italy: Mobility and Cultural Change*. London and New York.

Lazzarini, L. (1987). 'I graniti dei monumenti italiani e i loro problem di deterioramento', in *Materiali lapidei: problem relative allo studio del degrade e della conservazione* (Bollettino d'Arte Suppl. 41). Rome, 157–72.

Lazzarini, L. (1992). 'Des pierres pour l'éternité', *Les Dossiers d'Archéologie* 173: 58–67.

Lazzarini, L. (ed.) (2002a). *Interdisciplinary Studies on Ancient Stone. ASMOSIA VI*. Padua.

Lazzarini, L. (2002b). 'A new grey marble from Gortyna (Crete) used in Greek and Roman antiquity', in L. Lazzarini (ed.), *Interdisciplinary Studies on Ancient Stone. ASMOSIA VI*. Padua, 227–32.

Lazzarini, L. (2002c). 'La determinazione della provenienza delle pietre decorative usate dai romani', in M. De Nuccio and L. Ungaro (eds), *I marmi colorati della Roma imperiale*. Padua, 223–75.

Lazzarini, L. (2004). 'La diffusione e il riuso dei piú importanti marmi romani nelle province imperiali', in L. Lazzarini (ed.), *Pietre e marmi antichi. Natura, caratterizzazione, origine, storia d'uso, diffusione, collezionismo*. Padua, 101–22.

Lazzarini, L. (2007). *Poikiloi Lithoi, Versiculores Maculae: i marmi colorati della Grecia antica. Storia, uso, diffusione, cave, geologia, caratterizzazione scientifica, archeometria, deterioramento*. Pisa and Rome.

Lazzarini, L. (2010). 'Considerazioni sul prezo dei marmi bianchi e colorati di età imperiale', in S. Camporeale, H. Dessales, and A. Pizzo (eds), *Arqueología de la construcción II. Los procesos constructivos en el mundo romano: Italia y provincias orientales* (Anejos de Archivo Español de Arqueología 57). Madrid, 485–90.

Lazzarini, L., Agus, M., and Cara, S. (2006). 'The ancient quarries of the *neri antichi* (black limestones) from Zeugitania (Tunisia)', *Marmora* 2: 59–70.

Lazzarini, L. and Antonelli, F. (2004). 'L'identificazione del marmo constituente manufatti antichi', in L. Lazzarini (ed.), *Pietre e marmi antichi. Natura, caratterizzazione, origine, storia d'uso, diffusione, collezionismo*. Padua, 65–72.

Lazzarini, L. Gorgoni, C., Pallante, P., and Turi, B. (1997). 'Identification of ancient white marbles in Rome. II: the Portico of Octavia', *Science and Technology for Cultural Heritage* 6.2: 185–98.

Lazzarini, L., Mariottini, M., Pecoraro, M., and Pensabene, P. (1988). 'Determination of the provenance of marbles used in some ancient monuments in Rome', in N. Herz and M. Waelkens (eds), *Classical Marble: Geochemistry, Technology and Trade* (NATO ASI series E: Applied Sciences 153). Dordrecht, 399–409.

Lazzarini, L., Moschini, G., Xusheng, H., and Waelkens, M. (1985). 'New light on some Phrygian marble quarries through a petrological study and the evaluation of Ca/Sr ratio', in P. Pensabene (ed.), *Marmi antichi: problemi d'impiego, di restauro e d'identificazione* (Studi Miscellanei 26). Rome, 41–6.

Lazzarini, L., Pensabene, P., Preite-Martinez, M., and Turi, B. (2007). 'La determinazione della provenienza dei marmi usati nella statuaria e nei rilievi', in P. Pensabene (ed.), *Ostiensum marmorum decus et decor: studi architettonici, decorativi e archeometrici* (Studi Miscellanei 33). Rome, 619–27.

Lazzarini, L., Ponti, G., Preite-Martinez, M., Rockwell, P., and Turi, B. (2002). 'Historical, technical, petrographic, and isotopic features of Aphrodisian marble', in

J. J. Herrmann Jnr, N. Herz, and R. Newman (eds), *ASMOSIA 5. Interdisciplinary Studies on Ancient Stone*. London, 163–8.

Lazzarini, L., Preite-Martinez, M., and Turi, B. (2007). 'La determinazione della provenienza dei marmi usati in architettura a Ostia', in P. Pensabene (ed.), *Ostiensum marmorum decus et decor: studi architettonici, decorativi e archeometrici* (Studi Miscellanei 33). Rome, 609–15.

Lazzarini, L. and Sangati, C. (2004). 'I piú importanti marmi e pietre colorati usati dagli antichi', in L. Lazzarini (ed.), *Pietre e marmi antichi. Natura, caratterizzazione, origine, storia d'uso, diffusione, collezionismo*. Padua, 73–100.

Lazzarini, L. and Visonà, D. (2009). '*Lapis sarcophagus* and the provenance of its Mediterranean sarcophagi', in P. Jockey (ed.), *Leukos lithos. Marbres et autres roches de la Méditerranée antique: études interdisciplinaries. ASMOSIA VIII.* (Collection l'atelier méditerranéen). Paris, 369–88.

Leach, E. W. (1990). 'The politics of self-presentation: Pliny's "Letters" and Roman portrait sculpture', *ClAnt* 9.1: 14–39.

Le Bohec, Y. (ed. 1991). *Le Testament du Lingon* (Collection du Centre d'Etudes Romaines et Gallo-romaines (New series) 9). Lyon.

Lee, A. (1888). *Marble and Marble Workers. A Handbook for Architects, Artists, Masons, and Students*. London.

Lefebvre des Noëttes, R. J. E. C. (1931). *L'attelage: le cheval de selle à travers les âges. Contribution à l'histoire de l'esclavage*. Paris.

Lendon, J. E. (1997). *Empire of Honour. The Art of Government in the Roman World*. Oxford.

Lenthéric, C. (1892). *Le Rhône. Histoire d'un fleuve*, vol. 2. Paris.

León, P. (1988). *Traianeum de Italica*. Seville.

Leone, A. (1988). *Gli animali da trasporto nell'Egitto greco, romano e bizantino*. Rome.

Lepsius, G. R. (1890). *Griechische Marmorstudien*. Berlin.

Lesquier, J. (1918). *L'armée romaine d'Égypte d'Auguste à Dioclétien* (Mémoirs publiés par les membres de l'Institut Français d'Archéologie Orientale du Caire 41). Cairo.

Leveau, P. (2007). 'The western provinces', in W. Scheidel, E. L. Morris, and R. P. Saller (eds), *The Cambridge Economic History of the Greco-Roman World*. Cambridge, 651–70.

Lewis, N. (1983). *Life in Egypt under Roman Rule*. Oxford.

Liddle, A. (2003). *Arrian: Periplus Ponti Euxini*. Bristol.

Linant de Bellefonds, P. (1985). *Sarcophages attiques de la nécropole de Tyr. Une étude iconographique* (Mémoire 52). Paris.

Lintott, A. (1993). *Imperium Romanum. Politics and Administration*. London and New York.

Lipps, J. (2010–11). 'Das Hadrianeum auf dem Marsfeld in Rom. Einige Beobachtungen zur Architekturdekoration', *BJ* 210–11: 103–38.

Liverani, P. (2010). *The Vatican Necropoles: Rome's City of the Dead*. Milan.

Lizop, R. (1931). *Histoire de deux cités gallo-romaines. Les Convenae et les Consoranni (Comminges et Couserans)*. Toulouse.

Lo Cascio, E. (2006). 'The role of the state in the Roman economy: making use of the new institutional economics', in P. F. Bang, M. Ikeguchi, and H. G. Ziche (eds), *Ancient Economies, Modern Methodologies. Archaeology, Comparative history, Models and Institutions* (Pragmateiai 12). Bari, 215–36.

Lo Cascio, E. (2007). 'The early Roman Empire: the state and the economy', in W. Scheidel, E. L. Morris, and R. P. Saller (eds), *The Cambridge Economic History of the Greco-Roman World*. Cambridge, 619–47.

Long, G. (1875). 'Locatio, Conductio', in W. Smith (ed.), *A Dictionary of Greek and Roman Antiquities*. London.

Long, L. (1985). 'L'épave de pierres de taille de Carry-le-Rouet', in P. Roy and G. Fredj (eds), *Deuxièmes journées d'étude sur la plongée scientifique* (Bulletin de l'Institut Océanographique, Monaco 4). Monaco, 143–7.

Long, L. (1999). 'Carte Archéologique. Camargue et Rhône', *Bilan scientifique de département des recherches archéologiques sous-marines*: 41–6.

Long, L. (2004). 'Bouches-du-Rhône. Carte Archéologique', *Bilan scientifique de département des recherches archéologiques sous-marines*: 53–9.

Long, L. (2008). *Secrets du Rhône: les trésors archéologiques du fleuve à Arles*. Arles.

Long, L. E. (2012a). *Urbanism, Art, and Economy: The Marble Quarrying Industries of Aphrodisias and Roman Asia Minor*. PhD dissertation, University of Michigan.

Long, L. E. (2012b). 'The regional marble quarries', in C. Ratté and P. De Staebler (eds), *The Aphrodisias Regional Survey Project* (Aphrodisias 5). Mainz, 165–201.

Lorenz, C. (1995). 'Pierres de construction et pierres de decoration: deux ensembles différents quant à l'extraction, l'approvisionnement, le transport et l'importance des volumes', in J. Cabanot, R. Sablayrolles, and J.-L. Schenk (eds), *Les marbres blancs des Pyrénées: approches scientifiques et historiques*. Toulouse, 87–92.

Łukaszewicz, A. (1986). *Les édifices publics dans les villes de l'Égypte romaine. Problèmes administratifs et financiers* (Studia Antiqua). Warsaw.

Mackensen, M. (2000). 'Erster Bericht über neue archäologische Untersuchungen im sog. Arbeits- und Steinbruchlager von *Simitthus*/Chemtou (Nordwesttunesien)', *MDAI(R)* 107: 487–503.

Mackensen, M. (2005). *Militärlager oder Marmorwerkstätten. Neue untersuchungen im Ostbereich des Arbeits- und Steinbruchlagers von Simitthus/Chemtou* (Simitthus 3). Mainz.

Mackie, N. (1990). 'Urban munificence and the growth of urban consciousness in Roman Spain', in T. F. C. Blagg and M. Millett (eds), *The Early Roman Empire in the West*. Oxford, 179–92.

MacMullen, R. (1986). 'Frequency of inscriptions in Roman Lydia', *ZPE* 65: 237–8.

Macro, A. D. (1979). 'A confirmed Asiarch', *AJPh* 100: 94–8.

Maischberger, M. (1997). *Marmor in Rom: Anlieferung, Lager- und Werkplätze in der Kaiserzeit* (Palilia 1). Wiesbaden.

Maischberger, M. (1999). 'Some remarks on the topography and history of imperial Rome's marble imports', in M. Schvoerer (ed.), *Archéomatériaux: marbres et autres roches. ASMOSIA IV*. Bordeaux, 325–34.

Malinowski, R. and Fahlbusch, H. (1981). 'Untersuchungen des Dichtungsmörtels von fünf geschichtlichen Rohrleitungen im ägäisch-anatolischen Raum', in *Vorträge der Tagung Wasser im antiken Hellas in Athen, 4./5. Juni 1981* (Leichtweiss-Institut für Wasserbau der Technischen Universität Braunschweig, Mitteilungen 71). Braunschweig: Technischen Universität, 205–36.

Mañas, I. and Fusco, A. (2008). 'Canteras de *Lusitania*. Un anális arqueológico', in T. Nogales and J. Beltrán (eds), *Marmora Hispania: explotación y uso de los materiales pétreos en la Hispania romana* (Hispania Antigua, Serie Arqueológica 2). Rome, 481–522.

Mangartz, F. (1998). *Die antiken Steinbrüche der Hohen Buche bei Andernach* (Vulkanpark-Forschungen: Untersuchungen zur Landschafts- und Kulturgeschichte 1). Mainz.

Mangartz, F. (2000). 'Römerzeitlicher Abbau von Basaltlava in der Osteifel: ein bedeutender Wirtschaftszweig der Nordwestprovinzen', in *Steinbruch und Bergwerk: Denkmäler römischer Technikgeschichte zwischen Eifel und Rhein*. Mainz, 6–16.

Mangartz, F. (2006). 'Zur Rekonstruktion der wassergetriebenen byzantinischen Steinsägemaschine von Ephesos, Türkei—Vorbericht', *AKB* 36.4: 573–90.

Mangartz, F. (2010). *Die byzantinische Steinsäge von Ephesos: Baubefund, Rekonstruktion, Architekturteile* (Monographien des RGZM, 86). Mainz.

Maniatis, Y. (ed. 2009). *ASMOSIA VII* (BCH Suppl. 51). Athens.

Maniatis, Y., Herz, N., and Basiakos, Y. (eds 1995). *The Study of Marble and Other Stones Used in Antiquity. ASMOSIA III*. London.

Mar, R. (2008). 'La construcción pública en la ciudades hispanas. Los agentes de la construcción', in S. Camporeale, H. Dessales, and A. Pizzo (eds), *Arqueología de la construcción I. Los procesos constructivos en el mundo romano: Italia y provincias occidentales* (Anejos de Archivo Español de Arqueología 50). Madrid, 176–90.

Mar, R. and Pensabene, P. (2010). 'Finanziamento dell'edilizia pubblica e calcolo dei costi dei material lapidei: il caso del foro superiore di *Tarraco*', in S. Camporeale, H. Dessales, and A. Pizzo (eds), *Arqueología de la construcción II. Los procesos constructivos en el mundo romano: Italia y provincias orientales* (Anejos de Archivo Español de Arqueología 57). Madrid, 509–37.

Marano, Y. A. (forthcoming). 'Marmo e committenze nell'Adriatico tardoantico (V–VI secolo d.C.)', *MEFRA Moyen-Age*.

Marc, J.-Y. (1995). 'Who owned the marble quarries of Thasos during the imperial period?', in Y. Maniatis, N. Herz, and Y. Basiakos (eds), *The Study of Marble and Other Stones Used in Antiquity. ASMOSIA III*. London, 33–8.

Marco Simón, F. (2003). '*Signa Deorum*: comparación y context histórico en Hispania y Galia', in T. Tortosa and J. A. Santos (eds), *Arqueología e iconografía: indagar en las imágenes*. Rome, 121–36.

Marichal, R. (1988). *Les graffites de La Graufesenque* (Gallia Suppl. 47) Paris.

Märki-Boehringer, J., Deichmann, F., and Klauser, T. (1966). *Frühchristliche Sarkophage in Bild und Wort* (Antike Kunst, Beiheft 3). Olten.

Marrou, H. A. (1939). 'Les portraits inachevés des sarcophages romains', *RA* 14: 200–2.

Marsden, P. (1967). *A Ship of the Roman Period, from Blackfriars, in the City of London*. London.

Marsden, P. (1994). *Ships of the Port of London: first to eleventh centuries AD* (English Heritage Archaeological Report 3). London.

Maršić, D. (2007). 'Novi Heraklov žrtvenik iz Trogira', *Archaeologia Adriatica* 1: 111–28.

Marvin, M. (2008). *The Language of the Muses. The Dialogue between Roman and Greek Sculpture*. Los Angeles.

Massy, J.-L. (2013). *Archéologie sous-marine en Corse antique* (Cahiers d'Archéologie Subaquatique 20). Fréjus.

Matthews, K. and Walker, S. (1990). 'Report on stable isotope analysis of the marble of the Esquiline group of sculptures in the Ny Carlsberg Glyptotek', in C. Roueché and K. Erim (eds), *Aphrodisias Papers I: Recent Work on Architecture and Sculpture* (JRA Suppl. 1). Ann Arbor, 147–51.

Mattingly, D. J. (2006). 'The imperial economy', in D. S. Potter (ed.), *A Companion to the Roman Empire*. Oxford, 282–97.

Mattingly, D. J. (2007). 'Supplying Rome and the empire: some conclusions', in E. Papi (ed.), *Supplying Rome and the Empire* (JRA Suppl. 69). Portsmouth, RI, 219–27.

Matz, F. (1968). *Die dionysischen Sarkophage, 1* (Die antiken Sarkophagreliefs 4.1). Berlin.

Mauzy, C. A. (2006). *Agora Excavations, 1931–2006: A Pictorial History*. Athens.

Maxfield, V. and Peacock, D. (2001a). *Survey and Excavation—Mons Claudianus, 1987–1993. Volume II: Excavations: Part I* (Fouilles de l'Institut Français d'Archéologie Orientale 43). Cairo.

Maxfield, V. and Peacock, D. (2001b). *The Roman Imperial Quarries: Survey and Excavation at Mons Porphyrites, 1994–1998. Volume 1: Topography and Quarries* (Egypt Exploration Society, 67th Excavation Memoir). Exeter.

Mayer, M. (1992). 'L'exploitation des ressources lapidaires en Hispania', *Les Dossiers d'Archéologie* 173: 16–20.

Mayer, M. and Rodà, I. (1998). 'The use of marble and decorative stones in Roman Baetica', in S. Keay (ed.), *The Archaeology of Early Roman Baetica* (JRA Suppl. 29). Portsmouth, RI, 217–34.

Mayer, M. and Rodà, I. (1999). 'El broccatello de Tortosa: testimonies arqueológicos', in *Mélanges C. Domergue* (Pallas 50). Toulouse, 43–52.

Mazeran, R. (1998). 'Le transport des marbres sous l'Empire romain: les données des tranches de sciage de l'épave de Porto Nuovo près de Porto-Vecchio (Corse du Sud)', in É. Rieth (ed.), *Méditerranée antique: pêche, navigation, commerce*. Paris, 135–8.

Mazeran, R. (2004). 'L'exploitation du porphyre bleu de l'Estérel à l'époque romaine', in P. Chardron-Picault, J. Lorenz, P. Rat, and G. Sauron (eds), *Les roches décoratives dans l'architecture antique et du Haut Moyen Âge* (Archéologie et d'histoire de l'art 16). Paris, 129–36.

McCann, A. M. and Oleson, J. P. (2004). *Deep Water Shipwrecks off Skerki Bank: The 1997 Survey* (JRA Suppl. 58). Portsmouth, RI.

McLean, B. H. (2002). *Greek and Latin Inscriptions in the Konya Archaeological Museum* (Regional Epigraphic Catalogues of Asia Minor 4). London.

Mees, A. and Pferdehirt, B. (2002). *Römerzeitliche Schiffsfunde in der Datenbank 'Navis I'* (Römisch-Germanisches Zentralmuseum, Kataloge vor- und frühgeschichtlicher Altertümer 29). Mainz.

Megaw, A. H. S. (1959). 'Archaeology in Cyprus, 1958', *Archaeological Reports* (JHS Suppl.): 25–34.

Meiggs, R. (1973). *Roman Ostia*. 2nd edn. Oxford.

Meijer, F. (1986). *A History of Seafaring in the Classical World*. London and Sydney.

Meijer, F. (2002). 'Wrecks in the Mediterranean as evidence of economic activity in the Roman empire', in W. Jongman and M. Kleijwegt (eds), *After the Past. Essays in Ancient History in Honour of H. W. Pleket* (Mnemosyne Suppl. 233). Leiden and Boston, 135–56.

Melchor Gil, E. (1994). *El mecenazgo cívico en la Bética. La contribución de los evergetas al desarrollo de la vida municipal.* Córdoba.

Mellink, M. (1977). 'Archaeology in Asia Minor', *AJA* 81: 289–321.

Mendel, G. (1909). 'Catalogue des monuments grecs, romains et byzantins du Musée Impérial Ottoman de Brousse', *BCH* 33: 245–435.

Mendel, G. (1912–14). *Catalogue des sculptures grecques, romaines et byzantines,* 3 vols. Istanbul.

Meneghini, R. and Santangeli Valenzani, R. (2007). *I Fori Imperiali: gli scavi del Comune di Roma (1991–2007).* Rome.

Menella, G. (1990). 'L'imprenditoria private nelle cave di Carrara alla luce di *CIL* XI 6946', in F. Rebecchi (ed.), *Miscellanea di Studi Archeologici e di Antichità,* vol. 3. Modena: 133–40.

Mérel-Brandenburg, A.-B., Blanc, A., and Blanc, P. (2009). 'De l'origine des matériaux utlisés dans les monuments sculptés de l'Antiquité tardive en Languedoc méditerranéen', in P. Jockey (ed.), *Leukos lithos. Marbres et autres roches de la Méditerranée antique: études interdisciplinaries. ASMOSIA VIII.* (Collection l'atelier méditerranéen). Paris, 421–38.

Michaelides, D. (1985). 'Some aspects of marble imitation in mosaic', in P. Pensabene (ed.), *Marmi antichi: problemi d'impiego, di restauro e d'identificazione* (Studi Miscellanei 26). Rome, 155–70.

Michaelides, D. (1996). 'The economy of Cyprus during the Hellenistic and Roman periods', in V. Karageorghis and D. Michaelides (eds), *The Development of the Cypriot Economy, from the Prehistoric Period to the Present Day.* Nicosia, 139–52.

Michaelides, D., Herz, N., and Foster, G. V. (1988). 'Marble in Cyprus: Classical times to Middle Ages', in N. Herz and M. Waelkens (eds), *Classical Marble: Geochemistry, Technology and Trade* (NATO ASI series E: Applied Sciences 153). Dordrecht, 159–60.

Mielsch, H. (1985). *Buntmarmore aus Rom in Antikenmuseum Berlin.* Berlin.

Mihajlović, I. (2011). 'A Roman shipwreck with sarcophagi near Sutivan on the island of Brač', *Submerged Heritage* 1: 32–5.

Miholjek, I. and Mihajlović, I. (2011). 'Antički brodolomi s teretom sarkofage na području Dalmacije', *Portal. Godišnjak Hrvatskog Restauratorskog Zavoda* 2: 215–21.

Millar, F. (1963). 'The fiscus in the first two centuries', *JRA* 53: 29–42.

Millar, F. (1984). 'The political character of the Classical Roman Republic', *JRA* 74: 1–19.

Millar, F. (1992). *The Emperor in the Roman World (31 BC–AD 337).* 2nd edn. London.

Mineo, S. and Santolini, R. (1985). 'Testimonianze e persistenze nel territorio della via Trionfale', *BCAR* 90: 184–213.

Mirković, M. (2004). 'Sirmium', in Š. Kos and P. Scherrer (eds), *The Autonomous Towns of Noricum and Pannonia* (Situla 42). Ljubljana, 145–56.

Mitchell, S. (1976). 'Requisitioned transport in the Roman Empire: a new inscription from Pisidia', *JRS* 66: 106–31.

Mitchell, S. (1987). 'Imperial building in the eastern Roman provinces', *HSPh* 91: 333–65.

Mitchell, S. (1990). 'Festival, games, and civic life in Roman Asia Minor', *JRS* 80: 183–93.

Mitchell, S. (1993). *Anatolia: Land, Men and Gods in Asia Minor*, 2 vols. Oxford.

Mitchell, S. and Katsari, C. (eds 2005). *Patterns in the Economy of Roman Asia Minor*. Swansea.

Mitteis, L. and Wilcken, U. (1912). *Grundzüge und Chrestomathie der Papyruskunde*. Leiden.

Mócsy, A. (1970). *Gesellschaft und Romanisation in der römischen Provinz Moesia Superior*. Amsterdam.

Mócsy, A. (1974). *Pannonia and Upper Moesia: A History of the Middle Danube Provinces of the Roman Empire*. London.

Moens, L., De Paepe, P., and Waelkens, M. (1997). 'An archaeometric study of white marble sculpture from an Augustan Heroon and a middle Antonine nymphaeum at Sagalassos (southwest Turkey)', in M. Waelkens and J. Poblome (eds), *Sagalassos IV. Report on the Survey and Excavation Campaigns of 1994 and 1995* (Acta Archaeologica Lovaniensia, Monographiae 9). Leuven: Leuven Univsersity Press, 367–84.

Moltesen, M. (1988). 'The use of marble analysis in collections of ancient sculpture: some examples from the Ny Carlsberg Glyptotek', in N. Herz and M. Waelkens (eds), *Classical Marble: Geochemistry, Technology and Trade* (NATO ASI series E: Applied Sciences 153). Dordrecht, 433–42.

Moltesen, M. (1990). 'The Aphrodisian sculptures in the Ny Carlsberg Glyptotek', in C. Roueché and K. Erim (eds), *Aphrodisias Papers I: Recent Work on Architecture and Sculpture* (JRA Suppl. 1). Ann Arbor, 133–46.

Moltesen, M. (1994). *The Lepsius Marble Samples*. Copenhagen.

Moltesen, M. (2000). 'The Esquiline Group: Aphrodisian statues in the Ny Carlsberg Glyptotek', *Antike Plastik* 27: 111–29.

Moltesen, M., Bald Romano, I., and Herz, N. (2002). 'Stable isotopic analysis of sculpture from the Sanctuary of Diana at Nemi, Italy', in L. Lazzarini (ed.), *Interdisciplinary Studies on Ancient Stone. ASMOSIA VI*. Padua, 101–6.

Money, D. K. (1990). 'Lions of the mountains: the sarcophagi of Balboura', *AS* 40: 29–54.

Monna, D. (1988). 'J. B. Ward-Perkins and the Marble Committee', in N. Herz and M. Waelkens (eds), *Classical Marble: Geochemistry, Technology and Trade* (NATO ASI series E: Applied Sciences 153). Dordrecht, 3–6.

Monna, D. and Pensabene, P. (1977). *Marmi dell'Asia Minore*. Rome.

Monna, D., Pensabene, P., and Sodini, J. O. (1985). 'L'identification des marbres: sa nécessité, ses méthodes, ses limites', in P. Pensabene (ed.), *Marmi antichi: problemi d'impiego, di restauro e d'identificazione* (Studi Miscellanei 26). Rome, 15–34.

Monthel, G. (2009). 'Sauvetage de colonnes de grande taille dans une carrière de cipolin à Karystos (Eubée)', in P. Jockey (ed.), *Leukos lithos. Marbres et autres roches de la Méditerranée antique: études interdisciplinaries. ASMOSIA VIII.* (Collection l'atelier méditerranéen). Paris, 703–10.

Monthel, G. and Lambert, P.-Y. (2002). 'La carrière gallo-romaine de Saint-Boil (Saône-et-Loire)', *Gallia* 59: 89–120.

Monthel, G. and Pinette, M. (1977). 'La carrière gallo-romaine de Saint-Boil', *RAE* 28: 37–61.

Moraux, P. (1961). 'Die Pläne Plinius des Jüngeren für einen Kanal in Bithynien', in F. Altheim, K. Von Fritz, and G. Rohde (eds), *Aparchai: Untersuchungen zur klassichen Philologie und Geschichte des Altertums 4 Band: Gedenkschrift für Georg Rohde*. Tübingen, 181–214.

Morey, C. R. (1924). *Roman and Christian Sculpture, Part 1: The Sarcophagus of Claudia Antonia Sabina and the Asiatic Sarcophagi* (Sardis 5). Princeton.

Morisot, J. M. (1820–4). *Tableaux détaillés des prix de tous les ouvrages de bâtiment.* 2nd edn. Paris.

Morley, N. (1996). *Metropolis and Hinterland: The City of Rome and the Italian Economy 200 BC–AD 200.* Cambridge.

Morley, N. (2007). 'The early Roman Empire: distribution', in W. Scheidel, E. L. Morris, and R. P. Saller (eds), *The Cambridge Economic History of the Greco-Roman World.* Cambridge, 570–91.

Müller Celka, S. and Dalongeville, R. (2009). 'Les calcarénites dunaires littorales en Méditerranée orientale', in P. Jockey (ed.), *Leukos lithos. Marbres et autres roches de la Méditerranée antique: études interdisciplinaries. ASMOSIA VIII.* (Collection l'atelier méditerranéen). Paris, 143–60.

Naour, C. (1978). 'Nouvelles inscriptions de Balboura', *AncSoc* 9: 165–85.

Napoleone, C. (2001). *'Delle pietre antiche' di Faustino Corsi romano.* Milan.

Nieto, J. (1997). 'Le commerce de cabotage et de redistribution', in P. Pomey (ed.), *La navigation dans l'Antiquité.* Paris, 146–60.

Nocita, M. (2007). 'Gli scultori a Rodi nelle testimonianze epigrafiche greche', in M. Mayer, G. Barrata, and A. Guzmán (eds), *XII Congressus Internationalis Epigraphicae Graecae et Latinae*, 2 vols. Barcelona, 1029–38.

Noël, P. (1965). *Technologie de la pierre de taille.* Paris.

Noelke, P. (1980). 'Zur Grabplastik im römischen Köln', in *Führer zu vor- und frühgeschichtlichen Denkmälern 37.1: Köln I.1.* Mainz, 124–50.

Nogales, T., Lapuente, P., and De La Barrera, J. L. (1999). 'Marbles and other stones used in *Augusta Emerita, Hispania*', in M. Schvoerer (ed.), *Archéomatériaux: marbres et autres roches. ASMOSIA IV.* Bordeaux, 339–45.

Nogales, T., Rodrigues, L. J., and Lapuente, P. (2008). 'Materiales lapídeos, mármoles y talleres en *Lusitania*', in T. Nogales and J. Beltrán (eds), *Marmora Hispania: explotación y uso de los materiales pétreos en la Hispania romana* (Hispania Antigua, Serie Arqueológica 2). Rome, 406–66.

Noguera, J. M. and Antolinos, J. A. (2002). 'Materiales y técnicas en la escultura romana de *Carthago Nova* y su entorno', in T. Nogales (ed.), *Materiales y técnicas escultóricas en Augusta Emerita y otras ciudades de Hispania* (Cuadernos Emeritenses 20). Mérida, 91–166.

Noguera, J. M. and Ruiz, E. (2006). 'La curia de *Carthago Nova* y su estatua de togato *capite uelato*', in D. Vaquerizo and J. F. Murillo (eds), *El concepto de lo provincial en el mundo antiguo. Homenaje a la Profesora Pilar León Alonso*, vol. 2. Córdoba, 195–232.

Nolte, S. (2006). *Steinbruch—Werkstatt—Skulptur: Unetrsuchungen zu Aufbau und Organisation griechischer Bildhauerwerkstätten* (Beihefte zum Göttinger Forum für Altertumswissenschaft 18). Göttingen.

Nylander, O. (1991). 'The toothed chisel', *ArchClass* 43: 1037–52.

Öğüş, E. (2008). 'Lahit üretimi: mermer ocağından mezar anıtına/Sarcophagus production: from quarry block to funerary monument', in R. R. R. Smith and J. L. Lenaghan (eds), *Aphrodisias'tan Roma Portreleri*. Istanbul, 169–83.

Öğüş, E. (2010). *Columnar Sarcophagi from Aphrodisias: Construction of Elite Identity in the Greek East*, PhD dissertation, Harvard Unversity.

Olszewski, E. J. (1986). 'Giovanni Martino Frugone, marble merchant, and a contract for the Apostle statues in the Nave of St John Lateran', *Burlington Magazine* 128.1002: 659–66.

Orlandos, A. K. (1968). *Les matériaux de construction et la technique architecturale des anciens Grecs*, vol. 2. Paris.

Orsi, P. (1921). 'Crotone. Nuove scoperte subacquee di marmi in parte scritti a Punta Scifo', *NSA*: 493–6.

Ørsted, P. (1994). 'From Henchir Mettich to the Albertini Tablets. A study in the economic and social significance of the Roman lease system (*locatio-conductio*)', in J. Carlsen, P. Ørsted, and J. E. Skydsgaard (eds), *Land use in the Roman Empire* (ARID Suppl. 22). Rome, 115–26.

Ørsted, P. (2000). 'Roman state intervention? The case of mining in the Roman Empire', in E. Lo Cascio and D. Rathbone (eds), *Production and Public Powers in Classical Antiquity* (Cambridge Philological Society Suppl. 26). Cambridge, 70–6.

Ortolani, G. (2001). 'Lavorazione di pietre e marmi nel mondo antico', in G. Borghini (ed.), *Marmi antichi*. 4th edn. Rome, 18–42.

Ovadiah, A. and Turnheim, Y. (1994). *'Peopled' Scrolls in Roman Architectural Decoration in Israel: The Roman Theater at Beth Shean, Scythopolis* (RdA Suppl. 12). Rome.

Özgan, R. (2003). *Die kaiserzeitlichen Sarkophage in Konya und Umgebung* (Asia Minor Studien 46). Bonn.

Packer, J. E. (1997). *The Forum of Trajan in Rome. A Study of the Monuments*, 2 vols. Berkeley.

Padilla, A. (1999). 'Algunas notas sobre canteras y mármoles en los siglos III–IV', *Gérion* 17: 519–32.

Pagello, E. (1992). 'Un capitello non finito da Leptis Magna', *QAL* 15: 235–52.

Palagia, O. (2010). 'Sculptures from the Peloponnese in the Roman period', in A. D. Rizakis and C. E. Lepenioti (eds), *Roman Peloponnese III. Society, Economy and Culture under the Roman Empire: Continuity and Innovation* (Meletēmata 63). Athens, 431–45.

Palagia, O. (2011). 'An unfinished Molossian hound from the Dioysos quarry on Mount Pentelicon', *Marmora* 7: 11–17.

Palagia, O. and Herz, N. (2002). 'Investigation of marbles at Delphi', in J. J. Herrmann Jnr, N. Herz, and R. Newman (eds), *ASMOSIA 5. Interdisciplinary Studies on Ancient Stone*. London, 240–9.

Papageorgakis, J. (1963). 'Die antiken Marmorbrüche von Thessalien', Πρακτικα της Ἀκαδημιας Ἀθηνων (*Praktika tes Akademias Athenon*) 38: 563–72.

Papageorgakis, J. (1964). 'Les carriers antiques du marbre karystien', *AA* 1964: 264–84.

Papathanasopoulos, G. A. (1963). 'Μεθωνη', Αρχαιολογικον Δελτιον (*Archaiologikon Deltion*) 18.2: 92–5.

Papathanasopoulos, G. A. and Schilardi, D. U. (1981). 'An underwater survey of Paros, Greece: 1979. Preliminary report', *IJNA* 10.2: 133–44.

Parker, A. J. (1992a). *Ancient Shipwrecks of the Mediterranean and Roman Provinces* (BAR International Series 580). Oxford.

Parker, A. J. (1992b). 'Cargoes, containers and stowage: the ancient Mediterranean', *IJNA* 21.2: 89–100.

Parker, A. J. (2008). 'Review: Bilan scientifique de département des recherches archéologiques sous-marines 2004', *IJNA* 37.2: 421.

Parlasca, K. (1998). 'Palmyrenische Sarkophage mit Totenmahlreliefs. Forschungsstand und ikonographische Probleme', in G. Koch (ed.), *Akten des Symposiums '125 Jahre Sarkophag-Corpus'* (Sarkophag-Studien 1). Mainz, 311–17.

Parsons, W. B. (1939). *Engineers and Engineering in the Renaissance.* Cambridge, MA.

Paskoff, R. and Trousset, P. (2004). 'Les activites littorales et halieutiques', in H. Slim, P. Trousset, R. Paskoff, and A. Oueslati (eds), *Le littoral de la Tunisie. Étude géoarchéologique et historique* (Études Archéologiques Africaines). Paris, 255–98.

Paterson, J. (1998). 'Trade and traders in the Roman world: scale, structure, and organisation', in H. Parkins and C. Smith (eds), *Trade, Traders and the Ancient City.* London and New York, 145–64.

Paton, S. and Schneider, R. M. (1999). 'Imperial splendour in the province: imported marble on Roman Crete', in A. Chaniotis (ed.), *From Minoan Farmers to Roman Traders. Sidelights on the Economy of Crete* (Heidelberger Althistorische Beiträge und Epigraphische Studien 29). Stuttgart, 279–304.

Paul, G. (1996). 'Die Anastylose des Tetrapylons in Aphrodisias', in C. Roueché and R. R. R. Smith (eds), *Aphrodisias Papers 3. The Setting and Quarries, Mythological and other Sculptural Decoration, Architectural Development, Portico of Tiberius, and Tetrapylon* (JRA Suppl. 20). Ann Arbor, 201–14.

Peacock, D. (1992). *Rome in the Desert. A Symbol of Power.* Southampton.

Peacock, D. (1993). 'Mons Claudianus and the problem of the "granito del foro"', in R. Francovich (ed.), *Archeologia delle attività estrattive e metallurgiche.* Florence, 49–70.

Peacock, D. (1995). 'The *Passio Sanctorum Quattuor Coronatorum*: a petrological approach', *Antiquity* 69: 362–8.

Peacock, D. (1997). 'Charlemagne's black stones: the re-use of Roman columns in early medieval Europe', *Antiquity* 71: 709–15.

Peacock, D. and Maxfield, V. (1997). *Survey and Excavation—Mons Claudianus, 1987–1993. Volume I: Topography & Quarries* (Fouilles de l'Institut Français d'Archéologie Orientale 37). Cairo.

Peacock, D. and Williams, D. F. (1986). *Amphorae and the Roman Economy. An Introductory Guide.* London and New York.

Peacock, D. and Williams, D. F. (1999). 'Ornamental coloured marble in Roman Britain: an interim report', in M. Schvoerer (ed.), *Archéomatériaux: marbres et autres roches. ASMOSIA IV.* Bordeaux, 353–8.

Pearl, Z. and Magaritz, M. (1991). 'Stable isotopes and the Roman marble trade: evidence from Scytholpolis and Caesarea, Israel', in H. P. Taylor, J. R. O'Neil, and I. R. Kaplan (eds), *Stable Isotope Geochemistry: A Tribute to Samuel Epstein* (Special Publication, Geochemical Society 3). University Park, PA, 295–303.

Pearson, A. (2006). *The Work of Giants. Stone and Quarrying in Roman Britain.* Stroud.

Pegoretti, G. (1843–4). *Manuale pratico per l'estimazione dei lavori architettonici, stradali, idraulici e di fortificazione per uso degli ingegneri ed architetti* (Biblioteca Scelta dell'Ingegnere Civile 29), 2 vols. Milan.

Pegoretti, G. (1863–4). *Manuale pratico per l'estimazione dei lavori architettonici, stradali, idraulici e di fortificazione per uso degli ingegneri ed architetti*, 2nd edn., 2 vols. Milan.

Pekáry, T. (1968). *Untersuchungen zu dem römischen Reichstrassen* (Antiquitas, Reihe 1: Abhandlungen zur alten Geschichte 17). Bonn.

Pelletier, A. (1996). 'Pour une nouvelle histoire de *Lugdunum*', in R. Bedon (ed.), *Les villes de la Gaula lyonnaise* (Caesarodonum 30). Limoges, 167–78.

Peña, J. T. (1989). '*P. Giss. 69*: Evidence for the supplying of stone transport operations in Roman Egypt and the production of fifty-foot monolithic column shafts', *JRA* 2: 126–32.

Pensabene, P. (1972). 'Considerazioni sul transporto di manufatti marmorei in età imperiale a Roma e in altri centri occidentali', *DArch* 6: 317–62.

Pensabene, P. (1973). *I Capitelli* (Scavi di Ostia 7). Rome.

Pensabene, P. (1978). 'A cargo of marble shipwrecked at Punta Scifo near Crotone (Italy)', *IJNA* 7.2: 105–18.

Pensabene, P. (1982). *Les chapiteaux de Cherchel: étude de la décoration architectonique* (Bulletin d'archéologie algérienne, Supplement 3). Algiers.

Pensabene, P. (1986). 'La decorazione architettonica, l'impiego del marmo e l'importazione di manufatti orientali a Roma, in Italia e in Africa (II–VI D. C.)', in A. Giardina (ed.), *Società romano e impero tardoantico, III: le merci, gli insediamenti*. Rome and Bari, 285–429.

Pensabene, P. (1992). 'The method used for dressing the columns of the Colosseum portico', in M. Waelkens, N. Herz, and J.-L. Moens (eds), *Ancient Stones: Quarrying, Trade and Provenance* (Acta Archaeologica Lovaniensia, Monographiae 4). Leuven, 81–92.

Pensabene, P. (1993). *Elementi architettonici di Alessandria e di altri siti egiziani*. Rome.

Pensabene, P. (1994). *Le vie del marmo: i blocchi di cava di Roma e di Ostia, il fenomeno del marmo nella Roma antica*. Rome.

Pensabene, P. (1995). 'Some problems related to the use of Luna marble in Rome and western provinces during the first century AD', in Y. Maniatis, N. Herz, and Y. Basiakos (eds), *The Study of Marble and Other Stones Used in Antiquity. ASMOSIA III*. London, 13–16.

Pensabene, P. (1997). 'Marmi d'importazione, pietre locali e committenza nella decorazione architettonica di età severiana in alcuni centri delle province *Syria et Palestina* e *Arabia*', *ArchClass* 49: 275–422.

Pensabene, P. (1998a). 'Il fenomeno del marmo nella Roma tardo-repubblicana e imperiale', in P. Pensabene (ed.), *Marmi antichi II: cave e tecnica di lavorazione, provenienze e distribuzione* (Studi Miscellanei 31). Rome, 333–90.

Pensabene, P. (1998b). 'Contributo allo studio delle cave di Lesbo', in P. Pensabene (ed.), *Marmi antichi II: cave e tecnica di lavorazione, provenienze e distribuzione* (Studi Miscellanei 31). Rome, 175–206.

Pensabene, P. (1998c). 'Le colonne sbozzate di cipollino nei distretti di Myloi e di Aetos (Karystos)', in P. Pensabene (ed.), *Marmi antichi II: cave e tecnica di lavorazione, provenienze e distribuzione* (Studi Miscellanei 31). Rome, 311–26.

Pensabene, P. (2001a). 'Pentelico e proconnesio in Tripolitania: coordinamento o concorrenza nella distribuzione? Contributo ad una nuova discussione dei modelli di Ward-Perkins sulla circolazione del marmo', *ArchClass* 52: 63–127.

Pensabene, P. (2001b). 'Amministrazione dei marmi e sistema distributive nel mondo romano', in G. Borghini (ed.), *Marmi antichi*. 4th edn. Rome, 43–54.

Pensabene, P. (2002a). 'Le principali cave di marmo bianco', in M. De Nuccio and L. Ungaro (eds), *I marmi colorati della Roma imperiale*. Padua, 203–22.

Pensabene, P. (2002b). 'Il fenomeno del marmo nel mondo romano', in M. De Nuccio and L. Ungaro (eds), *I marmi colorati della Roma imperiale*. Padua, 3–68.

Pensabene, P. (2003). 'Sul commercio dei marmi in età imperiale: il contributo dei carichi naufragati di Capo Granitola (Mazara)', in G. Fiorentini, M. Caltabiano, and A. Calderone (eds), *Archeologia del Mediterraneo. Studi in onore di Ernesto de Miro* (Bibliotheca Archaeologica 35). Rome, 533–43.

Pensabene, P. (2004). 'La diffusione del marmo lunense nelle province occidentali', in S. F. Ramallo (ed.), *La decóracion arquitectónica en las ciudades romanas de Occidente*. Murcia, 421–43.

Pensabene, P. (2005). 'Marmi e committenza negli edifici di spettacolo in Campania', *Marmora* 1: 69–143.

Pensabene, P. (2006). 'Marmi e pietre colorate nell'architettura della Cirenaica in età imperiale', in E. Fabbricotti and O. Menozzi (eds), *Cirenaica: studi, scavi e scoperte. Parte I: nuovi dati da città e territorio*. (BAR International Series 1488). Oxford, 231–46.

Pensabene, P. (2007a). 'Gli elementi marmorei della scena. Classificazione tipologica e inquadramento nella storia della decorazione architettonica in Asia Minore', in D. De Bernardi, G. Ciotta, and P. Pensabene (eds), *Il teatro di Hierapolis di Frigia. Restauro, architettura ed epigrafia*. Genoa, 229–338.

Pensabene, P. (2007b). 'Marmi e committenza nelle Grandi Terme di Cirene', in L. Gasperini and S. M. Marengo (eds), *Cirene e la Cirenaica nell'antichità* (Ichnia 9). Tivoli, 551–90.

Pensabene, P. (ed. 2007c). *Ostiensum marmorum decus et decor: studi architettonici, decorativi e archeometrici* (Studi Miscellanei 33). Rome.

Pensabene, P. (2008). 'I marmi di Roma allo stato attuale della ricerca', in T. Nogales and J. Beltrán (eds), *Marmora Hispania: explotación y uso de los materiales pétreos en la Hispania romana* (Hispania Antigua, Serie Arqueológica 2). Rome, 13–56.

Pensabene, P. (2010). 'Cave di marmo biano e pavonazzetto in Frigia. Sulla produzione e sui dati epigrafici', *Marmora* 6: 71–134.

Pensabene, P. (2012). 'The quarries at Luni in the 1st century AD: final considerations on some aspects of production, diffusion and costs', in A. Gutiérrez, P. Lapuente, and I. Rodà (eds), *Interdisciplinary Studies on Ancient Stone. ASMOSIA IX* (Documenta 23). Tarragona, 731–43.

Pensabene, P., Antonelli, F., Lazzarini, L., and Cancelliere, S. (2012). 'Archaeometric analyses of white marbles from Hadrian's Villa (Tivoli, Italy) and the use of Pentelic and Dokymaean marbles in the statuary of the so-called Canopus', in A. Gutiérrez,

P. Lapuente, and I. Rodà (eds), *Interdisciplinary Studies on Ancient Stone. ASMOSIA IX* (Documenta 23). Tarragona, 104–8.

Pensabene, P. and Bruno, M. (1998). *Il marmo e il colore. Guida fotografica. I marmi della Collezione Podesti*. Rome.

Pensabene, P. and Lazzarini, L. (1998). 'Il problema del bigio antico e del bigio morato: contributo allo studio delle cave di Teos e di Chios', in P. Pensabene (ed.), *Marmi antichi II: cave e tecnica di lavorazione, provenienze e distribuzione* (Studi Miscellanei 31). Rome, 141–74.

Pensabene, P., Mar, R., and Cebrián, R. (2012). 'Funding of public buildings and calculation of the costs of the stone materials. The case of the Forum of Segobriga (Cuenca, Spain)', in A. Gutiérrez, P. Lapuente, and I. Rodà (eds), *Interdisciplinary Studies on Ancient Stone. ASMOSIA IX* (Documenta 23). Tarragona, 161–75.

Pensabene, P., Semeraro, T., Lazzarini, L., Turi, B., and Soligo, M. (1999). 'A historical study and characterization of the marbles of the depository of the Temple of the *Fabri Navales* at Ostia', in M. Schvoerer (ed.), *Archéomatériaux: marbres et autres roches. ASMOSIA IV*. Bordeaux, 147–56.

Pensuti, M. (1925). *Il Tevere nei ricordi della sua navigazione attraverso i secoli*. Rome.

Perret, V. (1956). 'Le Capitole de Narbonne', *Gallia* 14: 1–22.

Peschlow-Bindoket, A. (1981). 'Die Steinbrüche von Milet und Heracleia am Latmos', *JDAI* 96: 157–235.

Peschlow-Bindoket, A. (1990). *Die Steinbrüche von Selinunt. Die Cave di Cusa und die Cave di Barone*. Mainz.

Petersen, L. H. (2003). 'The baker, his tomb, his wife and her breadbasket: the monument of Eurysaces in Rome', *Art Bulletin* 85: 230–57.

Petriaggi, R. and Davidde, B. (2010). 'The sarcophagi from the wreck of San Pietro in Bevagna (Taranto): the subject of new works by the Istituto Superiore per la Conservazione ed il restauro', *Archaeologia Maritima Mediterranea* 7: 131–7.

Petrović, P. (1993). 'Naissus: foundation of emperor Constantine', in D. Srejović (ed.), *Roman Imperial Towns and Palaces in Serbia* (Gallery of the Serbian Academy of Sciences and Arts 73). Belgrade, 55–81.

Pétry, F. (1978). 'Informations archéologiques de la circonscription d'Alsace', *Gallia* 36.2: 347–78.

Petsalis-Diomidis, A. (2008). 'The body in the landscape: Aristides' *Corpus* in the light of *The Sacred Tales*', in W. V. Harris and B. Holmes (eds), *Aelius Aristides between Greece, Rome, and the Gods*. Leiden, 131–50.

Pettinau, B. (1983). 'Prezzi di marmi preziosi e tariffe dei lavori da muratori: 1805', *Xenia* 6: 87–99.

Petzl, G. (1987). *Die Inschriften von Smyrna, Teil II,1* (Inschriften griechischer Städte aus Kleinasien 24,1). Bonn.

Peyras, J. (1991). *Le Tell nord-est tunisien dans l'antiquité. Essai de mongraphie régionale* (Études d'Antiquités Africaines). Paris.

Pfanner, M. (1989). 'Über das Herstellen von Porträts. Ein Beitrag zu Rationalisierungsmassnahmen und Produktionsmechanismen von Massenware im späten Hellenismus und in der römischen Kaiserzeit', *JDAI* 104: 157–257.

Pflaum, H.-G. (1978). 'Les salaires des magistrats et fonctionnaires du Haut-Empire', in *Les dévaluations à Rome: époque républicaine et impériale* (Collection de l'École Française de Rome 37), 2 vols. Paris, 311–15.

Pflug, H. (1989). *Römische Porträtstelen in Oberitalien. Untersuchungen zur Chronologie, Typologie und Ikonographie.* Mainz.

Pichon, M. (2002). 'Le transport par voie navigable: l'example du site du Tendu (Indre)', *Gallia* 59: 83–8.

Pietrogrande, A. L. (1930). 'Sarcofagi decorati della Cirenaica', *Africa Italiana* 3: 107–40.

Pike, S. (1999). 'Preliminary results of a systematic characterization study of Mount Pentelikon, Attica, Greece', in M. Schvoerer (ed.), *Archéomatériaux: marbres et autres roches. ASMOSIA IV.* Bordeaux, 165–70.

Pike, S., Herrmann Jnr, J. J., and Herz, N. (2002). 'A provenance study of calcitic marble from the Archaeological Museum of Thessaloniki', in J. J. Herrmann Jnr, N. Herz, and R. Newman (eds), *ASMOSIA 5. Interdisciplinary Studies on Ancient Stone.* London, 263–73.

Pizzo, A. (2010). 'El approvisionamiento de los materiales constructivos en la arquitectura de *Augusta Emerita*: las canteras de granito', in S. Camporeale, H. Dessales, and A. Pizzo (eds), *Arqueología de la construcción II. Los procesos constructivos en el mundo romano: Italia y provincias orientales* (Anejos de Archivo Español de Arqueología 57). Madrid, 571–88.

Pochmarski, E. (1998). 'Überlegungen zur Chronologie der pannonischen Sarkophage', in G. Koch (ed.), *Akten des Symposiums '125 Jahre Sarkophag-Corpus'* (Sarkophag-Studien 1). Mainz, 182–200.

Poggi, D. and Lazzarini, L. (2005). 'Il granito sardo: cave e cavatura, usi, diffusione e aspetti archeometrici', *Marmora* 1: 49–68.

Pomey, P. and Tchernia, A. (1978). 'Le tonnage maximum des navires de commerce romains', *Archaeonautica* 2: 233–51.

Ponti, G. (1995). '*Marmor Troadense.* Granite quarries in the Troad', *Studia Troica* 5: 291–320.

Ponti, G. (1996). 'Ancient quarrying at Aphrodisias in the light of geological configuration', in C. Roueché and R. R. R. Smith (eds), *Aphrodisias Papers 3. The Setting and Quarries, Mythological and other Sculptural Decoration, Architectural Development, Portico of Tiberius, and Tetrapylon* (JRA Suppl. 20). Ann Arbor, 105–10.

Ponti, G. (2002). 'Techniche di estrazione e di lavorazione delle colonne monolitiche di granito troadense', in M. De Nuccio and L. Ungaro (eds), *I marmi colorati della Roma imperiale.* Padua, 291–8.

Ponza di San Martino, L. (1841). *Prontuario di stima ad uso degli ingegneri e degli architetti nella direzione de' lavori pubblici.* Turin.

Popović, V. (1993). 'Sirmium: a town of emperors and martyrs', in D. Srejović (ed.), *Roman Imperial Towns and Palaces in Serbia* (Gallery of the Serbian Academy of Sciences and Arts 73). Belgrade, 13–26.

Porteous, J. D. (1977). *Canal Ports: The Urban Achievement of the Canal Age.* London.

Poulsen, F. (1951). *Catalogue of Ancient Sculpture in the Ny Carlsberg Glyptothek.* Copenhagen.

Pounds, N. J. G. (1969). 'The urbanization of the classical world', *Annals of the Association of American Geographers* 59: 135–57.

Prada, J. L. (1995). *Caracterización de formas y procesos de alteración observadas en la piedra de construcción de edad miocénica del àrea monumental de Tarragona.* PhD thesis, Universitat de Barcelona.

Pralong, A. (1980). 'Trouvailles dans une carrière phrygienne inconnue: une inscription rupestre et un sarcophage "in situ"', *RA*: 251–62.

Price, M. (2007). *Decorative Stones: The Complete Sourcebook*. London.

Pritchard, F. (1986). 'Ornamental stonework from Roman London', *Britannia* 17: 169–89.

Prochaska, W. and Grillo, S. M. (2012). 'The marble quarries of the metropolis of Ephesos and some examples of the use of marbles in Ephesian architecture and sculpturing', in A. Gutiérrez, P. Lapuente, and I. Rodà (eds), *Interdisciplinary Studies on Ancient Stone. ASMOSIA IX* (Documenta 23). Tarragona, 584–91.

Pucci, G. (1973). 'La produzione della ceramica aretina. Note sull' "industria" nella prima età imperiale romana', *DArch* 7: 255–93.

Pullen, H. W. (1894). *Handbook of Ancient Roman Marbles*. London.

Purchase, W. R. (1903). *Practical Masonry. A Guide to the Art of Stone Cutting*. 4th edn. London.

Purpura, G. (1977). 'Un relitto con un carico di marmo a Capo Granitola (Mazara)', *Sicilia Archaeologica* 10.33: 55–9.

Quaß, F. (1993). *Die Honoratiorenschicht in den Städten des griechischen Ostens. Untersuchungen zur politischen und sozialen Entwicklung in hellenistischer und römischer Zeit*. Stuttgart.

Raban, A. (1992). 'Archaeological park for divers at Sebastos and other submerged remnants in Caesarea Maritima, Israel', *IJNA* 21.1: 27–35.

Rădulescu, A. (1972). 'Aspecte privind exploatarea pietrei în Dobrogea română', *Pontica* 5: 177–204.

Rădulescu, A., Coman, E., and Stavru, C. (1973). 'Un sarkofago di eta romana scoperto nella necropoli tumulare di Callatis (Mangalia)', *Pontica* 6: 247–66.

Raepsaet, G. (2005). 'Land transport', in *Brill's New Pauly. Encyclopaedia of the Ancient World*, Vol. 7. Leiden and Boston, 200–9.

Raepsaet, G. (2008). 'Land transport, part 2: riding, harnesses, and vehicles', in J. P. Oleson (ed.), *The Oxford Handbook of Engineering and Technology in the Classical World*. Oxford, 580–605.

Rakob, F. (1984). 'Deutsche Ausgrabungen in Karthago. Die punischen Befunde', *MDAI(R)* 91: 1–22.

Rakob, F. (ed.) (1993). *Simitthus I: die Steinbrüche und die antike Stadt* (Mainz am Rhein: Verlag Philipp von Zabern).

Rakob, F. (ed.) (1994a). *Simitthus II: der Tempelberg und das römische Lager* (Mainz am Rhein: Verlag Philipp von Zabern).

Rakob, F. (1994b). 'Das römische Steinbruchlager (Praesidium) in Simitthus', in F. Rakob (ed.), *Simitthus II: der Tempelberg und das römische Lager*. Mainz, 51–140.

Rakob, F. (1995a). 'Chemtou/Simitthus: the world of labour in ancient Rome', in M. Horton and T. Wiedemann (eds), *North Africa from Antiquity to Islam*. Bristol, 39–44.

Rakob, F. (1995b). 'Les carriers antiques en Tunisie', *Les Dossiers d'Archéologie* 200: 62–9.

Rakob, F. (1997). 'Chemtou: Aus der römischen Arbeitswelt', *AW* 28.1: 1–20.

Rambaldi, S. (2009). *L'edilizia pubblica nell'impero romano all'epoca dell'anarchia militare (235–284 D.C.)* (Studi e Scavi 22). Bologna.

Rauzier, M. (2001). 'Hérault. Au large de Mauguio', *Bilan scientifique de département des recherches archéologiques sous-marines*: 47.

Rawson, E. (1975). 'Architecture and sculpture. The activities of the Cossutii', *PBSR* 43: 36–47.

Rayet, O. (1888). *Études d'archéologie et d'art*, ed. S. Reinach. Paris.

Rea, J. T. (1902). *How to Estimate, Being the Analysis of Builders' Prices*. London.

Reinsberg, C. (2006). *Die Sarkophage mit Darstellungen aus dem Menschenleben: Vita Romana* (Die antiken Sarkophagreliefs 1.3). Berlin.

Reynolds, J. M. (1982). *Aphrodisias and Rome*. London.

Reynolds, J. M. (1996). 'Honouring benefactors at Aphrodisias: a new inscription', in C. Roueché and R. R. R. Smith (eds), *Aphrodisias Papers 3. The Setting and Quarries, Mythological and other Sculptural Decoration, Architectural Development, Portico of Tiberius, and Tetrapylon* (JRA Suppl. 20). Ann Arbor, 121–6.

Reynolds, J. M. and Roueché, C. (2007). 'The inscriptions', in F. Işik (ed.), *Girlanden-Sarkophage aus Aphrodisias* (Sarkophag-Studien 5). Mainz, 147–92.

Riccetti, L. (1988). 'Il cantiere edile negli anni della Paese Nera', in L. Riccetti (ed.), *Il duomo di Orvieto*. Bari, 139–215.

Ricci, A. (1895). *Manuale del marmista*. 2nd edn. Milan.

Rich, J. C. (1974). *The Materials and Methods of Sculpture*. New York.

Rieth, É. (1997). 'L'épave d'Yvoire (Haute-Savoie)', *Cahiers d'Archéologie Subaquatique* 13: 75–95.

Rieth, É. (1998). *Des bateaux et des fleuves. Archéologie de la batellerie du néolithique aux temps modernes en France*. Paris.

Ritti, T., Grewe, K., and Kessener, P. (2007). 'A relief of a water-powered stone saw mill on a sarcophagus at Hierapolis and its implications', *JRA* 20.1: 139–63.

Rižnar, I. and Jovanović, D. (2006). 'Stone material of regional provenance from Sirmium', *Starinar* 56: 139–51.

Roaf, M. (1983). *Sculptures and Sculptors at Persepolis* (Iran 21). London.

Robert, C. (1890). *Mythologische Cyklen* (Die antiken Sarkophagreliefs 2). Berlin.

Robert, L. (1937). *Études anatoliennes. Recherches sur les inscriptions grecques de l'Asie Mineure* (Études Orientales 5). Paris.

Robert, L. (1960). *Hellenica. Recueil d'épigraphie, de numismatique et d'antiquités grecques*, vols. 11–12. Paris.

Robert, L. (1962). 'Les Kordakia de Nicée, le combustible de Synnada et les poissons-scies. Sur des lettres d'un métropolite de Phrygie au Xe Siècle. Philologie et réalités, II', *Journal des Savants*: 5–74.

Rockwell, P. (1987–8). 'Carving instructions on the Temple of Vespasian', *RPAA* 60: 53–69.

Rockwell, P. (1990). 'Finish and unfinish in the carving of the Sebasteion', in C. Roueché and K. Erim (eds), *Aphrodisias Papers I: Recent Work on Architecture and Sculpture* (JRA Suppl. 1). Ann Arbor, 101–18.

Rockwell, P. (1991). 'Unfinished statuary associated with a sculptor's studio', in R. R. R. Smith and K. Erim (eds), *Aphrodisias Papers 2* (JRA Suppl. 2). Ann Arbor, 127–43.

Rockwell, P. (1993). *The Art of Stoneworking. A Reference Guide*. Cambridge.

Rockwell, P. (1996). 'The marble quarries: a preliminary study', in C. Roueché and R. R. R. Smith (eds), *Aphrodisias Papers 3. The Setting and Quarries, Mythological and other Sculptural Decoration, Architectural Development, Portico of Tiberius, and Tetrapylon* (JRA Suppl. 20). Ann Arbor, 81–104.

Rockwell, P. (2008). 'The Sculptor's Studio at Aphrodisias: the working methods and varieties of sculpture produced', in Y. Z. Eliav, E. A. Friedland, and S. Herbert (eds), *The Sculptural Environment of the Roman Near East: Reflections on Culture, Ideology, and Power.* Leuven, 91–115.

Rodà, I. (1997). 'Los mármoles de Itálica. Su comercio y origen', in A. Caballos and P. León (eds), *Italica MMCC. Actas de las jornadas del 2,200 aniversario de la fundación de Itálica.* Seville, 156–80.

Rodà, I. (1998). 'Sarcófagos cristianos de Tarragona', in G. Koch (ed.), *Akten des Symposiums '125 Jahre Sarkophag-Corpus'* (Sarkophag-Studien 1). Mainz, 150–61.

Rodà, I. (2001). 'Producción, materiales y circulación de sarcófagos en el Imperio Romano', in J. M. Noguera and E. Conde (eds), *El sarcófago romano. Contribuciones al estudio de su tipología, iconografía y centros de producción.* Murcia, 51–77.

Rodà, I., Pensabene, P., Domingo, J. Á. (2012). 'Columns and *rotae* in Tarraco made with granite from the Troad', in A. Gutiérrez, P. Lapuente, and I. Rodà (eds), *Interdisciplinary Studies on Ancient Stone. ASMOSIA IX* (Documenta 23). Tarragona, 210–27.

Rodenwaldt, G. (1933). 'Sarcophagi from Xanthos', *JHS* 53: 181–213.

Rodenwaldt, G. (1942). 'Ein Typus römischer Sarkophage', *BJ* 147: 217–27.

Röder, G. (1988). 'Numidian marble and some if its specialities', in N. Herz and M. Waelkens (eds), *Classical Marble: Geochemistry, Technology and Trade* (NATO ASI series E: Applied Sciences 153). Dordrecht, 91–6.

Röder, G. (1992). 'Felsberg granite as a substitute for Claudianus granite', in M. Waelkens, N. Herz, and J.-L. Moens (eds), *Ancient Stones: Quarrying, Trade and Provenance* (Acta Archaeologica Lovaniensia, Monographiae 4). Leuven, 131–5.

Röder, G. (1993). 'Die Steinbrüche des Numidischen Marmors von Chemtou', in F. Rakob (ed.), *Simitthus I: die Steinbrüche und die antike Stadt.* Mainz, 17–54.

Röder, J. (1957). 'Die antiken Tuffsteinbrüche der Pellenz', *BJ* 157: 213–71.

Röder, J. (1959). 'Zur Steinbrüchgeschichte des Pellenz und Brohltal', *BJ* 159: 4–88.

Röder, J. (1960). 'Die Reiter von Breitfurt. Technische Betrachtungen', in K. Schultz (ed.), *Pfälzisches Museum Festschrift. Des Historischen Museums der Pfalz in Speyer zum 50-jährigen Bestehen seines Neubaues* (Mitteilungen des historischen Vereins der Pfalz 58). Speyer, 96–109.

Röder, J. (1965). 'Zur Steinbruchgeschichte des Rosen-granits von Assuan', *AA* 1965: 467–552.

Röder, J. (1967). 'Die antiken Steinbrüche in der Mareotis', *AA* 1967: 118–31.

Röder, J. (1970). 'Die mineralischen Baustoffe der römischer Zeit im Rheinland', *Bonner Universitätsblätter*: 7–19.

Röder, J. (1971). '*Marmor phrygium*. Die antiken Marmorrüche von Iscehisar in Westanatolien', *JDAI* 86: 253–312.

Röder, J. and Röder, G. (1993). 'Die antike Turbinenmühle in Chemtou', in F. Rakob (ed.), *Simitthus I: die Steinbrüche und die antike Stadt.* Mainz, 95–102.

Rodríguez, O. (2008). 'Los *marmora* en el programa arquitectónico y decorative del teatro romano de Itálica: antiguas hipótesis, nuevas propuestas y posibles certezas a la luz de las aportaciones de los análisis de microscopía óptica de polarización', in T. Nogales and J. Beltrán (eds), *Marmora Hispania: explotación y uso de los materiales pétreos en la Hispania romana* (Hispania Antigua, Serie Arqueológica 2). Rome, 229–59.

Rodríguez, O., Beltrán, J., López Aldana, P., Ontiveros, E., and Taylor, R. (2012). 'The quarries of Almaden de la Plata (Seville, Spain): new data from the recent archaeological interventions', in A. Gutiérrez, P. Lapuente, and I. Rodà (eds), *Interdisciplinary Studies on Ancient Stone. ASMOSIA IX* (Documenta 23). Tarragona, 645–50.

Rodríguez, P. (2001). 'Talleres locales de sarcófagos en la Bética', in J. M. Noguera and E. Conde (eds), *El sarcófago romano. Contribuciones al estudio de su tipología, iconografía y centros de producción*. Murcia: 129–56.

Rogge, S. (1993). 'Tektonik und Ornamentik attischer Sarkophage. Studien zur Chronologie dieser Denkmälergattung', in G. Koch (ed.), *Grabeskunst der römischen Kaiserzeit*. Mainz, 111–32.

Rogge, S. (1995). *Die attischen Sarkophage, 1: Achill und Hippolytos* (Die antiken Sarkophagreliefs 9.1.1).

Rohmann, J. (1998). *Die Kapitellproduktion der römischen Kaiserzeit in Pergamon* (Pergamenische Forschungen 10). Berlin and New York.

Ronchetta, D. (1987). 'Necropoli', in *Hierapolis di Frigia, 1957–1987*. Turin.

Rondelet, J. (1867). *Traité théorique et pratique de l'art de bâtir*, 3rd edn., 5 vols. Paris.

Rook, T., Walker, S., and Denston, C. B. (1984). 'A Roman mausoleum and associated marble sarcophagus and burials from Welwyn, Hertfordshire', *Britannia* 15: 143–62.

Rosenbaum, E. (1960). *A Catalogue of Cyrenaican Portrait Sculpture*. Oxford.

Roueché, C. and Erim, K. (1982). 'Sculptors from Aphrodisias: some new inscriptions', *PBSR* 50: 102–15.

Rougé, J. (1952). 'La navigation hivernale sous l'Empire romain', *REA* 54: 316–25.

Rougé, J. (1966). *Recherches sur l'organisation du commerce maritime en Méditerranée sous l'empire romain*. Paris.

Rougé, J. (1981). *Ships and Fleets of the Ancient Mediterranean*. Middletown, Connecticut.

Roussel, P. and Launey, M. (1937). *Inscriptions de Délos: décrets postérieures a 166 av. J.-C. (Nos 1497–1524), dédicaces postérieures a 166 av. J.-C..* Paris.

Roux, G. (1966). 'Les comptes du IVe siècle et la reconstruction du temple d'Apollon à Delphes', *RA*: 245–96.

Royal, J. G. (2008). 'Discovery of ancient harbour structures in Calabria, Italy, and implications for the interpretation of nearby sites', *IJNA* 38.1: 49–66.

Rudolf, E. (1989). *Attische Sarkophage aus Ephesos* (Österreichische Akademie der Wissenschaften, Philosophisch-Historische Klasse, Denkschriften 209). Vienna.

Rudolf, E. (1992). *Der Sarkophag des Quintus Aemilius Arisitides* (Österreichische Akademie der Wissenschaften, philosophisch-historische Klasse, Denkschriften 230). Vienna.

Rüger, C. B. (1997). 'Zu Marmorschalen in Chemtou', *MDAI(R)* 104: 379–85.

Russell, B. J. (2008). 'The dynamics of stone transport between the Roman Mediterranean and its hinterland', *Facta* 2: 107–26.

Russell, B. J. (2010). 'Sarcophagi in Roman Britain', in H. Di Giuseppe and M. Dalla Riva (eds), *Meetings between Cultures in the Ancient Mediterranan. Proceedings of the 17th International Congress of Classical Archaeology* (Bollettino di Archeologia On-Line I, Volume Speciale E, E10, 10): 14–23.

Russell, B. J. (2011a). '*Lapis transmarinus*: stone-carrying ships and the maritime distribution of stone in the Roman empire', in D. J. Robinson and A. I. Wilson (eds), *Maritime Archaeology and Ancient Trade in the Mediterranean. Proceedings of the 2008 OCMA Conference, Madrid* (OCMA Monographs 7). Oxford, 139–56.

Russell, B. J. (2011b). 'The Roman sarcophagus "industry": a reconsideration', in J. Elsner and J. Huskinson (eds), *Life, Death and Representation. Some New Work on Roman Sarcophagi* (Millennium Studies 29). Berlin and New York, 119–47.

Russell, B. J. (2012). 'Shipwrecks and stone cargoes: some observations', in A. Gutiérrez, P. Lapuente, and I. Rodà (eds), *Interdisciplinary Studies on Ancient Stone. ASMOSIA IX* (Documenta 23). Tarragona, 533–9.

Russell, B. J. (2013). 'Roman and Late Antique shipwrecks with stone cargoes: a new inventory', *JRA* 26: 169–99.

Russell, B. J. (forthcoming). 'Supplying stone and the production of production-to-stock', in A. I. Wilson, M. Flohr, and B. Russell (eds), *Art and the Roman Economy* (OSRE). Oxford.

Russell, B. J. and Fachard, S. (2012). 'New work on quarrying in the territory of Eretria, Euboea', in A. Gutiérrez, P. Lapuente, and I. Rodà (eds), *Interdisciplinary Studies on Ancient Stone. ASMOSIA IX* (Documenta 23). Tarragona, 612–18.

Salamagne, A. (1991). 'L'approvisionement et la mise en oeuvre de la Pierre sur les chantiers du sud des anciens Pays-Bas méridionaux', in J. Lorenz and P. Benoit (eds), *Carrières et constructions en France et dans les pays limitrophes*. Paris, 79–91.

Saleh, H. and Sourouzian, H. (1987). *Official Catalogue: The Egyptian Museum, Cairo.* Mainz.

Salmojraghi, F. (1892). *Materiali naturali da costruzione*. Milan.

Salzman, L. F. (1967). *Building in England down to 1540. A Documentary History*. 2nd edn. Oxford.

Sanpaolesi, P. (1977). *La cupola di Santa Maria del Fiore: il progetto, la costruzione.* Florence.

Sartre, M. (1991). *L'Orient Romain. Provinces et sociétés provinciales en Méditerranée orientale d'Auguste aux Sévères (31 avant J.-C.–235 après J.-C.)*. Paris.

Savay-Guerraz, H. (1997). 'La "Pierre de Seysel" et l'évolution des carrières de Franclens (Haute-Savoie)', in J. Lorenz, P. Benoit, and D. Obert (eds), *Pierres & Carrières. Géologie–Archéologie–Histoire. Textes réunis en hommage à Claude Lorenz.* Paris, 239–46.

Saxer, R. (1967). *Untersuchungen zu den Vexillationen des römischen Kaiserheeres von Augustus bis Diokletian* (Epigraphische Studien 1). Cologne and Graz.

Sayce, A.-H. (1888). 'Les anciennes carrières de Ptolémais', *REG* 1: 311–17.

Scardozzi, G. (2010). '*Hierapolis* di Frigia, dalle cave ai cantieri di demolizione: l'approvvigionamento di material lapidei nella città di età imperiale e proto-bizantina', in S. Camporeale, H. Dessales, and A. Pizzo (eds), *Arqueología de la construcción II. Los procesos constructivos en el mundo romano: Italia y provincias orientales* (Anejos de Archivo Español de Arqueología 57). Madrid, 351–74.

Scardozzi, G. (2012). 'Ancient marble and alabaster quarries near Hierapolis in Phrygia (Turkey): new data from archaeological surveys', in A. Gutiérrez, P. Lapuente, and I. Rodà (eds), *Interdisciplinary Studies on Ancient Stone. ASMOSIA IX* (Documenta 23). Tarragona, 573–83.

Schaaff, H. (2000). 'Antike Tuffbergwerke in der Pellenz', in *Steinbruch und Bergwerk: Denkmäler römischer Technikgeschichte zwischen Eifel und Rhein. Kataloghandbuch zu den Austellungen in den Museen von Mayen und Andernach*. Mainz, 17–30.

Schattner, T. G. and Ovejero, G. (2008). 'Mármol en *Munigua*', in T. Nogales and J. Beltrán (eds), *Marmora Hispania: explotación y uso de los materiales pétreos en la Hispania romana* (Hispania Antigua, Serie Arqueológica 2). Rome, 285–312.

Schauenburg, K. (1967). 'Perückenträgerin im Blattkelch', *Städel-Jahrbuch* (new series) 1: 45–63.

Scheidel, W. (2007). 'Demography', in W. Scheidel, E. L. Morris, and R. P. Saller (eds), *The Cambridge Economic History of the Greco-Roman World*. Cambridge, 38–86.

Scheidel, W., Morris, E. L., and Saller, R. P. (eds) (2007). *The Cambridge Economic History of the Greco-Roman World*. Cambridge.

Schilardi, D. U. (2000). 'Observations on the quarries of Spilies, Lakkoi and Thapsana on Paros', in D. U. Schilardi and D. Katsonopoulou (eds), *Paria Lithos: Parian Quarries, Marble and Workshops of Sculpture*. Athens, 35–60.

Schliemann, H. (1880). *Ilios. The City and the Country of the Trojans*. London.

Schmidt-Colinet, A. (1990). 'Considérations sur les carrières de Palmyre en Syrie', in M. Waelkens (ed.), *Pierre Éternelle du Nil au Rhin. Carrières et Prefabrication*. Brussels, 87–92.

Schmidt-Colinet, A. and al-As'ad, K. (2007). 'Zwei neufunde palmyrenischer Sarkophage', in G. Koch (ed.), *Akten des Symposiums des Sarkophag-Corpus 2001* (Sarkophag-Studien 3). Mainz, 271–8.

Schneider, R. M. (1990). 'Kolossale Dakerstatuen aus grünem Porphyr', *MDAI(R)* 97: 233–60.

Schneider, R. M. (2002). 'Nuove immagini del potere romano. Sculture in marmo colorato nell'impero romano', in M. De Nuccio and L. Ungaro (eds), *I marmi colorati della Roma imperiale*. Padua, 83–105.

Schneider, R. M. (2006). 'Marble', in *The New Pauly Encyclopaedia of the Ancient World*, Vol. 8. Leiden and Boston, 281–91.

Schoep, I. (2004). 'Assessing the role of architecture in conspicuous consumption in the Middle Minoan I–II Periods', *OJA* 23.3: 243–69.

Schvoerer, M. (ed. 1999). *Archéomatériaux: marbres et autres roches. ASMOSIA IV*. Bordeaux.

Schwander, E.-L. (1991). 'Der Schnitt im Stein. Beobachtungen zum gebrauch der Steinsäge in der Antike', in A. Hoffmann, E.-L. Schwander, W. Hoepfner, and G. Brands (eds), *Bautechnik der Antike* (Diskussionen zur archäologischen Bauforschung 5). Mainz, 216–23.

Schwertheim, E. (2003). 'Die Inschriften', in R. Özgan (ed.), *Die kaiserzeitlichen Sarkophage in Konya und Umgebung* (Asia Minor Studien 46), Bonn, 85–92.

Scigliano, E. (2005). *Michelangelo's Mountain. The Quest for Perfection in the Marble Quarries of Carrara*. New York.

Seigne, J. (2002). 'A sixth-century water-powered sawmill at Jerash', *Annual of the Department of Antiquities of Jordan* 26: 205–13.

Serdaroğlu, Ü. (1990). 'Zur Geschichte der Stadt Assos und ihrer Ausgrabungen', in Ü. Serdaroğlu, R. Stupperich, and E. Schwertheim (eds), *Ausgrabungen in Assos* (Asia Minor Studien 2). Bonn, 1–6.

Shadmon, A. (1972). *Stone in Israel.* Jerusalem.

Shaw, B. D. (2001). 'Challenging Braudel: a new vision of the Mediterranean', *JRA* 14: 417–53.

Shaw, I. (2010). *Hatnub: Quarrying Travertine in Ancient Egypt* (Egypt Exploration Society Excavation Memoir 88). London.

Sichtermann, H. (1992). *Die mythologischen Sarkophage. Apollon, Ares, Bellerophon, Daidalos, Endymion, Ganymed, Giganetn, Grazien* (Die antiken Sarkophagreliefs 12.2). Berlin.

Sidebotham, S. E. (1996). 'Newly discovered sites in the Eastern Desert', *JEA* 82: 181–92.

Sidebotham, S. E., Branard, H., Harrell, J. A., and Tomber, R. S. (2001). 'The Roman quarry and installations in the Wadi Umm Wikala and Wadi Semna', *JEA* 87: 135–70.

Silvestrini, M. (1994). 'La documentazione epigrafica', in M. Mazzei (ed.), *Bovino. Studi per la storia della città antica. La collezione museale* (Archeologia del Mediterraneo Antico 1). Taranto, 135–60.

Sim, D. (1995). 'Weapons and mass production', *Journal of Roman Military Equipment Studies* 6: 1–3.

Şimşek, C. (2011). 'Sculpture from Laodikeia (Laodicea ad Lycum)', in D'Andria and I. Romeo (eds), *Roman Sculpture in Asia Minor* (JRA Suppl. 80). Portsmouth, RI, 336–45.

Sirano, F., Balasco, A., Beste, H.-J., D'Avino, V., and Neudecker, R. (2002). 'Il teatro di Teanum Sidicinum: attraverso un progetto di rivalutazione', *MDAI(R)* 112: 317–36.

Sirano, F. and Beste, H.-J. (2005). 'Studi sul teatro di Teano: rassegna preliminare', *MDAI(R)* 109: 399–423.

Skeat, T. C. (1964). *Papyri from Panopolis in the Chester Beatty Library, Dublin.* Dublin.

Škegro, A. (2006). 'The economy of Roman Dalmatia', in D. Davison, V. Gaffney, and E. Marin (eds), *Dalmatia. Research in the Roman Province 1970–2001: Papers in Honour of J. J. Wilkes* (BAR International Series 1576). Oxford, 149–74.

Skyring, W. H. (1831). *Skyring's Builders' Prices.* 21st edn. London.

Slim, H., Trousset, P., Paskoff, R., and Oueslati, A. (eds 2004). *Le littoral de la Tunisie. Étude géoarchéologique et historique* (Études d'Antiquités Africaines). Paris.

Smith, R. R. R. (1996). 'Typology and diversity in the portraits of Augustus', *JRA* 9: 30–47.

Smith, R. R. R. (1998). 'Cultural choice and political identity in honorific portrait statues in the Greek East in the second century AD', *JRS* 88: 56–93.

Smith, R. R. R. (2002). 'The use of images: visual history and ancient history', in T. P. Wiseman (ed.), *Classics in Progress. Essays on Ancient Greece and Rome.* Oxford: 59–102.

Smith, R. R. R. (2006). *Roman Portrait Statuary from Aphrodisias* (Aphrodisias 2). Mainz.

Smith, R. R. R. (2007). 'Statue life in the Hadrianic baths at Aphrodisias, AD 100–600. Local context and historical meaning', in F. A. Bauer and C. Witschel (eds), *Statuen in der Spätantike*. Wiesbaden, 203–35.

Smith, R. R. R. (2008). 'Sarcophagi and Roman citizenship', in C. Ratté and R. R. R. Smith (eds), *Aphrodisias Papers 4: New Research on the City and its Monuments* (JRA Suppl. 70). Portsmouth, RI, 347–94.

Smith, R. R. R. (2011). 'Marble workshops at Aphrodisias', in F. D'Andria and I. Romeo (eds), *Roman Sculpture in Asia Minor* (JRA Suppl. 80). Portsmouth, RI, 62–76.

Snodgrass, A. M. (1983). 'Heavy freight in Archaic Greece', in P. Garnsey, K. Hopkins, and C. R. Whittaker (eds), *Trade in the Ancient Economy*. London, 16–26.

Sodini, J. O., Lambraki, A., and Koželj, T. (1980). 'Les carrières de marbre d'Aliki a l'époque paléochrétienne', in *Aliki, I* (Études Thasiennes 9). Athens, 81–137.

Solano, A. (1985). 'Su una cava romana di granito a Nicotera', in P. Pensabene (ed.), *Marmi antichi: problemi d'impiego, di restauro e d'identificazione* (Studi Miscellanei 26). Rome, 83–96.

Soler, B. (2005). 'Algunas consideraciones sobre el empleo privado del mármol en *Carthago Nova*', *Mastia* 2: 149–87.

Soler, B. (2008). 'Los marmora de la Tarraconense y su difusión en Carthago Nova. Balance y perspectivas', in T. Nogales and J. Beltrán (eds), *Marmora Hispania: explotación y uso de los materiales pétreos en la Hispania romana* (Hispania Antigua, Serie Arqueológica 2). Rome, 121–65.

Spawforth, A. J. and Walker, S. (1985). 'The world of the Panhellion. I. Athens and Eleusis', *JRS* 75: 78–104.

Speidel, M. A. (1994). 'Scribonius Proculus: *Curator aedium sacrarum et operum publicorum* in Rome oder in Luna? Überlegungen zu CIL XI 1340', *ZPE* 103: 209–14.

Spruytte, J. (1983). *Early Harness Systems. Experimental Studies*. London.

Srejović, D. (1992–3). 'A porphyry head of a tetrarch from Romuliana (Gamzigrad)', *Starinar* 43–4: 40–7.

Stanier, P. (2000). *Stone Quarry Landscapes: The Industrial Archaeology of Quarrying*. Stroud.

Starac, A. (2007). 'A marble slab with relief of a stonemason', *Marmora* 3: 135–6.

Stefanidou-Tiveriou, T. (2009). 'Thasian marble: a connection between Thasos and Thessaloniki', in Y. Maniatis (ed.), *ASMOSIA VII* (BCH Supplement 51). Athens, 19–29.

Stewart, P. (2006), 'The image of the Roman emperor', in R. Maniura and R. Shepherd (eds), *Presence. The Inherence of the Prototype within Images and Other Objects*. Aldershot: 243–58.

Stewart, P. (2008). *The Social History of Roman Art*. Cambridge.

Stinsky, A. (2011). 'Kaiser oder Honoratioren? Die römischen Reiterstatuen von Breitfurt', *AW* 42.5: 40–6.

Stokes, A. (1934). *Stones of Rimini*. London.

Stoll, O. (1998). '"Silvaus im Steinbruch". Kulturtransfer durch Soldaten der *legio IIII Scythica* in Syrien?', in L. Schumacher (ed.), *Religion—Wirtschaft—Technik. Althistorische Beiträge zur Entstehung neuer kultureller Strukturmuster im historischen*

Raum Nordafrika/Kleinasien/Syrien (Mainzer Althistorischer Studien 1). St Katherinen, 99–146.

Stone, I. and Stone, J. (1962). *I, Michelangelo, Sculptor. An Autobiography through Letters.* Garden City, NY.

Story, J., Bunbury, J., Felici, A. C., Fronterotta, G., Piacentini, M., Nicolais, C., Scacciatelli, D., Sciuti, S., and Vendittelli, M. (2005). 'Charlemagne's black marble: the origin of the epitaph of Pope Hadrian I', *PBSR* 73: 157–90.

Stowel Pearson, L. and Herz, N. (1992). 'Isotopic analysis of a group of Roman gorgon sarcophagi', in M. Waelkens, N. Herz, and J.-L. Moens (eds), *Ancient Stones: Quarrying, Trade and Provenance* (Acta Archaeologica Lovaniensia, Monographiae 4). Leuven, 283–5.

Strauss, J. (2007). *Roman Cargoes: Underwater Evidence from the East*, PhD dissertation, University College London.

Strobel, K. (1991). 'Handwerk im Heer—Handwerk im zivilen Sektor', *Ktema* 16: 19–32.

Strocka, V. M. (1971). 'Kleinasiatische Klinensarkophage-Deckel', *AA* 1971: 62–86.

Strong, D. and Claridge, A. (1976). 'Marble sculpture', in D. Strong and D. Brown (eds), *Roman Crafts.* London, 195–207.

Stroszeck, J. (1998). *Die Dekorativen römischen Sarkophage: Löwen-Sarkophage* (Die antiken Sarkophagreliefs 6.1). Berlin.

Strubbe, J. (1975). 'A group of imperial estates in central Phrygia', *AncSoc* 6: 229–50.

Strubbe, J. (1987). 'The sitonia in the cities of Asia Minor under the principate', *EA* 10: 45–82.

Strubbe, J. (1989). 'The sitonia in the cities of Asia Minor under the principate (II)', *EA* 13: 99–122.

Sumaka'i Fink, A. (2000). 'Quarries and quarrying methods at Ramat Hanadiv', in Y. Hirschfeld (ed.), *Ramat Hanadiv Excavations. Final Report of the 1984–1998 Seasons.* Jerusalem, 628–36.

Świderek, A. (1957–8). 'Deux papyrus de la Sorbonne relatifs à des travaux effectués dans des temples de l'Heracléopolite', *JJP* 11–12: 59–91.

Talbert, J. A. (ed. 2000). *Barrington Atlas of the Greek and Roman World.* Princeton.

Taylor, R. (2003). *Roman Builders: A Study in Architectural Process.* Cambridge.

Tchernia, A. (1997). 'Le commerce maritime dans la Méditerranée romaine', in P. Pomey (ed.), *La navigation dans l'Antiquité.* Paris, 115–45.

Temin, P. (2006). 'Estimating GDP in the early Roman Empire', in E. Lo Cascio (ed.), *Innovazione tecnica e progresso economico nel mondo romano* (Pragmateiai 10). Bari, 31–54.

Thomas, C. M. and İçten, C. (2007). 'The *ostothekai* of Ephesos and the rise of sarcophagus inhumation: death, conspicuous consumption, and Roman freedmen', in G. Koch (ed.), *Akten des Symposiums des Sarkophag-Corpus 2001* (Sarkophag-Studien 3). Mainz, 335–44.

Thompson, D. J. (1983). 'Nile grain transport under the Ptolemies', in P. Garnsey, K. Hopkins, and C. R. Whittaker (eds), *Trade in the Ancient Economy.* London, 64–75.

Thonemann, P. (2011). *The Maeander Valley: A Historical Geography from Antiquity to Byzantium.* Cambridge.

Throckmorton, P. (1969). 'Ancient shipwreck yields new facts—and a strange cargo', *National Geographic* 135: 282–300.

Throckmorton, P. (1972), 'Romans on the sea', in G. F. Bass (ed.), *A History of Seafaring based on Underwater Archaeology.* London, 66–112.

Throckmorton, P. (1989). 'The ship of Torre Sgarrata', in H. E. Tzalas (ed.), *Tropis I: 1st International Symposium on Ship Construction in Antiquity.* Athens, 263–74.

Throckmorton, P. and Bullitt, J. (1963). 'Underwater surveys in Greece: 1962', *Expedition* 5.2: 16–23.

Toma, N. (forthcoming). 'Von Marmorblock über Halbfabrikat zu korinthischem Kapitell. Zur Kapitellproduktion in der Kaiserzeit', in J. Lipps and D. Maschek (eds), *Antike Bauornamentik: Möglichkeiten und Grenzen ihrer Erforschung.*

Tomasello, E. (1983). 'Un prototipo di capitello corinzio in Sabratha', *QAL* 13: 87–103.

Tomović, M. (1991). 'Prokoneski sarkofag sa girlandama iz Viminaciuma', *Viminacium* 6: 69–81.

Tomović, M. (1993). *Roman Sculpture in Upper Moesia* (Archaeological Institute, Belgrade, Monograph 24). Belgrade.

Torelli, M. (1980). 'Industria estrattiva, lavoro artigianale, interessi economici: qualche appunto', in J. D'Arms and E. C. Kopff (eds), *The Seaborne Commerce of Ancient Rome: Studies in Archaeology and History* (MAAR 36). Rome, 313–23.

Toubal, A. (1995). 'Les mines et les carrières en Numidie. Exploitations antiques', in P. Trousset (ed.), *Production et exportations africaines. Actualités archéologiques en Afrique du Nord antique et medieval.* Paris, 57–64.

Touchais, G. (1981). 'Chronique des fouilles en 1980', *BCH* 105: 771–889.

Toynbee, J. M. C. (1934). *The Hadrianic School: A Chapter in the History of Greek Art.* Cambridge.

Toynbee, J. M. C. (1951). *Some Notes on Artists in the Roman World* (Collection Latomus 6). Brussels.

Toynbee, J. M. C. (1962). *Art in Roman Britain.* London.

Toynbee, J. M. C. (1964). *Art in Britain under the Romans.* Oxford.

Traversari, G. (1993). *La Tyche da Prusias ad Hypium e la 'scuola' microasiatico di Nicomedia* (RdA Supplementi 11). Rome.

Tréziny, H. (2009). 'La pierre de construction à Marseille de l'antiquité aux temps modernes', in P. Jockey (ed.), *Leukos lithos. Marbres et autres roches de la Méditerranée antique: études interdisciplinaries. ASMOSIA VIII.* (Collection L'atelier méditerranéen). Paris, 203–12.

Triantafillou, C. (forthcoming). *Imperial Building in Trajanic Rome: A Study of the Construction and Economics of Public Building.* DPhil. thesis, University of Oxford.

Trigger, B. G. (1990). 'Monumental architecture: a thermodynamic explanation of symbolic behaviour', *World Archaeology* 22.2: 119–32.

Trimble, J. (2000). 'Replicating the body politic: the Herculaneum Women statue types in Early Imperial Italy', *JRA* 13: 41–68.

Trimble, J. (2011). *Women and Visual Replication in Roman Imperial Art and Culture.* Cambridge.

Tsafrir, Y. and Foerster, G. (1997). 'Urbanism at Scythopolis-Bet Shean in the fourth to seventh centuries', *DOP* 51: 85–146.

Tschira, A. (1948–9). 'Eine römische Grabkammer in Kephissia', *AA* 1948–9: 83–98.

Tsoflias, P. (1982). 'Les carrières antiques de marbre de l'Eubée du Sud', in *Troisièmes Journées de l'Industrie Minérale: le Marbre* (Bulletin des Musées Royaux d'Art et d'Histoire, Bruxelles 53.2). Brussels, 71–80.

Tufi, S. R. (1983). *Yorkshire* (Corpus Signorum Imperii Romani: Great Britain I.3). Oxford.

Türk, N., Çakıcı, S., Uz, D. M., Akça, S., and Geyik, K. (1988). 'The geology, quarrying technology and use of Beylerköy marbles in western Turkey', in N. Herz and M. Waelkens (eds), *Classical Marble: Geochemistry, Technology and Trade* (NATO ASI series E: Applied Sciences 153). Dordrecht, 85–90.

Turnheim, Y. and Ovadiah, A. (1996). 'Miscellaneous ornamental architectural elements in Roman Caesarea', in A. Raban and K. G. Holum (eds), *Caesarea Maritima. A Retrospective after Two Millennia.* Leiden, 262–304.

Tykot, R. H., Herrmann Jnr, J. J., Van der Merwe, N. J., Newman, R., and Allegretto, K. O. (2002). 'Thasian marble sculptures in European and American collections: isotopic and other analyses', in J. J. Herrmann Jnr, N. Herz, and R. Newman (eds), *ASMOSIA 5. Interdisciplinary Studies on Ancient Stone.* London, 188–95.

Vakoulis, T., Polykreti, K., Saatsoglou-Paliadeli, C., and Maniatis, Y. (2002). 'Marble quarries in central and western Macedonia, Greece: survey and proven determination with EPR spectroscopy', in L. Lazzarini (ed.), *Interdisciplinary Studies on Ancient Stone. ASMOSIA VI.* Padua, 247–58.

Valbruzzi, F. (1998). 'Su alcune officine di sarcophagi in Campania in età romano-imperiale', in G. Koch (ed.), *Akten des Symposiums '125 Jahre Sarkophag-Corpus'* (Sarkophag-Studien 1). Mainz, 117–28.

Van der Merwe, N., Herrmann Jnr, J. J., Tykot, R. H., Newman, R., and Herz, N. (1995). 'Stable carbon and oxygen isotope source tracing of marble sculptures in the Museum of Fine Arts, Boston and the Sackler Museum, Harvard', in Y. Maniatis, N. Herz, and Y. Basiakos (eds), *The Study of Marble and Other Stones Used in Antiquity. ASMOSIA III.* London, 187–97.

Vanhaverbeke, H. and Waelkens, M. (2002). 'The northwestern necropolis of Hierapolis (Phrygia). The chronological and topographical distribution of the travertine sarcophagi and their way of production', in D. De Bernardi (ed.), *Hierapolis. Scavi e ricerche, IV: Saggi in onore di Paolo Verzone.* Rome, 119–46.

Vanhove, D. (1989). 'À propos d'un fût de colonne dans une carrière de Krio Nero près de Styra en Eubée', *AC* 58: 226–30.

Vanhove, D. (1996). *Roman Marble Quarries in Southern Euboea and the Associated Road Systems* (Monumenta Graeca et Romana 8). Leiden.

Van Keuren, F., Attanasio, D., Herrmann Jnr, J. J., Herz, N., and Gromet, L. P. (2011). 'Multimethod analyses of Roman sarcophagi at the Museo Nazionale Romano, Rome', in J. Elsner and J. Huskinson (eds), *Life, Death and Representation. Some New Work on Roman Sarcophagi* (Millennium Studies 29). Berlin and New York, 149–88.

Van Keuren, F., Trillmich, W., Trillmich, C., Ghezzi, A., and Anderson, J. C. (2003). 'Unpublished documents shed new light on the Licinian Tomb, discovered in 1884–1885, Rome', *MAAR* 48: 53–119.

Van Minnen, P. (2002). 'Hermopolis in the crisis of the Roman Empire', in W. Jongman and M. Kleijwegt (eds), *After the Past. Essays in Ancient History in Honour of H. W. Pleket* (Mnemosyne Suppl. 233). Leiden and Boston, 285–304.

Van Tilburg, J. A. and Ralston, T. (1999). 'Engineers of Easter Island', *Archaeology* 52.6: 40–5.

Van Voorhis, J. A. (1998). 'Apprentices' pieces and the training of sculptors at Aphrodisias', *JRA* 11: 175–92.

Van Voorhis, J. A. (1999). *The Sculptor's Workshop at Aphrodisias*, PhD dissertation, Institue of Fine Arts, New York University.

Varène, P. (1975). *Sur la taille de la pierre antique, médiévale et moderne*. 2nd edn. Dijon.

Vasić, C. (1993). 'Felix Romuliana: Galerius' palace at Gamzigrad', in D. Srejović (ed.), *Roman Imperial Towns and Palaces in Serbia* (Gallery of the Serbian Academy of Sciences and Arts 73). Belgrade, 118–47.

Vasić, M. (2000). 'On the porphyry head from Niš once more', *Starinar* 50: 245–9.

Velkov, V. (1966). 'Ratiaria. Ein römische Stadt in Bulgarien', *Eirene* 5: 155–75.

Ventriglia, U. (1971). *La geologia della città di Roma*. Rome.

Ventura y Solsona, S. (1949). 'El sarcófago de Hipólito, de la "Punta de la Mora" del mar tarraconense', *AEA* 75: 147–74.

Vetters, W. (1990). 'Ancient quarries around Ephesus and examples of ancient stone-technologies', in P. G. Marinos and G. C. Koukis (eds), *The Engineering Geology of Ancient Works, Monuments and Historical Sites: Preservation and Protection*. 4 vols. Rotterdam, 2067–78.

Viaene, W., Ottenburgs, R., Muchez, P., and Waelkens, M. (1993). 'The building stones of Sagalassos', in M. Waelkens (ed.), *Sagalassos I. First General Report on the Survey (1986–1989) and Excavations (1990–1991)* (Acta Archaeologica Lovaniensia, Monographiae 5). Leuven, 85–92.

Vigneron, P. (1968). *Le cheval dans l'Antiquité gréco-romaine* (Annales de l'Est, Mémoire 35). Nancy.

Vitti, M. (2002). 'L'uso del marmo nelle pavimentazioni dei Fori Imperiali', in M. De Nuccio and L. Ungaro (eds), *I marmi colorati della Romai Imperiale*. Padua, 139–42.

Vrsalović, D. (1974). *Istraživanja i Zaštita Podmorskih Arheoloških Spomenika u S. R. Hrvatskoj*. Zagreb.

Vulić, N. (1905). 'Antike Denkmäler in Serbien', *JÖAI Beiblatt* 8: 1–24.

Vulić, N. (1909). 'Antike Denkmäler in Serbien', *JÖAI Beiblatt* 12: 147–203.

Vulić, N. (1931). 'Антигк и споменици наше земље', *Spomenik* 71: 1–259.

Vulić, N. (1941–8). 'Антигки споменици наше земље', *Spomenik* 98: 1–337.

Waelkens, M. (1982a). *Dokimeion. Die Werkstatt der repräsentativen kleinasiatischen Sarkophage. Chronologie und Typologie ihrer Produktion* (Archäologische Forschungen 11). Berlin.

Waelkens, M. (1982b). 'Carrières de marbre en Phrygie (Turquie)', in *Troisièmes Journées de l'Industrie Minérale: le Marbre* (Bulletin des Musées Royaux d'Art et d'Histoire, Bruxelles 53.2). Brussels, 33–56.

Waelkens, M. (1985). 'From a Phrygian quarry. The provenance of the statues of the Dacian prisoners in Trajan's forum at Rome', *AJA* 89: 641–53.

Waelkens, M. (1986). *Die kleinasiatischen Türsteine. Typologische und epigraphische Untersuchungen der kleinasiatischen Grabreliefs mit Scheintür*. Mainz.

Waelkens, M. (1988). 'Production patterns of sarcophagi in Phrygia', in N. Herz and M. Waelkens (eds), *Classical Marble: Geochemistry, Technology and Trade* (NATO ASI series E: Applied Sciences 153). Dordrecht, 139–44.

Waelkens, M. (1990). 'Technique de carrière, préfaçonnage et ateliers dans les civilisation classiques (mondes grec et romain)', in M. Waelkens (ed.), *Pierre éternelle du Nil au Rhin. Carrières et prefabrication*. Brussels, 53–72.

Waelkens, M. (1997). 'Interdisciplinarity in Classical archaeology. A case study: the Sagalassos Archaeological Research Project (Southwest Turkey)', in M. Waelkens and J. Poblome (eds), *Sagalassos IV. Report on the Survey and Excavation Campaigns of 1994 and 1995* (Acta Archaeologica Lovaniensia Monographiae 9). Leuven, 225–52.

Waelkens, M., De Paepe, P., and Moens, L. (1986). 'Survey in the white quarries of Anatolia', *Araştırma Sonuçları Toplantısı* 4: 113–26.

Waelkens, M., De Paepe, P., and Moens, L. (1988). 'Quarries and the marble trade', in N. Herz and M. Waelkens (eds), *Classical Marble: Geochemistry, Technology and Trade* (NATO ASI series E: Applied Sciences 153). Dordrecht, 11–28.

Waelkens, M., Herz, N., and Moens, J.-L. (eds 1992). *Ancient Stones: Quarrying, Trade and Provenance* (Acta Archaeologica Lovaniensia, Monographiae 4). Leuven.

Waelkens, M., Muchez, P., Loots, L., Degryse, P., Vandeput, L., Ercan, S., Moens, L., and De Paepe, P. (2002). 'Marble and the marble trade at Sagalassos (Turkey)', in J. J. Herrmann Jnr, N. Herz, and R. Newman (eds), *ASMOSIA 5. Interdisciplinary Studies on Ancient Stone*. London, 370–80.

Waelkens, M., Paulissen, E., Vanhaverbeke, H., Öztürk, İ., De Cupere, B., Ali Ekinci, H., Vermeersch, P.-M., Poblome, J., and Degeest, R. (1997). 'The 1994 and 1995 surveys on the territory of Sagalassos', in M. Waelkens and J. Poblome (eds), *Sagalassos IV. Report on the Survey and Excavation Campaigns of 1994 and 1995* (Acta Archaeologica Lovaniensia, Monographiae 9). Leuven, 11–102.

Walda, H. and Walker, S. (1984). 'The art and architecture of Lepcis Magna: marble origins by isotopic analysis', *LibStud* 15: 81–92.

Walker, S. (1979). 'Corinthian capitals with ringed voids: the work of Athenian craftsmen in the 2nd century AD', *AA* 1979: 103–29.

Walker, S. (1984). 'Marble origins by isotopic analysis', *World Archaeology* 16.2: 204–21.

Walker, S. (1985a). *Memorials to the Roman Dead*. London.

Walker, S. (1985b). 'The marble quarries of Proconnesos: isotopic evidence for the age of the quarries and for the lenos-sarcophagus carved at Rome', in P. Pensabene (ed.), *Marmi antichi: problemi d'impiego, di restauro e d'identificazione* (Studi Miscellanei 26). Rome, 57–68.

Walker, S. (1988). 'From West to East: evidence for a shift in the balance of trade in white marbles', in N. Herz and M. Waelkens (eds), *Classical Marble: Geochemistry, Technology and Trade* (NATO ASI series E: Applied Sciences 153). Dordrecht, 187–96.

Walker, S. (1990a). *Catalogue of Roman Sarcophagi in the British Museum* (Corpus Signorum Imperii Romani: Great Britain 2.2). London.

Walker, S. (1990b). '*Dignam Congruentque Splendori Patriae*. Aspects of urban renewal under the Severi', in M. Henig (ed.), *Architecture and Architectural Sculpture in the Roman Empire*. Oxford, 138–42.

Walker, S. and Matthews, K. J. (1997). 'The marbles of the Mausoleum', in I. Jenkins and G. B. Waywell (eds), *Sculptors and sculpture of Caria and the Dodecanese* London, 49–59.

Wallace, M., Keller, D., Wickens, J., and Lamberton, R. (2006). 'The Southern Euboea Exploration Project: 25 years of archaeological research', in M. Chidiroglou and A. Chatzidimitriou (eds), *Antiquities of Karystia*. Karystos, 18–51

Wallace-Hadrill, A. (2008). *Rome's Cultural Revolution*. Cambridge.

Walser, E. (1956). *Les marbres de la région Apuane*. Montreux.

Ward, P. (1970). *Sabratha. A Guide for Visitors*. Harrow.

Warden, P. G. and Romano, D. G. (1994). 'The course of glory: Greek art in a Roman context at the Villa of the Papyri at Herculaneum', *Art History* 17: 228–54.

Ward-Perkins, J. B. (1951). 'Tripolitania and the marble trade', *JRS* 41: 89–104.

Ward-Perkins, J. B. (1956). 'The Hippolytus sarcophagus from Trinquetaille', *JRS* 46: 10–16.

Ward-Perkins, J. B. (1960). 'A carved marble fragment at Riom (Pays-de-Dôme) and the chronology of the Aquitanian sarcophagi', *AntJ* 40: 25–34.

Ward-Perkins, J. B. (1963). 'Il commercio dei sarcofagi in marmo fra Grecia e Italia settentrionale', in *Atti del I Congresso Internazionale di Archeologia dell'Italia Settentrionale, Torino 1961*. Turin, 119–24.

Ward-Perkins, J. B. (1969). 'The imported sarcophagi of Roman Tyre', *BMB* 22: 109–45.

Ward-Perkins, J. B. (1971). 'Quarrying in antiquity. Technology, tradition and social change', *PBA* 57: 3–24.

Ward-Perkins, J. B. (1975). 'Dalmatia and the marble trade', *Disputationes Salonitanae* 1970: 38–44.

Ward-Perkins, J. B. (1975–6). 'Workshops and clients: the Dionysiac sarcophagi in Baltimore', *RPAA* 48: 191–238.

Ward-Perkins, J. B. (1976). 'Columna Divi Antonini', in *Mélanges d'histoire ancienne et d'archéologie offerts à Paul Collart*. Lausanne, 345–52.

Ward-Perkins, J. B. (1980a). 'The marble trade and its organization: evidence from Nicomedia', in J. H. D'Arms and E. C. Kopff (eds), *The Seaborne Commerce of Ancient Rome: Studies in Archaeology and History* (MAAR 36). Rome, 325–36.

Ward-Perkins, J. B. (1980b). 'Nicomedia and the marble trade', *PBSR* 48: 23–69.

Ward-Perkins, J. B. (1981). *Roman Imperial Architecture*. 2nd edn. London.

Ward-Perkins, J. B. (1992a). 'Materials, quarries and transportation (First Shuffrey Lecture)', in H. Dodge and B. Ward-Perkins (eds), *Marble in Antiquity: Collected Papers of J. B. Ward-Perkins* (Archaeological Monographs of the British School at Rome 6). London, 13–22.

Ward-Perkins, J. B. (1992b). 'The Roman system in operation (Second Shuffrey Lecture)', in H. Dodge and B. Ward-Perkins (eds), *Marble in Antiquity: Collected Papers of J. B. Ward-Perkins* (Archaeological Monographs of the British School at Rome 6). London, 23–30.

Ward-Perkins, J. B. (1992c). 'The trade in sarcophagi (Third Shuffrey Lecture)', in H. Dodge and B. Ward-Perkins (eds), *Marble in Antiquity: Collected Papers of J. B. Ward-Perkins* (Archaeological Monographs of the British School at Rome 6). London, 31–8.

Ward-Perkins, J. B. (1992d). 'Taste and technology: the Baltimore sarcophagi (Fourth Shuffrey Lecture)', in H. Dodge and B. Ward-Perkins (eds), *Marble in Antiquity: Collected Papers of J. B. Ward-Perkins* (Archaeological Monographs of the British School at Rome 6). London, 39–54.

Ward-Perkins, J. B. (1992e). 'Nicomedia and the marble trade', in H. Dodge and B. Ward-Perkins (eds), *Marble in Antiquity: Collected Papers of J. B. Ward-Perkins* (Archaeological Monographs of the British School at Rome 6). London, 61–105.

Ward-Perkins, J. B. (1993). *The Severan Buildings of Lepcis Magna: An Architectural Survey*. London.

Ward-Perkins, J. B. and Throckmorton, P. (1965). 'The San Pietro wreck', *Archaeology* 18.3: 201–9.

Waterhouse, H. and Simpson, R. H. (1961). 'Prehistoric Laconia, Part II', *ABSA* 56: 114–75.

Wattenbach, W. (ed. 1870). *Passio Sanctorum Quattuor Coronatorum*. Leipzig.

Weaver, P. R. C. (1972). *Familia Caesaris. A Social Study of the Emperor's Freedmen and Slaves*. Cambridge.

Weber, T. (1990). 'A survey of Roman sculpture in the Decapolis: a preliminary report', *Annual of the Department of Antiquities of Jordan* 34: 351–4.

Wegner, M. (1966). *Die Musensarkophage* (Die antiken Sarkophagreliefs 5.3). Berlin.

Weigall, A. E. P. (1909). *Travels in the Upper Egyptian Deserts*. Edinburgh.

Weil, M. (1974). *The History and Decoration of the Ponte S. Angelo*. University Park, PA.

Weinberg, G. D., Grace, V. R., and Edwards, G. R. (1965). *The Antikythera Shipwreck Reconsidered* (TAPhS 55.3). Philadelphia.

Westermann, W. L. (1928). 'On inland transportation and communication in antiquity', *Political Science Quarterly* 43: 364–87.

White, D. (1977). 'Excavations in the Demeter Sanctuary at Cyrene 1971. Second preliminary report', *Libya Antiqua* 9: 171–95.

White, K. D. (1984). *Greek and Roman Technology*. London.

Wiegartz, H. (1965). *Kleinasiatische Säulensarkophage. Untersuchungen zum Sarkophagtypus und zu den figürlichen Darstellungen*. Berlin.

Wiegartz, H. (1974). 'Marmorhandel, Sarkophagherstellung und die Lokalisierung der kleinasiatischen Säulensarkophage', in E. Akurgal and U. Bahadir Alkim (eds), *Mansel'e Armağan/Mélanges Mansel*, 3 vols. Ankara, 345–83.

Wiegartz, H. (1977). 'Zu Problemen einer Chronologie der attischen Sarkophage', *AA* 1977: 383–8.

Wielgosz, D. (2000). 'Le sculture in marmo proconnesio a Palmira', *RdA* 24: 96–105.

Wielgosz, D. (2008). 'Marbles sculptures from the Archaeological Museum of Bosra', *Marmora* 4: 57–64.

Wielgosz, D. and Degryse, P. (2008). 'Provenance of the imperial marble group from Philippopolis (Shahba, Syria). Archaeometric evidence', *Marmora* 4: 65–74.

Wielgosz, D., Lazzarini, L., Turi, B., and Antonelli, F. (2002). 'The origin of the marble sculptures from Palmyra', in L. Lazzarini (ed.), *Interdisciplinary Studies on Ancient Stone. ASMOSIA VI*. Padua, 389–402.

Williams, D. F. and Peacock, D. (2002). 'The use of Purbeck marble in Roman and Medieval Britain', in L. Lazzarini (ed.), *Interdisciplinary Studies on Ancient Stone. ASMOSIA VI*. Padua, 135–40.

Williams, J. H. (1971a). 'Roman building-materials in South-East England', *Britannia* 2: 166–95.

Williams, J. H. (1971b). 'Roman building materials in the South-West', *Bristol and Gloucestershire Archaeological Society* 90: 95–119.

Williams-Thorpe, O. (2008). 'A thousand and one columns: observations on the Roman granite trade in the Mediterranean area', *OJA* 27.1: 73–90.

Williams-Thorpe, O. and Henty, M. H. (2000). 'The sources of Roman granite columns in Israel', *Levant* 32: 155–70.

Williams-Thorpe, O. and Potts, P. J. (2002). 'Geochemical and magnetic provenancing of Roman granite columns from Andalucía and Extramadura, Spain', *OJA* 21.2: 167–94.

Williams-Thorpe, O. and Rigby, I. J. (2006). 'Roman granites of Sardinia: geochemical and magnetic characterisation of columns and quarries, and comments on distributions in the Mediterranean area', *Marmora* 2: 8–112.

Williams-Thorpe, O., Webb, P. C., and Thorpe, R. S. (2000). 'Non-destructive portable gamma ray spectrometry used in provenancing Roman granitoid columns from Leptis Magna, North Africa', *Archaeometry* 42.1: 77–99.

Wilson, A. I. (1997). *Water Management and Usage in Roman North Africa. A Social and Technological Study.* DPhil. thesis, University of Oxford.

Wilson, A. I. (2007). 'Urban development in the Severan empire', in S. Swain, S. Harrison, and J. Elsner (eds), *Severan Culture.* Cambridge, 290–326.

Wilson, A. I. (2008). 'Large-scale manufacturing, standardization, and trade', in J. P. Oleson (ed.), *The Oxford Handbook of Engineering and Technology in the Classical World.* Oxford, 393–417.

Wilson, A. I. (2009). 'Approaches to quantifying Roman trade', in A. K. Bowman and A. I. Wilson (eds), *Quantifying the Roman Economy. Methods and Problems* (Oxford Studies on the Roman Economy 1). Oxford, 213–49.

Wilson, A. I. (2011). 'Developments in Mediterranean shipping and maritime trade from the Hellenistic period to AD 1000', in D. J. Robinson and A. I. Wilson (eds), *Maritime Archaeology and Ancient Trade in the Mediterranean. Proceedings of the 2008 OCMA Conference, Madrid* (Oxford Centre for Maritime Archaeology 7). Oxford, 33–59.

Wilson, R. J. A. (1988). 'Ancient granite quarries on the Bocche di Bonifacio', in N. Herz and M. Waelkens (eds), *Classical Marble: Geochemistry, Technology and Trade* (NATO ASI series E: Applied Sciences 153). Dordrecht, 103–12.

Wilson Jones, M. (1989). 'Designing the Roman Corinthian order', *JRA* 2: 35–69.

Wilson Jones, M. (1991). 'Designing the Roman Corinthian capital', *PBSR* 61: 89–150.

Wilson Jones, M. (2000). *Principles of Roman Architecture.* New Haven.

Winckler, A. (1895). 'Description de la voie romaine de Simittu-Colonia (Chemtou) à Tabraca (Tabarka)', *Revue Tunisienne* 5: 38–47.

Wiseman, J. (1968). 'An unfinished colossus on Mt. Pendeli', *AJA* 72.1: 75–6.

Wood, J. (1806). *A Series of Plans for Cottages or Habitations of the Labourer.* 2nd edn. London.

Woolf, G. (1998). *Becoming Roman. The Origins of Provincial Civilization in Gaul.* Cambridge.

Worssam, B. C. and Tatton-Brown, T. (1990). 'The stone of the Reculver columns and the Reculver Cross', in D. Parsons (ed.), *Stone: Quarrying and Building in England, AD 43–1525*. Chichester, 51–69.

Wrede, H. (2001). *Senatorische Sarkophage Roms: der Beitrag des Senatorenstandes zur römischen Kunst der hohen und späten Kaiserzeit* (Monumenta Artis Romanae 29). Mainz am Rhein.

Wright, G. R. H. (2005a). *Ancient Building Technology. Volume 2: Materials* (Technology and Change in History 7/1), Part 1: Text. Leiden and Boston.

Wright, G. R. H. (2005b). *Ancient Building Technology. Volume 2: Materials* (Technology and Change in History 7/1), Part 2: Illustrations. Leiden and Boston.

Wurch-Koželj, M. and Koželj, T. (1995). 'Roman quarries of apse-sarcophagi in Thasos of the second and third centuries', in Y. Maniatis, N. Herz, and Y. Basiakos (eds), *The Study of Marble and Other Stones Used in Antiquity. ASMOSIA III*. London, 39–50.

Wurch-Koželj, M. and Koželj, T. (2009). 'Quelques sarcophages rectangulaires d'époque impériale, des carrières thasiennes aux nécropoles de Thasos', in Y. Maniatis (ed.), *ASMOSIA VII* (BCH Supplement 51). Athens, 289–307.

Ximénès, S. and Moerman, S. (1993). 'Port romain des Laurons: épaves lapidaries', *Cahiers d'archéologie subaquatique* 11: 159–66.

Yacoub, M. (1970). *Musée du Bardo. Musée antique*. Tunis.

Yavuz, A. B., Attanasio, D., Elçi, H., Brilli, M., and Bruno, M. (2009). 'Discovery and preliminary investigation of the Göktepe marble quarries (Muğla, Turkey): an alternative source of Aphrodisian marbles', in P. Jockey (ed.), *Leukos lithos. Marbres et autres roches de la Méditerranée antique: études interdisciplinaries. ASMOSIA VIII*. (Collection l'atelier méditerranéen). Paris, 93–109.

Yavuz, A. B., Bruno, M., and Attanasio, D. (2011). 'An updated, multi-method database of Ephesos marbles, including white, *greco scritto* and *bigio* varieties', *Archaeometry* 53.2: 215–40.

Yavuz, A. B., Bruno, M., and Attanasio, D. (2012). 'A new source of bigio antico marble: the ancient quarries of Iznik (Turkey)', in A. Gutiérrez, P. Lapuente, and I. Rodà (eds), *Interdisciplinary Studies on Ancient Stone. ASMOSIA IX* (Documenta 23). Tarragona, 255–62.

Yeo, C. A. (1946). 'Land and sea transport in imperial Italy', *TAPhA* 77: 221–44.

Younès, A., Gaied, E., and Gallala, W. (2012). 'Identification of stone blocks used for the building of the *Thysdrus* and *Thapsus* amphitheatres in Tunisia', *Archaeometry* 54.2: 213–29.

Younès, A. and Ouaja, M. (2009). 'The ancient underground quarries between Sullecthum and Leptiminus', in P. Jockey (ed.), *Leukos lithos. Marbres et autres roches de la Méditerranée antique: études interdisciplinaries. ASMOSIA VIII*. (Collection l'atelier méditerranéen). Paris, 229–37.

Young, G. K. (2001). *Rome's Eastern Trade. International Commerce and Imperial Policy, 31 BC–AD 305*. London and New York.

Youtie, H. C. (1978). 'Supplies for soldiers and stonecutters (P. Mich. Inv. 6767)', *ZPE* 28: 251–4.

Zanker, P. (1975). 'Grabreliefs römischer Freigelassener', *JDAI* 90: 267–315.

Zezza, U. and Lazzarini, L. (2002). 'Krokeatis Lithos (*Lapis Lacedaemonius*): source, history of use, scientific characterization', in L. Lazzarini (ed.), *Interdisciplinary Studies on Ancient Stone, ASMOSIA VI.* Padua, 259–64.

Zimmer, G. (1982). *Römische Berufsdarstellungen* (Archäologische Forschungen 12). Berlin.

Zimmer, G. and Wesch-Klein, G. (1989). *Locus datus decreto decurionum: zur Statuenaufstellung zweier Forumsanlagen im römischen Afrika* (Bayerische Akademie der Wissenschaften, philosophisch-historische Klasse. Abhandlungen, neue Folge 102). Munich.

Zimmermann, N. and Landstätter, S. (2011). *Wall Painting in Ephesos from the Hellenistic to the Byzantine Period.* Istanbul.

Zuiderhoek, A. (2009). *The Politics of Munificence in the Roman Empire: Citizens, Elites and Benefactors in Asia Minor.* Cambridge.

Index